TCP/IP

SIGNATURE SERIES

TCP/IP
Architecture, Protocols, and Implementation with IPv6 and IP Security

Dr. Sidnie Feit

Signature Edition

McGraw-Hill
New York San Francisco Washington, D.C.
Auckland Bogotá Caracas Lisbon London
Madrid Mexico City Milan Montreal New Delhi
San Juan Singapore Sydney Tokyo Toronto

Library of Congress Cataloging-in-Publication Data

Feit, Sidnie.
    TCP/IP : architecture, protocols, and implementation with IPv6
and IP security / Sidnie Feit.—Signature ed.
       p.   cm.
    Includes bibliographical references and index.
    ISBN 0-07-022069-7
    1. TCP/IP (Computer network protocol) I. Title.
TK5105.585.F45   1998
004.6'2—dc21
                                                98-42075
                                                  CIP

McGraw-Hill

A Division of The McGraw-Hill Companies

1 2 3 4 5 6 7 8 9 0 DOC/DOC 9 0 3 2 1 0 9 8

ISBN 0-07-022069-7

*The sponsoring editor for this book was Steven Elliot, the editing supervisor
was Curt Berkowitz, and the production supervisor was Claire Stanley. This
book was set in Century Schoolbook by Priscilla Beer of McGraw-Hill's Professional Book Group composition unit, in cooperation with Spring Point Publishing Services.*

Printed and bound by R. R. Donnelley & Sons Company.

McGraw-Hill books are available at special quantity discounts to use as pre-
miums and sales promotions, or for use in corporate training programs. For
more information, please write to the Director of Special Sales, McGraw-Hill,
11 West 19th Street, New York, NY 10011. Or contact your local bookstore.

 This book is printed on recycled, acid-free paper containing a minimum
of 50% recycled, de-inked fiber.

This book is dedicated to my husband and friend,
Walter.

CONTENTS

Contents

Contents

Contents

Contents

Contents

PREFACE

Like the two earlier editions, this book presents a general introduction to TCP/IP and its most important applications. It also contains a body of reference information for those who will continue to use and support TCP/IP.

This book is intended to be a practical guide to TCP/IP and contains detailed information on how to get started on a real network—how to tie together existing local and wide area networks, how to choose system names and assign network addresses, how to optimize networked application performance, and how to administer and manage a network. The book is intended for those who need to learn about TCP/IP: planners, network managers, network administrators, software developers, technical support, webmasters, or end users who want to understand their operating environment.

This book explains TCP/IP terminology, concepts, and mechanisms. It describes the standards that make up the TCP/IP protocol suite. Wherever possible, concepts are introduced by means of figures that summarize the main ideas in a single snapshot. These are supplemented by real-world interactive dialogs that clarify what is going on in the background. For those who need a detailed level of understanding, there are easy-to-read traces that reveal the structure of network messages and the interactive flow of these messages.

What's New?

Several completely new topics are covered in this edition. Multicasting technology is gaining in importance, and an entire chapter is devoted to multicast groups, multicast routing, and the Resource Reservation Protocol (RSVP). Another new chapter is devoted to directory systems and the Lightweight Directory Access Protocol (LDAP). The TCP material has been expanded significantly to cover TCP extensions for high performance and Transactional TCP.

Security is given a lot of attention in this edition. An introduction to security technologies now fills an entire chapter. The Domain Name System chapter includes a description of Secure DNS, which will shore up the Internet security infrastructure. And the network management chapter explains how security finally has been added to the Simple Network Management Protocol (SNMP) in version 3 of SNMP.

Much material has been extended and brought up to date to match changes to the TCP/IP suite. The IP version 6 standards have been completely revamped since the last edition. World Wide Web sites are migrating to HTML 4.0, HTTP 1.1, and XML. WebNFS has been introduced to carry NFS file service onto wide area networks. This third edition (Signature edition) presents the most current versions of the protocols.

Many new dialogs and traces have been added since the last edition, and several topics have been expanded. For example, the routing chapter contains traces that show RIP, RIP-II, and OSPF interactions, and the configuration chapter presents a detailed Dynamic Host Configuration protocol interaction.

Welcome to the world of TCP/IP! We hope that your journey through this book is smooth and pleasant.

—SIDNIE M. FEIT

ACKNOWLEDGMENTS

I would like to thank the Yale University mathematics department for their invitation to spend a term as visiting faculty, which led to the first edition of this book. The opportunity to use the diverse computer systems on the Yale computer network and to study their documentation was invaluable. Since that time, H. Morrow Long, Yale University Information Security Officer, has continued to point out security problems and solutions, interesting new software, and significant happenings on the Internet. Morrow also has been a reliable source for hard facts about real implementations.

Graham Yarbrough has provided insights based on his vast knowledge of the real world of business computing and network equipment.

Jay Ranade, editor of this series, always has offered positive encouragement.

Netmanage, Inc. provided a version of *Chameleon NFS*. Network management scenarios were executed with the help of *HP OpenView for Windows*. Network General provided a *Sniffer* monitor, extensive documentation, monitoring tips, and many megabytes of protocol traces. Netscape Communications Corporation provided directory server software. GN Nettest supplied WinPharoah monitor software and many interesting traces. Ashmount Research Ltd. provided a Windows-based *NSLookup* program.

Many other vendors contributed product and technical information. FTP Software, Inc. contributed software and documentation for their Windows product. Vendors, including, among others, Cisco Systems and Bay Systems, answered questions diligently, and responded quickly with product information.

TRADEMARKS

AT&T is a trademark of AT&T. Banyan VINES is a trademark of Banyan, Inc. BBN is a trademark of Bolt, Beranek, and Newman. Cabletron and Spectrum are trademarks of Cabletron Systems. Chameleon and NewtWatch are trademarks of NetManage, Inc. Cisco is a trademark of Cisco Systems, Inc. Clarinet is a trademark of Clarinet News Service. Cylink is a trademark of Cylink Corporation. DEC, VAX, VMS, ULTRIX, DIGITAL, and DECnet are trademarks of Digital Equipment Corporation. EIT is a trademark of Enterprise Integration Technologies. Ethernet is a registered trademark of Xerox Corporation. Fetch is a copyright of Dartmouth College. Gauntlet is a trademark of Trusted Information Systems. Verio Northeast is a trademark of Verio, Inc. Hewlett-Packard, HP, and HP OpenView are registered trademarks of Hewlett-Packard Company. IBM, VM, MVS, and OS/2 are trademarks of International Business Machines Corporation. IBM PC and LAN Server are registered trademarks of International Business Machines Corporation. Intel Inside is a trademark of Intel Corporation. LANrover is a trademark of Shiva, Inc. LAN Workplace is a trademark of Novell, Inc. MCI is a trademark of MCI, Inc. Macintosh is a trademark of Apple Computer, Inc. MacTCP is a copyright of Apple Computer, Inc. Microsoft, Microsoft Windows, Windows 95, and Windows NT are trademarks of Microsoft Corporation. MS DOS and LAN Manager are trademarks of Microsoft Systems, Inc. Netscape and Netscape Communicator are trademarks of Netscape Communications Corporation. NetWare and Novell are trademarks of Novell, Inc. NSLookup for Windows is copyrighted by Ashmount Research Ltd. OnNet and PC/TCP are trademarks of FTP Software. PC DOS is a trademark of International Business Machines Corporation. PC Quote is a trademark of PC Quote. Pkzip is a trademark of PKWARE. Reuters is a trademark of Reuters News Service. RSA is a trademark of TSA Data security, Inc. Shiva and Shiva LANRover are trademarks of Shiva, Inc. Sun is a trademark of Sun Microsystems. UNIX is a technology trademark of X/Open Company, Ltd. WAIS is a trademark of WAIS, Inc. XEROX is a trademark of Xerox Corporation. WinPharoah is a trademark of GN Nettest, Inc. All trademarks and copyrights mentioned are the properties of their respective owners.

Introduction

Today, an organization's computer network is its circulatory system. It has become a necessity of day-to-day operation that systems must be able to communicate when they need to, without regard for where they may be located in a network.

The first generation of commercial TCP/IP implementations linked an organization's branch offices, district offices, and headquarters into an integrated whole. Then traveling users were attached to the network via dial-up and wireless remote access connections. More recently, organizations have turned outward, first using the Internet as a valuable source of information, and then conducting mission-critical transactions across the Internet and other extranets. Adoption of TCP/IP "standards" has made all of these changes possible and TCP/IP has won almost universal acceptance.

Why is the TCP/IP protocol family so widely used? Its ability to glue heterogeneous local and wide area networks together makes it a capable integrator. Equally important, TCP/IP was designed from the start to support client/server communications.

TCP/IP is very democratic. An application at any TCP/IP system can act as a client, a server, or both. Whether a host is a handheld microcomputer or a massive supercomputer, it has equal standing in a TCP/IP network. TCP/IP operates in a peer-to-peer manner—any pair of computers has the potential to talk to one another. If this seems strange, then think of the telephone network. You can call any number you like. Of course, the party at the other end may choose not to talk to you.

The open peer-to-peer structure that gives TCP/IP the flexibility needed for distributed computing also exposes systems to a number of security hazards. Active defense strategies are required to protect systems.

TCP/IP Applications

TCP/IP is not just communications plumbing. The suite includes end-user applications as well as invisible utilities that keep the network operating properly. From the beginning, TCP/IP was packaged with several important generic application services:

- Terminal access to any host
- The ability to copy files from one host to another
- Exchange of electronic mail between any pair of users

Over the years, many other useful applications were added to the TCP/IP protocol suite, such as:

- Remote Printing
- Network File System
- Network News

The World Wide Web caused a lot of excitement when it was introduced, especially when the first graphical user interface appeared on the scene. However, not even its most avid fans predicted that the news of the world would appear first on the Web, that millions of people would play the stock market from their desktops, that Internet Web sites would become a business necessity, and that Web servers would spark a revolution in application development technologies.

TCP/IP Utilities

TCP/IP includes an expanding set of utilities that support network administration and maintenance. A few are:

- Directory service for mapping user-friendly host names to network addresses
- Dynamic Host Configuration
- Network Management for hosts, routers, and other network devices

The TCP/IP family is alive, well, and growing. Its user community is expanding at an almost explosive rate, and new services are being developed and modularly integrated into TCP/IP product offerings.

Terminology

Like many technical disciplines, data communications has a language all its own. Everyone in the field seems to use a similar vocabulary. The only problem is that groups within the profession use the same words to mean different things, and different words to mean the same thing!

We have made an effort to select a fairly simple vocabulary and use it consistently within this book. In the sections that follow, we describe some of the terminology and graphic conventions that are used.

Protocols, Units, Stacks, and Suites

A *protocol* is a set of rules governing the operation of some communications functions. For example, IP consists of a set of rules for routing data, and TCP includes rules for reliable, in-sequence delivery of data.

A *message, protocol data unit* (PDU) or *packet* is a formatted unit of data that is transmitted across a network. The information carried in a PDU is often called its *payload*.

A *protocol stack* is a layered set of protocols that work together to provide communication between applications. For example, TCP, IP, and Ethernet make up a protocol stack.

A *protocol suite* is a family of protocols that work together in a consistent fashion. The TCP/IP protocol suite encompasses a large number of functions, ranging from dynamic discovery of the physical address on a network interface card to a directory service that reveals how electronic mail should be routed.

Hosts

A *host* is a computer that runs applications and has one or more users. A host that supports TCP/IP can act as the endpoint of a communication. Note that personal digital assistants, personal computers (PCs), workstations, minicomputers, and mainframes all satisfy the definition of host, and all can run TCP/IP.

This book also uses the terms *station, computer,* and *computer system* synonymously with *host*.

Routers

A *router* routes data through a network. Back in the early days, TCP/IP standards writers adopted the word *gateway* for what the commercial marketplace now calls a router. Elsewhere in the communications world, the term *gateway* came to mean a system that performs some kind of protocol translation.

We use the term *router* throughout this book. However, some TCP/IP standards documents and some computer screen displays use the term gateway instead of router.

Internetwork

An *internetwork* is a set of network facilities (local and/or wide area networks) connected by routers. The *Internet* is a very special internetwork, connecting thousands of networks together.

Network Node, System, and Network Element

The terms *network node, system,* and *network element* are used to refer to a communicating entity in a network without specifying whether it is a host, a router, or another device, such as a switch or bridge. For example: *The goal of network management is to control and monitor all of the nodes in a network.*

LANs, WANs, and Links

In this book, the term *local area network* (LAN) is applied to Ethernet, Token-Ring, and FDDI multiaccess networks. A *wide area network* (WAN) covers a large geographical area and usually is constructed using serial telephone lines and shared packet-switching facilities.

The more general term *link* is used for any medium—local or wide area—over which nodes can communicate. For example, a link might be an Ethernet LAN, a cellular telephone data connection, a leased line, or a frame relay circuit.

People

The term *hacker* is sometimes used in admiration, describing someone who has a high degree of computer or network skill. At other times, it is used disparagingly, to mean someone who tries to break into private computer resources. In this text, we apply the term *cracker* to someone who tries to break into private computer resources.

Bytes and Octets

In this text, the word *byte* means an 8-bit quantity. Standards writers prefer to use the term *octet*. The reason for this is that in earlier times, computer designers used the term byte to denote the smallest addressable unit in a computer, and produced machines whose "bytes" had odd sizes, such as 10 or 11 bits. In this edition, we have given up use of "octet."

Big Endians and Little Endians

Some computers store data with the most significant byte first. This is called the *Big Endian* style of data representation. Other computers store data with the least significant byte first, in a *Little Endian* style.

Similarly, there are Big Endian data communications standards that represent transmitted data with the most significant bit of a byte first, while other Little Endians reverse the order.

Internet protocol standards writers are Big Endians. However, keep in mind that there are other groups (such as the Institute for Electrical and Electronics Engineers or IEEE) that represent transmitted data with the least significant bit or byte first.

Implementation in a Multivendor Environment

Unlike the proprietary networking protocols used in the past, TCP/IP is implemented by dozens of computer vendors and independent software companies.

Implementations are based on written standards and on free software that has been made available by volunteers. Strong guidance is provided in additional *Host Requirements* and *Router Requirements* documents.

The degree of internetworking that has been achieved is impressive, and end users generally find that their applications work very well.

However, if you look behind the scenes, you can find vendors who have taken shortcuts and omitted features that would provide better performance or improve error recovery. Sometimes software developers simply have misunderstood some detail in the specification and, as a result, have not provided some beneficial feature. Hence, you cannot assume that every mechanism described in this book is actually implemented in a given software package.

For readers of this book who are implementers, this text can help you to understand the *why* and *how* of many protocols. But no book should ever be used as a basis for implementation. TCP standards are free and are available online (see Appendix A). The documentation is continuously updated in order to add new features or describe more efficient ways to implement functions. Features that are not useful are declared obsolete.

Dialogs

There are many interactive dialogs in this text that demonstrate how TCP/IP components work. The text dialogs were generated on several Sun Microsystems and Windows computers. Many demonstrations were run at *katie.vnet.net,* a server operated by VNET Internet Access, an Internet Service Provider (ISP). The network performance statistics generated at *katie* are particularly interesting, since *katie* communicates with Internet hosts all over the world. Some demonstrations were run at *tigger.jvnc.net,* another busy host located in Princeton, New Jersey. *Tigger* is a server operated by Verio New Jersey, another Internet Service Provider.[1] A few of the text-based demonstrations were run at Yale computers.

TCP/IP has been implemented with very similar text-based user interfaces and command sets across many types of computers. Hence, the text dialogs are close to or identical to what you can experience for a wide range of systems (including Windows). In the text dialogs, end-user input is represented in bold text, whereas computer prompts and responses appear without emphasis.

There also are screens showing Graphical User Interfaces (GUIs) for TCP/IP applications running on Windows 95 and NT computers. Several Windows screens show Netmanage *Chameleon* applications. There are some screens from Hewlett-Packard's *HP OpenView for Windows Workgroup Node Manager* and Ashmount Research Ltd.'s *NSLookup for Windows.* A Qualcomm *Eudora* Macintosh electronic mail screen is displayed.

Recommended Reading

Appendix A lists useful documents and identifies several document archives that contain TCP/IP standards and other relevant information.

---

[1]Verio New Jersey formerly was Global Enterprise Services. Global Enterprise Services formerly was called *JVNC,* which is why its hosts have names that end with *jvnc.net.*

Appendix B describes the services provided by the Internet Assigned
Numbers Authority and by Network Information Centers (NICs) and
indicates where they are located. It describes how the *whois* databases
can be used to retrieve registration information and identify network
administrators. Appendix B also presents information about the CERT
Coordination Center, which coordinates responses to Internet security
threats.

Appendix C contains examples that show how IP addresses can be
assigned very efficiently (by using variable-length subnet masks).

Appendix D is a Glossary that contains definitions of terms. Like
many works whose subject is data communications, this book is pep-
pered with acronyms. Appendix E contains a list of acronyms and their
translations. Appendix F contains tables that translate between binary
and decimal numbers, including a useful subnet mask translation table.

TCP/IP: What It Is and Where It Came From

Introduction

In the short period of time since the first edition of this book was published, TCP/IP has evolved from being the protocol of choice for college campuses and research labs to a near-universal standard. The Internet has turned into the world's Main Street: millions of business and financial transactions occur each day, news breaks fast and first on the Internet, and the Internet has become an indispensable educational tool.

TCP/IP always is in transition, but the pace has quickened significantly since the previous edition of this book. The World Wide Web has gone through several generations of changes. Security is being taken seriously. Multicasting technology is maturing. The Lightweight Directory Access Protocol has given directory services a big boost. Some important new capabilities have been added to TCP. Both evolutionary and revolutionary transitions are in the works for IP.

Important changes to the administrative structure of the Internet also are taking place; new organizations are taking charge of naming, addressing, and other administrative functions.

We deal with many of the alterations to the TCP/IP and to the Internet in this book. However, this chapter begins at the beginning of the story.

Background

In the late 1960s, the Advanced Research Projects Agency of the U.S. Department of Defense, or ARPA (later changed to DARPA), began a partnership with U.S. universities and other research organizations to investigate new data communications technologies.

Together, the participants built the Advanced Research Projects Agency Network (ARPANET), the first packet-switching network. An experimental four-node version of the ARPANET went into operation in 1969. The experiment was a success, and the testbed facility evolved into a network spanning the United States from coast to coast. In 1975, the Defense Communications Agency (DCA) assumed responsibility for operating the network, which still was considered a research network.

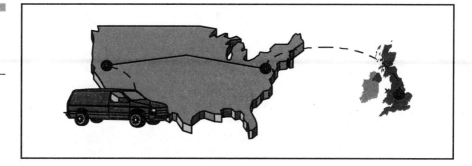

Figure 1.1
Demonstration of
TCP/IP across a mix-
ture of technologies.

The Birth of TCP/IP

The early ARPANET protocols were slow and subject to frequent network crashes. In 1974, a paper by Vinton G. Cerf and Robert E. Kahn
proposed a new set of core protocols.[1] The Cerf/Kahn design provided the
basis for the subsequent development of the *Internet Protocol* (IP) and
the *Transmission Control Protocol* (TCP). Starting in 1980, it took three
years to convert the ARPANET hosts, then numbering over 100, to the
new protocol suite.

The versatility of the new protocols was demonstrated in 1978 when a
terminal in a mobile van driving along California's Highway 101 transmitted data via packet radio to a node at SRI International, across the
continent via ARPANET, and then over a satellite network to a host in
London (see Figure 1.1).

During the early 1980s, the ARPANET was converted to the new protocols. By 1983, the ARPANET included over 300 computers and had
become an invaluable resource to its users. In 1984, the original
ARPANET was split into two pieces. One, still called ARPANET, was
dedicated to research and development. The other, called MILNET, was
an unclassified military network.

---

[1]"A Protocol for Packet Network Interconnections," *IEEE Transactions of Communications,*
May 1974.

Acceptance of the Protocols

In 1982, the U.S. Department of Defense (DOD) issued a policy statement adopting a single set of communications protocols based on the ARPANET protocols and created the Defense Data Network (DDN) as the parent entity uniting its distributed operational networks.

In 1983, the Department of Defense adopted the TCP/IP protocol suite as its standard. Acceptance of TCP/IP spread to other government departments, creating a large market for the technology.

TCP/IP Characteristics

TCP/IP has some unique characteristics that account for its durability. The TCP/IP architecture glues clusters of networks together, creating a larger network called an *internetwork*. To a user, an internetwork simply appears to be a single network, composed of all of the hosts connected to any of the constituent parts.

The TCP/IP protocols were designed to be independent of host hardware or operating system, as well as media and data-link technologies. The protocols were required to be robust, surviving high network error rates and supporting transparent adaptive routing in case network nodes or lines were lost.

Availability of TCP/IP

When the TCP/IP protocols became a requirement in computer procurements by the U.S. Department of Defense and other government agencies, vendors needed to implement TCP/IP in order to compete in government bids. Figure 1.2 illustrates how different systems, local area networks (LANs), and wide area networks (WANs) can be combined in a TCP/IP environment.

The U.S. Department of Defense encouraged the availability of TCP/IP by funding Bolt, Beranek, and Newman (BBN) to implement TCP/IP for Unix, and the University of California at Berkeley to incorporate the BBN code into the Berkeley Software Distribution (BSD) 4.2 Unix operating system. This operating system and its successors were migrated to many hardware bases. Later, TCP/IP was added to AT&T's System V Unix.

Figure 1.2
TCP/IP multivendor
and multinetwork
environment.

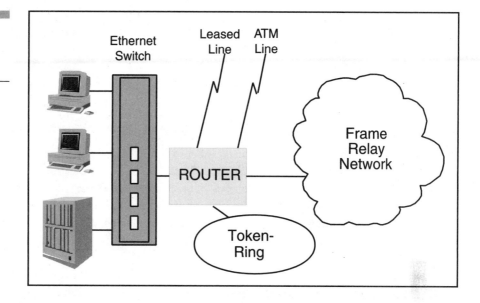

In the 1990s, TCP/IP moved into the commercial world. It is the most universally available networking software. TCP/IP routinely is bundled into computers ranging from mainframes to desktop and notebook systems.

In addition, there is support for TCP/IP over an ever-increasing selection of transmission technologies. We explore a number of these technologies in Chapter 4.

The Internet

The ease of gluing TCP/IP networks together combined with an open door policy that allowed academic and commercial research networks to connect to the ARPANET spawned the supernetwork called the *Internet*. Throughout the 1980s, the ARPANET was maintained as a backbone of this flourishing network.

Because of the characteristics of the TCP/IP protocols, Internet growth was steady and nondisruptive. The Internet became the world's largest internetwork, comprising substantial government, military research, academic, and commercial networks, each containing hundreds of subnetworks. In 1985, a new backbone net, the National Science Foundation Net (NSFNET), was incorporated to accommodate high-speed links to research sites and supercomputer facilities.

With the help of government support, an infrastructure of *regional Service Providers* mushroomed in areas all over the United States. Universities and research labs connected to the nearest regional provider, which in turn connected to the backbone.

The Internet spread across the globe, with Service Providers appearing in dozens of countries around the world. By 1994, millions of computers were interconnected, and the Internet was ready for the commercial marketplace. The National Science Foundation (NSF) gave up its role as provider of a central backbone. Service Providers in the United States connected to one another at large switching centers scattered across the country. The flow of traffic across international links increased, and Service Provider organizations mushroomed all over the world.

The Internet continues to be an incubator for new technology. Its mail, news, bulletin board services, and Web Servers provide a public forum in which ideas are debated and refined. Researchers, systems programmers, and network administrators exchange software bug corrections, solutions to interworking problems, and hints for improving performance. Software vendors publish free copies of their beta software at public sites and invite users to download, try, and comment on their new products.

Registration Services

For many years, the Department of Defense retained an important coordination role for the Internet. Its DDN Network Information Center (DDN NIC) provided registration and information services to users, site administrators, site technical support staff, and network managers.

In the spring of 1993, civilian Internet support functions were turned over to the National Science Foundation. The National Science Foundation (NSF) established a five-year contract with Network Solutions, Inc. for Internet name and address registration. Network Solutions established the InterNIC registration service, which was in charge of a major part of Internet host name allocation and supervised a big part of the Internet address space. Regional address registration centers also were set up in Europe (RIPE) and Asia (APNIC). Additional name registration centers were established in many countries.

In 1998, the National Science Foundation contract with the InterNIC expired. A separate, nonprofit address registration center (called the American Registry for Internet Numbers or ARIN) was spun off from the InterNIC. At the time of writing, a new method of administering generic names such as *abc.com* is under consideration.

See Appendix B for more information about registration centers.

IAB, IETF, and IESG

TCP/IP "standards" are very different from any prior standards. A small, elite group does not define them. Thousands of people are involved in the effort. The only prerequisite to participation is a serious willingness to work. TCP/IP standards evolve through rough-and-tumble public discussion and are tested by the marketplace. The TCP/IP suite is not fixed, but changes and grows. We never know what result a flash of inspiration may bring us.

Development of new TCP/IP protocols and maintenance of old protocols is coordinated by an organization called the Internet Architecture Board (IAB). The IAB identifies technical areas that need to be addressed. For example, in recent years, the IAB has spearheaded efforts to develop new network management protocols, more functional routing protocols, and a next generation version of IP.

In 1992, the *Internet Society* was formed, and the IAB was absorbed into the society. The Internet Society is an international professional organization created to promote the growth and successful operation of the Internet.

The IAB oversees some important groups. The *Internet Engineering Task Force* (IETF) writes and implements new protocols. Activities of the IETF working groups are supervised and reviewed by the *Internet Engineering Steering Group* (IESG).

Task Forces and Protocol Development

IETF members are volunteers. To tackle a specific problem, a working group whose members have appropriate technical expertise is formed. Participants in a working group use a methodology that combines theory with immediate implementation.

In fact, the validity and completeness of a protocol specification are tested by creating at least two independent implementations. An iterative *design-implement-experiment-review* process is used to evolve and enhance protocols and to improve the performance of the implementations.

This practical, hands-on approach to protocol development uncovers many flaws and oversights before a protocol is adopted. Features that make impossible demands on system resources or cause very poor performance are prevented from being incorporated into a protocol's architecture.

Source code for new protocols often is placed in public databases on the Internet. Vendors can use this code as the starting point for new products. This has many benefits. Product development is rapid and less costly. Starting from a common source framework promotes interoperability. Users also may copy and install public code on their own systems.

Other Sources of Internet Protocols

Although many of the protocols in the TCP/IP suite were designed and implemented by IETF working groups, university research groups and commercial organizations also have made significant contributions. To be accepted, contributions must be useful and usable.

There are some software packages that implement services that are critical to the correct operation of a TCP/IP network. Increasingly, the work of improving a package, fixing bugs, and providing customer support is performed by a consortium funded by a mixture of vendor, end-user, and government organizations. Several of these consortia are mentioned in the text.

Requests for Comments

A new protocol's specification is circulated in a document called a *Request For Comments* (RFC). RFC documents are numbered in sequence. Hundreds of these documents have been written.

RFC documents are stored at many Web sites around the world and are available at no cost (see *http://www.ietf.org/*).

Sometimes protocol specifications are updated to correct errors, improve performance, or add new features. Updated protocols are published with new, larger RFC numbers.

An index of RFCs is maintained in a document called *rfc-index.txt*. In the index, entries for obsolete RFCs contain the numbers of the superseding documents. For example, the index entry below announces that RFC 1098 obsoletes the original Simple Network Management Protocol standard and has itself been updated by a later document, RFC 1157:

```
1098 Case, J.D.; Fedor, M.; Schoffstall, M.L.; Davin, C.
Simple Network Management Protocol (SNMP). 1989 April; 34 p.
(Format: TXT571563 bytes) (Obsoletes RFC 1067; Updated by RFC 1157)
```

Not all RFCs describe protocols. Some just organize and present insights that have evolved within the Internet community. For example, there is an RFC that gives advice on selecting names for computers. Other RFCs provide guidance on how to administer a TCP/IP network and how to implement security procedures. There are RFCs that suggest implementation strategies for better performance, describe experimental algorithms, and discuss ethics on the Internet. After review, some of these are classified as *Best Current Practices* (BCP) documents.

State and Status of Standards

The IAB periodically publishes information on the progress of protocols as they move through several *states* that reflect their maturity level:

Experimental	Not on the standards track. Reflects ongoing research.
Proposed	On the standards track, but revision is likely.
Draft	Under consideration as a standard. Further testing and comment are needed.
Standard	Established as an official protocol.
Informational	Developed by vendors or other standards groups. Published to inform the community.
Historical	Superseded or not useful.

Protocols also are classified according to their requirement levels. Some protocols are required standards, while others are used where there is some special need. Some have outlived their usefulness and have been retired. The formal requirement *status* of a protocol is defined by one of the levels:

- Required
- Recommended

- Elective
- Limited use
- Not recommended

The current state and status of Internet protocols is described in an RFC called *Internet Official Protocol Standards*. This document is updated periodically and released with a new RFC number.

Assigned Numbers

The Internet Assigned Numbers Authority (IANA) has played a very important supporting role for TCP/IP. First of all, the IANA has overall control of IP address numbers. However, the IANA does not issue numbers to individual organizations. The IANA delegates parts of the address space to regional registries.

In addition, the IANA oversees TCP/IP parameters, which are standardized through registration with the IANA. These parameters are diverse and include option identifiers, error codes, service names, standard identifiers for terminals and computer systems, security algorithms, and much more. Many separate files containing parameter values currently are available at the IANA Web site (*http://www.iana.org/*).

For years, the IANA was located at the University of Southern California's Information Services Institute (ISI) under the direction of Dr. Jon Postel. It was supported by grants from the U.S. government. As part of the current restructuring of the Internet infrastructure, IANA functions are moving to a new not-for-profit organization with an international board of directors.

RFCs That Promoted Multivendor Interworking

The expectation that users would have needs that could not be met by one computer architecture was a strong motivation for adoption of the TCP/IP communications standards by U.S. government organizations. These groups wanted to be able to purchase equipment in a competitive market, with several vendors able to satisfy requirements. They believed that the effort to establish and maintain standards would be repaid in lower costs and better service.

However, there are problems that can arise in a multivendor environment:

- Standards sometimes include optional features. By implementing different options, vendors can make interoperability very difficult.

- Vendors sometimes misunderstand the standards, and their products operate incorrectly.

- There are mistakes in standards specifications.

- Some implementations, although fairly accurate, are inflexible and don't allow a system administrator to tune configuration parameters to improve performance.

- A single system that uses poorly designed algorithms for pacing data transmission and retransmission can degrade performance for all of the systems on a network.

Two RFCs published in October 1989 addressed many of these problems, correcting errors, clarifying definitions, specifying option support, listing configuration parameters, and identifying high-performance algorithms. Most important, these RFCs stated specific conformance requirements for host implementations. This was a major deficiency in the past. Correct operation, interworking, and performance are greatly improved by adherence to these RFCs, which are:

RFC 1122, Requirements for Internet Hosts—Communication Layers. This document deals with link layer, IP, and TCP issues.

RFC 1123, Requirements for Internet Hosts—Application and Support. This document covers remote login, file transfer, electronic mail, and various support services.

An RFC published in 1995 dealt with equally important issues relating to the operation of routers:

RFC 1812, Requirements for IP Version 4 Routers

Related Documents

A series of RFCs that do not contain protocol specifications also were published as a separate set of *For Your Information* (FYI) documents. For example, RFC 2196 is an FYI: *Site Security Handbook.*

Another series, the *Internet Engineering Notes* (IEN) contains a set of discussion papers written in the early years of Internet protocol development.

Information Resources

There are many World Wide Web servers and public file systems located at universities, research institutes, and commercial organizations attached to the Internet. These systems offer a wealth of networking information, such as copies of RFCs, papers discussing new algorithms, performance test results, source code for protocols network management tools, free software, and product information. Any Internet user who can operate a World Wide Web browser or perform file transfer can copy documents or code from these sites. Pointers to a number of key sources are included in later chapters. Sites of particular interest include:

The Internet Engineering Task Force:	*http://www.ietf.org/*
The RFC Editor:	*http://www.rfc-editor.org/*
The Internet Society:	*http://www.isoc.org/*
The Internet Assigned Numbers Authority:	*http://www.iana.org/*
The World Wide Web Consortium:	*http://www.w3.org/*

TCP/IP Architecture

Introduction

TCP/IP was designed for an environment that was quite unusual in the 1970s but now is the norm. The TCP/IP protocols had to connect equipment from different vendors. They had to be capable of running over different types of media and data links. They had to unite sets of networks into a single internetwork, all of whose users could access a set of generic services.

Furthermore, the academic, military, and government sponsors of TCP/IP wanted to be able to plug new networks into their internetworks without interruption of service to the rest of the network.

These requirements shaped the protocol architecture. The need for independence of media technology and plug-and-play network growth led to the decision to move data across an internetwork by chopping it into pieces and routing each piece as an independent unit.

The functions that guarantee reliable data transmission were placed into source and destination hosts. Because of this, router vendors could focus their efforts on improving performance and keeping up with new communications technologies.

As it happens, the TCP/IP protocols turned out to scale very well, running on systems ranging from mainframes to PCs. In fact, a useful subset that supports network management routinely is ported to "dumb" network devices such as bridges, multiplexers, and switches.

In this chapter, we present a very brief overview of the TCP/IP architecture.

Layering

In order to achieve a reliable exchange of data between computers, there are many separate procedures that must be carried out:

- Package the data
- Determine the path that the data will follow
- Transmit the data on a physical medium
- Regulate the rate of data transfer according to the available bandwidth and the capacity of the receiver to absorb data
- Assemble incoming data so that it is in sequence and there are no missing pieces

- Check incoming data for duplicated pieces
- Notify the sender of how much data has been received safely
- Deliver data to the right application
- Handle error or problem events

The result is that communications software is complicated! Following a layered model makes it easier to group related functions together and implement communications software in a modular manner.

The specific structure selected for the TCP/IP protocols was dictated by requirements that evolved in the academic and defense communities. IP does what is needed to glue different types of networks into an internetwork. TCP provides reliable data transfer.

Open Systems Interconnection

Open Systems Interconnection (OSI) was an international effort to create standards for computer communications and generic application services. OSI was an activity of the *International Organization for Standardization* (ISO), founded to promote trade and cooperative advances in science and technology. Standards promoting OSI are published as ISO documents.

The *OSI model* for computer communications became a standard part of any networking professional's education. It provided a framework for identifying where the functionality of various protocols fit into the overall scheme of things.

OSI protocols are used at some European sites, and the IETF has published a number of RFCs that deal with internetworking between TCP/IP and OSI environments. However, use of the OSI protocols is waning.

Figure 2.1 contrasts the TCP/IP and OSI layers. Let's take a brief look at what happens within each of the TCP/IP layers, starting from the bottom.[1]

---

[1]TCP/IP does not implement formal session and presentation layers.

Figure 2.1
TCP/IP and OSI
layers.

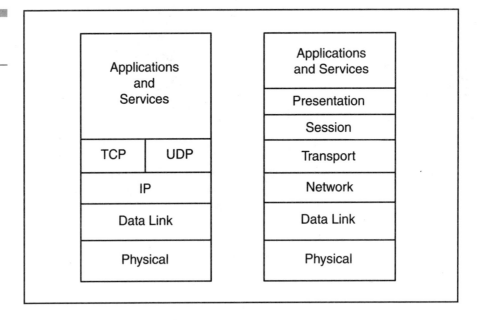

Physical Layer

The physical layer deals with everything required to place 0s and 1s on a medium—physical media, connectors, and the signals that represent the 0s and 1s. For example, Ethernet and Token-Ring network interface cards and cables implement physical layer functions.

Data Link Layer

Recall that a *link* is a local area network, a point-to-point line, or some other facility across which systems communicate by means of a data link layer protocol. At the data link layer, data is organized into units called *frames*. As shown in Figure 2.2, each frame has a header that includes address and control information and a trailer that is used for error detection.

For example, a Local Area Network (LAN) frame header contains source and destination "physical addresses" that identify the source and destination network interface cards on the LAN. The header for a frame that will be transmitted across a frame relay Wide Area Network (WAN) contains a circuit identifier in its address field.

Figure 2.2
Frame format.

Frames carry any type of protocol data across a link—NetWare IPX, Digital DECnet, IBM, SNA, and more. The data link layer is neutral territory. It is at layer 3, the network layer, that major differences between protocol families appear.

Links and their frames are described in Chapter 4.

Network Layer

The Internet Protocol performs network layer functions. IP routes data between systems. Data may traverse a single link or may be relayed across several links in an internetwork. Data is carried in units called *datagrams.*

As shown in Figure 2.3, a datagram has an IP header that contains layer 3 addressing information. Routers examine the destination address in the IP header in order to direct datagrams to their destinations.

The IP layer is called *connectionless* because every datagram is routed independently and IP does not guarantee reliable or in-sequence delivery of datagrams. IP routes its traffic without caring which application-to-application interaction a particular datagram belongs to.

Figure 2.3
IP datagram.

```
┌─────────────────┬────────────────────┐
│ IP  Header:     │                    │
│ Dest. IP Address│   I N F O R M A T I O N │
│ Source IP Address│                   │
└─────────────────┴────────────────────┘
```

IP runs on top of just about any kind of link—from gigabit Ethernet to ISDN[2] or POTS[3] dial-ups.

Transport Layer—TCP

The Transmission Control Protocol performs transport layer functions. TCP provides reliable data connection services to applications. TCP contains the mechanisms that guarantee that data is delivered error-free, without omissions and in sequence.

An application (such as file transfer) passes data to TCP. TCP adds a header, forming a unit that is called a *segment*.

TCP sends segments by passing them to IP, which routes them to the destination. TCP accepts incoming segments from IP, determines which application is the recipient, and passes data to that application in the order in which it was sent.

Transport Layer—UDP

An application sends a stand-alone message to another application by passing the message to the User Datagram Protocol (UDP). UDP adds a header, forming a unit called a *UDP Datagram* or *UDP message*.

UDP passes outgoing UDP messages to IP. UDP accepts incoming UDP messages from IP and determines which application is the recipient.

UDP is a "connectionless" communication service that often is used by simple database lookup applications. What we mean by the term "connectionless" is that no persistent session is set up. An application sends a stand-alone message at any time that it deems appropriate.

Packaging Data for Transmission

Figure 2.4 shows how application data is packaged for transmission. Starting from the top, an application produces some data to be transmitted. A series of headers is added before the information is placed onto a

---

[2]Integrated Services Digital Network.
[3]Plain Old Telephone Service.

Figure 2.4
Packaging data for
transmission.

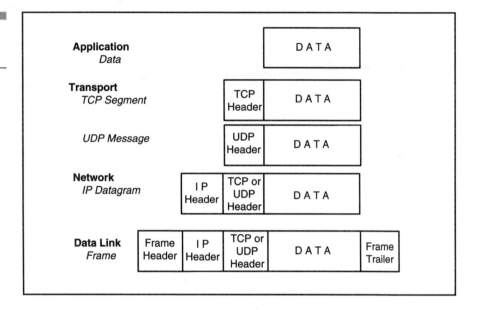

medium packaged in a frame. At the receiving end, an incoming frame is peeled, layer by layer. Each header is processed, and finally data are delivered to the destination application.

The generic term for information combined with an appropriate layer header is *Protocol Data Unit* (PDU). For example, a TCP segment is a transport layer PDU, and an IP datagram is a network layer PDU. Standards writers like formal terms like PDU. We will rarely use the term in this book.

TCP/IP Topology

The TCP/IP protocol suite can be used on stand-alone LANs and WANs or on complex internetworks created by gluing many networks together. Figure 2.5 illustrates stand-alone network links. Any hosts that are equipped with TCP/IP can communicate with one another across a LAN, point-to-point line, or wide area packet network.

Networks are joined into an internetwork by means of *IP routers*. Figure 2.6 shows an internetwork that was created by connecting the stand-alone networks together via IP routers.

Modern router products are equipped with multiple hardware interface

Figure 2.5
Stand-alone
networks.

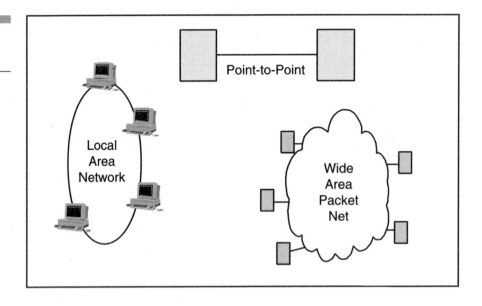

Figure 2.6
Gluing networks
together with
routers.

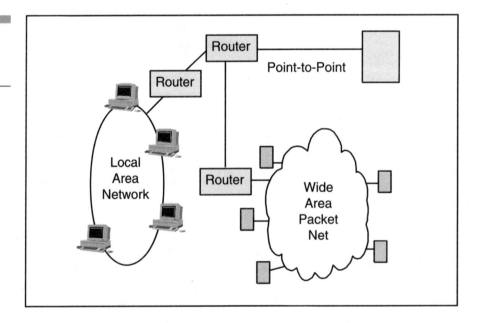

slots that can be configured with the combination of attachments that the customer needs: Ethernet, Token-Ring, Fiber Distributed Data Interface (FDDI), point-to-point synchronous, frame relay, ATM, or whatever.

Internetworks can be built up with arbitrarily messy topologies. However, when an internetwork has a coherent structure, it is easier for routers to do their job efficiently and to react quickly to a failure in some part of the network, altering paths so that datagrams avoid a trouble spot. An easy-to-understand logical design also helps network managers to diagnose, locate, and repair network faults.

The robust and competitive IP router market has helped to promote TCP/IP architecture. Router vendors are quick to implement new LAN and WAN technologies, widening their customers' connectivity options. The router price/performance ratio has decreased steadily over the past few years.

IP

IP software runs in hosts and in IP routers. If the destination for a datagram is not on the same link as the source host, IP in the host directs the datagram to a local router. If that router is not directly connected to the destination link, the datagram must be sent on to another router. This continues until the destination link is reached.

IP routes to remote locations by looking up the destination network in a routing table. A routing table entry identifies the next-hop router to which traffic should be relayed in order to reach a destination. Not all destinations need to be explicitly listed. An entry labeled "default" can point traffic toward a more powerful router that has more information, or toward a router that connects an organization to the Internet.

IP is described in Chapter 6. The closely related Internet Control Message Protocol (ICMP) is presented in Chapter 7. ICMP provides some error handling and query facilities associated with IP.

IP Version 6

The version of IP that runs in desktops and servers all over the world today is IP version 4 (IPv4). At the time that IPv4 was designed, no one could have dreamed that there would be millions (and someday billions) of networked computers in the world. IPv4 uses a skimpy address format that cannot meet the expanding needs of the Internet.

A new version of IP is needed in order to solve the address shortage problem. IP version 6 (IPv6) has been designed to do this—and to do many other things, for example:

- Build networks that automatically configure themselves.
- Support flows of data, such as audio and video.

At the time of writing, IP version 6 is still under construction, and is in a state of experimentation and change. Many parts of the TCP/IP suite must be modified in order to rebuild the protocol stack on top of IPv6. For example, applications must be rewritten to work with and display the new addresses.

Chapters 22 and 23 are devoted to IP version 6. Other IPv6 information is sprinkled through the book, wherever it is relevant.

Routing Protocols

In a small, static internetwork, routing tables can be entered and maintained manually. In larger internetworks, routers keep their tables up to date by exchanging information with one another. Routers can dynamically discover facts such as:

- A new network has been added to the internetwork.
- The path to a destination has been disrupted, and the destination cannot be reached at this time.
- A new router has been added to the internetwork. This router provides a shorter path to certain destinations.

There is no single required standard for router-to-router information exchange. An organization can use any protocol it wishes within its own boundaries. A routing information exchange protocol used within an internetwork is called an *Interior Gateway Protocol,* or IGP. The freedom to choose the most convenient protocol has stimulated competition and has led to great improvements in these protocols.

The *Routing Information Protocol* (RIP) is a popular standard Interior Gateway Protocol. RIP is popular because it is simple and widely available. However, the newer *Open Shortest Path First* (OSPF) protocol has a rich set of useful features.

Although all routers support one or more standard protocols, some router vendors also provide a proprietary protocol for router-to-router information exchange. For example, Cisco's Enhanced Interior Gateway Routing Protocol (EIGRP) is popular with its customers.

Routing protocols are described in Chapter 8.

TCP

TCP is implemented in hosts. The TCP entity at each end of a connection must ensure that the data delivered to its local application is:

- Accurate
- In sequence
- Complete
- Free of duplicates

The basic mechanism for doing this has been used since the dawn of data communications. The sending TCP:

- Numbers each segment
- Sets a timer
- Transmits the segment

The receiving TCP has to keep its partner informed of how much correct data has arrived by means of acknowledgments (ACKs). If an ACK for a segment does not arrive within a timeout period, TCP resends the segment. This strategy is called *retransmission with positive acknowledgment.*

TCP is described in Chapter 9, the longest chapter in this book.

UDP

UDP is implemented in hosts. UDP makes no promise of guaranteed delivery, and it is up to the peer applications to exchange information that confirms that data has arrived safely.

An application that wants to send data via UDP passes a block of data to UDP. UDP simply adds a header to the block and transmits it.

An application participating in UDP communications may send and receive UDP messages at any time. It is up to the clients and servers that are built on top of UDP to keep track of any relationship between the User Datagrams that are exchanged.

UDP also is described in Chapter 9.

Application Services

Implementations of TCP/IP are expected to provide several application services: terminal access, file transfer, electronic mail and remote printing always are supported. Most products also include World Wide Web clients and servers.

Terminal Access

In the early 1970s, most computer vendors built proprietary terminals that could be used only with their own computer systems. The U.S. Department of Defense (DOD) purchased systems from many different vendors but wanted every user to be able to connect to any host on their network from a single terminal. The *telnet* terminal access protocol was created to make this possible. *Telnet* terminal access was the first TCP/IP application. Over the years *telnet* has been enhanced to work with a large assortment of terminal displays and operating system types.

Telnet is described in Chapter 13.

File Transfer

File transfer was among the earliest services added to TCP/IP. The *File Transfer Protocol* (FTP) enables users to copy entire files from one system to another. FTP deals with simple types of files such as American National Standard Code for Information Interchange (ASCII) text or unstructured binary data. FTP also lets a user access a remote file system to perform housekeeping functions such as renaming files, deleting files, or creating new directories.

The File Transfer Protocol and a simplified Trivial File Transfer Protocol are described in Chapter 14.

Mail

Mail has attracted many end users to TCP/IP. Two aspects of mail are standardized:

- The format of the mail passed between users. There are formats for simple text and for multipart, multimedia messages.
- The mechanisms needed for direct or store-and-forward transfer of mail between hosts. The *Simple Mail Transfer Protocol* (SMTP) has been used to transmit mail since the earliest days of the Internet. Recent extensions have added new functionality.

Many proprietary mail systems have been linked to Internet mail, enlarging the community of potential mail partners. Electronic mail protocols are discussed in Chapter 16.

World Wide Web Service

The World Wide Web is the most versatile of all of the TCP/IP client/server applications. Users can view attractive documents enhanced by images and sounds, navigate effortlessly from site to site with the click of a mouse, and search huge archives of information.

Chapter 18 presents the component protocols used by World Wide Web clients and servers.

Additional Services

Other services have been added to the TCP/IP suite. The sections that follow describe those that are most popular and widely available.

File Access

File servers let users access remote files as if they are local. File servers first became popular in personal computer LAN environments as a means to share valuable disk resources and centralize maintenance and backup chores. Many TCP/IP products include the Network File System (NFS). The products support one or both of the NFS roles:

File access client. Lets a computer access remote files as if they are local. End users and local programs will be unaware of the actual location of these files.

File server. Maintains directories that can be accessed by specified computers on a network.

Clients usually access a file server located on their own LAN. A new version of NFS called WebNFS works well across wide area networks—including the Internet. NFS and WebNFS are discussed in Chapter 15.

News

The electronic news application started out as a way to support local bulletin board services and to exchange bulletin board information between sites.

Many organizations publish their own internal information or operate Internet bulletin boards using free TCP/IP news server software. Others access Internet news groups that discuss topics ranging from sports to plasma physics. A news client also can be used to retrieve news that comes from commercial wire services, such as Reuters, AP, and UPI. See Chapter 17 for a description of news internals.

Domain Name System Name Service

In order to use network services, you must be able to identify remote computers. Users and programs can identify computers by names that are easy to remember and easy to type.

To set up communication with a host, its name must be translated to a numeric IP address. In earlier times, each TCP/IP host kept a complete list of all of the names and addresses of all hosts on its network. It was impossible to keep these lists up to date on a dynamically growing network like the Internet, with its hundreds—then hundreds of thousands, and then millions—of hosts.

The *Domain Name System* (DNS) was invented to solve this problem. The Internet Domain Name System is a database of host names and addresses distributed across thousands of servers. DNS protocols enable a user to submit a query to a local server and receive a response that may have been obtained from a remote server.

In addition to translating between host names and addresses, DNS servers also provide information that is needed to route electronic mail to its destination. The Domain Name System is being expanded to hold information that will enhance the overall security of the TCP/IP network and application environment. The Domain Name System is introduced in Chapter 5 and studied in depth in Chapter 12.

Network Management

Over the years, many network management tools have been developed for use with the TCP/IP protocol suite. For example, there are commands that enable a network manager to see whether systems are active, view their current load, list logged-in users, and list services that are available.

These commands are very useful, but a lot more was needed to provide a consistent and comprehensive platform for centralized network management. The Internet community developed the *Simple Network Management Protocol* (SNMP) to manage everything from simple devices to host operating systems and application software. SNMP is described in Chapter 20.

Commercial Software

Many third-party vendors have built applications that run on top of TCP/IP. For example, database vendors link desktop clients to their servers by means of TCP/IP. New application servers designed to provide a robust environment for reliable business computing have appeared on the market. Application servers communicate with clients, peer application servers, and backend database servers using TCP/IP.

Host Client and Server Roles

Figure 2.7 illustrates interactions between hosts on a network. Note that TCP/IP truly is a peer-to-peer network architecture. Any host may act as a client, a server, or both.

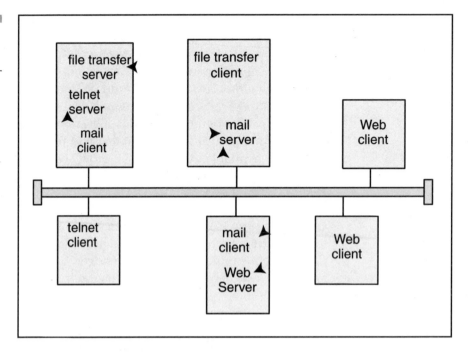

Figure 2.7
Application services
on a TCP/IP network.

Application Programming Interfaces

Operating systems that implement TCP/IP usually offer a communications programming interface for software developers. Most of these are based on the *socket programming interface,* first created for the Berkeley Unix operating systems.[4] The socket programming interface includes:

- Simple subroutines that create, transmit, and receive the stand-alone messages used in connectionless UDP communication

- Routines that set up TCP connections, send and receive data, and close the connection

- Routines that can be used to access IP directly, and send datagrams with any type of content.

---

[4]The Windows version of the socket programming interface is called WinSock.

Socket programming calls are described in Chapter 21, which also contains some sample programs.

There are many toolkits that simplify the development of distributed client/server applications by providing built-in communications software. They hide the detailed network calls and allow developers to concentrate on program logic. For example, database vendors offer tools for developing client/database server applications. There are two competing *Remote Procedure Call* (RPC) client/server programming interfaces that are widely available. RPC toolkits simplify communications and security programming. Object-oriented programming toolkits hide the details of remote object access.

The most successful tool is World Wide Web client and server software. Most new applications are being built around Web clients and servers. It is very easy to add or download a program or a script to a Web client, or to add application components to a Web server. In this case, the user interface, communications software, security, a rich client/server protocol (HTTP), and components that access backend data stores all are prepackaged. Additional prepackaged components are available and can be plugged in.

Protocol Components Overview

Figure 2.8 shows the relationship between common TCP/IP applications and the components of the TCP/IP protocol suite. The five applications at the top left—World Wide Web, electronic mail, file transfer, news, and telnet terminal access—are interactive client/server applications that run on top of TCP sessions.

End users are generally oblivious to the three applications on the right. The Network File System (NFS) makes remote files look as if they are located at the user's computer. In other words, NFS is a standardized file server. Client programs consult the Domain Name System (DNS) in order to translate server computer names to addresses; and Simple Network Management Protocol (SNMP) software in hosts, routers, and other network devices enables a network manager to extract information that is needed for capacity management and troubleshooting. NFS traditionally ran on top of UDP, but TCP use is on the rise today. The Domain Name System makes use of both UDP and TCP. UDP is the preferred protocol for the Simple Network Management Protocol, but it can run on top of anything.

Figure 2.8
TCP/IP protocol suite
components.

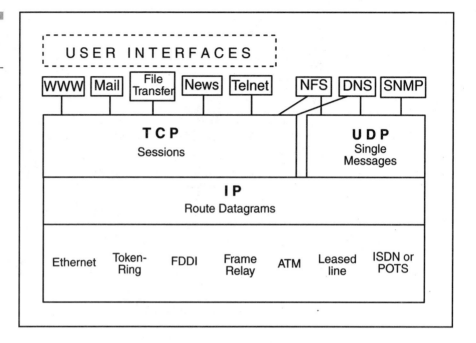

Client Programs

End users can choose from a rich array of products that offer graphical user interfaces for these applications. In a pinch, most systems provide simple, free built-in text-based clients for file transfer and terminal access.

Although these text-based user interfaces have not been formally standardized, all of them are based on Berkeley Software Distribution Unix end-user interfaces. Users who work in text command mode on two or more types of hosts find it very helpful that the user interface stays pretty much the same as they move from system to system.

Other Components of TCP/IP

Chapter 3 contains an overview of security technologies. Chapter 24 describes security capabilities that are being built into IP. Naming and addressing are dealt with in Chapter 5. Chapter 10 presents a series of protocols associated with multicasting. These relate to multicast clients, routing, and the RSVP reservation service. Chapter 11 describes the automatic configuration of TCP/IP systems via a BOOTP or DHCP server. Directories and the Lightweight Directory Access Protocol are discussed in Chapter 19.

CHAPTER **3**

Security Concepts

Introduction

TCP/IP has succeeded very well in opening up communications between computers on a LAN, across an organization's network, and even globally. But connectivity gives rise to new concerns about the security of information. The basic security issues in a networked environment are the same as those in a central host environment:

- Authenticating users
- Integrity—ensuring that data is not changed
- Confidentiality—preventing unwanted disclosure of information

TCP/IP has moved into the business world, and businesses have moved onto the Internet. Improved security has become a critical requirement. Fortunately the enabling technologies exist and are being integrated into the TCP/IP infrastructure. This chapter examines these technologies, and describes some of the ways in which they are used.

There are many acronyms that litter the road to security. We hope that the reader will not stumble over these, but will leap over them and focus on the concepts.

Message Digest Authentication

The most basic aspect of computer security is knowing who is who. In the past we have relied on usernames and passwords to identify interactive users. We have relied on the "From:" field in an electronic mail message to identify the sender. But eavesdroppers can capture passwords and electronic mail can be forged.

If we are going to conduct any serious transactions on our TCP/IP networks, we will need some way to identify originators reliably. Reliable identification is called *authentication.*

Many of the authentication mechanisms that currently are being adopted are based on calculations that are called *message digests, cryptographic checksums,* or *secure hash algorithms.* We will call them *message digests* in this chapter. As shown on the left side of Figure 3.1, a message digest is a calculation performed on a message. A message digest has some special characteristics:

- Altering even one bit of the data causes a big change in the answer.

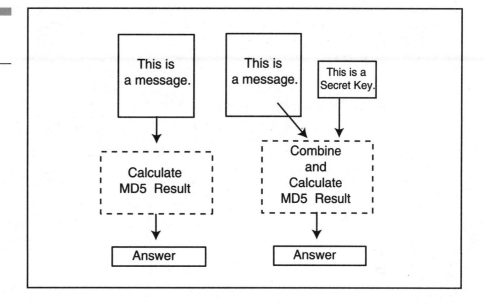

Figure 3.1
Using a message digest.

■ It is not feasible to engineer a message that produces a prespecified answer.

Two formulas are popular: Message Digest 5 (MD5), which was developed by Ronald Rivest of RSA Data Security, and the Secure Hash Algorithm (SHA-1), which was developed at the National Institute for Standards and Technology (NIST) and published as a federal information processing standard.

A message digest on data that has been combined with a secret password or secret key often is used in authentication procedures. The right side of Figure 3.1 illustrates this type of calculation.

During the past few years, data has been combined with a password in many different ways. Sometimes the password was concatenated at the beginning, sometimes at the beginning and end, and sometimes extra padding was added somewhere. Finally, a specific formulation was nailed down in RFC 2104. It was called Hashing for Message Authentication Code or HMAC.[1]

---

[1] The actual HMAC formula is H(Key XOR outer-padding, H(Key XOR inner-padding, data)), where H is a message digest. See RFC 2104 for a detailed description of how the HMAC calculation is performed.

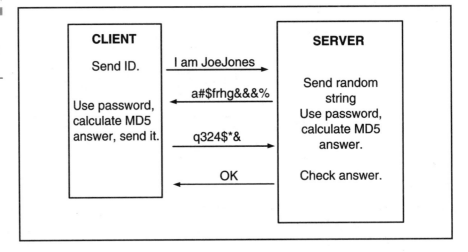

Figure 3.2
Using a message
digest in a challenge
handshake.

Challenge Handshake

A *challenge handshake* illustrates one way that message digests are used. Just as with conventional authentication, a user is given a password (or longer pass phrase) that is registered at a host. However, the password never will be sent across a network. Instead, the user's desktop system will perform a message digest calculation using the password as the secret key. As shown in Figure 3.2:

1. The user sends a username to a host.
2. The host sends a random message to the user.
3. The host and the user's desktop system both perform a message digest calculation on the random message combined with the user's secret password.
4. The user's system sends the answer to the host.
5. The host compares answers. If the user's system sent the right answer, the user is authenticated.

S/Key and One-Time Passwords

There are several variations on the basic challenge handshake authentication scheme. The Bellcore S/Key method that is outlined below provides extra protection; a user's password does not need to be stored at an authenticating host. As a result, a cracker who has broken into a host will not gain access to password information. The S/Key method is unusual; an authenticating host works its way backward through a series of responses that are created by applying a message digest calculation a large number of times. The outline below omits some of the protocol details, which can be found in RFC 1760.

Before S/Key can be used, an administrator has to decide how many times a user's password should be used before it must be changed. Let's suppose that a limit of 1,000 uses has been set:

1. The host combines a challenge phrase with the password and repeats a message digest calculation 1,001 times.

2. The host stores the result of the calculation, the challenge phrase, and a count of 1,000. The host discards the password.

3. The first time that the user connects, the host sends a challenge consisting of the challenge phrase and the count value, 1,000.

4. The user's client combines the challenge phrase with the password, applies the message digest 1,000 times, and sends the result.

5. The host applies the message digest to this result once and compares the result with the stored value (which was calculated with 1,001 repeats).

6. If the answer matches, the host discards the 1,001-repeat answer, stores the 1,000-repeat answer that it has received from the client, and decreases the count.

7. Every time the user connects, the host sends the challenge phrase and the current count.

Note that the authenticating host only needs to be initialized with the result of 1,001 message digest calculations. It does not really need to know the password at all. This is a very useful feature. An administrator can control a user's access to a set of servers by choosing a different challenge phrase for each server. The initial calculations for each server can be done at the administrator's system, and the various results can then be loaded into the servers.

The challenge handshake and S/Key are examples of *one-time password* authentication. This simply means that different authenticating data are exchanged every time the user accesses a host. A cracker who eavesdrops on a network will not learn anything helpful.

The Bellcore S/Key method has been refined and updated. The current version is called OTP (for One Time Password). One important change is that S/Key uses an older message digest, MD4, while OTP is designed so that an administrator can choose a message digest formula from several available selections. The OTP challenge identifies the message digest that is in use. This makes OTP easy to upgrade when superior message digest formulas are introduced.

Message Digests and Data Integrity

A message digest and a shared secret key also can be used to detect whether data has been changed in transit. Standard HMAC message-digest based data integrity verification is illustrated in Figure 3.3:

1. A message digest calculation is performed on the data combined with the secret key.

2. The data and the resulting message digest are sent to the partner.

3. The partner performs a message digest calculation on the data combined with the secret key.

4. The partner compares the answer with the enclosed message digest. If they match, the data has not been changed.

Note that without knowing the secret key, an attacker cannot forge or change data without detection. This mechanism is used for secure electronic mail and for client/server transactions that need to be protected.

Figure 3.3
Protecting message data using a message digest.

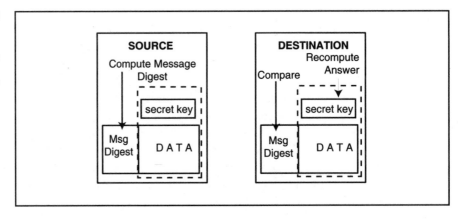

It is used with Secure Sockets Layer (SSL) security, which is described later in this chapter.

Confidentiality via Symmetric Encryption

To prevent snoopers from reading and using your data, the data must be encrypted. The classic way to do this is for the sender and receiver to agree on a secret key. The data is encrypted using this key before it is sent. Often a message digest is enclosed so that the receiver can check that the entire message is received exactly as it was sent. As shown in Figure 3.4, once the data has been encrypted, it looks like a string of gibberish.

This is the traditional *symmetric* method of encryption. Symmetric encryption uses the *same* key to encrypt and decrypt data. Both users must know the key and keep it secret. Disadvantages are:

- For safety, a separate key is needed for each pair of entities that communicate.

- Updating keys is difficult.

Figure 3.4
Symmetric
encryption.

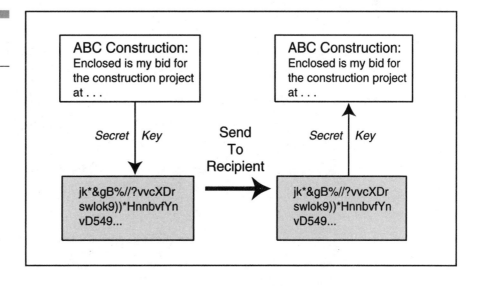

Figure 3.5
Using different keys
to lock and unlock.

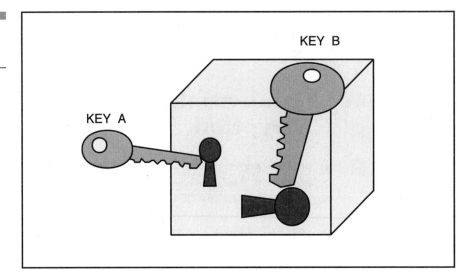

Asymmetric Public Key Encryption

In recent years, *asymmetric* encryption methods have been introduced. Asymmetric encryption uses *different* keys to encrypt and decrypt data.[2]

To understand this, suppose that you had a box with two different keys, A and B, as shown in Figure 3.5.

- If you lock the box using A, you must unlock it using B.
- If you lock the box using B, you must unlock it using A.

Asymmetric encryption also is called *Public Key* encryption because it enables you to manage your encryption keys in a very convenient way. Key A can be your *public key*. You can give it to your friends or print its value in a directory.

- All partners can use your public key to encrypt data sent to you.
- *No one else knows your private key, so no one else can decrypt the data that is sent to you.*[3]

Managing public/private keys is much easier than managing symmetric keys. But we need a reliable third party who will vouch for the fact that a

---

[2]The idea is due to Diffie, Hellman, and Merkle.

[3]The popular RSA public/private scheme that currently is in use is based on the fact that numbers that are the product of two large primes appear to be very difficult to factor. It took a worldwide team several months to factor a 129-digit number. However, computer speeds are increasing. Experts advise the use of keys that are at least 1024 bits in length for data that must remain secret for several years.

key published as "Jane Jones' Public Key" really belongs to Jane Jones, and not an impersonator. These third-party authenticators are called *Certification Authorities*. Certification Authorities are discussed later.

In actuality, private keys are not used to encrypt data. The asymmetrical encryption methods known today are very slow.

For this reason, a combined asymmetric/symmetric method is preferred.

Combined Encryption

Combined encryption works as follows:

1. A random symmetric key is chosen. This is called the *session key*.
2. Data is encrypted with this key.
3. Then the random key is encrypted using the recipient's public key and included in the message. (This is like putting the new random key inside a container that has been locked with the recipient's public key.)
4. The recipient uses its *private* key to decrypt the temporary random key and then uses the temporary key to decrypt the data.

As shown in Figure 3.6, the recipient's public key puts an impenetrable envelope around the random key. The recipient is the only one who can

Figure 3.6
Enclosing a key used to decrypt a message.

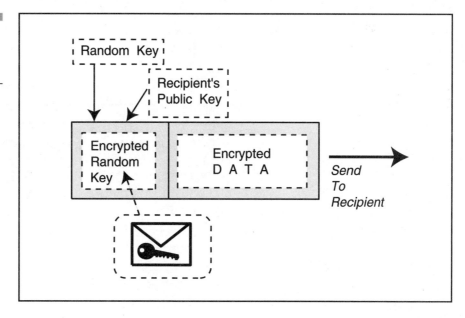

unlock this envelope. Using a public key to ship an encryption key to a recipient is an example of a *key exchange algorithm*.

Authenticating the Data and the Source

Combined encryption is an efficient method of ensuring that only the intended recipient will be able to decrypt and read the enclosed data. However, we have not authenticated the data—everyone knows the recipient's public key, so a cracker could substitute bogus data for the original message. Also, we have not authenticated the source of the data—we do not know who sent it. Both problems are solved using a message digest:

- The originator includes its identity in the data.
- The originator computes the message digest of the data.
- The originator uses its *private key* to encrypt the message digest of the data.
- The encrypted message digest is concatenated with the data and the result is encrypted with the session key (see Figure 3.7).

Figure 3.7
Authenticating with a
message digest.

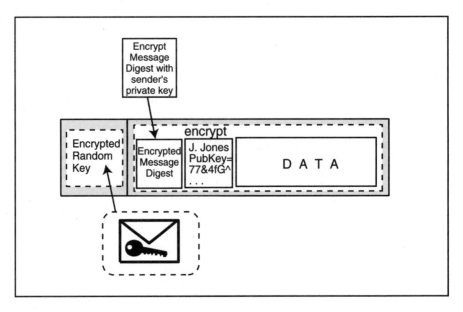

The authenticating information is called an *electronic signature* or *digital signature*. The important fact about a digital signature is that only one person in the whole world could have created it—the person who owns that specific public/private key pair. To verify a digital signature, the receiver:

1. Uses its private key to unwrap the session key.

2. Uses the session key to decrypt the overall message. The message has two parts: the encrypted message digest and the data.

3. Looks up the sender's public key and uses it to extract the message digest.

4. Recalculates the message digest and compares the result with the enclosed message digest.

When the receiver has unwrapped all of the pieces, the receiver knows:

- Only the owner of that public/private key pair could have sent this data.

- The data has not been altered.

The trend today is for each partner to use two public/private key pairs. One pair is used for digital signatures. (This is called a *signature* key pair.) The other pair is used to encrypt and decrypt session keys. (This is called a *key-exchange* key pair.)

Certification

How can you be sure that a public key really belongs to a specific person or business entity? Friends who meet with one another face-to-face can exchange their public keys on floppy disks. Bringing public keys into the world of impersonal electronic transactions requires more structure.

We need a trusted third party that can establish and vouch for identities. Use of a third party is common in business transactions. A credit card company establishes the identity of a cardholder before issuing a card. A business uses its bank as a reference when executing a major transaction.

The trusted third parties used in electronic transactions are called *Certificate Authorities* (CAs). Several companies, including Verisign, GTE, and IBM, offer CA services. Other Certificate Authorities include banks, credit card issuers, companies that certify their own employees, and other organizations.

A CA verifies an applicant's identity. It then creates a formatted certificate that contains information about the applicant, a unique serial number, and the applicant's public key.[4]<[FR 4]> The Certificate Authority then uses its own private key to create an electronic signature for the certificate. This electronic signature is attached to the certificate. This scheme works because CA public keys are widely advertised and well known. For example, the public keys of many CAs are bundled into Netscape and Microsoft browsers. As a result, they are stored on millions of desktops.

Applying Certificates

Certificates are used to:

- Validate signature and key-exchange public keys for Web servers, email servers, and other types of servers.
- Validate signature and key-exchange public keys associated with users.
- Authenticate the source of programs, Java applets, or ActiveX applets that you may wish to download to your computer.
- Identify parties engaged in electronic commerce transactions.

Key and Certificate Storage and Smart Cards

Today, private keys and certificates usually are stored on a hard disk in encrypted form. A user can back up personally owned keys and certificates onto a floppy disk. The disk must be locked away in a secure location.

Some organizations have advanced to a higher level of security. They issue smart cards that hold employee keys and certificates. An employee must insert the key-card into a card reader connected to a computer and enter a password that unlocks the card before connecting to the company network. Keys stored on a card tucked into a wallet are safer than keys on the hard disk of a computer that may have been left unguarded. A card also is convenient, because a user can plug a card reader into any computer and access the network from any location.

---

[4]Certificates have a format defined in an international standard called X.509.

Certificate Revocation Lists

A certificate indicates that a trusted third party has validated the identity of a key-pair owner. The owner might lose its keys or may turn out to be a dishonest person. It is important to be able to revoke certificates. A CA provides a directory of certified public keys as well as lists of revoked public keys.

An organization's network servers can protect themselves from inappropriate access by periodically obtaining revocation lists from a central directory.

Secure Web Transactions: SSL

The most important utilization of the mechanisms that have been described previously is the Secure Sockets Layer (SSL) protocol, which authenticates and encrypts information exchanged between an individual client and server. SSL was created by Netscape and later made available to other vendors. The IETF has taken responsibility for future versions of SSL.[5]

SSL originally was used for secure interactions between Web clients and Web servers, but also has been applied to file transfer, telnet, news, or other applications. Most commercial transactions that take place on the Internet today are protected by SSL. SSL enables servers and clients to:

- Exchange certified public keys
- Set up a session key
- Encrypt their data
- Authenticate their data using digital signatures

When you click on a link that starts a secure Web transaction, you will see *https* instead of *http* in the window at the top of your screen.

In SSL version 3, a server authenticates itself to the client and the client chooses a symmetric encryption key to be used to encrypt the data for the transaction. The server optionally can ask the client to authenti-

---

[5]The next version of SSL is called *Transport Layer Security* (TLS).

Figure 3.8
An SSL interaction.

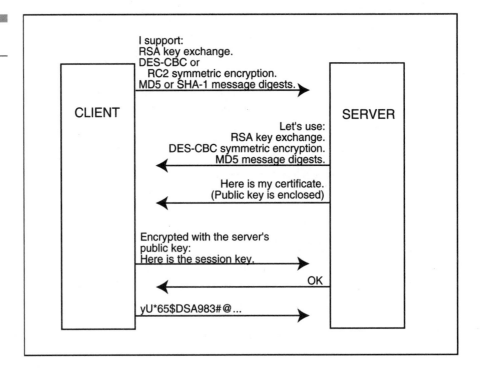

cate itself. In the dialog below (also, see Figure 3.8), a public key is used to encrypt a symmetric session key. The steps are:

- The client sends a "hello" announcing the cryptographic methods that it supports: one or more public key algorithms,[6] symmetric encryption algorithms, and types of message digests.

- The server responds, selecting a specific key exchange algorithm, symmetric key encryption method, and message digest algorithm from the lists presented by the client.

- The server sends its certified public key to the client.

- Optionally, the server can ask the client to provide a certificate.

- The client checks the server's certificate.

- The client generates a random key (the session key) to be used for symmetric encryption of the data.

---

[6]Currently, RSA public key encryption is the most commonly used method of sending a session key to a recipient.

- The client encrypts the symmetric key with the server's public key and sends the result to the server.
- The server acknowledges that it has received the session key and that the negotiation is complete.
- Data exchanged between the client and server is encrypted using the session key.

When you fill out a form at an Internet Web server, you either are warned that you are about to send data to an unauthenticated server, or else your browser indicates that it has successfully checked the server's certificate by displaying a security icon that indicates that a secure SSL session is in progress. An "https" introducing the current page location also indicates that a secure session is in progress.

Kerberos

The authentication methods that we discussed earlier were carried out by means of direct interaction between a client and a server. The Kerberos authentication technology, which was invented at the Massachusetts Institute of Technology, brings a third party—a Kerberos authentication server—into the picture.

A Kerberos security server is a trusted third party that performs secure "introductions" between users and servers. Users and servers that participate in Kerberos authentication are called "principals." Secret keys for all principals are stored at the Kerberos security server. These secret keys are used in an authentication procedure. They also are used to distribute random session keys to clients and servers. The session keys are used to encrypt the data passed between a user's computer and the servers accessed by the user.

Typically, a user initiates the Kerberos authentication procedure at the start of each workday. Kerberos supports strong central administrative control because a security administrator can cut a user off from all server access by removing the user's account from the security server.

In the standard version of Kerberos, a user's secret key is an ordinary password. Even though the password never is sent across the network, this leaves Kerberos open to password-guessing attacks. However, some implementations support an authentication procedure based on public/private keys. This adds considerable strength to Kerberos, but prevents a user from logging on to the network from any workstation other than one owned by the user.[7]

Kerberos provides the framework for a single sign-on, and this is a big benefit. A Kerberos security server can authenticate a user to any Kerberos-enabled (*Kerberized*) service. Kerberos came from the Internet community, and the first applications that were Kerberized were Internet standbys—NFS, telnet, file transfer, and mail server access via POP or IMAP. Kerberized access to a number of commercial applications has been made available without much fanfare. Another significant feature of Kerberos is that user access privileges can be set up and controlled centrally at the Kerberos Security server.

Kerberos security server products have gone through several versions, gaining stability and good administrative tools. The current IETF version, Kerberos 5, is a proposed standard.

How Kerberos Works

The steps involved in using Kerberos are described below. There are two stages:

- A client interacts with the Kerberos *Authentication Service* to obtain a "ticket" that will introduce the client to a Kerberos *Ticket Granting Service*.
- The client sends requests to the Kerberos Ticket Granting Service, asking for tickets that will enable the client to access specific servers.

A more complete scenario is sketched out below:

- A user logs into its local Kerberos client by entering a username and password. The client sends the username to the Authentication Service at the Kerberos security server. This is the only unencrypted information that passes between the client and Kerberos.
- The Kerberos Authentication Service sends back a block of information that has been encrypted with the user's password.[8] The

---

[7]This will change when keys are stored on portable smart cards and smart card readers are commonplace.

[8]Recall that the password is replaced with a signed certificate in some implementations. In this case, a public key could be used for the encryption.

user's client decrypts this block with the locally entered user password.

■ The block contains a randomly chosen session key, an expiration time, and a "ticket" that introduces the user to the Ticket Granting Service (TGS). This ticket has been encrypted with the Ticket Granting Service's password key, and cannot be read by the user. The ticket contains a copy of the session key, the expiration time, and credentials that identify the user.

■ When the client needs to communicate with a server, the client sends this encrypted ticket to the Ticket Granting Service. The TGS extracts the user authentication information and the session key. Now the client and the TGS are ready to have an encrypted conversation.

■ The client requests a new session key and ticket that will enable it to access a network server. The TGS sends back the ticket. Optionally, the ticket can contain client access privilege information. The ticket is encrypted so only the targeted server can read it.

■ The client saves all of its unexpired tickets in a secure local cache. The client can reuse tickets until they expire.

■ If the user is going to leave the workstation, the user logs out of Kerberos. All of the tickets will then be wiped out of the cache.

Each server ticket establishes a separate session key that is valid for a limited period of time and is used to encrypt data exchanged between the client and the server. Data integrity is protected by means of message digest calculations on the data combined with the session key. Kerberos uses symmetric encryption for all of its privacy operations.

Simple Authentication and Security Layer

We have seen that there are many different authentication and privacy procedures. Just a few of these include:

■ S/Key

■ OTP

■ Kerberos

Confronted with too many solutions and no clear rules on how to launch any of them, developers have been slow to add any security features to their applications. What has been missing is a protocol framework that:

- Enables a client to tell a server that it supports a security protocol and if so, which one.

- Enables a server to indicate whether it supports the method, and if it does, to continue the security interaction in a well-defined manner.[9]

The IETF has proposed a solution called the *Simple Authentication and Security Layer* or SASL, which is just a framework for the exchange of security information. The SASL specification (RFC 2222) lays down rules for security protocol designers to follow so that the exchange of security information starts out in a well-defined manner.

The protocol designers register their SASL methods with the Internet Assigned Numbers Authority (IANA), which assigns a unique identifier to each method. The SASL framework:

- Enables a client to identify one of the registered authentication mechanisms.

- Gets the conversation between the client and the server rolling.

Just to clarify the way this would work for a typical client/server interaction, the dialog below shows what the SASL version of S/Key looks like:

- The session is set up and the server sends a prompt showing that it is ready.

- The client sends a command that announces that it would like to authenticate using S/Key.

- The server responds accepting the method.

- The client sends a username.

- The server sends a challenge, which consists of a count and the challenge phrase.

- The client calculates the result based on the count, challenge phrase, and password, and sends it to the server.

- The server announces that the authentication was successful.

---

[9]This type of negotiation is not needed for SSL because a client announces that it wants to use SSL by connecting to a port that has been assigned to the SSL version of the application.

Security procedures that include encryption in addition to authentication also can be launched using SASL.

IP Security

The encryption and message digest mechanisms described earlier can be used to set up "secure tunnels" between sites. A router on the boundary of a site authenticates and encrypts every datagram that is addressed to a second site. A new IP header, containing the address of the router on the boundary of the destination site, is added to each datagram. Figure 3.9 shows two routers that are tunneling data across the Internet.

Up-to-date tunnel implementations are based on IP Security, which adds authentication and privacy to each individual IP datagram. Chapter 24 describes how IP Security works. IP Security is an option that is available for some implementations of IP version 4, and it is required for all implementations of IP version 6.

Figure 3.9
Tunneling between two sites.

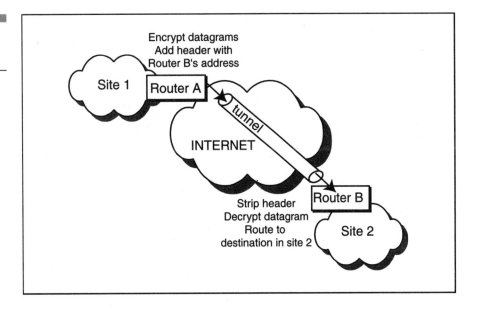

Firewalls

This chapter has focused on authentication, data integrity, and privacy. Later, in Chapter 6, we discuss firewalls, which protect sites (or individual hosts) by inspecting traffic and applying rules that determine whether it should be passed through the firewall or discarded.

Recommended Reading

RFC 2104 describes hashed message authentication codes (HMAC). RFC 2085 presents HMAC-MD5 authentication. RFC 2222 describes the Simple Authentication and Security Layer (SASL) framework for defining and registering security schemes. S/Key is described in RFC 1760 and the updated version, One-Time Password, is presented in RFC 2289.

SSL documentation is available from Netscape. The successor TLS specification was still in draft form at the time of writing.

RSA Data Security publishes an excellent free reference document called "Answers to Frequently Asked Questions About Today's Cryptography" at its Web site, *http://www.rsa.com/*.

CHAPTER 4

Physical and Data Link Technologies

Introduction

During the past few years, an unprecedented number of innovative LAN and WAN technologies have been introduced and quickly absorbed into the marketplace. The increase in twisted pair capacity and installation of fiber media have proceeded at a pace that no one could have predicted. Integrated Services Digital Network (ISDN), frame relay, T1, fractional T1, T3, SONET[1] fiber-optic lines, Switched Multimegabit Data Service (SMDS), cable connections, xDSL, and Asynchronous Transfer Mode (ATM) promise wide area connections that are faster and cheaper.

As each new technology has emerged, the Internet Engineering Task Force (IETF) has responded quickly, writing specifications for running IP—along with other protocols—over the new medium. Then, with almost no delay, router vendors have produced hardware interfaces and software drivers that have enabled users to take advantage of the new technology.

The efforts of the IETF can be seen in the long series of Request For Comment (RFC) documents with titles like:

> *The Point-to-Point Protocol (PPP) for the Transmission of Multiprotocol Datagrams over Point-to-Point Links*
>
> *Standard for the transmission of IP datagrams over IEEE 802 networks*
>
> *Transmission of IP and ARP over FDDI Networks*
>
> *Classical IP and ARP over ATM*

Physical, MAC, and Data Link Functions

This chapter describes how IP runs on top of various lower-layer technologies. Let's take a moment to recall what happens at these lower layers, which are represented in Figure 4.1.

The physical layer deals with everything that is required to impress 0s and 1s upon a medium. Physical layer standards describe cables, con-

---

[1]*Synchronous Optical Network,* a telephony standard for the transmission of information over fiber-optic channels.

Figure 4.1
Lower layer
functions.

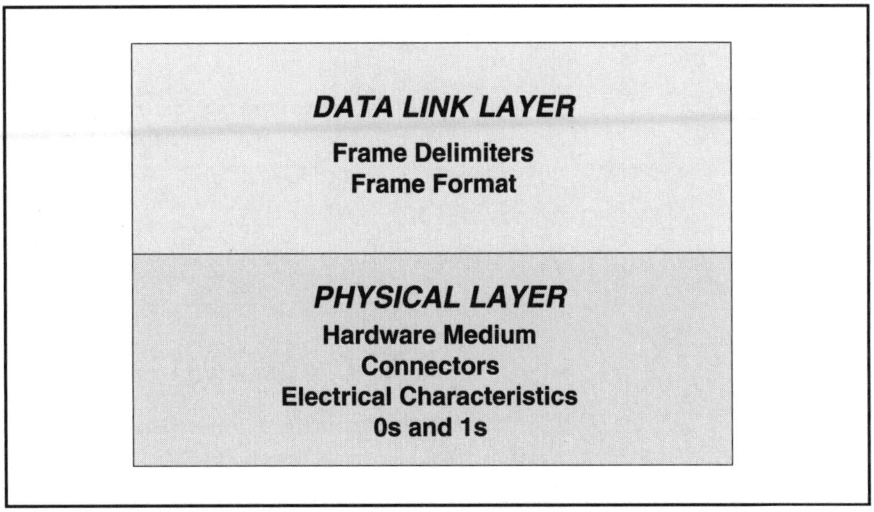

DATA LINK LAYER

Frame Delimiters
Frame Format

PHYSICAL LAYER

Hardware Medium
Connectors
Electrical Characteristics
0s and 1s

nectors, and electrical or optical components of a medium; they also describe how 0s and 1s will be represented and recognized on reception.

To enable us to make sense out of the data that we transmit, we package it into units called *frames*.[2] A frame carries information across a single link. To reach its final destination, an IP datagram may need to be carried across several links.

The description of a frame's format belongs to the data link layer. The frame format differs depending on the underlying technology used for the link (e.g., a T1 line, frame relay circuit, or an Ethernet LAN). Each frame has a header that provides the information needed to deliver the frame across a link. The format of the header depends on the technology used.

Network Technologies

Network technologies break down roughly into four categories:

1. Wide area point-to-point lines

2. LANs

3. Wide area packet delivery services

4. Cell switching services

---

[2]Note that some authors refer to these units as *packets*.

Figure 4.2
Multiple protocols
sharing a medium.

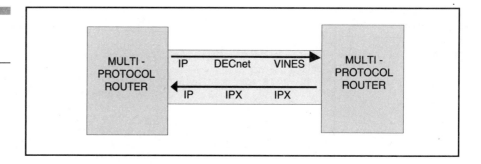

For each technology, we need mechanisms to:

- Identify the destination when a single interface leads to multiple systems (for example, for a LAN interface)
- Detect errors when the data becomes corrupted in transit

Today, both local and wide area media are *multiprotocol* environments. As shown in Figure 4.2, a link often is shared by several protocols such as TCP/IP, Novell IPX/SPX, DECnet, Vines—and even bridged traffic. Multiprotocol hosts and routers need a way to sort out the various types of traffic, so we also need a mechanism to:

- Identify the protocol type for the Protocol Data Unit (PDU) carried within each frame

Identifying a protocol type does not sound like it should be a difficult job. You just get a standards body to make a list of protocols, assign a number to each, and put that number into a field in the frame header.

And it is that easy—except that several standards bodies have done the job, and each uses different introducers for the fields and different numbers to identify the protocols. In this chapter, we describe the various formats used for the major transmission technologies.

Repackaging

You might start a business trip by taking a train to the airport, then flying between cities on a plane, and finally taking a bus to your destination. Each hop of the trip uses a different form of transportation, and each requires a separate ticket. After your train trip is over, the train ticket is useless—you throw it away. When your flight is complete, the boarding pass is useless and is discarded. And the bus ticket will not be good for any more rides, so it is not kept.

Figure 4.3
Repackaging
datagrams.

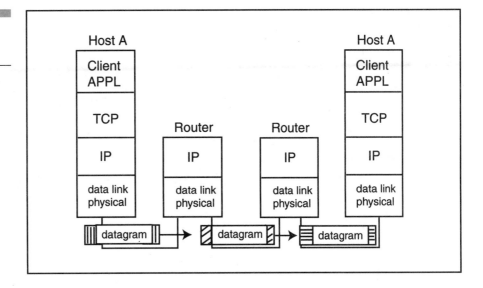

IP works the same way. Internet designers built IP so that datagrams could be relayed across a sequence of different links to reach their destination. Before a datagram is transmitted across a link, it is wrapped in frame packaging appropriate to the link. When a router receives a frame (see Figure 4.3):

- The router strips off the frame wrapping and extracts the datagram. The frame wrapping (the "ticket") is discarded.

- The router looks at the datagram's destination IP address and chooses the next-hop medium.

- The router then repackages the datagram in a new frame wrapping for its trip across the next link and transmits the datagram on its way.

Now we are ready to get down to the specifics. In the sections that follow, we discuss the way that data is packaged for the various types of network technology. We start off with point-to-point links.

Point-to-Point Protocols

IP datagrams can be sent across a point-to-point link between a pair of hosts, a pair of routers, or a host and a router. IP will transmit data-

Figure 4.4
Multiple clients and
servers sharing a link.

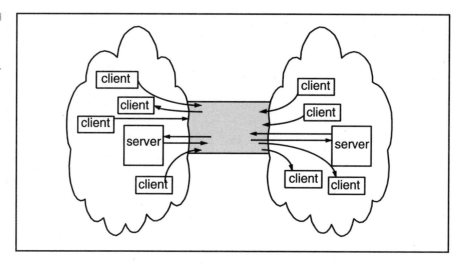

grams for many different TCP and UDP interactions across a single
point-to-point link.

IP does not know or care about the identities of source or destination
applications. Every time that IP is handed an outgoing datagram, it
transmits the datagram as soon as it can. As illustrated in Figure 4.4,
the traffic for many different client/server interactions shares a link—
just as riders who have many different destinations share a subway
ride.

Today, IP traffic is carried across point-to-point links packaged in several different ways:

- Using one of the conventional versions of the High-level Data
  Link Control (HDLC) point-to-point protocol
- Via the Internet standard Point-to-Point Protocol (PPP)
- Using the old Serial Line Interface Protocol (SLIP)

Little by little, implementations are migrating over to the Internet PPP
standard, which offers many advanced features.

HDLC

The *High-level Data Link Control* (HDLC) protocol, written in the
1960s, is an international standard for point-to-point links. HDLC sends

Figure 4.5
HDLC bit-stuffing.

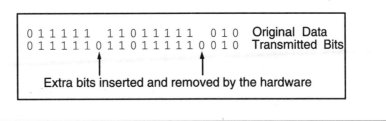

serial data as a clocked stream of bits, partitioned into frames. Every frame is delimited by the special *flag* pattern:

0 1 1 1 1 1 1 0

This flag pattern appears one or more times between frames. In order to recognize this pattern, it is necessary to prevent the flag pattern from appearing within the user's data. To accomplish this, after transmitting the opening flag, the sending hardware will insert a 0 after any five consecutive 1s in the data. This procedure is called *zero-bit insertion* or *bit-stuffing*.

At the receive end of the link, after recognizing the beginning of a frame, the receiving hardware will remove any zero which appears after five consecutive 1s within the frame.

Figure 4.5 shows some sample data before and after bit-stuffing is executed.

HDLC Frame Format

The HDLC protocol established a basic pattern that has influenced all subsequent frame formats. As shown in Figure 4.6, an HDLC information frame is made up of a header, some data, and, at the end, a trailer that contains a *Frame Check Sequence* (FCS). Flag bytes are used as delimiters at the beginning and end of the frame.

The frame check sequence is the result of a mathematical computation performed on the frame at its source.[3] The same computation is performed at the destination end of the link. If the answer does not agree

---

[3]The calculation itself is called a *Cyclic Redundancy Check* (CRC). Some authors call the value placed in the trailer the CRC instead of calling it the *frame check sequence*.

Figure 4.6
Format of an HDLC
frame, with flag
delimiters.

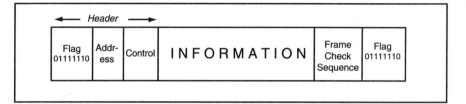

with the value in the FCS field, some bits of the frame have been altered in transmission, and so the frame is discarded.

The use of a frame check sequence to detect transmission errors was a very successful idea. We will see an FCS field in all but one of the WAN and LAN frames.

The HDLC frame header contains a *destination address* field. This field is needed for *multipoint* versions of HDLC (such as IBM's Synchronous Data Link Control, or SDLC) that enable many systems to share a single line. Each system is assigned an address, and traffic is directed to a system by putting its address in the header.

IP does not make use of multipoint line technology, and IP datagrams are carried in an HDLC frame whose address is set to the binary value 11111111 (X'FF in hexadecimal) which is known as the *All-Stations,* or broadcast, address.

The HDLC frame header also contains a *control* field. Some link protocols[4] put frame numbers and acknowledgment numbers into the control field. These link protocols retransmit numbered frames that are not acknowledged within a timeout period.

Frames that carry IP—and many other protocols (including IPX and DECnet)—do not require numbering and acknowledgment. For IP (and these other protocols), the control field is set to X'03, which identifies an HDLC *Unnumbered Information* frame.

Thus, an IP datagram wrapped in an HDLC frame has the format shown in Figure 4.7.

To summarize, when an HDLC frame carries an IP datagram:

- The All-Stations address, X'FF, is used.

- The control field is set to X'03, meaning unnumbered information.

---

[4]For example, IBM's SDLC and the X.25 Link Access Protocol Balanced (LAPB) link layer are based on HDLC and use the control field for numbering, acknowledgment, and retransmission at the link layer.

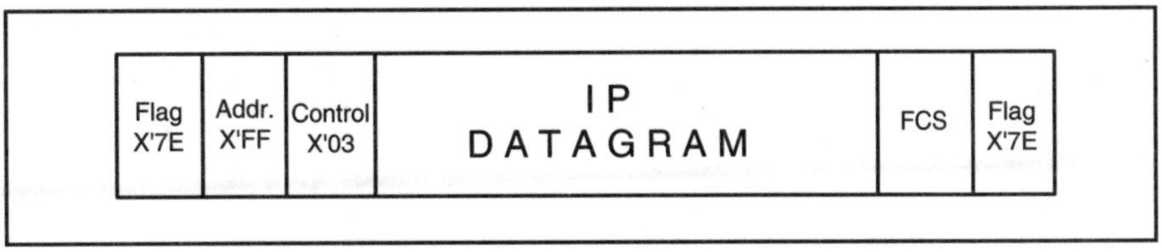

▬▬ ▬▬ ▬▬ ▬▬

Figure 4.7
Format of an HDLC
frame carrying an IP
datagram.

Flag X'7E	Addr. X'FF	Control X'03	I P DATAGRAM	FCS	Flag X'7E

Problems with HDLC

The fact that HDLC is a "standard" does *not* mean that you can run a point-to-point line between any two HDLC interfaces and expect them to communicate successfully with one another.

There are many options defined within the HDLC standard—and many different "standard" versions of HDLC have been implemented. Just to confuse things even more, many vendors have implemented their own versions of HDLC point-to-point interfaces.

As a result, for a long time there was no single standard for point-to-point communication, making it difficult to interwork equipment from different vendors.

HDLC was designed before the days of multiprotocol networking. Today, point-to-point lines often carry traffic for several protocols. This causes another problem, because the recipient of a frame needs to know the network protocol for the data that is carried in the frame.

An IETF committee was given the job of solving these problems.

The Internet Point-to-Point Protocol

The IETF working group's solution was the *Point-to-Point Protocol,* more frequently called *PPP.* PPP can be used over any full-duplex circuit—either synchronous bit-oriented or asynchronous (start/stop) byte-oriented. It can be used on slow dial-ups, fast leased lines, ISDN, or even on SONET fiber-optic lines. And PPP was designed to carry PDUs for many protocols—IP, IPX, DECnet, ISO, and others. PPP even carries bridged data.

PPP includes several subprotocols. For example:

■ The *Link Control Protocol* sets up, tests, configures, and closes down a link.

■ *Network Control Protocols* are used to initialize, configure, and terminate use of a particular network protocol. A separate Network Control Protocol is defined for each of IP, IPX, DECnet, ISO, and so forth.

A typical PPP scenario is:

1. An originating PPP sends a *Link Control* frame to start things going. The partners exchange additional Link Control frames to establish the options to be used for the link.

2. *Network Control Protocol* frames are exchanged to choose and configure the network layer protocols to be used.

3. Data for the selected protocols is sent across the link in PPP frames. Each frame includes a header field that identifies what type of protocol data is enclosed.

4. Network Control and Link Control Protocol frames are used to close the link down.

A PPP frame header looks like an HDLC header that contains one extra field which identifies the next-layer protocol. Figure 4.8 shows the format of a PPP frame containing an IP datagram. The address field contains X'FF ("all stations") and the control field contains X'03 ("unnumbered information"). The additional *protocol field* contains X'00-21, a value that indicates that the frame is carrying an IP datagram. Protocol numbers to be used with PPP are published by the Internet Assigned Numbers Authority (IANA).

PPP Compression

It may seem wasteful to include the same address and control bytes in every frame. In fact, the partners at each end of the PPP link can

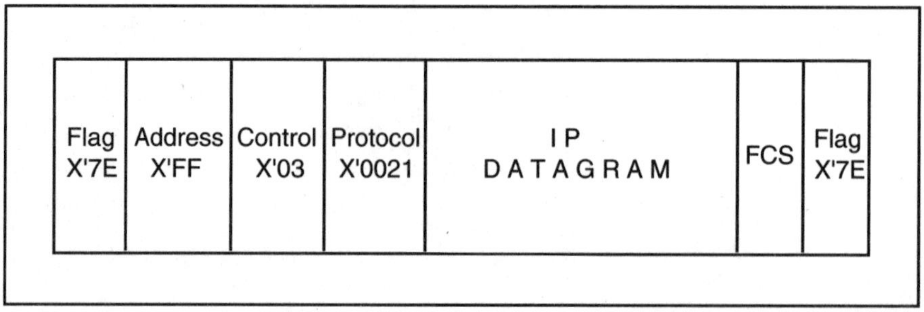

Figure 4.8
Format of a PPP frame carrying an IP datagram.

Flag X'7E	Address X'FF	Control X'03	Protocol X'0021	IP DATAGRAM	FCS	Flag X'7E

Figure 4.9
PPP frame with compressed format.

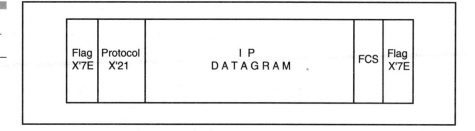

Flag X'7E	Protocol X'21	I P D A T A G R A M	FCS	Flag X'7E

negotiate to operate in a *compressed* mode that eliminates these fields.

The value in the protocol field indicates whether the information content is a Link Control message, a Network Control message, or information, such as an IP datagram. At PPP link setup time, the protocol field starts out as 2 bytes in length, but the size of the protocol field used when information is transferred can be negotiated down to 1 byte. Hence, a datagram can be wrapped in the efficient packaging shown in Figure 4.9.

Van Jacobson compression is another PPP option that saves transmission bytes for TCP sessions. IP and TCP headers together account for 40 or more bytes of overhead. Van Jacobson compression reduces a typical 40-byte combination to 3, 4, or 5 bytes, which is a significant saving.[5]

Additional PPP Capabilities

The PPP working group tackled some other problems that can arise when using a point-to-point link.

Authentication

PPP is popular for Internet dial-up service. PPP also is used to connect a telecommuting or traveling user to an IP network via a dial-up connection. PPP dial-ups sometimes are used to connect a small branch office workgroup LAN to a headquarters site.

---

[5]The way that this is done is that both partners save the initial headers. These are updated during the TCP session by sending only the changes to header values. Since most header information is static, the saving is substantial.

Before permitting an external system to connect to your network via a dial-up link, you might wish to authenticate that system! Currently, PPP supports two forms of authentication:

- The simple *Password Authentication Protocol* (PAP). A cleartext userid and password are packaged inside a frame sent across the link during the link setup procedure.
- The *Challenge Handshake Authentication Protocol* (CHAP).

The challenge handshake (which was described in Chapter 3) is quite clever. Recall, as shown in Figure 4.10, that:

1. A cleartext username is sent across the link.

2. The remote partner sends back a random challenge message.

3. The local system performs a message digest computation (using the challenge message and the user's password as inputs) and sends the answer back.

4. The remote partner looks up the password, does the same calculation, and compares the answers.

An eavesdropper will see different garbage bytes each time the link is set up. When a solid 16-byte password is used, it is virtually impossible to figure out the password by watching the link.

Figure 4.10
The PPP challenge handshake.

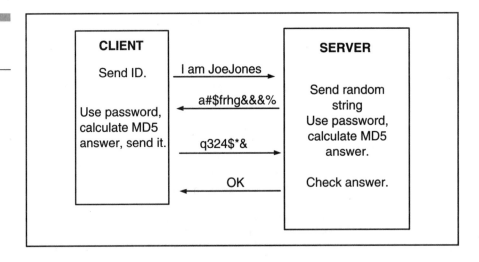

Automatic Link Quality Monitoring

PPP often is used between a pair of routers. Sometimes the quality of a link degrades for some reason. It would be helpful to have early warning of the condition of the link so that some action could be taken automatically. For example, a router could terminate a dial-up connection and redial. Or if the problem is occurring on a leased line, the router could send an alert to management personnel and possibly shunt traffic onto an alternative link temporarily.

PPP provides a very simple and effective way to check up on link quality. The link monitoring process simply counts the number of transmitted and received frames and bytes. (Incoming discards and errors also are counted.) Periodically, a report is sent to the peer at the other end of the link.

This information gives a good picture of what is happening on the link. For example, if I have sent 100,000 bytes during a time interval, but my partner reports that it has received only 50,000 of them successfully, something is very wrong with the link.

Serial Line Interface Protocol

The *Serial Line Interface Protocol* (SLIP) was invented before PPP was available and provides a rudimentary method for transmitting IP datagrams across a serial link.

SLIP is surely the most primitive protocol ever invented. An IP datagram simply is transmitted, byte by byte, on a serial line. SLIP marks the end of a datagram with the delimiter byte, 11000000 (X'C0). What happens when X'C0 appears inside a datagram? The transmitting SLIP uses escape sequences that the receiving SLIP translates back to the data that actually was sent:

C0 in data —> DB DC

DB in data —> DB DD

SLIP typically is used to connect a PC, Macintosh, or Unix computer to an IP network via a dial-up link. Note that SLIP provides no frame check sequence and leaves all error checking to higher layers. SLIP cannot carry any protocol other than IP.

Compressed SLIP (CSLIP) is an improved version of SLIP that com-

Figure 4.11
ASCII terminal and
SLIP connections.

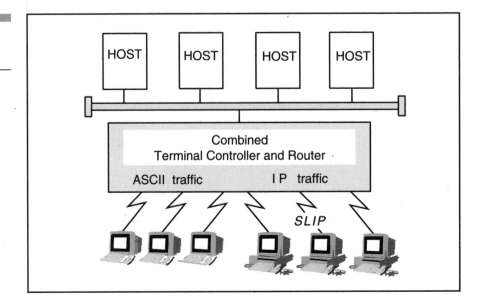

presses TCP/IP headers via the Van Jacobson algorithm. CSLIP provides much better link performance than SLIP.

SLIP can be used for host-to-host, host-to-router, or router-to-router
communications. Figure 4.11 shows a communications server that supports both "dumb" ASCII terminal dial-ins and SLIP dial-ups. The
device acts as an IP router for the SLIP traffic.

SLIP's most appealing feature is that it is widely available. Its most
annoying feature is that the workstation user needs to write a script
that will read prompts sent by the communications server and send a
userid, password, and other information at appropriate points in the
dialog. PPP is more functional, does not require scripts, and is rapidly
displacing SLIP.

Local Area Networks

Next, we examine how IP and other protocols are packaged in frames that
are sent across LANs. Classical LAN design includes several factors:

- Stations share a physical medium.
- There are *Media Access Control* (MAC) rules that determine
  when a station can transmit data.
- Data is carried in frames.

We look at the *Ethernet* technology first, since it provides a very simple example of a LAN implementation.

DIX Ethernet

Ethernet LANs were the first to carry IP datagrams. Digital Equipment Corporation (DEC), Intel Corporation, and Xerox Corporation defined the original *DIX* Ethernet specification in 1980. This was revised as version 2 in 1982, and sometimes is called Ethernet 2 or Ethernet II.

DIX Ethernet Media Choices

The traditional backbone medium for this technology was baseband coaxial cable. Originally, only a heavy half-inch 50-ohm cable was used. Later, a thinner, more flexible quarter-inch grade of coaxial, called *thinnet* or *cheapernet,* was introduced. Finally, most sites switched over to twisted pair wiring. A 10-megabit-per-second signaling rate was prevalent for quite a long time, but now speeds of 100 megabits per second are becoming commonplace, and gigabit speeds are available. Ethernet also runs on broadband and fiber-optic media.

To distinguish between the many different flavors of Ethernet implementations, the following type of notation is used:

```
[Data rate in megabits per second] [medium type] [maximum cable
segment in hundreds of meters]
```

Thus 10BASE5 means BASEband coax with a data rate of 10 megabits per second and a maximum cable segment length of 500 meters. The thin cable specification is 10BASE2, which means BASEband coax with a data rate of 10 megabits per second and a maximum cable segment size of 200 meters.

Similarly, 10BROAD36 is BROADband coaxial, 10 megabits per second, and a maximum cable segment length of 3600 meters.

The twisted pair and fiber specifications do not quite match the pattern. 10 megabits per second over twisted pair and fiber are identified as 10BASET and 10BASEF. At 100 megabits per second, there are serious differences between the lengths of cable runs for different types of cables:

- 100BASE-T4 is the implementation for category 3 unshielded twisted pair.

- 100BASE-TX is the implementation for category 5 unshielded or shielded twisted pair.

- 100BASE-FX multimode is a fiber-optic implementation.

- 100BASE-FX single mode is a fiber-optic implementation.

A station attaches to a transmission medium via a Network Interface Card (NIC).

DIX Ethernet Media Access Control Protocol

Traditional DIX Ethernet uses a very simple Media Access Control procedure with a long title: *Carrier Sense Multiple Access with Collision Detection* (CSMA/CD).

An interface with data to send wraps the data in a frame and listens to the medium. As shown in Figure 4.12, if the medium is available, the interface transmits.

The frame header contains the physical address of the destination interface. (The physical address also is called the MAC address or NIC address.) The system with that physical address absorbs the frame and processes it. If two or more stations transmit at the same time, they detect the collision, back off for a random amount of time, and try again.

LAN frames often are called MAC frames.

Figure 4.12
Ethernet media
access control.

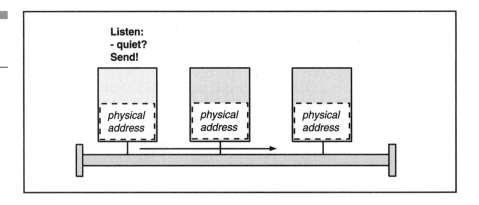

Figure 4.13
DIX Ethernet frame
carrying an IP
datagram.

Destination Physical Address (6 octets)	Source Physical Address (6 octets)	Protocol Type X'0800	IP DATAGRAM	FCS

DIX Ethernet Frame Format

The format of a DIX Ethernet frame that is carrying an IP datagram is shown in Figure 4.13.

The destination and source MAC addresses are 6 bytes long. The *Ethernet type* code, X'08-00, signals that the information content of this frame is an IP datagram.

There are Ethernet type codes that identify many other protocols.[6] The medium can be shared by several of these protocols because the Ethernet type code identifies the protocol for each frame, enabling the destination station to pass the frame's information to an appropriate procedure.

The display below shows a Windows NT monitor trace of a DIX Ethernet frame. The 6-byte source and destination addresses are shown in hexadecimal notation. The addresses are administered by the IEEE. A vendor that wishes to manufacture Ethernet interface cards obtains one or more 3-byte prefixes from the IEEE. The vendor is responsible for making sure that it assigns a different address to each if its interface cards. For example, the destination address below starts with 0020AF, which indicates that the card was manufactured by 3COM. The display states that the destination address is "Universally administered." This means that the address shown is the original address assigned by the vendor. An administrator can override the original address and assign a different one—for example, an address coded to show the building, floor, and wiring closet for this computer.

The destination address is described as an "Individual address." This is the address that identifies this interface uniquely. Later we will see that frames can be sent to a broadcast address that reaches every system on the LAN, or a multicast address[7] that reaches a group of systems.

---

[6]The IANA publishes a document that contains all Ethernet parameters.

[7]See Chapter 10.

```
ETHERNET: Destination address : 0020AF3BD450
       ETHERNET: .......0 = Individual address
       ETHERNET: ......0. = Universally administered address
+ ETHERNET: Source address : 00A024A6EDE4
       ETHERNET: Frame Length : 58 (0x003A)
ETHERNET: Ethernet Type : 0x0800 (IP: DOD Internet Protocol)
ETHERNET: Ethernet Data: Number of data bytes remaining = 44
(0 x 002C)
```

In order to operate correctly, the CSMA/CD protocol requires frames to be at least 64 bytes in length. Therefore, it is necessary to add padding after a very short datagram.

Frame Format for IPv6

The only change to the frame format of a DIX Ethernet frame when its payload is an IPv6 datagram is that the Ethernet type code must be set to X'86-DD.

802 Networks

After DIX Ethernet and other LAN technologies had proved their usefulness in the marketplace, the IEEE established the *802 committee*, which was given the task of designing and publishing standards for LAN technologies.

Standards in the 802 series have guided many vendor implementations. These standards have been republished by the International Standards Organization with ISO document numbers.

The 802 standards deal with physical media, media access controls, and frame formats for many types of LANs. For example:

- 802.3 describes a slightly modified version of Ethernet.
- 802.4 describes a broadband token-passing LAN that was designed for use in factories. It is now obsolete.
- 802.5 describes Token-Ring technology.
- 802.6 describes a Distributed Queue Dual Bus subnetwork of a Metropolitan Area Network (MAN). Parts of this protocol were adopted for the Switched Multimegabit Data Service (SMDS).

802.2 LLC Header

A separate IEEE 802.2 standard defines a *Logical Link Control* (LLC) header to be used with all 802 LAN technologies. The LLC header has two jobs:

■ For OSI frames, it identifies the source and destination protocols for the frame.

■ It includes a control field.

How are these fields used? The IEEE description involves a lot of formal language, but the purpose of each element is very simple.

The *Destination Service Access Point* (DSAP) and *Source Service Access Point* (SSAP) ISO codes define the destination and source protocol entities for the frame.

DSAP/SSAP values have been assigned to ISO protocols but not to IP or to a flock of other protocols that are in daily use. For IP and the other common protocols, the DSAP and SSAP are set to X'AA, meaning that another header follows that will tell you what kind of protocol data the frame is carrying. The additional header is called a *Subnetwork Access Protocol,* or *SNAP,* subheader.

What does the SNAP subheader contain? An introducer, followed by our old friend, the Ethernet type code. The introducer has a fancy title— *Organizationally Unique Identifier* (OUI). The OUI identifies who was responsible for assigning the protocol numbers.

The OUI introducer for Ethernet type codes is X'00-00-00 (see Figure 4.14). A separate OUI of X'00-80-C2 is used to introduce protocol numbers for various bridge protocols.

802.3 and 802.2

The 802.3 standard includes specifications for Ethernet media, the CSMA/CD Media Access Protocol, and a MAC frame format. According

Figure 4.14
802.3 frame with 802.2 LLC and SNAP subheader.

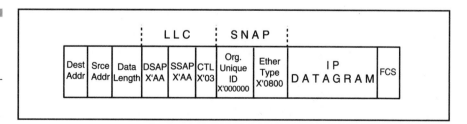

to 802 committee standards, an 802.2 header must be included within an 802.3 MAC frame.

Figure 4.14 shows the result of putting an IP datagram into an 802.3/802.2 frame.

- Note that unlike DIX Ethernet, the third field of the 802.3 frame header contains the *length* of the information that follows[8] (exclusive of padding) instead of an Ethernet type code. We see later that an IP header includes a datagram length field, so, for IP, this information is redundant.

- The DSAP and SSAP are set to X'AA, signaling that a SNAP subheader will follow.

- The control field is X'03, meaning unnumbered information—just as in HDLC.

- The X'00-00-00 introducer in the SNAP field indicates that an Ethernet type follows. The Ethernet type is X'08-00.

Other protocols such as IPX and DECnet have similar frames—you just insert the appropriate value for their Ethernet type.

Note that using 802.3/802.2 adds 8 bytes of overhead without adding any functionality for IP. For this reason, there are many implementations that still use the older DIX Ethernet format. Ethernet Network Interface Cards and their software drivers usually support both protocols—customers can select their preferred configuration.

People frequently use the term *Ethernet* indiscriminately for either the older DIX or newer IEEE 802.3/802.2 implementations. Sometimes it is important to know which you are talking about. A system configured to talk DIX usually cannot communicate with a system configured to talk 802.3/802.2.

Layering for 802 Networks

Let's spend a little more time exploring the IEEE view of the world. With the advent of 802 LANs, the IEEE divided layer 2, the link layer, into two sublayers, as shown in Figure 4.15.

The MAC sublayer provides the rules for accessing the medium—such as "listen and send" for 802.3 or "wait for the token" in 802.5. The

---

[8]The length includes the 8 bytes in the LLC and SNAP fields.

Figure 4.15
Layering for 802
LANs.

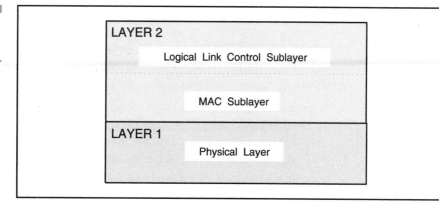

MAC layer also defines the first part of the frame header, which includes the destination and source physical (MAC) addresses.

The Logical Link Control sublayer defines the format of the LLC header. It also defines fairly complicated rules for communicating when frame numbering, acknowledgments, flow control, and retransmission are used at the data link level. A link that provides these capabilities is called a *Type 2* link. There are several protocols, including SDLC, LAPB, and LAPD that perform Type 2 communication across a LAN.

Of course, for IP datagrams, the only requirement is that the Logical Link sublayer should indicate that an IP datagram is enclosed in the frame. IP normally runs over a *Type 1* link protocol.

Other LAN Technologies

Token-Ring, token bus, and Fiber Distributed Data Interface (FDDI) LANs follow IEEE conventions and *must* include an 802.2 LLC header and SNAP subheader in order to carry IP and the other protocols identified via Ethernet type codes. There is no shortcut format for these LANs.

The same LLC and SNAP fields used in Figure 4.14, namely:

X'AA-AA-03-00-00-00 (*Ethernet type*)

are used to identify the enclosed protocol. The type X'08-00 identifies IP version 4 and X'86-DD identifies IP version 6.

802.5 Token-Ring Configuration and Media

Token-Ring LANs were introduced by IBM, and the IEEE later published a standardized version of the protocol as 802.5. Stations on a Token-Ring are configured as a physical ring.

802.5 Media Access Control Protocol

The idea behind token-based Media Access Control for Token-Rings is simple. A special frame called the *token* is passed from station to station, around the ring. When a station receives the token, it has the right to transmit data for a limited period of time. When that time expires, the token-holder must pass the token to the next station.

Although the basic idea is straightforward, a ring protocol needs many more mechanisms than Ethernet does. In particular, the MAC layer protocol for 802.5 includes procedures for joining or leaving the Token-Ring, identifying neighbors, detecting a dead station or lost token, preventing data from cycling forever, and signaling problems. There are different MAC layer headers defined for the various special 802.5 functions. The protocol type of a frame that carries data is identified via LLC and SNAP headers, which follow the Token-Ring Routing Information Field.

802.4 Token Bus

The 802.4 standard described a broadband coaxial-based bus LAN that used token-passing to control access to the medium. 802.4 was part of the *Manufacturing Automation Protocol* suite, which was devised for use in industrial facilities. Signals on a broadband coaxial medium are not disrupted by the electronic emissions common in a factory environment. The use of a token-passing protocol provided predictable scheduling of LAN access. However, 802.4 never attained widespread use.

Fiber Distributed Data Interface

FDDI 100-megabit-per-second LANs frequently are used as backbone networks, interconnecting slower local area networks.

- FDDI primarily is intended for use with fiber-optic cable, although twisted pair cables also can be part of the network.

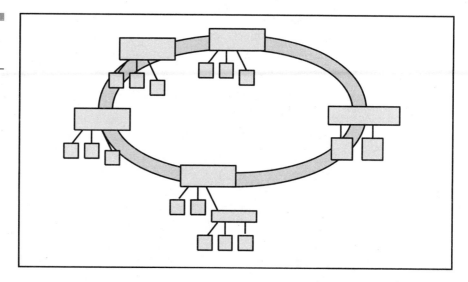

Figure 4.16
Topology of an FDDI network.

■ As shown in Figure 4.16, the core of an FDDI network consists of a single or double ring called the *trunk*. Stations can connect directly to the trunk or to concentrators attached to the trunk. Optionally, tree-shaped networks can sprout from concentrators on the trunk.

■ When the trunk is a dual ring, the LAN can be set up to recover from a break in the cable. Normally, traffic circulates on one ring. If there is a failure, the second ring is used to shunt traffic around the fault and keep the network running.

FDDI media access is based on token-passing. In fact, the MAC protocol is modeled closely on the 802.5 Token-Ring.

An FDDI frame has a MAC header and trailer and, when used to carry IP, uses the same 802.2 LLC and SNAP headers that were described earlier to identify the fact that a frame contains an IP datagram.

Use of Hubs

Ethernets, Token-Rings, and FDDI LANs started out with very different cabling topologies, but over time, most organizations chose to connect their systems to centralized hubs via twisted pair or fiber-optic cable. Hubs simplified LAN administration and repair. Thus the actual physical topology of the various types of LANs has been converging to a single physical topology—a star or a chain of stars.

Switching

All of the LAN technologies that we have been discussing have one feature in common—a frame sent across the LAN can be "heard" by any station on the LAN. Although the rules say that a frame should be accepted only by an interface with a particular physical address, a system owner often has the power to set a computer's network interface to a promiscuous mode that captures all of the data that appears on the LAN segment.

A desire for improved performance as well as concerns about security have led to the introduction of frame switching.

LAN Switches

Inexpensive Ethernet switches are taking the place of the traditional shared-media LANs. A station attached to a switch hears only its own traffic, and does not have to contend with other stations for access to the medium—it owns the full bandwidth. In fact, 10-megabit, 100-mebabit, or gigabit connections to a switch can be used in full-duplex mode, so that systems can send and receive at the full bandwidth rate simultaneously. The classical Ethernet frame formats have been maintained through all of these speed and technology changes.

Although Ethernet switches predominate, Token-Ring, FDDI, and multiprotocol switches are available.

Broadcasting and Multicasting

A multiaccess LAN technology supports broadcasting. An all-1s destination physical address is used to indicate that every interface attached to a LAN should absorb a frame. The hexadecimal representation of a broadcast address may be written as:

X'FF-FF-FF-FF-FF-FF

An interface also can be configured to absorb frames sent to one or more physical *multicast* addresses. Multicasting allows frames to be sent to a group of systems.

There are lots of multicast addresses—in fact, half of the LAN addresses are multicast addresses. There is a "multicast bit" in the low-order bit of the first address byte—that is, in position:

X'01-00-00-00-00-00

If the value of the multicast bit is 1, then the address is a multicast address. The other bits will be set to values that have been picked for some multicast-based service.

The Internet Assigned Numbers Authority maintains a list of reserved multicast physical addresses. For example, the block of addresses in the range from 01-00-5E-00-00-00 to 01-00-5E-7F-FF-FF has been set aside for Internet multicasts. Other individual addresses have been reserved by vendors for use by their network devices. For example, a multicast address is used to send a message to every bridge on an Ethernet LAN. In Chapter 10, we see how layer 3 multicasts across an IP network get mapped onto layer 2 LAN multicasts.

The term *unicast address* is used to distinguish a unique physical address assigned to a single interface from broadcast and multicast addresses. If a frame header contains a unicast address, the frame is supposed to be delivered to one specific interface.

Now it is time to leave LANs and look at several special wide area technologies.

Packet Networks

The packet-switching technology that was introduced in the experimental ARPANET has been reshaped and used in many types of data communications facilities. X.25 packet networks gained wide use in the 1980s. More recently, many users have adopted the newer frame relay packet-switching technology, which provides a wide range of bandwidth options.

X.25 Networks

Our telephone network lets any telephone instrument place a call to any other phone in the world. There is an international standards organization that is responsible for uniting national telephone networks into a global network. For a long time, this organization was called the *International Telegraph and Telephone Consultative Committee,* or *CCITT.* The name has since been changed to the *Telecommunication Standardization Sector of the International Telecommunications Union,* or, more simply, *ITU-T.*

During the 1970s, the CCITT started work on a set of recommendations intended to create a global *data* network. These recommendations reached maturity during the 1980s. The most important of these is *X.25,* which lays down the rules for connecting a computer to a data network. More specifically, X.25 defines the interface between a computer (called *data terminal equipment,* or *DTE*) and a network communications element (*data circuit-terminating equipment,* or *DCE*) that is part of a private or service provider data network.

X.25 sets up reliable data circuits between computers. These are called *virtual circuits* because, unlike the phone system, a fixed path for the exclusive use of the call is *not* reserved throughout a call. Real links are shared by many concurrent virtual circuits. However, the link sharing that takes place is invisible to the users of the circuits.

X.25 is popular worldwide, and there are many public X.25 data networks connecting computers around the globe.

X.25 data networks offer two types of circuits. *Switched virtual circuits* are data calls that are set up just like a phone call. Participating computers are assigned numbers.[9] A caller enters the number of the computer to be reached, and the call is put through. Alternatively, a customer may acquire *permanent virtual circuits* that behave like dedicated leased lines.

The CCITT recommendations do not place constraints on the *internal* structure of a regional X.25 data network. However, many X.25 data networks use an internal packet-switching technology. Packet switches can choose paths dynamically according to current network conditions.

X.25 Layering

X.25 is a three-layer protocol. Its link layer is called *Link Access Protocol Balanced* (LAPB), and its network layer is called the *X.25 Packet*

---

[9]The 14-digit numbers used in X.25 calls are described in CCITT recommendation X.121.

Level. User premise DTE equipment sets up a link to an X.25 provider's DCE. This link is used to carry data for *multiple* layer 3 virtual circuits. A switched virtual circuit is initiated by sending a *Call Request* packet.

X.25 and IP

X.25 is one of the many wide area technologies used to transport IP datagrams. IP uses an X.25 virtual circuit in the same way that it uses a telephony point-to-point line. That is, IP traffic exchanged by hosts or routers is carried across an X.25 virtual circuit.

The X.25 link (layer 2) and packet (layer 3) protocols go to a lot of trouble to make sure that data are transmitted in order and free of errors. An X.25 circuit is intended to provide a reliable end-to-end data connection.

It might seem rather strange to run an unreliable IP datagram service on top of a hard-working protocol like X.25. It may seem even stranger when one realizes that both X.25 and IP provide layer 3 protocols. However, considerations of cost or convenience always override purity of layering. Layer 3 protocol units for VINES, DECnet, and Systems Network Architecture (SNA) also can be carried on X.25 circuits. Even layer 2 bridged frames sometimes are carried on an X.25 circuit.

Figure 4.17 illustrates how IP traffic from multiple sources is routed across a single X.25 virtual circuit and forwarded to multiple destinations.

Figure 4.17
Using an X.25 network to carry IP datagrams.

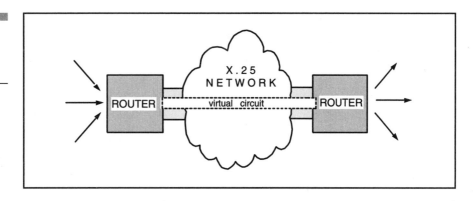

Multiprotocol over X.25

There are two methods of carrying multiprotocol traffic across an X.25[10] network:

1. Set up a *separate* virtual circuit for each protocol. During call setup, notify the partner of the protocol that will be carried.

2. Set up a *single* virtual circuit that is shared by several protocols. During call setup, indicate that multiple protocols will appear. Notify the partner of the protocol carried in each packet by adding a header to each packet.[11]

The method that is selected depends on how much the service provider charges for additional circuits and on how long it takes to set up a new circuit.

Depending on the economics of the situation, a system may set up a switched X.25 connection on demand, when there is some traffic waiting to be forwarded to a remote site. The call will be closed after a period of inactivity. Call setup sometimes is a very slow process, which makes multiprotocol use of the circuit more attractive.

IP on a Separate X.25 Virtual Circuit

If IP traffic exclusively will be carried on a separate switched virtual circuit, this fact is indicated in the X.25 *Call Request* packet that initiates the circuit. There is an optional *Call User Data* field in the X.25 Call Request, and this is set to X'CC to indicate that IP traffic will be carried.

The value X'CC is a *Network Layer Protocol ID* (NLPID) that was assigned to IP traffic by the International Standards Organization.

Other Protocol on a Separate X.25 Virtual Circuit

A few other protocols have been assigned NLPID codes by ISO, but proprietary commercial protocols do not have ISO codes. However, as we

---

[10]The same methods and formats are used for ISDN in the packet mode.

[11]The X.25 community calls its layer 3 protocol data unit a *packet*.

have seen, many commercial protocols were assigned 2-byte type codes for the first multiprotocol environment—Ethernet. For example, AppleTalk traffic has Ethernet type code X'80-9B.

To run a single protocol that has an assigned Ethernet type code across a virtual circuit, the NLPID code X'80, followed by the SNAP subheader for the Ethernet type, is sent in the Call User Data field in the X.25 Call Request. For example, to set up a virtual circuit for AppleTalk traffic, send:

X'80-00-00-00-80-9B

Multiprotocol on a Virtual Circuit

If a virtual circuit will carry multiple protocols, the Call User Data field is set to X'00, and an extra header is placed in *each* packet in order to identify the protocol type for its contents. IP datagrams are identified quite efficiently by using the IP NLPID identifier, X'CC, as this extra header.

For protocols that must be identified by an Ethernet type code, the message header starts with an NLPID value of X'80 that indicates that a SNAP subheader follows. For example, *each* AppleTalk PDU on a multiprotocol circuit would be preceded by the header:

X' 80-00-00-00-80-9B

Packets Versus Protocol Data Units

There is one small complication in the way that X.25 transfers information. Some X.25 networks transmit very small packets. However, they transmit entire higher-layer PDUs (such as IP datagrams) by sending them as contiguous *packet sequences* which are put back together into a single PDU at the other end of the circuit.[12] The protocol identifier is needed only in the header of the first X.25 packet of the sequence.

---

[12]A "more/nomore" flag is used to signal where a packet sequence ends.

Frame Relay

X.25 networks provide reliable, in-sequence transmission of data. There is a great deal of overhead involved in assuring the level of quality offered by X.25. When IP traffic is streamed across an X.25 virtual circuit, much of the X.25 overhead is wasted effort.

The frame relay technology is better suited to TCP/IP use. Frame relay is a layer 2 protocol. When using frame relay, only a simple link layer frame header and error checking trailer are added to an IP datagram.

X.25 saves messages until they are acknowledged and retransmits if an Acknowledgment (ACK) is not received. Unlike X.25, frame relay does *not* save messages, it does *not* wait for ACKs, and it does *not* retransmit data. This results in the efficient use of the bandwidth that is available.

The initial frame relay standard defined service only for *permanent* virtual circuits. This meant that a user would contract with a service provider to obtain connectivity to prespecified sites at a set of agreed bandwidths. Many service providers offer bandwidths up to the T1 (1.544 megabits per second) rate.[13] Generally, a customer pays a fixed monthly fee based on a preagreed bandwidth.

Switched frame relay service enables systems that have been assigned global addresses to set circuits up dynamically—in much the same way that you would set up a switched telephone call. Supporting a switched service is more of a challenge because it is hard to predict how much traffic users will present to the service at any given time, and networks may occasionally be flooded with sudden bursts of traffic.

Frame relay offers good performance when compared to X.25 and has been very well received. Some organizations have bought their own frame relay equipment and have built private networks.

Frame Relay Frames

As was done for the protocols discussed earlier, an IETF committee has specified the format that allows multiprotocol routed and bridged traffic to share a frame relay circuit. The encapsulation for an IP datagram is shown in Figure 4.18.

---

[13]E1 rates of 2.048 megabit per second rates are supported at many locations outside of North America and Japan.

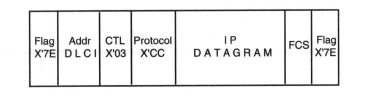

Figure 4.18
Frame relay encapsu-
lation for an IP
datagram.

A frame relay address field usually is 2 bytes long and includes a 10-bit *Data Link Connection Identifier* (DLCI) that identifies a specific circuit. A few bits in the address field are used to signal congestion and to indicate whether this frame should be given preferential treatment when frames are discarded due to congestion. (If a service provider needs more addresses, the address field can be extended to 3 or 4 bytes.)

The control field is X'03, to denote unnumbered information. The protocol identifier X'CC indicates that this frame contains an IP datagram.

The frame is transmitted across the Service Provider's network. Frames whose frame check sequence values reveal that data has been corrupted are discarded.

For protocols (such as AppleTalk) that must be identified by an Ethernet type code, the message header has the format shown in the example in Figure 4.19. To improve the alignment of the message, an X'00 pad byte is inserted after the control field. The Network Layer Protocol ID value of X'80 indicates that a SNAP subheader follows. In this example, the SNAP subheader contains the Ethernet type code for AppleTalk.

Except for the pad byte, the header that is inserted is identical to the one used for multiprotocol X.25 circuits.

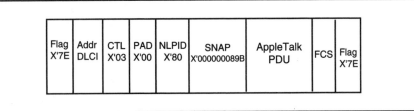

Figure 4.19
Frame relay header
with an Ethernet type
code.

SMDS

The *Switched Multimegabit Data Service* (SMDS) is yet another public packet-switched data service. It was designed by the Regional Bell Operating Companies. The purpose of the service is to offer a large range of wide area bandwidth choices, including very high bandwidth options (e.g., 155 megabits per second).

An interesting characteristic of SMDS is that data can be sent without opening a virtual circuit—it supports *connectionless* operation. In fact, a logical IP subnetwork can be constructed using wide area facilities, and (as shown in Figure 4.20) this logical wide area subnetwork will behave very much like a high-speed LAN. This makes SMDS an interesting option for a wide area backbone.

The official *SMDS Interface Protocol* (SIP) is based on an IEEE standard, 802.6.

IP over SMDS

Figure 4.21 shows the format of the header inserted after the SMDS SIP header, to signal the fact that the frame contains an IP datagram.

The format is identical to that used for IEEE 802 LANs. The first 3 bytes are an IEEE 802.2 LLC header, and the SNAP subheader contains X'08-00, the Ethernet type code for IP.

Figure 4.20
SMDS wide area backbone.

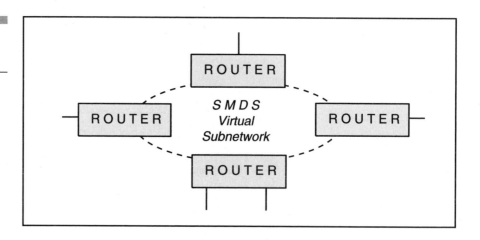

Figure 4.21
LLC and SNAP used
to identify IP carried
by SMDS.

SIP Header	DSAP X'AA	SSAP X'AA	CTL X'03	Org. Unique ID X'000000	Ether Type X'0800	IP DATAGRAM

LLC : SNAP

Asynchronous Transfer Mode

Asynchronous Transfer Mode (ATM) is a cell-switching technology suitable for use in both WANs and LANs. ATM combines the security benefits of switching with high performance and flexible choices of bandwidth. Characteristics of the technology include:

- ATM data is switched in 53-byte cells.
- Each cell contains a 5-byte header that includes cell routing information.
- Frames are split into cells at the source and combined back into frames at the destination by the *ATM Adaptation Layer* (AAL).
- There are several AAL frame formats, but the one that is relevant for IP datagram transmission is AAL5.
- The job of segmenting and reassembling frames for wide area transmission is done by a Data Exchange Interface (DXI), a piece of equipment analogous to a telephone line digital interface.

Like X.25 and frame relay, ATM communication is carried out by setting up a virtual circuit and sending frames across that circuit.

There are two methods of carrying multiprotocol traffic across an ATM network:

- Set up a separate virtual circuit for each protocol.
- Set up a single virtual circuit shared by several protocols.

The method chosen will depend on cost factors and the speed with which circuits can be set up and taken down.

If a separate virtual circuit is used for each protocol, just as for X.25, the protocol type for a switched circuit will be announced in a call request message.

Figure 4.22
LLC and SNAP used
to identify IP carried
by ATM AAL.

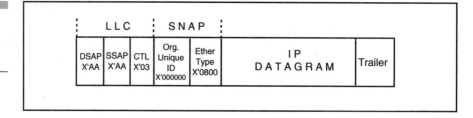

When a single virtual circuit carries multiple routed protocols, as shown in Figure 4.22, the AAL5 frame will start with the familiar LLC and SNAP headers. The IP Ethernet type is enclosed in the SNAP sub-header shown in the figure. The header can be omitted when the exclusive use of IP has been established during call setup.

Note that the AAL5 frame does not have a header with destination and source address fields. This is because an end-to-end virtual circuit is established when the "call" is set up, and information needed to switch data from the source to the destination along that circuit path is included in the 5-byte cell headers.

The AAL5 trailer contains padding bytes (for alignment), a user data field, a *payload length* field, and a frame check sequence. The payload length covers the LLC and SNAP headers and the datagram.

Maximum Transmission Unit

Each of the technologies that we have discussed has a different maximum limit on the size of its frames. After subtracting away the size of the frame header, trailer, and the LLC and SNAP headers (if they are present), the residue defines the maximum size of the datagrams that can be carried across the medium. The maximum datagram size is called the *Maximum Transmission Unit,* or *MTU*.

For example, the maximum frame size for an 802.3 Ethernet network is 1518 bytes. Subtracting the MAC header and trailer (18 bytes) and the Type 1 link control and SNAP headers (8 bytes), we get a maximum datagram size of 1492 bytes.

Table 4.1 summarizes maximum datagram sizes for a range of technologies.

Point-to-point lines are a special case. There really is no inherent limitation on datagram size for a point-to-point line. The optimum size

TABLE 4.1

Maximum
Transmission Units

Protocol	Maximum Datagram Bytes (MTU)
Default for Point-to-Point	1500
Point-to-Point (low delay)	296
SLIP	1006 (original limit)
X.25	1600 (differs for some networks)
Frame Relay	Usually at least 1600
SMDS	9180
Ethernet Version 2	1500
IEEE 802.3/802.2	1492
IEEE 802.4/802.2	8166
16 Mb IBM Token-Ring	Maximum 17914
IEEE 802.5/802.2 4 Mb Token-Ring	Maximum 4464
FDDI	4352
Hyperchannel	65535
ATM	Default 9180, Maximum 65535

depends on the error characteristics of the line. (If the error rate is high, better throughput can be obtained by using shorter units.) The default is 1500 bytes and this size is often used.

SLIP was specified with a maximum datagram size of 1006 bytes. This is a very inconvenient size.

The MTU values shown for Token-Rings are the largest allowed for 4-megabit and 16-megabit per second rings. Actual Token-Ring MTUs depend on a number of factors, including the token holding time for the ring.

MTUs for IPv6

MTU values have been assigned for IP version 6 datagrams for some media types. The default DIX Ethernet MTU remains 1500 for IPv6 datagrams. The default MTU size for IPv6 frames on an FDDI network has not been changed either, and remains 4352 octets. Similarly, the default of 9180 still is recommended for ATM. Even though far larger sizes are possible, currently, a default MTU size of 1500 is recommended for Token-Rings, to ease interworking with Ethernets. However, different values can be established according to the local environment.

Tunneling

Adhering to a layered structure is a worthy goal, but sometimes the easiest way to get data from one place to another is to hitch a ride with another protocol. This process is called *tunneling,* probably because data temporarily disappears into the depths of another protocol until it pops out at some exit point.

Making tunneling work is not complicated—you simply wrap one or more headers for another protocol around your data unit, route it using the other protocol, and unwrap it at the far end of the tunnel.

In fact, we already have seen some examples of tunneling. In Chapter 3, encrypted datagrams were wrapped in a fresh IP header in order to be forwarded across an insecure IP network. When IP datagrams are moved across an X.25 network, they are wrapped inside X.25 network layer headers. In this case, IP traffic is tunneled through X.25.

There are many other examples of tunneling in current use. Sometimes Novell NetWare IPX traffic is tunneled through an IP network. A NetWare message is wrapped in IP and UDP headers, routed through the IP network, and delivered to a remote NetWare server. A number of vendors offer products that tunnel SNA traffic through an IP network.

Tunneling always imposes a burden of extra overhead. Because it hides part of a network's path inside a foreign protocol, tunneling can degrade the ability to control and manage a network and sometimes creates bursts of traffic that are not subject to normal flow control.

Sharing a Network Interface

As we already have seen, it is not unusual to find that a LAN or WAN is being used for several protocols at once. In fact, a single node sometimes sends and receives a mixture of protocols on its network interface. How can this be done?

To keep the discussion simple, let's consider a specific interface—say for an Ethernet LAN. A PC or server may wish to use an Ethernet inter-

Figure 4.23
Protocols sharing a
network interface.

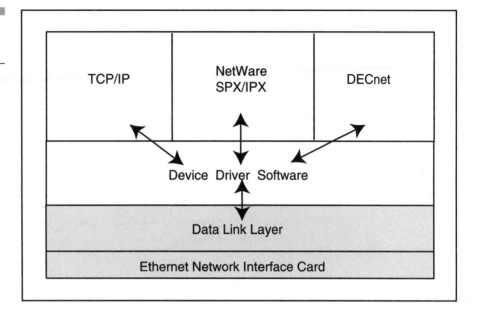

face for TCP/IP, IPX, and DECnet. Can these protocols coexist? We already have seen some evidence that they can. The link layer header will contain a field that identifies the network layer protocol for the message. Figure 4.23 shows an Ethernet interface that is shared by TCP/IP, IPX, and DECnet protocol stacks.

Device Driver

The intervening layer of *device driver* software hides the detailed hardware I/O interactions from the higher-level protocol stacks:

- IP sends and receives data by interacting with a *device driver.*
- Device driver software is supplied by each interface card vendor, and is changed whenever a card is updated.
- There is a standard programming interface between IP and device-driver software, so that the same version of IP can be used with many different interface cards.
- The device driver passes outgoing data to the interface card and accepts incoming data from an interface card.

■ The device driver plays a role in creating the frame headers and trailers that are wrapped around a datagram.

Link Layer Issues

The percentage of a datagram that is header information has an impact on throughput. Obviously, when bulk data is being transmitted, it is most efficient to carry as much data as possible in a datagram.

However, we have seen that there are different maximum datagram sizes for various network types. In Chapter 6, we see that IP provides a mechanism for fragmenting large IP datagrams when passing data into a network with a small maximum datagram size. This feature ensures that data can be delivered, even when an incompatible MTU size is encountered. However, as might be expected, the fragmentation and reassembly mechanisms slow down network response time.

When a pair of communicating hosts are attached to the same LAN, they will wish to optimize data transfers by using the largest possible datagrams. But when transmitting data to a remote host across unknown network types, a default maximum 576-byte MTU is the fallback size used to prevent fragmentation.

Later, in Chapter 7, we see that there is a procedure that automatically discovers the biggest datagram that can be used along a given path. This avoids fragmentation and enables bulk data to be transferred efficiently in optimally sized datagrams.

Trailers

A troublesome problem is the use of nonstandard protocol formats by some obsolete versions of TCP/IP. The Berkeley Software Distribution 4.2 implementation introduced a nonstandard format for Ethernet MAC frames that moved the frame type field and layer 3 and 4 header information into a *trailer*. The purpose of this rearrangement was to speed up the processing of incoming frames by reducing the number of times that data is copied. Some commercial products incorporated this feature.

The use of Berkeley trailers can lead to interworking problems. Fortunately, Berkeley trailers are becoming rare. However, if you need to use this feature, see RFC 1122 for advice on how to use trailers safely.

Recommended Reading

RFC 1661 and RFC 2153 describe the Point-to-Point Protocol. PPP authentication protocols are explained in RFC 1994, and automatic link quality monitoring is presented in RFC 1989. There are several RFCs that describe how to transmit IP datagrams over lower-layer facilities. See:

RFC 1356 for X.25

RFC 1490 for frame relay

RFC 1209 for SMDS

RFC 1390 for FDDI

RFC 1483, 1755, 1932, and 2225 for ATM

RFC 1055 for SLIP

RFC 1042 for IEEE 802 networks

RFC 894 for Ethernet

RFC 1201 for ARCNET

RFC 1149 for avian carriers

Information about HDLC can be found in ISO 3309, 4335, and 7809. The IEEE 802 series and ISO 8802 series describe physical, media access, and logical link protocols for LANs and metropolitan area networks.

Naming
and Addressing

Introduction

Every node in a network needs to be given a name and IP address. How should this be done? It may not be much of a problem for a stand-alone LAN with a handful of hosts, but when dealing with hundreds or thousands of hosts, starting off with a good name and address plan saves a ton of headache remedies when hosts, routers, and networks are added, removed, or relocated.

Internet administrators have had to cope with name and address management for a worldwide internetwork whose size has doubled every year or so. They came up with a practical strategy—delegate.

The TCP/IP Internet scheme of name and address management:

■ Makes it possible to delegate name and address assignment to someone in charge of all or part of a particular network

■ Allows names to reflect the logical structure of an organization

■ Assigns addresses that reflect the physical topology within an organization's network

We shall see that the Internet uses a hierarchical naming method that enables administrators to construct descriptive, easy-to-remember names.

Examples of Internet Names

Some names are whimsical, such as a group of hosts at the Yale Medical school that have been called:

blintz.med.yale.edu

couscous.med.yale.edu

lasagne.med.yale.edu

paella.med.yale.edu

strudel.med.yale.edu

Servers often are given names that make it easy for people to find them. For example:

www.whitehouse.gov

ftp.microsoft.com

By the way, Internet node names are not case sensitive. For example, *www.whitehouse.gov* could have been written *WWW.WHITEHOUSE. GOV* or *WWW.Whitehouse.Gov*.

Usually an end user will type host names in lowercase, while some tables list names in uppercase. In this text, you see uppercase, lowercase, and mixed-case node names.

Hierarchical Structure of Names

It is easy to understand the hierarchical structure for these names. Each organization has a descriptive top-level name, such as *yale.edu, whitehouse.gov,* or *microsoft.com.* The organization then is free to design any convenient naming scheme. For example, Yale, like most universities, delegates naming responsibility to each department or division. Hence, there are names that end with:

> *cs.yale.edu*
>
> *math.yale.edu*
>
> *geology.yale.edu*

Some departments create further subnames. For example, computers for Yale computer science majors are located in a room in the basement of the computer science (CS) building called *The Zoo.* The *Zoo* computers have names like:

> *lion.zoo.cs.yale.edu*
>
> *tiger.zoo.cs.yale.edu*
>
> *leopard.zoo.cs.yale.edu*

All of the *Zoo* computers happen to be located on a single LAN. However, names can be assigned in any way that is *administratively* convenient. For example, another family of subnames at the Yale computer science department is:

> *olive.theory.cs.yale.edu*
>
> *walnut.theory.cs.yale.edu*

These machines are *not* located on a single LAN.

Formal Structure of Names

A name is made up of a series of labels separated by dots. It is not uncommon to see names made up of two, three, four, or five labels. Each label must start with a letter. The characters that may be used for the rest of the label are letters, digits, and the hyphen (-) character. All of the following are legitimate computer names:

bellcore.com

www.apple.com

A.ROOT-SERVERS.NET

lion.zoo.cs.yale.edu

Names that are longer than this may be difficult for users to remember and type. However, Internet naming standards permit each label to have up to 63 characters, and a name can contain up to 255 characters.

Worldwide Naming Tree

Internet names are structured in a tree, as shown in Figure 5.1. Each node in the tree is assigned a label. Each node in the tree also has a name, called its *domain name*. A node's domain name is made up of the sequence of labels that lead *from* the node *to* the top of the tree. A node's domain name is written as the sequence of labels separated by dots.

A *domain* is defined to be a chunk of the naming tree that consists of a node and all of the nodes below it. In other words, a domain is made up of all names with a common ending. Examples of domains include:

- *edu* and all names under it (i.e., ending in *edu*)
- *yale.edu* and all names under it (i.e., ending in *yale.edu*)
- *cs.yale.edu* and all names under it (i.e., ending in *cs.yale.edu*)

The *top-level domains* (as shown in Figure 5.1) are:

edu   Four-year, degree granting institutions

Figure 5.1
The worldwide
naming tree.

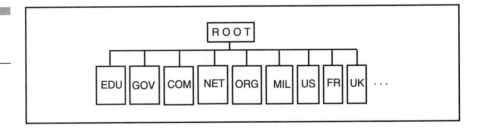

gov	United States federal government agencies
com	Commercial organizations
net	Originally used for Internet network service organizations. Now extended to general-purpose names.
org	Originally used for not-for-profit organizations. Now extended to general-purpose names.
int	International organizations (*www.nato.int*)—rarely used (and not shown in the figure)
mil	Military organizations (*army.mil, navy.mil*).
us	U.S. state and local government agencies, schools, libraries, and museums
countries	Two-character ISO country codes

The domains *edu, com, net, org, edu, gov, mil,* and *int* are "generic" top-level domains, as opposed to the remaining country code domains. The country codes identify dozens of other top-level domains: *fr* for France, *uk* for the United Kingdom, *de* for Germany, and so forth. The structure of the tree under the country code is delegated to administrators for that country. Domains *yale.edu, whitehouse.gov,* and *ibm.com,* shown in Figure 5.2, are called *second-level domains.*

There is one more formality. The label for the *root* of the naming tree is a period. Hence the complete name of the *lion* system in the Yale Computer Science network actually is:

lion.zoo.cs.yale.edu.

Most users (and authors) omit the final period when typing a name.

Figure 5.2
Second-level
domains.

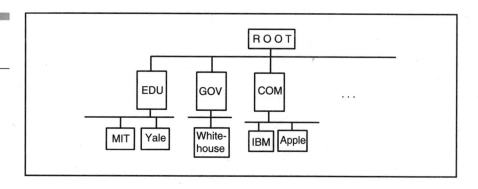

Administration of Names

Using a hierarchical name structure makes it easy to ensure that all of your computer names are unique, while delegating the job of administering computer names to appropriate personnel. Note how the administration of a name like *lion.zoo.cs.edu* can be delegated:

lion   It is up to the administrator of the Computer Science *Zoo* facility to make sure that every *Zoo* computer is assigned a different name (*lion, tiger,* etc.).

.zoo   The Yale CS department administrator must use different names for each departmental subgroup (*zoo, theory,* etc.).

.cs   As long as Yale's network administrator has assigned a different name to each department (*cs, math, geology*), every computer at Yale will have a unique name.

.yale.edu   A central registration service makes sure that every organization obtains a unique name (e.g., *yale.edu, microsoft.com*). Hence, each computer in the world can be given a unique name.

To ensure the worldwide uniqueness of names on the Internet, it was necessary to set up a registration service that makes certain that *every* business or organization uses a different name. Initially, the Internet was sponsored by the U.S. Department of Defense (DOD). The DOD funded the *Department of Defense Network Information Center (DDN NIC)*, which was responsible for administering the registration of all names.

In 1993, the National Science Foundation assumed responsibility for nonmilitary names. The National Science Foundation granted a five-year contract to Network Solutions, which was placed in charge of top-level names *com, net, org,* and *edu.* That contract has expired. At the time of writing, the Network Solutions InterNIC continues to perform this function. However, a new administrative structure is under consideration.

There are other organizations that administer parts of the naming tree:

us   The United States tree is administered by the U.S. Domain Registry at the Information Sciences Institute of the University of Southern California, at *http://www.isi.edu/in-notes/usdnr/*.

gov, fed.us, and *fed.gov*   The United States government registration service is at *http://www.registration.fed.gov/*.

Mil   The Department of Defense Network Information Center (DoD NIC) registration service is at *http://www.nic.mil/*.

Other countries operate their own registries for names within their own subtrees. Currently, pointers to these registries may be found at *http://rs.internic.net/faq/other_registries.html*.

Configuring a System's Name

The way that a system's name is configured varies from system to system. Most often, the administrator either types the name into a menu or invokes a command.

On *tigger*, which is a Unix system running *SunOS*, the *hostname* command is used to set or display the name of the host

```
> hostname
tigger.jvnc.net
```

Some systems separate names into two parts—the initial label and the rest of the domain name. This is done so automatic nicknames can be used for systems under the same domain node. For example, if a user working at a computer in domain *jvnc.net* types *minnie*, the name automatically is completed to *minnie.jvnc.net*.

A Windows 95 user enters a computer's name by selecting:

```
Start/Settings/Control Panel/Network/TCP/IP -> (binding)/Proper-
ties/DNS Configuration
```

The Windows 95 configuration menu is shown in Figure 5.3. A similar sequence is used to configure Windows NT systems.

Windows 95 configuration information can be viewed quickly by typing *winipcfg* at a command prompt. For NT, the text command that displays configuration data is *ipconfig*.

Addresses

The IP protocol uses IP addresses to identify hosts and route data to them. Every host must be assigned a unique IP address that can be used in actual communications. A host name is translated into its IP address by looking up the name in a database of name-address pairs.

Figure 5.3
Configuring a
system's name.

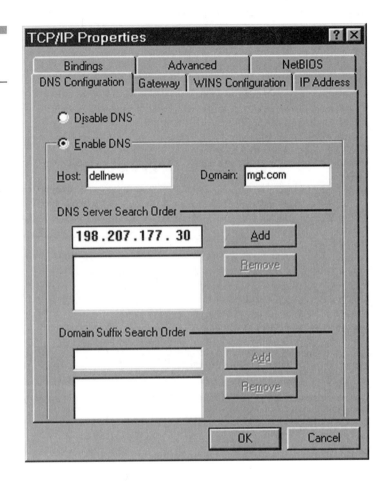

When IP addresses were designed, no one dreamed that there would be millions of computers and other devices that would want or need an IP address. The designers thought that they had to satisfy the needs of a modest community of universities, research groups, and military and government establishments.

They chose a design that seemed reasonable to them at the time. An IP address is a 32-bit (4-byte) binary number. Clearly, the address was chosen to fit conveniently into a 32-bit computer register. The resulting *address space* (which is the set of all possible address numbers) contains 2^{32} (4,294,967,296) numbers.

The *dot* notation was invented as a way of reading and writing IP addresses easily. Each byte (8 bits) of the address is converted into a decimal number, and the numbers are separated by dots. For example, the address for *blintz.med.yale.edu* in 32-bit binary and in dot notation is:[1]

10000010 10000100 00010011 00011111

130 . 132 . 19 . 31

Note that the biggest number that can appear in any position of a dotted address is 255, which corresponds to the binary number 11111111.

Address Formats

As shown in Figure 5.4, an IP address has a two-part format consisting of a *network address* and a *local address*. The network address identifies the network to which the node is attached. The local address identifies an individual node within the organization's network.

Every computer must have an IP address that is unique within the range of systems with which it will communicate.

The Internet Assigned Numbers Authority (IANA) has overall control of the IP address space. The IANA allocates big blocks of addresses to regional registries. Currently, there are three:

1. *The American Registry for Internet Numbers (ARIN).* ARIN currently is in charge of addresses for North America, South America, the Caribbean, sub-Saharan Africa, and a few other regions not covered by the other two registries. ARIN can be accessed at *http://www.arin.net/*.

2. *The Reseaux IP Europeens (RIPE) Network Coordination Center.* RIPE is the Internet address registry for Europe and surrounding areas. RIPE can be accessed at *http://www.ripe.net/*.

---

[1]See Appendix F for a complete tabulation of binary byte to decimal number translations.

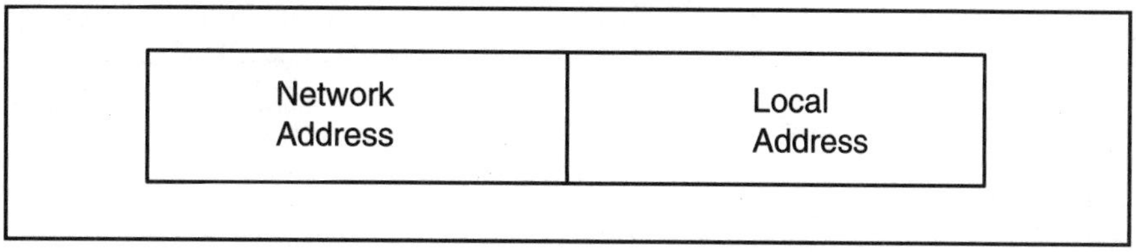

Figure 5.4
Format of an IP
address.

Network Address	Local Address

3. *The Asia-Pacific Network Information Center (APNIC).* APNIC coordinates address registrations for the Pacific basin countries. APNIC can be accessed at *http://www.apnic.net/*.

Each of these registries assigns blocks of addresses to large Internet Service Providers, who in turn assign subblocks of addresses to their customers.

An organization that plans to connect to the Internet must obtain a block of unique IP addresses. Addresses are obtained from a suitable registration authority.

As we saw earlier, a registration authority delegates large blocks from its IP address space to Service Providers. Most organizations must obtain their public addresses from their Service Providers instead of a registration NIC.

Address Classes

For many years, there were only three address block sizes—large, medium, and small. There were three different network address formats for the three block sizes. The address formats were:

Class A for very large networks

Class B for medium-sized networks

Class C for small networks

These Class A, B, and C formats are displayed in Figure 5.5. Note that the address classes have the characteristics shown in Table 5.1.

Figure 5.5
Traditional address classes.

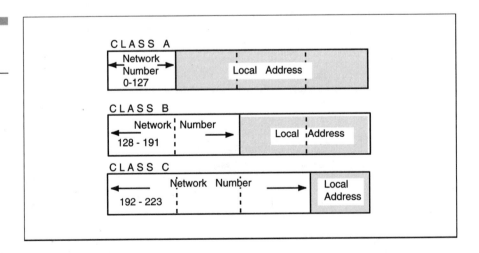

TABLE 5.1	Class	Length of Network Address	First Number	Number of Local Addresses
Address Class Characteristics	A	1 byte	0-127	16,777,216
	B	2 bytes	128-191	65,536
	C	3 bytes	192-223	256

In the early days of the Internet, organizations with very large networks—such as the United States Navy or Digital Equipment Corporation—were given Class A addresses. The network part of a Class A address is 1 byte long. The remaining 3 bytes of a Class A address belong to the local part and are used to assign numbers to nodes.

There are very few Class A addresses, and most fairly big organizations have had to be content with a medium-sized Class B block of addresses. The network part of a Class B address is 2 bytes long. The remaining 2 bytes of a Class B address belong to the local part and are used to assign numbers to nodes.

Smaller organizations receive one or more Class C addresses. The network part of a Class C address is 3 bytes long. This leaves only 1 byte in the local part that is used to assign numbers to nodes.

It is easy to spot the class of an IP address. You just look at the first number in the dotted address. The number ranges for each class are shown in Table 5.1 and Figure 5.5.

In addition to Classes A, B, and C, there are two special address formats, Class D and Class E. Class D addresses are used for IP *multicasts*. Multicasting distributes a single message to a group of computers dispersed across a network. Multicast addresses, which support conferencing applications, are discussed later in this book.

Class E addresses are reserved for experimental use.

- Class D addresses start with a number between 224 and 239.
- Class E addresses start with a number between 240 and 255.

Addresses Not Connected to the Internet

Several blocks of addresses have been reserved for use for networks that will *not* be connected to the Internet. These addresses include:

10.0.0.0–10.255.255.255

172.16.0.0–172.31.255.255

192.168.0.0–192.168.255.255

Note that *many* organizations will use these addresses. If your company merges with another company at some future date, or decides to communicate with clients or suppliers via the Internet, address conflicts could occur. However, you can register a public Class C network and use it for any needed external communications. You can obtain a firewall that relays information between organizations or between internal computers and the outside world via your registered Class C network.

The pros and cons of using these reserved addresses are discussed in RFC 1918, *Address Allocation for Private Internets.*

Addressing Examples

In this section, we take a look at some examples of globally unique Class A, B, and C addresses. Later on, we examine the new *classless* method of assigning network addresses.

Assigning Class A Addresses to Networks

Some very large organizations have Class A addresses. In this case, the registration authority assigns a fixed value to the first byte of the address and the last 3 bytes are managed by the organization. For example, the following addresses and host names belong to Hewlett-Packard, which was assigned Class A address 15.

15.255.59.2   *hplb.hpl.hp.com*

15.81.168.10   *palrel1.hp.com*

Hewlett-Packard owns the numbers from 15.0.0.0 to 15.255.255.255. These numbers make up the organization's *address space.*

Assigning Class B Addresses to Networks

The registration authority assigns a fixed value to the first 2 bytes of a Class B address. The last 2 bytes are managed by the organization. For example, the following addresses and host names belong to the Global Enterprise Systems Service Provider, which was assigned the Class B address 128.121.

128.121.50.145	*tigger.jvnc.net*
128.121.50.7	*nisc.jvnc.net*
128.121.50.2	*r2d2.jvnc.net*

Global Enterprise Systems owns the numbers from 128.121.0.0 to 128.121.255.255.

Class B addresses are very popular and many organizations have requested and received them. Unfortunately, although there are more than 16,000 possible Class B network identifiers, the supply is running out.

Assigning Class C Addresses to Networks

An organization with a small network that needs globally unique addresses is given one or more Class C addresses. This means that the registration authority assigns fixed values to be used in the first 3 bytes of the organization's addresses. The organization has control of the last byte. For example, Excite, Inc., was assigned the Class C address 198.3.98. Some of its addresses and host names are:

198.3.98.250	*NS00.excite.com*
198.3.98.251	*NS01.excite.com*

Translating Names to Addresses

End users like to type easy-to-remember names, while IP needs to know the addresses of destination systems. Many computers are configured with a small file called *hosts,* which lists the names and addresses of local systems. Here is part of a *hosts* file stored at the Global Enterprise Systems host *tigger.jvnc.net:*

```
128.121.50.2     r2d2.jvnc.net     r2d2
128.121.50.7     nisc.jvnc.net     nisc
128.121.50.141   minnie.jvnc.net   minnie
128.121.50.144   donald.jvnc.net   donald
128.121.50.145   tigger.jvnc.net   tigger
128.121.50.148   chip.jvnc.net     chip
```

The demonstrations in the next few sections of this chapter are run at *tigger.jvnc.net*.

Recall that the distributed Internet Domain Name System (DNS) database is used for global name-to-address translation. Below, the *nslookup* application sends name translation queries to a Domain Name Server called *r2d2.jvnc.net*.[2] We will look up the address of a World Wide Web Server for the White House and a file transfer server at Novell, Inc.:

```
> nslookup
Default Server: r2d2.jvnc.net
Address: 128.121.50.2

> www.whitehouse.gov.
Server: r2d2.jvnc.net
Address: 128.121.50.2

Name: www.whitehouse.gov
Address: 198.137.240.92

> ftp.novell.com.
Server: r2d2.jvnc.net
Address: 128.121.50.2

Name: ftp.novell.com
Address: 137.65.2.108
Aliases: ftp.novell.com
```

Alias Names

Often, it is convenient to assign one or more aliases (nicknames) to a computer, in addition to its real name. For example, the computer *RA.DEPT.CS.YALE.EDU* provides World Wide Web service for the Yale computer science department. It has been assigned the nickname *www.cs.yale.edu*. The computer *DEPT-GW.CS.YALE.EDU* provides file transfer service for the department, and has been assigned the nickname *ftp.cs.yale.edu*.

```
> www.cs.yale.edu.
Server: r2d2.jvnc.net
Address: 128.121.50.2

Name: RA.DEPT.CS.YALE.EDU
Address: 128.36.16.1
Aliases: www.cs.yale.edu
```

---

[2]This *nslookup* dialog is being run at a Unix computer. However, *nslookup* also can be run in an NT command window.

```
> ftp.cs.yale.edu.
Server: r2d2.jvnc.net
Address: 128.121.50.2

Name: DEPT-GW.CS.YALE.EDU
Address: 128.36.0.36
Aliases: ftp.cs.yale.edu
>
```

If the load on DEPT-GW gets too heavy, its FTP service—and the service nickname—can easily be transferred to a bigger host. This enables users to reach the service by means of the same name, even if the home site for the service has been changed. A host's true name is called its *canonical name*.

Inefficiency Caused by Address Classes

A Class A network spans 16,777,216 addresses, whereas Class B supports 65,536 and Class C includes only 256 numbers. The large gaps between these numbers led to very inefficient address block allocations and contributed to the depletion of the IP address space.

Later we describe the more efficient *classless* method of allocating addresses to organizations.

TCP/IP Networks and Subnets

An organization that has a Class A or Class B network address is very likely to have a fairly complex network made up of many LANs and several WAN links. It makes sense to partition the address space in a way that matches the network's structure as a family of subnetworks. To do this, the local part of the address is broken into a *subnet part* and a *system part* in any convenient way, as illustrated in Figure 5.6.

The size of the subnet part of an address and the assignment of numbers to subnets is the responsibility of the organization that "owns" that part of the address space.

Subnet addressing often is done at a byte boundary. An organization

Figure 5.6
Breaking the local
address into subnet
and system parts.

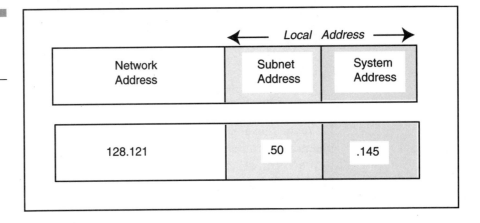

Figure 5.6
Breaking the local
address into subnet
and system parts.

that owns a Class B address such as 128.21 might use its third byte to
identify subnets. For example:

128.121.1

128.121.2

128.121.3

The fourth byte would then be used to identify individual hosts on a
subnet.

On the other hand, an organization with a Class C address has only a
1-byte address space. It might choose to do no subnetting at all or perhaps might use 4 bits for subnet addresses and 4 bits for host addresses,
as shown in Figure 5.7. In the figure, the local address, 61, is expressed
in binary as 0011 1101. The first 4 bits identify a subnet and the last 4
bits identify a system.

Subnet Masks

Traffic is routed to a host by looking at the network and subnet part of
its IP address. For example, suppose that a router inside network
128.121 needs to forward a datagram toward destination address
128.121.1.5. If the third byte is the subnet number, the router would
check its routing table to find a path to LAN 128.121.1.

A Class A, B, or C network part has a fixed size. But organizations
can choose their own subnet field sizes, so how can their hosts and
routers recognize this field? The answer is that systems must be configured to know the size of the subnet part of the address.

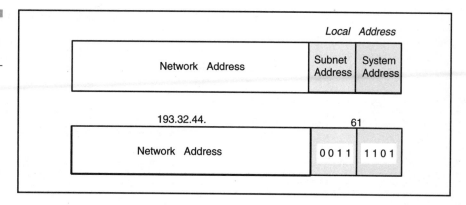

Figure 5.7
A 4-bit subnet part in a Class C address.

The fact we care about is "how many bits are in the subnet part?" By tradition, this is expressed in an unfriendly looking manner. The subnet field size is expressed indirectly using a configuration parameter called the *subnet mask*. The subnet mask is a sequence of 32 bits. The bits corresponding to the network and subnet fields of an address are set to 1, while the bits for the host part of the address are set to 0.

For example, when we use the third byte of addresses starting with 128.121 to identify subnets, the mask is:

11111111 11111111 11111111 00000000

Subnet masks often are expressed in dotted decimal notation. The mask above can be written as:

255.255.255.0

Sometimes they are written in hexadecimal characters. The mask above can be written as:

ff ff ff 00

Role of Subnet Masks

Subnet masks play an important role in routing IP datagrams. They are used to figure out whether a destination is on the same LAN as the source. For example:

SOURCE: 128.121.50.145
DESTINATION: 128.121.50.100
SUBNET MASK: 255.255.255.0

We use the 0s in the subnet mask to zero out the host part of the address and then compare what is left. The remaining parts both are 128.121.50, so both systems are on the same LAN.

But suppose that we have:

SOURCE: 128.121.50.145

DESTINATION: 128.121.50.100

SUBNET MASK: 255.255.255.128

The host part is only 7 bits long. In binary, the last byte of each address is:

$$145 = \mathbf{1}\,0\,0\,1\,0\,0\,0\,1$$
$$100 = \mathbf{0}\,1\,1\,0\,0\,1\,0\,0$$

The bits shown in bold type belong to the subnet part of the address. The last bit of the subnet part does not match and the systems are not on the same LAN.

Choosing and Writing Subnet Masks

The number of bits that you use as the subnet part of addresses depends on the shape of your network.

- If you have a few big LANs, you do not need many subnet bits, but you need a lot of host bits.
- If you have a lot of very small LANs, you need more subnet bits and fewer host bits.

Table 5.2 shows the ways in which the local addresses in a Class B network can be partitioned into subnets. It also shows the number of subnets and hosts for each partition. The number of hosts and subnets each will be 2 less than you would expect because of some restrictions that we describe in the sections that follow.[3] We also explain why 1/15 (1 subnet bit and 15 host bits) and 15/1 splits of the address bits are not allowed.

---

[3]The subnet counts in the table obey the "official" rules. However, in real implementations, use of an all zeros subnet number is common, resulting in one more subnet than is shown (i.e., 3 instead of 2, 7 instead of 6, etc.).

TABLE 5.2

Subnets for a Class
B Network.

Subnet Bits	Number of Subnets	Host Bits	Number of Hosts	Mask
0	0	16	65,534	255.255.0.0
1	—	15	—	Not allowed
2	2	14	16,382	255.255.192.0
3	6	13	8,190	255.255.224.0
4	14	12	4,094	255.255.240.0
5	30	11	2,046	255.255.248.0
6	62	10	1,022	255.255.252.0
7	126	9	510	255.255.254.0
8	254	8	254	255.255.255.0
9	510	7	126	255.255.255.128
10	1,022	6	62	255.255.255.192
11	2,046	5	30	255.255.255.224
12	4,096	4	14	255.255.255.240
13	8,190	3	6	255.255.255.248
14	16,382	2	2	255.255.255.252
15	—	1	—	Not allowed

The table shows that if you use 6 subnet bits, you can have up to 62 subnets, each containing up to 1022 hosts. The subnet mask bit pattern is:

11111111 11111111 11111100 00000000

This translates to 255.255.252.0.

Most networks are made up of a mixture of large, medium, and small LANs. In Appendix C, we provide examples that illustrate how you can use several different subnet masks within a single network. Using several mask sizes enables you to assign your addresses very efficiently.

Special Reserved Addresses

Some IP addresses have been set aside for special uses. These include:

- Broadcast addresses
- The zero host address, 0.0.0.0

- The loopback address, 127.0.0.1
- Zero-filled addresses used in routing tables

Broadcasts

A *broadcast* is a message that goes to every system on a LAN or on a network. There are several IP address patterns that are used for broadcasts. To distinguish an ordinary IP address from a broadcast, an ordinary IP address is called a *unicast* address.

LAN Broadcast and Zero Address

Manually configuring hundreds or thousands of desktop systems is a big job. Many organizations use a boot server that automatically assigns startup parameters to desktop hosts. When a system starts up, it transmits a broadcast message onto its LAN with destination IP address 255.255.255.255[4] (i.e., an address consisting of 32 ones). An unconfigured system uses 0.0.0.0 as the IP source address.

A LAN broadcast is executed by wrapping the IP datagram in a frame whose header contains the all-1s physical broadcast address as its destination address. The request is picked up and processed by a boot server.

Because of this special usage, neither 0.0.0.0 nor 255.255.255.255 may be used as the real IP address of any host.

Broadcast Directed to a Subnet

A broadcast also can be directed to a specific LAN. This might be a system's directly connected LAN or could be a LAN that is remote from the source host. For example if 131.18.7 is a subnet of a Class B network, address 130.18.7.255 is used to broadcast a message to all nodes on this subnet.

If the destination LAN is remote, the result of sending an IP datagram to the broadcast LAN address is that one copy of the datagram

---

[4]Berkeley 4.2 TCP/IP and some products based on it used 0s instead of 1s for broadcasting. This is a nonstandard practice and, over time, these operating systems should be obsoleted or replaced.

will be relayed across the network until it reaches a router attached to LAN 131.18.7. The router would then wrap the datagram in a frame whose header contains the all-1s physical broadcast address as its destination address.

Because an all-1s host field denotes a broadcast, an all-1s host IP address is forbidden. For example, no host on subnet 7 could be assigned the reserved IP address 130.18.7.255.

Broadcasts to Networks

It is possible to send an IP datagram to every host on a selected remote network. This is done by setting the entire local part of the destination address to 1s. For example, suppose that an administrator wanted to send an announcement to all nodes on a Class C Ethernet network 201.49.16.0. The IP address used for the broadcast is:

201.49.16.255

Because 201.49.16.255 is reserved for broadcasts, no host can be given this address.

Address 131.18.255.255 could be used to aim a message at every node in an entire Class B network. Note that if we assigned subnet number 255 to one of the subnets, we would have a problem. It would not be clear whether a broadcast to 130.15.255.255 was intended for that subnet or for the whole network. The way to avoid this is never to use an all-1s field (like 255) as a subnet number.[5]

Zero-filled Addresses Used in Routing Tables

Administrators have always found it convenient to use a dotted address format to refer to a network. By convention, this is done by filling in the local part of the address with zeroes. For example, 5.0.0.0 identifies a Class A network, 131.18.0.0 identifies a Class B network, and 201.49.16.0 identifies a Class C network.

---

[5]However, note that sending a broadcast to a subnetted network is a potentially disastrous action since it could generate a "broadcast storm." We can expect routers to screen out destination addresses like this.

The same type of notation is used to identify subnets. For example, if network 131.18.0.0 uses an 8-bit subnet mask, 131.18.5.0 and 131.18.6.0 refer to subnets.

In earlier times, an organization would use a single subnet mask throughout an entire network. LAN destinations were entered into routing tables by simply typing in an address that had a zero host part. Use of 0 as a subnet number was forbidden because there would be no way to tell whether an entry for a destination such as 130.15.0.0 referred to network 130.15 or subnet 130.15.0.

Routing Prefixes

Today's routing tables tell you how many bits in a routing table entry need to be matched up. One result of this is that even though the official rules say it should not be done, use of 0 as a subnet number is common today. An entry for 130.15.0.0 (16 bits) tells you the quickest path to external network 130.15. An entry for 130.15.0.0 (24 bits) tells you the quickest path to subnet 130.15.0.

The set of address bits that need to be matched for routing purposes is called the *routing prefix*. For "130.15.0.0 (16 bits)" the routing prefix is 130.15. For "130.15.0.0 (24 bits)" the routing prefix is 130.15.0. Currently, a slash followed by a number denotes a prefix length. For example: 130.15.2.0/24.

Result of Restrictions on IP Addresses

The set of usable IP addresses is diminished slightly because of the restrictions on all-0s and all-1s address fields.

- A host field cannot consist entirely of 0s.
- A host field cannot consist entirely of 1s.
- A subnet field cannot consist entirely of 1s.

One result is that a 1-bit host address field would be completely nonsensical—there would be no usable addresses. A 1-bit subnet field would provide only one subnet, and so it also does not make sense. Thus, to be usable, a host or subnet field must contain at least 2 bits.

Table 5.2 showed that an 8-bit host field provides 254 usable IP addresses. You can write numbers ranging from 0 to 255 using 8 bits, and the usable numbers are the ones from 1 to 254.

Loopback Address

At the opposite extreme of broadcasts are messages that never leave the local host. There are many hosts that contain both client and server processes. The local clients and servers communicate via IP within the host. To do this, they use a special address called the *loopback* address. By convention, any address starting with 127 is reserved for this purpose. In practice only the address 127.0.0.1 is used. (Note that an entire Class A address space of 2^{16} numbers was reserved for loopback addresses.)

It is easy to see the loopback address in action. Before running the dialog below, we started a NetManage Chameleon file transfer server on a Windows 95 system. We then opened a command window and started the text-based file transfer client that is bundled with Windows 95. The user interface is far from pretty, but it is possible to see what is going on by focusing on the commands that are entered; these are shown in bold-face. The steps are:

- Open a file transfer session between the local client and the local server.
- Login with a username and password.
- Ask the server to change to a directory called *data*.
- List the files in that directory.
- Ask the client to change to a directory called *info* (using the *lcd* command).
- Get file *alaska.txt* from the directory called *data* and copy it to the directory called *info*.

```
C:\WINDOWS> ftp 127.0.0.1
Connected to 127.0.0.1.
220 newdell Windows NT NetManage Chameleon32 FTP Server (Version
6.0) ready

User (127.0.0.1:(none)): sidnie
331 sidnie, please enter your password.
Password:
230 User sidnie logged in.

ftp> cd data
200 CWD command successful.

ftp> dir
200 PORT command successful.
150 Opening data connection.
04-28-98 03:22PM              305 alaska.txt
04-20-98 08:43AM              193 Tips.txt
```

```
226 Transfer complete.
236 bytes received in 0.33 seconds (0.72 Kbytes/sec)

ftp> lcd \info
Local directory now C:\info

ftp> get alaska.txt
200 PORT command successful.
150 Opening ASCII mode data connection for alaskatrip.txt.
226 File transfer complete.
305 bytes received in 0.33 seconds (0.92 Kbytes/sec)

ftp> !dir
 Volume in drive C is NEWDELL
 Volume Serial Number is 3347-11D8
 Directory of C:\info

 .             <DIR>       06-22-98 7:30p .
 ..            <DIR>       06-22-98 7:30p ..
ALASKA TXT    305         06-22-98 7:34p alaska.txt
              1 file(s)   305 bytes
              2 dir(s)    1,001,324,544 bytes free

ftp> quit
221 Goodbye.
```

The upshot of this long dialog is that we copied a file from one directory at our PC to another. This is not an impressive achievement. Nonetheless, the loopback address is a terrific feature of TCP/IP. Someone who has just developed a new client/server application can install the client and the server on a single computer and test their interactions without even using a network. This simplifies and speeds up the whole testing procedure. Using a loopback connection between a local browser and Web server also is an excellent way to build and test a Web server.

Summary of Special Reserved Addresses

Various types of special addresses are summarized in Table 5.3.

Classless Addresses

The A, B, C method of handing out blocks of addresses was very inefficient. A Class C address provided at most only 254 usable addresses. (Recall that 0 and 255 cannot be used to address a node.) On the other

TABLE 5.3

Special Addresses

Addresses	Description
0.0.0.0	Used as source address in a boot configuration request. Also denotes the default route in a routing table.
127.0.0.0	Reserved.
127.0.0.1	Loopback. Client and server are in the same host.
127.0.0.2-127.255.255.255	Reserved
255.255.255.255	Broadcast on locally attached LAN.

hand, if an organization that needed a few hundred or a few thousand addresses was given a Class B address, many addresses would be wasted.

It makes a lot more sense to assign organizations the number of bits that they really need. This is done very easily. For example, if an organization needs 4000 addresses, it is given 12 bits to use as the local part of its addresses. The initial 20 address bits are a fixed prefix used as the "network" or routing prefix part of the address. The conventional way to denote the size of this "classless" network part is /20. Many classless address allocations are being taken from the available Class C number space. Obtaining a 20-bit prefix is equivalent to obtaining 16 contiguous Class C addresses. Table 5.4 shows various address prefix sizes and

TABLE 5.4

CIDR Blocks from Class C Address Space

Size of Network Part	Number of Local Part Bits	Equivalent Number of Class C Networks	Number of Addresses in the Block
/26	6	1/4	64
/25	7	1/2	128
/24	8	1	256
/23	9	2	512
/22	10	4	1024
/21	11	8	2048
/20	12	6	4096
/19	13	32	8192
/18	14	64	16384
/17	15	128	32768

address block sizes. Pieces of the Class A address space can be handed out in the same way.

Role of the Internet Service Providers

Instead of assigning addresses to end-user customers directly, it is much more efficient for ARIN and the other address registries to give big blocks of addresses to major Internet Service Providers, and then let them take care of the needs of their customers.

This leads to efficient routing across the Internet. Backbone routing tables need to list only the routing prefixes that have been handed out to the Internet Service Providers. After a datagram has been routed into an ISP's network, the ISP's routers can check its destination against the list of longer routing prefixes that have been given to its customers. For example, a provider might be given the block starting with the 10-bit prefix **11000001 11,** and then might give one of its customers the block starting with the 18-bit prefix **11000001 11**011111 01.

The whole procedure is called *Classless Internet-Domain Routing* (CIDR). All that is needed to make it work is to enter routing prefixes that do not end on byte boundaries into routing tables. For example, in an Internet backbone table, the 10-bit routing prefix 11000001 11 would be filled out with zeroes to produce 193.192.0.0. The prefix is expressed as:

193.192.0.0/10

or alternatively, using a mask,

(193.192.0.0, 255.192.0.0)

which is another way of saying "match 10 bits." The customer's 18-bit routing prefix would be entered into the ISP's internal routing table and can be expressed as:

193.223.64.0/18 or (193.223.64.0, 255.255.192.0)

CIDR *Whois* Example

The Internet *whois* information store provides a good way to explore Internet number assignments. This is a set of databases whose information is entered by the various domain name and address registries. Most Unix systems provide a text-based *whois* client. Various nicer desktop graphical user interfaces are available.

Figure 5.8
A Netmanage
Chameleon *whois*
client.

Whois can map the name of an organization to information about the addresses that it owns, the locations of its domain name servers, and information about its network administrators. *Whois* also can work backward, mapping a network address to its owner.

Figure 5.8 shows the simple user interface for the Chameleon *Whois*. The query result in the window shows that the Interop exposition owns Class A address 45.0.0.0.

The dialog below was produced using a Unix *whois*. The statement *-h whois.arin.net* indicates that the query should be sent to a *whois* server operated by ARIN. The responses are very big, so we will show only parts of each response.

Below, we see that MCI owns a block of 1024 Class C addresses ranging from 205.216.0 to 205.219.255 and another block of 256 Class C addresses ranging from 204.71.0 to 204.71.255. These blocks sometimes are called "supernets."

```
> whois -h whois.arin.net mci
. . .
MCI Telecommunications Corporation (NETBLK-MCI-NETBLK04)
MCI-NETBLK04
205.216.0.0 - 205.219.255.255
. . .
```

```
MCI Telecommunications Corporation (NETBLK-MCI-PROVIDER)
MCI-PROVIDER
204.71.0.0 - 204.71.255.255
. . .
```

The response to the next query shows that Yahoo is an MCI customer. (Yahoo also uses other service providers. They want to be sure that they have access, even if there is an outage at one provider.) Yahoo has obtained several address blocks from MCI:

```
> whois -h whois.arin.net yahoo
Yahoo (NETBLK-NET-MV-YAHOO2)      NET-MV-YAHOO2
205.216.146.0 - 205.216.146.63
Yahoo (NETBLK-NET-MV-YAHOO3)      NET-MV-YAHOO3
205.216.146.64 - 205.216.146.127
Yahoo (NETBLK-NET-YAHOO-CORP1)    NET-YAHOO-CORP1
205.216.162.0 - 205.216.162.255
Yahoo (NETBLK-NET-SNV-YAHOO1)     NET-SNV-YAHOO1
204.71.200.0 - 204.71.201.255
. . .
```

Note that the first block of Yahoo addresses is 1/4 of a Class C address. Then they obtained another 1/4. The next block is a full Class C address, and the next is a pair of Class C addresses.

To route to any address in the range 205.216.0 to 205.219.255, an Internet backbone router would need a routing table entry for 205.216.0.0 /14. Any address that matches the first 14 bits of 205.216.0.0 will be in that range. To see this, we write the addresses and the corresponding "mask" in binary:

205.216.0.0 = 11001101 11011000 00000000 00000000

205.217.0.0 = 11001101 11011001 00000000 00000000

205.218.0.0 = 11001101 11011010 00000000 00000000

205.219.0.0 = 11001101 11011011 00000000 00000000

mask = 11111111 11111100 00000000 00000000
(14 1s in the mask)

The Need for IP, Next Generation

The introduction of classless, supernetted addresses and classless routing is a stopgap measure to extend the life of the current IP addressing scheme.

When IP addresses were originally designed, no one anticipated the computer technologies that would put computers on desks, into homes, and into commonplace devices—and network them together. The current addresses are inconvenient and inadequate for the job that needs to be done.

Unlike the hierarchical structure used for telephone numbers, the addresses were designed without country or area codes. This makes routing especially burdensome. Internet routers still store routing entries for thousands of separate networks.

IP version 6 (*Next Generation*) is designed to solve these problems by introducing bigger (16-byte) addresses, and also to prepare for new ways of using computers and computer networks. Version 6 is described in Chapters 22 and 23.

Unfortunately, the road to IP version 6 is a rough ride. Application programs need to be rewritten in order to work with 16-byte addresses instead of 4-byte addresses.

IP Addresses, Interfaces, and Multihoming

Identifying networks and subnets within an IP address has many benefits:

- It simplifies the job of assigning addresses. A block of addresses can be delegated to the administrator of a particular network or subnet.

- It simplifies the job of routing. Table lookups of network or subnet numbers can be carried out quickly and efficiently.

These are important advantages. However, there is an important consequence of this addressing scheme. Consider Figure 5.9. The router in the figure has three different interfaces and is connected to two LANs and a leased line.

The router is connected to internal subnets 128.36.2 and 128.36.18. It also is connected to an external network, 193.92.45. What is "the" IP address of the router?

The answer is that *systems* do not have IP addresses, their *interfaces* do. Each interface has an IP address that starts with the network and subnet number of the attached LAN or wide area link. A router with three interfaces must be assigned three IP addresses.

Figure 5.9
Assigning IP address-
es to interfaces.

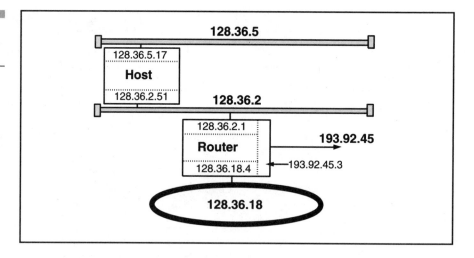

A host also may be connected to more than one subnet or network. The host in Figure 5.9 has interfaces to two Ethernets. This host also has two IP addresses—128.36.2.51 and 128.36.5.17.

A system that is attached to more than one subnet is called *multi-homed*. A multihomed host introduces some complications into IP routing. Data will be routed to a multihomed host differently depending on which of its IP addresses is chosen for communication. It may in fact be helpful to associate multiple names to the host, corresponding to its various inter-faces. For example (see Figure 5.9), users on LAN 128.36.2 might be told a different host name from the one told to users on LAN 128.36.5.

In spite of the drawbacks that result from multihomed hosts, the inclusion of network and subnet identifiers within an address has con-tributed greatly to the efficiency of routers and to the ease with which a TCP/IP Internet can be enlarged.

Configuring Addresses and Subnet Masks

Figure 5.10 shows the Windows NT Server menu used to enter a sys-tem's IP address and the size of the subnet field. Note that this IP address and subnet mask are associated with a 3Com Etherlink Ether-net adapter interface. This menu is reached via the commands:

```
Start/Settings/Control Panel/Network/Protocols/TCP/IP
Protocol/Properties/IP Address
```

Figure 5.10
Configuring an IP
address and subnet
mask.

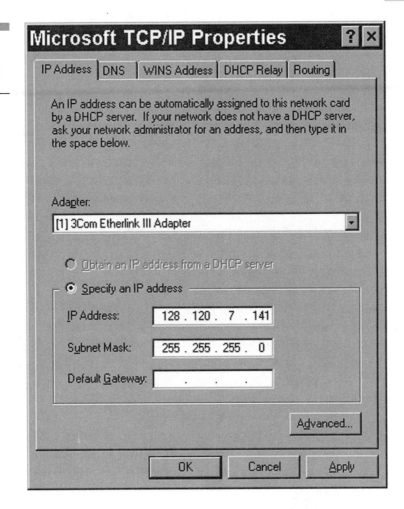

An almost identical menu is used on other Windows systems. The subnet mask must be entered into the menu in dotted decimal form.

On a Unix system, the *ifconfig* command is used to set or display IP address and subnet mask parameters.[6] The dialog below displays the IP address and subnet mask at host *tigger.jvnc.net* for Ethernet LAN interface 0 (le0):

```
> ifconfig le0
le0:    flags563,UP,BROADCAST,NOTRAILERS,RUNNING.
        inet 128.121.50.145 netmask ffffff00 broadcast
128.121.50.255
```

---

[6]The *ifconfig* configuration command must be repeated every time the system boots, and hence must be included in a startup script.

The IP address for the interface is 128.121.50.145. Its subnet mask is expressed in hex, ffffff00. The appropriate broadcast address for the subnet is 128.121.50.255.

Relationship Between Names and Addresses

Users who look at a system name like *fermat.math.yale.edu* and its IP address in dot format, 128.36.23.3, can easily get the idea that parts of names actually correspond to numbers in the dotted address. This definitely is not the case.

It is true that sometimes systems on a LAN are assigned names that *appear* to match an address hierarchy. However:

- Completely unrelated names *may* appear on the same LAN.
- Hosts with similar name structures *may* be located on different LANs or even on different networks.

For example, consider the following names and addresses:

macoun.cs.yale.edu   128.36.2.5

bulldog.cs.yale.edu   130.132.1.2

Addresses reflect network points of attachment and are bound to locations. But system names do not depend on their physical network attachments.

The best illustration of this fact is that a Web server such as *www.abc.com* can be located in an Internet Service provider's network instead of within ABC's own network. Traffic is routed to a system based on its address, not its name, and a system's address always is looked up before data is sent to it. Thus, organizations are free to design a flexible naming plan that best meets their needs.

Address Resolution Protocol

Before a datagram can be sent between two stations on a LAN, it must be wrapped up in a frame header and a frame trailer. The frame is delivered to the Network Interface Card whose physical address matches the destination physical address in the frame header.

Therefore, to deliver a datagram across a LAN, the physical address of the destination node must be discovered.

Fortunately, there is a procedure that automatically discovers physical addresses. The *Address Resolution Protocol* (ARP) provides a broadcast-based method for dynamically translating between IP addresses and physical addresses.

The systems on the local network use ARP to discover physical address information for themselves.[7] When a host wants to start communicating with a local partner, it looks up the partner's IP address in its ARP table, which is kept in RAM memory. If there is no entry for that IP address, the host broadcasts an ARP request containing the destination IP address (see Figure 5.11).

The target host recognizes its IP address and reads the request. The first thing that the target host does is update its own ARP address translation table with the IP and physical addresses of the sender. This is prudent because it is likely that the target soon will be conversing with the sender. The target host then sends back a reply containing its own hardware interface address.

When the source receives the reply, it updates its ARP table and is ready to transmit data across the LAN.

---

[7]An administrator also can manually enter some permanent address translation entries into an ARP table, if desired. However note that this could create a big maintenance hassle.

Figure 5.11

Finding the physical address of a system.

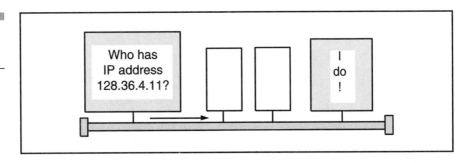

ARP Message Contents

ARP initially was used on Ethernet LANs, but its design is general, so it can be used with other types of networks such as Token-Rings, Fiber Distributed Data Interface (FDDI) LANs, and Switched Multimegabit Data Service Wide Area Networks (SMDS WANs). A variant of ARP has been designed for use with wide area virtual circuits (such as frame relay).

An ARP message is placed in the data field of a frame, immediately following the layer 2 headers. The protocol type of the frame is identified to be ARP via Ethernet type code X'0806. The display that follows shows an NT monitor trace of an ARP request.

```
ETHERNET: ETYPE = 0x0806 : Protocol = ARP: Address Resolution Protocol
ARP_RARP: ARP: Request, Target IP: 198.207.177.9
    ARP_RARP: Hardware Address Space = 1 (0x1)
    ARP_RARP: Protocol Address Space = 2048 (0x800)
    ARP_RARP: Hardware Address Length = 6 (0x6)
    ARP_RARP: Protocol Address Length = 4 (0x4)
    ARP_RARP: Opcode = 1 (0x1)
    ARP_RARP: Sender's Hardware Address = 00A024A6EDE4
    ARP_RARP: Sender's Protocol Address = 198.207.177.41
    ARP_RARP: Target's Hardware Address = 000000000000
ARP_RARP: Target's Protocol Address = 198.207.177.9
```

Table 5.5 explains the ARP message fields. The field in the preceding message trace that is labeled "Protocol Address Space" indicates that the higher-layer address in the query is an IP address.

TABLE 5.5

Format of an ARP Message

Number of Bytes	Field
2	Type of hardware address
2	Higher layer addressing protocol
1	Length of hardware address
1	Length of higher layer address
2	Type of message
	00 01 = request, 00 02 = response
*	Source hardware address
*	Source higher layer (IP) address
*	Destination hardware address
*	Destination higher layer (IP) address

The designers of ARP were very forward thinking. ARP use is not exclusively restricted to IP. They made it possible to use ARP for different higher-layer protocols, protocol address lengths, and hardware address lengths. Thus the lengths of the last four fields depend on the technology and protocol in use. Hardware addresses for 802.X LANs contain 6 bytes, and IP (version 4) addresses are 4 bytes long.

The source and destination roles are reversed in the reply shown below. For example, the source protocol address is 198.207.177.9 in the reply. The information that the ARP requester wanted is in the field labeled "Sender's Hardware Address."

```
ETHERNET: ETYPE = 0x0806 : Protocol = ARP: Address Resolution Protocol
ARP_RARP: ARP: Reply, Target IP: 198.207.177.41 Target Hdwr Addr:
00A024A6EDE4
    ARP_RARP: Hardware Address Space = 1 (0x1)
    ARP_RARP: Protocol Address Space = 2048 (0x800)
    ARP_RARP: Hardware Address Length = 6 (0x6)
    ARP_RARP: Protocol Address Length = 4 (0x4)
    ARP_RARP: Opcode = 2 (0x2)
    ARP_RARP: Sender's Hardware Address = 0020AF3BD450
    ARP_RARP: Sender's Protocol Address = 198.207.177.9
    ARP_RARP: Target's Hardware Address = 00A024A6EDE4
    ARP_RARP: Target's Protocol Address = 198.207.177.41
    ARP_RARP: Frame Padding
```

Since the original ARP request is broadcast, any system on the LAN could use the information in the ARP message to update its table entry for the requester. Normally, a host system enters an update only when it is the target of an ARP message. However, smart switches cache ARP information and use it to direct frames to the correct outgoing line.

ARP Table

Most systems provide a command that allows an administrator to:

- View the local ARP table
- Manually add or delete table entries
- Load a table with entries from a configuration file

The dialog below uses the *arp -a* command to show how *tigger*'s ARP table changes after a *telnet* connection is set up to host *mickey*, which is not currently in the table. Note that the output displays the name of each system, its IP address in dot format, and the 6 bytes of its physical address as hexadecimal numbers separated by a : delimiter.

```
>arp -a
nomad-eth0.jvnc.net (128.121.50.50) at 0:0:c:2:85:11
r2d2.jvnc.net (128.121.50.2) at 8:0:20:a:2c:3f
jim-mac.jvnc.net (128.121.50.162) at 8:0:7:6f:a6:65
tom-mac.jvnc.net (128.121.50.163) at 8:0:7:ff:96:9e
chip.jvnc.net (128.121.50.148) at 0:0:3b:86:6:4c
nisc.jvnc.net (128.121.50.7) at 8:0:20:11:d2:b7
nicol.jvnc.net (128.121.50.10) at 0:0:3b:80:32:34
minnie.jvnc.net (128.121.50.141) at 8:0:20:7:b5:da
>
> telnet mickey.jvnc.net
Trying 128.121.50.143 ...
Connected to mickey.jvnc.net.
Escape character is '@]'.

SunOS UNIX (mickey.jvnc.net)

login:
. . .

logout

> arp -a
nomad-eth0.jvnc.net (128.121.50.50) at 0:0:c:2:85:11
R2d2.jvnc.net (128.121.50.2) at 8:0:20:a:2c:3f
jim-mac.jvnc.net (128.121.50.162) at 8:0:7:6f:a6:65
tom-mac.jvnc.net (128.121.50.163) at 8:0:7:ff:96:9e
chip.jvnc.net (128.121.50.148) at 0:0:3b:86:6:4c
nisc.jvnc.net (128.121.50.7) at 8:0:20:11:d2:b7
nicol.jvnc.net (128.121.50.10) at 0:0:3b:80:32:34
minnie.jvnc.net (128.121.50.141) at 8:0:20:7:b5:da
mickey.jvnc.net (128.121.50.143) at 8:0:20:7:53:8f
>
```

Reverse ARP

A variant of ARP called *reverse ARP* (RARP) was designed to help a node to find out its *own* IP address. It was intended for use by diskless workstations and other devices that need to get configuration information from a network server.

A station using the reverse ARP protocol broadcasts a query stating its physical address and requesting its IP address. A server on the network that is configured with a table of physical addresses and matching IP addresses can respond to the query.

Reverse ARP has been superseded by the BOOTP protocol and its improved version, the `Dynamic Host Configuration Protocol* (DHCP). These protocols are far more powerful and are used to provide a complete set of configuration parameters to a TCP/IP system. BOOTP and DHCP are discussed in Chapter 11.

Multiple Addresses for One Router Interface

Router vendors allow you to assign *multiple* IP addresses to a single router interface. Why would anyone want to do this? Multiple subnet addresses might be needed for a LAN that has a very large number of systems. Or, separate subnet numbers might be used to apply different traffic filtering rules to systems belonging to two different workgroups. Each workgroup would belong to a separate *logical* subnet, although both share the same *physical* medium.

Figure 5.12 shows a LAN with two logical subnets, 128.36.4.0 and 128.36.5.0. The router's LAN interface has been assigned the two IP addresses, 128.36.4.1 and 128.36.5.1. Traffic *to* this LAN will be routed correctly. However, some extra work needs to be done to route datagrams originating at a LAN host correctly.

Suppose that system A has an 8-bit subnet field. When A wants to send a datagram to B, it will pass the datagram to the router. To avoid this, the hosts on the LAN could be configured with 7-bit subnet masks, since 4 corresponds to 0000 0100 and 5 is 0000 0101.

Figure 5.12
A router interface with two IP addresses.

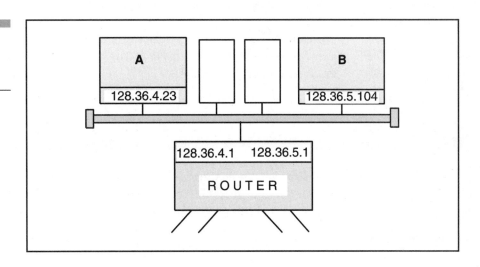

Multiple Addresses for One Host Interface

You also can assign multiple IP addresses to a host interface. The most common reason to do this is to locate Web servers for multiple domain names on a single computer. For example, all traffic for *www.abc.com* could be directed to IP address 192.4.1.50, whereas traffic for *www.xyz.com* could be directed to IP address 192.4.1.51. Requests sent to either server would be delivered to the same network interface, but the data that is returned would depend on the IP address that was used for the request.

Proxy ARP

Suppose that adjacent subnet numbers were not available for use on the LAN. For example, suppose that 128.36.4.0 and 128.36.20.0 were sharing the medium. In this case, hosts on the LAN could be configured with the mask 255.255.0.0—which means "no subnetting." Hosts would then use ARP for *all* destinations on network 128.36. This will work perfectly for systems that share the medium, but what about traffic to subnets of 128.36 that are not on the LAN?

The LAN router will handle external traffic if it supports *Proxy ARP.* When a router that supports Proxy ARP sees an ARP request for a destination that is external to the LAN,[8] the router sends an ARP response containing the *router's* physical address. The host wraps a frame around the datagram and forwards it to the router, which unwraps the datagram and sends it onward.

Recommended Reading

The address classes are defined in the IP standard, RFC 791. Subnetting is defined in RFC 950, and supernetting is discussed in RFC 1519. Broadcasts are described in RFC 919 and RFC 922.

---

[8]If there are multiple routers on the LAN, then the router that has the best path to the destination answers.

The Address Resolution Protocol is defined for Ethernets in RFC 826. Reverse ARP is described in RFC 903.

RFC 1178 contains both sound and entertaining advice on how to choose a name for your computer. RFCs 1034 and 1101 contain detailed explanations of domain naming. RFC 1918 explains the address allocations for private networks.

The Hosts Requirements standard, RFC 1122, provides further details about naming and addressing and corrects errors in the defining standards.

Internet Protocol

Introduction

Recall that an internetwork is a set of networks connected by routers,[1] and the Internet Protocol is a network layer protocol that routes data across an internetwork. The researchers and designers who created IP were responding to U.S. Department of Defense (DOD) requirements for a protocol that could:

- Accommodate the use of hosts and routers built by different vendors
- Encompass a growing variety of network types
- Enable the network to grow without interrupting service
- Support higher-layer sessions and message-oriented services

The IP network layer architecture was designed to meet these needs.

It turned out that IP also gave network builders exactly what they needed in order to integrate the local area network (LAN) "islands" that had spread across their organizations. Furthermore, new islands could be plugged in without disrupting what already was in place.

These features eventually caused IP to become the network protocol of choice for government agencies, universities, and businesses.

IP Datagrams

The IP protocol provides the mechanisms needed to transport units called *IP datagrams* across an internetwork. As shown in Figure 6.1, an IP datagram is made up of an IP header and a chunk of data to be delivered.

---

[1]Recall that sometimes the term *gateway* rather than *router* is used.

Figure 6.1
Datagram format.

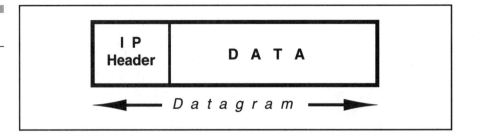

Figure 6.2
IP best effort delivery.

Figure 6.2
IP best effort delivery.

IP is a "best effort" protocol. This means that IP does not guarantee that a datagram will be delivered safely to its destination. All that is guaranteed is that a best effort will be made (see Figure 6.2). A datagram may be destroyed along the way because:

- Bit errors occurred during transmission across a medium.
- Temporarily, there was no usable path to the destination.
- A congested router discarded the datagram because of a shortage of buffer space.

All of the features that ensure reliability have been concentrated within the TCP layer. Recovery from destroyed data depends on TCP actions.

Primary IP Function

The primary IP function is to accept data from TCP or the User Datagram Protocol (UDP), create a datagram, route it through the network, and deliver it to a recipient application. Each IP datagram is routed independently. IP relies on two tools to help it to route datagrams:

1. The *subnet mask*
2. The IP *routing table*

How the Subnet Mask Is Used

We briefly review the use of the subnet mask, which was presented in Chapter 5. Suppose that your computer has IP address 130.15.12.131 and is attached to a LAN. If you have data to be sent:

From: 130.15.12.131

To: 130.15.12.22

You might guess that both systems are on the same subnet. However, your computer needs to check whether this is true. The way to do this is to *throw away the host part of each IP address and compare what is left* (the network and subnet parts). You cannot be sure of exactly which bits are the host part until you look at the subnet mask. Suppose that your host has subnet mask:

  255.255.255.0

This means that the mask consists of 24 ones and 8 zeros:

  11111111 11111111 11111111 00000000

The 0s correspond to the host part of the address, and the 1s identify the network and subnet portions of the address. After dropping the host part, we can see that the network and subnet part of both the source and destination address is 130.15.12, and so both computers are on the same subnet.[2]

For this example, routing is *direct*. This means that the datagram must be wrapped in a frame and transmitted directly to its destination on the LAN, as shown in Figure 6.3.

The destination address that is placed in the frame header must be the physical address of the destination system. The Address Resolution Protocol (ARP) table will be checked to see if there is an entry that provides the physical address for 130.15.12.22. If there is not yet an entry, the ARP protocol will be used to create one.

A small change in the subnet mask for our example shows how important the subnet mask is:

From: 130.15.12.131

To: 130.15.12.22

Subnet mask: 255.255.255.128

---

[2]Your computer actually performs a logical AND between the mask and each of the IP addresses. The effect is that the 0s in the subnet mask zero out the host part of the address, leaving just the network and subnet parts.

Figure 6.3
Framing and trans-
mitting a datagram.

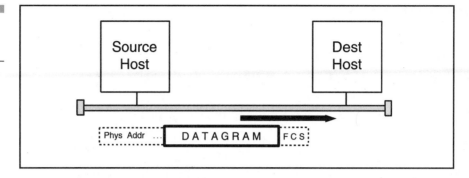

This means that the mask consists of 25 ones and 7 zeros:

11111111 11111111 11111111 10000000

The host part consists of the last 7 bits of the IP address. If we write the
two addresses in binary, they are:

10000010 00001111 00001100 *1*0000011

10000010 00001111 00001100 *0*0010110

The last bit of the subnet parts does not match. These hosts are not on
the same LAN.

Host IP Routing Table

Suppose that you have data to be sent:

From: 130.15.12.131

To: 192.45.89.5

A quick subnet mask check would show that this destination is *not* on
the local subnet. In this case, IP must consult its local routing table.

A host's routing table usually is very simple. Figure 6.4 shows a LAN
that is connected to remote sites by means of a single router. If a destination is not on the local network, a host does not have any choice. The
only way to leave the local net is via that router.

Each host and desktop computer on this LAN contains a routing table
that tells IP how to route datagrams to systems that are not connected
to the LAN. To point the way to remote locations, this routing table
needs the single entry:

default 130.15.12.1

Figure 6.4
Forwarding traffic via
a default router.

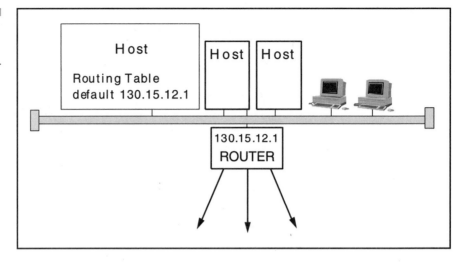

In other words, *forward any nonlocal datagrams to the default router,
which has IP address 130.15.12.1.* (Note that destination address 0.0.0.0
is used to mean *default* in routing tables.)

Next-Hop Routing

The reason that host routing tables can be kept simple is that IP does not
need to look at the complete route that will be followed to a destination.
It only needs to find out the next hop and forward the datagram there.

To forward a datagram to the router interface at 130.15.12.1, the
datagram must be wrapped in a frame whose header contains the physical address of the router's interface card.

When the router receives the frame, it will strip off the frame header
and trailer and examine the IP datagram header in order to decide
where it should go next.

Another Host Routing Table
Example

Sometimes a host routing table is a bit more complicated. For example, there are two routers on the subnet 128.121.50.0 in Figure 6.5.

Figure 6.5
Routing decisions.

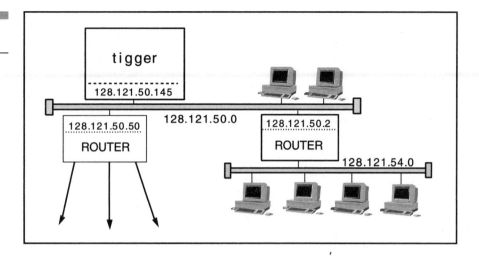

The second router leads to a small LAN that is the home of several workstations.

Tigger has a route to such a LAN. We can view *tigger*'s routing table[3] with the *netstat -nr*[4] command.

```
> netstat -nr
Routing tables
Destination      Gateway           Flags   Refcnt   Use       Interface
127.0.0.1        127.0.0.1         UH      6        62806     lo0
default          128.121.50.50     UG      62       2999087   le0
128.121.54.0     128.121.50.2      UG      0        0         le0
128.121.50.0     128.121.50.145    U       33       1406799   le0
```

The *netstat* output discloses quite a lot of information about how and where *tigger*'s traffic is being routed:

- We can see that the first destination in the table is the *loopback* address, 127.0.0.1. It is a placeholder for traffic between clients and servers within *tigger*.

- The *default* entry is used to route to any destination that is not explicitly listed in the table. Traffic should be forwarded to the router interface at IP address 128.121.50.50.

---

[3]Note the use of the term *gateway* rather than *router* at the head of column 2 in the display.

[4]Other computers may respond with tables that are formatted a little differently. They will contain similar but not necessarily identical information.

- Datagrams to any system on subnet 128.121.54.0 should be forwarded to the router interface at IP address 128.121.50.2.

- The last entry is a placeholder that says "to route to any system on subnet 128.121.50.0, route via 128.121.50.145." But 128.121.50.145 is *tigger*'s own address, and 128.121.50.0 is *tigger*'s own LAN. Although this entry does not provide new routing information, it does let us view some interesting statistics about local traffic.

Netstat displays quite a lot of additional information:

- *Flags* tell whether a route is up (usable) and whether the next hop is a host (H) or gateway (G).

- *REFcnt* tracks the number of currently active uses of the route.

- The *Use* column counts the number of datagrams that have been sent on the route (since the last initialization).

- Interface *lo0* is a *logical* interface used for loopback traffic. All traffic to and from *tigger* passes through the single Ethernet interface, *le0*.

Note that by including the local subnet, 128.121.50.0, in the report, we have discovered that more than twice as much traffic was sent to the outside world than to systems on the local area network.

Rule for Routing Table Lookups

Each entry in a routing table provides information about routing to an individual destination. A routing table destination can be an individual host, a subnet, a network, a supernet, or *default*.

There is a general rule that applies to the way that IP uses a routing table, whether that table is in a host or a router. The entry chosen should be based on the *most precise match* to the destination IP address. In other words, when IP looks up the address of a destination host, conceptually, it is as if:

- The table is first searched to see if there is an entry that matches the complete IP address. If there is, this entry is used to route traffic.

- If not, the table is searched for an entry corresponding to the destination subnet.

- If not, the table is searched for the destination network.
- If not, the table is searched to see if there is a supernet routing prefix entry that matches.
- If this cannot be found, the default route is used.

Of course, a real implementation would search the table just once, throwing away a match when a more precise match was found.

Router Routing Tables

Host routing tables can be very simple, but the tables in routers often will contain a lot more information. A router has two or more interfaces, and each datagram must be transmitted through the appropriate interface. The router may need to record next-hop selections for many different subnets and networks, as shown in Figure 6.6.

Branch Office Routing Table

Some routers have very simple routing tables. For example, the branch office router in Figure 6.7 directs incoming traffic from headquarters to

Figure 6.6
Routing to many
locations.

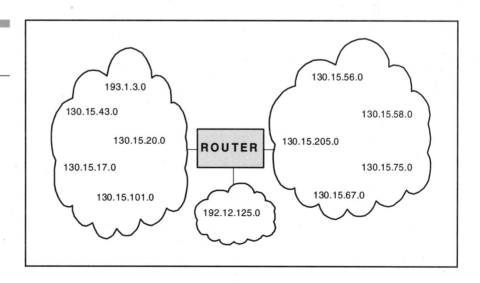

Figure 6.7
Branch office routing.

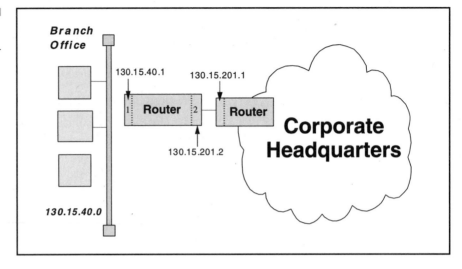

the site's LAN and forwards all outgoing traffic across a wide area link to a router in company headquarters.

This router has two interfaces:

Interface	IP Address
1	130.15.40.1
2	130.15.201.2

Routing table information would include:

Destination	Interface	Next Hop	Type	Protocol
130.15.40.0	1	130.15.40.1	Direct	Manual
0.0.0.0	2	130.15.201.1	Indirect	Manual

The first entry just describes the direct connection to the locally connected subnet, 130.15.40.0. The subnet is reached *directly* through its own interface.

The second entry provides the default route to the rest of the network. The next-hop router is 130.15.201.1, and it is reached via interface 2. The headquarters destinations are reached *indirectly,* via the next-hop router. Both of these routes were entered manually.

Global Routing Operations

So far, we have been concentrating on a single routing decision. Figure 6.8 illustrates a global IP routing operation. When TCP or UDP at Host A wishes to send data to its peer at Host B, the sender passes its data to IP, along with the destination host's IP address. IP adds a header containing the destination IP address to the data.

- IP at Host A examines the destination address to see if the destination is on the local subnet. It isn't, so IP performs a routing table lookup.

- The table indicates that the next hop is Router X. The datagram is framed, and the LAN physical address for Router X is placed in the frame header.

- When the datagram arrives at Router X, the framing is removed. IP at Router X compares the destination IP address with all of its own IP addresses (using the subnet masks) to see if the destination is on a locally connected subnet.

- It isn't, so IP performs a routing table lookup. The next hop is Router Y. The datagram is framed for serial transmission and sent to Router Y.

Figure 6.8
Global routing.

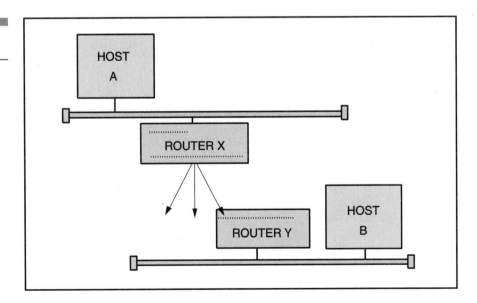

- When the datagram arrives at Router Y, the framing is removed. IP at Router Y compares the destination IP address with all of its own IP addresses (using the subnet masks) to see if the destination is on a locally connected subnetwork. It is, and Router Y frames the datagram for delivery to Host B.

This route from Host A to Host B consists of three hops: A to X, X to Y, and Y to B.

IP Features

There are a number of features that contribute to IP's flexibility and ability to fit into many different environments. Among these features are *adaptive routing* and *datagram fragmentation and reassembly*.

Adaptive Routing

Ordinarily, datagram routing is *adaptive*. That is, a node checks its routing table and chooses the next hop that is best at the current instant. Routing table entries depend on network conditions and can change at any time.

For example, if a link goes down, datagrams will be switched to a different route if one is available (see Figure 6.9).

Figure 6.9
Adaptive routing.

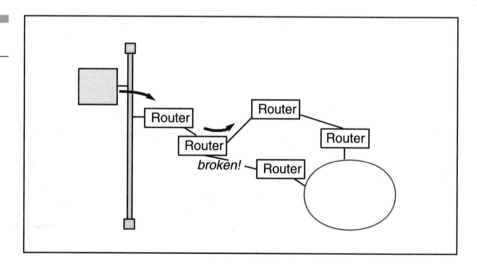

> *A change in network topology just causes datagrams to be rerouted automatically.*

Adaptive routing builds in flexibility and robustness. On the other hand, an IP header *can* contain a strict source route to be followed to a destination. This might be done in order to route sensitive traffic along a secure path.

MTU, Fragmentation, and Reassembly

Before a datagram can be transmitted across a network hop, it must be encapsulated within the layer 2 header(s) required for the network technology, as shown in Figure 6.10. For example, to traverse an 802.3 or 802.5 network, a Media Access Control (MAC) header, Logical Link Control (LLC) header, Sub-Network Access Protocol (SNAP) subheader, and MAC trailer are added.

As we have seen in Chapter 4, each LAN and WAN technology imposes a different size limit on its frames. A datagram has to fit inside a frame, and so the maximum frame size restricts the size of the datagrams that IP can send across a medium.

The maximum datagram size for a medium is computed by subtracting the size of the frame header, frame trailer, and data link layer header from the total maximum frame size:

Max frame size − frame header size − frame trailer size − link layer header size

Recall that the biggest datagram size for a medium is called the *Maximum Transmission Unit,* or MTU. For example, DIX Ethernet has an MTU of 1500 bytes, 802.3/802.2 has an MTU of 1492 bytes, Fiber Distributed Data Interface (FDDI) has an MTU of 4352 bytes, and Switched Multimegabit Data Service (SMDS) has an MTU of 9180 bytes.

Figure 6.10
Transmission format for a LAN header.

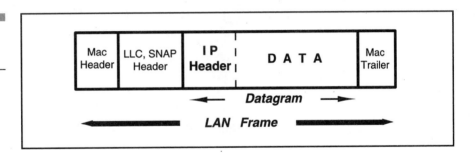

In a large internetwork, an originating host may not know all of the size limits that a datagram will meet along its path. What happens if the source host has sent out a datagram that is too large for some intermediate network?

When the datagram arrives at the router that is attached to that intermediate network, IP solves the size problem by chopping the datagram into several smaller datagrams called *fragments*. It is up to IP *in the destination host* to gather up the incoming fragments and rebuild the original datagram.

Fragmentation most often is performed in a router. However, a UDP application might initiate a large message that causes the sending host to fragment a datagram. Unfortunately, fragmentation is a performance killer. Later, we will find out about several methods that are used to avoid fragmentation.

IP Header

Now we are going to take a close look at what makes IP tick. We examine the IP header and learn the rules for handling a datagram as it traverses a network. Figure 6.11 shows the fields in the IP header. The display below shows a trace of a header that was obtained using Microsoft NT Network Monitor.

```
IP: ID = 0x2400; Proto = TCP; Len: 1500
        IP: Version = 4 (0x4)
        IP: Header Length = 20 (0x14)
        IP: Service Type = 0 (0x0)
        IP:     Precedence = Routine
        IP:     ...0.... = Normal Delay
        IP:     ....0... = Normal Throughput
        IP:     .....0.. = Normal Reliability
        IP: Total Length = 1500 (0x5DC)
        IP: Identification = 9216 (0x2400)
+ IP: Flags Summary = 2 (0x2)
        IP: Fragment Offset = 0 (0x0) bytes
        IP: Time to Live = 32 (0x20)
        IP: Protocol = TCP - Transmission Control
        IP: Checksum = 0x414A
IP: Source Address = 198.207.177.9
IP: Destination Address = 198.207.177.41

IP: Data: Number of data bytes remaining = 1480 (0x05C8)
```

An IP header typically is 20 bytes long, although if options are included, a header can be as big as 60 bytes. The most important fields in the

Figure 6.11
Format of an IP
datagram.

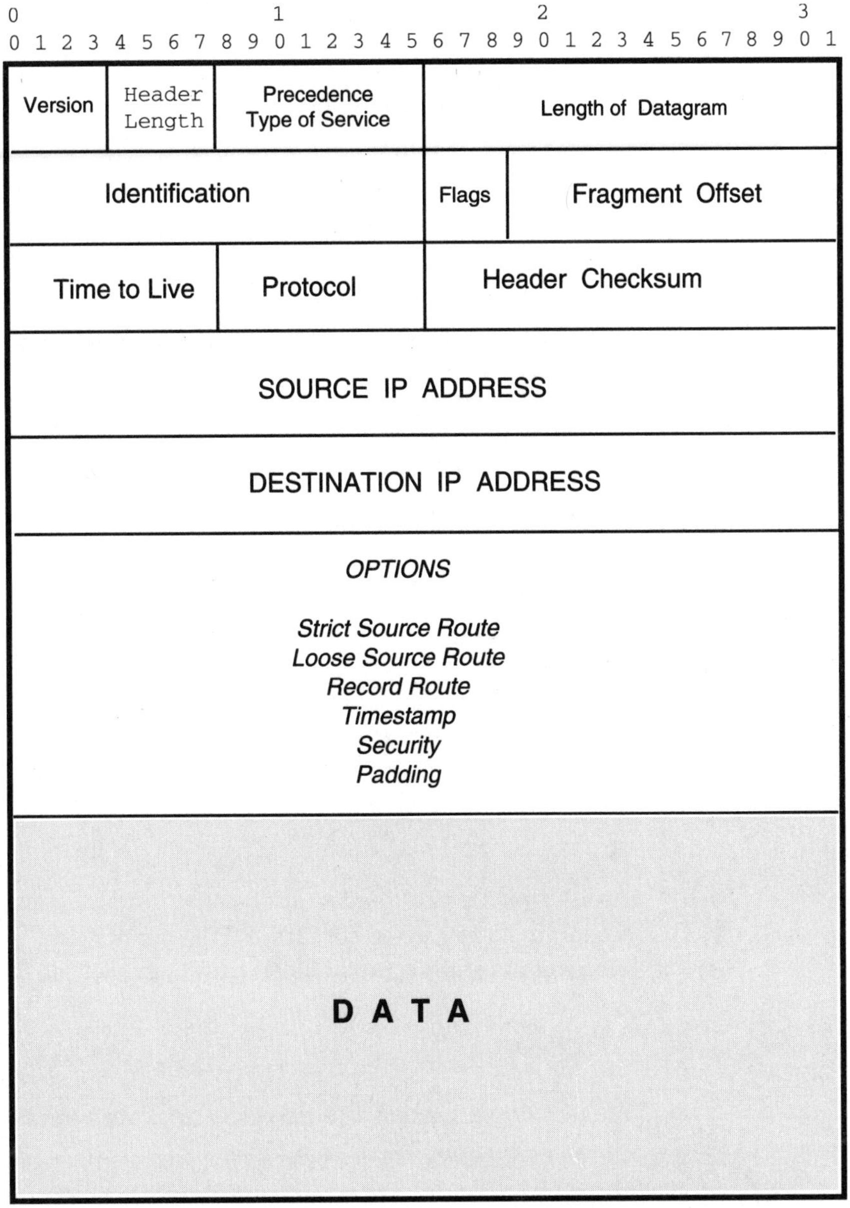

0		1		2		3

0 1 2 3 4 5 6 7 8 9 0 1 2 3 4 5 6 7 8 9 0 1 2 3 4 5 6 7 8 9 0 1

Version	Header Length	Precedence Type of Service	Length of Datagram		
Identification			Flags	Fragment Offset	
Time to Live		Protocol	Header Checksum		
SOURCE IP ADDRESS					
DESTINATION IP ADDRESS					
OPTIONS *Strict Source Route* *Loose Source Route* *Record Route* *Timestamp* *Security* *Padding*					
D A T A					

header are *Destination IP Address, Source IP Address,* and *Protocol.* The destination IP address enables IP to route the datagram. Once the datagram has reached its destination host, the *Protocol* field enables IP to deliver the datagram to the appropriate service—such as TCP or UDP. The value in the Protocol field is 6 in the preceding example, meaning that the datagram contains a TCP segment. Checking through the remaining fields in the sample IP header:

- This is a version 4 datagram. This is the currently prevalent version of IP. (The "Next Generation" version number is 6.)

- The header length is 20 bytes, the most common value.

- This datagram was taken from a file transfer across a DIX Ethernet, so it is not surprising that its total length (including the IP header) is 1500, the biggest size for DIX Ethernet.

- The next field is used to indicate whether special handling is needed. The sending application could set a priority level from 0 (low) to 7 (high). The application also could ask for a special service such as improved delay, better throughput, or superior reliability. This is zeroed out in the example, as is common. However, sophisticated routers can implement these features.

- The next three fields enable fragmentation to work. We discuss them in detail later.

- The Time-To-Live is implemented as a hop counter. It is set when the datagram is initially launched, and then counts down at each router. If the value hits 0 at a router, the datagram has been wandering around the network too long, and it is discarded. The value in the captured datagram is 32.

- Finally, the checksum field contains a checksum value computed against all of the other fields in the IP header.

As is typical, the header shown previously contains no options. The remaining 1480 bytes contain a TCP header and file transfer data. The sections that follow provide bits-and-bytes details for the IP header.

Version

As was noted earlier, the currently deployed version of IP is 4 and the "Next Generation" version number is 6.

Header Length and Datagram Length

The IP header length must be a multiple of 4 bytes. In practice, almost all datagram headers have the minimum length, which is 20 bytes. If one or more options are included, the header will be longer. The maximum size for an IP header is 60 bytes.

Note that the header fields displayed in Figure 6.11 are arranged as a sequence of 32-bit (4-byte) "words." (The bits in a word are numbered from 0 to 31.) The value in the header length field actually indicates the number of 32-bit words. If there are no options, the length is five words (20 bytes). If one or more options are included, the header may need to be padded with 0s so that it ends at a 32-bit word boundary.

The *Datagram Length* field contains the total length of the datagram measured in bytes. The measurement includes both the header and the data portions of the datagram. This 16-bit field can express values up to a maximum of $2^{16} - 1$ (65,535) bytes.

Network maximum frame sizes are not the only reason to limit datagram size. The diverse types of devices that support IP have different limits on the sizes of the memory buffers that they use for network traffic. The IP version 4 standard is very undemanding and imposes the modest requirement that all hosts must be able to accept datagrams consisting of up to 576 bytes.[5] Unfortunately, it turns out that if a host actually limits itself to datagrams that are this small, its performance will suffer badly. Later, we see that there are times when a performance-killing 576-byte default size limit will kick in automatically unless suitable action is taken to prevent it.

Protocol Field

There are several other protocols besides TCP and UDP that send and receive datagrams. The Internet Assigned Numbers Authority (IANA) is responsible for coordinating the assignment of TCP/IP parameter values, including values that can be used in the IP *Protocol* field. Some of the numbers that have been assigned for the IP *Protocol* field relate to proprietary, vendor-specific protocols.

Table 6.1 shows some of the commonly used IP *Protocol* field numbers.

Precedence and Type of Service

The Department of Defense was the original sponsor of the TCP/IP protocol suite, and the ability to assign precedence (priority) levels to datagrams was important to the DOD. Many of today's routers do a good job

---

[5]Currently, a minimum MTU of 1280 bytes has been set for IPv6.

TABLE 6.1

Common IP
Protocol Field
Numbers

#	Title	Protocol	Description
1	ICMP	Internet Control Message Protocol	Carries error messages, and supports some network utilities.
2	IGMP	Internet Group Management Protocol	Supports multicasting groups.
6	TCP	Transmission Control Protocol	Supports sessions.
8	EGP	Exterior Gateway Protocol	Older protocol used to establish routing to external networks.
9	IGRP	Private Interior Gateway Protocol	Used by Cisco for IGRP. Enables Cisco routers to exchange routing information.
17	UDP	User Datagram Protocol	Provides delivery of stand-alone blocks of data.
46	RSVP	Reservation Protocol	Supports quality of service for a flow of data.
50	ESP	Encapsulating Security Payload	Announces that a header used with encrypted data follows.
51	AH	Authentication Header	Announces that a header containing authentication information follows.
88	EIGRP	Cisco's Enhanced Interior Gateway Routing Protocol	Enables Cisco routers to exchange routing information using an improved protocol.
89	OSPF	Open Shortest Path First	Enables OSPF routers to exchange routing information.

of handling datagrams according to their precedence levels, and organizations that wish to prioritize their traffic make use of this feature. There are three precedence bits, providing eight different precedence levels.

The *Type of Service* (TOS) bits contain quality of service information that can affect how a datagram is handled. For example, when a router runs short of memory, it has to discard some datagrams. A router might consider a datagram whose reliability bit is set to 1 to be less eligible for discard than one whose reliability bit is equal to 0.

The position of the precedence and Type of Service bits in the field is:

Bits	Type	Description
0-2	Precedence:	Levels 0-7.
		Level 0 is normal.
		Level 7 provides the highest priority.
3-6	Type of Service	Delay, reliability, throughput, cost, or security.
7	Reserved for future use.	

The Type of Service values, as described in the current *Assigned Numbers* document, are shown in Table 6.2. Settings are mutually exclusive—only one TOS value can be requested in any one IP datagram. The *Assigned Numbers* standard recommends specific values to be used for various applications. For example, minimize delay for *telnet,* maximize throughput when copying a file, and maximize reliability when delivering network management messages.

Some routers ignore the Type of Service field entirely, while others can use the field in making routing decisions or in deciding which traffic should be protected against discard when memory is in short supply. It is believed that Type of Service will play a bigger role in the future. The *Assigned Numbers* document recommends using the values in Table 6.3.

Time-To-Live

When a topology change occurs in an IP internetwork—such as a link down or a new router initializing—some datagrams may wander around during the short period that new routes are being selected. More serious

TABLE 6.2

Type of Service
Values

TOS Value	Description
0000	Default
0001	Minimize Monetary Cost
0010	Maximize Reliability
0100	Maximize Throughput
1000	Minimize Delay
1111	Maximize Security

TABLE 6.3

Recommended
Type of Service
Values

Protocol	TOS Value	Description
Telnet and other login protocols	1000	Minimize delay.
FTP control session	1000	Minimize delay.
FTP data session	0100	Maximize throughput.
TFTP	1000	Minimize delay.
SMTP command phase	1000	Minimize delay.
SMTP DATA phase	0100	Maximize throughput.
Domain Name Service UDP Query	1000	Minimize delay.
Domain Name Service TCP Query	0000	No special handling.
Domain Name Service Zone Transfer	0100	Maximize throughput.
Network News Transfer Protocol	0001	Minimize monetary cost.
ICMP Errors	0000	No special handling.
ICMP Requests	0000	Normally 000, but sometimes sent with other value.
ICMP Responses		Same as request being answered.
Any Interior Gateway Protocol	0010	Maximize reliability.
Exterior Gateway Protocol	0000	No special handling.
Simple Network Management Protocol	0010	Maximize reliability.
Boot Protocol	0000	No special handling.

misrouting problems can result from human error when routing information is entered manually. A mistake can cause datagrams to get "lost" or locked into circular paths for a long time.

The Time-To-Live (TTL) field limits the amount of time that a datagram will be allowed to remain in an internetwork. The TTL is set by the originating host and is decremented at each router that handles the datagram. A datagram that has not yet reached its destination host when the TTL reaches zero is discarded.

Although formally defined as a time in seconds, the TTL actually is implemented as a simple hop counter that is decremented—usually by 1—at each router. (Optionally, a larger decrement could be applied to a datagram that has just crossed a very slow link or has been queued for transmission for a long time.)

The current recommended default TTL is 64.

Header Checksum

This 16-bit field contains a checksum that is computed on the fields[6] of the IP header. The checksum must be updated as the datagram is forwarded because the Time-To-Live field changes at each router. (Other header values also may change because of fragmentation or due to values written into option fields.)

Fragmentation

The Identification, Flags, and Fragment Offset fields enable datagrams to be fragmented and reassembled. Let's examine an example that shows how this works. We'll generate a fragmented datagram using the *ping* function, which is familiar to most users. *Ping* can be used to check whether a remote system is active. We will use *ping* to launch a big datagram that actually is fragmented at its source host. Many different versions of *ping* have been written. The one shown below is available on Windows 95 and Windows NT systems. This command transmits a single *ping* message (-n 1) containing a 4500 byte data field (-l 4500) and an 8-byte protocol header:[7]

```
C:\WINDOWS> ping -n 1 -l 4500 198.207.177.9
```

This produced four datagrams whose headers contained the following fields:

```
1.  IP: Total Length = 1500 (0x5DC)
    IP: Identification = 24320 (0x5F00)
    IP: ......1 = More fragments in datagram after this one
    IP: ......0. = May fragment datagram if necessary
    IP: Fragment Offset = 0 (0x0) bytes

2.  IP: Total Length = 1500 (0x5DC)
    IP: Identification = 24320 (0x5F00)
    IP: ......1 = More fragments in datagram after this one
    IP: ......0. = May fragment datagram if necessary
    IP: Fragment Offset = 1480 (0x5C8) bytes
```

---

[6]The checksum is the 16-bit 1s complement of the 1s complement sum of all 16-bit words in the header. Prior to the calculation, the checksum field is set to 0.

[7]*Ping* is built on top of an ICMP message (the echo message). ICMP messages are described in the next chapter. The ICMP header for the message is 8 bytes long.

```
3.  IP: Total Length = 1500 (0x5DC)
    IP: Identification = 24320 (0x5F00)
    IP: .......1 = More fragments in datagram after this one
    IP: ......0. = May fragment datagram if necessary
    IP: Fragment Offset = 2960 (0xB90) bytes

4.  IP: Total Length = 88 (0x58)
    IP: Identification = 24320 (0x5F00)
    IP: .......0 = Last fragment in datagram
    IP: ......0. = May fragment datagram if necessary
    IP: Fragment Offset = 4440 (0x1158) bytes
```

The total unfragmented payload was 4508 bytes. This was made up of the 8-byte header and 4500 bytes of data. Each of the first three datagrams has length of 1500 bytes. This consists of 20 bytes of IP header and 1480 bytes of the payload. The last datagram is 88 bytes long and carries 68 bytes of payload.

$$3 \times 1480 + 68 = 4508 = \text{size of the original unfragmented payload}$$

Note that:

- Each of the datagram fragments has the same identification number.
- Each of the first three fragment headers contain a flag that says "more follows."
- The fragment offsets identify where each piece fits: 0, 1480, 2960, and 4440 bytes from the start of the original payload.

Let's examine the steps that an IP router follows when processing an incoming datagram whose size is larger than the MTU for the next link:

1. The first step is to check the Flags field. There is a "Don't Fragment" bit in the Flags field. If the "Don't Fragment" flag is set to 1, nothing can be done—the datagram must be discarded.

2. If the "Don't Fragment" flag is 0, the data portion is broken into pieces consistent with the next-hop MTU. Each break must be aligned on an 8-byte boundary.

3. Each piece is given an IP header similar to the header for the original datagram. In particular, each piece will have the same source, destination, protocol, and Identification field value. However, the following fields need to be set separately for each piece:
   a. Length of datagram. This is the length of the datagram holding the current piece.

b. There is a "More" flag in the Flags field. This must be set to 1 in all but the final piece.

c. The Fragment Offset field is set to indicate the position of this piece relative to the beginning of the original datagram. The start position is 0. The fragment offset is actually the true offset divided by 8.

d. Separate checksums must be calculated for each of the fragments.

Now let's look at the individual fields.

Identification Field

The *Identification* field contains a 16-bit number. This number helps the destination host to recognize datagram fragments that belong together.

Flags Field

The *Flags* field contains three bits, as shown below:

Bit 0	Bit 1	Bit 2
0 = Reserved	0 = May Fragment	0 = Last Fragment
	1 = Don't Fragment	1 = More Fragments

Bit 0 is reserved, and must be 0. The sender can set the next bit to 1 to prevent the datagram from being fragmented. If a datagram cannot be delivered without fragmentation and this bit is set to 1, the datagram would have to be discarded and an error message would be sent back to the source.

Bit 2 is set to 0 if this is the last—or the only—piece of a datagram. Bit 2 is set to 1 to indicate that this datagram is a fragment and more fragments follow.

Fragment Offset Field

An 8-byte chunk of data is called a *fragment block*. The number in the *Fragment Offset* field reports the size of the offset in fragment blocks. The

Fragment Offset field is 13 bits long, so offsets can range from 0 to 8191 fragment blocks—corresponding to offsets of from 0 to 65,528 bytes.

A recipient host can tell that an incoming datagram was not fragmented when an offset of 0 shows that it contains the start of the data, while the flag set to "last" shows that it contains the end of the data.

Reconstructing a Fragmented Datagram

A fragmented datagram is reconstructed at the recipient host. The pieces of a fragmented datagram can arrive out of order. When the earliest fragment arrives at the destination host, IP allocates some memory for reassembling the datagram. The *Fragment Offset* field indicates the starting point of the data in this fragment.

Fragments with matching *Identification, Source IP Address, Destination IP Address,* and *Protocol* fields belong together and are merged as they arrive. There is one inconvenient omission in the IP protocol; the recipient has no way of knowing how long the entire datagram will be until the end fragment arrives. The *Total Length* field in a fragment's header field reveals the length of only *that* datagram fragment.

This means that the recipient system has to do some guesswork about how much buffer space to reserve for an incoming datagram. Vendors handle this problem in different ways. Some allocate small incremental buffers to hold incoming fragments, while others use a single, fixed-sized buffer.

The original IP standard imposed a very modest requirement on recipient hosts. They must be able to reassemble datagrams with total length of up to 576 bytes. Clearly, an implementation really should be able to handle fragmented datagrams whose total size is at least the MTU for the interface on which they arrive. The ability to handle bigger datagrams is needed for applications such as the Network File System (NFS), when it runs over UDP. An NFS file server typically sends an 8K block of data in a single UDP datagram.

Reassembly Timeout

Now imagine the scenario:

- A datagram is transmitted.
- The sending process crashes.
- The datagram is fragmented.
- One of the fragments is destroyed along the way.

The receiving host could wait forever, but the missing piece will never arrive. Obviously, the receiving host needs to set a *reassembly timeout*. When the timeout expires, the destination host gives up, discards the received fragments, and sends an error message back to the originator. The reassembly timeout sometimes is configurable, and the recommended value is 60 to 120 seconds.

To Fragment or Not to Fragment

After having gone to all of this trouble to support fragmentation, the procedure turns out to be a real performance bottleneck. As a result, most programmers carefully design their applications so that datagrams are small enough so that they will not be fragmented.

In Chapter 7, we find out about a protocol called *Path MTU Discovery*. Path MTU Discovery prevents fragmentation by finding out the size of the biggest datagram that can be carried all of the way to the destination.

Looking at IP Statistics

We can get an idea of how IP behaves by checking some rough statistics. The *netstat -sp ip* command provides counts of IP statistics. The report that follows was run at a Windows 95 desktop connected to the Internet by a dial-up connection.

```
C:\WINDOWS> netstat -sp ip

IP Statistics

        Packets Received                   = 17529
        Received Header Errors             = 0
        Received Address Errors            = 583
        Datagrams Forwarded                = 0
        Unknown Protocols Received         = 0
        Received Packets Discarded         = 0
        Received Packets Delivered         = 16946
        Output Requests                    = 17592
        Routing Discards                   = 0
        Discarded Output Packets           = 0
        Output Packet No Route             = 0
        Reassembly Required                = 0
        Reassembly Successful              = 0
        Reassembly Failures                = 0
        Datagrams Successfully Fragmented  = 0
        Datagrams Failing Fragmentation    = 1
        Fragments Created                  = 0
```

The *netstat* command produces somewhat more information at a Unix host. The report below was generated at *katie.vnet.net,* which is a server that is accessed by hosts all over the Internet. The variable names that are displayed (such as ipForwarding) have been defined in network management standards documents.

```
Katie> netstat -sP ip

IP    ipForwarding          = 2          ipDefaultTTL         = 255
      ipInReceives          = 14961509   ipInHdrErrors        = 0
      ipInAddrErrors        = 0          ipInCksumErrs        = 1
      ipForwDatagrams       = 0          ipForwProhibits      = 0
      ipInUnknownProtos     = 150        ipInDiscards         = 0
      ipInDelivers          = 14862388   ipOutRequests        = 13124999
      ipOutDiscards         = 0          ipOutNoRoutes        = 0
      ipReasmTimeout        = 60         ipReasmReqds         = 1146
      ipReasmOKs            = 1114       ipReasmFails         = 32
      ipReasmDuplicates     = 19         ipReasmPartDups      = 9
      ipFragOKs             = 1102       ipFragFails          = 0
      ipFragCreates         = 2792       ipRoutingDiscards    = 0
```

The results show that *katie* does not act as a router (ipForwarding = 2). By default, *Katie* will launch datagrams with Time-To-Live hop counter value set to 255. *Katie*'s reassembly timeout is 60 seconds, which is a little short for an Internet server. And in fact, we see that *katie* failed to reassemble datagrams 32 times. There are counts of incoming and outgoing datagrams. The only errors reported are a single bad IP header checksum and 150 datagrams that arrived with protocol fields that identified protocols that *katie* does not support.

Options

Up to 40 extra IP header bytes are available to carry one or more options.[8] The options that are included in a datagram are chosen by the sending applications. Many options were defined in the early years of IP use. A few of these have survived and show up from time to time:

- Strict Source Route
- Loose Source Route
- Record Route

---

[8]The complete list of options is available from the Internet Assigned Numbers Authority.

- Timestamp
- No Operation
- End of Option List (Padding)

Padding is used as needed to make the header length a multiple of 4 bytes when the options do not end on a 4-byte boundary.

The Department of Defense and some other government agencies use security options.

- Department of Defense Basic Security
- Department of Defense Extended Security

A useful new option has recently been defined:

- Router Alert

This option lets a router know that it should examine the datagram carefully because it will need some special processing by the router.

Source Routes

Two source route options are provided. A *Strict Source Route* describes a complete path that must be followed to a destination. A *Loose Source Route* identifies milestones along the way. Any path can be used between identified milestones.

Strict source routes sometimes are used to improve data security. Unfortunately, as we see a little later, source routes also are part of the cracker's arsenal and are used in attempts to thwart network security.

Occasionally, source routes are used for network testing purposes. Loose Source Routes were intended to help out with routing to distant locations.

The mechanisms for strict and loose source routing are the same. The only difference is that *only* systems on the list may be visited when using a strict source route.

Reverse Route

When source routing is used, the traffic flowing back from the destination to the source must follow the same path (i.e., must visit the same set of routers in reverse order).

Figure 6.12
Routes from the point
of view of Host A and
Host B.

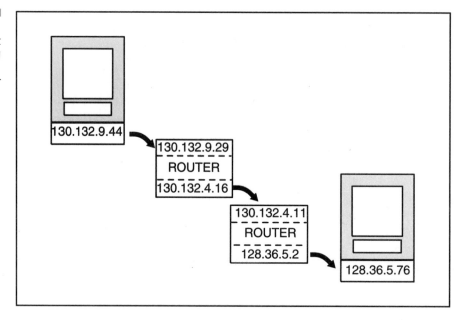

There is one complication: the source and destination views of a router's address are not the same. Figure 6.12 shows a path through two routers. The route from Host A to Host B traverses routers whose IP addresses are known to Host A as 130.132.9.29 and 130.132.4.11. The route from Host B to Host A traverses routers whose IP addresses are known to Host B as 128.36.5.2 and 130.132.4.16. The addresses at each of a router's interfaces differ because the interfaces connect to different subnets, as shown in the figure.

The solution is simple. As each router is visited, the incoming address is replaced in the source route by its outgoing address. The destination takes the resulting list, reverses its order, and uses it as the source route in the opposite direction.

Describing the Route

You might expect the source route to be implemented by listing the routers *between* the source and destination, but this is not what is done. Table 6.4 shows the contents of the *Source IP Address, Destination IP Address,* and *Source Route* fields at each step along the path:

■ At Step 1, the *Destination IP Address* field contains the address of the first router. There is a pointer in the *Source Route* field that points to the next hop (shown in bold print).

TABLE 6.4

Source Routing

Step	Source IP Address	Destination IP Address	Source Route Field
1	130.132.9.44	130.132.9.29	**130.132.4.11** 128.36.5.76
2	130.132.9.44	130.132.4.11	130.132.4.16 **128.36.5.76**
3	130.132.9.44	128.36.5.76	130.132.4.16 128.36.5.2

- At Step 2, the *Destination IP Address* field contains the address of the second router. The pointer in the *Source Route* field points to the next hop along the way. In this example, the next hop is the actual destination for the datagram.

- At Step 3, the datagram has arrived. Its *Source* and *Destination IP Address* fields have the true values, and the *Source Route* field lists the routers to be visited on the way back.

Source Routes and Security

Source Routes have become part of the network cracker's arsenal of burglary tools. They have been used to reach across the Internet into networks that administrators thought were safe.

Routers that filter traffic entering an organization have to be configured either to discard all source-routed traffic or to examine the *Source Route* field for the *real* destination of the datagram.

Another problem arises because multihomed hosts, which are connected to two or more subnetworks, can be targeted to carry source-routed datagrams, providing back door access for traffic. Multihomed hosts should be configured to discard source-routed datagrams, and should never route any traffic.

You can test source routing using *ping*. From a Microsoft Windows system, try:

```
ping -n 1 -k host-list destination
```

Record Route

A *Record Route* field contains a list of IP addresses of routers visited by the datagram. Each router along the way will try to add its outgoing IP address to the list.

The sender presets the length of the Record Route field, and it is possible that all of the space will be used up before the datagram reaches its destination. In this case, the router simply forwards the datagram without adding its address.

You can use *ping* to try out the Record Route option. Below, we record the route for *www.bbnplanet.com,* which is the nickname of a host called *web180b.bbnplanet.com.* We request space for nine addresses, which is the maximum number that the IP options field can hold. Note that there are seven addresses on the outgoing route, and two of the addresses for the return trip are included.

```
C:\WINDOWS> ping -a -n 1 -r 9 www.bbnplanet.com
Pinging web180b.bbnplanet.com [207.121.185.180] with 32 bytes of data:

Reply from 207.121.185.180: bytes = 32 time = 208ms TTL = 248
        Route: core-nwrk1-atm5/0.5.grid.net [206.80.180.129] ->
               mae-e.grid.net [192.41.177.68] ->
               maeeast.bbnplanet.net [4.0.1.94] ->
               vienna1-nbr2.bbnplanet.net [4.0.5.41] ->
               cambridge1-br1.bbnplanet.net [206.34.78.20] ->
               cambridge1-colo1.bbnplanet.net [199.94.217.7] ->
               web180b.bbnplanet.com [207.121.185.180] ->
               cambridge1-colo1.bbnplanet.net [206.34.78.45] ->
               cambridge1-br1.bbnplanet.net [4.0.5.42]
```

Some versions of *ping* for Unix also record routes.

Timestamp

There are three formats for a *Timestamp* field. It may contain:

- A list of 32-bit timestamps.
- A list of IP address and corresponding timestamp pairs.
- A list of preselected addresses provided by the source, each followed by space in which to record a timestamp. A node records a timestamp only if its address is next on the list.

Space may run out if the first or second format is used. There is an overflow subfield that contains a count of the number of nodes that could not record their timestamps.

Department of Defense Basic and Extended Security

The *Basic Security* option is used to assure that the source of a datagram is authorized to transmit it, intermediate routers may appropriately relay it, and the destination should be allowed to receive it.

The *Basic Security* option parameters consist of a classification level that ranges from Unclassified to Top Secret and flags that identify the protection authorities whose rules apply to the datagram. Protection authorities include organizations such as the U.S. National Security Agency, Central Intelligence Agency, and the Department of Energy.

A datagram carrying the Basic Security option may also include an *Extended Security* option field. There are several different formats for this option, depending on the needs of various defining authorities.

A host or router must discard information that it has not been authorized to handle. Secure systems are configured with the range of classification levels that they may transmit and receive and the authority or authorities that are valid. Note that there are many commercial products that do not support secure operation.

End of Option List and No Operation

The *No Operation* option is used as filler between options. For example, it is used if it is desirable to align the next option on a 16- or 32-bit boundary.

The *End of Option List* option is used to pad the end of the options field to a 32-bit boundary.

Encoding Options

There are two single-byte options that are encoded as follows:

No Operation   00000001

End of Option List   00000000

The remaining options consist of several bytes. Each starts with a *type* byte and a *length* byte.

One issue must be considered for these options: should the option be copied into the header of each fragment of a fragmented datagram? This must be done for *Security, Strict Source Routing,* and *Loose Source Routing. Record Route* and *Timestamp* fields appear only in the first fragment.

The type byte can be broken down as follows:

Bits	Function	Description
0	Copy flag:	Set to 1 if copied on fragmentation.
1-2	Option Class	0 for datagram or network control. 2 for debugging and measurement.
3-7	Option Number	Unique value for each option.

Table 6.5 shows the value of the type byte, as well as its breakdown into Copy, Class, and Option Number, for each standard option. The formats for the common option fields are displayed in Figure 6.13.

Encoding a Strict Source Route

A Strict Source Route option contains a pointer and a list of addresses. The pointer contains the position of the next address to be processed. Initially, the pointer starts out with a value of 4. It is incremented by 4 at each hop.

Encoding a Loose Source Route

A Loose Source Route option contains a pointer and a list of addresses. Here again, the pointer starts out with a value of 4. The pointer is incremented when the next address on the list is reached.

Table 6.5

Copy, Class, and Option Number

Value	Copy	Class	Number	Name
0	0	0	0	End of Options List
1	0	0	1	No Operation
137	1	0	9	Strict Source Route
131	1	0	3	Loose Source Route
7	0	0	7	Record Route
68	0	2	4	Timestamp
130	1	0	2	Security
133	1	0	5	Extended Security
148	1	0	20	Router Alert

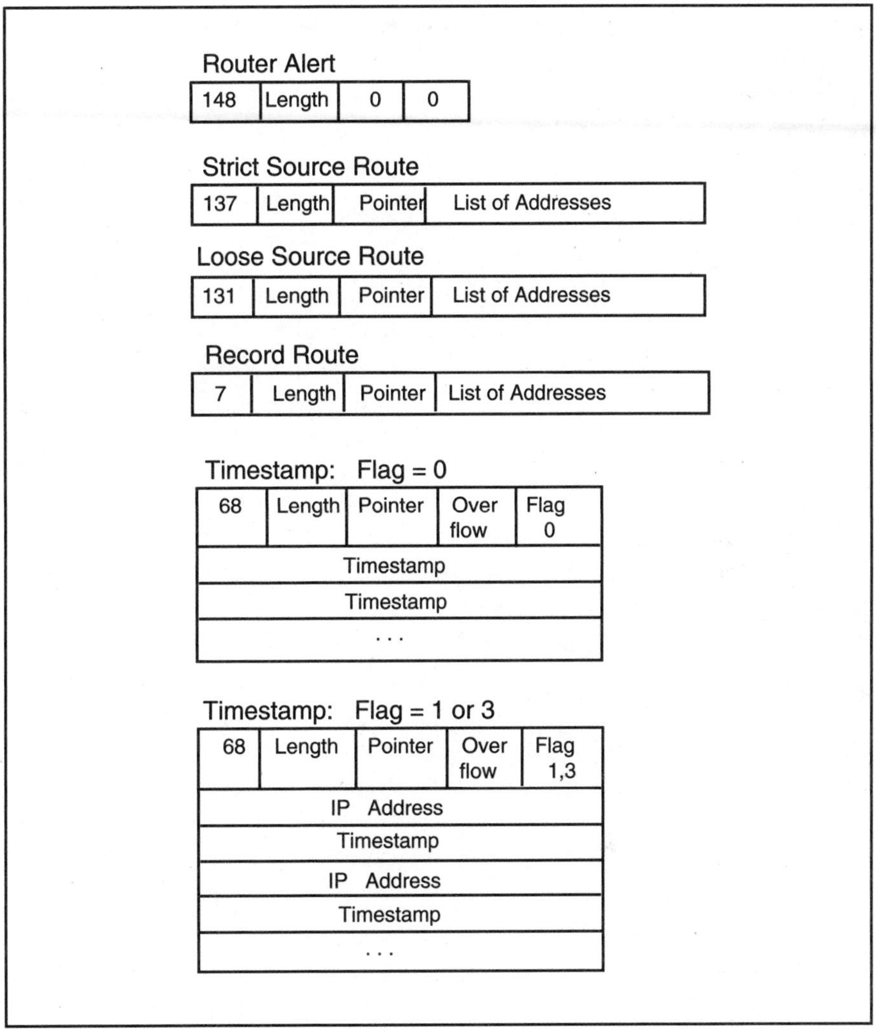

Figure 6.13
Formats for option
fields.

Router Alert

| 148 | Length | 0 | 0 |

Strict Source Route

| 137 | Length | Pointer | List of Addresses |

Loose Source Route

| 131 | Length | Pointer | List of Addresses |

Record Route

| 7 | Length | Pointer | List of Addresses |

Timestamp: Flag = 0

68	Length	Pointer	Over flow	Flag 0
Timestamp				
Timestamp				
. . .				

Timestamp: Flag = 1 or 3

68	Length	Pointer	Over flow	Flag 1,3
IP Address				
Timestamp				
IP Address				
Timestamp				
. . .				

Encoding Record Route

A Record Route option contains a pointer and space for addresses. Initially, the value of the pointer is set to 4. This is followed by unused space that has been set aside to hold addresses.

As each router is visited, its address is recorded at the location indicated by the pointer, and the pointer is incremented by 4. If all of the reserved space gets used up, the datagram is routed to the destination, and no more addresses are recorded.

Encoding a Timestamp

A *Timestamp* option contains a pointer, an overflow subfield, and a flag subfield. The flag field indicates which of the three possible formats is to be used in this timestamp option.

If the flag subfield contains a 0, at each hop a timestamp will be recorded in preallocated space and the pointer will be incremented by 4. If the preallocated space has been used up, the overflow field will be incremented by 1. What happens if the overflow count overflows? The datagram is discarded.

If the flag subfield contains a 1, at each hop an IP address and a timestamp will be recorded in the preallocated space and the pointer will be incremented by 8. If the preallocated space has been used up, the overflow field will be incremented by 1.

Suppose that the sender wants to record timestamps at a list of preselected nodes. In this case, the flag field is set to 3, and the sender fills in the selected addresses.

If the pointer is currently set at a router's address, the router fills in the timestamp value and increments the pointer by 8.

Encoding Basic and Extended Security Options

These options are under the control of military and government agencies. See RFC 1108 for further information.

Sample IP Header

The display in Figure 6.14 shows a fully detailed analysis of a DIX Ethernet MAC frame header and an IP header obtained using a Network General *Sniffer.*

The MAC header starts out with the 6-byte physical addresses of the destination and source stations. Note that the *Sniffer* analyzer has replaced the first 3 bytes of each physical address with the name of the board manufacturer, which in this case is *Sun.* The type field contains the characteristic X'0800 code that says "deliver this information to IP."

In the display, an IP datagram follows immediately after the short DIX Ethernet MAC header. Recall that if this were an 802.3 frame, an 8-byte LLC header with a SNAP subheader would follow the MAC frame header.

■■ ■■ ■■ ■■

Figure 6.14

Interpretation of MAC and IP headers.

```
DLC:    — DLC Header —
DLC:
DLC:    Frame 14 arrived at 10:26:10.5797; size is 61 bytes.
DLC:    Destination = Station Sun    076A03, Sun Atlantis
DLC:    Source      = Station Sun    07FD89, Sun Jupiter
DLC:    Ethertype   = 0800 (IP)
DLC:

IP:     — IP Header —
IP:
IP:     Version = 4, header length = 20 bytes
IP:     Type of Service = 00
IP:         000. .... = routine
IP:         ...0 .... = normal delay
IP:         .... 0... = normal throughput
IP:         .... .0.. = normal reliability
IP:     Total length = 47 bytes
IP:     Identification = 4458
IP:     Flags = 0X
IP:     .0.. .... = may fragment
IP:     ..0. .... = last fragment
IP:     Fragment offset = 0 bytes
IP:     Time to Live = 30 seconds/hops
IP:     Protocol = 6 (TCP)
IP:     Header checksum = 12F4 (correct)
IP:     Source address = [192.42.252.1]
IP:     Destination address = [192.42.252.20]
IP:     No options
IP:

HEX

MAC Header
08 00 20 07 6A 03      (Destination physical address)
08 00 20 07 FD 89      (Source physical address)
08 00                  (Protocol Type for IP)

IP Header
45 00 00 2F (Version, Hdr Length, Prec/TOS, Total Length)
11 6A 00 00 (Identification, Flags, Fragment Offset)
1E 06 12 F4 (Time to Live, Protocol, Header Checksum)
C0 2A FC 01 (Source IP Address)
C0 2A FC 14 (Destination IP Address)
```

The frame size is 61 bytes. This includes the 14-byte MAC frame header but does not include the 4-byte MAC trailer, so the complete frame originally was 65 bytes long. Ethernet or 802.3 frames on coaxial media must have a length of at least 64 bytes, so this frame barely exceeds the minimum size. The datagram in this frame has a total length of only 47 bytes.

Like most IP headers, this one carries no options and therefore has the standard 20-byte length. As is frequently the case, the *Type of Service* field has been set to 0.

We can tell that this datagram is not a fragment of a larger datagram because its *Fragment Offset* field is 0—showing that this is the start of a datagram—and the second flag is set to 0—indicating that this is the end of a datagram.

This datagram has 30 hops left in its *TTL* field. The *Protocol* field has value 6, which means that the datagram will be delivered to TCP at the destination host.

The *Sniffer* has translated the source and destination IP addresses into the convenient dot format.

The hexadecimal bytes that made up the original MAC header and IP header are shown at the bottom of the display. The original *Sniffer* display of the hex fields has been altered to make it easier to match the hex codes to their interpretation.

Datagram Processing Scenarios

To get a better understanding of IP, it is useful to walk through the operations carried out when a datagram is processed at a router and at a recipient host. Figure 6.15 outlines the steps.

Problems or errors generally are handled by discarding the datagram and sending an error report back to the source. These reports are described in Chapter 7, which discusses the *Internet Control Message Protocol* (ICMP).

Router Processing

When a router receives a datagram, the first thing it does is to go through a series of checks to see if the datagram should be discarded. The header checksum is recomputed and compared to the checksum field.

The *Version, Header Length, Total Length,* and *Protocol* fields are screened to see that they make sense. The Time-To-Live value is decremented. A checksum error, parameter error, or zero Time-To-Live value cause the datagram to be discarded. Of course, the datagram also could get discarded if the router did not have enough free buffer space to continue processing the datagram.

The next step is to perform security screening. A series of preconfigured tests is applied to the datagram. For example, a router might

Figure 6.15
Datagram
processing.

ROUTER	HOST
Remove frame header and trailer.	Remove frame header and trailer.
Compute Header Checksum. Discard if invalid.	Compute Header Checksum. Discard if invalid.
Check parameters. Discard if invalid.	Check parameters. Discard if invalid.
Decrement the Time to Live. Discard if 0.	Check Destination. Here? Keep it.
Perform security screening. Discard if datagram fails any test.	(Perform security screening.)
Select next hop from routing table. Discard if fragmentation is needed and "don't fragment" flag=1.	Source routed? Check whether allowed to forward.
Process options, if present. Update fields for options such as such as source routing.	Not Fragmented? Deliver to higher layer service.
Update datagram header (or headers for fragments). Compute new header checksum(s).	Fragment? Insert. If datagram is complete, deliver to upper layer service.
Wrap in a fresh frame.	Fragmentation timer expired? Discard fragments.
Transmit to next hop system.	

restrict incoming traffic so that only a small number of destination servers were accessible.

Next, the router executes the routing procedure. A strict or loose source routing option will be consulted if it is present. An advanced router might take the Type of Service value into consideration. If the datagram cannot be routed without fragmentation and the "don't fragment" field is set to 1, the datagram will be discarded. If allowed and necessary, the datagram will be fragmented.

If options are present, they are processed. An updated header must be built for each datagram (or datagram fragment). Finally, the header checksum is recalculated, and the datagram is forwarded to its next-hop system.[9]

---

[9]This is the common scenario for datagram processing at a router. However, there are times when a router will be the final destination for a datagram. For example, a request for network management information may be sent to a router.

Routers, Switches, and Switching Routers

Why are switches faster than routers? A switch is a layer 2 device that operates by examining frame headers. It builds a switching table by recording the source MAC addresses of each incoming frame and the switch interface on which the frame arrived. For example, if a frame with MAC address *m* arrives on interface 2, the switch records this fact. The switch then will be able to deliver all frames with destination MAC address *m* by transmitting them out of interface 2. The switch does not remove the frame header and trailer. It examines the frame header and then transmits the frame. Switches are simple, and can operate at blinding speed.

Routers are pretty fast, but as Figure 6.15 illustrated, they need to perform a substantial amount of computing on each datagram. A router removes the frame wrapping on the way in and must rewrap on the way out. A router computes a checksum, consults a routing table, and performs security screening.

Some organizations are speeding up network performance by flattening out their networks and doing more switching and less routing. However, there are several disadvantages to large, switched networks. Broadcasts go everywhere. Switches cannot tolerate a topology that contains loops, so there cannot be two active paths to the same destination.

The happy compromise is a routing switch technology. A network is broken up into virtual LANs in order to keep broadcasts under control. When a flow of datagrams is sent between two virtual LANs, the first datagram is routed and a special table entry is created. The rest can be switched using the destination MAC frame address. Some routing switch interfaces operate purely as routers. This allows a robust, redundant topology to be built.

Destination Host Processing

At the destination host, the checksum is computed and compared to the *Header Checksum field*. The destination address is checked to make sure it is valid for this host. The *Version, Header Length, Total Length,* and *Protocol* fields are screened for correctness. A datagram will be discarded if any of these are in error or if the host does not have buffer space available to process the datagram.

The ability to perform security screening on incoming datagrams has been added to many server hosts. Traffic from unauthorized source addresses can be discarded, and a set of permissible applications can be established. This is a valuable feature that should be used when it is available.

If the datagram is a fragment, the host checks four fields: *Identification, Source Address, Destination Address,* and *Protocol.* Fragments with identical values in all of these fields belong to the same datagram. Next, the Fragment Offset value is used to position this fragment correctly within the whole.

Complete datagrams are delivered to the appropriate higher-layer service, such as TCP or UDP.

A host cannot wait indefinitely to complete the reassembly of a datagram. When the initial fragment arrives, a timer is set at a locally configured value—usually between 1 and 2 minutes. The fragments of the incomplete datagram are discarded when the timer expires.

Firewalling and Security

A site may need protection from the outside world. Everyone wants to enjoy the benefits of communication. But prudent network managers know that their computer resources must be protected from crackers. A filtering router has become the most popular defense weapon in a network manager's arsenal.

A filtering router is set up to admit or discard traffic based on the security needs of a site. As shown in Figure 6.16, a filtering router can be configured to enable or disable traffic based on:

- Source IP address
- Destination IP address
- Protocol
- Application

For example, internal users might be permitted to send and receive electronic mail and to access external World Wide Web (WWW) servers. External users might be allowed to access a small selection of servers at the site.

The trouble with a simple filtering firewall is that it only can make decisions based on the single datagram that it currently is inspecting. Adding a smart firewall can enhance security. There are two types of firewall—*stateful* and *proxy*. Either type may be integrated with a

Figure 6.16
A firewall router.

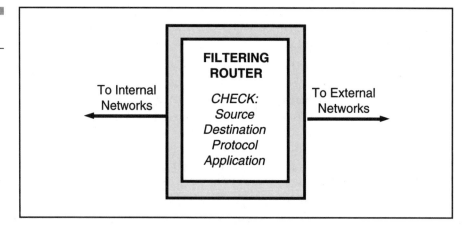

router or operate as a standalone system placed in the path between a site and other networks.

A stateful firewall maintains awareness of what is going on in each session. For example, it can correlate a file that is being transferred to a client with the client's earlier request for that file.

Some firewall hosts act as proxies. When an internal user requests information from the outside world, the proxy firewall actually communicates with the external system, gets the information, and then relays the information to the internal user.

For some implementations, internal users must connect to the firewall and authenticate themselves before they will be allowed to connect to or from the outside world. Users can be assigned privileges on an individual basis. All traffic exchanged with the outside world is filtered through the firewall system and can be screened carefully.

To be well protected, a site can set up a "demilitarized zone" LAN that places a firewall host and all externally accessible application servers on a LAN that is protected by filtering routers. Figure 6.17 shows a demilitarized zone LAN that is used to protect a site from Internet intruders.

Figure 6.17
Protecting a site with a demilitarized zone.

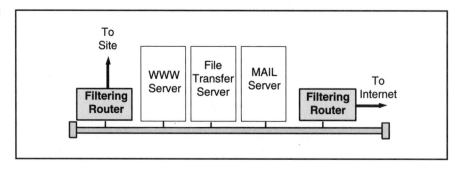

Firewalls enable clients in a network that uses private addresses to communicate across the Internet. The firewall has a public address and replaces the internal client addresses with its own address. The firewall's address is the only one visible to systems in the outside world.

IP Performance Issues

The performance of an internetwork depends on the quantity of available resources in its hosts and routers and on how efficiently the resources are used. These resources are:

- Transmission bandwidth
- Buffer memory
- Central Processing Unit (CPU) processing

Perfect protocol mechanisms are unknown. Protocol design involves tradeoffs between gains and losses in efficiency.

Transmission Bandwidth

IP makes efficient use of bandwidth. Datagrams queued for transport to their next hop can be transmitted as soon as any bandwidth is available. There is no waste due to having to reserve bandwidth for specific traffic or waiting for acknowledgments.

Furthermore, there are very capable IP routing protocols that can split traffic over multiple paths and can choose routes dynamically so that they avoid a congested router or an overloaded link. Use of these protocols will help to maintain the best possible use of the available transmission resources.

There is little overhead due to control messages. ICMP error messages are the only source of control traffic.

There are some potentially negative features. When a load of traffic is directed from one or more high-speed LANs to a lower bandwidth point-to-point line, datagrams start to pile up in a queue at the router. Delivery time from source to destination increases, and some datagrams will be discarded. This will cause TCP to retransmit datagrams, increasing the load and decreasing the effective throughput.

Note that once a network becomes congested, datagram delivery becomes slower and less reliable. TCP retransmissions could have had the effect of keeping the network congested. Fortunately, some very effective algorithms cause TCP to respond to congestion immediately by throttling back the amount of data that is sent and slowing down the retransmission rate. These algorithms have a significant impact on network performance and have become a required part of the TCP standard. They are discussed in Chapter 9.

Router vendors are competing vigorously in offering ever more capable products, able to process millions of datagrams per second.

Buffer Utilization

Once an IP router has transmitted a datagram, its responsibility for that datagram is over. The buffer that was occupied by the datagram is available for immediate reuse. However, IP at a destination host will have to tie up some of its buffer space if it is reassembling a fragmented datagram.

Buffer Memory and Congestion

As we noted earlier, when a router connects one or more fast links to a slow link, datagrams from the fast links can pile up and fill an outgoing router memory queue (see Figure 6.18). When a queue is almost full, the router will discard all of the datagrams.[10]

Router congestion is the most common cause of datagram loss.

CPU Processing

There is little CPU overhead in processing datagrams. Header analysis is straightforward. There is no need for elaborate software to manage timeouts and retransmissions. Because it is connectionless and dynamic, IP requires routing to be executed at each hop. But this is accomplished by simple table lookups, which can be accomplished quickly even for very large tables.

---

[10]An alternative strategy is to selectively start discarding some datagrams as soon as a pileup starts. There is debate on which strategy works best.

Figure 6.18
Fast links feeding into
a slow link.

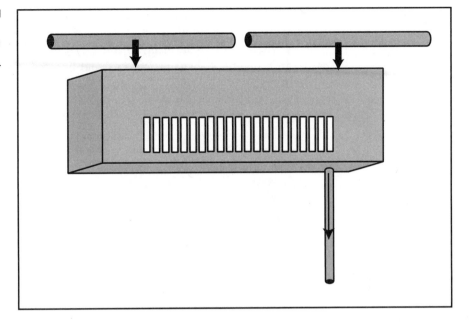

In spite of this, a single central CPU may have trouble keeping up with the 100 megabit and gigabit per second transmission rates that are available today. A new generation of routers and routing switches process datagrams in parallel in multiple hardware modules.[11] Routers have accelerated so that they can keep up with gigabit-per-second wire speeds.

Note that security screening performed by routers can slow down processing, especially if there is a very long list of conditions to be checked for each datagram. Some routers include extra processing modules dedicated to filtering and inspecting traffic.

Recommended Reading

The IP protocol was defined in RFC 791. Updates, corrections, and conformance requirements are specified in RFC 1122. RFC 1812 details the requirements for IP version 4 routers and explains many details about the operation of these routers.

---

[11]These are built with Application Specific Integrated Circuits or ASICs.

The Router Alert option is defined in RFC 2113. Department of Defense security options are discussed in RFC 1108. RFCs 1071, 1141, and 1624 discuss computation of the Internet checksum. RFC 815 presents an efficient algorithm for reassembling fragmented datagrams at a recipient host.

Internet Control
Message Protocol

Introduction

IP has a simple, elegant design. Under normal conditions IP makes very efficient use of memory and transmission resources. But what happens when things go wrong? After a router has crashed and disrupted the network, what notice is given that datagrams are wandering around until their Time-To-Lives (TTLs) expire? What warning is provided so that applications don't persist in sending information to an unreachable destination?

The *Internet Control Message Protocol* (ICMP) keeps traffic sources updated on a number of network problems. ICMP also plays the role of network helper, assisting hosts with their IP routing and enabling network managers to discover the status of network nodes. ICMP's functions are an essential part of IP. All hosts and routers must be able to generate ICMP messages and process the ICMP messages that they receive. Properly used, ICMP messages can contribute to smoother network operation.

ICMP messages are carried in IP datagrams with ordinary IP headers (see Figure 7.1) with the *Protocol* field set to 1.

Figure 7.1

Packaging for an ICMP message.

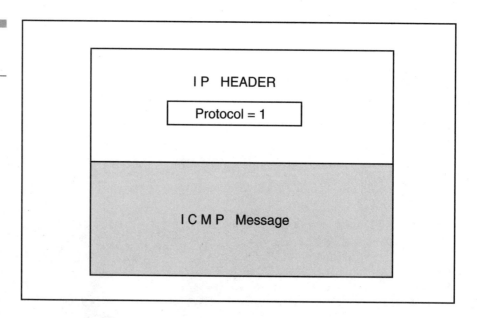

ICMP Error Messages

There are a number of situations that cause IP datagrams to be discarded. For example, a destination may be unreachable because a link is down. The Time-To-Live hop count may have expired. It might be impossible for a router to forward a large datagram because fragmentation was not enabled. When a datagram has to be discarded, ICMP messages are used to report the problem to the source that sent the datagram. Figure 7.2 shows an ICMP message traveling to a datagram source.

ICMP notifies systems of problems quickly. ICMP is a very robust protocol because error notification does not depend on the existence of a network management center.

There also are disadvantages. For example, if a destination is not reachable, messages will be propagated to sources all over the network, rather than to a network management station.

In fact, ICMP has no facilities for reporting errors to a designated network operations center. This is left up to the Simple Network Management Protocol (SNMP), which is presented in Chapter 20.

Figure 7.2
ICMP message directed to a traffic source.

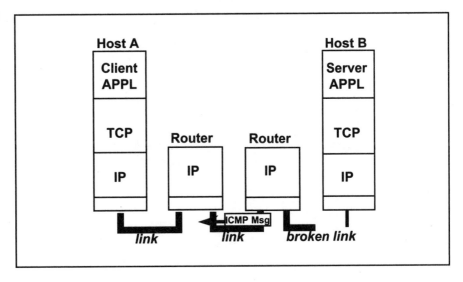

Figure 7.3
Types of ICMP error
messages.

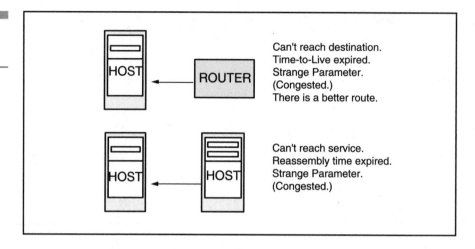

Types of Error Messages

Figure 7.3 summarizes the messages that routers and destination hosts send in order to report problems. Table 7.1 lists the formal names for the ICMP error messages.

Obligation To Send ICMP Error Messages

The ICMP protocol does not require *every* error to trigger an ICMP message. This makes very good sense. The first priority of a router is to forward datagrams. And a busy recipient host should give more attention to delivering datagrams to its applications than to remote

TABLE 7.1

ICMP Error
Messages

Message	Description
Destination Unreachable	A datagram cannot reach its destination host, utility, or application.
Time Exceeded	The Time-To-Live has expired at a router, or the Fragment Reassembly Time has expired at a destination host.
Parameter Problem	There is a bad parameter in the IP header.
Source Quench	A router or destination is congested. (It is strongly recommended that systems should not send Source Quench messages.)
Redirect	A host has routed a datagram to the wrong local router.

error notifications. It won't hurt if occasionally some discards are not reported.

In fact, some network administrators prefer to turn off all but the most essential ICMP messages.

Incoming ICMP Messages

What happens when a host receives an ICMP message? Let's look at an example. We'll try to connect to an address at one of the reserved—and therefore unreachable—networks:

```
> telnet 10.1.1.1
Trying 10.1.1.1 …
telnet: connect: Host is unreachable
```

Note that we've been told exactly what happened. To find out *which* router sent the ICMP message(s), we can use a handy tool called *traceroute* on most systems (but called *tracert* on Windows systems):

```
> traceroute 10.1.1.1
traceroute to 10.1.1.1 (10.1.1.1), 30 hops max,   40 byte packets
1 nomad-gateway              (128.121.50.50)   2 ms 2 ms 2 ms
2 liberty-gateway            (130.94.40.250) 91 ms 11 ms 78 ms
3 border2-hssi2-0.NewYork.mci.net (204.70.45.9)    !H !H !H
```

The New York router has sent *Destination Unreachable* messages which are reported on the screen as the "!H" responses.

The *traceroute* function itself is based on ICMP *Time Exceeded* messages. The procedure is:[1]

- ▣ A UDP message containing a small amount of text data is constructed. The message is given an IP header whose Time-To-Live field is set equal to 1.

- ▣ The datagram is transmitted three times.

- ▣ The first router (*nomad-gateway* in the preceding example), decrements the Time-To-Live value to 0, discards the datagram, and sends an ICMP Time Expired message back to the source.

- ▣ The *traceroute* function identifies the router that sent the messages and prints the three round-trip times.

---

[1]The Unix *traceroute* program uses UDP messages. However, the Windows version, *tracert*, sends ICMP echo messages, which are described later in this chapter.

- The Time-To-Live is set to 2, and the messages are sent again.
- The process is repeated, increasing the Time-To-Live at each step.

If the destination can be reached, eventually the full route will be displayed.

When *Not* To Send ICMP Messages

ICMP messages can be useful to end users and network troubleshooters within your own intranet. However, many sites that are connected to the Internet block out almost all incoming ICMP messages that arrive from the Internet. This is a wise precaution. Hackers have attacked sites by streaming in ICMP messages that clog links and disrupt network operations. Most ICMP messages are not essential; if datagrams cannot be delivered, then the communication will terminate anyway after a time out period.

In addition, many sites do not send ICMP messages back to Internet sources. If someone is trying to break into your site, you do not want to provide information on why their traffic is not getting through, and what system is blocking them.

The ICMP protocol includes some obvious limits on when systems may send ICMP error messages. We can expect to receive error messages when a network is under stress. It is important to ensure that the ICMP traffic does not flood the network, making the situation much worse. Therefore ICMP messages will not report problems caused by:

- Routing or delivering ICMP messages
- Broadcast or multicast datagrams
- Datagram fragments other than the first
- Messages whose source address does not identify a unique host (e.g., a source IP address such as 127.0.0.1 or 0.0.0.0)

ICMP Message Format

Recall that an ICMP message is carried in the data part of an IP datagram. Each ICMP message starts with the same three fields: a *Type* field, a *Code* field, and a *Checksum* field.

- The Type field is a 1-byte number that identifies the kind of ICMP message that will follow.
- The Code field is a 1-byte number that sometimes provides a more specific description of an error.
- The ICMP checksum is applied to the ICMP message (starting from its *Type* field).

The type determines the format of the rest of the message.

ICMP error messages enclose the IP header and first 8 bytes of the datagram that caused the error. This information can be the basis for problem solving since the original IP header includes the intended destination and the target layer 4 protocol. When we study TCP and UDP, we will discover that the extra 8 bytes include information that identifies the communicating application entities.

Destination Unreachable Message

There are many stages at which delivery of a datagram can fail. Because of a broken link, a router may be physically unable to reach a destination subnet or to execute the next hop in a source route. A destination host may be unavailable because it is down for maintenance.

As we have seen in Chapter 6, modern routers have powerful security features. A router can be configured so that it screens the traffic entering a network. Thus, datagrams may be undeliverable because communication with the destination has been administratively prohibited.

The format of the *Destination Unreachable* message is shown in Figure 7.4. The *Type* (3 in this case) identifies this as a *Destination Unreachable* message. The *Code* indicates the reason. The full list of

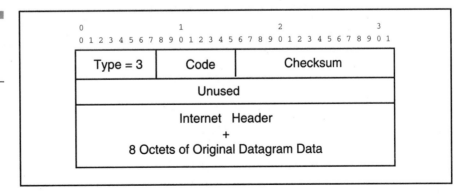

Figure 7.4
Format of the Destination Unreachable ICMP message.

TABLE 7.2

Destination
Unreachable Error
Codes

Code	Meaning
0	Network is unreachable.
1	Host is unreachable.
2	Requested protocol is unreachable (possibly not supported at the destination).
3	Port is unreachable. (Remote application may be unavailable.)
4	Fragmentation is needed but the "Don't Fragment" flag is set.
5	Source route has failed.
6	Destination network is unknown.
7	Destination host is unknown.
8	Source host is isolated.
9	Communication with destination net is administratively forbidden.
10	Communication with destination host is administratively forbidden.
11	Network is unreachable for specified Type of Service.
12	Host is unreachable for specified Type of Service.
13	Communication Administratively Prohibited by router filtering.
14	Host Precedence Violation. Sent by the first-hop router. The requested precedence is not permitted (based on source/destination IP address, port, or protocol).
15	Precedence cutoff in effect. The requested precedence is below a minimum set by network operators.

codes is quite extensive and is shown in Table 7.2. The trace below describes a typical Destination Unreachable message. Unreachable code x0D (13) means that communication was administratively prohibited because of router filtering.

```
ICMP: Destination Unreachable: 10.1.1.1
ICMP: Packet Type = Destination Unreachable
ICMP: Unreachable Code = 0x0D
ICMP: Checksum = 0xA796
ICMP: Unused Bytes = 0 (0x0)
ICMP: Data: Number of data bytes remaining = 28 (0x001C)
        (Original IP header + 8 bytes follows)
```

Time Exceeded Message

A datagram may time out because the Time-To-Live reached zero while the datagram was in transit. Another kind of timeout occurs when a

Figure 7.5
Format of the Time
Exceeded ICMP
message.

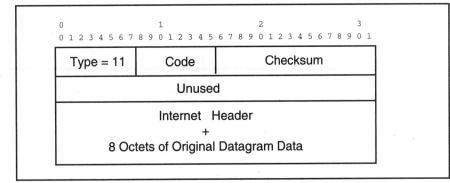

destination host's reassembly timer expires before all of the pieces have arrived. In either case, an ICMP *Time Exceeded* message is sent to the datagram source. The format of the *Time Exceeded* message is shown in Figure 7.5. The code values (shown in Table 7.3) indicate the nature of the timeout. The trace below describes a typical Time Exceeded message.

```
ICMP: Time Exceeded while trying to deliver to 166.82.01.07
ICMP: Packet Type = Time Exceeded
ICMP: Time Exceeded Code = Time To Live Exceeded In Transit
ICMP: Checksum = 0x9FA3
ICMP: Data: Number of data bytes remaining = 28 (0x001C)
        (Original IP header + 8 bytes follows)
```

Parameter Problem Message

The ICMP *Parameter Problem* message is used to report problems not covered by any of the other error messages. For example, there may be some inconsistent information in an options field that makes it impossible to process the datagram correctly. Most often, parameter problems arise because of implementation errors at the system that wrote the parameter into the IP header. Parameter problem errors are rare today.

TABLE 7.3

Time Exceeded
Codes

Code	Meaning
0	Time-To-Live exceeded.
1	Fragment Reassembly Time exceeded.

Figure 7.6
Format of the Parameter Problem ICMP message.

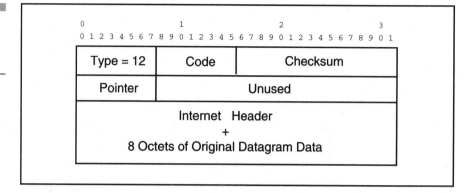

The Pointer field in the ICMP Parameter Problem message identifies the byte at which the error was detected. Figure 7.6 displays the format of the *Parameter Problem* message. Table 7.4 displays the *Parameter Problem* code values.

Congestion Problems

The IP protocol is very simple; a host or router processes a datagram and sends it on as quickly as possible. However, delivery does not always proceed smoothly. A slow wide area connection, such as a T1 link between two 10-megabit-per-second LANs, can create a bottleneck. Congestion causes a router to discard a batch of datagrams. This can trigger retransmissions that produce even more traffic.

Fortunately, TCP does an excellent job of traffic control. TCP slows down when a network gets congested. TCP also is careful never to overflow the destination host's buffer space. However, UDP provides no traffic or flow control service. Heavy UDP traffic can put a router into a persistent state of congestion. UDP traffic arriving at a slow server may

TABLE 7.4

Parameter Problem Codes

Code	Meaning
0	The value in the pointer field identifies the octet where an error occurred.
1	A required option is missing (used in the military community to indicate a missing security option).
2	Bad length.

flood the server with UDP traffic. This will cause the server to discard the overflow traffic.

Source Quench

Unfortunately, we cannot look to ICMP to solve congestion problems. The *Source Quench* message shown in Figure 7.7 was intended to help cure congestion. Unfortunately, no one ever was able to figure out:

> *When—and to whom—should a router or host send a Source Quench message, and what should the receiver do about it?*

Usually, ICMP error messages tell a source host why one of its datagrams has been discarded. However, in a congestion situation, it is possible that many of the datagrams that happen to be discarded do not come from the hosts that are generating very heavy traffic.

Also, the wisdom of loading extra messages onto a congested network is questionable. The current *Router Requirements* document (RFC 1812) stipulates that in fact, *Source Quench* messages *should not* be sent. Then what is the cure for congestion? There is no substitute for solid network administration:

- Keeping the network design up-to-date and removing unnecessary bottlenecks.
- Performing capacity planning and upgrading equipment and transmission levels when needed.
- Checking application activity and rescheduling tasks (such as big file transfers) to off-peak times.
- Prioritizing traffic.

Figure 7.7
Format of the Source Quench message.

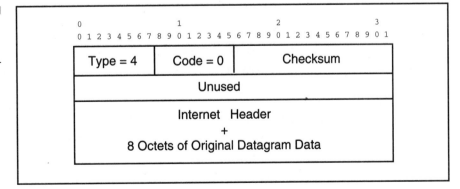

0	1	2	3
0 1 2 3 4 5 6 7	8 9 0 1 2 3 4 5	6 7 8 9 0 1 2 3	4 5 6 7 8 9 0 1

Type = 4	Code = 0	Checksum

Unused

Internet Header + 8 Octets of Original Datagram Data

Figure 7.8
Correcting host
routing via a Redirect
message.

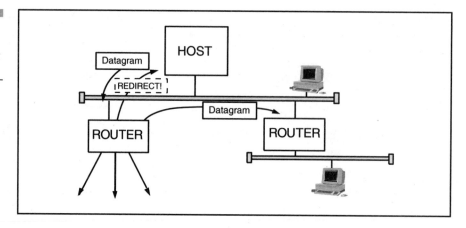

Redirect

More than one router might be attached to a LAN. If a local host sends a datagram to the wrong router, the router forwards the datagram but sends a *Redirect* message to the source host, as shown in Figure 7.8. The host should switch subsequent traffic to the shorter route.

Redirect messages cut down on manual network administration chores. A host can be configured with a single default router and then will dynamically learn about paths that pass through other routers. For example, there are several routers on *katie*'s LAN. However, *katie*'s routing table, shown below, only has been configured with a default router.

```
> netstat -nr

Routing Table:
  Destination    Gateway        Flags    Ref        Use         Interface
  166.82.1.0     166.82.1.7     U        3          143559      1e0
  224.0.0.0      166.82.1.7     U        3          0           1e0
  default        166.82.1.1     UG       01181512
  127.0.0.1      127.0.0.1      UH       0          52568       1o0
```

However, pinging a host on subnet 82 produces an interesting result. Note that a route to 166.82.82.2 via router 166.82.1.116 has been added. This entry is temporary. It will be discarded after a timeout period.

```
> ping 166.82.82.2
ICMP Host redirect from gateway rtr-char1.vnet.net (166.82.1.1)
to rtr-char6.vnet.net (166.82.1.116) for chrissy.vnet.net
(166.82.82.2)

> netstat -nr
```

Figure 7.9
Format of the Redirect ICMP message.

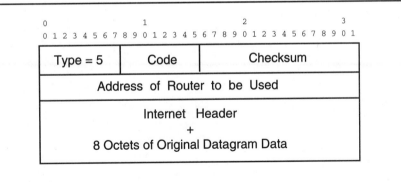

Figure 7.9
Format of the Redirect ICMP message.

```
Routing Table:
  Destination    Gateway        Flags   Ref        Use      Interface
166.82.82.2      166.82.1.116   UGHD    0          2
166.82.1.0       166.82.1.7     U       3          143569   le0
224.0.0.0        166.82.1.7     U       3          0        le0
default          166.82.1.1     UG      01181585
127.0.0.1        127.0.0.1      UH      0          52568    lo0
```

The format of the Redirect message is shown in Figure 7.9. Redirect codes are listed in Table 7.5. Codes 2 and 3 reflect the fact that sometimes routers choose a delivery path based on a datagram's *Type of Service* (TOS) field.

Handling of Incoming ICMP Error Messages

When ICMP error messages arrive at a source host, what happens to them? Vendors vary greatly in the way that they implement networking

TABLE 7.5

Redirect Codes

Code	Meaning
0	Redirect datagrams for the Network.
1	Redirect datagrams for the Host.
2	Redirect datagrams for the Type of Service and Network.
3	Redirect datagrams for the Type of Service and Host.

software, and TCP/IP standards try to allow for a lot of leeway. The guidelines given for the various message types are:

Destination Unreachable The ICMP message is delivered to the transport layer. For TCP, if the problem is transient, TCP will retry for a period of time. Otherwise the application will be notified. The application may pass the information on to the user via a message shown on the user's screen.

Redirect The host must update its routing table.

Time Exceeded The ICMP message is delivered to the transport layer. TCP will retry for a period of time. UDP can notify the application.

Parameter Problem The ICMP message is delivered to the transport layer; which may notify the application.

Path MTU Discovery

When performing a function (such as a file transfer) which carries bulk data from one host to another, the size of the datagrams that are used can have a big impact on performance. IP and TCP headers use up at least 40 bytes of overhead.

- If data is sent in 80-byte datagrams, overhead is 50 percent.
- If data is sent in 400-byte datagrams, overhead is 10 percent.
- If data is sent in 4000-byte datagrams, overhead is 1 percent.

To minimize overhead, we would like to send the biggest datagrams that we can. But recall that there are limits on the biggest datagram size [the Maximum Transmission Unit (MTU)] that can be transmitted across each medium. If datagrams are too large, they will be fragmented, and fragmentation slows performance.

For many years, hosts avoided fragmentation by setting the MTU to 576 for traffic to any nonlocal destination. But experiments have shown that using 576-byte datagrams significantly reduces data transfer performance.

Fortunately, when setting up a TCP session, most hosts will announce the size of the biggest message that they can receive. On modern networks, this prevents the use of peewee 576-byte datagrams.

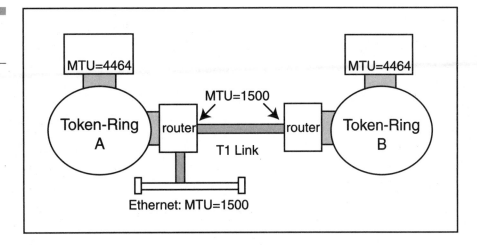

Figure 7.10
An intermediate link
with a small MTU.

However, as Figure 7.10 shows, using a destination's MTU can lead to fragmentation when there is an intermediate link with a smaller datagram size limit. In the figure, Token Ring A is connected to Token Ring B by a wide-area T1 link. The Token-Ring interfaces can transmit and receive 4464-byte datagrams. However, the T1 link cannot carry any datagram containing more than 1500 bytes. Any datagram larger than this will be fragmented.

Clearly, it would be very helpful to know the biggest datagram size that can be sent along a path and delivered intact. There is a very simple mechanism called *Path MTU discovery* that determines this size. The way that it works is:

- The *Don't Fragment* flag in IP headers is set equal to 1.
- For TCP, the initial Path MTU corresponds to the smaller of the values announced for the local and remote ends of the connection.[2] Unfortunately, if a remote partner has not announced a value, then TCP must start with the default 576-byte Path MTU, and cannot increase the MTU size above this value. For UDP, the initial Path MTU size is the MTU for the local interface.
- If the datagram is too large for some router to forward, the router will send back an ICMP *Destination Unreachable* message with code = 4.
- The sending host reduces the datagram size and tries again.

---

[2]TCP partners usually announce their MTU sizes at session startup.

Figure 7.11
Destination Unreach-
able message report-
ing MTU size.

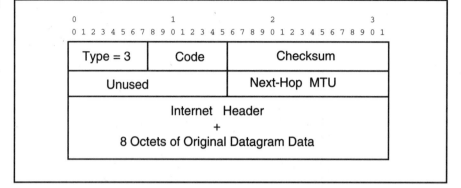

What size should the source host try next?[3] If the router has up-to-date software, its *Destination Unreachable* message will include the MTU size that would have worked for the next hop (see Figure 7.11).[4]

Because paths can change dynamically, the *Don't Fragment* flag can be left on throughout the communication. Routers will send corrections as needed. Of course, a change of path might actually increase the size that could be used. Some hosts periodically try a larger value to see if improvement is possible.

If old router software is used, the router can send back a Destination Unreachable message, but will not provide the next-hop MTU size. However, a host can make a reasonable guess by picking the next lower level from a list of common MTU "plateau" sizes, as shown in Table 7.6. The resizing procedure continues until a feasible value has been found and the destination is reached. Note that a single smallest plateau value is used for a cluster of nearby MTU values.

Not all ICMP messages signal errors. Some are used to probe the network for useful information. Is host X up? Is router Y running? How long does it take for a round trip to Z and back? What is my address mask?

Specifically, the ICMP query messages include:

- *Echo* request and reply messages that can be exchanged with hosts and routers.

- *Timestamp* request and reply messages that track round-trip time and also retrieve the clock setting at a target system.

- *Address Mask* request and reply messages that enable a system to discover the address mask that should be assigned to an interface.

---

[3]The Path MTU specification suggests that IP should store Path MTUs that have been discovered for recently accessed destinations. and make this information available to TCP and UDP.

[4]Sometimes firewalls are configured to discard *all* incoming ICMP messages. Path MTU discovery will not work if these Destination Unreachable messages cannot be received.

TABLE 7.6

Path MTU Plateaus

Plateau	MTU	Description
	65535	Official Maximum MTU
65535	65535	Hyperchannel
32000	32000	Just in case
17914	17914	16 Mb IBM Token-Ring
8166	8166	IEEE 802.4
	4464	4 Mb IEEE 802.5, Maximum value
4352	4352	FDDI
	2048	Wideband Network
2002	2002	4 Mb IEEE 802.5, Recommended value
	1500	DIX (Ethernet II) Networks
	1500	Default for Point-to-Point
1492	1492	IEEE 802.2/802.3
1006	1006	SLIP
	576	Some X.25 Networks
	544	DEC IP Portal
	512	NETBIOS
	508	IEEE 802/Source-Routing Bridge
508	508	ARCNET
296	296	Some Point-to-Point lines
68	68	Official Minimum MTU

Figure 7.12 summarizes the ICMP query services. The *ping* program, which sends "Are you alive?" echo messages, is used on a daily basis by network managers. *Address Mask* queries are used occasionally, while *Timestamp* messages rarely are seen.

Echo Request and Reply

The *Echo Request* and *Echo Reply* are used to check whether systems are active. Type = 8 is used for the request and Type = 0 for the reply. The number of bytes in the data field is variable and can be selected by the sender.

The responder must send back the same data that it receives. The

Figure 7.12
ICMP Query
messages.

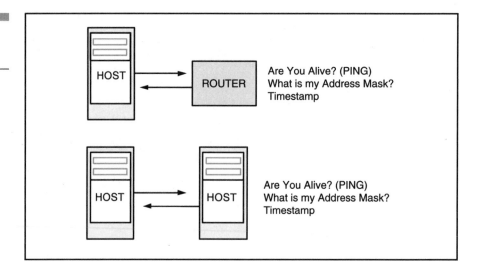

Identifier field is used to match a reply with its original request. A sequence of echo messages can be sent to test whether the network is dropping messages and to estimate the average round-trip time. To do this, the identifier is held fixed while the sequence number (which starts at 0) is incremented for each message. The format of the echo message is shown in Figure 7.13.

The famous *ping* command, available on just about every TCP/IP system, is built on the ICMP echo request and reply messages. In the dialog below, we first test that host *ring.bell.com* is alive. Then we send it a sequence of 14 messages, each containing 64 bytes of data. Note that messages 0, 1, and 2 were dropped. Round-trip times are displayed at the right.

Figure 7.13
Format of Echo
Request or Reply
messages.

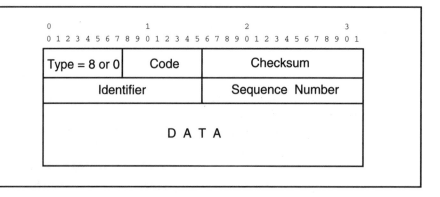

```
> ping ring.bell.com
ring.bell.com is alive

> ping -s ring.bell.com 64 14

64 bytes from ring.bell.com: icmp_seq = 3. time = 21. ms
64 bytes from ring.bell.com: icmp_seq = 4. time = 18. ms
64 bytes from ring.bell.com: icmp_seq = 5. time = 17. ms
64 bytes from ring.bell.com: icmp_seq = 6. time = 19. ms
64 bytes from ring.bell.com: icmp_seq = 7. time = 17. ms
64 bytes from ring.bell.com: icmp_seq = 8. time = 17. ms
64 bytes from ring.bell.com: icmp_seq = 9. time = 17. ms
64 bytes from ring.bell.com: icmp_seq = 10. time = 18. ms
64 bytes from ring.bell.com: icmp_seq = 11. time = 17. ms
64 bytes from ring.bell.com: icmp_seq = 12. time = 17. ms
64 bytes from ring.bell.com: icmp_seq = 13. time = 17. ms

—ring.bell.com PING Statistics—
14 packets transmitted, 11 packets received, 21% packet loss
round-trip (ms) min/avg/max = 17/17/21
```

Ping has always been a useful tool, but newer versions of *ping* have made it even better. The dialogs below were obtained using the Windows 95/NT version of *ping*. "Ping - n 1 - i 2" requests one ICMP echo message to be sent to *katie* with a Time-to-Live value of 2. Since *katie* is more than 2 hops away, a TTL Expired ICMP message is returned.

```
C:\ > ping -n 1 -i 2 katie.vnet.net
Pinging katie.vnet.net [166.82.1.7] with 32 bytes of data:
Reply from 206.80.173.254: TTL expired in transit.
```

"Ping -n 1 -f -l 2000" turns on the *don't fragment* flag (-f) and sets the length of the message to 2000 bytes. The result is that the datagram cannot be delivered.

```
C:\ > ping -n 1 -f -l 2000 katie.vnet.net
Pinging katie.vnet.net [166.82.1.7] with 2000 bytes of data:
Packet needs to be fragmented but DF set.
```

Below, we send one *ping* message to an address that does not exist on the Internet, and are informed that the destination network is unreachable.

```
C:\ > ping -n 1 10.1.1.1
Pinging 10.1.1.1 with 32 bytes of data:
Reply from 206.80.180.38: Destination net unreachable.
```

Finally, we send an ICMP echo message to *www.microsoft.com*. Microsoft screens out incoming ICMP messages, and sends no response so hackers cannot pinpoint the firewall location.

```
C: > ping -n 1 www.microsoft.com
Pinging www.microsoft.com [207.46.130.165] with 32 bytes of data:
Request timed out.
```

In the first three examples, note that the *ping* application has received the appropriate ICMP messages and has printed the ICMP information for the end-user.

Address Mask

An address mask is one of the essential pieces of information that a system must know in order to function on a TCP/IP network. Today, it is common practice to configure server hosts manually and use a Dynamic Host Configuration Protocol (DHCP) server to automatically configure desktop clients. A single DHCP message holds all of the essential data needed to get a TCP/IP host going—IP address, subnet mask, address of a default router, and one or more Domain Name Server addresses.

However, many networks contain hosts and network devices that were installed before DHCP existed. They depend on some older mechanisms that obtained configuration information in a piecemeal fashion. These systems live on as long as they are doing their job in a satisfactory manner. The result is that some obsolete methods survive into the present.

ICMP Address Mask messages are among these old survivors. When a system boots, it can broadcast an *Address Mask Request.* Typically, a neighboring router acts as address mask server and provides an *Address Mask Reply.*

Figure 7.14 displays the format of the *Address Mask Request* and *Reply.* The type is 17 for the request and 18 for the reply. The subnet address mask is returned in the Address Mask field in the Reply message. Usually, the identifier and sequence number can be ignored.

Figure 7.14
Format of an Address Mask message.

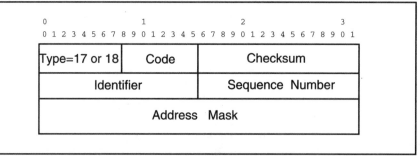

If you are monitoring a network, you may occasionally see a broadcast message that contains an unsolicited Address Mask Reply. The system acting as an address mask server can be configured so that if it has been offline for a while, it will broadcast an *Address Mask Reply* as soon as it becomes active. This is done for the benefit of systems that started up while the server was unavailable.

Timestamp and Timestamp Reply

Timestamp messages can be used to calculate the network round-trip time. The also were intended to give a sense of how long the remote system spends buffering and processing a datagram. Note the fields:

Originate timestamp	Time that the sender last touched the message
Receive timestamp	Time that the echoer first touched it
Transmit timestamp	Time that the echoer last touched it

In fact, most recipients put the same value into the Receive and Transmit timestamp fields. The time that is returned is supposed to be measured in milliseconds since midnight, Universal Time (formerly Greenwich Mean Time).

Although this protocol looks as if it could provide a very simple way for one system to synchronize its clock with another, the synchronization would be a rough one because of possible network delays. There is a far more capable *Network Time Protocol* that has been defined for Internet time synchronization.

Type 13 is used for the *Timestamp Query* and type 14 is used for the *Timestamp Reply*. The format of the message is shown in Figure 7.15.

Figure 7.15
Format of a Timestamp Request or Reply message.

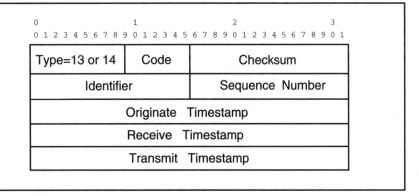

Viewing ICMP Activities

Below we show *netstat* ICMP protocol statistics for *katie*. This report shows ICMP activity since the last initialization.

```
> netstat -sP icmp

ICMP   icmpInMsgs = 71959              icmpInErrors = 0
       icmpInCksumErrs = 0            icmpInUnknowns = 0
       icmpInDestUnreachs = 493       icmpInTimeExcds = 1259
       icmpInParmProbs = 0            icmpInSrcQuenchs = 26
       icmpInRedirects = 6            icmpInBadRedirects = 0
       icmpInEchos = 69901            icmpInEchoReps = 274
       icmpInTimestamps = 0           icmpInTimestampReps = 0
       icmpInAddrMasks = 0            icmpInAddrMaskReps = 0
       icmpInFragNeeded = 2           icmpOutMsgs = 72115
       icmpOutDrops = 68836           icmpOutErrors = 0
       icmpOutDestUnreachs = 2202     icmpOutTimeExcds = 12
       icmpOutParmProbs = 0           icmpOutSrcQuenchs = 0
       icmpOutRedirects = 0           icmpOutEchos = 274
       icmpOutEchoReps = 69901        icmpOutTimestamps = 0
       icmpOutTimestampReps = 0       icmpOutAddrMasks = 0
       icmpOutAddrMaskReps = 0        icmpOutFragNeeded = 0
       icmpInOverflows = 0
```

Katie has sent 2202 *Destination Unreachable* messages. These notified clients that *katie* did not support some protocol or service that was requested. *Katie* received 69,901 *Echo Requests,* and all were answered. Users at *katie* sent 274 echo (*ping*) messages, and an equal number of responses were received. A fairly large number of Time-to-Live exceeded messages arrived. These probably resulted from use of the *traceroute* function. There were only 493 incoming *Destination Unreachable* messages; and 26 *Source Quenches* that were received by *katie*, showing that not all systems have disabled this function as yet.

Router Discovery

Although many LANs have a single default router, there are a substantial number of LANs that have two or more routers. What happens when a router is added to a LAN? Redirect messages will notify systems of new routes. But suppose that the default router has crashed?

A host can be configured with a list of default routers, in order of preference. A list of default routers also can be learned from a DHCP server. A third method, the *Router Discovery* protocol, allows default routers to announce themselves. Router Discovery is based on ICMP messages.

The essential idea is that routers will periodically advertise their presence. Hosts need to listen for these advertisements.

The preferred way for a router to announce its presence is to send advertisements to the *all-systems multicast address,* 224.0.0.1. But not all host systems support and can receive multicast addresses, so sometimes the broadcast address, 255.255.255.255, must be used.

A host that is coming up may not want to wait around to find out about the routers on its LAN. The host can ask routers to send their advertisements right away. The preferred way to do this is for the host to send a *Router Solicitation* message to the *all-routers multicast address,* 224.0.0.2. Again, since not all systems support multicast addresses, sometimes the broadcast address, 255.255.255.255, must be used instead.

A typical scenario for a router is:

- Each router interface is configured with the *advertisement address* that it should use to send its advertisement messages—either 224.0.0.1 or 255.255.255.255.

- When the router initializes, if multicasting can be used, the router starts listening for host solicitation requests on the all-routers multicast address (224.0.0.2). (Of course, the router also listens for broadcasts.)

- The router announces its presence to hosts on a connected LAN by transmitting a Router Advertisement to the advertisement address. The advertisement lists the router's IP address for that interface, and also announces the preference level that has been assigned to its IP address.[5] A higher number indicates a more preferred address.

- The router shows that it is still alive by periodically multicasting another Router Advertisement. (A seven to ten minute period is suggested.)

- The router also sends an advertisement when a host asks it to do so.

For a host, the scenario is:

- Any host that supports multicasting automatically will be a member of the all-systems multicast group, 224.0.0.1. However,

---

[5]A single interface can actually be assigned multiple IP addresses. In this case, each address—and its preference number—is included in the advertisement.

if there are LAN hosts that do not support multicasting, then routers will use broadcasts to announce their presence.

- When a host initializes, it starts to listen for Router Advertisements.

- At start-up, a host optionally can send a Router Solicitation message asking routers to announce themselves. The message is sent to the preconfigured solicitation address, which is either 224.0.0.2 or 255.255.255.255.

- When a host hears from a new router, the host adds one or more default routes via this router to its routing table. The host also records the preference number for this entry. The entry is assigned a lifetime timeout value (typically, 30 minutes), which was announced in the Router Advertisement.

- The lifetime timeout is reset whenever a fresh advertisement is received from the router. If the timeout expires, the router's entry is removed from the host's routing table.

- To tell the world that it is about to shut down gracefully, a router can send an advertisement with a lifetime of 0.

If more than one router is present, how does a host choose the entry that it should use as its default? The host chooses a default entry with the highest preference level. If that router does not in fact provide the best path, it will send back an ICMP redirect message.

Router Advertisements are Type 9 ICMP messages and *Router Solicitations* are Type 10.

Dead Routers

Router discovery will help a host find out that a local router has crashed, but only after a very long timeout—possibly 30 minutes. Good host TCP/IP implementations include built-in detection algorithms to detect whether a router is dead. Positive clues are easy. For example:

- The existence of active TCP sessions connected via the router
- Receipt of an ICMP redirect message from the router

Negative clues include:

- Many consecutive TCP retransmission timeouts
- Failure to respond to ARP requests

The TCP/IP standards currently leave it up to implementers to decide exactly how their system will detect a dead router when multiple default routers are available. For example, on a Windows NT system, TCP will ask IP to switch to the next default on its list when TCP has sent $\frac{1}{2}$ of its maximum allowed retransmissions on a session without receiving any response.

IP version 6 provides a better method of discovering whether a local router—or local host—has ceased to communicate.

ICMP Type Numbers

Table 7.7 lists the currently defined ICMP types. Some of these types relate to ICMP version 6, and some are experimental.

TABLE 7.7

ICMP Types

Type	Description
0	Echo Reply
1	Unassigned
2	Unassigned
3	Destination Unreachable
4	Source Quench
5	Redirect
6	Alternate Host Address
7	Unassigned
8	Echo Request
9	Router Advertisement
10	Router Selection
11	Time Exceeded
12	Parameter Problem
13	Timestamp
14	Timestamp Reply
15	Information Request
16	Information Reply
17	Address Mask Request
18	Address Mask Reply

TABLE 7.7

ICMP Types
(Continued)

Type	Description
19	Reserved (for Security)
20-29	Reserved (for Robustness Experiment)
30	Traceroute (experimental)
31	Datagram Conversion Error (experimental)
32	Mobile Host Redirect
33	IPv6 Where-Are-You
34	IPv6 I-Am-Here
35	Mobile Registration Request
36	Mobile Registration Reply
37	Domain Name Request
38	Domain Name Reply
39	SKIP
40	Photuris (session-key management protocol for use with IP Security)
41-255	Reserved

Recommended Reading

ICMP is defined in RFC 792. RFC 1122, the Host Requirements document, and RFC 1812, Router Requirements, contain some extremely useful clarifications. Router discovery is described in RFC 1256.

Path MTU discovery is explained in RFC 1191, and additional Path MTU advice is available in RFC 1435. ICMP version 6 is described in Chapter 23.

CHAPTER **8**

IP Routing

Introduction

Routing is the most important function that IP does. In large networks, IP routers exchange information that keeps their routing tables up to date. How is this done?

> *There is no single required protocol for updating IP routing table information.*

Instead, network administrators always have been free to select any routing information protocol that meets their own internal requirements. Over the years, numerous protocols have been designed—and improved—by standards groups and by vendors. By long tradition, these protocols are called *Interior*[1] *Gateway Protocols,* or IGPs.

Separating the way that routing tables get updated from the rest of IP was a very good idea. Routing has become more and more sophisticated and efficient, while the basic IP protocol has remained unchanged.

Today, there are several IGPs in common use. Currently, the venerable *Routing Information Protocol* (RIP) is still popular. RIP chooses routes based on simple hop count estimates.

Sites that have selected Cisco routers often opt for Cisco's proprietary *Internet Gateway Routing Protocol* (IGRP) or *Enhanced IGRP* (EIGRP). (E)IGRP uses sophisticated cost measurements that take many factors—including current load and reliability—into consideration.

The more complex *Open Shortest Path First* (OSPF) has become quite popular. OSPF is an IETF standard. And there are some organizations that use OSI's *Intermediate System to Intermediate System* (IS-IS) protocol, which can route both OSI and IP traffic. Both OSPF and IS-IS build detailed maps for at least part of a network and generate paths before choosing a route.

Allowing free choice of protocols within an end-user organization has worked quite well. However, a standard *is* needed when routing across the chains of Internet Service Provider networks that connect end-user sites together. Although there still is occasional use of the older *Exterior Gateway Protocol* (EGP), many Service Providers have converted to the *Border Gateway Protocol* (BGP).

Many router products can run several routing protocols at the same time. In this chapter, we look at how each of these protocols work and examine their distinguishing features.

---

[1]Also called *Internal* Gateway protocols.

IP Routing

An IP datagram follows a path made up of a sequence of hops. A node is one hop away—or adjacent—if there is a direct Local Area Network (LAN) or Wide Area Network (WAN) connection to the node. Routers that are separated by one hop are called *neighbors*.

A datagram is routed by choosing its *next-hop* destination at each router along its path. The next hop may be a router or it may be the final destination. Next-hop routing is flexible and robust.

The two tools used in routing are the subnet mask and routing table. A routing protocol is simply a method used to gather information that helps to build the routing table.

Manual Routing

The simplest routing protocol is manual routing:

The administrator types entries into the routing table at each router.

This may not be elegant, but sometimes it is exactly the right thing to do. For example, the network in Figure 8.1 has a simple hub and spokes design. There is a leased or dial-up line from the central headquarters site out to each branch office. The branch office LANs are "stubs," which means that no additional LANs are reached through them.

When router A needs to deliver a datagram, the choices are not complicated. Either the datagram has come down the line from headquarters and is addressed to a system on LAN A, or the datagram is addressed to a destination that is not on LAN A and should be forwarded to headquarters. One default entry pointing to headquarters is all the router A needs to know. The same procedure works for routers B, C, and D.

To complete the job, the administrator adds four entries to the headquarters routing table. The syntax for doing this varies according to the type of router, but the information is similar in all cases. The command below adds a default route to an NT server that has been configured to act as a headquarters router. The command:

- Identifies destination LAN 130.15.1.0
- Provides a subnet mask
- Identifies the neighboring interface (139.15.100.1) at router A
- Assigns a metric to the route.

Figure 8.1
A simple branch
office network.

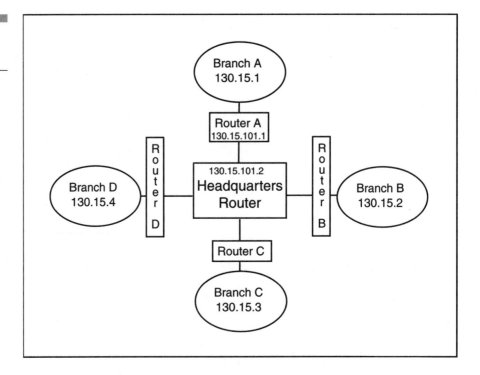

The metric value 2 reflects the fact that to get to a destination on LAN A, you traverse one hop to router A and one hop to the destination. The -p flag makes this route persistent—it will be remembered between system boots.

```
route -p add 130.15.1.0 mask 255.255.255.0 130.15.100.1 metric 2
```

Manual routing does not work if a network:

- Is growing.
- Is changing.
- Provides more than one path to a destination.

In this case, it is best to allow routers to exchange information with one another so that they can:

- Discover new links and LANs that have been added to the network.
- Choose the path that is best at the current time.

 # Routing Metrics

How do we decide that one route is better than another? There has to be some kind of *metric* (distance measurement) that can be used to compare routes.

Distance Vector Protocols

Very simple routing protocols just use end-to-end hop counts to compare routes. Some improvement is gained by using *weighted* hop counts; for example, a hop across a high-speed LAN could be given weight 1, while a hop across a slow medium (such as a 56-kilobit-per-second point-to-point line) could be given a weight of 10. This assures that a path across fast links will be preferred to a path across slow links. *RIP* chooses routes based on a simple "hop count" metric.

More sophisticated protocols combine several separate metrics such as bandwidth, delay, reliability, current load, or dollar cost into the calculation of an overall route cost. (E)IGRP uses multiple metrics.

Algorithms that base routing decisions on metric values alone are called *distance vector* algorithms.

Link State Protocols

Recently, a lot of attention has been focused on *link state* routing algorithms. A link state router builds a map of the network and discovers paths from the router to any destination.

A cost metric is assigned to each link in the map. A total cost is computed for each path starting at the router by combining the link costs. Then the best path or paths for carrying traffic are selected.

The routers send updates to one another whenever the topology changes. After a change, all paths are recalculated. *OSPF* and *IS-IS* are link state protocols.

Link state algorithms are sometimes called *Shortest Path First,* or SPF. This refers to the name of the computer science algorithm that is used to calculate the shortest paths from one node to all other nodes in a network, when the map of the network is known.

Routing Tables

Recall that a host or a router consults its routing table in order to forward datagrams toward a remote destination. This table matches each destination with the address of the router to be used as the next hop.

> *Destinations listed in a routing table can include supernets,[2] networks, subnets, and individual systems.*

A default destination entry also can be included. It is represented as destination 0.0.0.0.

There is no standard format for routing tables, but a simple table entry would contain items such as:

- Address of a destination network, subnet, or system
- Mask for this destination
- IP address of the next-hop router to be used
- Network interface to be used to reach the next-hop router
- Distance to the destination (e.g., number of hops to reach the destination)
- Number of seconds since the route was last updated

It is unusual to include an individual host address in a routing table. Routing entries typically identify destination supernets, networks, or subnets. The idea is that if you can get to a router on a host's network, and then to a router on the host's subnet, you will be able to get to that host. Occasionally a few entries that contain the complete IP addresses of some systems are included in a routing table.

Let's look at a couple of sample routing tables to get a feel for how they work.

A RIP Routing Table

The routing entries in Table 8.1 come from a RIP router owned by a university. The routing table was obtained in response to an SNMP request sent from an *HP OpenView for Windows Workgroup Node Manager.* The

---

[2]Recall that a supernet is a classless block of IP addresses which have a common prefix.

table lists destinations and tells you the next-hop router to which you should forward datagrams heading for that destination. The table also contains the metric (distance) information that helped the router to choose the next hop. Note that a metric of 0 is shown for the directly connected LAN. Some implementations never use a 0 metric and assign a value of 1 to a directly connected LAN.

The routing table includes entries for many different subnets of network 128.36.0.0, along with routes to the three networks 130.132.0.0, 192.31.2.0, and 192.31.235.0. The table display is split into two parts because of the large number of columns.

Using the Route Mask

To find a match for a destination address such as 128.36.2.25, you would compare 128.36.2.25 with each entry's *Route Destination*. The entry's *Route Mask* tells you how many bits of 128.36.2.25 must match corresponding bits in the Route Destination—in other words, the Route Mask tells you the length of the routing prefix. For example, the third entry in Table 8.1 has Route Mask 255.255.255.0, which means that the first 3 bytes, 128.36.2, need to match—and they do.[3]

What happens if we get a match with two or more different entries? The one with the longest routing prefix is preferred.

Default Route

The first entry in Table 8.1 is the *default* route. It announces that if no match is found, traffic should be forwarded to the neighbor router with address 128.36.0.2.

Using Subnet 0

By the way, the administrators of this network are doing something that is frowned upon by the standards writers. They have assigned subnet number 0 to the LAN that this router lives on. Recall that you are not supposed to use 0 as a subnet number. However, some facilities

---

[3]More formally, the result of performing a logical *AND* of the destination address and entry's Route Mask is compared with the entry's Route Destination.

TABLE 8.1

Routing Table in a
RIP Router

ip Route Dest	ip Route Mask	ip Route NextHop	ip Route Type	ip Route Proto
0.0.0.0	0.0.0.0	128.36.0.2	indirect	rip
128.36.0.0	255.255.255.0	128.36.0.62	direct	local
128.36.2.0	255.255.255.0	128.36.0.7	indirect	rip
128.36.11.0	255.255.255.0	128.36.0.12	indirect	rip
128.36.12.0	255.255.255.0	128.36.0.21	indirect	rip
128.36.13.0	255.255.255.0	128.36.0.12	indirect	rip
128.36.14.0	255.255.255.0	128.36.0.21	indirect	rip
128.36.15.0	255.255.255.0	128.36.0.21	indirect	rip
128.36.16.0	255.255.255.0	128.36.0.36	indirect	rip
128.36.17.0	255.255.255.0	128.36.0.12	indirect	rip
128.36.19.0	255.255.255.0	128.36.0.10	indirect	rip
128.36.20.0	255.255.255.0	128.36.0.10	indirect	rip
128.36.21.0	255.255.255.0	128.36.0.5	indirect	rip
128.36.22.0	255.255.255.0	128.36.0.5	indirect	rip
128.36.126.0	255.255.255.0	128.36.0.41	indirect	rip
130.132.0.0	255.255.0.0	128.36.0.2	indirect	rip
192.31.2.0	255.255.255.0	128.36.0.1	indirect	rip
192.31.235.0	255.255.255.0	128.36.0.41	indirect	rip

need to use every number that they can get their hands on. Router vendors understand this, and the router can handle these addresses. Since the subnet mask is included in the routing table (as the Route Mask), the router has no problem recognizing that 0 is being used as a subnet number.

Direct and Indirect Destinations

Note that the second table entry says that LAN 128.36.0 is of type *direct,* which means that this subnet is directly connected to this router. The protocol is *local,* which indicates that this route was learned by looking at the configuration of the router.

TABLE 8.1

Routing Table in a
RIP Router
(Continued)

ip Route Dest	ip Route Metric 1	ip Route Metric 2	ip Route Metric 3	ip Route Metric 4	ip Route Metric 5	ip Route If Index	ip Route Age (secs)
0.0.0.0	2	−1	−1	−1	−1	1	153836
128.36.0.0	0	−1	−1	−1	−1	1	0
128.36.2.0	1	−1	−1	−1	−1	1	30
128.36.11.0	1	−1	−1	−1	−1	1	13
128.36.12.0	1	−1	−1	−1	−1	1	15
128.36.13.0	1	−1	−1	−1	−1	1	14
128.36.14.0	1	−1	−1	−1	−1	1	16
128.36.15.0	1	−1	−1	−1	−1	1	17
128.36.16.0	12	−1	−1	−1	−1	1	24
128.36.17.0	1	−1	−1	−1	−1	1	16
128.36.19.0	14	−1	−1	−1	−1	1	27
128.36.20.0	1	−1	−1	−1	−1	1	28
128.36.21.0	1	−1	−1	−1	−1	1	5
128.36.22.0	1	−1	−1	−1	−1	1	5
128.36.126.0	1	−1	−1	−1	−1	1	23
130.132.0.0	4	−1	−1	−1	−1	1	25
192.31.2.0	3	−1	−1	−1	−1	1	10
192.31.235.0	2	−1	−1	−1	−1	1	25

The remainder of the entries list remote subnets and networks that are reached indirectly, by forwarding traffic to other routers. These routes were learned via RIP.

Routing Metrics

Looking at the second part of the table, we see that it has space for several metrics. RIP only uses one metric, a simple hop count reporting the distance to a destination. The unused columns are set to −1. Note that a 0 metric is assigned to subnet 128.36.0, which is directly connected to the router. Many of the other destinations are one hop away. However, subnet 128.36.16.0 is 12 hops away and 128.36.19.0 is 14 hops away.

TABLE 8.2

IGRP and BGP
Routing Entries

ip Route Dest	ip Route Mask	ip Route NextHop	ip Route Type	ip Route Proto
0.0.0.0	0.0.0.0	130.94.40.250	indirect	ciscoIgrp
128.121.50.0	255.255.255.0	128.121.50.50	direct	local
128.121.52.0	255.255.255.0	128.121.50.55	direct	local
128.121.54.0	255.255.255.0	128.121.50.50	direct	local
128.6.0.0	255.255.0.0	130.94.0.49	indirect	ciscoIgrp
128.96.0.0	255.255.0.0	130.94.40.250	indirect	ciscoIgrp
130.33.0.0	255.255.0.0	130.94.16.2	indirect	ciscoIgrp
130.44.0.0	255.255.0.0	130.94.0.49	indirect	ciscoIgrp
130.68.0.0	255.255.0.0	130.94.0.49	indirect	ciscoIgrp
130.94.1.24	255.255.255.248	130.94.0.49	indirect	ciscoIgrp
130.94.1.32	255.255.255.248	130.94.0.49	indirect	ciscoIgrp
130.94.2.8	255.255.255.248	130.94.0.49	indirect	ciscoIgrp
130.94.2.16	255.255.255.248	130.94.0.49	indirect	ciscoIgrp
130.94.7.0	255.255.255.248	130.94.0.49	indirect	ciscoIgrp
130.94.7.8	255.255.255.248	130.94.0.49	indirect	ciscoIgrp
44.0.0.0	255.0.0.0	130.94.15.201	indirect	bgp
128.3.0.0	255.255.0.0	130.94.40.201	indirect	bgp
129.210.0.0	255.255.0.0	130.94.15.201	indirect	bgp
13.0.0.0	255.0.0.0	130.94.15.201	indirect	bgp

Route Age

The *Route Age* column tracks the number of seconds since each route was updated or validated. Entries that have been learned via RIP will age out and be invalidated if they are not reconfirmed within 3 minutes.

An IGRP/BGP Routing Table

The routing entries in Table 8.2 come from a Cisco Internet router owned by an Internet Service Provider (ISP). The table lists destinations

TABLE 8.2

IGRP and BGP
Routing Entries
(Continued)

ip Route Dest	ip Route Metric 1	ip Route Metric 2	ip Route Metric 3	ip Route Metric 4	ip Route Metric 5	ip Route If Index	ip Route Age (secs)
0.0.0.0	10647	1170	21000	0	255	6	12
128.121.50.0	0	−1	−1	−1	−1	1	0
128.121.52.0	0	−1	−1	−1	−1	1	35
128.121.54.0	0	−1	−1	−1	−1	1	0
128.6.0.0	12610	1536	61000	2	255	3	11
128.96.0.0	14647	1170	61000	2	255	6	16
130.33.0.0	8710	1536	22000	1	255	2	18
130.44.0.0	16610	1536	101000	4	255	3	37
130.68.0.0	12710	1536	62000	3	255	3	39
130.94.1.24	82125	128	40000	0	255	3	41
130.94.1.32	182571	56	40000	0	255	3	42
130.94.2.8	10510	1536	40000	0	255	3	42
130.94.2.16	10510	1536	40000	0	255	3	43
130.94.7.0	10610	1536	41000	1	255	3	2
130.94.7.8	12510	1536	60000	1	255	3	3
44.0.0.0	0	−1	−1	−1	−1	6	51766
128.3.0.0	0	−1	−1	−1	−1	6	42049
129.210.0.0	0	−1	−1	−1	−1	6	586765
13.0.0.0	0	−1	−1	−1	−1	6	224463

and identifies the next-hop router to be used for datagrams heading for each destination. The table includes several metrics that are used to select the best routes. These metrics are combined using a formula that can be adjusted by the router administrator.

The routing table includes entries for many different networks and subnets. (These entries also were retrieved using an HP *OpenView* management system.)

Using the Route Mask

Just as before, the Route Mask is used to match up a destination with a table entry. For example, to find a match for destination 128.121.54.101, we apply the Route Mask for each entry to 128.121.54.101 and compare the result with the Route Destination. Applying the mask 255.255.255.0 in the fourth entry, we get 128.121.54.0, which matches the entry's Route Destination.

IGRP can produce ties—there might be multiple entries with the same destination and mask. In this case, the route with the best metric is used. Or, if the metrics are close, IGRP can split traffic across two or more paths.

Default Route

The first entry in the table is the *default* route. If no match is found, traffic is forwarded to the neighbor router with address 130.94.40.250.

Direct and Indirect Destinations

The next three destinations are of type *direct,* which means that they are subnets that are directly connected to the router. Their protocol is *local,* which indicates that the routes were learned via the router's manually entered configuration information.

Next, there are several entries for remote (indirect) destinations whose routes were learned via Cisco's proprietary IGRP protocol.

Small Subnets

The set of destinations starting with entry 130.94.1.24 look like host addresses at first glance, but the Route Mask shows that all of these entries actually represent small subnets. The host part occupies only the last 3 bits of the address. For example, the binary representation of 24 is 00011000, and so all of the bits for 24 actually lie within the subnet part of the address. The hosts on this subnet would have addresses ranging from 130.94.1.25 to 130.94.1.30.

Border Gateway Protocol Entries

Finally, the table ends with a list of remote destinations that were learned via the *Border Gateway Protocol,* which provides information used to route between different networks on the Internet.

Routing Metrics

If we examine the second part of Table 8.2, we see that a 0 metric is assigned to destinations that are reached on three directly connected subnets. As before, unused metric values in the table are set equal to −1.

Values have been assigned to all five metrics for Cisco's IGRP. However, there is no attempt to display meaningful metrics for Internet remote destination networks, which were learned via the Border Gateway Protocol.

All of the interfaces on the router are numbered, and a datagram is sent via the interface identified in the *IfIndex* column.

Route Age

For IGRP, the *Route Age* column tracks the number of seconds since the route was updated or validated. Entries that have been learned via a protocol will age out if they are not reconfirmed from time to time. For BGP, the Route Age is used to track the stability of long distance routes.

Protocols That Maintain Routing Tables

How did these routers learn their table entries? How are entries kept up to date? How is the best choice for the next-hop router discovered? These chores are the job of the routing protocol. The simplest routing protocol is:

- Study diagrams of your network to find the best paths. Choose the next hop so that these paths are followed.
- Enter data into your routing tables manually.
- Update your routing tables manually.

This is exactly what was recommended for the simple branch office network that was shown in Figure 8.1.

Manual routing can be used for a very small network. But for a complex network that is growing and changing and has multiple potential routes to a destination, manual routing will turn into a nightmare. At some point it becomes impossible for humans to analyze and respond to network conditions. A routing protocol is then needed to automate:

- Exchange of information between routers about the current state of the network
- Recomputation of the best next-hop selection as changes occur

Over the years, there has been substantial research into routing protocols. Many have been implemented and their merits have been hotly debated. What are the characteristics of a winning protocol?

- When the network changes, it should respond quickly.
- It should compute optimal routes.
- It should scale up well as your network grows.
- It should be frugal in its use of computer resources.
- It should be frugal in its use of transmission resources.

But computing optimal routes in a large network may require considerable CPU and memory, and quick response may require immediate flooding of information across the network. A good protocol design has to provide good value in return for computing and network resources. We'll start off our study of routing protocols by looking at a very simple one—RIP.

Routing Information Protocol

RIP is derived from the venerable Xerox Network Systems (XNS) routing protocol. RIP's popularity is based on its simplicity and availability.

RIP was included in the Berkeley Software Distribution TCP/IP implementation and still is distributed with Unix systems as program *routed*. RIP was in widespread use for several years before being standardized in RFC 1058. Version 2 of RIP was completed in 1994. RIP version 1 has been declared "historical" which means obsolete, but still is used at some sites.

RIP computes routes using a simple distance vector routing algorithm. Every hop in the network is assigned a cost (usually 1). The total

Figure 8.2
Discovering hop
counts to a
destination.

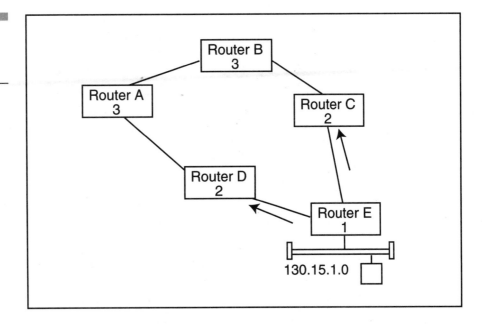

metric for a path is the sum of the hop costs. RIP chooses the next hop
so that datagrams will follow a least-cost path.

Figure 8.2 shows how distance estimates propagate across a network.
For this example, we will count the distance to a directly connected net-
work as 1, which is recommended in the RIP standard. (Recall that the
Cisco routers examined earlier set this distance to 0.)

Suppose that Router E has just been connected to the network:

- Router E advertises a metric of 1 to LAN 130.15.1.0, meaning
  that Router E can reach any host on this directly connected LAN
  in 1 hop. The route is sent to neighbor routers C and D.

- Router C checks its routing table and notes that it has no route
  to this destination. Router C adds an entry with a metric that is
  equal to 2 (after adding on a cost of 1 for crossing the link
  between Router C and Router E). Router D follows the same procedure.

- Router C reports the entry to Router B and Router D reports the
  entry to Router A. Each adds 1 to the metric and places an entry
  in its own table.

- When Router A reports this entry to Router B, B notes that the
  path through A would require 4 hops. Router B has a better 3-
  hop path via neighbor C, so B discards the information.

- If one of the links connecting Router B to Router E failed, then B would set the entry for this destination to 16, meaning, "I can't get there." A fresh report from Router A would be welcomed, and Router B would start to use the 4-hop path through Router A.

RIP's strong points are its simplicity and availability. Often there is no reason to use more functional—and complicated—methods for a small network or a network with a simple topology. However, for large, complex networks, RIP has some serious shortcomings. For example:

- The maximum metric for any path is 15. Sixteen means *"I can't get there!"* Because it is easy to run out of hops on a big network, RIP usually is configured with a cost of 1 for each hop, whether that hop is a slow dialup or a high-speed fiber link.
- After a disruption in the network, RIP often is slow to reestablish optimal routes. In fact, after a disruption, datagram traffic may run around in circles for a while.
- RIP cannot respond to changes in delay or load across links. It cannot split traffic to balance the load.

Initializing RIP

To get started, each router only needs to know the networks to which it is connected. A RIP version 1 router broadcasts this information to each of its LAN neighbor routers. It also sends the routing information to neighbors at the other end of a point-to-point line or virtual circuit.

As shown in Figure 8.3, the news spreads like gossip—each router passes the information to its own neighbors. For example, Router B would discover its distance to subnet 130.34.2.0 very quickly.

By the way, just because RIP is used in a network does not mean that it needs to be used at every router. Router C really has no routing choices—any destination that is not directly connected to C must be reached via router D. A single manual entry that defines a default route is sufficient for Router C. There is no reason to clutter its link to D with routing table updates.

Like all automated routing protocols, RIP has to send routing updates, receive routing updates, and recompute routes. A RIP router sends information to its neighbor routers every 30 seconds. Sending out routing information is called "advertising" routes.

A host on a LAN could eavesdrop on RIP broadcasts and use them to

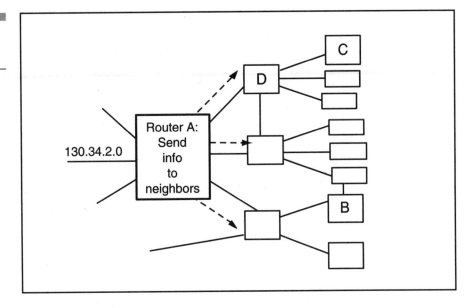

Figure 8.3
Propagating routing information.

update its own routing table—or at least assure itself that its routers are alive. This used to be a fairly common practice, but now is unusual.

The display below shows some columns from an NT monitor trace of RIP broadcasts from a router. Note that the messages are sent at approximately 30-second intervals. The RIP update message is called a "response." In addition to the automatic, timed response messages, a response also can be invoked by an explicit "request" message.

Time	Dst MAC Addr	Prot	Description
2.710	*BROADCAST 198.207.177.255	RIP	Response, 4 Entries (ver. 1)
32.727	*BROADCAST 198.207.177.255	RIP	Response, 4 Entries (ver. 1)
62.745	*BROADCAST 198.207.177.255	RIP	Response, 4 Entries (ver. 1)

Updating a RIP Table

As shown in Figure 8.4, Router A has been sending traffic to network 136.10.0.0 through Router B. Router A receives an update from Neighbor D that announces a shorter route and therefore changes its routing table. Note that the hop from Router A to Router D is added to D's metric to compute the distance (2) from A to 136.10.0.0.

Figure 8.4
Updating routing
tables with RIP.

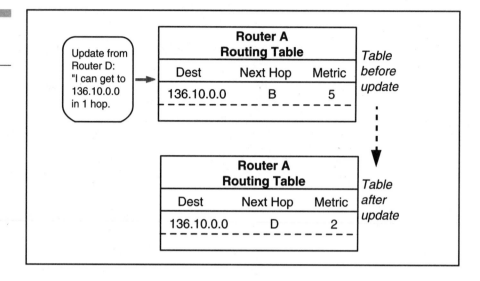

RIP Version 1 Mechanisms

Now let's walk through the formal steps for RIP version 1 routing. We start our routing table with distances that we know about. Then, whenever an update arrives from a neighbor, we recheck our table and see if any entries can be added or improved:

1. A cost is assigned to traversing each directly attached subnetwork.

2. A router sends its current routing table to its neighbors every 30 seconds.

3. When a router receives a neighbor's table, it checks each incoming entry. The cost assigned to the subnetwork on which the update arrived is added to each metric.

4. If a destination is new, it is added to the local routing table.

5. If a destination already is in the table, but the update provides a shorter route, the entry is replaced.

It would be nice if routes always got better and better, but sometimes a link or a router will go down, and our traffic will have to take a longer path. We find out about bad news two ways:

1. Router A has been sending traffic to a destination via Router X, and X sends an update that announces that the number of hops to that destination has increased (or perhaps that the destination cannot be reached). Router A changes its entry accordingly.

2. Router A has been sending traffic to a destination via Router X but has not received any updates for 3 minutes. Router A has to assume that Router X has crashed and mark all routes through X as unreachable (by giving them a metric value of 16). If no new route to an unreachable destination is discovered within 2 minutes, its entry is deleted.[4] In the meantime, Router A's updates tell other systems that Router A cannot reach the destination.

RIP Version 1 Update Messages

As we mentioned earlier, update messages are sent between RIP routers at regular intervals. In addition, request messages may be sent to a neighbor to ask for routing information. Typically, a system would send out a request:

- During system initialization

- When performing a network monitoring function

The format of the RIP version 1 request or response/update message is shown in Figure 8.5. A command field of 1 indicates a request and 2 indicates a response or spontaneous update.

The display that follows shows the first two entries in a RIP update that contains four entries. Note that the RIP message is carried in a UDP datagram, and the source and destination ports both are 520.[5] The 4-byte introductory field indicates that this is a version 1 response. Each of the entries that follow occupy 20 bytes, 10 of which are unused.

```
UDP: Src Port: RIP, (520); Dst Port: RIP (520); Length = 92
UDP: Data: Number of data bytes remaining = 84

   (RIP: Response, 4 Entries (ver. 1))
      RIP: Command = Response
      RIP: Version = 1 (0x1)
      RIP: Unused = 0 (0x0)
         RIP: Address Family Identifier = 2 (0x2)
         RIP: Unused = 0 (0x0)
         RIP: IP Address = 198.207.200.0
         RIP: Unused = 0 (0x0)
         RIP: Unused = 0 (0x0)
         RIP: Metric = 2 (0x2)
```

---

[4]This is called *garbage collection.*

[5]Ports will be described in Chapter 9.

Figure 8.5

Format of a RIP version 1 message.

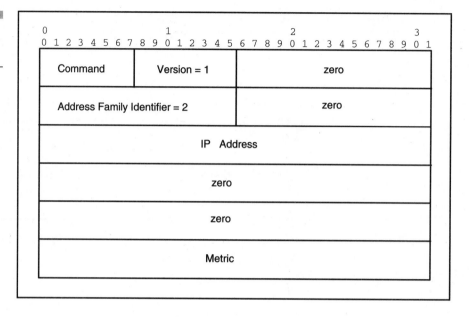

```
RIP: Address Family Identifier = 2 (0x2)
RIP: Unused = 0 (0x0)
RIP: IP Address = 198.207.201.0
RIP: Unused = 0 (0x0)
RIP: Unused = 0 (0x0)
RIP: Metric = 2 (0x2)
      . . .
```

RIP Version 1 Message Details

When the original RIP RFC was written, it was anticipated that these routing messages would be used for other network protocols besides IP, and so an *address family identifier* field and space for up to 14 bytes per address were included.

The address family, IP address, and metric fields can be repeated, and a single message can contain up to 25 address entries. The maximum message size is 512 bytes. If more than 25 entries need to be sent, multiple messages are used.

An update contains all destinations and metrics in the sender's routing table. A request contains an entry for each address for which a metric is desired. A single entry with address 0 and a metric of 16 asks for a complete routing table update.

As we have seen, automatic RIP updates are sent via the User Datagram Protocol (UDP) from source port 520 to port 520 at destination routers. However, requests can be sent from any port, and the response would then be sent back to the requesting port.

Fine-Tuning RIP

The preceding sections have described the basic RIP protocol. However, RIP implementations need some additional features in order to solve some problems:

- With a 30-second interval between updates, it could take a long time for changes to percolate through a big network.
- After a change—especially if some connectivity has been lost—there is a tendency for traffic to run around in circles.

The next sections describe how these problems can be handled.

Triggered Updates and Hold Down

Triggered updates speed up the process of discovering changes. Whenever a router changes its metric for a route, it sends updates announcing the change. Note that one new update will trigger others that may trigger others. However, this spurt of messages will prevent a lot of user traffic from wandering along bad routes.

Since there will be a tendency for a lot of updates to be sent at the same time, each system waits for a short random time period before sending. Sending only those entries that actually have changed, rather than the entire routing table reduces the bandwidth used by triggered updates.

While adjustments are going on, a router that has discovered that a destination is unreachable may receive an obsolete update that indicates that a defunct route is available. If this update were accepted, not only would the router replace good information with bad, it would trigger updates that spread the misinformation.

For this reason, most implementations include a *hold down* rule that sets a period of time during which updates are ignored for a destination that has just been marked unreachable.

Split Horizon and Poisoned Reverse

Why does RIP traffic sometimes run around in circles? The reason is that after a change, it can take a while for all of the routers to get

Figure 8.6
Routing after a net-
work disruption.

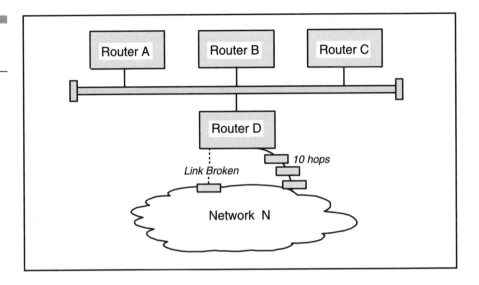

updated to accurate information. Figure 8.6 shows a very simple example.[6] Router D has two paths to *Network N*. One is a 2-hop path, and the
other is a long 10-hop path. When the short path is disrupted, Router D
replaces the route with the alternate, which has a metric of 10.

But the routing entries for *Network N* in the RIP messages sent by
Routers A, B, and C would have the form:

Network N   Metric = 3

These messages would *not* have any way to say that the route is through
Router D. What would happen if Router D got a scheduled update from
A before it has had a chance to tell Router A about its own change? D
would update its routing table entry to:

Destination	Next Hop	Metric
Network N	A	4

- ■ D would start sending its traffic to A (who would send it back).
- ■ D also would send updates to A, B, and C announcing that it can
  get to *Network N* in four hops.

---

[6]The example is based on one in RFC 1058.

- A would reply that it now can get to *N* in five hops. Routers B and C would be equally confused and, depending on the timing of updates, might send traffic for *N* to each other, to A, or to D.
- RIP updates would bounce back and forth.

The good news is that the metrics at A, B, and C would be increased by each update message until they finally reached 11 and the correct route would be discovered. The bad news is that datagrams would wander around in circles until the routes settled down. A couple of simple mechanisms can prevent the period of confusion from occurring.

Split Horizon means that a router should not report a route to the next-hop system for that route. For the example in Figure 8.6, this says that Routers A, B, and C must not tell Router D that they have a route to *Network N,* because that route actually passes through D.

Poisoned Reverse goes further. With Poisoned Reverse, Routers A, B, and C in Figure 8.6 prevent misunderstanding by sending updates across the LAN that say "Don't try to get there through me!" Specifically, the updates would include the entry:

$$\text{Network N} \qquad \text{Metric} = 16$$

This cures the problem for the configuration shown above, but for networks containing big loops, traffic may run around in circles for a while, even if the destination actually can't be reached at all. Fortunately, the metrics will eventually increase to 16, and correct routing will be restored. The process is called *counting to infinity*.

Up-to-date versions of RIP provide hold down, Split Horizon, and Poisoned Reverse. However, there are dozens of versions of RIP, written for every sort of box. When in doubt about what a particular router does, move that router into a branch office and configure it manually.

There are several obvious deficiencies in the RIP version 1 message protocol. These are described in the sections that follow.

No Subnet Mask

Note that masks are not included in RIP version 1 messages (see Figure 8.5), so a RIP version 1 router cannot tell whether an address represents a subnet or a host address.

For a long time, router vendors solved this problem by requiring users to choose one subnet mask and use it for an entire network. A

router connected to that network would learn the subnet mask by checking the configuration of its interface to the network.

A router that was not directly connected to a network would have no
way to learn the network's subnet mask. If it received a routing entry
for a subnet of the remote network, the entry would be useless. For this
reason, version 1 routers do not send subnet or host entries for a network to routers that are not connected to that network. An external
router is sent a single entry for an entire network (e.g., for 145.102.0.0).

Note that this can result in *extra* entries as well as too few entries. If
a network has Classless Inter-Domain Routing (CIDR) addressing, a
separate entry must be provided for each of the class C addresses in the
bunch. In contrast, one entry that included a mask could have represented the entire CIDR network.

LAN Broadcasts

Version 1 messages are broadcast onto LANs. Every network interface
must therefore absorb and examine the message. The use of LAN *multicasts* would make a lot more sense.

Lack of Authentication

Another worrying problem in version 1 is the lack of authentication for
RIP messages. Suppose that someone with access to a network injected
false routing messages (using forged source addresses) that reported
that most destinations were unreachable? This would cause serious disruption of service.

Can't Distinguish Fast from Slow Links

A network administrator is allowed to manually assign a hop count to a
link. Thus a 9600-bit-per-second point-to-point link could be assigned a
hop count of, say, 5 to indicate that it has less capacity than a
10,000,000-bit-per-second LAN link.

Unfortunately, when hops add up to more than 15, destinations
become unreachable. Therefore, administrators usually must assign the
same hop count, 1, to slow and fast links.

There is one advantage to having a small maximum hop count. Recall that an unreachable destination sometimes causes a temporary routing loop to form. The metrics in update messages for the loop increase up to 16 fairly quickly, and this breaks the loop. A bigger limit would slow down recovery from looping.

Excessive Traffic

Routing tables grow to a substantial size on large networks. Sending entire routing tables in updates can impose a heavy overhead on a network. Routers also are slowed down by having to process dozens or hundreds of entries, most of which have not changed.

Even small periodic messages are a problem for switched long distance connections. Dialups or X.25 circuits may be used for links with only occasional, sporadic traffic. To save money, these circuits are closed when there is no traffic to send. Whenever possible, manual configuration is used to describe the remote networks, but sometimes this is not feasible. One solution that many vendors support for slow or switched lines is to send complete tables at start-up time, but disable further automatic RIP messages. Updates may be manually requested at later times. A more robust proposed standard method restricts message contents to new or modified entries, and only sends a message when there is something new to report.[7]

Newer routing protocols (like OSPF and EIGRP) use this kind of strategy all of the time, on all types of links. They send updates only after a change and report only the changed routes. Routers exchange periodic (*Hello*) messages to show that they are alive, except across switched links, where the neighbor is assumed to be alive until an attempted transmission fails.

RIP Version 2

It took ten years before RIP version 1 was updated to version 2 (RIP-2). In that time, a lot of work had been accomplished in designing complex new protocols that solved all of the problems. But many organizations liked the simplicity, ease of installation, and ease of use of RIP.

---

[7]These messages need to be acknowledged, since they will not be repeated periodically.

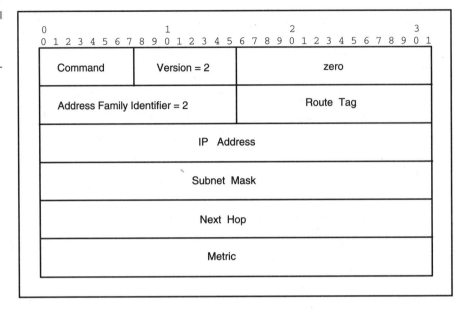

Version 1 of RIP has been declared "historic," and users should upgrade to version 2. RIP-2 offers simple solutions for a few of RIP's problems. However, to preserve interworking with RIP version 1 routers, the changes are modest. The maximum hop count remains at 15, and complete routing tables still are exchanged every 30 seconds. But tables can be multicast, rather than broadcast.

Most RIP-2 enhancements are based on packing more information into the update messages. RIP-2 routing updates have the format shown in Figure 8.7. The additional information includes:

Subnet Mask	Put it into the message.
Next Hop	Used to report routes through *other* routers. For example "go to *Network N* via Router B." Figure 8.8 shows how a single "bilingual" router (Router A) translates between RIP and IGRP and passes next-hop information between the two sets of routers.
External Routes	The *Route Tag* field indicates that this is information about an external network. It may have been learned by means of an external protocol, such as EGP or BGP.[8]

---

[8]A popular use for the tag is to hold an identifier called an "Autonomous System number" that is associated with an entire internetwork. See the discussion of Autonomous Systems later in this chapter.

Figure 8.8

Using the *Next-Hop*
field to report routes.

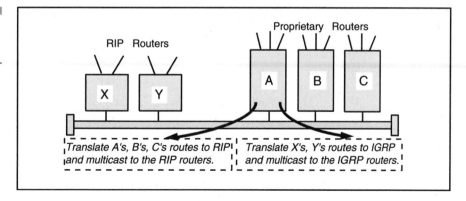

Figure 8.8

Using the *Next-Hop*
field to report routes.

The display below shows a RIP-2 message trace obtained with an NT monitor:

```
IP: ID = 0xC807; Proto = UDP; Len: 112

    UDP: Src Port: RIP, (520); Dst Port: RIP (520); Length = 92
    UDP: Data: Number of data bytes remaining = 84

(RIP: Response, 4 Entries (ver. 2))
    RIP: Command = Response
    RIP: Version = 2 (0x2)
    RIP: Routing Domain = 0 (0x0)
    RIP: Data Frame: IP Address = 198.207.200.0, Metric = 2
      RIP: Address Family Identifier = 2 (0x2)
      RIP: Route Tag = 0 (0x0)
      RIP: IP Address = 198.207.200.0
      RIP: Subnet Mask = 255.255.255.0
      RIP: Next Hop = 0.0.0.0
      RIP: Metric = 2 (0x2)
```

RIP Version 2 Authentication

Optionally, the space for the first entry in an update can be used for authentication. The space is identified as an authentication field by using X'FFFF as the Address Family Identifier. The type of authentication being used is named in the next field. A RIP-2 message can be authenticated by a simple password or by a message digest computed on the message data combined with a secret. Currently, the MD5 message digest is used.

The remaining 16 bytes contain the authentication information. Figure 8.9 shows the format of a message that starts with an authenticator.

Figure 8.9
RIP version 2 message starting with an authenticator.

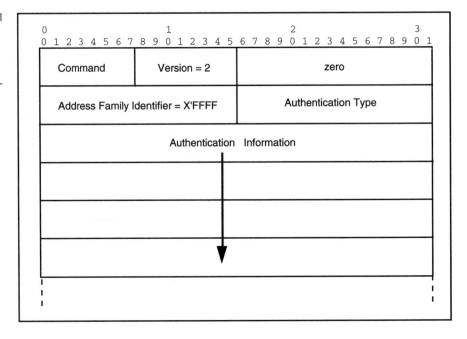

The display below shows a RIP-2 message that contains an authentication field and one entry. Note that a simple password, "SafeRIP," is used for authentication. Someone eavesdropping on the network could discover this password. Authentication based on HMAC message digests would be a better choice.

```
IP: ID = 0x2F11; Proto = UDP; Len: 72

    UDP: Src Port: RIP, (520); Dst Port: RIP (520); Length = 52
    UDP: Data: Number of data bytes remaining = 44 (0x002C)
    (RIP: Response, 0 Entries (ver. 2))
        RIP: Command = Response
        RIP: Version = 2 (0x2)
        RIP: Routing Domain = 0 (0x0)
        RIP: Authentication Frame
            RIP: Address Family Identifier = 65535 (0xFFFF)
            RIP: Authentication Type = 1 (0x1)
            RIP: Authentication = SafeRIP
        RIP: Data Frame: IP Address = 198.207.200.0, Metric = 2
            RIP: Address Family Identifier = 2 (0x2)
            RIP: Route Tag = 0 (0x0)
            RIP: IP Address = 198.207.200.0
            RIP: Subnet Mask = 255.255.255.0
            RIP: Next Hop = 0.0.0.0
            RIP: Metric = 2 (0x2)
```

RIP for IP Next Generation

RIP-2 has survived almost unchanged for use with IPv6. However, there are some important modifications:

- UDP port 521 is used instead of port 520.
- Message lengths are limited only by MTU restrictions.
- RIP authentication has been dropped because security capabilities are built into IPv6.
- The message format has been redesigned to hold the new 16-byte addresses.

Figure 8.10 shows the format of the new RIP messages. As before, the message is introduced by a 4-byte header that contains the command code (request or response) and the version of this protocol (currently 1).

Each routing table entry in a RIP message occupies 20 bytes, just as before. The first 16 bytes hold the destination. Instead of using a 16-byte mask, a 1-byte field announces the length of the routing prefix. A zero length is used to indicate that this is a default route.

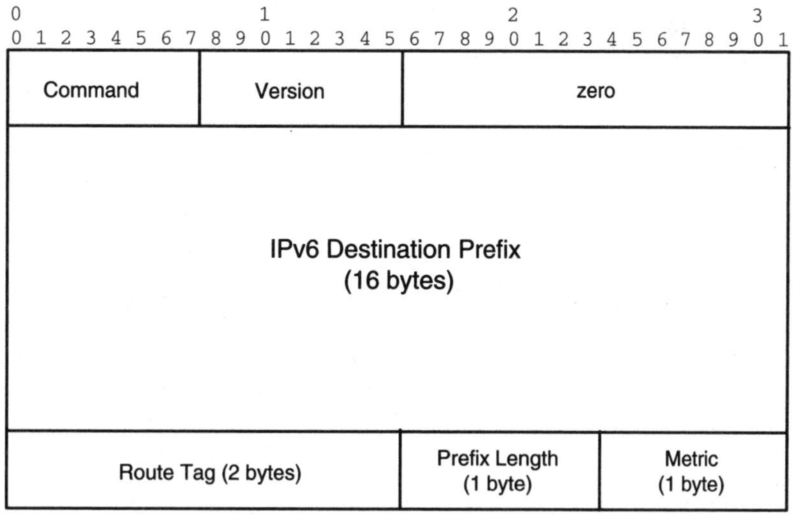

Figure 8.10
Format of a RIP message for IP version 6.

The route tag is used just as before, to indicate that this is a route to an external network. The metric is the usual RIP hop counter.

A separate 20-byte entry must be used in order to include a next-hop pointer. The metric for this entry is set to X'FF to indicate the fact that the entry contains next-hop information. The route tag and prefix fields are set to 0. A next hop pointer applies to all of the entries that follow it up to the end of the message or until another next hop pointer entry appears.[9]

Moving to More Sophisticated Protocols

Two approaches have been taken in developing more advanced protocols. Like RIP, Cisco's proprietary IGRP is a distance vector protocol, but IGRP fixes RIP's shortcomings. OSPF and OSI's IS-IS are Link State protocols. They create network maps, discover all routes to a destination, and then compare the route metrics to choose the best paths.

These protocols all support advanced features, such as the ability to split traffic among several roughly equivalent routes.

IGRP and EIGRP

Although IGRP is a distance vector protocol, IGRP's cost metric is computed using a formula that takes many factors into account, including the network's delay and bandwidth. In addition, IGRP can base routes on the current load level ("occupancy") of each link, as well as the current end-to-end error rate.

IGRP can split traffic across paths that are equally—or almost equally—good. When there are several paths to a destination, more of the traffic is sent along the paths that have higher bandwidth.

A Service Provider's boundary IGRP router can gather information from several external internetworks. Routes to external internetworks

---

[9]A 0 next-hop address indicates that routing for the entries that follow should go back to the normal practice of using the source address of the report as the next hop.

are reported to internal routers. Thus, IGRP can support routing between different organizations.

EIGRP uses the same metrics and routing formulas as IGRP, but it introduces some important improvements. EIGRP cuts down greatly on routing traffic by sending updates only after a change and sending only the altered entries. EIGRP also includes an algorithm that prevents loops from forming.

In the sections that follow, we first describe IGRP and then discuss the EIGRP enhancements.

IGRP Routing

Like RIP, an IGRP router would broadcast its routing table to its neighbors at periodic intervals. And like RIP, an IGRP router starts up with routing table entries for its directly connected subnetworks. Its table is enlarged by updates sent by neighboring routers. IGRP update messages do not include subnet masks. In place of the simple hop counts used in RIP, IGRP routing updates carry several types of metric information, namely:

Delay	The delay is the time (in units of 10 microseconds) that it takes a bit to reach a destination when there is no load on the network.
Bandwidth	The metric is 10,000,000 divided by the smallest bandwidth on the path (measured in kilobits per second). For example, the smallest bandwidth of 10 kilobits per second yields a metric of 1,000,000.
Load	The load is the proportion of the path's bandwidth that currently is in use. It is coded on a scale from 0 to 255; 255 means 100 percent loaded.
Reliability	This is the fraction of the datagrams that are arriving undamaged. It is coded on a scale from 0 to 255; 255 means that 100 percent are arriving undamaged.
Hop count	The number of hops to the destination.
Path MTU	The biggest Maximum Transmission Unit (MTU) that can be carried across every link on the path.

The delay, bandwidth, and MTU are derived from router configuration information. The load and reliability are computed dynamically, from information exchanged by the routers. Table 8.3 shows some examples of coded delay and bandwidth values.

TABLE 8.3

IGRP Delay and
Bandwidth
Measurements

Medium	Default Delay Values (10 microsecond units)	Bandwidth Metric (10,000,000 ÷ bandwidth in kilobits per second)
Satellite (500 megabit per second)	200,000 (2 seconds)	20
Ethernet (10 megabit)	100 (1 millisecond)	1,000
1.544 megabit	2000 (20 milliseconds)	6,480
64 kilobit	2000	156,250
56 kilobit	2000	178,570
10 kilobit	2000	1,000,000
1 kilobit	2000	10,000,000

Recall that Table 8.2 displayed metric values returned by a Simple Network Management Protocol (SNMP) poll of a Cisco router. For example:

ip Route Dest	ip Route Metric 1	ip Route Metric 2	ip Route Metric 3	ip Route Metric 4	ip Route Metric 5	ip Route If Index	ip Route Age (secs)
128.6.0.0	12610	1536	61000	2	255	3	11
128.96.0.0	14647	1170	61000	2	255	6	16
128.112.0.0	10667	1170	21200	1	255	6	23

For IGRP/EIGRP the metric values have the following meanings:

Metric1   Overall route metric

Metric2   Bandwidth metric

Metric3   Sum of interface delays

Metric4   Route hop count

Metric5   Interface reliability (255 means 100 percent)

The display that follows shows the format of an IGRP update message.[10] Part of the IP header is included.

```
IP header length = 5 (32-but words, or 20 bytes)
Time to live = 2
Protocol = 9 (IGRP Cisco Inter-Gateway Routing Protocol)
Source address = 134.141.25.1
Destination address = 134.141.255.255
-----------------------------------
Version = 1
Opcode = 1 (Update)
Edition = 55
Autonomous System number = 100
Subnets in Local Net = 43
Networks in Autonomous System = 0
Networks outside of Autonomous System = 0
Checksum = E9AE
IGRP routing entry #1
  IP address = 134.141.13.0
  Delay (tens of microseconds) = 200
  Bandwidth 91Kbit/sec = 1000
  MTU = 1500 Bytes
  Reliability = 255/255
  Load = 1/255
  Hop count = 1
  . . .
```

Other Configured IGRP Values

Configuring an IGRP router is fairly straightforward. In addition to the IP addresses, subnet masks, MTUs, bandwidths, and link delays, you can specify:

- A variance factor V. If M is the smallest path metric, all paths with metric less than M $\times$ V will be used.
- Whether hold downs are enabled or disabled.

Timers also are configurable, although the defaults frequently are used. The default values are:

- Updates are broadcast every 90 seconds.
- If no update is received from a next-hop router within 270 seconds, its entries are timed out. If there is no alternative route, the destination is marked unreachable.

---

[10]This trace was obtained using a WinPharoah monitor from GNNettest.

- A hold down, during which no new path for an unreachable destination will be accepted, will last 280 seconds.

- If no update for a destination has been received for 540 seconds (the *flush* time), it is removed from the routing table.

IGRP Protocol Mechanisms

Cisco IGRP messages are carried directly in IP datagrams whose header protocol field is set to 9.[11] Like RIP, an IGRP router sends periodic updates to its neighbors. The updates include the entire current routing table, with all metrics.

A hold down prevents a defunct route from being reinstalled by a stale message. No new route to the destination is accepted during the hold down period. (Hold downs can be disabled if desired.)

Split horizon is used to prevent advertising a path to an inappropriate neighbor, and IGRP also provides its own version of route poisoning. If the metric for a route increases by more than a factor of 1.1, it is very likely that a loop is building, and so the route is removed.

Triggered updates are sent after a change—such as removal of a route. A route is removed when:

- Communication to a neighbor times out. Routes via the neighbor are removed.

- A next-hop router sends a notification that a route is unusable.

- The metric has increased sufficiently so that route poisoning is invoked.

Exterior Routing

One reason that IGRP has been popular with Internet Service Providers is that it handles routing between Service Provider networks. IGRP updates can include multiple routes to outside networks. A default route to the outside world can be selected from several proposed external routes.

---

[11]Actually, 9 was set aside for any private interior routing protocol. Cisco chose to use it for IGRP.

Enhanced IGRP Features

Enhanced IGRP messages are carried in IP datagrams whose protocol header field is set to 88. EIGRP uses the same metrics and distance calculations found in IGRP. However, it improves IGRP significantly by supporting subnet masks and doing away with periodic updates. Only changes are sent, and an EIGRP sender makes sure that these changes have been received by requiring them to be acknowledged. Simple periodic *Hello* messages are used to discover neighbors and check that they are still active. Another important enhancement is use of the *Diffusing Update ALgorithm* (DUAL), which guarantees loop-free routing.

EIGRP DUAL

The basic idea behind DUAL is simple. It is based on the observation:

> *If a path consistently takes you closer to a destination, then the path cannot be a loop.*

Turning the statement around, if a path is a loop, it will contain a router whose distance to the destination is bigger than the previous router's distance (as illustrated in Figure 8.11).

DUAL is designed to find paths that have the property that each router along the way is closer to the destination. Router E in Figure 8.11

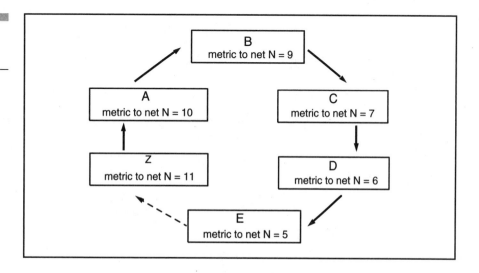

Figure 8.11
Routing around a loop.

will view with great suspicion an update from its *downstream* neighbor Z that reports a much bigger metric than is in E's own current table.

DUAL Topology Table

To implement DUAL, EIGRP saves information that IGRP would have thrown away. EIGRP saves the route information that each neighbor has sent in its updates. (IGRP would have discarded information about any routes that were not optimal.) The information is stored in a side table called the *Topology Table*. The Topology Table contains a set of entries for each destination:

Neighbor

Neighbor's metric

Neighbor

Neighbor's metric

. . .

My current best metric

DUAL Feasible Successors

The interesting entries in the Topology Table are the ones that describe *feasible successors*. My *feasible successors* are neighbors who are closer to the destination than I am (currently).

As long as there is at least one feasible successor, I have a route to the destination and am in *Passive* state for DUAL. However, when an update changes the picture so that I have no feasible successor, I start to query my neighbors to find out whether traffic has simply been switched to a longer route or a loop is forming. Let's walk through the process a little more formally:

1. Suppose that I have reached the point where I have only one feasible route to a destination, via router Z.

2. An update arrives from Z that increases Z's metric. Furthermore, the new distance from Z to the destination is *greater* than my current distance. This could indicate that a loop is forming.

3. I go into *Active* state and start a *route recomputation*.

4. But while the recomputation is in progress, I will continue to route through Z.

5. I send an update message (which is called a "query") to all neighbors except Z. The message announces my new, bigger metric distance for the destination.

6. If a neighbor has one or more feasible routes, it sends a reply and announces its good routes to the destination.

7. A neighbor that does not have a feasible route will enter *Active* state (if it is not already in it) and send queries to *its* neighbors. (Optionally, it can report back immediately that it already is in *Active* state and is recomputing.)

8. Queries will "diffuse" through the network until either a feasible route is found or a router that knows that the destination is unreachable is contacted.

9. When a router has found a feasible route or established unreachability, it sends back replies to the queries that it has received.

10. When all of its own queries have been answered, a router returns to passive state.

EIGRP has proven that distance vector routing is far from dead. In the next sections, we will look at its competitor, link state routing.

Open Shortest Path First

In 1988, the Internet Engineering Task Force (IETF) started work on a new standard protocol to replace RIP. The result was the *Open Shortest Path First* (OSPF) Interior Gateway Protocol, a routing protocol intended for use within internetworks of all sizes. In 1990, OSPF was recommended as a proposed standard. The protocol is a nonproprietary public technology.

Recall that a link state router discovers paths by building a map of the network and using the map to build a tree of paths with the router as its root. A metric value is computed for each path, and then the optimal path or paths are selected.

OSPF uses link state paths with distance metrics. OSPF is designed to scale well and to spread accurate routing information quickly. In addition, OSPF supports:

  ■ Quick detection of topology changes and very rapid reestablishment of loop-free routes

- Low overhead, using updates that report changes rather than all routes
- Traffic splitting across multiple equivalent paths
- Use of multicast on LANs
- Masks for subnetting and supernetting
- Authentication

In April of 1990, when the very large NASA Science internetwork converted to OSPF, routing overhead traffic decreased dramatically. After a change or disruption in the network, globally correct routing information was reestablished very quickly—typically within a few seconds, as compared to minutes for older protocols.

Version 2 of OSPF originally was published in mid-1991. The current specification, RFC 2328, was published in mid-1998. This is a 244-page document, so the description below should be considered a rough outline of the protocol.

Areas and Networks

In the OSPF standard, the term *network* means an IP network, a subnet, or CIDR supernet. Similarly, a *network mask* identifies a network, subnet, or CIDR supernet. An *area* is a set of contiguous networks and hosts, along with any routers having interfaces to the networks. We use the term *OSPF internetwork* for the set of components that make up an entire OSPF network.

An OSPF internetwork is made up of one or more areas. Each area is assigned a number. Area 0 is a connected *backbone* that links to all of the other areas and glues the OSPF internetwork together. Figure 8.12 illustrates this topology.

OSPF Area Routing

Routing within an area is based on a complete link state map for the area. OSPF scales well because a router needs to know detailed topology and metric information *only* about an area that it belongs to.

Every OSPF router in an area keeps an identical *routing database* describing the topology and status of all of the elements in the area. The database is used to construct the area map. This database includes the state of every router, each router's usable interfaces, its connected net-

Figure 8.12
OSPF backbone and
areas.

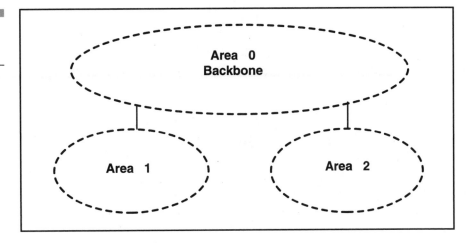

works, and its neighbor routers. Routers learn about neighbors via *Hello* messages. *Hello* messages are repeated periodically to announce that a system is still alive and active.

Whenever a change occurs (such as a link going down), update information is propagated through the area. This promotes accurate routing and quick response to trouble. For example, if OSPF routing were used in the network in Figure 8.13, Router A would quickly be informed that the link to B was down and would realize immediately that there was no usable route to *Network N*.

A router that is initializing obtains a copy of the current routing database from an adjacent neighbor. After that, only changes need to be communicated. Changes get known quickly because OSPF uses an efficient flooding algorithm to spread update information through the area.

Figure 8.13
Using complete route
information.

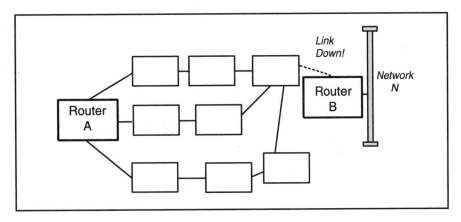

OSPF Area Shortest Paths

A router uses its area database to construct a tree of shortest paths with itself as the root. This tree is used to build the routing table.

The OSPF Backbone, Borders, and Boundaries

Areas are glued together by the backbone. The backbone contains all routers that belong to multiple areas, as well as any networks and routers not assigned to any other area. Recall that areas are numbered, and the backbone is area 0.

A *border* router belongs to one or more areas and to the backbone. If the OSPF internetwork is connected to the outside world, *boundary* routers learn routes to external networks.

In Figure 8.14, backbone area 0 includes Routers A, B, C, F, and G. Area 1 includes Routers B and D. Area 2 includes Routers C, E, and F. Routers B, C, and F are border routers. Router G is a boundary router. Router B knows the full topologies of area 1 and of the backbone. Similarly, Routers C and F know the full topologies of area 2 and of the backbone.

Figure 8.14
Routers and areas in an OSPF network.

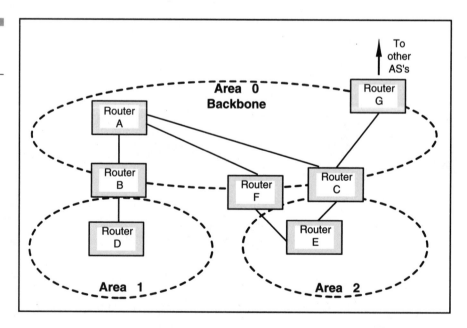

Figure 8.15
Defining a virtual
link.

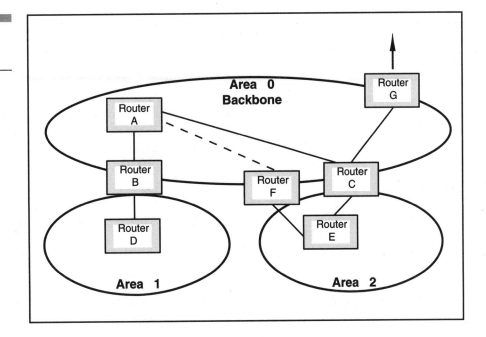

The backbone must be contiguous. What happens if a restructuring of
the network or an equipment failure causes the backbone to be broken?
Sometimes *virtual links* can be used to tie together the pieces of the
backbone.

A virtual link can be defined between two backbone routers that
interface to the same area. The virtual link is treated like an unnumbered point-to-point link. The cost of the virtual link is the total path
cost of the route between the two routers.

As shown in Figure 8.15, if the link from A to F were lost, Router F
would no longer be connected to the other backbone routers via a backbone link. The virtual link F-E-C could be used to restore the connected-
ness of the backbone.

Routing Across an OSPF Area Border

A border router knows the complete topology of each area to which it
connects. Recall that every border router belongs to the backbone, and
so it also knows the full backbone topology.

Using Summarized Information Inside an OSPF Area

Each border router summarizes area information and tells the other backbone routers how far it is from networks within its own area(s). This enables every border router to calculate distances to destinations outside its own areas and then pass that information into its own areas.

The summarized information includes a network, subnet, or supernet identifier; a network mask; and the distance from the router to the external network.

For example, in Figure 8.16, suppose that Router E wants to choose a path to *Network M*. Router E uses its area database to find the distances d_c and d_f to the border Routers C and F. Each of these has reported its distance m_c and m_f to *Network M*. Router E can compare $d_c + m_c$ with $d_f + m_f$, and pick the shortest route.

Note that Router B should not bother to pass summarized distance information into area 1. There is only one path out of this area, and so one simple default route entry suffices for all external destinations. If an area has a single border router, or if it just doesn't matter which border

Figure 8.16
Routing between areas.

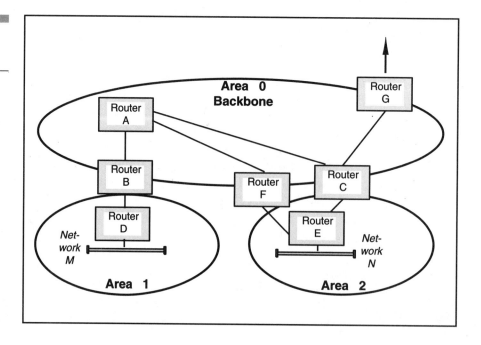

router is used, it is called a *stub* area, and one or more default routes can be provided to reach external destinations.

External OSPF Destinations

Many OSPF internetworks are connected to the Internet or to other OSPF internetworks. OSPF boundary routers provide information about distances to external networks.

There are two types of OSPF external distance metrics. Type 1 is equivalent to the local link state metric. Type 2 metrics are long distance metrics—they are measured at a greater order of magnitude. If an analogy is made with driving distances, think of Type 2 routes as being derived from a national road map and measured in hundreds of miles, while Type 1 metrics use a local distance measurement in miles.

Figure 8.17 shows two routes to an external network N. The Type 1 metrics would be ignored in the distance calculation, and the route with Type 2 metric equal to 2 would be chosen.

Another feature of OSPF (especially convenient for Service Providers) is that a router on the boundary of an OSPF internetwork can act as a *route server* and can advertise entries that identify routes through other boundary routers. Information would include:

Destination, Metric, Boundary Router to be used

Figure 8.17
Choosing routes using Type 2 metrics.

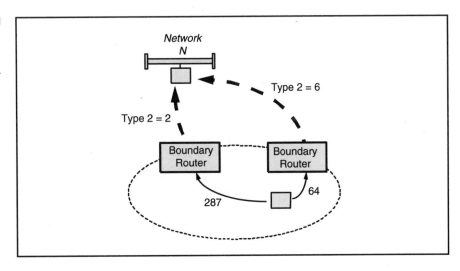

Designated Router

On a multiaccess network, *Hello* messages also are used to select and identify a *Designated Router.* The Designated Router has two jobs:

- It is responsible for reliably updating its adjacent neighbors with the latest network topology news.
- It originates *networks links advertisements,* which list all routers connected to the multiaccess network.

A backup Designated Router also is selected.

Hello messages are sent to the "all OSPF routers" multicast address, 224.0.0.5. After a Designated Router and its backup have been selected, they can receive messages sent to the "Designated Routers" multicast address 224.0.0.6.

In Figure 8.18, Designated Router A exchanges information with Routers B, C, and D on its LAN as well as with Router E, which is connected by a point-to-point link.

Adjacencies

Designated Router A acts as the local expert and keeps up to date on the complete local topology. It then communicates this topology to adjacent routers.

Figure 8.18
A Designated Router updates its neighbors.

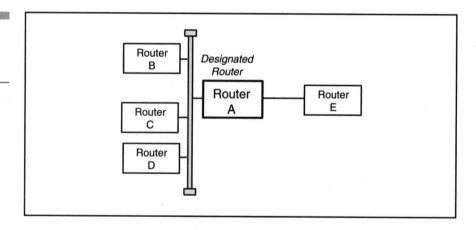

B, C, and D keep their databases synchronized by talking to A. They do not have to talk to one another. Two routers that synchronize databases with one another are called *adjacent*. B and C are *neighbors,* but they are not adjacent to one another.

Clearly, this is an efficient method of keeping the LAN router databases synchronized. It can also be used on frame relay or X.25 networks. Routers can exchange *Hellos* across virtual circuits, choose a Designated Router, and synchronize their databases with the Designated Router. This speeds up synchronization and cuts down on network traffic.

The loss of a Designated Router would be a pretty disruptive event. For this reason, a backup Designated Router always is selected and is ready to take over immediately. An automatic election process is used to choose a Designated Router and its backup.

Initializing a Routing Database

Now suppose that Router B has just been restarted after being offline for maintenance. First B listens to *Hellos,* discovers its neighbors, and finds out that Router A is the Designated Router. Next, B brings itself up to date by talking to A.

More specifically, A and B will exchange *Database Description* messages. These messages contain a list of what each has in its database. Each item has a sequence number that is used to establish which router has the freshest information for the item. (The sequence number of a routing entry is increased[12] whenever the entry is updated.)

After this exchange of information is complete, each knows:

- Which items are not yet in its local database
- Which items are present but out of date

Link State Request messages are used to ask for entries that are in need of an update. *Link State Update* messages respond to these requests. After a full (and acknowledged) exchange of information, the databases are synchronized. Link State Update messages also are used to report changes in the area topology. Topology updates are flooded through an area so that all databases are kept in synchronization.

---

[12]Numbers eventually roll around to 0.

OSPF Protocol

Now we are ready to look at some of the internals of the OSPF protocol.

OSPF Message Types

The five message types used in the OSPF protocol exchanges that we have described are:

Hello	Used to identify neighbors, to elect a Designated Router for a multiaccess network, to find out about an existing Designated Router, and as an "I am alive" signal.
Database Description	During initialization, used to exchange information so that a router can find out what data is missing from its database.
Link State Request	Used to ask for data that a router has discovered is missing from its database or is out of date.
Link State Update	Used to reply to a Link State Request and also to dynamically report changes in network topology.
Link State ACK	Used to confirm receipt of a Link State Update. The sender will retransmit until an update is ACKed.

OSPF Messages

OSPF messages are carried directly in IP datagrams, with protocol number 89. All OSPF messages start with the 24-byte header that is shown in Figure 8.19. The current version is 2. The *type field* contains a number that identifies the message type. The length is the total length, including the header.

OSPF Authentication types are registered with the IANA. Currently, both simple password authentication and cryptographic authentication are defined. Cryptographic authentication is based on the use of a shared secret key and a Message Digest. Secure and authenticated transmission of routing information is especially important to the robustness of networks.

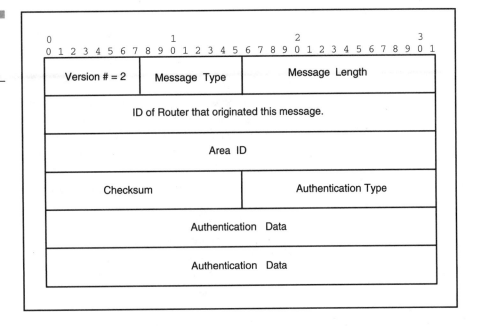

Figure 8.19
The standard 24-byte OSPF message header.

Hello Messages

Each OSPF router is configured with a unique identifier that is included in messages. Usually, the router's smallest IP address is used as its unique ID.

A router periodically multicasts *Hello* messages to address 224.0.0.5 on a multiaccess network [such as an Ethernet, Token-Ring, or Fiber Distributed Data Interface (FDDI) LAN] to let other routers know that it is active. It also sends *Hello* messages to peers attached by point-to-point links or virtual circuits to let these neighbors know that it is awake.

One reason that *Hello* works well is that on a multiaccess network, a *Hello* message contains a list of IDs of neighbors whose *Hellos* the sender already has heard. That way, every router knows whether its messages are getting through.

The *Hello* message below was multicast to the all-routers address, 224.0.0.5 by router R1 that is connected to the backbone area. Router R1 has address 198.207.177.30. A simple password is included in the message.

The router announces that it will send *Hellos* every 10 seconds. All routers on a LAN should be configured with the same *Hello* interval. R1 indicates that a neighbor is declared dead after no *Hello* has been received for 40 seconds. The "dead" interval often is selected to be 4 times the *Hello* interval.

Router R1 has priority number 1. The priority number is used to select the Designated Router. The system with the biggest priority number wins the election. An administrator can assign priority numbers that assure that a selected system will win. If there is a tie, the system with the largest ID is chosen. The ID is a manually configurable number, but recall that it usually is selected to be one of the router's IP addresses. In the trace below, the router's ID is the IP address associated with the router's Ethernet interface.

A flag in the Options field indicates that this router is capable of exchanging external routes. There is another router attached to this LAN, but it is inactive. Therefore, this router becomes the Designated Router.

```
OSPF: Message = Hello
OSPF: Version = 2 (0x2)
OSPF: OSPF Packet Type = Hello
OSPF: Packet Length = 44 (0x2C)
OSPF: Source Router ID = 198.207.177.30
OSPF: Area ID = 0 (0x0)
OSPF: Checksum = 0x0CC1
OSPF: Authentication Type = Simple Password
OSPF: Authentication = 0x726365734650534F
OSPF: Netmask = 255.255.255.0
OSPF: Hello Interval = 10 (0xA) seconds
OSPF: Hello Options = 2
OSPF: Router Priority = 1 (0x1)
OSPF: Dead Interval = 40 (0x28) seconds
OSPF: Designated Router = 198.207.177.30
OSPF: Backup Designated Router = 0.0.0.0
```

Some time later, router R2 whose IP address is 109.207.177.50 wakes up and announces its presence. Note that R2 has a higher priority number.

```
OSPF: Message = Hello
OSPF: Version = 2 (0x2)
OSPF: OSPF Packet Type = Hello
OSPF: Packet Length = 44 (0x2C)
OSPF: Source Router ID = 198.207.177.50
OSPF: Area ID = 0 (0x0)
OSPF: Checksum = 0x849A
OSPF: Authentication Type = Simple Password
OSPF: Authentication = 0x726365734650534F
OSPF: Netmask = 255.255.255.0
OSPF: Hello Interval = 10 (0xA) seconds
OSPF: Hello Options = 2
OSPF: Router Priority = 2 (0x2)
```

```
OSPF: Dead Interval = 40 (0x28) seconds
OSPF: Designated Router = 0.0.0.0
OSPF: Backup Designated Router = 0.0.0.0
```

After further exchanges of *Hellos,* the pecking order has been established. R1 is the Designated Router and R2 is the backup. Usually we expect the router with the biggest priority number to become the designated router. However, R2 was inactive when R1 took on that role, and it is better for network stability to allow R1 to remain designated router than to make a change.

Using *Hellos,* all neighbor routers on a LAN are detected and appear on each router's neighbor list. In this case, there only are two routers on the LAN.

```
OSPF: Message = Hello
OSPF: Version = 2 (0x2)
OSPF: OSPF Packet Type = Hello
OSPF: Packet Length = 48 (0x30)
OSPF: Source Router ID = 198.207.177.50
OSPF: Area ID = 0 (0x0)
OSPF: Checksum = 0x1CB7
OSPF: Authentication Type = Simple Password
OSPF: Authentication = 0x726365734650534F
OSPF: Netmask = 255.255.255.0
OSPF: Hello Interval = 10 (0xA) seconds
OSPF: Hello Options = 2
OSPF: Router Priority = 2 (0x2)
OSPF: Dead Interval = 40 (0x28) seconds
OSPF: Designated Router = 198.207.177.30
OSPF: Backup Designated Router = 198.207.177.50
OSPF: Neighbor = 198.207.177.30
```

Contents of an OSPF Link State Update

Every OSPF router maintains a detailed database of information needed to build its area routing tree, such as descriptions of:

- Each router's interfaces, connections, and associated metrics
- Each multiaccess network and a list of all routers on the network

The information that builds these databases is transmitted in Link State Update messages. Updates are sent between "adjacent" routers. When the Designated Router on a broadcast network receives an update, it multicasts it to the other routers on the network. Updates propagate through an area quite efficiently. Every newly received link state update must be acknowledged.

A Link State Update message contains items that are called *Advertisements*. Each message can include the following types of Advertisements:

Router Links	The state of each of the interfaces on a router.
Network Links	The list of routers connected to a multiaccess net. This is provided by the Designated Router on the net.
Summary Link to a Network	A route to a network outside the local area but in the internetwork. This is provided by a border router.
Summary Link to a Boundary Router	A route through the internetwork to the boundary of the internetwork. This is provided by a border router.
AS External Link	A route to a destination in another internetwork. This information is provided by a boundary router.

A Link State Update message begins with the standard 24-byte header. The remainder of the message is made up of advertisements of the various kinds just listed.

OSPF Enhancements

There has been a steady flow of enhancements for OSPF. For example, to decrease cost, it is desirable to disconnect dial-up lines and virtual circuits when there is no traffic to send. The original protocol was modified so that periodic *Hellos* can be turned off, so these lines do not need to be kept up all of the time. Numerous other small enhancements and bug fixes have been incorporated into the protocol. OSPF also has been extended to support IP multicasting.

OSI Routing

OSI uses the term *Intermediate System* rather than router or gateway. The OSI routing protocol, *IS-IS,* originally was defined to support OSI routers but then was extended to IP.

Like OSPF, IS-IS is a link state protocol and supports hierarchical routing, splitting of traffic on multiple paths, and authentication.

IS-IS has two types of routers: level 1 for routing within an area and level 2 for routing to destinations outside an area. (Level 2 routers could be viewed as analogous to routers in the OSPF backbone.) A level 1 Intermediate System router forwards traffic bound for destinations outside of its area to its nearest level 2 router. Traffic is then routed to a level 2 router that is connected to the destination area.

Many of the mechanisms used in OSPF were based on similar (but not identical) mechanisms in IS-IS, for example, the use of link state advertisements, flooding, and sequence numbers.

Some IS-IS proponents believe that it is better to route IP and OSI traffic using this single integrated protocol instead of using separate router-to-router protocols.

Exterior Protocols

You can use any routing protocol that you wish within your own network, but standards are needed to route data across the Internet. These standard protocols define how information will be exchanged with external networks. The two protocols in common use are the Exterior Gateway Protocol (EGP) and the Border Gateway Protocol (BGP).

Autonomous Systems

The Internet is made up of many separate pieces, with each piece under the control of some administering organization (such as UUNET, MCI, or AT&T). The standard exterior protocols are used to obtain the information required in order to pass data between these pieces.

First we, need a way to define these pieces. This is done using the concept of an Autonomous System:

An Autonomous System (AS) is a connected group of IP networks which have a single and clearly defined routing policy.

An Internet Service Provider network and a set of attached customer sites make up a typical Autonomous System. The Internet Service Provider obtains one or more chunks of address space and doles out smaller subchunks to customers. Routing to and from the Service Provider is based on the prefixes that define the blocks of addresses. The provider chooses how traffic within its own network will be routed, and is responsible for routing data between its customers and the rest of the Internet.

Internet routing is based on selecting a chain of Autonomous Systems that connect the source to the destination. To define these chains, each Autonomous System is labeled with a unique 16-bit identifier. AS numbers are administered by the American Registry for Internet Numbers (ARIN). Autonomous System numbers are included in EGP and BGP messages.

Figure 8.20 shows a set of connected Autonomous System networks. Usually, customer networks are bundled into their ISP's Autonomous System. However, a customer connected to multiple ISPs needs its own registered IP addresses and its own AS number. If a customer has a routing policy that does not agree with the policy of its ISP, it also needs its own AS number. (For example, a customer might not be willing to have its traffic routed across some external Autonomous System that its ISP judged to be acceptable.) The Autonomous Systems in the figure use whatever internal routing protocol they like, but exchange information using BGP and EGP.

Recall that the Internet Assigned Numbers Authority (IANA) has set aside blocks of IP addresses for private use. Just in case anyone needs them, the IANA also has reserved AS numbers 64,512 through 65,535 for private use. Two or more companies that wish to exchange data across a private extranet (not connected to the Internet) can use these

Figure 8.20
Autonomous Systems and routing protocols.

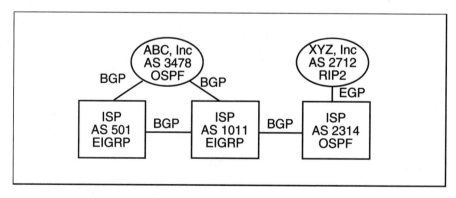

private Autonomous System numbers and one of the exterior protocols to route traffic between them.

EGP

For many years, the simple Exterior Gateway Protocol (EGP) was used on the Internet to enable an Autonomous System to route information to external networks. EGP is widely available. A very simple design is used. EGP routers in neighboring Autonomous Systems tell one another what networks they can reach.

EGP was designed in the early 1980s when the Internet was still fairly small and had a simple topology consisting of a backbone and a set of networks directly connected to the backbone. As the Internet evolved into its present, meshlike topology, EGP began to pass reachability information through a chain of Autonomous Systems, as shown in Figure 8.21.

EGP does not disclose the routes that are followed by datagrams that are traveling to external locations. It even hides which Autonomous Systems are traversed along the way. EGP's simple reachability information has proved to be inadequate in the modern environment. Use of EGP is diminishing rapidly. The protocol is described very briefly here.

Figure 8.21
Simple EGP messages in a complex network.

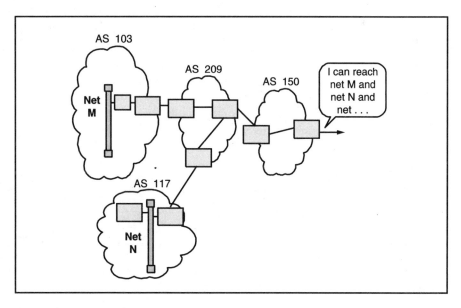

EGP Model

An EGP router is configured with the IP addresses of one or more exterior neighbor EGP routers. Usually, exterior neighbors are connected to a common multiaccess network or are joined by a point-to-point link.

EGP enables a router to find out which networks can be reached through its exterior neighbors. EGP has the following ingredients:

Neighbor Acquisition	A router sends a *Neighbor Acquisition Request.* The receiver sends back both a *Neighbor Acquisition Response* and a *Neighbor Acquisition Request* message.
Neighbor Release	To terminate being a neighbor, a router sends a *Neighbor Cease* message. The receiver sends back a *Neighbor Cease* message.
Neighbor Reachability	The relationship between acquired neighbors is kept alive by periodic exchanges of *Hello* and *I Heard You* messages.
Network Reachability	A router sends a poll to the exterior neighbor, requesting information on reachable networks. The neighbor responds with a *Network Reachability* message.

The content of *Network Reachability* messages needs a little more explanation. If the exterior neighbors are connected by a point-to-point link, the message will identify networks that can be reached via the sender. A hop count to each destination also is provided. Figure 8.22 illustrates this configuration—Router A reports reachable networks to Router X.

Figure 8.22
Network Reachability messages.

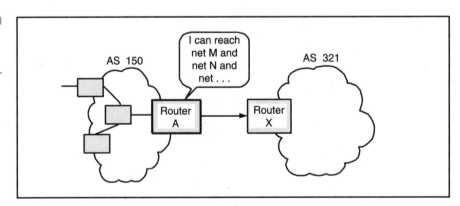

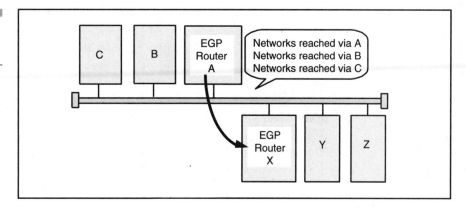

Figure 8.23
Efficient exchange of
EGP information.

As shown in Figure 8.23, sometimes several routers from different Autonomous Systems share a common multiaccess network. In this case, EGP Router A will inform EGP Router X of the networks reached via A, B, and C, respectively (and the hop counts for each, if known). Similarly, EGP Router X will inform EGP Router A of the networks reached via X, Y, and Z, respectively.

Routers A and X are *direct* neighbors, but Routers B and C are *indirect* neighbors of Router X. If Router A were to crash, Router X could try to acquire one of its indirect neighbors, B or C, as a direct EGP neighbor.

EGP messages are carried directly inside IP datagrams whose protocol field is set to 8.

BGP

The Border Gateway Protocol (BGP) is used for large-scale routing. BGP is in wide use on the Internet. The current version is BGP-4.

To get an idea of how BGP works, think of automobile travel between the countries in Europe. If you wanted to drive from Spain to Denmark, you could take a look at a map of Europe and see that there is a path via the chain of countries: Spain, France, Germany, and Denmark. If you have a taste for ferry rides, you might prefer an alternate route: Spain, France, England, and Denmark. Because countries wish to protect their borders, there are a few well-defined entry/exit points. Once you have planned your overall route strategy, you would need to select the most convenient entry/exit points. Once in a country, you would use internal maps to plot your route from an entry point to the next exit point.

The BGP routing strategy is similar. In today's Internet, there are many Service Providers, and they are joined together by well-defined entry/exit points. Traffic often transits the networks of several different Service Providers on the way to its destination. For example, the route below starts within VNET, passes to Gridnet (whose routers are not assigned names), crosses Alternet (which is the same as UUNET), and takes several hops across AT&T's network before entering the University of Texas campus.

```
> traceroute www.utexas.edu
traceroute to www.utexas.edu (128.83.40.17), 30 hops max, 40 byte
packets
 1 rtr-char1.vnet.net (166.82.1.1) 5.525 ms 5.144 ms 3.743 ms
 2 206.80.168.230 (206.80.168.230) 69.939 ms 79.050 ms 46.474 ms
 3 Fddi9-0.BR2.TCO1.alter.net (198.32.186.249) 44.079 ms 35.864 ms
   29.817 ms
 4 112.atm10-0-0.xr2.tcO1.alter.net (146.188.160.94) 0.712 ms
   33.585 ms 42.204 ms
 5 292.atm7-0.xr2.dca1.alter.net (146.188.160.125) 26.054 ms 76.398
   ms 99.080 ms
 6 194.atm11-0-0.gw1.dca1.alter.net (146.188.161.29) 87.815 ms
   134.270 ms 81.721 ms
 7 att-dc-gw.customer.alter.net (157.130.32.22) 75.325 ms 184.399
   ms 207.495 ms
 8 br2-a350s5.wswdc.ip.att.net (192.205.31.166) 213.592 ms 130.774
   ms 91.829 ms
 9 br1-h20.n54ny.ip.att.net (12.127.15.221) 95.970 ms 105.070 ms
   71.250 ms
10 12.127.14.122 (12.127.14.122) 95.278 ms 67.822 ms 61.071 ms
11 br1-h00.dlstx.ip.att.net (12.127.15.246) 99.642 ms 110.883 ms
   102.237 ms
12 ar1-a300s1.dlstx.ip.att.net (12.127.2.5) 103.292 ms 162.783 ms
   154.502 ms
13 12.127.176.74 (12.127.176.74) 140.643 ms 205.645 ms 240.715 ms
14 utx1-a1-0-0-1.tx-bb.net (192.12.10.17) 298.156 ms 195.087 ms
   164.024 ms
15 ut5-fe1-0-0.tx-bb.net (192.12.10.29) 183.675 ms 224.930 ms
   206.791 ms
16 ser2-fe11-1-0.gw.utexas.edu (129.117.38.98) 264.799 ms 195.192
   ms *
17 com-rsm-v4.gw.utexas.edu (128.83.4.5) 268.264 ms 212.592 ms
   220.467 ms
18 web3.cc.utexas.edu (128.83.40.17) 164.496 ms 186.433 ms 203.151 ms
```

The purpose of BGP is to support routing across a chain of Autonomous Systems while preventing loops from forming. To do this, BGP systems exchange information that describes paths to the networks that they can reach. Unlike EGP, BGP reveals the entire chain of Autonomous Systems that must be traversed to reach a network.

For example (as shown in Figure 8.24), a BGP system in Autonomous System 34 reports to AS 205 that *Networks M* and *N* are in the AS. AS 205

Figure 8.24
A BGP chain of
Autonomous
Systems.

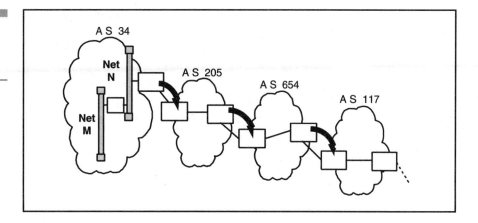

reports a path to *M* and *N* through itself *and* AS 34. Then AS 654 reports a path to *M* and *N* through itself *and* AS 205 *and* AS 34. The path grows along the way, and the full path is reported to the next system. Thus, BGP reachability information includes the entire chain of Autonomous Systems that are crossed on the way to a destination network.

The path is reported in the order that would be used to reach the destination, that is:

AS 654, AS 205, AS 34

If AS 117 passes the information on, it would add itself in front:

AS 117, AS 654, AS 205, AS 34

Note how easy it is to detect and prevent loops. If an AS receives an advertisement and sees its own ID on a path, it simply throws the advertisement away.

In addition to reporting paths to individual networks, BGP can identify aggregate sets of networks using CIDR prefixes.

BGP Route Aggregation

An Internet *route* consists of a destination network and instructions on how to get there. There has been explosive growth in the number of routes because of the rapid increase in the number of networks.

An interim solution has gotten routing under control. The current method of route reduction is to assign a block of addresses with a common prefix to a Service Provider. The provider assigns subblocks to its customer networks.

The size of the Service Provider prefix is identified by a number that indicates the length in bits of the IP address prefix. Traffic can be sent from external Autonomous Systems to the provider and its customers by means of a single route that corresponds to the prefix. The provider can then use longer prefixes to forward the traffic to each of its customers.

This is simple for incoming traffic, but we have to reverse the scenario to see what a Service Provider must do on an ongoing basis with outgoing advertisements. Customers will inform their Service Provider of routes to their internal networks. The Service Provider will *aggregate* routes with a common prefix into single routing entries before advertising them to the outside world.

BGP Mechanisms

A BGP system opens a TCP connection to well-known port 179 at a BGP neighbor. Each opening message identifies the sender's Autonomous System and BGP identifier and may include authentication information.

Once the connection is open, the peers exchange their route information. The connection remains open, and updates are sent as needed. To make sure that they still are in contact, the systems periodically exchange *Keep-alive* messages (usually every 30 seconds).

A Service Provider network carries traffic between Autonomous Systems, and is very likely to include multiple systems that speak BGP. These systems will communicate with one another via *internal* BGP connections. An *external* BGP connection is used to communicate to a BGP peer system in a different Autonomous System. (These connections are referred to as *links,* even though they are TCP connections that might possibly pass through intermediate routers.)

One big difference between BGP and other routing protocols is that the systems that exchange BGP routing information can be hosts—they do not have to be routers. One possible configuration is to give a host the job of talking to all external BGP systems in neighboring Autonomous Systems. The host could then be used as a route server, passing information to boundary routers in its own Autonomous System.

Contents of BGP Update Messages

A BGP update message can contain at most one feasible route. But it also can include a list of one or more *withdrawn* routes, which are routes that should no longer be used.

A route description is made up of a sequence of *path attributes,* which include:

Origin of Path Information	One of: Source was the IGP of the original AS; source was EGP; other.
AS Path	The path along which this update was carried.
Next Hop	IP address of the boundary router that should be used as the next hop to the destination. This might be a router belonging to the local Autonomous System or an external router that is directly connected to both the sender and to the recipient for this update.
Multiexit Discriminator	If I have multiple exit points that connect me to my neighbor's Autonomous System, my neighbor can assign numbers to indicate which exit is better. The neighbor's *smallest* number indicates a better route.
Local Preference	Purely internal information, used when sending BGP updates to systems in the local AS. When there are multiple BGP routes to a destination, a *bigger* number is preferred.
Atomic Aggregate	Indicates that an Autonomous System has aggregated several destinations into a single route entry.
Aggregator	The IP address and AS number of the last system that aggregated several routes into this one.
Reachable Nets	A list of prefixes for networks that can be reached via this route.

Making Choices

Figure 8.25 illustrates the difference between the Multi-exit Discriminator and Local Preference. Systems in AS 117 want to reach *Network* N in AS 433. AS 654 has two routes to that destination, and AS 654 announces that the one through Router E is better. However, AS 117 has an internally assigned local preference for the route to *Network N* via AS 119.

Figure 8.25
Preferred routes.

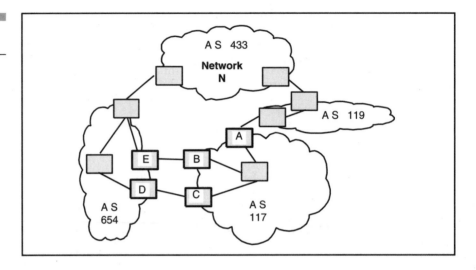

Using Aggregation

The purpose of route aggregation is to avoid including a lot of unnecessary information in remote routing tables. A Service Provider can aggregate the routes reported by its client Autonomous Systems.

As shown in Figure 8.26, BGP routers in AS 650, 651, and 652 can report their routes, but the provider in AS 117 aggregates them into one entry. The fact that this has been done is signaled by the *Atomic Aggregate* attribute.

Figure 8.26
Aggregating routes.

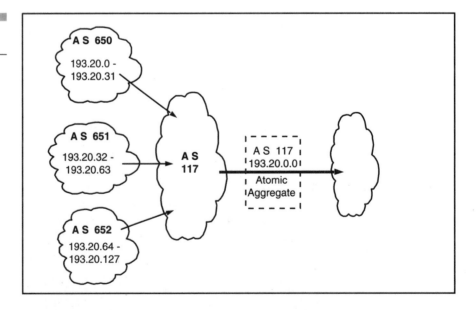

Note that AS 652 might be a local Service Provider and might already be aggregating its customer's routes, so it is possible that more of the route is hidden from remote systems. Each of the aggregating Autonomous System routers will forward traffic to the customer destinations based on their own routing tables.

Withdrawing BGP Routes

A route is terminated when:

- It is on a list of withdrawn routes sent in an update.
- An update provides a replacement route.
- The BGP system closes its connection. All routes learned via that system are voided.

GateDaemon Consortium

Most vendors need to offer and support several routing protocols. The addition of IP version 6 and the increasing popularity of multicast routing protocols[13] adds to the vendor development burden. Vendors also need to worry about whether their routing software will interwork with software written by other vendors.

Fortunately, help is just a mouse click away, in typical Internet fashion. The Merit GateDaemon Consortium at *http://www.gated.org/* writes and maintains "GateD" packages of routing software for:

- RIP (versions 1 and 2)
- OSPF
- ISO IS-IS
- Two other protocols not discussed in this chapter: Hello and slsp
- Versions of the above that run over IPv6
- Several multicast routing protocols

The packages include management modules that enable a network management station to control and troubleshoot a router running GateD software.

The consortium grew out of an earlier project at Cornell University funded by the National Science Foundation. The work now is funded by

---

[13]See Chapter 10.

membership payments from vendors who wish to use the GateD software in their commercial products. Free academic and research memberships are available.

Recommended Reading

Routing is a very important function, and many RFCs have been written on the subject. Some of the most important and useful ones are listed below. Check the RFC index for the most current versions.

RIP:

RFC 1058 *Routing Information Protocol*

RFC 1723 RIP *Version 2 Carrying Additional Information*

RFC 1582 *Extensions to RIP to Support Demand Circuits*

RFC 2080 *RIPng for IPv6*

RFC 2081 *RIPng Protocol Applicability Statement*

RFC 2091 *Triggered Extensions to RIP to Support Demand Circuits*

OSPF:

RFC 2178 *OSPF Version 2*

RFC 1793 *Extending OSPF to Support Demand Circuits*

RFC 1586 *Guidelines for Running OSPF Over Frame Relay Networks*

RFC 1584 *Multicast Extensions to OSPF*

RFC 1403 *BGP OSPF Interaction*

BGP:

RFC 1771 *A Border Gateway Protocol 4 (BGP-4)*

RFC 1773 *Experience with the BGP-4 Protocol*

RFC 1772 *Application of the Border Gateway Protocol in the Internet*

RFC 2283 *Multiprotocol Extensions for BGP-4*

RFC 2042 *Registering New BGP Attribute Types*

See Cisco's online documentation at *www.cisco.com* for technical information on IGRP and EIGRP.

User Datagram Protocol and Transmission Control Protocol

Introduction

Now that we have dealt with the physical movement of bits across media and the routing of datagrams across an internet, we are ready to turn to the services that applications will use directly for the transfer of data. The first of these, *User Datagram Protocol* (UDP), is very simple. UDP enables applications to send individual messages to one another.

The second service, TCP, supports reliable sessions. Although its basic mechanisms are straightforward, many performance-boosting features have been added to TCP. These features make TCP work better, but also make it more complicated to explain. Most of this chapter is devoted to TCP.

At the end of the chapter, we present two enhancements to TCP that have recently been added to implementations:

- *TCP extensions for high performance:* These extensions smooth the way for gigabyte per second transmissions. They also boost performance on paths that have a long round-trip delay, for example, paths that include a satellite link.

- *Transactional TCP:* Improves efficiency for applications that need to complete a very large number of transactions per second using brief, reliable sessions.

Purpose of UDP

Why was a UDP service created? There are many applications that can be built on top of User Datagrams in a very natural way. For example, a simple exchange of User Datagrams can be used to execute a quick database lookup. We already have encountered an important service that is based on UDP, namely the *Domain Name System* (DNS) (see Figure 9.1).

The overhead of sending and receiving the many messages required to set up and take down a connection is avoided by simply sending a query and a response. UDP also is a perfect building block for creating monitoring, debugging, management, and testing functions.

UDP is a very basic service, simply passing individual messages to IP for transmission. Since IP is unreliable, there is no guarantee of delivery. If an application sends a query in a UDP Datagram and a response does not come back within a reasonable amount of time, it is up to the application to retransmit the query.

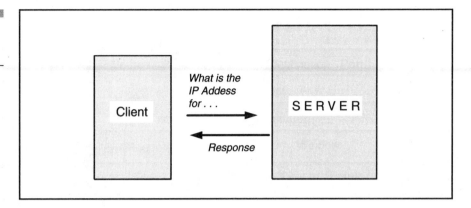

Sometimes this results in duplicate queries showing up at a server. If the application includes a transaction identifier with its query message, the server will be able to recognize duplicates and discard them. This mechanism is the application's responsibility, not UDP's.

Another advantage of UDP is that it can be used by applications that need to broadcast or multicast messages. For example, a DHCP or BOOTP client broadcasts a request for configuration parameters.

Application Port Numbers

What happens to data when it arrives at a destination host? How does it get delivered to the appropriate process?

As shown in Figure 9.2, for each layer there is a protocol identifier that indicates what should be done with incoming data. At layer 2, an Ethernet type of X'08-00 in a frame header indicates that the frame should be passed to IP. At layer 3, the *Protocol* field in the IP header identifies the layer 4 protocol to which datagrams should be passed (e.g., 6 for TCP, 17 for UDP).

A host can be expected to participate in many simultaneous communications at any time. How do UDP datagrams get sorted out and delivered to appropriate application layer processes?[1] The answer is that every UDP communication endpoint is assigned a 16-bit identifier called a *port* number.[2]

---

[1]This process of passing data to the correct process is sometimes referred to as *demultiplexing*.

[2]The term *port* probably was a poor choice for this identifier. Application port numbers identify clients and servers, and have *nothing* to do with systems hardware or the physical path that data follows.

Figure 9.2
Passing data up to
the application layer.

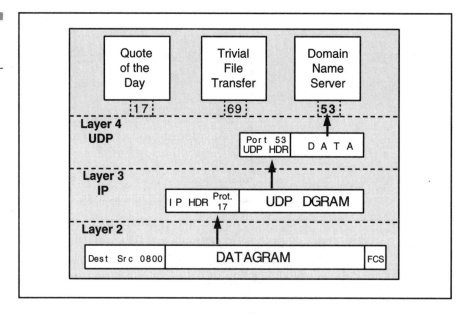

Port numbers from 0 to 1023 are reserved for standard services. Standard ports are called *well-known* ports. The use of a well-known port enables a client to identify the service that it wishes to access. For example, the UDP-based Domain Name Service is accessed at well-known port 53.

How do well-known ports get assigned? As you might guess, the Internet Assigned Numbers Authority (IANA) is in charge of this function. Port numbers for specific applications are registered with the IANA and published at the IANA Web site, *http://www.iana.org/*. A partial list of UDP ports is displayed in Table 9.1.

Several of these well-known services provide building blocks for testing, debugging, and measurement. For example, the *echo* service at port 7 does what its name implies—it returns any datagram that is sent to it. *Discard* at port 9, on the other hand, just throws datagrams away. A *character generator* responds to any message with a datagram containing between 0 and 512 bytes. The number of bytes is randomly chosen.

The *quote of the day* service responds to any datagram by sending back a message—for example, some fortune cookie wisdom to brighten your day when you log off. On many systems, you can run a *fortune* program that requests a quote:

TABLE 9.1

Examples of Well-known UDP Ports

Service	Port/Protocol	Description
Echo	7/udp	Echo User Datagram back to sender.
Discard	9/udp	Discard User Datagram.
Daytime	13/udp	Report time in a user-friendly way.
Quote	17/udp	Return a "quote of the day."
Chargen	19/udp	Character generator.
Nameserver	53/udp	Domain name server.
Bootps/DHCPs	67/udp	Server port used to download config. info.
Bootpc/DHCPc	68/udp	Client port used to receive config. info.
TFTP	69/udp	Trivial File Transfer Protocol port.
SunRPC	111/udp	Sun Remote Procedure Call.
NTP	123/udp	Network Time Protocol.
SNMP	161/udp	Used to receive net management queries.
SNMPtrap	162/udp	Used to receive network problem reports.

```
> fortune
Churchill's Commentary on Man:
  Man will occasionally stumble over the truth, but most of the
  time he will pick himself up and continue on.
```

A *daytime* server responds to any datagram with a message containing the current date and time in a readable ASCII format. In contrast, the *Network Time Protocol* (NTP) provides a robust method for synchronizing the clocks at computers across a network.

The DHCP server and client are used for system configuration. A system can grab a software download using the *Trivial File Transfer Protocol*.[3] We already have talked to the *Nameserver* at port 53 via the *nslookup* command. Ports 161 and 162 are used by the *Simple Network Management Protocol*.

Apart from the official number assignments, any system running TCP/IP may reserve a range of numbers for important network services and applications.

---

[3]The Trivial File Transfer Protocol is described in Chapter 14.

The remaining port numbers (above 1023) are allotted to clients by a host's networking software on an as-needed basis. The scenario that follows indicates how this happens:

1. A user invokes a client program (such as *nslookup*).

2. The client process executes a system routine that says "I want to perform UDP communication. Give me a port."

3. The system routine selects an unused port from the pool of available ports and gives it to the client process.

We shall see that TCP also identifies its sources and destinations with its own 16-bit port identifiers. For example, port 21 is used to reach a *File Transfer* service and port 23 is used to reach a *telnet* login service.

TCP and UDP numbers are independent of each other. One process may be sending messages from UDP port 1700 while another is engaged in a session at TCP port 1700. There are some services that can be accessed via both TCP and UDP. In this case, the IANA makes an effort to assign the same numbers to the UDP and the TCP ports assigned to the service. However, as endpoints of communication, these still are different "places."

Writing Port Numbers

Port numbers occupy 16-bit fields in UDP and TCP headers. Most of the time, a port number is displayed as an integer in the range from 0 to 65,535 (the largest number that can be written using 16 bits). Occasionally, a screen report will present a port number as two integers separated by a comma. In this case, each of the bytes in the port number has been translated to a number in the range from 0 to 255.

Socket Addresses

The combination of the IP address and port used for a communication is called a *socket address*. Note that a socket address provides all of the information a client or server needs in order to identify its communicating partner.

The IP header contains the source and destination IP addresses. The UDP header contains the source and destination port numbers. Thus every IP datagram containing a UDP message carries the socket addresses for its source and destination.

UDP Protocol Mechanisms

What mechanisms are needed to make the User Datagram Protocol work? First of all, UDP has been assigned its unique protocol identifier, 17. This number is placed in the IP *Protocol* field of outgoing UDP messages. Incoming messages with 17 in the IP *Protocol* field are delivered to UDP. UDP forms a message by adding a simple header to application data. This header contains the source and destination port numbers.

UDP Header

Figure 9.3 displays the UDP header format. The header contains the 16-bit source and destination port numbers that identify the endpoints of the communication. A length field indicates the total number of bytes in the UDP header and data part of the message. A checksum field is provided to validate the contents of the message.

Checksum

Recall that the IP header contained a checksum field used to validate the fields in the IP header. The purpose of the UDP checksum is to validate the *contents* of a UDP message.

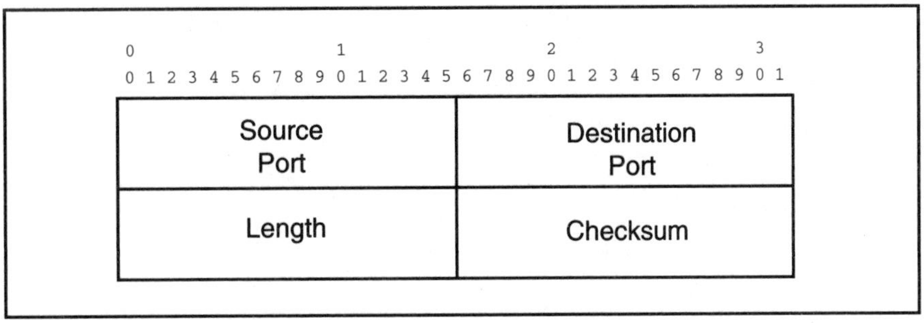

Figure 9.3
The UDP header.

0	1	2	3
0 1 2 3 4 5 6 7 8 9	0 1 2 3 4 5 6 7 8 9	0 1 2 3 4 5 6 7 8 9	0 1

Source Port	Destination Port
Length	Checksum

Figure 9.4
Pseudo header fields
included in the UDP
checksum.

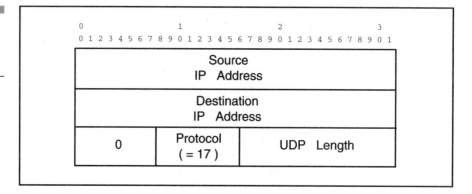

The UDP checksum is computed on the combination of a specially constructed *pseudo header* containing some IP information, the UDP header, and the message data.

The format of the pseudo header that is put together by the checksum function is shown in Figure 9.4. Note that the source address, destination address, and protocol field are taken from the IP header.

Calculation of the UDP checksum in a particular communication is optional. If unused, the field is 0. If a checksum has been computed and the value turns out to be 0, this is represented as a field of 1s.

Sample UDP Messages

The following display shows the IP and UDP portions of a query and its corresponding response. The displays were generated by a Network General *Sniffer* LAN monitor. The query contains a request for status information and was sent to a host by a network management station. The data portions of the query and response messages are not shown here.

The request was sent from source IP address 128.1.1.1 and UDP port 1227 to destination IP address 128.1.1.10 and UDP port 161. (Network management queries always are sent to UDP port 161.)

In both IP headers, the IP *Protocol* field was set to 17, meaning "UDP." A UDP checksum was not computed for the request, but a UDP checksum was included in the response.

```
IP:      --- IP Header ---
IP:
IP:      Version = 4, header length = 20 bytes
IP:      Type of service = 00
```

```
IP:                    000. .... = routine
IP:                    ...0 .... = normal delay
IP:                    .... 0... = normal throughput
IP:                    .... .0.. = normal reliability
IP:      Total length = 131 bytes
IP:      Identification = 21066
IP:      Flags = 0X
IP:      .0.. .... = may fragment
IP:      ..0. .... = last fragment
IP:      Fragment offset = 0 bytes
IP:      Time to live = 60 seconds/hops
IP:      Protocol = 17 (UDP)
IP:      Header checksum = 2A13 (correct)
IP:      Source address = [128.1.1.1]
IP:      Destination address = [128.1.1.10]
IP:      No options
IP:
UDP:     —- UDP Header —-
UDP:
UDP:     Source port = 1227 (SNMP)
UDP:     Destination port = 161 (SNMP)
UDP:     Length = 111
UDP:     No checksum
UDP:
```

The response was sent from IP address 128.1.1.10 and port 161 to IP address 128.1.1.1 and port number 1227, which was the source port for the request.

```
IP:      —- IP Header —-
IP:
IP:      Version = 4, header length = 20 bytes
IP:      Type of service = 00
IP:                    000. .... = routine
IP:                    ...0 .... = normal delay
IP:                    .... 0... = normal throughput
IP:                    .... .0.. = normal reliability
IP:      Total length = 160 bytes
IP:      Identification = 2015
IP:      Flags = 0X
IP:      .0.. .... = may fragment
IP:      ..0. .... = last fragment
IP:      Fragment offset = 0 bytes
IP:      Time to live = 64 seconds/hops
IP:      Protocol = 17 (UDP)
IP:      Header checksum = 7061 (correct)
IP:      Source address = [128.1.1.10]
IP:      Destination address = [128.1.1.1]
IP:      No options
IP:
UDP:     —- UDP Header —-
UDP:
UDP:     Source port = 161 (SNMP)
UDP:     Destination port = 1227
UDP:     Length = 140
UDP:     Checksum = 4D4F (correct)
UDP:
```

UDP Overflows

When an application acquires a UDP port, the networking software will reserve some memory buffers to hold a queue of User Datagrams arriving at that port. A UDP-based service has no way to predict or control how many datagrams will be sent to it at any time.

If the service is bombarded with more datagrams than it can handle, the overflow simply will be discarded. The fact that this has happened will show up in networking error statistics reports. (Sometimes the memory shortage is reported under a heading such as "UDP Socket Overflows.")

The brief UDP statistics report below was produced by the *netstat* command at Unix host *katie*. The "-s" flag requests statistics and "p udp" specifies UDP protocol statistics.

```
> netstat -sP udp
UDP
        udpInDatagrams      = 91237      udpInErrors  =   0
        udpOutDatagrams     = 101689
```

A similar UDP statistics report is available at Windows 95 and NT systems using the same command:[4]

```
C:\WINDOWS>netstat -sP udp

UDP Statistics

  Datagrams Received    = 8637
  No Ports              = 3466
  Receive Errors        = 0
  Datagrams Sent        = 1467
```

TCP Introduction

IP was kept simple so that the network layer could focus on performing one important function—routing data from its source to its destination. The job of turning an exchange of datagram traffic into a solid, reliable application-to-application data connection is carried out by TCP, which is implemented in the end hosts. Services such as the World Wide Web (WWW), terminal login, file transfer, and mail transfer run on top of TCP connections.

---

[4]The fact that the "P" in -sP is uppercase does not matter for Windows, but it does matter for Unix.

First we discuss the classic version of TCP, universally available today. Then we present some fairly recent enhancements that are being added to implementations.

Major TCP Services

We may view TCP as providing *data calls,* analogous to voice telephone calls. A caller identifies the destination. At the other end, a listening application is alerted that there is an incoming call and picks up the connection. The two ends exchange information for a while. When they are finished, both parties say "good-bye" and hang up.

IP makes a best-effort attempt to deliver datagrams, but some may be destroyed along the way, while others can arrive out of order. A datagram may wander around the network for a fairly long time and turn up unexpectedly. It is up to TCP to assure that data is delivered to an application *reliably, in sequence, and without confusion or error.*

An application in a fast, powerful host could swamp a slow recipient with data. TCP provides the *flow control* that enables the *receiver* to regulate the rate at which the sender may transmit data. TCP also has mechanisms that let it respond to network conditions, adjusting its own behavior to optimize performance.

TCP and the Client/Server Model

TCP operates very naturally in a client/server environment (see Figure 9.5). A server application listens for incoming connection requests. For example, World Wide Web, file transfer, and terminal access servers lis-

Figure 9.5
A client calling a
server.

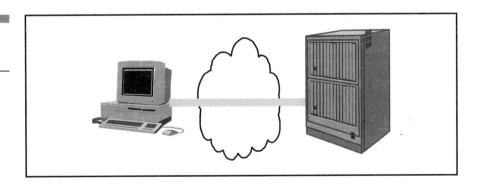

ten for incoming clients. A client application initiates TCP communication by invoking communications routines that establish a connection with a server.[5]

The "client" may actually be another server; for example, a mail server connects to a peer mail server in order to transfer mail between computers. The party that initiates the call plays the "client" role.

TCP Concepts

How does an application pass data to TCP? How does TCP pass data to IP? How do sending and receiving TCPs identify the application-to-application connection that a unit of data belongs to? These questions will be answered in the sections that follow.

Outgoing and Incoming Data Streams

A loose conceptual model for a TCP connection is that an application sends a stream of data to a peer application—and, at the same time, the application receives a stream of data from its peer,[6] as shown in Figure 9.6. Occasionally it is convenient to visualize TCP data transmission as an outgoing and incoming stream of data. However, we are going to present a far more detailed and accurate picture of what is going on.

---

[5]Chapter 21 describes the socket programming interface.

[6]This is just a model. In reality, applications pass pieces of data of varying size to TCP for transmission.

Figure 9.6
Applications
exchanging streams
of data.

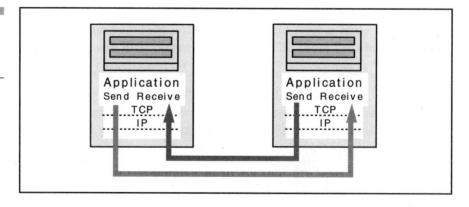

Application Port Numbers

A client must identify the service that it wants to reach. This is done by specifying the service host's IP address and its TCP port number. Just as for the User Datagram Protocol (UDP), TCP port numbers range from 0 to 65,535. Recall that ports in the range 0 to 1023 are well-known ports, used to access standard services.

Some sample well-known TCP ports and their applications are listed in Table 9.2. *Discard* at port 9 and *chargen* at port 19 are TCP versions of the utilities already described for UDP. Keep in mind that traffic sent to TCP port 9 will be totally separate from traffic sent to UDP port 9. The remaining ports listed belong to the most popular TCP applications.

SSL Ports

Recall that Secure Sockets Layer (SSL), described in Chapter 3, can be used with just about any TCP application. The way that it works is that

TABLE 9.2

Well-known TCP Ports and Their Applications

Service	Port/Protocol	Description
Discard	9/tcp	Discard all incoming data.
Chargen	19/tcp	Exchange streams of characters.
FTP-Data	20/tcp	File Transfer data transfer.
FTP	21/tcp	File Transfer control session.
telnet	23/tcp	Telnet remote login.
SMTP	25/tcp	Simple Mail Transfer Protocol.
http	80/tcp	World Wide Web.
POP3	110/tcp	POP mail download service.
IMAP	143/tcp	IMAP mail server.
ftps	990/tcp	FTP over SSL.
ftps-data	989/tcp	FTP data over SSL.
telnets	992/tcp	Telnet over SSL.
SMTPs	465/tcp	SMTP over SSL.
https	443/tcp	Web HTTP over SSL.
POP3s	995/tcp	POP3 over SSL.
IMAPs	993/tcp	IMAP over SSL.

a client that wishes to use SSL security connects to a special port that has been assigned to the SSL version of the application. For example, if a client connects to port 995, the POP3 mail server will expect the client to start an SSL security negotiation. The entire mail download will be encrypted, so no eavesdropper will be able to view the client's mail. Unfortunately, although every major Web server supports SSL, many *telnet,* mail, and file transfer servers do not, and connecting to the secure port may only get you an error message.

Client Ports

What about the ports used by clients? There are a few exceptional instances in which a client will operate out of a well-known port, but most of the time, a client that wants to open a connection just asks the operating system to assign it an unused, unreserved port number. When the connection ends, the client will relinquish the port back to the system, and it can be reused by another client. Since there are more than 64,000 TCP ports in the pool of unreserved numbers, there is no shortage of ports for clients.

Socket Addresses

Recall that the combination of the IP address and the port used for communication is called a *socket address*. The IP header contains the source and destination IP addresses. The TCP header contains the source and destination TCP port numbers. Thus, every TCP message carries the socket addresses for its source and destination.

A TCP connection is completely identified by the socket addresses at its two ends. Figure 9.7 shows a connection between a client with socket address (128.36.1.24, port = 3358) and a World Wide Web server with socket address (130.42.88.22, port = 80).

Usually a server is capable of handling many clients at the same time. The server's unique socket address is accessed simultaneously by all of its clients, as shown in Figure 9.8. Since a datagram containing a segment for a particular TCP connection identifies both of the IP addresses and both of the ports, it is easy for a server to keep track of multiple client connections. The next section provides a worm's-eye look of how this works.

Figure 9.7
Socket addresses.

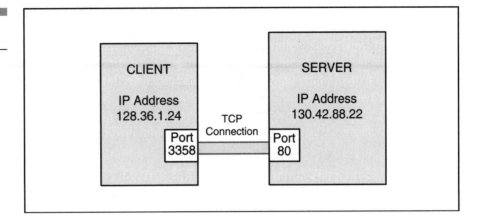

Parking Lot Full of Buffers

Let's examine what is happening at a World Wide Web server that is taking care of many clients. As shown in Figure 9.9, TCP operates a port 80 "parking lot" for the data arriving from and going to clients. When a new client connects to the server, TCP creates two memory buffers (parking spaces) for the client's traffic—one for incoming data and the

Figure 9.8
Multiple clients connecting to a server socket address.

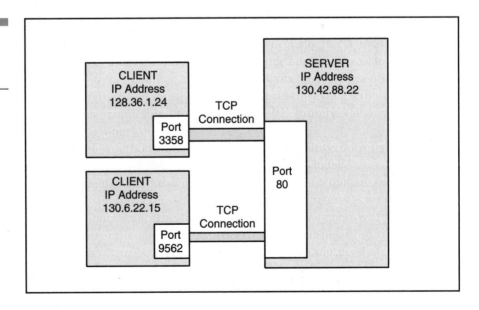

Figure 9.9
TCP send and receive
windows.

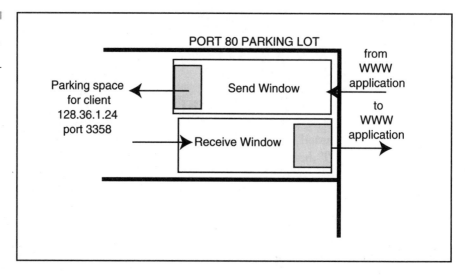

other for outgoing data. The buffers reserved for a particular client are
marked with the client's socket address.

■ When data arrives from the client, the data is stored briefly in
the client's TCP receive buffer parking space until the server
application program requests the incoming data.

■ When the Web server passes data to TCP to be sent to this
client, the data is stored briefly in the client's TCP send buffer
parking space until it can be packaged and sent across the network.

The *netstat -a* display below presents part of a report that shows active
TCP sessions at *katie*. The report gives us a snapshot of TCP parking
spaces.

```
Local Address      Remote Address        Swind Send-Q Rwind Recv-Q State
166.82.1.7.23      166.82.194.51.4148    32120 0      8760  0      ESTABLISHED
166.82.1.7.23      166.82.175.142.2084   32120 0      8759  1      ESTABLISHED
166.82.1.7.23      208.151.233.2.4154    8760  22     10136 0      ESTABLISHED
166.82.1.7.23      207.76.136.178.1910   7389  1137   8760  0      ESTABLISHED
166.82.1.7.48040   166.82.1.9.119        33580 0      8760  0      ESTABLISHED
166.82.1.7.23      207.205.149.242.1027  7683  0      8760  0      TIME_WAIT
```

■ The first column displays socket addresses at *katie*. These are
made up of *katie*'s IP address (166.82.1.7) and the port number
for each session. *Katie* is acting as a *telnet* server (port 23) for
five of the sessions. The fifth row shows that a client application

at *katie* is accessing a remote *news* server using client port 48,040.

■ The second column shows the remote partner's socket address. (119 is the news server port.)

■ The size of each send buffer is the sum of the values in the "Swind" and "Send-Q" columns. The send window (Swind) is the amount of unused send space and the send queue (Send-Q) is the amount of data currently waiting to be sent. For example, on the fourth line, 7389 bytes are free and 1137 bytes are queued to be sent. The total send buffer size is 8526.

■ The size of each receive buffer is the sum of the values in the "Rwind" and "Recv-Q" columns. Rwind is the amount of empty receive space and Recv-Q is the amount of data that has arrived but has not yet been delivered to its application. Note that there is 1 byte on the receive queue for the second session.

■ The last column shows the state of each session. The first five are active. The fifth session is ending.

Cloning the Server

Many servers clone a new "valet" to take care of each incoming client. The "valet" is a fresh copy of the service program. Thus, if there are 200 Web clients, there will be 200 service instances running.[7] See Chapter 21 for a sample program that shows how this could be done.

Segments

TCP must convert an application's outgoing stream of data into a form that can be delivered in datagrams. How is this done?

The application passes data to TCP and TCP places this data into a send buffer. TCP slices off a chunk of data and adds a header, forming a segment. Figure 9.10 shows how data in a TCP send buffer is packaged into a segment. TCP passes the segment to IP for delivery in a single

---

[7]This used to be implemented by starting a fresh "process" for each client. Starting a process takes a fair amount of time, and processes need a lot of computer resources. Today, often "threads" are used. Threads are preloaded and ready to go, and require modest computer resources.

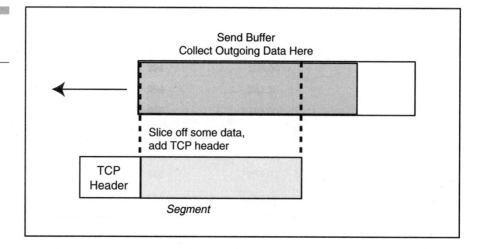

datagram. Packaging data in good-sized chunks makes efficient use of transmission facilities, so TCP likes to wait until a reasonable amount of data has collected before creating a segment.

Push

Sometimes big, efficient data chunks are not appropriate for a particular application. For example, suppose that an end user's client program has initiated an interactive session with a remote server, and the user has just typed a command and pressed the *return* key. The user's client program wants to let TCP know that this data should be sent to the remote host and delivered to the service application promptly. The *push* feature makes this happen

If you view a trace of an interactive session, you will see many segments that contain very little data. The headers for these segments will contain a flag that indicates that they have been pushed. On the other hand, push would not be used during a file transfer (except for the very last segment), allowing TCP to pack data into segments as efficiently as possible.

Urgent Data

Recall that application data transmission is modeled as an ordered stream of bytes flowing to its destination. But using the example of an interactive session again, suppose that a user has pressed an *attention* or *break* key. The remote application should be able to jump over intervening bytes and notice this as soon as possible.

There is an *Urgent Data* mechanism that flags specific information in a segment as *urgent*. TCP can signal its peer that a segment contains urgent data and can point to where that data is. The peer TCP can pass this information to the destination application.

TCP Reliability Mechanisms

The sections that follow describe the mechanisms that TCP uses to deliver data reliably, in order, and without loss or duplication.

Numbering and Acknowledgment

TCP employs numbering and acknowledgment (ACKs) to transfer data reliably. The TCP numbering scheme is unusual: *every byte* sent on a TCP connection is viewed as having a sequence number. A segment's TCP header contains the sequence number *of the first byte of data in the segment*.

The receiver is expected to ACK received data. If an ACK does not arrive within a timeout interval, the data is retransmitted. This strategy is called *positive acknowledgment with retransmission*. Figure 9.11 shows an oversimplified view of TCP timeout and retransmission.

Figure 9.11
TCP timeout and
retransmission.

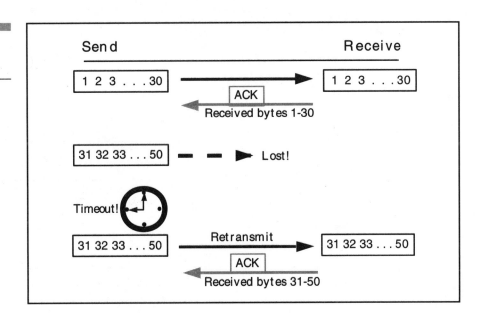

The receiving TCP keeps a close watch on incoming sequence numbers in order to arrange arriving data in order and to make sure that no data is missing. Sometimes the same data arrives twice. This is because the sender has timed out and retransmitted, even though the data was not lost. This happens because occasionally ACKs are late or lost. The sequence numbers pinpoint which data has been duplicated so that it can be discarded.

TCP Header Fields for Ports, Sequencing, and ACKs

As shown in Figure 9.12, the first few fields of the TCP header provide space for the source and destination ports, the sequence number of the first byte of enclosed data, and the acknowledgment value, which contains the sequence number of the *next* byte expected from the other end. In other words, if TCP has received all bytes up to 30 from its partner, it would write 31 into the acknowledgment field of the segment that it is about to transmit.

One small detail should be noted. Suppose that TCP has transmitted bytes 1 through 50 and currently has no more data that needs to be sent. If some data arrives from the partner, TCP needs to acknowledge it. To do this, TCP will send a header without any data attached. That header must contain a sequence number, even though no data is enclosed. The sequence number field would contain 51, the number of the next byte that TCP *intends* to send. When TCP sends data later on, the new TCP header also will have 51 in the sequence number field.

Figure 9.12
Initial fields of the TCP header.

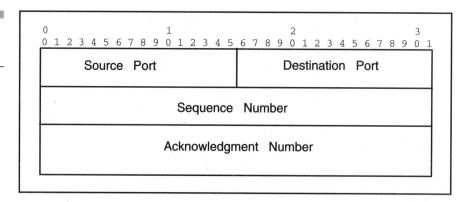

■ ■ Establishing a Connection

How does a TCP/IP connection get set up? TCP/IP is based on client/server communications. After a server starts up it tells TCP that it is ready to communicate. The server application then waits for incoming clients. Clients initiate sessions. A client asks TCP to open a session and identifies the server's IP address and port number. The client TCP and server TCP then exchange a set of messages that set up the session.

Three-Way Handshake

The setup procedure is called a *three-way handshake* because three messages (called SYN, SYN, and ACK) are used to start the connection. Three important pieces of information are exchanged during connection setup. Each side notifies its partner of:

1. How much buffer space it has available to receive data.

2. (Optionally) the maximum amount of data that any incoming segment may carry. This is called the Maximum Segment Size.

3. The initial sequence number it will use for numbering outgoing data.

Note that each side uses items 1 and 2 to *set limits on what the other side can do,* saying "don't send me data in chunks that are too big, and don't send me more than my buffer can hold."

> *The ability to control how the partner sends data is an important feature in the scalability of TCP/IP.*

The Maximum Segment Size and the size of the receive buffer space often have a huge impact on performance, as we soon shall see.

Rather than starting their byte numbering at 1, each side generates a fresh initial sequence number by reading a clock value and adding a number that is secret and/or random. The goal is to produce a start number that is increasing and is unpredictable. Later, we explain why this is a good idea.

Connection Scenario

Figure 9.13 shows a sample connection scenario. Very simple initial sequence numbers are shown, to promote easy readability. The steps are:

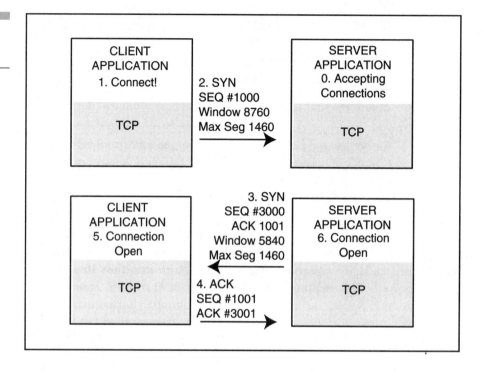

0. The server initializes and is ready to accept connections from clients. (This is called a *passive open.*)

1. The client asks TCP to open a connection to a server at a given IP address and port. (This is called an *active open.*)

2. The client TCP picks an initial sequence number (1000 in the example). The client TCP sends a *synchronize segment* (SYN) carrying this sequence number, the size of the receive window (8760 bytes), and the size of the biggest segment that the client can receive (1460 bytes).

3. When the SYN arrives, the server TCP picks *its* initial sequence number (3000). The server TCP sends a SYN segment containing its initial sequence number (3000), an ACK 1001 (meaning that the server expects that the first data byte sent by the client will be numbered 1001), the size of the server's receive window (5840 bytes), and the size of the biggest segment that the server can receive (1460 bytes).

4. When the client TCP receives the server's SYN/ACK message, the

client TCP sends back an ACK 3001, meaning that the client expects that the first data byte sent by the server will be numbered 3001.

5. The client TCP notifies its application that the connection is open.

6. When the server TCP receives the client TCP's ACK, the server TCP notifies its application that the connection is open.

The client and server have announced their rules for receiving data, have synchronized their sequence numbers, and are ready to exchange data.[8] Note that each partner has chosen a receive buffer size that is a multiple of the Maximum Segment Size. It makes good sense to choose a size that can hold some number of maximum-size chunks.

The announced Maximum Segment Size is based on the MTU of the interface card:

$$MSS = MTU - 40$$

The Maximum Segment Size is the largest amount of data that can be carried. Hence, 40 bytes for the combined TCP and IP headers is subtracted from the MTU to estimate that value. 1460 is a popular value, because it is the Ethernet MTU (1500) minus 40.

The Listen Queue

When a new client arrives at a server, the client must wait in a "Listen Queue" until the handshake is complete. A Listen Queue has a limited size. If you have ever accessed a Web server and seen a "Connecting" message flashing on your screen for a long time, it is likely that the Web server's Listen Queue is packed, and you are having trouble getting into it.

A rarely used application can get by with a small Listen Queue. (Five is a popular default length.) A busy Web server needs a huge Listen Queue. The size of an application's Listen Queue may be set in several ways:

■ The application designer provides a way for a server administrator to set the value to be used.

■ The application designer hard-codes a specific value.

---

[8]The TCP specification also allows for an unlikely scenario in which peer applications perform an active open to each other at the same time.

■ The application designer ignores the issue, so a system default has to be used.

A Listen Queue that is too small can kill performance. Clients may be unable to get through the doorway and into a server, even though the server is very lightly loaded.

Data Transfer

Data transfer begins after completion of the three-way handshake.[9] Figure 9.14 shows a straightforward exchange of data. In order to keep the numbering simple, 1000-byte messages are used. *Each segment's TCP header includes an ACK field that identifies the sequence number of the next byte expected from the partner.*

In the figure, the first segment sent by the client contains bytes 1001 to 2000. Its ACK field announces that 3001 is the sequence number of the next byte expected from the server.

The server responds with a segment that contains 1000 bytes of data (starting at 3001). The ACK field in the TCP header indicates that bytes 1001 to 2000 have been received in perfect condition, so the sequence number of the next byte expected from the client is 2001.

---

[9]The TCP standard actually allows inclusion of data in the handshake segments. For traditional TCP, data will not be delivered to an application until the handshake is complete. There is a TCP extension that allows immediate delivery.

Figure 9.14
Simple flow of data and ACKs.

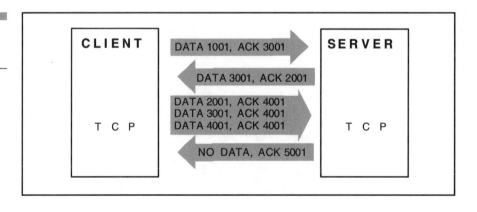

Figure 9.15
Data loss and retrans-
mission.

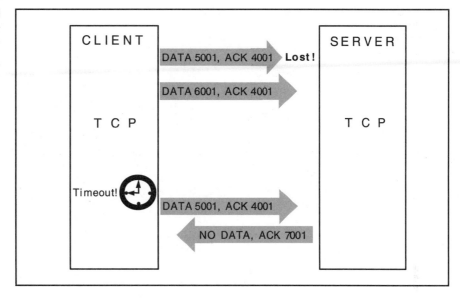

Next, the client sends segments starting at bytes 2001, 3001, and 4001 in quick succession. Note that the client did not have to wait for an ACK after each segment. Data can be sent to a partner as long as the partner has some unused buffer space available.

The server saves bandwidth by using a single ACK to indicate that all of the segments were received in perfect condition.

Figure 9.15 shows a transfer of two segments in which the first segment is lost. After a timeout period, the segment is retransmitted. Note that once the missing segment arrives, the receiver can send a single ACK that confirms that both segments have arrived safely.

Fast Recovery with Duplicate ACKs

Failure to receive an ACK may mean that the network is congested and a lot of data is being lost. If the network has gotten badly congested, it is a good idea to wait out the retransmission timeout and avoid overloading the network with retransmitted data.

On the other hand, maybe just a single segment met with a mishap,

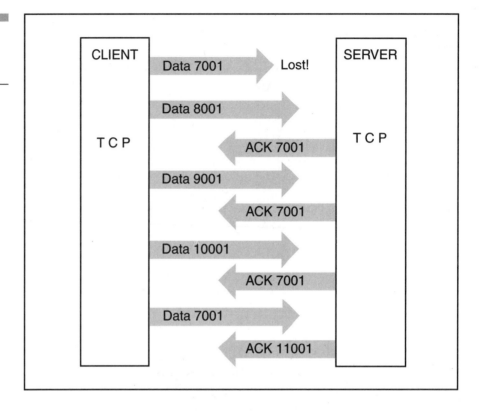

or perhaps that one segment simply is a little late. There may not really be any reason to bog down your session with a long wait.

How can you tell what really is going on? Actually, there is a simple mechanism that works well when there is a steady flow of data from a sender. In Figure 9.16, the client is sending a series of segments. Unfortunately, the segment with sequence number 7001 has been lost. When the other segments arrive, the server cannot acknowledge them—remember that an ACK says that all data up to the ACK number has been received.

The solution is that every time a new segment comes in, the server keeps ACKing the missing piece—essentially saying "I am waiting for the segment starting with 7001!" After receiving several of these duplicate ACKs (typically 3) the partner retransmits the missing segment. The server can now ACK all of the data that has been received and the data flow can proceed without interruption. (However, since loss of even one segment is a symptom that indicates that there may be some congestion, the sending TCP will temporarily throttle back its rate of transmission.)

Closing a Connection

The normal termination of a connection is carried out by means of a handshake similar to the connection opening. Either side can launch the close, which usually follows the pattern:

A: "I'm finished. I have no more data to send."

B: "OK."

B: "I'm finished too."

A: "OK."

The following pattern also is valid but is seldom seen:

A: "I'm finished. I have no more data to send."

B: "OK. But here is some data..."

B: "I'm finished too."

A: "OK."

In the example in Figure 9.17, the server initiates the close, as is often the case in real client/server interactions. For example, after a *telnet*

Figure 9.17
Closing a
connection.

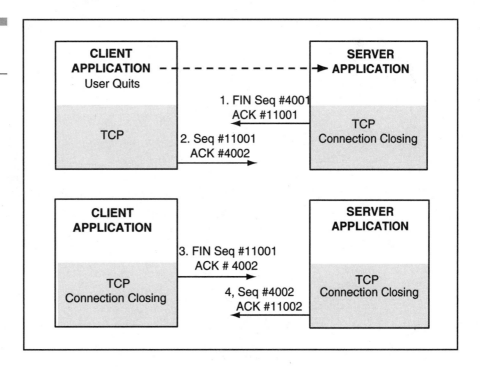

user types "logout," the *telnet* server invokes a call to close the connection.[10] The steps in Figure 9.17 are:

- The server application tells TCP to close the connection.
- The server TCP sends a FIN, informing the partner that it will send no more data.
- The client TCP sends an ACK of the FIN segment.
- The client TCP notifies its application that the server wishes to close.
- The client application tells its TCP to close.
- The client TCP sends a FIN message.
- The server TCP receives the client's FIN, and responds with an ACK.
- The server TCP notifies its application that the connection is closed.

Note that in step 2, the client ACKs 4002 instead of 4001. Advancing the number lets the server know that the client has seen the FIN segment. (Otherwise, the client might just be ACKing the previously received data.) Similarly, in step 4, the server ACKs 11002 instead of 11001. This is called "ACKing the FIN."

The closer is responsible for waiting around for a while to make sure that:

- The partner received the final ACK. (If not, the partner will send a duplicate FIN and the closer has to be around to respond with an ACK.)
- Incoming late duplicate data is disposed of gracefully.

To be sure that all stragglers have been cleaned up, the closer stays in an end-of the road TIME-WAIT state for quite a long time—twice the maximum time that a datagram could possibly survive in the network. By long convention, this maximum time is assumed to be 2 minutes, so the TIME-WAIT is set at 4 minutes. Actually, a TIME-WAIT state can last longer. If the partner sends a duplicate FIN, the TIME-WAIT period starts all over again.

---

[10]According to the rules, both sides could initiate a close simultaneously. This would be very unusual, but if it did happen, the close would be completed when each party had sent an ACK.

TIME-WAITs can be a big drag on a server. Some of the memory resources assigned to a terminating session are frozen and unusable until the TIME-WAIT is over. Busy application services that have been designed so that they initiate session closes may become paralyzed periodically because their memory fills up with frozen sessions in TIME-WAIT state. The first version of the World Wide Web protocol required Web servers to close every session, leaving them vulnerable to TIME-WAIT paralysis.

Abrupt Close

Either side can call for an abrupt close. Originally, this was conceived as a way of bailing out of a connection that was in trouble—either because of miscommunication between the client and server at the application level, or because of some network problem. An abrupt close is requested by sending one or more "resets" to the partner. A reset is signaled by means of a flag in the TCP header.

Today, resets also are used as a weapon that can torpedo a TIME-WAIT state. For example:

- A server announces "I am going to send you 10,500 bytes."
- The server transmits the data and receives ACKs for all of it.
- The server sends a reset and breaks off the session.

Or alternatively:

- A server sends a FIN, announcing "I have no more data to send."
- The client sends an ACK and then sends a reset, releasing the server.

Session Trace

The display below shows an NT monitor trace of a World Wide Web session from an NT client at port 1049 to an Internet Web server at port 80.

Note the opening SYN/SYN/ACK handshake. The NT monitor appears to report that the SYNs each contain 4 bytes of data. In fact, the monitor gets its "data" count by subtracting 20 from the total payload size. The opening SYN headers each contain a 4-byte Maximum Segment Size option field, so the headers actually are 24 bytes long. The monitor reports the 4 extra header bytes as data.

The client's request is sent in two pieces (283 bytes followed by 115 bytes). The client ACKs each segment received from the server. Note that no segments were lost. The server sends a FIN to indicate that the download is complete and the client ACKs and resets the connection to prevent the server from entering a TIME-WAIT state.

```
....S., len:  4, seq:1739551-1739554,       ack: 0, win: 8192, src: 1049 dst:   80
.A..S., len:  4, seq:7916495-7916498, ack:1739552, win: 8760, src:   80 dst: 1049
.A...., len:  0, seq:1739552-1739552, ack:7916496, win: 8760, src: 1049 dst:   80
.AP..., len:283, seq:1739552-1739834, ack:7916496, win: 8760, src: 1049 dst:   80
.A...., len:  0, seq:7916496-7916496, ack:1739835, win: 8760, src:   80 dst: 1049
.AP..., len:115, seq:7916496-7916610, ack:1739835, win: 8760, src:   80 dst: 1049
.A...., len:  0, seq:1739835-1739835, ack:7916611, win: 8645, src: 1049 dst:   80
.A...., len:1460,seq:7916611-7918070, ack:1739835, win: 8760, src:   80 dst: 1049
.A...., len:  0, seq:1739835-1739835, ack:7918071, win: 8760, src: 1049 dst:   80
.AP..., len:1460,seq:7918071-7919530, ack:1739835, win: 8760, src:   80 dst: 1049
.A.!.., len:  0, seq:1739835-1739835, ack:7919531, win: 8760, src: 1049 dst:   80
.A...., len:1460,seq:7919531-7920990, ack:1739835, win: 8760, src:   80 dst: 1049
.A...., len:  0, seq:1739835-1739835, ack:7920991, win: 8760, src: 1049 dst:   80
.AP..., len:1460,seq:7920991-7922450, ack:1739835, win: 8760, src:   80 dst: 1049
.A...., len:  0, seq:1739835-1739835, ack:7922451, win: 8760, src: 1049 dst:   80
.A...., len:1460,seq:7922451-7923910, ack:1739835, win: 8760, src:   80 dst: 1049
.A...., len:  0, seq:1739835-1739835, ack:7923911, win: 8760, src: 1049 dst:   80
.AP..., len:867, seq:7923911-7924777, ack:1739835, win: 8760, src:   80 dst: 1049
.A...., len:  0, seq:1739835-1739835, ack:7924778, win: 7893, src: 1049 dst:   80
.A...., len:1460,seq:7924778-7926237, ack:1739835, win: 8760, src:   80 dst: 1049
.A...., len:  0, seq:1739835-1739835, ack:7926238, win: 8760, src: 1049 dst:   80
.A...., len:1460,seq:7926238-7927697, ack:1739835, win: 8760, src:   80 dst: 1049
.A...., len:  0, seq:1739835-1739835, ack:7927698, win: 8760, src: 1049 dst:   80
.A...., len:1460,seq:7927698-7929157, ack:1739835, win: 8760, src:   80 dst: 1049
.A...., len:  0, seq:1739835-1739835, ack:7929158, win: 8760, src: 1049 dst:   80
.A...., len:1460,seq:7929158-7930617, ack:1739835, win: 8760, src:   80 dst: 1049
.A...., len:  0, seq:1739835-1739835, ack:7930618, win: 8760, src: 1049 dst:   80
.A...., len:1460,seq:7930618-7932077, ack:1739835, win: 8760, src:   80 dst: 1049
.A...., len:  0, seq:1739835-1739835, ack:7932078, win: 8760, src: 1049 dst:   80
.A...F, len:746, seq:7932078-7932823, ack:1739835, win: 8760, src:   80 dst: 1049
.A...., len:  0, seq:1739835-1739835, ack:7932825, win: 8014, src: 1049 dst:   80
...R.., len:  0, seq:1739835-1739835, ack:7932825, win:    0, src: 1049 dst:   80
```

Transmission Control Block and Sockets

There is a lot of information associated with a session: the source and destination IP addresses, port numbers, current sequence number, next ACK expected, Maximum Segment Sizes, current session state, and more. TCP stores the information for a session in a data structure called a *Transmission Control Block* (TCB) that is associated with the session. One could visualize the *Transmission Control Block* as a chart pinned to a fence next to the two parking lot spaces used for a session's incoming and outgoing data.

The Berkeley researchers who wrote the famous "Socket" programming interface use the word "socket" to identify an endpoint of a connection. A *socket* is a pair of parking lot spaces and its Transmission Control Block.

Flow Control

The TCP data receiver is in charge of its incoming flow of data. The receiver decides how much data it is willing to accept, and the sender must stay within this limit. The discussion that follows describes the way that this is done at a conceptual level. Vendors can implement these mechanisms in any way that is convenient for them.

Recall that during connection setup, each partner assigns receive buffer space to the connection and announces, "Here's how many bytes you can send me." This number usually is an integer multiple of the maximum segment size.

Incoming data flows into the receive buffer and stays there until it is absorbed by the application associated with that TCP port. Figure 9.18 shows a receive buffer that can hold 4K bytes.

Figure 9.18
The receive window within a receive buffer.

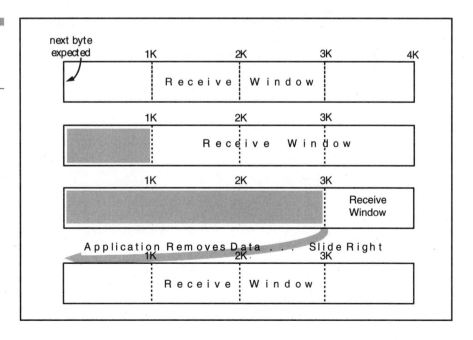

Buffer space is used up as data arrives. When the receiving application tion removes data, space is cleared for more incoming data.

Receive Window

The *receive window* consists of any space in the receive buffer that is not occupied by data. Data will remain in a receive buffer until the targeted application accepts it. Why wouldn't an application remove its data immediately?

A simple scenario should help to explain this. Suppose that a client is sending a file to a file transfer server that is running at a very busy multiuser computer. The file transfer server program will read data from the receive buffer and write it out to disk. When the server performs its disk Input/Output (I/O), the program will have to wait for the I/O to complete. In the meantime, other programs will be scheduled and run by the operating system. More data can arrive while the file transfer server process is waiting to run again.

The receive window extends from the last acknowledged byte to the end of the buffer. In Figure 9.18, initially the whole buffer is available, and so there is a 4K-byte receive window. 1K bytes arrive, and the receive window shrinks to 3K.[11] Two more segments containing 1K bytes each arrive, causing the receive window to shrink to 1K bytes.

Finally, the application absorbs the 3K bytes of data in the buffer, making space available for more incoming data. This can be visualized as *sliding* the window to the right. Now all 4K buffer bytes are free.

Every ACK sent by the receiver contains an update on the current status of its receive window. The flow of data from the sender is regulated according to these window updates.

Most of the time, the receive buffer size set at start-up is maintained throughout the connection. However, the TCP standard does not restrict the way that an implementation manages its buffers. The receive buffer size can grow or shrink, as long as the receiver never "takes back" an allowance that it has granted the sender.

What happens when segments arrive which are in the window but are out of order? Virtually all implementations hold onto any data falling within the window and ACK the entire block of contiguous data

---

[11]For simplicity, all of the segments in this example contain 1K bytes of data. For real sessions, actual amounts will, of course, vary, depending on the needs of the application.

when the missing bytes arrive. This is fortunate, since throwing away good data would lead to poor performance.

Send Window

The data sender needs to keep track of:

- How much data it has sent
- How much has been acknowledged
- The current size of the partner's receive window.

Figure 9.19 shows an example of how these change during data transmission.

1. The sender starts out with a 4K-byte send window. The size of the send window is the amount of fresh data that the partner currently is willing to receive.

2. The sender transmits 1K bytes. A copy of these bytes (shown in the shaded area) must be kept until the bytes have been acknowledged, since they may need to be retransmitted. The total *send space* is still 4K, but the send window has shrunk to 3K.

Figure 9.19
Send window.

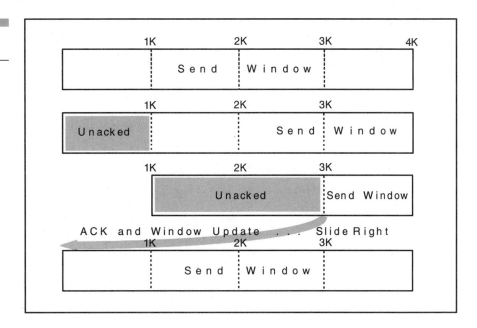

3. An ACK arrives for the first 1K bytes, but it does not change the right edge of the send window. Another 2K bytes are sent. The result is shown in the third part of Figure 9.19. The 2K bytes in the shaded area have to be kept. The send space is 3K bytes and the send window now is 1K bytes.

4. An ACK arrives that reports that all of the transmitted bytes have been received. The receiving application has read all of the data out of its receive buffer, so the ACK message also updates the window size to 4K.

There are some interesting features of the way that a sender operates:

- The sender does not have to wait for an ACK for each segment of data that is transmitted before sending more. The only limitation on transmission is the size of the receive partner's window. (For example, it is legal for the sender to transmit 4K 1-byte segments!)

- Suppose that a sender has to retransmit data that was sent in several short (e.g., 80-byte) segments? The data can be repackaged in the most efficient way for retransmission. As many chunks of data as possible would be packed into a segment.

TCP Header

Figure 9.20 displays the format of a TCP segment—that is, a TCP header and data. A sample NT trace of a TCP header taken from a data transfer session is shown here:

```
TCP: Source Port = FTP [default data] (20)
TCP: Destination Port = 0x04FB (1275)
TCP: Sequence Number = 602685556 (0x23EC4074)
TCP: Acknowledgement Number = 16889768 (0x101B7A8)
TCP: Data Offset = 20 (0x14)
TCP: Reserved = 0 (0x0000)
TCP: Flags = 0x18 : .AP...
TCP: ..0..... = No urgent data
TCP: ...1.... = Acknowledgement field significant
TCP: ....1... = Push function
TCP: .....0.. = No Reset
TCP: ......0. = No Synchronize
TCP: .......0 = No Fin
TCP: Window = 8760 (0x2238)
TCP: Checksum = 0xA63A
TCP: Urgent Pointer = 0 (0x0)
TCP: Data: Number of data bytes remaining = 1460 (0x05B4)
```

Figure 9.20
TCP segment.

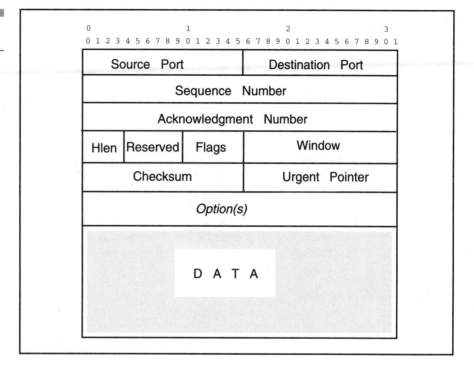

The TCP header starts with its source and destination port identifiers (20 and 1275). The *Sequence Number* field identifies the position in the outgoing data stream held by the data in this segment. The *ACK* field identifies the position (16889768) in the incoming data stream for the next byte. The receive window field indicates that there is room for 8760 more bytes (starting from 16889768).

The *Data Offset* field contains the TCP header length.[12] There are six flags:

URG	1 if urgent data is included
ACK	1 for all but the initial SYN segment
PSH	1 indicates that data should be delivered promptly
RST	1 indicates an error; also used to abort a session
SYN	Set to 1 during connection setup
FIN	Set to 1 during graceful close

---

[12]The number in the field actually is 5, because the size is measured in multiples of 4 bytes.

Even though this segment is chock full of data, the application has pushed it.

Maximum Segment Size Option

The *maximum segment size* (MSS) option is used to announce the size of the biggest chunk of data that can be received by the system. The name is quite misleading. Normally, a *segment* is defined as a TCP header plus data. In spite of its title, a system's *maximum segment size* is defined as:

The size of the biggest datagram that can be received − 40

In other words, the MSS reports the receiver's biggest *data payload* size when the TCP and IP headers each are 20 bytes long. If there are any header options, their lengths must be subtracted. Thus, to find out how much data really can be stuffed into a segment, a sending TCP needs to calculate:

Announced MSS + 40 − (size of TCP and IP headers)

It is a very good idea for partners to exchange their MSS values in the initial "SYN" messages that start up a TCP connection. Remember that if a system does not announce its maximum segment size, a default (and inefficient) MSS of 536 bytes will be assumed.

The maximum segment size is encoded with a 2-byte introducer followed by a 2-byte value, so the biggest size possible is $2^{16} - 1$, or 65,535 bytes.

The MSS imposes a strict top limit on the segment size that TCP can send—the recipient cannot handle anything bigger. But the sending TCP might possibly have to send *smaller* segments because of the Path MTU size for the connection.

Use of Header Fields in the Connection Request

The first segment sent to start a connection has the SYN flag set to 1 and the ACK flag set to 0. The initial SYN is the *only* segment that will have an ACK flag of 0. Note that firewalls use this fact to screen incoming TCP session requests.

The *Sequence Number* field contains the *initial sequence number*. The *Window* field contains the initial *receive window* size. The only option currently defined for TCP is the maximum segment size that this TCP is willing to receive. The maximum segment size usually is included in the connection request (in the *Options* field). The length of a TCP SYN header that contains the MSS option is 24 bytes. The following display shows the opening SYN for a data transfer session.

```
TCP: Source Port = FTP [default data]
TCP: Destination Port = 0x04FB
TCP: Sequence Number = 602685555 (0x23EC4073)
TCP: Acknowledgement Number = 0 (0x0)
TCP: Data Offset = 24 (0x18)
TCP: Reserved = 0 (0x0000)
TCP: Flags = 0x02 : ....S.
TCP: ..0..... = No urgent data
TCP: ...0.... = Acknowledgement field not significant
TCP: ....0... = No Push function
TCP: .....0.. = No Reset
TCP: ......1. = Synchronize sequence numbers
TCP: .......0 = No Fin
TCP: Window = 8760 (0x2238)
TCP: Checksum = 0x0763
TCP: Urgent Pointer = 0 (0x0)
TCP: Options
TCP: Option Kind (Maximum Segment Size) = 2 (0x2)
TCP: Option Length = 4 (0x4)
TCP: Option Value = 1460 (0x5B4)
```

Use of Header Fields in the Connection Response

In a response accepting the connection, both the SYN and ACK flags are 1. The responder's initial sequence number is in the *Sequence Number* field, and the receive window size is in the *Window* field. We have seen that this is at most 65,535.

The maximum segment size that the responder is willing to receive usually is included in the connection response (in the *Options* field). This can be different from the initiator's size. A connection request can be rejected by sending a response whose reset flag, RST, is equal to 1.

The display below shows a connection response:

```
TCP: Source Port = 0x04FB
TCP: Destination Port = FTP [default data]
TCP: Sequence Number = 16889767 (0x101B7A7)
TCP: Acknowledgement Number = 602685556 (0x23EC4074)
TCP: Data Offset = 24 (0x18)
TCP: Reserved = 0 (0x0000)
TCP: Flags = 0x12 : .A..S.
TCP: ..0..... = No urgent data
TCP: ...1.... = Acknowledgement field significant
```

```
TCP:  ....0... = No Push function
TCP:  .....0.. = No Reset
TCP:  ......1. = Synchronize sequence numbers
TCP:  .......0 = No Fin
TCP:  Window = 8760 (0x2238)
TCP:  Checksum = 0x4EA9
TCP:  Urgent Pointer = 0 (0x0)
TCP:  Options
TCP:  Option Kind (Maximum Segment Size) = 2 (0x2)
TCP:  Option Length = 4 (0x4)
TCP:  Option Value = 1460 (0x5B4)
```

Choosing the Initial Sequence Number

During connection start-up, each end of the connection is supposed to choose an initial sequence number in a rather complicated way. First of all:

- Set up a 32-bit clock that ticks roughly every 4 microseconds.
- Compute the message digest of the (local socket address, remote socket address).

The basic recommended method is:

Add the message digest to the current clock time.

Why bother to do this? The worry is that an old stale segment from a closed (or possibly aborted) session may wander in and be confused with segments from a new, current session. The goal is to choose a start number that minimizes this likelihood.

Another concern is that systems that use predictable sequence numbers can be open to a cracker attack. Some users are foolish enough to accept connections from a "trusted" system without requiring a password. They base their trust on the IP address of the source. A cracker can give its system any IP address. If the cracker uses the trusted IP address, the only glitch is that datagrams sent back to the trusted address will never make it back to the cracker. They will indeed go to the trusted system.[13] But if the cracker can guess the partner's start sequence number, he doesn't care. He can get the target system to accept a string of commands that can do his dirty work:

SYN → To target

Target's SYN, ACK goes to the real trusted system

---

[13]The cracker "jams" that system by flooding it with data.

ACK → To target: "I heard your sequence number."

DATA → To target: "Username: John-Q-Owner. Erase all of the files on the hard disk."

An even stronger start sequence number formula than the one shown previously is recommended if you want an extra secure barrier against cracker attacks. The message digest can be computed on the source and destination socket addresses, a secret password, and some random data.

General Header Field Usage

Let's review the elements of the TCP header. To prepare a TCP header for transmission, the sequence number of the first byte of enclosed data is entered into the *Sequence Number* field.

The number of the next byte expected from the partner is filled into the *Acknowledgment Number* field, and the ACK bit is set to 1. The *Window* field contains the current size of the receive window, that is: *The number of bytes, starting from the acknowledgment number, that can be received.* Note that this provides extremely precise flow control. The partner is told the exact status of the receive window throughout the session.

If the application has signaled a push to TCP, the PUSH flag is set to 1. The receiving TCP is supposed to react to the PUSH flag by delivering the data to its application promptly when the application is willing to receive it.

An URGENT flag set to 1 indicates that urgent data is pending, and the Urgent Pointer points to the last byte of urgent data. Recall that a typical use of urgent data is to send a break or interrupt signal from a terminal. Urgent data is sometimes referred to as *out-of-band* data. This term is misleading. Urgent data is sent within the TCP data stream. It is up to the receiving TCP implementation to provide some mechanism that warns an application that urgent data is waiting and lets an application examine urgent data before it has read all of the bytes that lead up to this data.

The RESET flag is set to 1 to abort a connection. It also can be set in response to a segment that does not make sense for any current connection that TCP is managing.

The FIN flag is set to 1 in the messages that are used to close a connection.

Figure 9.21
Pseudo header fields
included in the TCP
checksum.

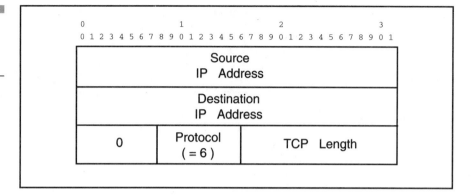

Checksum

The IP checksum was applied only to the IP header. The checksum in the TCP header is applied to the entire TCP segment,[14] as well as to a pseudo header made up of information extracted from the IP header. The pseudo header shown in Figure 9.21 is similar to that used for the UDP checksum. The TCP length used in the calculation is computed by adding the length of the TCP header to the length of the data. The TCP checksum is *required,* not optional as in UDP. The checksum for an incoming segment is computed and compared to the content of the checksum field in the TCP header. If the values do not match, the segment is discarded.

Detecting a Lost Connection

A partner's system may crash, or the route to the partner may be totally disrupted by loss of a gateway or link. What happens then?

If TCP is trying to send some data to the partner, the problem will be detected pretty quickly. The retransmission timer will cause data to be resent repeatedly. After a preconfigured threshold, TCP will send a reset and the connection will be declared dead. (The default maximum number of retransmissions varies from system to system.)

---

[14] The checksum field in the TCP header is set to 0 during the checksum computation.

Window Probes

An active sender and a sluggish receiver can lead to a 0-byte receive window. This also is called a *closed window*. When space opens up, an ACK will be sent updating the window size. But what if the ACK is lost? Both sides could wait forever.

To avoid this, the sender sets a *persist timer*[15] when the receive window closes. When the timer expires, a segment called a *window probe* is sent to the partner. (Some implementations include data in the probe.) The probe causes the partner to send back an ACK that reports the current window status.

If the window is still 0, the persist timer is doubled. This repeats until the timer value reaches a maximum of 60 seconds. TCP will continue to send probes every 60 seconds forever—or until the window opens or a user interrupts the process or a timeout imposed by the application expires.

Keep-Alives

What happens to a connection when neither end has any data to send for a long time? TCP was designed to keep an idle session going unless it was told otherwise. Smart application developers set their own timers in the application program and have the program kill off worthless sessions. For example, most of us have been automatically disconnected from a *telnet* login or a file transfer server because we have not made any requests for a few minutes.

If the application developer does not define any timeout, a connection could be maintained in an idle state indefinitely. During the period that it is idle, the network could crash or wires could be cut and sewn together again. As long as the network is up when the partners start to exchange data again, they will not lose their session. This design suited the Department of Defense (DOD) sponsors very well.

But any connection—even an idle one—uses up a block of RAM memory in a computer. Some administrators would like to reclaim resources that are unused. Hence, many TCP implementations allow the administrator to turn on *keep-alive* messages that test idle connections by default.

---

[15]Its value is set equal to the retransmission timeout.

In this case, TCP sends keep-alives to an idle partner periodically, to check that it is still there. A keep-alive triggers an ACK in response. The suggested minimum default value of the timeout is 2 hours! If no response is received, TCP will retransmit several times after a short (e.g., 75-second) timeout period. If the other end does not respond, TCP finally transmits a reset and officially kills the connection.

Performance Issues

How well can TCP perform? There are many factors that affect performance. Most basic are resources such as memory and bandwidth. Figure 9.22 summarizes the elements that have an impact on performance.

The bandwidth and delay of the underlying network impose limits on throughput. Poor transmission quality causes lots of discarded datagrams. Discards provoke retransmissions, with the result that effective bandwidth is cut.

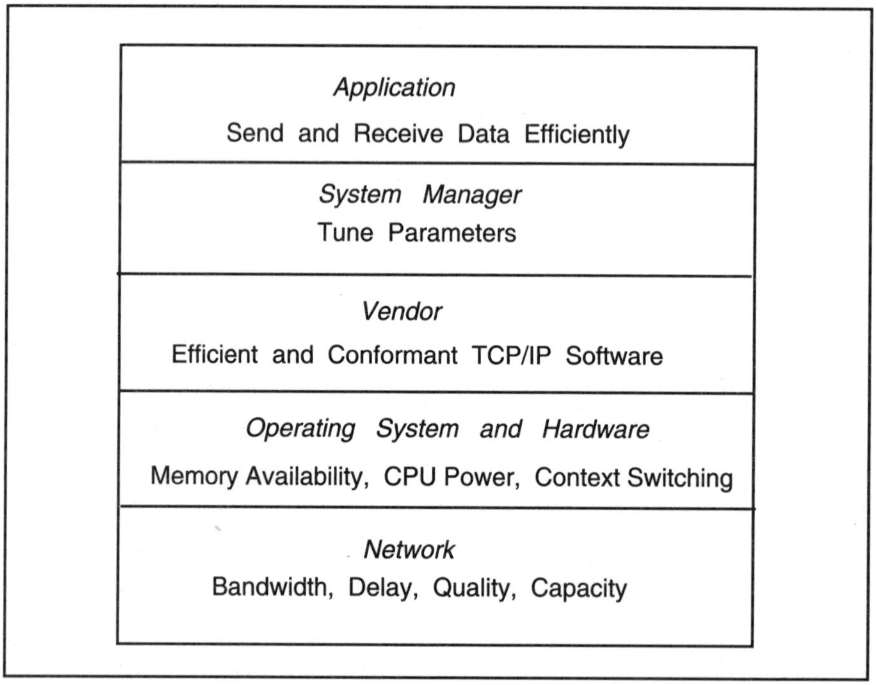

Figure 9.22
TCP performance factors.

| *Application* |
| Send and Receive Data Efficiently |

| *System Manager* |
| Tune Parameters |

| *Vendor* |
| Efficient and Conformant TCP/IP Software |

| *Operating System and Hardware* |
| Memory Availability, CPU Power, Context Switching |

| *Network* |
| Bandwidth, Delay, Quality, Capacity |

A receiver that provides lots of input buffer space allows a sender to keep transmitting without pause. This is especially important for networks with large delays, where a long time elapses between sending data and receiving an ACK and window update. To support a steady flow of data from a source, the destination needs a receive window whose size is at least (bandwidth×delay).

For example, if you can send data at 10,000 bytes per second, and it takes 2 seconds for an ACK to arrive, the receiver must provide a receive buffer of at least 20,000 bytes in order to maintain a steady flow of data. A receive buffer that could hold only 10,000 bytes would cut throughput in half.

Another factor that has an impact on performance is a host's ability to react to high-priority events and rapidly *switch context*—that is, stop doing one thing and take care of another. A host may be supporting many local interactive users, background batch processes, and dozens of communications connections. Switching context to take care of communications housekeeping is a hidden overhead. An implementation that does a good job of integrating TCP/IP with the operating system kernel can cut back significantly on context switching overhead.

Capable CPU resources are needed to quickly carry out the steps required to process the TCP header. Choosing a good network interface card that offloads some of the processing work also can make a big difference.

Finally, vendors should make it easy to set configuration parameters so that network managers can tune TCP to local conditions. For example, the ability to match buffer sizes to bandwidth and delay can improve throughput substantially. Unfortunately, there are some implementations that hard code fixed configuration choices into the networking software.

Now suppose that your environment is perfect—lots of resources and the host switches contexts faster than Billy the Kid ever drew his gun. Will you get wonderful performance?

Maybe. The quality of the TCP software is important. Over the many years of TCP experience, many performance problems have been diagnosed and solved. Software that conforms to RFC 1122, which defines requirements for the communications layers in Internet hosts, encompasses these solutions.

Silly Window Syndrome (SWS) avoidance and the algorithms of Jacobson, Karn, and Partridge are especially important. These important algorithms are discussed in the sections that follow.

And finally, software developers can make a big difference by writing programs that do not perform unnecessarily small sends and receives and have built-in timeouts that free network resources when no useful work is being accomplished.

Performance Algorithms

Now we come to the most complex part of TCP. Many mechanisms that improve performance or solve bottleneck problems have been discovered. We introduce several of them in this chapter.

- The delayed ACK cuts down overhead by reducing the number of stand-alone acknowledgment messages.
- The slow start prevents a new session from piling large amounts of traffic onto a network that might already be congested.
- Curing the Silly Window Syndrome prevents poorly designed applications from loading the network with overhead messages.
- Computing retransmission timeouts based on session's real round-trip times reduces unnecessary retransmissions but does not delay too long when a retransmission really is needed.
- Throttling back TCP transmissions when the network is congested allows routers to get back to normal and provides a fair share of the network resources to all of its sessions.

Delayed ACK

Since ACKs are based on sequence numbers, and, as we already have seen, it is easy for TCP to acknowledge several segments at once. The idea behind the delayed ACK is that a receiver should not acknowledge a segment immediately, but instead should wait a little while. If the receiver delays a little before sending an ACK, there is a chance that:

- The receiver can acknowledge multiple segments with a single ACK message.
- The receiver's application may get some data to send within the timeout period, in which case the ACK will be contained in the outgoing header and a separate message won't be needed.

Cutting down on the number of ACKs that are sent saves bandwidth that can be used for other traffic.

To avoid delaying a stream of full-sized segments (e.g., while performing a file transfer), an ACK usually is sent for every second full segment. However, some systems will acknowledge more than two segments at a time when there is a fast, steady flow of data.

Many implementations use a 200-millisecond timeout. But note that delaying the ACK will not slow down transmission. If tiny segments are arriving, there will be plenty of buffer space, and the transmitter can keep sending. If full segments are arriving, every second one usually immediately triggers an ACK.

Slow Start

What would happen if you turned on every appliance in your house at the same time? This is not very different from what happens every morning when everyone arrives at the office and races for their electronic mail. However, the *slow start* prevents the network from blowing its fuse.

A connection that immediately starts to transfer bulk data across a congested network could cause a severe problem. The idea behind slow start is that a new connection starts out carefully, increasing its rate of transfer gradually according to network conditions. Here is how it is done.

- At connection setup, the partner announces its receive window. The TCP sender calculates a second *congestion window* size for the purpose of throttling transmissions to match network conditions. The sender is limited by the congestion window rather than the (larger) receive window.

- The congestion window starts off at one segment. For each ACK that is received, the congestion window is increased by one segment—as long as it still is smaller than the receive window.

- If the network is not overloaded, the congestion window soon will reach the size of the receive window. During normal steady state transmission, the size of the congestion window is identical to the size of the receive window.

Note that slow start is not really very slow. After one ACK, the congestion window equals two segments. If separate ACKs for two segments arrive successfully, the window will increase to four segments. If these are ACKed successfully, the window could increase to eight segments. In other words, the window might grow to its natural size exponentially.

Suppose a timeout occurs instead of an ACK. We'll discuss what TCP does after a timeout a little later.

Silly Window Syndrome

In the earliest implementations of TCP/IP, a phenomenon called *Silly Window Syndrome* (SWS) was observed to happen fairly frequently. To understand SWS, let's look at a worst-case (and, one hopes, unlikely) scenario:

1. A sending application is transmitting data quickly.
2. The receiving application is reading 1 byte of data at a time out of the receive buffer—slowly.
3. The receive buffer fills up.
4. The receive application reads 1 byte, and TCP sends an ACK saying "I have room for 1 byte of data."
5. The sending TCP packages 1 byte and transmits it.
6. The receive TCP sends an ACK saying "Thanks. I got it, and I have no more room."
7. The receive application reads 1 byte, sends an ACK, and the process repeats.

The slow receive application already has plenty of data waiting for it, and hustling those bytes into the right edge of the window performs no useful function—but it does add a lot of unnecessary traffic to the network.

The situation does not have to be this extreme to cause trouble. A fast sender, a slow receive application that reads chunks of data that are small relative to the maximum segment size, and an almost full receive buffer can trigger it. Figure 9.23 shows a buffer whose condition could trigger Silly Window Syndrome.

Figure 9.23
Buffer with a very small receive window.

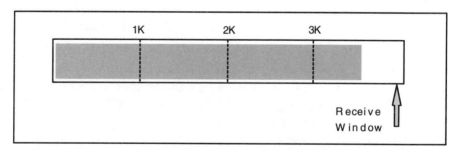

TCP's solution is simple. Once the receive window has shrunk to less than a given target size, TCP starts to lie. TCP must not tell the sending partner about insignificant amounts of window space that open up when the receive application performs small reads. Instead, TCP must keep the extra resources a secret until the target amount of buffer space is available. The recommended amount is one segment—except for the case where the whole receive buffer holds only one segment, in which case one-half of the buffer will do. The target size at which TCP tells the truth is:

Minimum (½ Receive-Buffer-Size, Maximum Segment Size)

TCP starts to lie when the window size is less than this amount and tells the truth when the window size is at least this amount. Notice that no harm is being done by holding back the sender since the receive application has not absorbed most of the data that already is waiting for it.

Of course, the best solution is to design applications that behave smarter than the ones that we have described. When an application reads in data from the TCP receive buffer, it should remove all of the data that is queued there, rather than asking for just a few bytes. The data will then be moved into memory owned by the application, and TCP's buffer will be ready to receive more segments.

Nagle Algorithm

So far we have blamed the receiver for encouraging TCP to send small, inefficient segments. Sometimes a sending application is to blame. For example, a *telnet* client connected to a Unix host will send lots of tiny segments. This can't be totally cured, but the Nagle algorithm introduces a very simple idea that can reduce the number of tiny datagrams presented to a network.

The Nagle method holds back transmission (even of pushed data) if the sender is waiting for an ACK of some previously transferred data. For example, this makes good sense for a typical *telnet* session to a Unix host, because characters cannot appear on the user's screen until they are echoed back from the host. Often the ACK segment will contain the echoed characters. (See Chapter 13 for more details on how *telnet* works.) When the ACK (and characters) arrive, another batch of characters is sent. This sometimes results in uneven screen response, but it can reduce network overhead.

The Nagle algorithm states that accumulated data is sent if the previous data is ACKed, if a full-sized segment can be sent, or if a preset timeout expires. The algorithm can be disabled for real-time applications that must send data as soon as possible.

Retransmission Timeout

After sending a segment, TCP sets a timer and listens for an ACK. If the ACK does not arrive within the timeout period, TCP retransmits the segment. But how long should the timeout be?

If the retransmission timeout is too short, the sender will clutter the network with unnecessary segments and burden the receiver with extraneous duplicates. But timeouts that are too long prevent brisk recovery when a segment really has been destroyed. Long waits decrease throughput.

How do you choose an ideal timeout? A value that works well on a high-speed Local Area Network would be disastrous for a multi-hop long-distance connection, so it is clear that "one size fits all" will not work here. Moreover, even during a single connection, network conditions may change and delays may increase or decrease.

Algorithms of Jacobson, Karn, and Partridge[16] enable TCP to adapt to changing conditions and are now mandated for TCP implementations. These algorithms are sketched below.

Common sense tells us that the best basis for estimating a good retransmission timeout for a particular connection is to keep a watch on the connection, recording the *round-trip times* that elapse between the transmission of data and the arrival of acknowledgment of that data.

Elementary statistics can suggest a good idea of what to do next (see Figure 9.24.) Obviously, it makes sense to compute the average round-trip time. But the average would be a bad choice for a timeout, because half of the round-trip values can be expected to be bigger than the average. However, if we add on a couple of deviations, we get an estimate that allows for normal variability without causing retransmission waits that are too long.

It is not necessary to perform the heavy-duty calculation involved in finding the formal statistical standard deviation. A simple rough estimate will do—use the absolute value of the difference between the latest value and the average:

[16]See "Congestion Avoidance and Control," Jacobson, and "Improving Round-Trip Time Estimates in Reliable Transport Protocols," Karn and Partridge.

Figure 9.24
Looking at a distribu-
tion of round-trip
times.

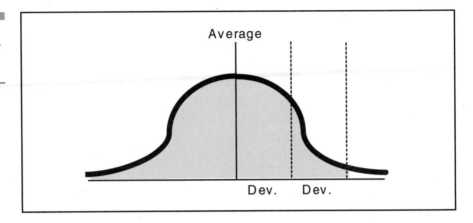

$$\text{Latest deviation} = |\text{ latest round trip} - \text{average round trip }|$$

Another factor needs to be considered in order to calculate a good retransmission timeout. That is the fact that round-trip times change depending on network conditions. What has happened in the last minute is much more important than what happened an hour ago.

For example, suppose that we kept a running average of round-trip times for a very long session. We'll assume that at the start the network was lightly loaded and there were 1000 small values, but then traffic built up and there was a significant increase in delays.

For example, if 1000 values with average 170 were followed by 50 values with average 282, the current average would be

$$170(1000/1050) + 282(50/1050) = 175$$

A more responsive measure, the *Smoothed Round-Trip Time* (SRTT), using weighting factors so that recent values dominate the result. The weighting formula most used today is:

$$\text{New SRTT} = \frac{7}{8}(\text{old SRTT}) + \frac{1}{8}(\text{latest Round-Trip Time})$$

Table 9.3 shows how quickly the SRTT formula adjusts if the current SRTT is 230, and a change in network conditions causes a sequence of longer Round-Trip Times.[17] The value calculated in column 3 is fed back into the next line of column 1 as the old SRTT.

---

[17]We are assuming that no timeouts occur.

TABLE 9.3

Computing the
Smoothed Round-
Trip Time

Old SRTT	Latest RTT	(7/8)(Old SRTT) + (1/8)(RTT)
230.00	294	238.00
238.00	264	241.25
241.25	340	253.59
253.59	246	252.64
252.64	201	246.19
246.19	340	257.92
257.92	272	259.68
259.68	311	266.10
266.10	282	268.09
268.09	246	265.33
265.33	304	270.16
270.16	308	274.89
274.89	230	269.28
269.28	328	276.62
276.62	266	275.29
275.29	257	273.00
273.00	305	277.00

Now what value should be chosen for the retransmission timeout? A look at the sample Round-Trip Times shows that there are fairly large deviations between individual times and the current average. It makes sense to allow a good-sized margin for deviations. If we can come up with a reasonable estimate for a smoothed deviation (SDEV), the formula below would provide a good retransmission timeout[18] value:

$$T = \text{RETRANSMISSION TIMEOUT} = \text{SRTT} + 2\,(\text{SDEV})$$

This is the formula referenced in RFC 1122. However, some implementations use:

$$T = \text{SRTT} + 4\,(\text{SDEV})$$

---

[18]Standards documents refer to this as the RTO (for Retransmission TimeOut).

To compute SDEV, first calculate the absolute value of the current deviation:

$$DEV = |\text{ latest Round-Trip Time} - \text{old SRTT }|$$

Next, use a smoothing formula to fold in this latest value[19]:

$$\text{New SDEV} = \frac{3}{4}\,(\text{old SDEV}) + \frac{1}{4}\,\text{DEV}$$

One question remains—how do we get started? Set:

$$\text{Initial Timeout} = 3 \text{ seconds}$$
$$\text{Initial SRTT} = 0$$
$$\text{Initial SDEV} = 1.5 \text{ seconds}$$

A separate retransmission timeout must be separately calculated for each TCP session. Van Jacobson has defined a fast algorithm that computes the retransmission timeout very efficiently.

Sample Retransmission Statistics

How well does this timeout work? Quite remarkable performance improvements were observed when this timeout was implemented. We can get a good indication of a worst-case level of retransmission overhead by looking at some simple *netstat* statistics from *katie*.

The *netstat* statistics include many 32-bit counters that roll over when they reach the maximum value ($2^{32} - 1$). Therefore, if a host has not rebooted recently, the numbers may not represent the real counts, but might be counts that have rolled around some unknown number of times. For long-lived hosts, you need to take two readings and subtract them. The two readings below were taken roughly one hour apart:

```
tcpOutDataSegs      = 32405922
tcpRetransSegs      = 1105227

tcpOutDataSegs      = 32502114
tcpRetransSegs      = 1108041
```

---

[19]Note that all of the divisors in Van Jacobson's formulas are powers of 2. This is because computers can divide by powers of 2 very quickly by shifting binary numbers to the right. Van Jacobson is a very good programmer as well as being a networking expert.

The differences between the values are:

```
tcpOutDataSegs   =    96192
tcpRetransSegs   =    2814
```

The rate of retransmission is almost 3 percent. This is higher than one would expect on a private network. However, *katie* is an Internet server and communicates with hosts all over the world, with irregular variations in round-trip times. Thus, we would expect *katie* to have a bigger timeout rate than a host on a private network, which is more likely to be in the 1.5-2 percent range.

Calculations After a Retransmission

The Round-Trip Time used in the calculations above is the time between transmission of a segment and receipt of its acknowledgment. But suppose that the acknowledgment does not arrive within the timeout period and the data must be retransmitted?

Karn observed that the Round-Trip Time cannot be updated when this happens. The current Smoothed Round-Trip Time and *Smoothed Deviation* have to be saved until some segment is acknowledged without an intervening retransmission. At that point, the calculations resume, using the saved values and the new measurements.

Actions After a Retransmission

But what should be done in the meantime? In fact, TCP's behavior should change quite drastically after a retransmission. The predominant cause of data loss is congestion. Hence, the reaction to a retransmission should be to:

- Slow down retransmissions
- Fight congestion by throttling back on the total traffic burden for the network

Exponential Backoff

After a retransmission, the timeout is doubled. What happens if the timer expires again? Data is retransmitted and the retransmission timeout is doubled again. This is called *exponential backoff.*

If failures continue, the timeout will continue to double until it latches at a prespecified maximum (e.g., 4 minutes). After a preconfigured number of retransmissions without an ACK, the connection will time out.

Curing Congestion by Reducing Data on the Network

Since the most common cause of lost datagrams is congestion, a retransmission throws a session into congestion avoidance mode. The amount of data that is sent needs to be reduced for a while.

The reduction in data level is a little complicated. It begins just like the Slow Start described earlier. But as we approach the threshold level of traffic that initially got us into trouble, we will really slow down, gradually adding one segment at a time to the congestion window. We now define a threshold value for slowing down. First compute the danger threshold:

$$\text{Threshold} = \frac{1}{2} \text{ minimum}$$

(current congestion window, partner's receive window)

If this is bigger than two segments, use it as the threshold. Otherwise, set the threshold to two segments. The complete recovery algorithm is:

- Initially, set the congestion window to one segment.
- For each ACK received, increase the congestion window by one segment until the threshold is reached. (This is like the usual Slow Start.)
- From now on, a small increment will be added to the congestion window each time an ACK arrives. The increment is chosen so that the rate of increase is at most one segment added per Round-Trip Time.[20]

The idealized scenario below gives a rough idea of how recovery proceeds. We assume that the partner's receive window (and our current congestion window) equaled eight segments when the timeout occurred, so the threshold is four segments. Also suppose that the

---

[20]The increment is (MSS/N) where N is size of the congestion window in segments.

receiving application reads data immediately, so the receive window stays at eight segments.

1. Send one segment. (Congestion window = one segment.)

2. ACK received, send two segments.

3. ACKs for two more segments received. Send four segments. (We have reached the threshold.)

4. ACKs for four more segments received. Send five segments.

5. ACKs for five more segments received. Send six segments.

6. ACKs for six segments received. Send seven segments.

7. ACKs for seven segments received. Send eight segments. (The congestion window now equals the receive window.)

As long as all data is ACKed within the retransmission timeout, this process will continue until the congestion window reaches the receive window size. Figure 9.25 illustrates what happens. The window size grows exponentially (doubling) during the initial "slow" start and then levels off to linear growth.

Figure 9.25
Limiting transmission during congestion.

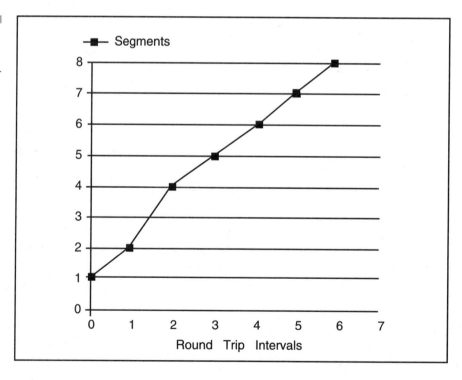

TCP Statistics

Finally, let's look at a complete *netstat* statistics report to see many of these mechanisms at work. *Katie* had not been running too long at the time that these were taken, and so they represent actual counts.

tcpRtoAlgorithm	= 4	tcpRtoMin	= 200
tcpRtoMax	= 240000	tcpMaxConn	= −1
tcpActiveOpens	= 23953	tcpPassiveOpens	= 20628
tcpAttemptFails	= 3416	tcpEstabResets	= 857
tcpCurrEstab	= 56	tcpOutSegs	= 43439957
tcpOutDataSegs	= 32502114	tcpOutDataBytes	= 1320940436
tcpRetransSegs	= 1108041	tcpRetransBytes	= 540857182
tcpOutAck	= 10933252	tcpOutAckDelayed	= 3148665
tcpOutUrg	= 28270	tcpOutWinUpdate	= 5899
tcpOutWinProbe	= 141676	tcpOutControl	= 104881
tcpOutRsts	= 12456	tcpOutFastRetrans	= 147896
tcpInSegs	= 49792883		
tcpInAckSegs	= 24703351	tcpInAckBytes	= 1320724788
tcpInDupAck	= 1098611	tcpInAckUnsent	= 0
tcpInInorderSegs	= 31043508	tcpInInorderBytes	= 2859850164
tcpInUnorderSegs	= 192484	tcpInUnorderBytes	= 205198463
tcpInDupSegs	= 179221	tcpInDupBytes	= 61161831
tcpInPartDupSegs	= 2145	tcpInPartDupBytes	= 1312588
tcpInPastWinSegs	= 78	tcpInPastWinBytes	= 225589922
tcpInWinProbe	= 1530	tcpInWinUpdate	= 140837
tcpInClosed	= 1359	tcpRttNoUpdate	= 729898
tcpRttUpdate	= 23942369	tcpTimRetrans	= 1397585
tcpTimRetransDrop	= 384	tcpTimKeepalive	= 3735
tcpTimKeepaliveProbe	= 1190	tcpTimKeepaliveDrop	= 77
tcpListenDrop	= 15	tcpListenDropQ0	= 0
tcpHalfOpenDrop	= 0		

We next examine a few of the values:

- The statement "tcpRtoAlgorithm = 4" means that the Van Jacobson retransmission timeout calculation is being used.
- RtoMin and RtoMax are measured in milliseconds and are lower and upper thresholds on the retransmission time. Note that the maximum is 4 minutes.
- *Katie* signaled urgent data 28,270 times, and sent 41,676 window probes to check whether the remote receive window still was full.
- Duplicate ACKs enabled *katie* to retransmit early 147,896 times.
- 179,221 duplicate (and 2145 partly duplicate) data segments arrived as a result of retransmission timeouts at remote partners.
- Some data arrived that was past the receive window. This was caused by incoming window probes that carried some data bytes. (If there actually was room in the window, they could have been accepted.)

- The round-trip time was calculated 23,942,369 times.
- 384 sessions were dropped because repeated retransmissions produced no ACK response.
- Keep-alives were used on some sessions; 1190 were sent.

TCP Functions

TCP is a protocol of considerable size. This chapter has dealt with the many jobs that TCP has to perform. The list below summarizes TCP's functions:

- Associating ports with connections
- Establishing connections by means of a three-way handshake
- Performing a slow start to avoid overloading the network
- Segmenting data for transmission
- Numbering data
- Handling incoming duplicate segments
- Computing checksums
- Regulating the flow of data with receive and send windows
- Terminating connections in an orderly fashion
- Aborting connections
- Signaling urgent data
- Positive acknowledgment with retransmission
- Calculating retransmission timeouts
- Throttling back traffic when the network is congested
- Detecting that segments have arrived out of order
- Probing closed receive windows

TCP States

A TCP connection passes through a number of stages. First the connection is set up by means of an exchange of messages, then data is transmitted, and then it is closed by means of an exchange of messages. Each step in the progress of a connection corresponds to a connection *state*.

TABLE 9.4

Server State
Transitions

Server State	Event	Description
CLOSED		A ficticious state, prior to starting the connection
	Passive Open by Server application.	
LISTEN		The server waits for a connection from a client.
	Server TCP receives SYN, sends SYN/ACK.	The server has received a SYN and has sent a SYN/ACK. It is waiting for an ACK.
SYN-RECEIVED	Server TCP receives ACK.	
ESTABLISHED		The ACK has been received and the connection is open.

The TCP software at each end of a connection keeps track of the state at its end of the connection at all times.

Below, we sketch a typical progression of states at the server and client ends of a connection. This is not intended to represent an exhaustive investigation of all possible state transitions. See RFC 793 and the *Host Requirements* document for a complete discussion of TCP states.

During connection setup, the sequence of states is slightly different at the server and client ends. The server states during setup are shown in Table 9.4. The client states during setup are shown in Table 9.5.

TABLE 9.5

Client State
Transitions

Client State	Event	Description
CLOSED		A ficticious state, prior to starting the connection
	Client application requests a connection. Client TCP sends SYN.	
SYN-SENT		The client TCP has sent a SYN to the server.
	Client TCP receives SYN/ACK and sends ACK.	The client has received a SYN/ACK from the server, and has sent back an ACK.
ESTABLISHED		Data transfer can proceed.

TABLE 9.6

Closer's State
Transitions

Closer State	Event	Description
ESTABLISHED	Local application requests a close.	
	TCP sends FIN/ACK.	
FIN-WAIT-1:		The closer is waiting for the partner's response. Recall that fresh data may still arrive from the partner at this stage.
	TCP receives ACK.	
FIN-WAIT-2:		The closer has received an ACK from the partner, but not a FIN. The closer waits for the FIN, accepting incoming data in the meantime.
	TCP receives FIN/ACK. Sends ACK.	
TIME-WAIT		The connection is held in limbo to allow all connection messages (e.g., late duplicates) that may still exist out in the network to arrive or be discarded. If any messages arrive, TCP will know that they belong to a defunct connection and will discard them. The timeout period is twice the estimated maximum segment lifetime.
CLOSED		All information about the connection is deleted.

In the unlikely case that partners simultaneously try to initiate a connection with each other, each would pass through the states CLOSED, SYN-SENT, SYN-RECEIVED, and ESTABLISHED.

The ends of a connection remain in ESTABLISHED state until one end initiates a *close* by sending a FIN segment. During a normal termination, the closer passes through the states shown in Table 9.6. The closer's partner passes through the states shown in Table 9.7.

TABLE 9.7

Partner's Closing
State Transitions

Closer's Partner's State	Event	Description
ESTABLISHED	TCP receives FIN/ACK.	
CLOSE-WAIT		A FIN has arrived.
	TCP sends ACK.	
		TCP waits for its application to issue a close. The application may optionally send more data.
	Local application issues close.	
	TCP sends FIN/ACK.	
LAST-ACK		TCP is waiting for the final ACK.
	TCP receives ACK.	
CLOSED		All information about the connection is deleted.

Viewing the States of TCP Connections

The *netstat -an* command can be used to examine the current state of connections. The display below shows a partial listing of *katie*'s connections in *listen, startup, established, close-wait,* and *time-wait* states.

Note that the connection port number is tacked onto the end of each local and foreign address. Port 512 is used by the *rexec* remote process execution service. Port 37 provides a time service. Port 515 is a print service.[21]

```
> netstat -an
Local Address    Remote Address      Swind Send-Q Rwind Recv-Q State
    *.111            *.*               0            0     0      0 LISTEN
    *.21             *.*               0            0     0      0 LISTEN
    *.23             *.*                      0     0      0      0 LISTEN
```

---

[21]The other port numbers can be checked by consulting the list published at *www.iana.org.*

```
*.512              *.*              0    0      0  0 LISTEN
*.37               *.*              0    0      0  0 LISTEN
*.7                *.*              0    0      0  0 LISTEN
*.9                *.*              0    0      0  0 LISTEN
*.13               *.*              0    0      0  0 LISTEN
*.515              *.*              0    0      0  0 LISTEN
166.82.1.7.1023   166.82.1.123.2049    8760   0   8760  0 ESTABLISHED
166.82.1.7.1022   166.82.1.5.2049      8760   0   8760  0 ESTABLISHED
166.82.1.7.33717  166.82.1.9.119       33580  0   8760  0 CLOSE_WAIT
166.82.1.7.34891  166.82.1.9.119       33580  0   8760  0 CLOSE_WAIT
166.82.1.7.513    166.82.177.55.1023   32120  0   8760  0 ESTABLISHED
166.82.1.7.23     166.82.194.51.4148   32120  0   8760  0 ESTABLISHED
166.82.1.7.23     166.82.175.142.2084  32120  0   8760  0 ESTABLISHED
166.82.1.7.23     204.146.167.231.1825 31680  16  10164 0 ESTABLISHED
166.82.1.7.23     208.151.233.2.4154   8760   0   10136 0 ESTABLISHED
166.82.1.7.23     199.72.84.158.2073   7915   0   8757  3 ESTABLISHED
166.82.1.7.23     192.135.215.6.4471   8192   0   9112  0 ESTABLISHED
166.82.1.7.47947  166.82.1.9.119       33580  0   8760  0 CLOSE_WAIT
166.82.1.7.23     192.58.204.204.4184  8576   0   8908  0 ESTABLISHED
166.82.1.7.48066  166.82.1.9.119       33580  0   8760  0 CLOSE_WAIT
166.82.1.7.48075  166.82.1.9.119       33580  0   8760  0 ESTABLISHED
166.82.1.7.513    166.82.101.200.946   2048   0   9112  0 ESTABLISHED
166.82.1.7.48076  170.140.4.6.6667     33600  0   9600  0 ESTABLISHED
166.82.1.7.48078  166.82.1.9.119       33580  0   8760  0 CLOSE_WAIT
166.82.1.7.513    166.82.9.2.827       2048   0   9112  0 ESTABLISHED
166.82.1.7.513    166.82.100.201.802   2048   0   9112  0 ESTABLISHED
166.82.1.7.48101  166.82.1.5.25        8760   0   8760  0 TIME_WAIT
166.82.1.7.113    166.82.1.5.42238     8760   0   8760  0 TIME_WAIT
166.82.1.7.48103  166.82.1.5.25        8760   0   8760  0 TIME_WAIT
166.82.1.7.23     207.205.149.242.1027 7683   0   8760  0 TIME_WAIT
166.82.1.7.113    166.82.1.5.42400     8760   0   8760  0 TIME_WAIT
166.82.1.7.113    166.82.1.5.42404     8760   0   8760  0 TIME_WAIT
```

Some Implementation Issues

From the beginning, TCP was intended for multivendor internetworking. The TCP protocol specification does not try to nail down exactly how the internals of an implementation will work. It is left to vendors to find the mechanisms that suit their own environment best. One result of this is that the ability of a network supervisor to tune TCP/IP networking parameters varies greatly across systems—in both its scope and method.

Operating systems that have separate end-user and system privilege levels restrict the use of well-known ports to privileged system processes. This is intended to make systems more secure by only permitting an authorized administrator to decide whether the system will run an application such as a file transfer or World Wide Web service. However, once a server has started up, running at a high privilege level is a security hazard. Crackers have sometimes been able to exploit a bug or oversight in the server application's software to gain access to the computer with the same privilege level as the application. The solution is to switch the server to a controlled user privilege level as soon as it has initialized and grabbed its port. Sometimes this switch must be configured by the server administrator.

The IETF did not define a standard application TCP/IP programming interface, as a matter of policy. The intention was to leave the field free for experimentation with different toolkits. However, this also could have led to different programming interfaces on every platform and to no portability of application software across platforms. In fact, vendors chose to base their toolkits on the Berkeley Socket programming interface. The value of a standard programming interface was proven when the WinSock (Windows Socket) programming interface was introduced. This led to a proliferation of desktop applications that could run on top of any WinSock conformant TCP/IP stack, including desktop Web browsers.

TCP Extensions for High Performance

TCP has weathered many changes over its long lifetime, but current high-speed networking technologies are beginning to strain its limits:

- When the TCP header was designed, it was hard to believe that anyone would ever need a receive buffer bigger than 65,535 bytes. Today, the 16-bit window size field in the TCP header is inadequate for the needs of high-speed or long-delay paths.

- The 32-bit sequence number field, which counts up to 4,294,967,295 bytes, appeared to provide a generous numbering space. As we move to gigabit and gigabyte speeds, these numbers wrap around too quickly.

- Ultra high speeds also can cause problems with the calculation of round-trip times.

An RFC document called *TCP Extensions for High Performance*[22] addresses the problems raised by today's high-speed networks. The

---

[22]RFC 1323, by V. Jacobson, R. Braden, and D. Borman.

extensions enable TCP to continue to operate correctly and efficiently and include:

- A Window Scale option, which speeds the smooth delivery of traffic by opening up big receive windows.
- The use of timestamps to detect old duplicate segments when data is streamed across the network at breakneck speeds that make the TCP sequence numbers wrap around quickly.
- The use of timestamps to improve the calculation of round-trip delay times.

Long Fat Pipes and Elephants

In order to understand the window size problem, let's suppose that we are trying to transfer a file via a satellite link. These days, satellite services offer lots of bandwidth. However, if the traffic passes through a high-flying satellite, delays can be long. Let's look at what happens during a file transfer if:

- Our session has exclusive use of a 125,000-byte (1-megabit)-per-second satellite link.
- Our partner has a 1000 byte receive window. We'll assume that the partner's application will empty the receive window as soon as a segment arrives.
- The total round-trip delay is 1 second.

As shown in Figure 9.26, after sending one segment we have to wait 1 second to receive an ACK. Because of the small window, we must wait

Figure 9.26
Long ACK delay.

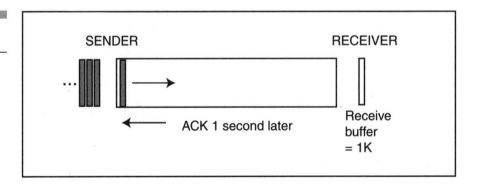

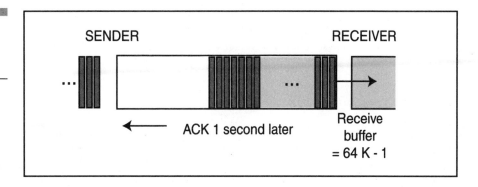

Figure 9.27
Improving through-
put with a bigger
receive window.

for the ACK before sending any more data. In spite of the very large bandwidth that is available, we only achieve a throughput of one segment per second. Almost all of the bandwidth is wasted.

We can improve our throughput if we enlarge the receive window to its maximum size, 64 kilobytes,[23] as shown in Figure 9.27. Now we can push 64 kilobytes per second through the pipe, but we still are wasting almost half of the bandwidth. The only way to fill the pipe is to have a 125,000 byte receive window.[24]

If the delay were 2 seconds, we would need a window that is twice as big—250,000 bytes—to keep the pipe filled during the entire delay time. In general, to make full use of a given bandwidth:

$$\text{Receive Window} = \text{Bandwidth} \times \text{Delay}$$

Satellites are not the only problem. Suppose that we perform a file transfer across a wide area T3 link that has a 200 millisecond round trip delay. A T3 link provides roughly 43 megabits (5,380,000 megabytes) of throughput. In order to fill the pipeline, we would need a window of:

$$\text{Bandwidth} \times \text{Delay} = 5{,}380{,}000 \times .2 = 1{,}076{,}000 \text{ bytes}$$

With a 64K window, we are limited to sending at most 64K each $\frac{2}{10}$ second, or a total throughput of 320K per second on an individual session.

---

[23]Actually, the window size is 64K-1 or 65,535, which is the largest number that can be written with 16 bits.

[24]For simplicity, we have ignored header and trailer bytes. However, for a PPP link with frame and Van Jacobson TCP/IP header compression, the total overhead per second would only be on the order of 1000 bytes.

T3 bandwidth does not increase the throughput for an individual file transfer. With a 64K window and 200-millisecond delay, we still are stuck at 320K bytes per second.

If we reduce delay to an absolute minimum, the round-trip speed-of-light,[25] the delay for a 6000-mile cross-country round-trip is 32 milliseconds. With a 64K window, the throughput is capped by:

Bandwidth/Delay = 64K/.032 = 2000K = 2 megabytes per second

Clearly, we need bigger receive windows. The authors of the TCP extensions have playfully named paths that have a large bandwidth $\times$ delay product "long fat pipes." A network containing such a pipe is called a "long fat network" (LFN), or "elephan(t)."

Window Scale Option

Changing the window field in the TCP header would introduce incompatibilities with existing installations. It makes better sense to add a TCP option field that increases the window size.[26] This has been done in a way that allows for huge growth in the future. Figure 9.28 shows the format of the Window Scale option.

The 1-byte scale is used as the exponent for a scaling factor. The steps in calculating the window size are:

■ Compute the scaling factor by raising 2 to the power that appears in the Window Scale option field. For example, $2^0 = 1$, $2^1 = 2$, $2^2 = 4$, $2^3 = 8$.

■ Multiply the value in Window field by the scaling factor.

Table 9.8 shows the possible scaling factors and the receive window sizes that result if the value in the Window field is 64,000 or 65,535.

---

[25]The speed of light is 186,000 miles per second.

[26]The processing rules will allow old implementations to simply ignore the option.

Figure 9.28
Format of the Window Scale option.

kind 3	length 3	Scale exponent

TABLE 9.8

Scale Factors

Window Scale Option Value = Exponent	Scaling Factor	Receive Window if TCP Window Field = 64,000 bytes	Receive Window if TCP Window Field = 65,535 bytes (64 Kilobytes)
0	1	64,000	65,535
1	2	128,000	131,070
2	4	256,000	262,140
3	8	512,000	524,280
4	16	1,024,000	1,048,560
5	32	2,048,000	2,097,120
6	64	4,096,000	4,194,240
7	128	8,192,000	8,388,480
8	256	16,384,000	16,776,960
9	512	32,768,000	33,553,920
10	1024	65,536,000	67,107,840
11	2048	131,072,000	134,215,680
12	4096	262,144,000	268,431,360
13	8192	524,288,000	536,862,720
14	16384	1,048,576,000	1,073,725,440

If the receive window were too big, we would not be able to distinguish between new sequence numbers and old duplicates. To prevent problems, 14 is the largest exponent that may be used. This corresponds to a maximum window scale factor of 16,384. The biggest possible window is $16,384 \times 65,535 = 1,073,725,440$, which is slightly less than 2^{30}.

Window Scale Protocol

A client that wishes to use scaled windows must include the window scale option in its opening SYN. A server that supports scaled windows will then include the option in its SYN, ACK. The option only may be included in SYN segments.

Figure 9.29 shows three opening handshake dialogs:

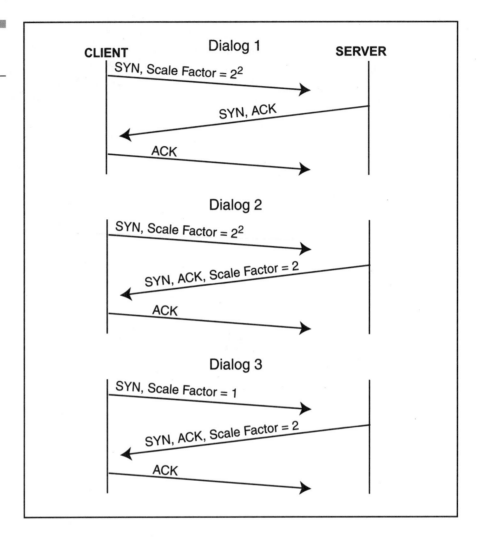

- In the first dialog, the client indicates that it is prepared to scale by sending a scale option. However, the server does not support scaling. The server ignores the option and sends back an ordinary SYN, ACK. Neither side will scale its window.

- In the second dialog, the client will scale its window by a multiple of 4. The server will scale its window by a multiple of 2.

- In the third dialog, the client plans to transfer a large file to the server. There is no reason for the client to scale its own window. However, the client must include a Window Scale option in order to show the server that it supports scaling—otherwise, the server will not be allowed to announce its own scaling value. The client's option value is 0, giving a scale factor of 1. This means that the size announced in the client's Window field should be used unchanged. The server announces that it will double its Window field value.

Window Scale Options and the TCB

The TCP Transmission Control Block (TCB) holds the parameters that TCP needs to track during a session, including the send and receive window sizes. Formerly, these would fit into a 2-byte field. When scaling is used, a window size field of 4 bytes is used. Earlier, we saw that any permissible window size is smaller than 2^{30}, so a 4-byte (32-bit) field can hold a window size value.

Wrapped TCP Sequence Numbers

TCP stores a record of the last incoming sequence number that it has ACKed, and examines incoming sequence numbers to see whether they are:

- Smaller, and hence represent old duplicate data.
- Larger, and hence should be new data.

But TCP numbers increase to 4,294,967,295 and then wrap to 0 (that is, values are counted modulo 2^{32}). How do we divide the number space into "bigger" and "smaller" values? This is not hard to do. The half of the numbers "to the right" are bigger and the half "to the left" are smaller.

Specifically, for a sequence number m, the rule is that:

$$m + 1, m + 2, m + 3,..., m + 2^{31} - 1 \text{ are bigger than } m$$

$$m - 1, m - 2, m - 3,..., m - 2^{31} - 1 \text{ are smaller than } m$$

Of course, when we add or subtract, we have to do it modulo 2^{32}. This will be clearer if we look at an example using 2^4 instead of 2^{32}. For this example, our number space ranges from 0 to 15.

If the current sequence number is 10, the 7 numbers to the left of 10 (3-9 shown in italics below) are smaller than 10. The 7 bold numbers (11-1) to the "right" of 10 are bigger than 10. When we count 7 numbers

Figure 9.30
"Smaller" and "larger"
number ranges.

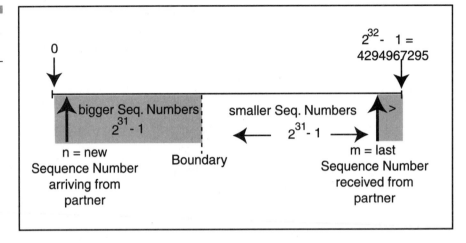

to the right, we wrap around after 15 to reach 0 and 1. The value 2 is the boundary that separates the bigger values from the smaller values.

0 1 |2| 3 4 5 6 7 8 9 10 11 12 13 14 15

Figure 9.30 gives a pictorial representation when the numbers range from 0 to $2^{32} - 1$.

- The gray areas include the values "bigger" than m, the last sequence number received from partner A.

- A boundary number separates the gray area from the rest of the sequence number space (the white area), which consists of numbers "smaller" than m.

Figure 9.31
Segment numbers for
recent segments.

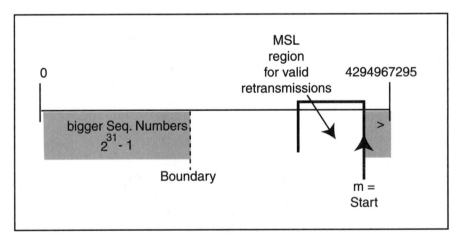

Occasionally, TCP will receive old duplicate segments whose numbers are in the white space. TCP will recognize that the sequence numbers are smaller than the current value and discard these segments. The duplicates are segments that have been sent within the last Maximum Segment Lifetime (MSL) time period. Figure 9.31 marks out an area that contains segment numbers sent during this time period. Anything that was sent earlier will either have already been delivered or will have been discarded because of an expired hop counter.

Numbers in the white area are supposed to correspond to old data. But if the transmission rate is faster than 2^{31} bytes per Maximum Segment Lifetime (MSL), then "live" numbers will race through the gray area and overlap into the white area. It no longer will be possible to distinguish between old duplicates and new data. Figure 9.32 shows what happens.

Could this happen? Table 9.9 shows how long it takes for the sequence numbers to wrap through 2^{31} bytes for various environments. Of course, we would expect any of these links to be shared by many concurrent TCP sessions. Even so, we clearly have reached transmission levels at which wrapped numbers are a real concern, especially when we use big, scaled receive windows.

Timestamps to Protect Against Wrapped Sequence Numbers

The discussion in the previous section showed that for high-speed links, we need a way to tell the difference between an old duplicate and a new

Figure 9.32
Overlapping
numbers.

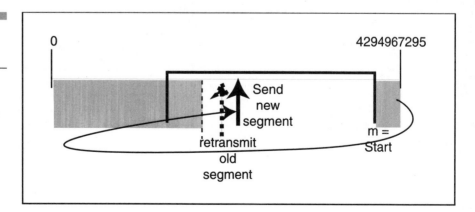

TABLE 9.9

Wrapping Times
for TCP Sequence
Numbers

Link	Megabits/Sec	Megabytes/Sec	Wrap Time
T1	1.5	.19	188 minutes
Ethernet	10	1.25	28 minutes
T3	45	5.63	6 minutes
Fast Ethernet	100	12.50	3 minutes
OC3	155	19.38	2 minutes
OC12	622	77.75	.5 minute
Gigabit Ethernet	1000	125.00	.3 minute

segment whose sequence number has wrapped into the white area that contains "smaller" numbers. The protocol that does this is called *Protecting Against Wrapped Sequence numbers* or PAWS. PAWS distinguishes between old and new segments by adding a Timestamps option to the TCP header. Figure 9.33 shows the format of the Timestamps option.

Each computer initializes a time counter when it boots up and advances its time counter at a regular interval. The PAWs standard suggests selecting an interval in the range of 1 millisecond to 1 second.

Figure 9.34 shows how timestamps are used. Both parties use an interval of 1 second. To keep the figure simple, the TCP sequence numbers are not shown. The timestamps are initialized in the SYN segments. The data receiver stores a partner's recent timestamp in order to:

- Compare it to the timestamp on an incoming segment from the partner.
- Echo it back to the partner.

Note how easily an old duplicate is detected and discarded. After discarding the segment, the client sends an ACK with current timestamps indicating the sequence number that is expected next. Normal sequence number processing is carried out on segments with valid timestamps.

Figure 9.33
Format of the Timestamps option.

kind 8	length 10	Sender's Timestamp	Timestamp Received from Partner

Figure 9.34
Using timestamps to
detect old duplicates.

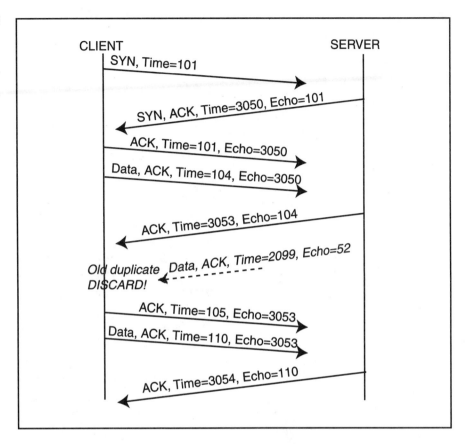

With a 1-second clock, it will take 24,855 days to count through 2^{31} timestamp numbers and almost 50,000 days to count through the whole timestamp number space. With a 1-millisecond clock, it will take 25 days to count through 2^{31} timestamp numbers and 50 days to count through the whole timestamp number space.[27]

Round-Trip Time Measurement

The Timestamp option gives you two functions for the price of one. Timestamps also enable TCP to compute good round-trip time (RTT)

---

[27]If a session had a quiet period of 25 days before sending its next segment, TCP would have to invalidate the saved timestamp. This is because the incoming timestamp would be a value in the "smaller" timestamp range.

Figure 9.35
Subtracting time-
stamps to compute
the round-trip time.

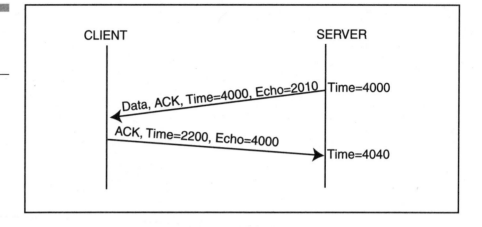

estimates. Round-trip estimates are used to calculate the Retransmission Timeout (RTO). Choosing a small timestamp clock interval will
make the round-trip time estimates more accurate: we use 1-millisecond
clock intervals in this section.

The round-trip time is the elapsed time between sending a data segment and receiving an ACK that covers that segment. The sender places
its current timestamp value into the header of each outgoing segment.

Figure 9.35 provides a simple illustration of how a round trip time is
calculated. The server sends a segment to the client at time 4000. The
ACK arrives at 4040. The client can subtract to compute that the round
trip time is 40 milliseconds.

Figure 9.36 shows two consecutive segments that are acknowledged
together by a delayed ACK. The time that elapses between sending the
first segment and receiving the ACK is the correct round trip time value.
For Figure 9.36, this value is $4150 - 4100 = 50$.

Figure 9.36
Computing the
round-trip time with
a delayed ACK.

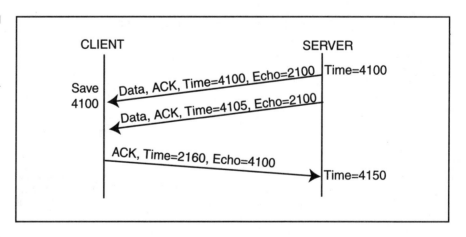

In general, the rules for computing a round trip time are:

- The sender saves the timestamp for the leftmost unacknowledged segment in its send window.

- The receiver saves and echoes the timestamp for the leftmost unacknowledged segment in its receive window.

- The round-trip time is computed when the sender receives an ACK that advances the left edge of its send window.

Figure 9.37 shows a more complicated exchange. The server sends four segments to the client.

- The first segment is sent at time 4600 and is ACKed at 4650, giving a round-trip time of 50 milliseconds.

Figure 9.37
Computing the round-trip time after loss of data.

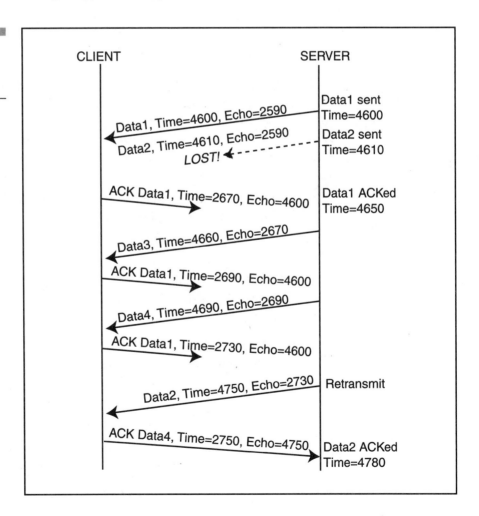

- The second segment is sent at 4610. The segment is lost. No round-trip time can be calculated until this missing data is delivered.

- The client receives two out-of-order segments (Data3 and Data4). The client responds to each by ACKing the first segment and reechoing the timestamp for the first segment (which is the last one that advanced the left edge of the send window).

- An acknowledgement for the second, third, and fourth segments arrives at 4780, giving a total round-trip time of 4780−4610 = 170 milliseconds. It is appropriate to use this value, which realistically reflects the fact that data has been lost and an intermediate router probably is somewhat congested.

Transactional TCP

While TCP provides all of the services needed for reliable sustained sessions, UDP is at the opposite end of the spectrum, offering a fast getaway for launching messages to a peer across a network, but no guarantee of reliable, in-sequence delivery of data. There are applications whose requirements fall halfway between TCP and UDP. These are applications for which:

- Clients perform uncomplicated transactions,[28] each consisting of a request and its corresponding response.

- Reliable, in-sequence delivery of data is important.

TCP for Transactions (T/TCP) fills the gap between classic TCP and UDP. T/TCP is not a separate stand-alone protocol. It is an extension to TCP that can be used selectively to speed up request/response exchanges by:

- Decreasing session setup time.

- Expediting the session close procedure.

- For short transactions, freeing up the closer's resources quickly.

---

[28]As used here, a "transaction" is a very simple interaction. For example, the retrieval of text or a graphic element of a Web page fits the model quite well. The term "transaction" has a different meaning for Online Transaction Processing Systems, which provide lots of special services, such as the automatic rollback of all data updates if any problem arises. No special application services are assumed for the transaction interactions that are discussed here.

UDP and TCP Response Times

The display below shows the timing of a sample DNS request and response. The client station was connected to the Internet via a dial-up connection and the messages passed through three intermediate routers. The request and response were carried in UDP datagrams.[29]

Frame	Time	Bytes	Source	Destination
Request	.000	32	207.205.163.57:1071	166.82.1.3:53
Response	.390	123	166.82.1.3:53	207.205.163.57:1071

The next display shows the timing of the messages used to retrieve a short World Wide Web text page. The Web site was accessed via the same dial-up connection immediately after the DNS lookup shown above. These messages passed through the same three intermediate routers.

The output illustrates the price of TCP's reliability. A "three-way handshake" (SYN, SYN, ACK) sets up the session. Some time is consumed while the server creates a Transmission Control Block and stores session parameters in the block. At the end of the closing sequence (at frame 8), the server goes into a TIME-WAIT state that typically lasts for at least 4 minutes. The server must maintain the session's Transmission Control Block during this time.

Frame	Time	Flags	Bytes	Source	Destination
SYN	.000	....S.	0	207.205.163.57:1079	166.82.8.12:80
SYN	.280	.A..S.	0	166.82.8.12:80	207.205.163.57:1079
ACK	.280	.A....	0	207.205.163.57:1079	166.82.8.12:80
Request	1.502	.AP...	238	207.205.163.57:1079	166.82.8.12:80
Response, FIN	2.093	.AP..F	1246	166.82.8.12:80	207.205.163.57:1079
ACK	2.273	.A....	0	207.205.163.57:1079	166.82.8.12:80
FIN	2.484	.A...F	0	207.205.163.57:1079	166.82.8.12:80
ACK (TIME-WAIT)	2.744	.A....	0	166.82.8.12:80	207.205.163.57:1079

[29]This trace and the one that follows were captured using the Microsoft Windows NT Server 4.0 network monitor.

T/TCP and the Three-Way Handshake

The rules of TCP allow data to be carried with the SYN handshake messages, but do not allow TCP to deliver this data to an application until the handshake sequence is completed and the session has been established. Prior to T/TCP, most TCP implementations did not carry any data in opening handshake messages, even though it was legal.

T/TCP allows data bundled with the handshake messages to be delivered immediately. The procedure is called a TCP Accelerated Open (TAO). Figure 9.38 shows a request/response interaction that has been expedited using an Accelerated Open:

- The request is included with the opening SYN request. The client has no further data to send, and so flags this message as a FIN as well as a SYN.

- The server accepts the request data immediately and starts to process it.

- If the server can complete the processing very quickly—within the time limit of a delayed ACK—the server can bundle the response with its SYN, ACK reply. If the whole response fits into one segment, a FIN also is signaled.

- The transaction has been completed within one round-trip time. The client sends an ACK and terminates the connection.

Figure 9.38
Accelerating a request/response interaction.

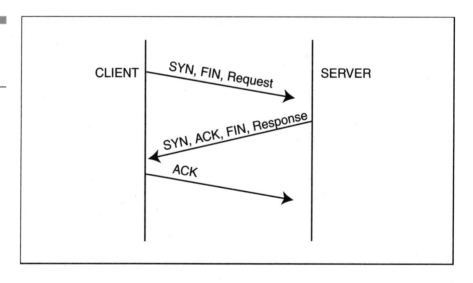

Not all transactions can be boiled down to two messages and an ACK. However, many can be speeded up by allowing the server to start to work on request data that arrives with the opening SYN. The savings in time and resources are not important for occasional, isolated request/response transactions. T/TCP is appropriate for applications that may generate tens or hundreds of thousands of simple transaction sessions per second.

Value of the Three-Way Handshake

Superficially, it looks as if the only change to TCP that is needed is to allow a recipient to accept and start processing data that arrives with a SYN or SYN, ACK segment. If that were the case, then this would be a very short topic. As you might guess, some new protocol elements are needed in order to make the TCP Accelerated Open work properly.

First of all, the client gets some very important information from the server during a normal three-way handshake—the server's window size and Maximum Segment Size. But note that in Figure 9.38:

- The client does not know the server's window size. The T/TCP specification suggests using a default start-up size of 4K.

- The client does not know the server's Maximum Segment Size (MSS). The T/TCP specification suggests caching server MSS values. Without a cached value, the client will be restricted to a maximum of 536-byte data segments for remote connections.

Also, as we saw earlier in this chapter, the three-way handshake provides a useful defense against forged source IP addresses. As Figure 9.39 shows, a cracker with a forged address would not receive the server's SYN, ACK, and would not be able to complete the handshake with a valid ACK. The normal rules of TCP prevent data from being accepted until a handshake has completed successfully, but a server using T/TCP would accept and process the initial request data.

A firewall that protects against T/TCP requests from external clients is a basic necessity in order to protect against cracker attacks. T/TCP interactions could be restricted to clients and servers located on a well-protected LAN, or some form of authentication information (such as Kerberos credentials or a digital signature) could be included with the data.

Finally, the three-way handshake at the start of a session has another

Figure 9.39
Danger of accepting
data with a SYN.

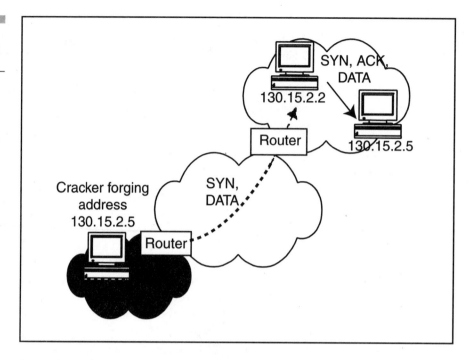

benefit; it prevents an old duplicate SYN from being confused with a new session initiation. For example, in Figure 9.40, a late duplicate SYN arrives from a client. The server thinks that this is a request for a new session and sends back a SYN, ACK. However, the client knows that there is no pending SYN request for this pair of socket addresses and

Figure 9.40
Protection against old
duplicate SYNs.

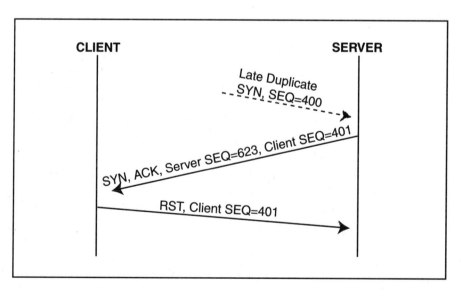

sequence number 400. The client is able to send a reset (RST) and clear up the confusion.

Without a three-way handshake, old duplicate SYNs could cause a lot of trouble—especially when there are lots of fast, short sessions. The T/TCP mechanism that solves this problem is described in the sections that follow.

T/TCP Connection Counter

T/TCP distinguishes between old, stale connections and new ones by numbering the connections in a commonsense manner.

- Each host maintains its own TCP Connection Counter (CC) variable.
- Each host stores the value of the last Connection Counter used by each of its partners.

A host's Connection Count is a 32-bit variable. Every time a new session is started, the host increments its counter and associates that value with the session. Connection Counts for a session are carried in options fields added to the TCP header.

If a server receives a SYN that contains a Connection Counter value that is bigger than the cached value for that client, then the connection is assumed to be new and the three-way handshake is bypassed. The server accepts the enclosed request data and starts to process the data.

The figures that follow show a series of connections between a client and server that support T/TCP. The figures display the flags and Connection Count option values. Segment and acknowledgment numbers are omitted to keep the pictures simple. Figure 9.41 shows an efficient client/server interaction:

- Client A increases its Connection Count to 25 and includes the value in its SYN, FIN segment.
- Server B checks that 25 is bigger than the last Connection Count value from Client A.
- Server B increases its own Connection Count to 101. The server includes this value in its SYN/ACK/FIN segment and also echoes back the client's value.
- The client's final ACK includes its Connection Count.

Figure 9.41
Exchanging Connec-
tion Counts.

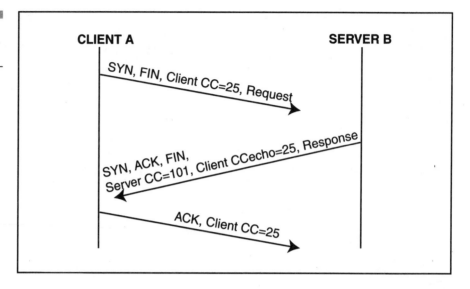

Not all transactions can be completed this quickly. For example, in Figure 9.42, it takes a while for the server to compute its response. The server is not able to piggyback its response on its SYN, ACK, and so it has to send a separate acknowledgment segment that does not contain data. Note that the only segment containing an echoed CC value is the

Figure 9.42
Dialog for a server
that cannot respond
immediately.

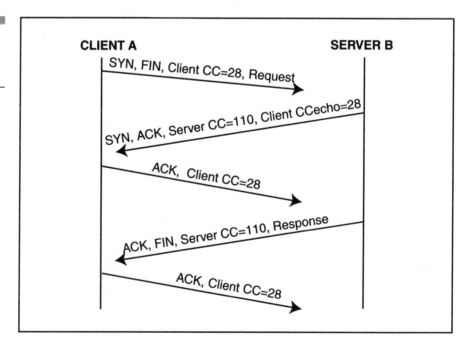

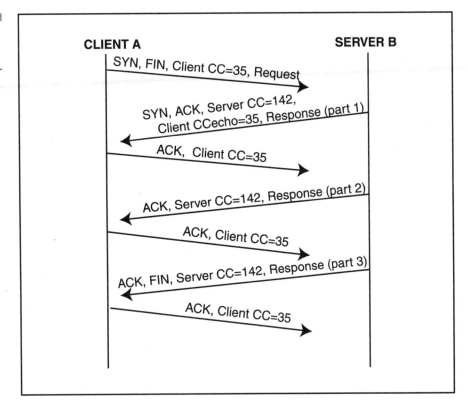

Figure 9.43
A response delivered
in multiple segments.

server's SYN response. Each party simply states its own CC value in
every segment except for the server's SYN response.

In Figure 9.42, the client's CC number has increased from 25 to 28
and the server's CC number has increased from 101 to 110. This is
because each has participated in sessions with other partners during the
period between the session in Figure 9.41 and this one. A host increments its counter every time it participates in a session that uses Connection Counts.

In Figure 9.43, three segments were needed to carry the information
in the response. The server signals its FIN in the last data segment.

Reverting to Three-Way Handshakes

Let's take a look at how T/TCP reacts when an incoming SYN segment has
a Connection Count value that is lower than expected. This might be:

Figure 9.44
Handling a SYN with
an unexpected CC
value.

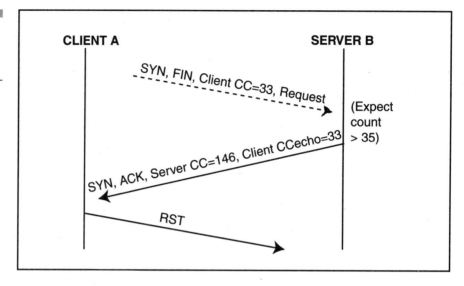

- An old duplicate.
- A valid out-of-order SYN for a new session.

It is not hard to handle this. T/TCP simply reverts to the normal three-way handshake in order to discover whether this is a valid new session. In Figure 9.44, the Connection Count value, 33, is smaller than the cached value, which is 35. The server replies with a SYN, ACK, and stores the incoming data. The ACK acknowledges the start sequence number; it does not acknowledge the data. The server will not acknowledge and process the data unless the client completes the handshake with an ACK. In the figure, the SYN is in fact an old duplicate SYN and the client responds with a reset (RST).[30] If the SYN had been valid, then the session would have proceeded in the normal manner.

A server also will revert to a three-way handshake if:

- It does not support T/TCP.
- It supports T/TCP, but has no cached value for the incoming client.

---

[30]The client easily checks whether it has a session with corresponding ports, sequence numbers, and Connection Count that is in a SYN-SENT state.

New Connection Counts

We have not yet described how a client notifies a server of its Connection Count value the first time (since its last reboot) that the client connects to the server. Start-up is accomplished by sending the CC number in a *CCnew* option field. Both sides then proceed with an ordinary three-way handshake for the connection. Any data included with the SYN segments will not be processed until the handshake is completed. However, the stage will be set for the subsequent use of efficient T/TCP connections. Figure 9.45 shows the connection setup interaction.

Another event can trigger the use of a CCnew three-way handshake. There might be a long time lapse before a client returns to a particular server. In the meantime, the client might engage in a large number of sessions with other servers, causing its sequence numbers to wrap around so that the new CC appears to be smaller than the old one, as shown in Figure 9.46. To detect this, a client caches the last CC that it sent to each server. If the server would interpret the new CC value as a smaller CC number, the client reinitializes with a CCnew. The next section describes how we determine whether a new CC number is "bigger" or "smaller."

Figure 9.45
Establishing the Connection Count after a reboot.

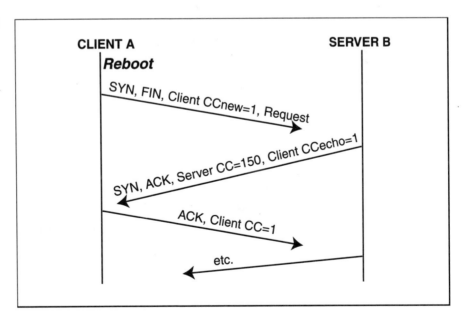

Figure 9.46
Using CCnew after
the CC numbers
have wrapped.

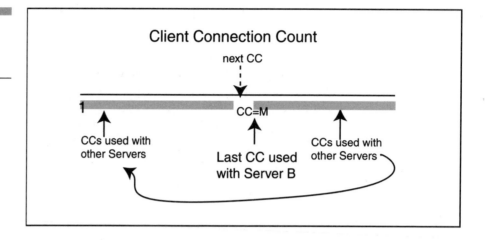

Comparing CC Numbers

For a given CC number m, which numbers are bigger and which are smaller? Just as for TCP sequence numbers, the rule is that the half to the right are bigger and the half to the left are smaller. Specifically:

$$m + 1, m + 2, m + 3,..., m + 2^{31} - 1 \text{ are bigger than } m$$

$$m - 1, m - 2, m - 3,..., m - 2^{31} - 1 \text{ are smaller than } m$$

Of course, when we add or subtract, we have to do it modulo 2^{32}. Figure 9.47 gives a pictorial representation of the full ranges of numbers. The

Figure 9.47
Recognizing new
and stale CC values.

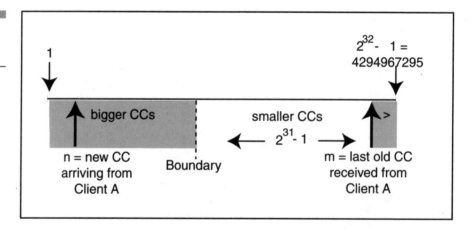

figure shows Server B's view of Client A's Connection Count values. The most recent count used by Client A was m. As shown in the figure, CC value m divides the numbering space into two pieces:

- The gray areas include the values to the "right" of m, the last CC received from partner A. The CC values spanned by the gray area are "bigger" than m.

- A boundary number separates the gray area from the rest of the CC number space which is to the "left" of m. The CCs in this area are "smaller" than m.

When a server receives a new SYN from Client A, the server checks whether the new CC is in a gray area and hence is bigger than m. For example, the new CC value equal to n in Figure 9.47 is bigger than m.

But how can Server A be sure that the SYN with CC value equal to n is not an old duplicate? We need to add one rule that is a critical part of the T/TCP protocol:

CC values must advance at a rate slower than 2^{31} counts per $2 \times MSL$.

Now we know that the SYN cannot be an old segment, because the old SYN would have been sent more than $2 \times MSL$ earlier in the past. Anything that old would have perished by now.

Truncating TIME-WAIT

Earlier we saw that the TCP partner that initiates a session close will enter a prolonged TIME-WAIT state at the end of the closing handshake.[31] Figures 9.41, 9.42, and 9.43 illustrated how a client initiates a FIN as soon as possible in order to minimize the number of round trip message exchanges in a session, and hence can be expected to be the T/TCP closer. The prolonged TIME-WAIT period (usually 4 minutes) freezes port numbers and bogs down control block resources. It does not fit the model of streamlined T/TCP transactions—it is like attaching a bulky trailer to a racing car.

Fortunately, it turns out that if the duration of a T/TCP transaction is less than the Maximum Segment Lifetime (MSL), the client can

---

[31]This enables the closer to handle old incoming duplicate segments or to retransmit its final ACK if the partner retransmits its FIN.

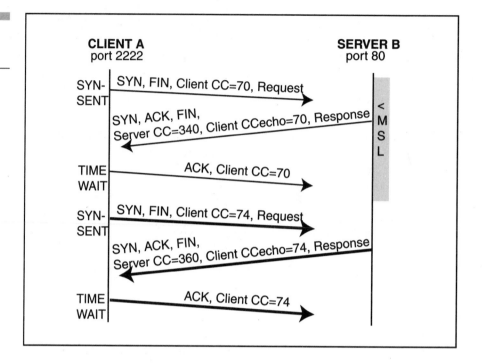

safely stop a TIME-WAIT after a far shorter period and start a new
session with the same source, destination and port numbers—and a
bigger CC. This is shown in Figure 9.48. The short TIME-WAIT will
be set to 8×the Retransmission Timeout,[32] if this is in fact less than
2 × MSL. Since Retransmission Timeouts ranging from less than a
second to just a few seconds are common, this is very likely to be the
case.

The reason that this works is that the CC numbers take the place of
the TIME-WAIT barrier. Recall that during TIME-WAIT, the closer's
TCP:

- Gracefully handles incoming duplicate segments that may still
  be in the network.

- Recovers if its own last ACK was lost. The closer will receive
  another FIN from its partner, ACK it, and restart the TIME-
  WAIT period.

---

[32]The multiplier of 8 was recommended at the time of writing.

When using T/TCP:

- Duplicates from old sessions can be recognized by their CC numbers.
- If the final ACK sent by the closer is lost, a T/TCP partner can use a new incoming SYN as an implicit final ACK for the previous connection.

To make this work, we have to be sure that CC numbers did not wrap around during a session. This is the reason that the TIME-WAIT is truncated only if the session completes in less time than the MSL.

Encoding the T/TCP Options

Three options are used for T/TCP: CC, CCnew, and CCecho. Figure 9.49 shows the encodings for these options. Each option is made up of:

- An option-kind identifier number (1 byte).
- The total length of the option (1 byte). The total length is 6 for each of these options.
- A Connection Count value that is 4 bytes in length.

Recall that a T/TCP host maintains a global 32-bit CC variable. The host selects a CC value for a fresh session by incrementing this variable by 1. Zero is never used as a Connection Count. If the CC variable reaches its maximum value (4,294,967,295), then the next value selected is 1. The send and receive Connection Counts for a session are stored in its Transmission Control Block.

Figure 9.49
T/TCP options.

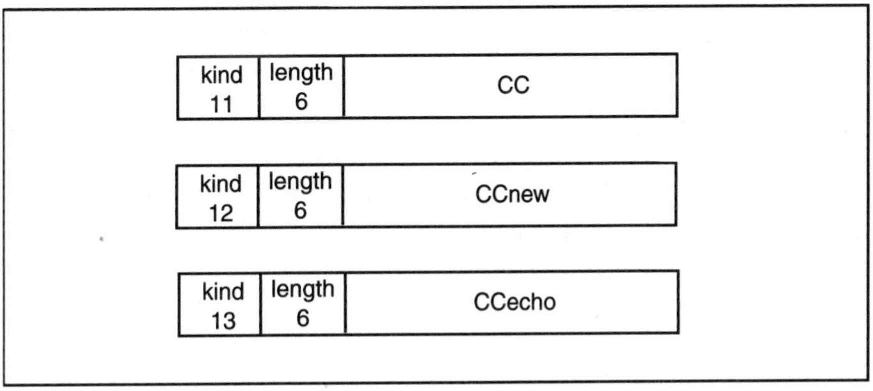

Bringing in New Options

TCP implementations are supposed to be designed with an eye to the future. This means that when receiving unfamiliar options, TCP should ignore them. When a new feature is added to TCP, the design always includes a fallback mode so that it is possible to interwork with partners that do not support the feature.

Unfortunately, instead of just getting on with their job, some implementations crash when they come across an unfamiliar option. It is wise to test carefully before deploying TCP extensions on your network.

Recommended Reading

User Datagram Protocol is defined in RFC 768. RFCs 862 to 865 discuss the *echo, discard, character generator,* and *quote of the day* UDP services. RFC 867 describes the *daytime* utility and RFC 1119 presents version 2 of the *network time service.* Additional UDP services are examined in other chapters.

The original TCP standard is defined in RFC 793. Updates, corrections, and conformance requirements are specified in RFC 1122. Karn and Partridge published their article, "Improving Round-Trip Estimates in Reliable Transport Protocols," in the *Proceedings of the ACM SIG-COMM 1987.* The Jacobson article, "Congestion Avoidance and Control," appeared in the *Proceedings of the ACM SIGCOMM 1988 Workshop.* Jacobson has published several RFCs refining performance algorithms. Additional RFC documents of interest include:

- RFC 2001 *TCP Slow Start, Congestion Avoidance, Fast Retransmit, and Fast Recovery Algorithms.*
- RFC 1948 *Defending Against Sequence Number Attacks.*

RFC 1323 describes the TCP extensions for high performance. Implementation details are discussed in *TCP/IP Illustrated, Volume 2,* by Wright and Stevens. T/TCP is described in RFC 1644. The protocol is described in great detail in *TCP/IP Illustrated, Volume 3* by W. Richard Stevens (Addison-Wesley).

Multicasts,
Multicast Routing,
and RSVP

What Good Is Multicasting?

Broadcasts generate a lot of overhead. Every time that a system receives a broadcast message, it must interrupt what it is doing and process the message. For example, if there are two RIP version 1 routers attached to a LAN, each will broadcast its routing table. A host will be interrupted by these broadcasts, even though it has no interest in the routing messages.

Multicasts have been used for quite a long time to cut down on the jabber. For example, OSPF routers multicast their messages so that they do not interrupt the activities of other stations. This is especially efficient on a switched LAN, which only will forward multicast traffic to participants, so that other stations do not even have to sacrifice any bandwidth to the multicast.[1]

Multicasts provide a very good way to locate the nearest server of a particular type. For example, an organization could replicate data at identical database servers that respond to a selected multicast address. A client could send a message with IP Time-To-Live set to 1 to the selected multicast address. If there was no response, the client could increase the Time-To-Live one step at a time until the nearest server was found.

Increasingly, multicasting is being used for conferences, distance learning, and entertainment applications. Vendors offer multimedia clients and servers, and multicast routers. Content providers are planning for the day when they will beam IP multicast channels to households down from satellites or across cable.

Multicast Issues

The big issues for multicasting are to establish methods for:

1. Joining and leaving a multicast.
2. Routing data from a sender to the receivers.
3. Finding out about multicast events.
4. Reserving resources for time-sensitive content, such as voice or video.

[1] IP version 6 replaces many broadcast messages with multicast messages, greatly reducing network overhead.

After introducing some general multicast concepts, we tackle version 2 of the Internet Group Management Protocol (IGMP), which enables systems to join and leave a multicast. Next, we discuss several schemes for routing multicast datagrams from a sender to receivers. This is followed by a brief discussion of issue 3, finding out about multicast events. Conferencing usually requires voice and video transmissions, and timely delivery of data is essential. The final topic in this chapter is the Resource Reservation Protocol (RSVP), which enables receivers to reserve network resources so that delay and delivery reliability are kept at acceptable levels.

Multicasting on a LAN

LAN multicasting is a good starting point for understanding how multicast technology works. Recall that in Chapter 4 we learned that a LAN MAC address contains a multicast bit located in position:

X'01-00-00-00-00-00

If the value of the multicast bit is 1, then the address is a multicast address.[2] The rest of the address will have a value that has been assigned to some multicast-based service. A number of LAN multicast addresses have been reserved by vendors and are used for communication between their network devices. For example:

- Spanning tree bridges use multicast address X"01-80-C2-00-00-00 to exchange topology information.
- DEC Lanbridge Traffic Monitors use X"09-00-2B-00-00-03 to communicate.

The block of addresses in the range from 01-00-5E-00-00-00 to 01-00-5E-FF-FF-FF has been set aside for Internet multicast applications. A host begins to listen to one of these addresses because a user has started an application that needs to receive data at that address. When the application terminates, the system will no longer accept data sent to that address.

The upper part of Figure 10.1 shows each member of a group of receivers absorbing a single multicast Ethernet frame. The lower part of

---

[2] Note that this means that there are lots of multicast addresses.

Figure 10.1
Delivering multicast
frames on a LAN.

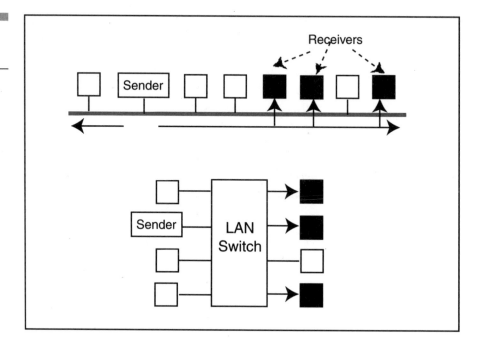

Figure 10.1 shows how an Ethernet switch propagates a multicast frame to precisely the three stations that have announced that they wish to receive traffic to that multicast MAC address.

IP Multicasting

LAN multicasting is a handy concept, but multicasting across a corporate network—or across the Internet—has the most exciting potential. Figure 10.2 shows a multicast datagram being delivered across a network to recipients that have joined a multicast. A copy of each datagram is sent down each link that leads to multicast participants. For delivery on a destination LAN, a single datagram is wrapped in a multicast frame and absorbed by all of the participants on that LAN. This system is efficient; a datagram is not forwarded along links that do not lead to recipients, and only one copy of each datagram crosses any wide-area link.

Figure 10.2
Propagating multicast
datagrams.

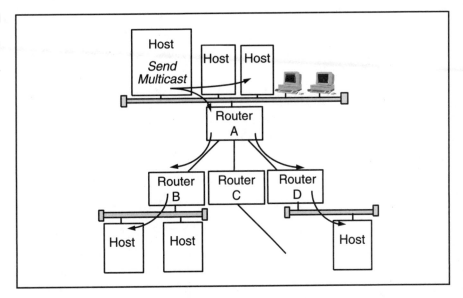

Multicast IP Addresses

An entire IP address class—Class D—has been set aside to support IP multicasting. Figure 10.3 shows the format of Class D addresses, which start with numbers in the range 224-239.

Some IP multicast addresses are reserved for specific purposes. Examples of permanently defined multicast IP addresses include:

224.0.0.1   All systems on a local subnet

224.0.0.2   All routers on a local subnet

224.0.0.5   All routers supporting the Open Shortest Path First (OSPF) routing protocol

224.0.0.9   All RIP-2 routers

Figure 10.3
Class D format for IP
multicast datagrams.

The Internet Assigned Numbers Authority (IANA) has reserved the entire range of addresses from 224.0.0.0 to 224.0.0.255 for the use of routing protocols and other low-level topology discovery or maintenance protocols.

The address range 239.52.0.0-239.255.255.255 is reserved for site-local multicasts. An organization can choose addresses from this range for its internal multicasts. Other ranges have been reserved by organizations that offer (or plan to offer) multicast support services or content. For example:

224.0.12.000-224.0.12.063   Microsoft and MSNBC

224.0.13.000-224.0.13.255   UUNET PIPEX Net News

A complete list of the current address assignments can be obtained from the IANA.

Multicast Groups

A *multicast group* is a set of systems that receives data at a specific multicast IP address. Members of the group retain their own IP addresses but also have the ability to absorb data that is sent to the multicast IP address. Any system may belong to zero, one, or many multicast groups. A rough scenario for a host participating in a multicast is:

- A user starts a conferencing client program.
- The program makes a system call that notifies IP that it wants to join the specific multicast group that has been associated with a conference.
- IP prepares the LAN interface card to receive multicasts at a corresponding physical address.
- IP notifies local routers that this system has joined the multicast group.
- The conferencing client receives and processes incoming multicast datagrams.
- The user quits the conference.
- The conferencing client notifies IP that it wants to quit the conference multicast group.
- (Optionally) IP notifies local routers that it has quit the multicast group.

Routers need special multicast routing software in order to propagate multicast IP datagrams to receivers across an internetwork.

Sending Multicast Traffic

The previous section dealt with multicast receivers. Obviously, someone needs to be sending this traffic. A talker does not have to be a listener. Stated more formally, a system that sends datagrams to a multicast group does not necessarily have to be a member of the group. In some applications (such as conference calls) everybody talks and listens. In other applications (lectures or video shows) senders do not also receive.

Multicast addresses are used only for destinations. A sender's source address must be a conventional unicast address.

Mapping Multicast IP Addresses to LAN Addresses

On a LAN, every member of a multicast group needs to watch for traffic addressed to the multicast IP address assigned to the group and absorb data sent to that address. This turns out to be easy because there is a mapping between a multicast IP address and a corresponding LAN multicast MAC address. When a host joins a group, its interface card is instructed to watch for the corresponding multicast LAN MAC address. The following translation rule is used for Ethernet and FDDI:

- The first 3 bytes of the physical multicast address are set to 01-00-5E.
- The next bit should be set to 0, and the final 23 bits should be set to the low-order 23 bits of the IP multicast address.

This mapping is illustrated in Figure 10.4:

- The final 23 bits in the IP multicast address have been marked "x." These bits are copied into the low-order bits of the physical multicast address.
- Positions marked "?" in the IP multicast address might be filled in with any bits. They are not copied into the physical multicast address.

Figure 10.4
Mapping part of the
IP address into the
physical address.

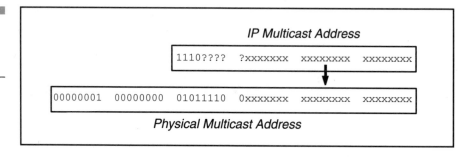

This means, for example, that all three multicast IP addresses:

    11100000 00010001 00010001 00010001 (224. 17.17.17)

    11100000 10010001 00010001 00010001 (224.145.17.17)

    11100001 10010001 00010001 00010001 (225.145.17.17)

map to the *same* physical multicast address:

    00000001 00000000 01011110 00010001 00010001 00010001

Interfaces on systems that belong to any of the three groups would capture multicasts for all of the groups. However, each host's IP layer would discard extraneous multicasts.

Translating Multicast Addresses to Token-Ring Addresses

The same scheme used earlier for Ethernet and FDDI usually cannot be used for Token-Ring. As originally implemented, Token-Ring hardware interfaces could not be configured with arbitrary multicast addresses. Any one of three translation methods is used, depending on the hardware available at a site:

1. Embed 23 bits of the IP multicast address, as before

2. Choose and use one of the Token-Ring *functional* addresses

3. Use a Token-Ring *all rings broadcast*

Method 1 is the best solution, if the hardware permits it. Alternatively, there are 31 *functional* physical addresses that have been set aside to identify systems that have a specific role, such as a bridge, ring wiring concentrator, or ring error monitor. When method 2 is selected, multicasts are sent to the functional physical address:

03-00-00-20-00-00

When a station receives a frame sent to this functional address, the IP address would have to be examined to see if this station really is a member of a multicast group.

Since one functional address is used for all multicast addresses, this method is not very efficient. However, it is better than the last alternative, method 3, which broadcasts to all stations.

IGMP Software

Before a site is ready for multicast applications, IP host software needs to be upgraded to a version that supports multicasting. IGMP is the extra component of IP that hosts need. IGMP is considered to be an integral part of IP. Current computers are being shipped with IGMP capability integrated into IP.

IGMP Functions

It does not make sense to send traffic addressed to a multicast group to a LAN unless some host on the LAN is participating in the group. Multicast routers cooperate with one another to send traffic to exactly those LANs that contain at least one host that wishes to receive the traffic.

To make this work, a LAN-attached router needs to know whether there are any local participants who need to receive datagrams addressed to the group. IGMP defines the messages and procedures that enable:

- Clients to join or leave multicast groups
- Routers to keep track of whether there are any active participants for a specific multicast on an attached LAN.

A router really does not care whether a LAN has one group member or 100 group members. The result is the same; traffic for the group must be delivered to the LAN. The protocol is rigged to keep the IGMP message traffic low. If one host has joined a group, the other hosts do not have to say "me too."

IGMP Destination Addresses

Some IGMP messages are sent to two of the special multicast addresses mentioned earlier:

224.0.0.1   All systems on a local subnet

224.0.0.2   All routers on a local subnet

Other IGMP messages are addressed to multicast group addresses at which LAN group members are receiving multicast application data.

IGMP datagrams are kept on the local LAN by setting their Time-To-Live to 1.

IGMP Overview

Before examining the details of the IGMP protocol, let's run through overviews of router and host activities.

Multicast Router Role

A multicast router needs to keep a list of the multicast group addresses for which there are active members on an attached LAN. The router checks up on active groups periodically by sending *general Query* messages. These messages ask active members of any multicast group to respond.

Occasionally, a router will receive a *Leave Group* message from a host that no longer is interested in traffic for a specific group. After receiving a Leave Group message, the router needs to check and see whether there are other members of the group still lurking on the LAN. The router does this efficiently by sending a *group-specific Query* message to the address for that group. The router will repeat its query once or twice because it is possible for any datagram to be lost or damaged. Repeating makes it very likely that the request will reach all of the local hosts.

Multiple routers may be connected to a LAN. There is no reason for all of them to send queries, so one is selected to be the active querier. The rest just listen to the queries and reports. Choosing the querier is easy. Each router sends a few general queries when it starts up. The router with the lowest IP address becomes the querier.

What happens if the querier router crashes? After a timeout, the other routers start to send queries again. They discover which router has the lowest IP address, and that one takes over.

Routers absorb and examine all multicast datagrams. When a multicast datagram arrives at a router, the router transmits the datagram onto each attached LAN that has a member in the group.[3] The router may also need to forward the datagram across wide-area links to other multicast routers.

Multicast Host Role

The rule for query responses is "don't all answer at once." Instead of answering a query immediately, a host sets a random timeout value for each relevant group address. A query message contains a field that sets a maximum response time, and random timeout values are bounded by this maximum response time. When a host's timer for a group address expires, the host sends two or three *Membership Reports* to that group address. This will:

- Tell local routers that there is at least one active host for that group.
- Tell all of the other group members to stop their timers. They don't need to reply. The presence of even one active host will keep the multicast traffic flowing.

The host repeats its report once or twice because it is possible for any datagram to be lost or damaged. Repeating makes it very likely that everyone will hear the response.

When a fresh host joins a multicast group, it will not want to wait around to find out whether there are other members. It automatically sends a Membership Report to the group.

A polite host that wants to leave a group and was the last one to reply to a query can notify routers of this fact by sending a *Leave Group* message.

The sections that follow fill in the protocol details.

---

[3]Of course, the router will not send the datagram back onto the network from which it was received.

Scope of the IGMP Protocol

Note that everything about IGMP is interface specific. A router becomes the querier for one of its interfaces. A host joins a group on an interface. Messages are sent across—and received from—the link connected to that interface.

IGMP Protocol Details

This section describes the IGMP messages that are used in host-router interactions. Additional IGMP messages may be defined in the future and used for other purposes.

IP Header

The IP header of a datagram that carries one of the IGMP messages used for host-router interactions:

- Has Time-To-Live set to 1, to make sure that the datagram is not forwarded out of the local LAN.
- Has protocol field set to 2, identifying the IGMP protocol.
- Includes the Router Alert option, so that routers immediately will be aware that these messages need special attention.

Use of the Router Alert option makes very good sense. It warns local routers to absorb and examine all IGMP multicast datagrams.

Message Format

All of the IGMP messages discussed in this chapter have the same format, which is shown in Figure 10.5.

There are four message types:

Type X"11: Membership Query

Type X"16: Version 2 Membership Report

Type X"17: Leave Group

Type X"12: Version 1 Membership Report

Figure 10.5
IGMP message for-
mat.

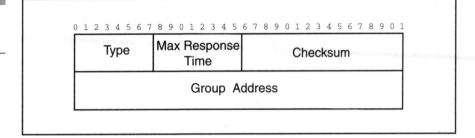

The last type is included for backward compatibility with version 1 hosts. It has the same purpose as the version 2 Membership Report.

General Membership Queries

A general Membership Query asks hosts to report all groups to which they belong.

- General queries are sent to the special all-systems multicast group IP address, 224.0.0.1.
- The group address field in a general query message is set to 0.

Specific Membership Queries

A router sends a specific Membership Query after it has received a Leave Group message. The query asks whether there are any active members left in the group.

- The router sends the query to the IP address of the group that was left.
- The group address field in the query message is set to the group address that was left.

Membership Report Messages

A host sends a Membership Report in response to a query after its query timer has expired.

- A host sends the Membership Report message to the IP address of the group that it is reporting. This ensures that all of the other hosts in the group will see the message.
- The group address field in the Membership Report message is set to the group address that the host is reporting.

Leave Group Messages

Recall that a host that is dropping out of a group sends a Leave Group message if it was the last member to send a Membership Report for that group.

- Leave Group messages are sent to the all-routers multicast address, IP address 224.0.0.2. There is no need for other hosts to see these messages.
- The group address field in the Leave Group message is set to the group address that the host is leaving.

Maximum Response Time

The maximum response time in query messages informs group members of the maximum time that may elapse before they respond with a report. The time is measured in tenths of a second. The default time is 10 seconds.

Multicast Routing

IGMP alone is not enough to make multicasting work. Special multicast routing software is needed so that routers can set up and prune back the paths followed by data flowing from sources to destinations. It is necessary to add multicast routing software to existing routers or buy new routers that can perform multicast routing. Multicast routing is our next topic.

Figure 10.6 shows a sender's datagram being delivered to network recipients that have joined a multicast. A copy of the datagram is transmitted down each link leading to one or more recipients. These are the thick black lines in the figure. Note that these links form a tree of paths.

Figure 10.6
Multicasts being for-
warded down a tree
of paths.

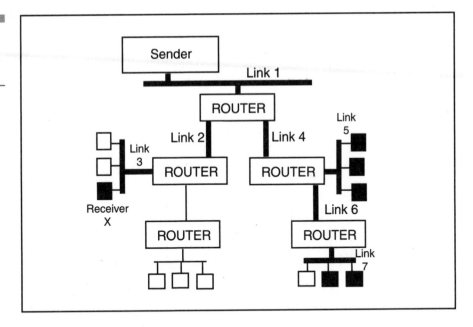

The tree that is shown is efficient; the datagram is not forwarded along links that do not lead to recipients. Note that if the data had been sent to each recipient separately, six copies of each datagram would be transmitted across Link 1 and five copies would have been sent across Link 4. Multicasting is an effective way to send identical data to a large number of recipients.

Paths change as receivers join or leave the multicast. For example, if Receiver X quits, then the path through Link 2 and onto Link 3 (which is the LAN at the left) no longer is needed. Link 2 and Link 3 would be "pruned" from the set of active links.

Figure 10.6 actually is simplified. First of all, a multicast can have any number of senders. For example, Figure 10.7 shows a wide area multicast that has two senders. Furthermore, any system could act as both sender and receiver. Figure 10.8 depicts a LAN voice conference in which every participant is both a sender and a receiver. And Figure 10.9 illustrates two different multicasts taking place on the same network. Participants and flows for the second multicast are shown using dotted lines. Every participant in the second multicast is both a sender and a receiver.

As even these simple examples show, keeping track of all of the multicast paths on a network requires more information than ordinary routing protocols can provide. Hosts and routers that support multicast services need software designed for this purpose.

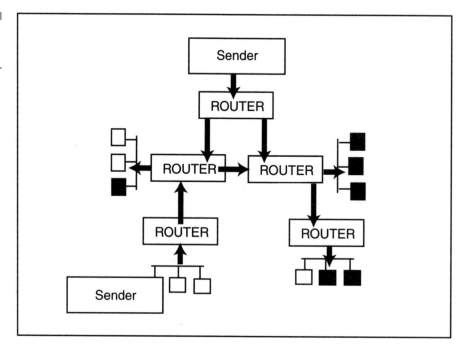

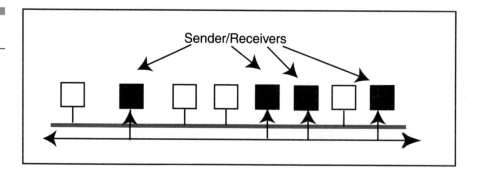

Multicast Routing Protocol Selections

Multicast routing is a young technology. There are several competing routing protocols, and changes to each can be expected. Implementers must make some choices and be prepared to update software that is still evolving. In this chapter we discuss four of these protocols:

Figure 10.9
Two concurrent conferences.

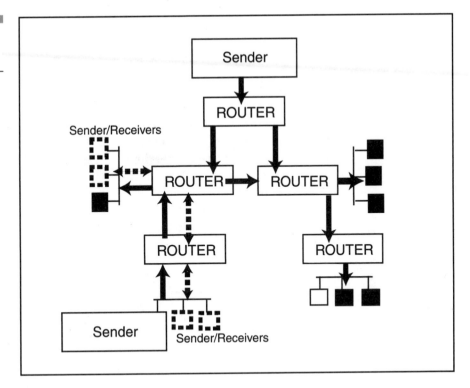

1. Distance Vector Multicast Routing Protocol (DVMRP)

2. Multicast Extensions to OSPF (MOSPF)

3. Protocol Independent Multicast-Dense Mode (PIM-DM)

4. Protocol Independent Multicast-Sparse Mode (PIM-SM)

Each of these protocols serves the same purpose. They enable network routers to exchange the information needed to forward multicast datagrams from a source to destinations along a reasonably efficient path. Each protocol does this job a little differently and has features that make it a good choice for some environments and a bad choice for others.

We outline the features of the Distance Vector Multicast Routing Protocol and Multicast Extensions to OSPF in the sections that follow. Only a very brief discussion of Protocol Independent Multicast-Dense Mode and Protocol Independent Multicast-Sparse Mode is included, since these protocols are still at an experimental stage.

Distance Vector Multicast Routing Protocol

The Distance Vector Multicast Routing Protocol (DVMRP) enables routers to exchange and use multicast routing information. It is completely separate from whatever protocol has been selected to route unicast datagrams (such as RIP, OSPF, or EIGRP). We start this section by presenting a big-picture overview of what DVMRP does, and hone in on the details later.

Figure 10.10 illustrates DVMRP routers in action. A host on LAN 1 starts to send multicast datagrams to a particular multicast group address. Routers in the internetwork use information obtained from one another via DVMRP messages to build a tree of paths that connects the source LAN to LANs that contain multicast group members. The black boxes in the figure represent the multicast group members.

If some sender on LAN 1 starts to transmit multicast datagrams to a different multicast group, it is likely that the recipient LANs will differ, and hence at least some of the paths that are used will be different. For

Figure 10.10
DVMRP routers building paths to recipients.

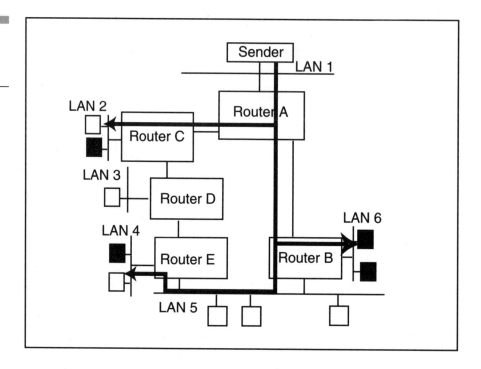

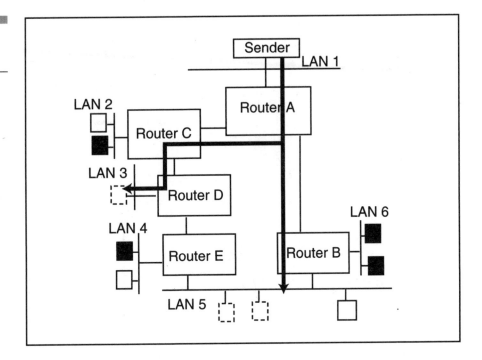

Figure 10.11
A second set of
paths.

example, Figure 10.11 shows the paths that are followed when a sender on LAN 1 transmits datagrams to a multicast group whose members are represented by the boxes with dotted outlines.

Upstream and Downstream

Data flows down a path through a sequence of routers. Adjacent routers on a path have an "upstream" or "downstream" relationship with one another. An upstream router is closer to the sender, while a downstream router is further from the sender. For example, in Figure 10.12:

- Router C is upstream from Router D.
- Routers B and C are downstream from Router A.

Note that even though Router E is adjacent to Router D, it is not on a downstream path. This is because there is a better path to Router E via Router B. Router E is downstream from Router B.

Figure 10.12
Upstream and down-
stream neighbors.

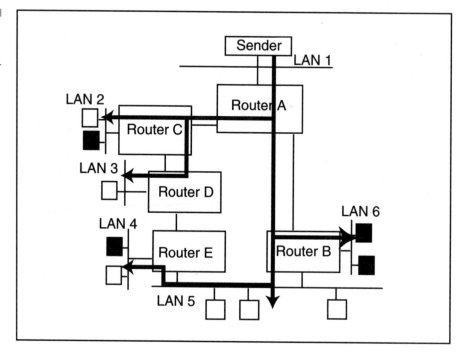

Building Paths from a Sender

How do multicast paths get built? When a sender starts to transmit, all multicast datagrams initially are forwarded to every router in the internetwork. The datagrams follow a tree of paths that connects the sender's LAN to *every* LAN in the internetwork. Figure 10.12 showed a complete tree for senders on LAN 1.

Pruning the Tree for a Group

Sending all datagrams for a multicast group to all LANs would be very wasteful. A multicast datagram only should be forwarded to LANs that contain hosts that have joined the group. Starting at the bottom of the tree, routers that do not lead to downstream group members prune themselves from the tree.

Efficient trees like the ones shown in Figure 10.10 and Figure 10.11 were created by pruning the complete tree. Paths in a pruned tree lead to LANs that contain active members of a specific group. For example, in Figure 10.12:

- No hosts on LAN 3 have joined the group, so Router D will send a prune request to Router C, asking to be removed from the tree.

- Router C has received an IGMP join message for the group from a host on LAN 2, so it will keep its path to the sender.

- Router B knows that there are no group members on LAN 5. However, Router B also knows that downstream neighbor Router E is reached via LAN 5. Router B must continue to send datagrams down this path until Router E asks for a prune.

Figure 10.10 showed the paths that remain after Router D has sent its prune request. If at a later time a host on LAN 3 joins the multicast group, Router D will send a graft request and reconnect to the tree.

Sender Network/Multicast Group Trees

The shape of a complete tree depends on the location of the sender. Figure 10.13 shows a complete tree when a sender is on LAN 3.

Figure 10.13
Tree for a sender on LAN 3.

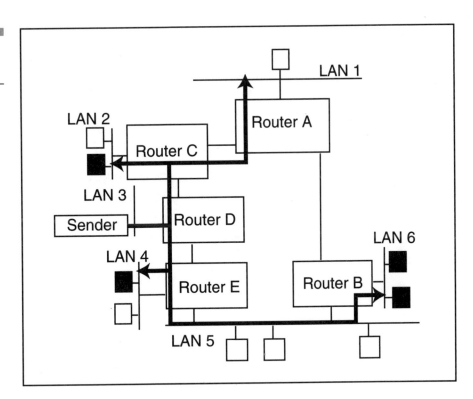

After a sender LAN has been identified, a new pruned subtree must be generated for each destination multicast group. In other words, a separate pruned tree is needed for each pairing:

(source network, multicast group)

DVMRP Overhead

Keeping track of all of this information could turn into a massive burden of work for a router. Fortunately, each router only learns and records what it needs to know. After a flow of datagrams from a sender network has started, each router will:

- Create an entry for the (source network, destination group) pairing.
- Record the identity of its unique upstream neighbor for that source network.
- Keep track of which of its downstream neighbors lead to recipients.

For example, in Figure 10.10 Router C learned that Router A is its upstream neighbor. Router C knows that Router D is a downstream neighbor, but Router D has sent a prune request, and so Router C will not forward datagrams further down the tree. This is a modest amount of data for a single (source network, multicast group) entry. Tracking DVMRP multicast routes becomes a burden if:

- The number of active source and destination LANs is very large.
- There are a lot of concurrent multicasts.
- Routers belong to many paths.
- Routes change fairly frequently.

DVMRP Mechanisms

Now it is time to examine some of the mechanisms behind DVMRP. DVMRP routers exchange hop-count metric information that is very similar to RIP routing information. The way that DVMRP (and other multicast routing protocols) use routing information may seem strange at first. Routers calculate the shortest path *back to sender LANs,* rather than the shortest path forward to destination LANs. This technique is called *Reverse Path Multicasting* (RPM).

Each LAN on the internetwork is viewed as a potential source (sender) LAN. Specifically, for each LAN, a router learns:

- How far the router is from the LAN. A simple hop-count metric is used.[4]
- The next-hop neighbor for a path to that LAN. This identifies the upstream neighbor and the interface used to reach that neighbor.

This information is used whenever a router receives a multicast datagram:

- The router notes the incoming interface on which the datagram arrives.
- The router looks up the datagram's source address in its DVMRP routing table.
- If the incoming interface does not lead to the shortest path to the datagram's source, the datagram is discarded.
- If the incoming interface leads to the shortest path to the datagram's source, the datagram is processed.

In summary:

- DVMRP computes shortest paths from destinations to sources.
- The path followed from a source to a destination is exactly this path—in reverse order.

Processing a Datagram

Let's walk through the steps that are followed when a multicast datagram is sent down the paths in Figure 10.14.

Step 1: The sender forwards the multicast datagram to adjacent Router A.

Step 2: Router A notes the incoming interface and checks that it leads to the shortest path back to the originating LAN. Router A then forwards the datagram to downstream Routers B and C.

---

[4]As in RIP, any link can optionally be assigned a value bigger than 1.

Figure 10.14
Processing a multicast
datagram.

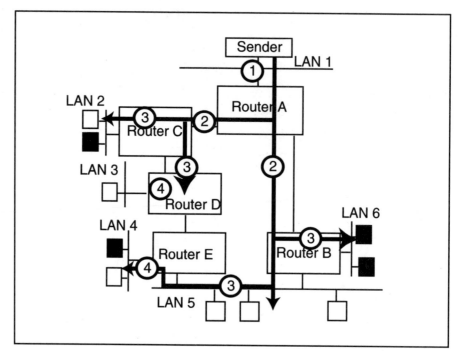

Step 3: Router B notes the incoming interface and checks that it leads to the shortest path back to the originating LAN. Router B forwards the datagram onto LAN 6 because it has multicast members. Router B also forwards the datagram onto LAN 5 because it leads to downstream Router E. Router C notes the incoming interface and checks that it leads to the shortest path back to the originating LAN. Router C forwards the datagram onto LAN 2 because it has multicast members. Router C also forwards the datagram to downstream Router D.

Step 4: Router D checks that the incoming interface leads to the shortest path back to the originating LAN. Then Router D discards the datagram because LAN 3 has no members for this multicast group, and there are no downstream neighbors. (Router E is not downstream because it has a different, shorter path back to LAN 1.) Router E checks that the incoming interface leads to the shortest path back to the originating LAN. Router E forwards the datagram onto LAN 4. Router E does not forward the datagram to neighbor D because it is not downstream.

The sections that follow describe how a router gathers the routing information that it needs in order to process multicast datagrams.

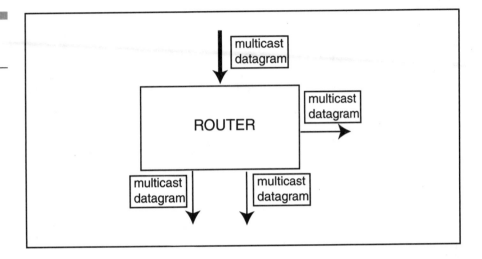

Figure 10.15
Initial forwarding strategy.

Start-up

When a router starts up, it has no network topology information on which to base multicast forwarding decisions. If a multicast datagram arrives before the router has established a route to the source, the router will forward a multicast datagram through every interface except for the one on which the datagram was received, as shown in Figure 10.15. At this point, the router has no way of knowing:

- Whether there are downstream recipients for the multicast group.
- Whether this router is on an optimal path from the source to recipients.

If the sending router is not upstream on an optimal path, a receiving router that has an up-to-date routing table will discard the datagram.

Getting To Know the Neighbors

The router will be able to make intelligent decisions after it has discovered its neighbor routers and has received routing information from them. The "hello" messages that routers use to announce themselves and discover their neighbor routers are called *DVMRP Probe* messages.

Probes enable a router to discover neighbors on an attached LAN. As shown in Figure 10.16, Router A discovers neighbors B, C, and D using

Figure 10.16
Using Probe
messages to find
neighbors.

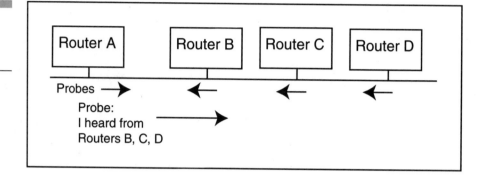

Probe messages, and announces that fact in subsequent Probes. Probes are sent to the All-DVMRP-Routers multicast address 224.0.0.4.

Routing Table

After a router and its neighbors have discovered one another, they begin to exchange DVMRP routing table entries. A routing table initially includes the networks to which a router is directly attached. The routing table grows as the router learns additional entries from its neighbors. A routing table entry includes:

- An address and mask that identify a network.
- A metric that corresponds to the distance to that network.

The term "network" is used loosely here:

- An address and mask might correspond to a conventional network, such as (198.202.100.0, 255.255.255.0), which identifies a particular Class C network.
- The address and mask might correspond to a subnet such as (130.15.1.0, 255.255.255.0) or (130,15.2.64, 255.255.255.192).
- Or the address and mask might identify a CIDR network, such as (197.1.16.0, 255.255.252.0) which includes all addresses starting with 197.1.16, 197.1.17, 197.1.18, and 198.1.19.

The protocol used to exchange information and build up the local routing table is quite similar to RIP. A cost metric (usually 1) is associated with each router interface. The metric associated with a path to a destination is the sum of the metrics along that path. The maximum metric for any path is 31. A value of 32 is called "infinity" and means "I can't get there."

Using the Routing Table To Identify Upstream Routers

The routers will build routing tables that have entries for each LAN in the internetwork. Recall that DVMRP looks at a routing table from a different point of view than we are used to. (You could think of DVMRP as upside-down routing.) Optimal routes *to* each potential *sender network* are computed. Then these are turned backwards and used to route traffic *from* the sender.

For example, Figure 10.17 shows the set of optimal paths from LANs 2, 3, 4, and 5 to LAN 1. Just as with RIP, an individual router will not be aware of the complete (backward) path, but will know its optimal next hop. From the point of view of the routers:

■ Router C can tell that its best route to LAN 1 is via upstream neighbor Router A.

Figure 10.17
Finding the best path back to a sender.

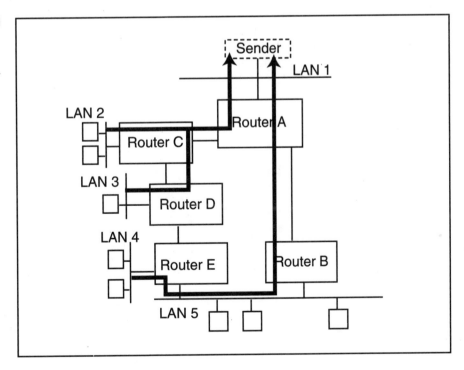

- Router D can tell that its best route to LAN 1 is via upstream neighbor Router C.

- Router B can tell that its best route to LAN 1 is via upstream neighbor Router A.

- Router E can tell that its best route to LAN 1 is via upstream neighbor Router B.

Poison Reverse

Each router now knows its upstream neighbor on the way to any LAN. However, it needs a way to notify the upstream router of this fact—in other words, say "I am downstream from you." This is done using a trick called "Poison Reverse." We'll explain Poison Reverse by looking at an example. In Figure 10.18, when Router A reports to Router C that it is 1 hop from LAN 1:

1. Router C verifies that its best route to LAN 1 is through Router A.

2. Router C echoes the route back to Router A with a metric of (32 + 1). This is the Poison Reverse.

Figure 10.18
Poison Reverses.

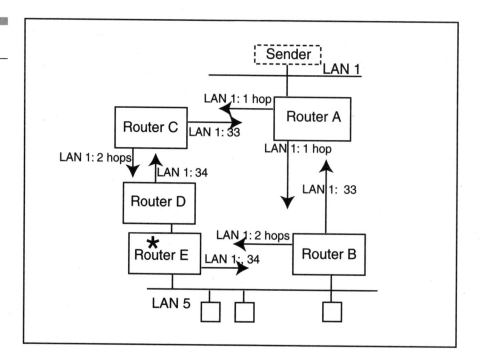

3. Router A then adds Router C to the list of dependent downstream routers for LAN 1.

4. If Router A receives multicast datagrams from a sender on LAN 1, Router A will forward them to Router C.

Similarly, after Router C reports to Router D that it is 2 hops from LAN 1, Router D verifies that its best route to LAN 1 is through Router C. Router D sends a Poison Reverse route entry to Router C whose metric is (32 + 2), and Router C adds Router D to its list of dependent downstream routers for LAN 1.

After Router D reports to Router E that it is 3 hops from LAN 1, Router E can verify that it has a better route through Router B. Therefore, Router E will send a Poison Reverse to Router B but it will not send one to Router D. Router E must discard any multicasts from a sender in LAN 1 that arrive through the interface marked with an asterisk symbol (*) in Figure 10.18.

Note that Router E will not transmit datagrams coming from LAN 1 onto LAN 5 because it knows that Router B is attached to LAN 5 and is closer to LAN 1. The router (Router B in this case) selected to forward datagrams onto a LAN is called the *designated forwarder* for the source.

Figure 10.18 shows the poison reverse messages for a single source LAN, LAN 1. Of course, every time a router receives a network entry from a neighbor that is its upstream hop for that network, the router will respond with a poison reverse message. For example, Router B is Router A's upstream neighbor for a source on LAN 5.

DVMRP Forwarding Cache Entries

The stage is now set for routing multicast traffic. When a router receives a multicast datagram with a new (source network, multicast group) combination, it creates a *forwarding cache* entry for this combination.

Initially, the router will forward the multicast datagrams for this pairing out of all of its downstream interfaces. This enables all of the downstream routers to find out about this new flow of traffic. The router uses the DVMRP poison reverse information that it receives to determine the routers that are downstream with respect to this source. The router places all of the routing information that it gathers for this (source network, multicast group) pairing into its forwarding cache entry.

The list of active downstream routers will change when the router receives prune requests from its downstream neighbors.

Pruning the Tree

A pruning procedure is used to cut unused branches off the tree of paths. However, before pruning, we need to understand the concept of a leaf network (relative to a particular source network).

A succinct way to describe a leaf network is that it is "the end of the road." A LAN connected to the world by only one router is a leaf. For example, in Figure 10.19, relative to source LAN 1:

- Router C has a leaf interface connecting to leaf LAN 2.

- Router D has a leaf interface connecting to leaf LAN 3.

- Router E has a leaf interface connecting to leaf LAN 4.

- Router B has a leaf interface connecting to leaf LAN 6.

- Router B does *not* have a leaf interface to LAN 5. LAN 5 is not a leaf network because it is a link on the path to downstream Router E.

It is important to keep in mind that you start by specifying the source network and then define leaf networks for that source. For example, LAN 1 is a leaf network for traffic that is sent from LAN 2.

Figure 10.19
Identifying leaf interfaces and leaf LANs.

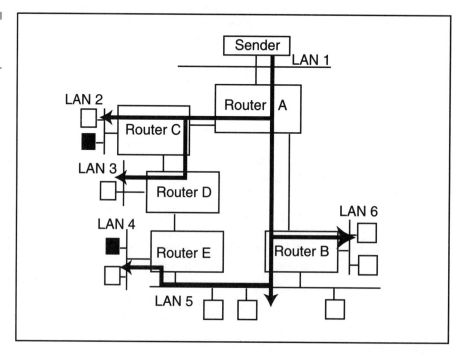

Pruning starts at the leaf networks for a given source and works its way back up the tree. An example may make this clearer. We will prune the tree shown in Figure 10.19 for source network LAN 1 and the group whose members are represented by the black boxes. Each router must check its leaf networks.

- Router C serves LAN 2. Router C checks its local IGMP group database and sees that a host on LAN 2 has signed up for this multicast. Hence Router C must continue to receive datagrams for this group.

- Router D makes a similar check. No hosts on LAN 3 have signed up for this multicast. Furthermore, there is no path from Router D to any downstream routers. Hence, Router D does not need to receive datagrams for this group. The stage now is set for a prune request.

- Router D sends a DVMRP Prune message to Router C, stating that it does not want traffic for this (source network, multicast group) pair. Router C will stop forwarding the traffic for this group to Router D, and will flag this downstream interface as pruned.

- Router B notes that no host on LAN 6 has signed up for the multicast. But Router B cannot ask to be pruned because it must forward traffic to downstream Router E.

- A host on leaf LAN 4 has signed up for the multicast. Hence this path is needed. However, if the host on LAN 4 quits the group, then Router E will send a prune message to Router B and Router B will send a prune message to router A.

Pruning is not permanent. A timeout is associated with each pruned interface. After the timeout, data to the group will start to flow down a pruned path again. If there still are no group members, the downstream routers repeat the prune requests.

Grafting onto the Tree

When a host that is connected to a pruned branch joins a multicast, the adjacent router will use graft messages to undo the prunes that are in place. The graft has to be sent to every upstream router that has been sent a prune.

Figure 10.20
Grafting a branch
back onto the tree.

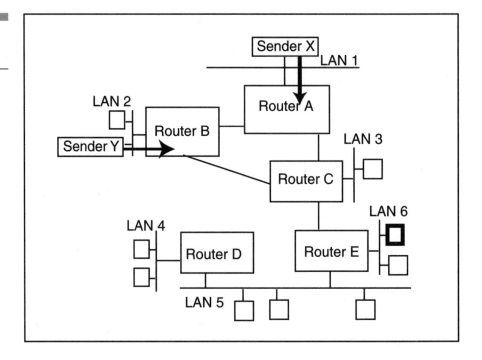

For example, in Figure 10.20, there are two senders, but currently there are no receivers. If a host on LAN 6 joins the multicast, then Router E must take action to undo the prunes. Earlier, Router E sent two separate prune messages to Router C for this group. One was used to roll back the path from Sender X and the other rolled back the path from Sender Y.

Router E starts the grafting process by sending a graft message to Router C.[5] Router C needs to send a graft message to Router A to cancel the prune for LAN 1 (Sender X) and a separate graft message to Router B to cancel the prune for LAN 2 (Sender Y). Grafts continue until paths to all of this multicast's senders have been restored.

Some DVMRP Protocol Details

DVMRP is considered to be part of IGMP. Its messages are carried by IP datagrams whose protocol field is set to 2, the IGMP protocol number. A DVMRP message starts immediately after the IP header.

---

[5]Since it is important to know whether or not a graft has been received, graft messages are acknowledged. A graft will be retransmitted if it is not acknowledged within a timeout period.

The protocol is similar to RIP in many ways. Every interface is configured with a metric equal to 1 or more. The total metric for a path is the sum of the metrics. Routers exchange routing table entries on a periodic basis.

There also are some important differences. The reporting period is 60 seconds. If there is a large number of routes to report, a router will split up its list into pieces and spread the transmission across subintervals of the 60-second period. To speed up the discovery of routing changes, additional "flash" updates can be sent as needed.

The DVMRP message types are listed below. The numbers at the left are the message type numbers.

1	DVMRP Probe	Discover neighbor routers.
2	DVMRP Report	Exchange route information.
7	DVMRP Prune	Ask a neighbor to prune the sending router from a multicast delivery list.
8	DVMRP Graft	Ask a neighbor to add the sending router to a multicast delivery list.
9	DVMRP Graft Ack	Graft requests need to be acknowledged.

Multicast Extensions to OSPF

DVMRP is a new and separate routing protocol that builds its own routing table. The sole purpose of DVMRP is to create and maintain multicast path information. The creators of Multicast Extensions to OSPF (MOSPF) took a different approach. They enlarged the OSPF protocol to perform multicast routing. OSPF enables routers to build a map that describes all of the routers and links in an area. MOSPF adds information that identifies where group members are located.

Initially, we can simplify the discussion by discussing multicasts that occur within a single OSPF area. (Also, we do not discuss the special considerations needed when a router is itself a member of a multicast group.)

Recall[6] that an OSPF router exchanges network topology information with other routers in its area that enables it to build a map of the area. The OSPF router then can calculate the shortest-path route to any destination in the area. MOSPF routers exchange some additional information. Each router announces whether it forwards datagrams onto LANs

---

[6]See Chapter 8.

that contain active members of a multicast group. All routers will receive this information, so any MOSPF router can calculate the shortest-path tree that connects a sender to the networks that contain active receivers.[7]

MOSPF Source-Rooted Trees

Like any OSPF path, an MOSPF path between a multicast datagram source and destination will be a least-cost path. The cost metric is based on factors such as bandwidth and delay.

An MOSPF router builds a tree of multicast paths on an as-needed basis. That is, when a router receives a datagram with a new (source network, multicast group) pairing, it will calculate the tree of paths leading from the source network to networks that contain active multicast receivers.

There is one technicality. Normally, OSPF allows traffic to be split across multiple paths to a destination. MOSPF has to choose a unique path between a sender's LAN and each destination network that contains multicast members. MOSPF paths are calculated by adding tie-breaking rules to the algorithm that computes the shortest paths for OSPF.

MOSPF Forwarding Cache Entries

MOSPF has one feature in common with DVMRP. When a router receives a multicast datagram for a new (source network, multicast group) combination, it creates a *forwarding cache* entry for this combination. After building a (source network, multicast group) tree, the router can easily extract the small amount of information that it actually needs in order to route an incoming multicast datagram. If the router is on a path in the tree, the router can store:

- The upstream node and the interface from which datagrams for the (source network, multicast group) pairing should be received.
- The list of outgoing interfaces leading to downstream branches of the tree.

Since MOSPF routing information identifies the remote networks that contain group members, the router can maintain up-to-date information on which downstream interfaces lead to group members.

---

[7]Like OSPF, separate trees could be built for each IP Type-of-Service value.

The forwarding cache contains entries for each (source network, destination group) pairing for which this router:

- Has received at least one datagram.
- Belongs to the corresponding tree for the (source network, multicast group) for the datagram.

A router discards its forwarding cache after a topology change because the trees must be recalculated. If there were no topology changes, cache entries could be kept indefinitely. (However, if available router memory runs low, the router can reclaim space occupied by entries that have not been used for a long time.)

MOSPF Designated Router

Recall that in order to cut out unnecessary replicated OSPF topology transmissions, a single Designated Router is elected to transmit routing updates onto a LAN. If the network contains a mixture of OSPF and MOSPF routers, an MOSPF-capable router must be selected as the OSPF Designated Router. This router then will be the only one configured to:

- Keep track of group memberships on the attached LAN.[8]
- Report the presence of active multicast group members to other routers
- Transmit multicasts onto the multiaccess network.

It is easy to assure that an MOSPF router is chosen to be the Designated Router. Selection is carried out via an election process that depends on configured priority numbers. If non-MOSPF routers are assigned a priority value of 0, the rules assure that none of them can be selected to be the Designated Router.

Multicasting Across Multiple Areas

An OSPF border router passes summary information about its attached area (or areas) to the OSPF backbone and routes datagrams between areas and the backbone. Similarly, selected MOSPF border routers need to play a role in routing multicast datagrams between areas.

---

[8]It does this by sending the periodic IGMP Membership Queries and listening for IGMP Host membership reports.

One or more of the MOSPF border routers for an area is configured to be an *inter-area multicast forwarder.* An inter-area multicast forwarder has two special responsibilities:

- It tells neighboring backbone routers which (area, multicast group) combinations have active members.
- It is responsible for transmitting multicast datagrams between areas.

As shown in Figure 10.21, backbone routers learn which areas contain active members of a group in a straightforward way. For example, Router A is an inter-area multicast forwarder for Area 1, and reports that the area contains receivers for group G1. This information will propagate to all MOSPF backbone routers. If multicast traffic addressed G1 originates outside of area 1, backbone routers will forward it to area 1.

Although the backbone is all knowing, it will not export this information to other areas. For example, routers internal to Area 1 will not learn that the backbone has receivers for groups G1 and G3, or that Area 2 has receivers for groups G2 and G3.

Then how does multicast traffic get forwarded out of an area? A somewhat odd mechanism called "wild-card receiver" routers is used:

- A wild-card receiver for an area automatically belongs to all multicast groups.
- Every inter-area multicast forwarder router is a wild-card receiver for any (nonbackbone) area that it belongs to.

Put another way, an inter-area multicast forwarder acts like a magnet for multicast datagrams in its area. For example, Router A in Figure

Figure 10.21
Reporting group
memberships to the
backbone.

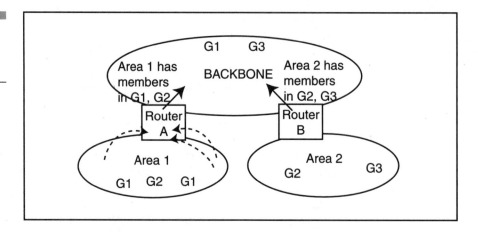

10.21 will receive all multicast traffic that originates in its area. Since Router A also belongs to the backbone, Router A knows that the backbone contains receivers for groups G1 and G2 and Area 2 contains receivers for groups G2 and G3. Whenever Router A receives datagrams addressed to G1, G2, or G3, it will forward them across the backbone to their destinations.

Mixed Environments

Only OSPF routers that have been upgraded to MOSPF can participate in multicast routing. This means that in a network that contains OSPF and MOSPF routers, the OSPF routers are invisible with respect to multicasts. The scope of a mixed network is restricted to the network spanned by contiguous MOSPF routers.

MOSPF Protocol Mechanisms

A number of OSPF protocol message additions have been defined in order to support multicasting. The most important addition is the Group-membership Link State Advertisement. This message reports one or more locations that contain members of one specific multicast group.

A router sends an advertisement for multicast group G if it is the Designated Router for one or more networks that contain hosts that have joined group G. The advertisement will include:

- The multicast address for group G.
- A list of router interface addresses for the attached networks containing members of group G. (The router must be the Designated Router for each attached network in the list.)

Two other features are small, but important:

- An extra option flag (called the Multicast Capable or MC-bit) in the OSPF Hello message enables a multicast OSPF router to announce that it is capable of performing MOSPF multicast routing.
- Recall that an OSPF router describes its attached links to other routers by means of a router Link State Advertisement message. A flag has been added to this message to enable an MOSPF router to announce that it is a wild-card multicast receiver.

Recall that routers that forward multicast datagrams between areas need to become wild-card receivers.

MOSPF Overhead

Every router needs to provide and maintain information that identifies the LANs that contain active group members. If a router lies on several paths that connect sources to destinations, it might need to calculate a large number of shortest path trees. In a large network with volatile group memberships, the computing overhead can be quite substantial.

Protocol Independent Multicast

You might think that two multicast routing protocols were more than enough, but there are other approaches that are being tried. As its name suggests, Protocol Independent Multicast (PIM) generates multicast routes using routing information gathered by any of the popular unicast routing protocols. There are two very different versions of PIM:

- *Protocol Independent Multicast-Dense Mode* (PIM-DM) works best when multicast members are densely distributed across an internetwork—in other words, when there are group members spread across many of the LANs on an internetwork.

- *Protocol Independent Multicast-Sparse Mode* (PIM-SM) is tailored for environments whose sender and receiver networks are sparsely distributed across an internetwork. The Sparse Mode mechanisms are especially helpful when there are wide-area links in the internetwork; multicast traffic will never be sent across these links when there are no active recipients at the remote end.

Protocol Independent Multicast-Dense Mode

Like DVMRP, Protocol Independent Multicast-Dense Mode (PIM-DM) initially floods traffic through a network to every router. In this way, every router becomes aware of (sender network, multicast group) pairings.

The routing table that has been built by whatever unicast protocol is in use is consulted when routing information is needed. A router uses that routing table to compute the path back to a sending source and identify the upstream interface for that path. The shortest path back from a destination to the source will be reversed and followed by traffic from the source to that destination. If two or more paths are equally good, the upstream router with the highest IP address is chosen and breaks the tie.

Unlike DVMRP, there is no poison reverse mechanism that enables downstream routers to announce themselves. Traffic arriving on a valid upstream interface is transmitted out of all other interfaces until the router receives prune requests from its neighbors. Branches are truncated using prune messages and regrown—either automatically after a prune timeout, or before the timeout, using PIM-graft messages.

Like DVMRP, routers connected to the same LAN announce themselves—in this case, using PIM-hello messages. A router attached to the LAN knows whether another router on the LAN is upstream, but it does not know whether any router on the LAN is downstream. As a result, a special procedure is required to figure out when to prune a branch that passes through the LAN. The procedure is illustrated in the simple configuration in Figure 10.22.

In the figure, a sender on LAN 1 is transmitting multicast datagrams to members of multicast group G, which are represented by the black boxes. LAN 4 has no more members, so Router D wishes to prune this

Figure 10.22
Staying aware of downstream links.

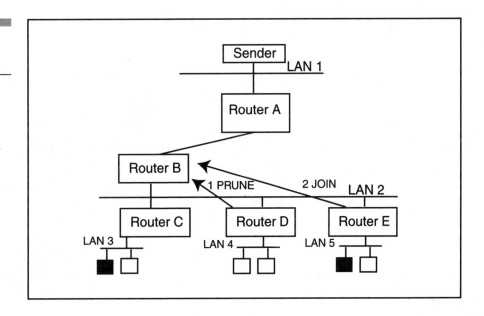

branch. Router D multicasts[9] a prune message onto LAN 2 so that it will be heard by all of the routers on the LAN. The message identifies Router B as its upstream router.

Now Router B has to decide whether to send a prune message upstream to remove LAN 2 from the tree. Router B is the upstream router for Router C and Router E and they still serve group members. It is up to them to prevent Router B from pruning LAN 2. After hearing Router D's prune request, each schedules a PIM-Join multicast request to nullify the prune. However, after the first request has been sent, the other one is not needed. Router B will know that LAN 2 must not be pruned.

Figure 10.23 illustrates another feature of Dense Mode PIM. There is more than one upstream path to a sender from LAN 2 and initially, both Router B and Router G will transmit the same multicast datagrams onto LAN 2. When a router receives datagrams on the same interface on which it is sending them, the router transmits a PIM-Assert LAN multicast message that announces its distance to the sender. The router with the shorter distance (Router B in this case) is

---

[9]The message is sent to the special PIM routers address 224.0.0.13.

Figure 10.23

Choosing the router that will forward multicasts from LAN 1.

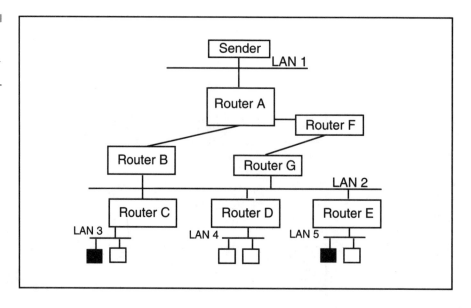

elected to be the one that will continue to forward datagrams from this sender.

Protocol Independent Multicast-Sparse Mode

The multicast protocols that we have discussed so far require a lot of active effort on the part of all routers and generate a fair amount of overhead traffic. Sparse Mode PIM was designed to reduce overhead when there are many multicast streams and there are relatively few recipient LANs for each stream. For example, sparse mode works well when there are many small separate conferences on an internetwork—especially when some wide-area links have to be crossed.

DVMRP and PIM-DM send multicasts throughout a network until told to stop by a prune request. Sparse Mode PIM is designed so that a no multicast datagrams ever are transmitted to a destination LAN that does not contain members of the group.

Sparse Mode Rendezvous Point

The trick that makes this work is to have a prespecified router act as a relay point between the senders and receivers for a group. This router is called a *Rendezvous Point* (RP) for the group. An RP must be known to every router in the internetwork ahead of time. Figure 10.24 shows the flow of traffic between senders and receivers.

Encapsulating and Sending to the Rendezvous Point

In Figure 10.24 when Sender 1 begins to transmit multicast datagrams to group G, adjacent Router A looks up the address of the Rendezvous Point for group G. Router A encapsulates the multicast datagrams within unicast datagrams addressed to the RP. The RP unwraps the multicast datagrams and forwards them down paths leading to recipients.

Router E follows the same procedure for multicasts to group G from Sender 2. The heavy black arrows in the figure represent encapsulated traffic.

Figure 10.24
Routing through a
Rendezvous Point.

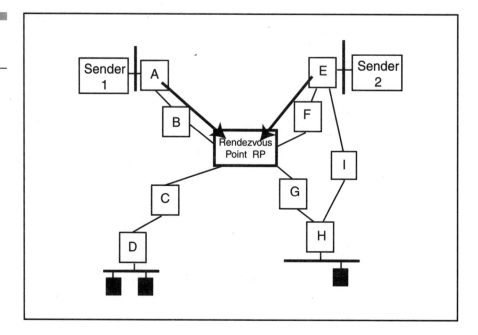

Building a Path Between the RP and a Receiver

Now we need to build the paths from an RP to the receivers for the group. In Figure 10.24, Router D knows that hosts on its adjacent LAN have joined Group G. Router D needs to build a path to the Rendezvous Point for the group and let the RP know that it wants to receive the datagrams for the group. The path between Router D and the RP is made up of the chain of upstream routers leading from Router D to the RP.

To get the ball rolling, Router D checks its routing table and sees that Router C is its upstream router on the way to RP. As shown in Figure 10.25:

- Router D sends a join message to Router C.
- Router C records the fact that downstream Router D leads to members of Group G.
- Router C sends a join to the Rendezvous Point.

Each node now has the information needed to transmit datagrams down the path to members adjacent to Router D. If later the members on LAN 1 quit the group, the Router D will send a prune message up the tree and lop off that branch.

Figure 10.25
Building a path to
the RP with join
messages.

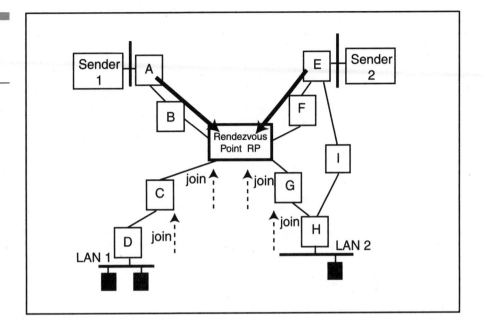

The same procedure is used to mark out a path from the RP to Router H—and to lop it off if there are no receivers. One advantage of using an RP is that if there are no receivers for Group G in the entire internetwork, the RP will know it. The RP will send messages to encapsulating routers cutting off transmission for a period of time.

Improving Performance Under Heavy Traffic

If a sender transmits steadily and at a high transmission rate, using an RP can cause performance problems:

- Encapsulation and decapsulation add overhead.
- The RP can become a bottleneck if there are several heavy senders.
- Traffic is not following the most efficient route to its destinations.

Performance can be improved in two stages:

- Build a transmission path from a heavy sender to the RP so that encapsulation is not needed.

■ Switch the entire path between a source and destination from the RP path to the optimal path.

The sections that follow describe these stages.

Building a Path Between the Sender and the RP

Based on some configured threshold, the RP can decide that a sender's traffic is too heavy and should not be encapsulated. The RP starts to build a normal multicast path between the RP and the sender by transmitting a join request to the upstream router on the path to the sender. The join is repeated until the path is established all the way to the router adjacent to the sender.

For example, suppose that in Figure 10.26, Sender 3 on LAN 5 transmits a heavy load of traffic:

■ The RP sends a join request for (Sender 3, Group G) to upstream Router F.

Figure 10.26

Replacing encapsulation with a path.

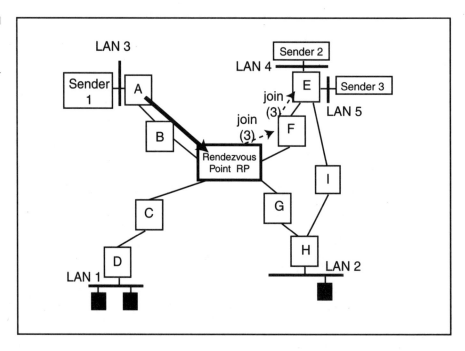

■ Router F sends a join request for (Sender 3, Group G) to upstream Router E.

This creates a path for traffic from Sender 3 to the RP. This sender's traffic will not be encapsulated, although traffic from other senders still may be encapsulated.

Switching the Entire Path

One result of building a path from the sender to the RP instead of encapsulating the datagrams is that a destination router will see the actual address of the sender. If the rate of traffic from the sender exceeds a local threshold, the destination router can send a join to the upstream router that leads to the sender.

For example, in Figure 10.27, Router H is receiving a heavy flow of traffic from Sender 3 to Group G.

■ Router H sends a join request for (Sender 3, Group G) to upstream Router I.

Figure 10.27
Bypassing the RP.

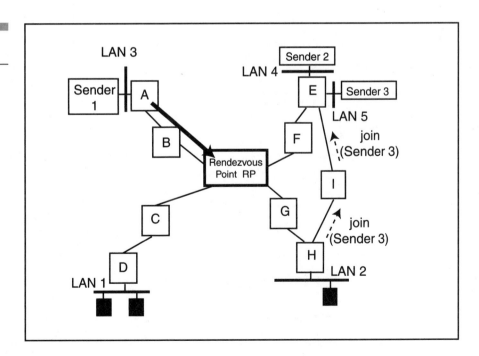

- Router I sends a join request for (Sender 3, Group G) to upstream Router E.

This establishes the optimal path for multicast datagrams from Sender 3 to Router H. When traffic starts to arrive down this path, the destination router can prune itself from the RP tree.

Some Sparse Mode Protocol Mechanisms

We list just a few of the mechanisms used for Sparse Mode PIM. Some of them are similar to those already described for Dense Mode PIM:

- Identifying LAN neighbors via *hello* messages.
- In case of conflict, electing a router that forwards datagrams for a group onto a LAN via Assert messages.
- Choosing a Designated Router for a LAN.

The Designated Router:

- Keeps track of group memberships for the LAN.
- Sends join and prune requests upstream. Joins and prunes are sent upstream very efficiently. All joins and prunes for all groups are gathered into a list and sent in a single join/prune message.
- Encapsulates outgoing traffic from local senders and transmits it to the RP.

Where Is the Group's Rendezvous Point?

Several methods have been suggested for propagating information about the location of RPs for given multicast groups. One method uses an election mechanism to choose a bootstrap router that selects RPs and notifies other routers of their existence. Candidate RPs then register with the bootstrap router. Currently, there is ongoing experimentation with several other setup methods.

MBONE

MBONE stands for *Multicast Backbone*. The Internet MBONE is a testbed for multicast protocols, and much of the multicast technology that currently is available was created for and tested on the MBONE.

Participants in multicast research are spread across the Internet. They solved the problem of creating a common testbed by building a "virtual network." Multicast routing protocols are supported in parts of the Internet that are connected by tunnel paths. A tunnel path consists of hops through a series of routers that do not support a given protocol.

Figure 10.28 depicts a tunnel between Router A and Router B. Router A encapsulates datagrams with an new IP header addressed to Router B. Router B discards the extra header and forwards the datagram to its destination.

Multicast traffic is forwarded by treating the tunnel as a single link. Multicast datagrams are wrapped in an extra IP header before they enter a tunnel. The destination address in the new IP header is the router at the other end of the tunnel. At the other end, the extra IP header is removed and multicast routing resumes.[10]

---

[10]In general, a tunnel can be used to build a connection between networks that support some given protocol across an intermediate network that does not support the protocol.

Figure 10.28
Tunneling between islands that support multicasting.

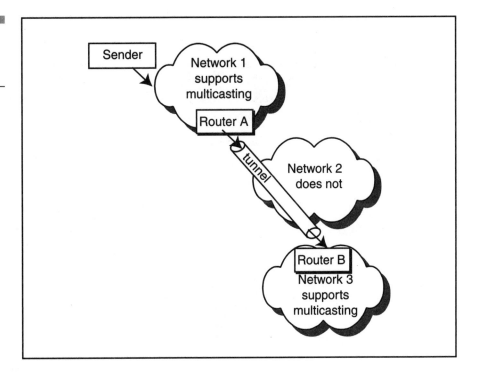

Finding Out About Multicasts

Multicast applications are truly distributed, so the problem is, how do we find them? Conference organizers need a way to announce their events, and users need a way to get information about these events. Several protocols are being developed to bring conference information to users—and bring users to conferences:

- The Session Announcement Protocol (SAP) enables users to listen to a multicast that announces multicast sessions.

- The Session Description Protocol (SDP) defines a format for information describing the time, address, and characteristics of a multicast session. SDP messages are carried in SAP announcements.

- The Session Initiation Protocol (SIP) is a protocol that invites users to join a conference and start their sessions. SIP is analogous to a telephone "conference call" setup capability.

The Session Announcement Protocol publishes events via repeated multicasts to IP address 224.2.127.254, and UDP application port 9875. Users can "tune in" to this multicast address and pick up information that has been formatted according to the rules of the Session Description Protocol.

Alternatively, formatted session description information can be made available in session description files stored at World Wide Web servers,[11] included in email messages, or distributed by means of other protocols.

The Session Description Protocol defines the format of announcement messages that include:

- The name of the conference and its purpose
- Contact information for the conference organizers
- The start and end time of the conference
- Types of media—for example, text, voice, video
- Transport protocol and format of each media type
- Multicast addresses and ports at which to receive each of the media types
- Bandwidth requirements

---

[11]At the time of writing, a URL design for session description files still was in an early draft stage.

IPv6 Multicast Listener Discovery Protocol

The job performed by IGMP for IP version 4 has been assigned to the version 6 *Multicast Listener Discovery* (MLD) protocol. The behavior of routers and hosts has not been changed. However, the IGMP messages are replaced with ICMP version 6 messages. The ICMPv6 messages are described in Chapter 23.

RSVP

We have studied many ways to route traffic from multicast senders to receivers. Next we examine the *Resource Reservation Protocol* (RSVP), which enables a receiver to request resources for an incoming flow of data. The goal of a reservation is to:

- Limit the delivery delay.
- Improve reliability.

RSVP's designers have focused most of their attention on multicast applications. That is why the topic is being presented within this chapter. However, RSVP can be used for ordinary client/server interactions. The material that will be presented will apply equally well to normal unicast traffic when you replace multicast addresses with unicast addresses and allow for the use of TCP.

We do not try to tell the whole story of RSVP here. The details are voluminous and are still changing. Along the way, we will set some boundaries on the discussion in order to keep it simple. The goal of the discussion that follows is to provide a solid understanding of the core of ideas that form and motivate the protocols. Details that would distract from the thread of explanation have been omitted intentionally.

Resource Reservation Protocol

Have you ever done a really big file download and been frustrated when the data transfer rate slowed to a crawl? Wouldn't it be nice to be able to tell the network to clear a path for you so that the data could zoom across the network to your system? That is a wish that RSVP could fulfill. RSVP enables a receiver to request that network resources be reserved for a particular data flow along a path from the sender to the receiver.

What RSVP Can Do

RSVP is designed to improve performance for a particular data receiver. RSVP:

- Enables a receiver to reserve network resources for selected data flowing toward the receiver.
- Automatically adapts to routing changes.
- Automatically adapts to changes in the population of senders and receivers.

RSVP has been designed so that it could work with protocol families other than TCP/IP. However, the discussion in this chapter is restricted to TCP/IP.

It is unlikely that an organization will update all of its routers overnight. In early stages of implementation, RSVP probably will be available for islands of hosts and routers. The RSVP specifications describe how tunneling can be used to tie these islands together. An RSVP tunnel path consists of hops through a series of routers that do not support RSVP. Figure 10.28 illustrated how a tunnel works.

Unfortunately, it often will be impossible to control packet loss and delay for datagrams that are tunneled across an intervening non-RSVP network. The remaining discussion in this chapter will ignore the use of tunnels.

RSVP Sessions

Previously in this book, "session" has meant a TCP session.[12] An RSVP "session" is different. It is a data flow to a destination address. Formally, a RSVP session is defined by the following parameters:

---

[12]A TCP session is identified by the unique pairing of the client and server source and destination IP addresses and port numbers.

- A destination IP address.

- Transport protocol used (UDP or TCP).

- Destination port number.[13] Some implementations may enable users to select a specific stream of data by specifying application level parameters—such as a MIME data type.

We will concentrate on the case when the destination IP address is a multicast address, UDP is the transport protocol used, and a destination port number identifies the flow. For a multicast address, an RSVP session can include traffic that flows from many different senders to many different receivers.

Moving to RSVP

It is RSVP's job to help receivers reserve network resources when the performance that they get from normal best-effort delivery is not good enough. But RSVP software must be installed in senders, receivers, and intermediate routers before RSVP can be used.

Users will not change the way that they establish sessions or tune in to multicasts. Users whose performance is satisfactory will not need to take any action at all. But we can expect that sometimes multimedia performance will need a boost. Those for whom sound fades in and out or images are poor can invoke RSVP to improve reception.

Using RSVP

RSVP software in a client will ask for enough "resources" to be set aside for a flow of data so that it can be delivered in a timely fashion at an acceptable level of reliability. But what are these "resources"?

- The most obvious is bandwidth. RSVP enables receiver clients to request that bandwidth be set aside for a flow.

- Priority queues are important resources. Even though bandwidth may have been reserved, datagrams may be prevented from getting onto the medium because there is a queue of data-

---

[13]The port number usually is included, although it is optional for multicasts.

Figure 10.29
Improving reservation
performance using
priority queuing.

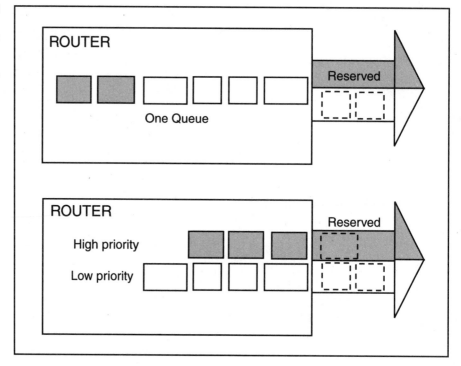

grams blocking their way, as shown in the upper half of Figure 10.29. Using separate queues identified according to priority smoothes the way, as shown in the lower half of Figure 10.29.

■ Extra queue memory set aside to prevent packet loss is another resource. Voice and video are very likely to be sent in compressed form, which means that the actual traffic will be bursty. Sometimes a short burst of traffic will arrive at a router at a higher rate than the outgoing reserved bandwidth could handle. To prevent packet loss, a router must be capable of storing some amount of overflow temporarily until it can be sent.

Throughput, delay, and controlled packet loss are factors that relate to the *Quality of Service* (QoS) for a flow of data. Delivering a desired Quality of Service is what RSVP is all about. But the exact characteristics that are needed for "good" service will vary from application to application.

For example, a user performing a file transfer wants the overall transmission time to be as short as possible. Traffic loss should be kept to a minimum to prevent retransmissions and slow starts. On the other hand, the most important factor for voice and video data is timely delivery. Loss of some data can be handled better than late arrival of a noticeable amount—"better never than late!" Clearly, an effective reservation service must offer several classes of QoS, each tailored to the needs of a kindred family of applications.

QOS Classes

Measuring and describing a Quality of Service in concise, quantitative terms is not a simple matter. At the time of writing, two classes of service have been defined:

- Guaranteed service provides a high level of protection against data loss and establishes a firm bound on queuing delays.
- Controlled-load service delivers a flow of data so that even on a busy network, the performance approximates that of an unloaded network.

Finding Out What Resources Are Needed

A receiver uses RSVP to ask for a specific Quality of Service and sufficient resources to improve performance. But there is no point in making a reservation that asks for more than is needed for a flow or is more than the network can deliver. To create a sensible reservation request, a receiver needs know:

- Which Quality of Service classes are supported by the network.
- The traffic characteristics of the flow of data coming from a sender.

Path Messages

Each sender provides key information in special RSVP "Path" messages. These messages are periodically transmitted downstream to all group recipients.[14] These Path messages contain the data that receivers—and routers along the way—need to know. A sender:

- Identifies a specific session (by destination IP address, protocol, and port).
- Describes the traffic characteristics of the flow of session data.
- Indicates which QoS classes it supports for the flow and adds parameters that may be needed in order to use a particular class of service.

The parameter information[15] in a Path message changes and grows as it makes its way through routers along the way:

- Routers indicate whether they also can support the QoS classes supported by the source.
- Routers update some of the parameter values. For example, a router updates the Path MTU, adds its own path latency to the sum of the path latencies,[16] and adds its own delays to several delay variables.

Information from the Path message is stored at each node traversed by the message:

- Each router and recipient stores a pointer to the neighboring upstream node from which the Path message was forwarded.
- Routers and recipients extract and store traffic and delay parameters.

Figure 10.30 illustrates what happens when a Path message is forwarded through the network. It is processed at every node along the way and leaves behind a back pointer to the previous node along with information about a flow of data.

A Path message that contains information about a data flow to a multicast group must be forwarded to every member of the group. Figure 10.31 shows how a path message is propagated to receivers spread

---

[14]The recipient IP address for a Path message is the receiver's (unicast or multicast) address. However, the message is briefly held and processed by each router along the way.

[15]This information is stored in a part of the Path message called the ADSPEC.

[16]Formally, what is computed is the "minimum path latency." The minimum path latency for a network node is the delay caused by packet processing and transmission across the next link. It does not include any queuing delay.

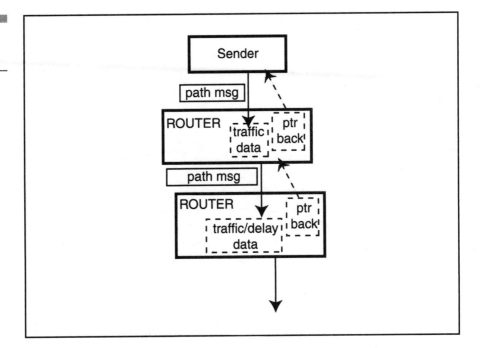

Figure 10.30
Processing a Path
message.

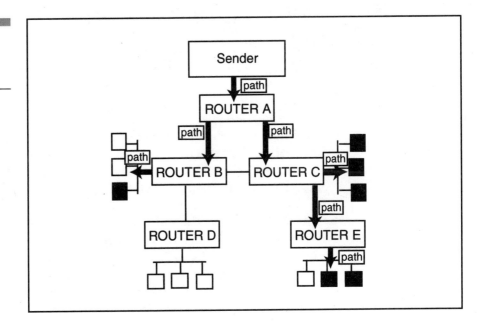

Figure 10.31
Propagating Path
messages to
receivers.

across the network. Router A is a *splitting point*—after receiving a Path message, Router A needs to generate two outgoing messages. Router C also is a splitting point. Routers that are splitting points for downstream Path messages will be "merging points" for upstream RSVP requests.

Timing Out Paths

An originating sender includes a refresh timeout value in a Path message. This indicates the approximate interval after which the sender will renew the Path information. Stored path information will expire unless the sender renews it within a configured multiple (often 3) times the refresh timeout.

The periodic transmission of fresh Path messages and the timing out of stale information automatically take care of route changes. Path messages sent after a route change will follow the new route and plant new path pointers. The timeout limit ensures that old data will age out and be discarded.

Making a Reservation

A client now is ready to construct an RSVP reserve (Resv) message. Recall that a session is defined by a destination IP address, protocol, and port number. A client's Resv message asks for resources and a specific QoS for a session.

When the traffic destination is a multicast IP address, there can be many different senders for a session. The Resv message can apply to all senders or can list exactly those senders that should be covered by the RSVP request.

For example, in Figure 10.32, Senders 1, 2, and 3 are transmitting video data to a group. Receiver X is a member of that group. Receiver X has no problem with the delivery performance for nearby Sender 3. Receiver X transmits a reservation that asks for enough resources to cover the traffic from both Sender 1 and Sender 2. Note that the link between Router A and Router B will have to carry the combined traffic from Senders 1 and 2. The bandwidth reserved on that link will be the sum of the bandwidths for Sender 1 and Sender 2.

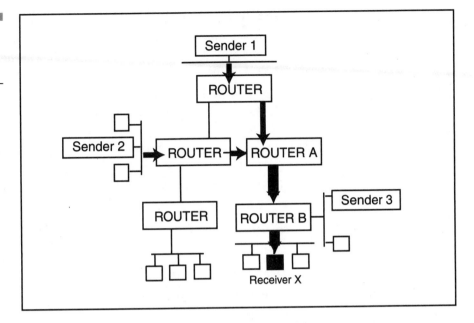

Figure 10.32
Reserving resources
for data from specific
senders.

The RSVP request message needs to be processed by:

■ Every sender covered by the reservation.

■ Every router on the backward path (or paths) between the receiver and the sender (or senders).

Fortunately, as was shown in Figure 10.30, prior Path messages will have left behind trails of pointers that mark out the paths to senders. A receiver transmits its request to the appropriate upstream router that leads to a sender. That router processes the request and either rejects it or forwards it upstream.

Resv Message

The required components of a Resv message include:

■ The session identifier—the destination address, protocol identifier, and the destination port.

■ The IP address of the node that forwarded the Resv message. For the first hop, this will be the client that originates the reservation. For later hops this field will contain the address of the prior neighbor router.

- A set of traffic and Quality of Service parameters for the flow.
- The reservation "style" which indicates whether separate bandwidth is being reserved for each sender or whether several senders will share one block of reserved bandwidth.
- Either a "wild card" indication that all senders should be included or the IP addresses and port numbers of each sender covered by the request.
- A refresh timeout that indicates the approximate time until the client will renew the reservation. A reservation will expire unless the client renews it within a configured multiple of the refresh timeout.

There are some optional parameters that can be included in the reservation request:

- Information that authenticates the client.
- A request for a confirmation of the reservation.
- An explicit list of sender hosts to which the information in the message is to be forwarded.
- Other information that enables a policy application to decide whether the reservation is administratively permitted.

Getting Permission from Policy Control

If bandwidth were free and infinite, then anyone could ask for reserved bandwidth and get it. But in the real world, limits need to be placed on the total amount of bandwidth that is available for reservations and on who has the right to get it. This means that two questions need to be answered as part of the reservation process:

- Are there enough resources available to meet this request?
- Is this user authorized to make this request?

In order to answer these questions, mechanisms are needed to:

- Configure limits on how much of the available bandwidth or memory can be reserved. Some resources need to be preserved for ordinary best effort traffic.

- Test a new request to see whether the node has enough reservable resources to satisfy the request. This is called "admission control."
- Establish authorization criteria.
- Test a new request against the authorization criteria. This is called "policy control."

Overall resource limits can be set up as part of host and router configuration. Policy control will be based on authentication information and policy control data that will (eventually) be included in reservation requests. At the time of writing, the structure and content of policy control data was still being developed.

Terminating a Reservation

As noted earlier, a reservation will automatically time out if it is not renewed in a timely fashion. However, systems that are good network citizens release reserved resources that they no longer need. They do this by sending an RSVP teardown message (ResvTear). There are two different types of teardown messages—a reservation teardown and a path teardown.

A receiver end-system sends a ResvTear message up the path tree towards servers. The message is forwarded only as far as it needs to go in order to prune back the flow tree. In Figure 10.33, Receivers X, Y, and Z have set up reserved resources for the same multicast flow. When Receiver X sends a teardown message up the path tree:

- Router B releases all of the resources reserved for the flow.
- Router A releases the bandwidth on Link 5 and the reserved queue memory for Link 5.

However, if Receiver Y sends a teardown message, no resources are freed. The previously reserved bandwidth resources for Links 1, 2, and 3 and queue memory in Routers A, C, and E still are needed to serve Receiver Z.

There is another way for resources to be released. One of the senders covered by a reservation may decide to stop transmitting data to the group. The sender frees resources by sending a PathTear message down the tree. A router also may send a PathTear message. This could be trig-

Figure 10.33
Pruning a
reservation.

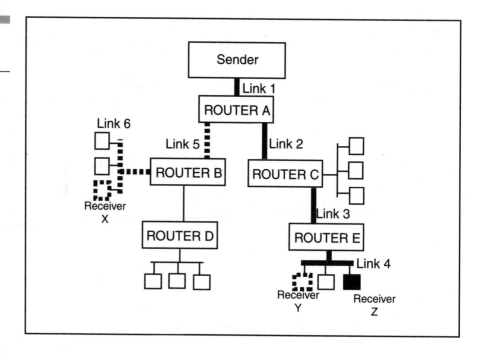

Figure 10.33
Pruning a
reservation.

gered by a timeout of Path or Resv information, or by the loss of resources due to an event such as operator intervention.

Reservation Styles

A receiver can choose from three different *styles* of reservation. The style determines whether resources will be reserved for a specific sender, will be shared by several selected senders, or will apply to all senders.

Wildcard-Filter Style

Suppose that you were setting up a reservation for a voice conference between yourself and two other participants who are at different remote locations. You expect that normally only one person will speak at a time (although occasionally two may overlap for a brief time). It makes sense to reserve resources for just one incoming voice flow. This makes economical use of any router or link that is on more than one path; a single

Figure 10.34
Sharing bandwidth
with a Wildcard-Filter.

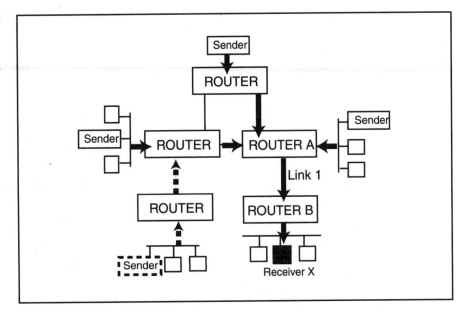

resource allocation can be shared by all of the senders since you expect traffic from only one of them at a time.

Figure 10.34 shows this configuration from the point of view of Receiver X. Note that all of the reserved flows carried to Receiver X must cross Link 1. On this link, one block of bandwidth will be shared by the traffic. Similarly, all senders will share the queue memory set aside for this reservation in Router A and Router B. This is called a *Wildcard-Filter* (WF) style. If a new party joins the group, the WF reservation made by Receiver X automatically is extended to the new sender, as shown by the dotted lines in Figure 10.34.

Shared-Explicit Filter Style

The situation depicted in Figure 10.35 is a little different. Sender 3 and Sender 4 are nearby and no reservation is needed in order to obtain excellent performance for their traffic. But Receiver X wants to set up a good path that can be shared by traffic from Sender 1 and Sender 2. In this case the Shared-Explicit (SE) style of reservation is used. Specific sources are identified and their traffic shares reserved resources at any common link or router. Currently, a sender is identified by its IP address and, optionally, the port number that is the source of the flow that it is sending.

Figure 10.35
A Shared-Explicit
reservation for
Sender 1 and
Sender 2.

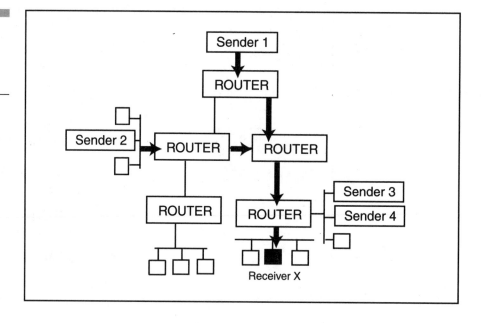

Fixed-Filter Style

Finally, Figure 10.32 showed a conferencing situation in which Sender 1 and Sender 2 transmitted video to the other participants. Receiver X wishes to make a reservation for the video data from these senders. Sender 1 and Sender 2 each must be assigned their own fixed bandwidth and memory resources. These resource allocations are added to compute the bandwidth that will be needed between Router A and Router B and the memory resources that are needed. This is called a Fixed-Filter (FF) style of reservation. Multiple Fixed-Filter allocations can be placed into the same RSVP request message. Each fixed filter sender is identified by its IP address and, optionally, source port number.

Style Summary

To summarize:

■ For the Wildcard-Filter style, all senders share the reserved resources.

■ For the Shared-Explicit style, the reserved resources are shared by a selected list of senders.

■ For the Fixed-Filter style, resources are not shared. A separate allocation is requested for each sender on a list.

Reservations and Path MTU

When a receiver makes a reservation, it applies to a specific flow of data from one or more senders. A destination port number often is used as part of the description of the flow; a source port number often is used as part of the description of a sending source.

After processing a Resv message, each router that handles the flow is supposed to give the datagrams in the flow that come from specified sources the preferred treatment that was set up by the reservation. Almost invariably, a router must examine destination—and sometimes source—port numbers in order to determine that a datagram is covered by a reservation. But if the datagram has been fragmented, fragments after the first will not carry the port numbers. The solution is to recognize that reservations and fragmentation don't mix, and prevent fragmentation.

Information in Path and Resv messages is used to avert fragmentation. A sender includes a Path_MTU parameter in its Path messages. This parameter is corrected along the way so that a multicast receiver obtains an MTU value that is small enough for every link between the sender and receiver.

A receiver that wants to reserve resources includes an MTU value in its reservation request. Since a reservation may apply to traffic generated by several senders, the MTU value in the reservation request is the minimum of the PATH_MTU values for the senders that will be included in the reservation.

Merging

A receiver's reservation request includes several parameters that describe the bandwidth and memory resources that will be needed. A router has to examine all of its current reservations when processing a new reservation request:

■ Sometimes no additional resources are needed to fulfill the request.

- Sometimes some or all of the requested resources must be added to those already set aside.

To understand this, let's look at some examples. In Figure 10.36 Receiver X has reserved separate Fixed-Filter resources for video transmissions from Sender 1 and Sender 2.

If Receiver Y asks for Fixed-Filter resources for the transmission from Sender 1:

- Router C needs to set aside resources for the reservation.
- Router B needs to set aside bandwidth on the link to Router C and reserve queue memory for the interface to that link.

The remaining routers on the path from Sender 1 (Router E and Router A) already have set aside the required bandwidth and memory. The same datagrams that they already are forwarding toward Receiver X can be sent on to Receiver Y.

If receiver Z asks for a Fixed-Filter reservation for traffic from Sender 3, totally fresh bandwidth and memory resources need to be locked in at Routers B, A, and D.

We can see that each router needs to figure out how to combine the bandwidth and memory resource parameters for a request with the parameters from other requests. This process is called *merging*.

Figure 10.36
Merging scenarios.

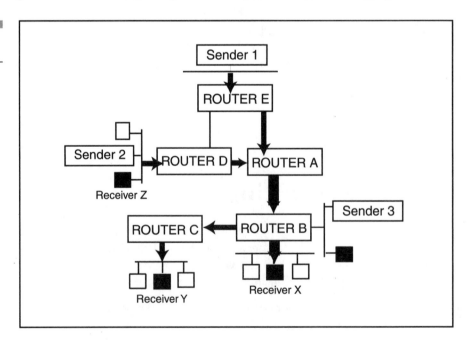

Merging the Path MTU

The Path MTU provides another example of a merged parameter. A sender must use the smallest MTU reported in RSVP requests from all RSVP receivers. Once a multicast datagram has been sent to an RSVP receiver it must not be fragmented, so the MTU size must be small enough to reach *any* RSVP receiver intact.

RSVP FLOWSPEC

The traffic parameters that determine the resources that will be needed are carried in a part of the reservation message called the FLOWSPEC. A router will replace the parameters in the FLOWSPEC with their merged values as the reservation makes its way toward the relevant senders. If possible, several incoming Resv messages are merged into one message that is forwarded up a path. The RSVP specification includes a detailed list of merging rules.

Quality of Service Classes

This section contains brief descriptions of two Quality of Service classes.

Controlled-Load Service

Users working on a healthy network that is not heavily loaded enjoy good response times and low rates of datagram loss. It is the goal of the controlled load service to approximate the behavior of an unloaded network for reserved flows, even when the network is quite busy. Specifically:

- The packet loss rate will approximate the basic packet error rate of the transmission medium.
- For a very high percentage of packets, the transit delay will not greatly exceed the minimum delay.

A client requesting a *controlled-load* reservation provides parameters that describe the traffic flow. These parameters are based on information received earlier in Path messages. Every node on the path will check whether it can reserve sufficient bandwidth, buffer memory, and computational resources so that the flow can be delivered with approximately unloaded performance.

The current controlled-load specification does not provide any quantitative description of how this should be done. It is up to individual implementers to find effective mechanisms. For example, a designer might:

- Set up a separate high-priority queue for controlled-load traffic.
- Reserve some pooled high-priority bandwidth that can be used to transmit traffic bulges that occasionally build up in flows.

Guaranteed QoS

The guaranteed service:

- Ensures that data will not be lost because of queue overflows (assuming that the flow stays within its announced traffic parameters).
- Provides a firm bound on the maximum delay for a path.

Every path has an intrinsic minimum delay that is the result of the link transmission times and datagram processing times. Real delay varies because of random queuing time in intermediate nodes. The guaranteed service provides an overall delay that has a known upper bound.

There are many factors involved in providing a guaranteed rate service, and their interaction is complex. We will examine just a few of the issues to give a sense of what is involved. Figure 10.37 shows a very simple scenario. A source transmits a flow of data at a steady rate r. There is a small, fixed processing delay at each router, and then the router forwards the data at steady state r.

Of course, the real world behaves nothing like this. Compressed voice or video data is bursty. Sometimes data is transmitted at above the average rate, sometimes below. Figure 10.38 illustrates more realistic transmission characteristics. Data sometimes is sent at below average rates and sometimes at above average rates. Queues of data that pile up in a router can cause more fluctuation, sometimes making a "bulge" larger than it was on the previous hop. However, if the average transmission rate and the sizes of incoming excess bursts are con-

Figure 10.37
Transmission with a
fixed delay.

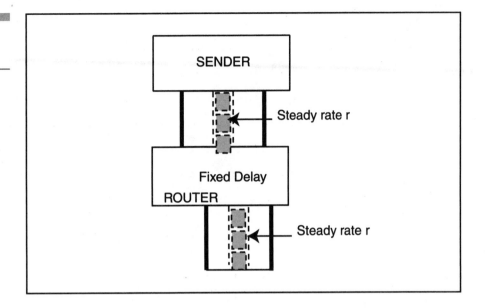

trolled, the lengths of delays and sizes of bulges will have a known maximum value.

Figure 10.39 shows traffic variations when they are averaged across time intervals of length T. Flow traffic is described by its average rate r, and the "bucket size" b which corresponds to the excess

Figure 10.38
Queued data causing
a bulge.

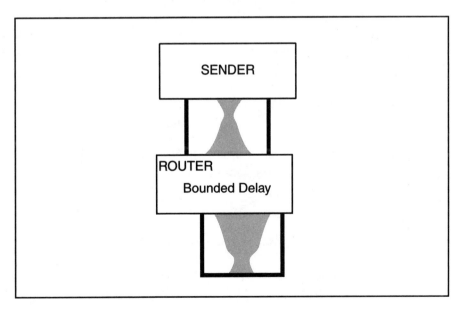

Figure 10.39
Traffic variations
averaged across time
intervals.

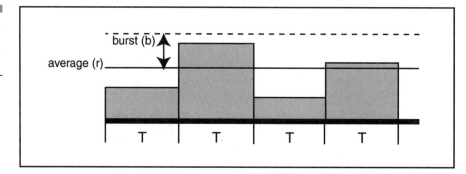

burst in the figure. Guaranteed delivery is implemented using the mechanisms:

- A bandwidth rate $R \geq r$ is reserved. Choosing a value for R that is somewhat larger than the average rate r helps to expedite the bulges on their way.

- At intermediate nodes, buffering space is reserved to take care of data bulges caused by delays along the path. Some nodes have enough buffering resources to reshape the traffic so that it fits back into its original limits.

Recall that senders describe the traffic characteristics in Path messages. Delay information is accumulated in Path messages as they make their way towards a receiver. This information is essential to providing the guaranteed service.

RSVP Message Types

We have discussed almost all of the RSVP message types. Table 10.1 contains the complete list.

Some Technical Issues

A bandwidth reservation capability is a welcome addition to the TCP/IP protocol family. However, the protocol is not entirely worry-free.

TABLE 10.1

RSVP Messages

Type	Name	Comments
1	Path	From sender. Reports sender traffic characteristics and capabilities of intermediate routers.
2	Resv	From receiver. Requests bandwidth and control of delay.
3	PathErr	Reports an error in processing a Path message. The message is forwarded toward the sender of the Path message.
4	ResvErr	Reports an error in processing a Resv message or the disruption of a reservation. The message is forwarded to appropriate receivers.
5	PathTear	From a sender with no more data to send, or a router when the refresh timer for Path data has expired. Requests deletion of stored Path variable information for a specific sender and session. The message is forwarded toward receivers.
6	ResvTear	From a receiver who wishes to terminate a reservation or a router when the refresh timer for reservation data has expired. The message is forwarded toward senders.
7	ResvConf	An acknowledgment of a Resv request, sent to systems whose Resv request asked for a confirmation. Senders provide the confirmation unless the reservation has been merged into a bigger reservation. In this case, the merging router sends the confirmation.

- At the time of writing, the protocol for inclusion of authentication information in reservation requests had not been completed. Forged reservation requests could be transmitted as part of a denial of service attack.

- Every node must play. For example, if a downstream router at one end of a point-to-point link does supports RSVP but its upstream partner does not, nothing works reliably.

- Further study is needed to define and implement policy data. Policy data is the basis for deciding whether a user has the right to reserve resources. Policy data may include authentication credentials, account numbers, limits, quotas, and so forth.

- Supporting many separate small reservation flows will drag down router performance. Even just a few big reservations may be hard to support while keeping up with very high speed interfaces.

- Organizations probably will need a chargeback system for reserved bandwidth. It is not clear how usage can be tracked and billed—especially in a multicast environment.

■ Some conference discussions will need to be private and protected. However, using the encryption capability of IP Security hides port numbers. One solution that has been suggested maps the IP Security Parameter Index (see Chapter 24) to a virtual port that is used to identify the flow.

Recommended Reading

RFC 1112 described version 1 of IGMP. RFC 2236 describes version 2. RFC 1584 presents MOSPF. DVMRP and the Protocol Independent Multicast routing protocols were still in draft form at the time of writing. RFC 2205 describes RSVP. Additional information relating to RSVP can be found in RFC 2206-2212, RFC 2215, and 2216. RFC 2327 contains the current version of the Session Description Protocol. Information about MBONE can be found at *www.mbone.com.*

11

Configuration with BOOTP and DHCP

Introduction

One of the most remarkable changes in the use of computers in recent years has been the spread of TCP/IP network connectivity to desktops across an entire enterprise. The infrastructure needed to support the growing network—routers, bridges, switches, and hubs—has been expanding at a similar rate.

Support staffs have struggled to keep up with the demand for connectivity and the frequent moves, changes, and network reconfigurations that characterize today's volatile environment. These circumstances created a need for a mechanism that could automate node configuration and distribute operating system and network software. The most effective way to do this is to store configuration parameters and software images at one or more network boot servers. At start-up time, systems interact with a boot server, get configuration parameters, and optionally retrieve an appropriate software download.

In this chapter, we describe the Bootstrap Protocol, BOOTP, and the Dynamic Host Configuration Protocol, DHCP. Both protocols are based on client/server interactions. A client requests configuration parameters and a BOOTP or DHCP server supplies them.

BOOTP was the original bootstrap configuration protocol. BOOTP did a pretty good job of providing systems with configuration parameters, but IP address configuration required a lot of tedious manual work on the part of the BOOTP server administrator. BOOTP's updated version, DHCP, can automate IP address assignment fully and has several other useful enhancements.

Configuration Protocol Requirements

Some computers require only a handful of configuration variables in order to get started. For others, it may be convenient to provide long, detailed lists of parameter values. Some systems need a software download in addition to configuration parameters in order to get going. For example, diskless computers, network computers, routers, and switches may need complete operating system software downloads.

A configuration protocol must be robust and flexible. Depending on network size, topology, and availability requirements, it might be most convenient to centralize boot information at a single server or disperse it across several servers.

Replicated servers would improve availability and response time. Unfortunately, neither BOOTP nor DHCP currently provide any support for replication.

BOOTP Capabilities

BOOTP was the first standard for automatic booting in a TCP/IP environment. After the protocol had undergone several rounds of extensions, BOOTP was able to provide systems with all of their basic configuration parameters—as well as quite a few special parameters.

BOOTP assigned IP addresses from a table of physical addresses and matching IP addresses. An administrator had to create the table at the BOOTP server manually.

The Need for DHCP

Field use of BOOTP made administrators aware that some more features were needed. Administrators wanted *automated* IP address configuration so that they would not have to type in (and maintain) long lists of hardware addresses and matching IP addresses. They also wanted foolproof IP address configuration so that if a user unplugged a system, moved it onto a desk in a different building, and plugged it into the network, the system would receive valid configuration data and could operate on the network immediately.

DHCP extended BOOTP to have these features, as well as many other capabilities. DHCP also cleaned up a number of ambiguities in BOOTP that sometimes led to less than optimal interworking.

DHCP evolved from BOOTP, and the easiest way to understand it is to start with an examination of BOOTP. BOOTP also is worth studying because there are many older systems that cannot use DHCP, and so still rely on BOOTP.

Figure 11.1
Local interaction
between a boot
client and server.

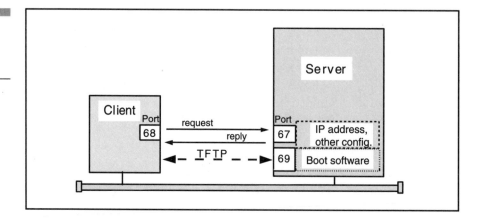

Initial Version of BOOTP

BOOTP was originally designed with diskless workstations in mind. The modest goal was to enable automatic booting even if the system started out with nothing more than some basic IP, UDP, and trivial file transfer code in Read-Only Memory. Hence, the original scenario (shown in Figure 11.1) was:

- The client broadcasts a request for information in a UDP message.
- The server returns the client's IP address, and optionally, the location of a file to be downloaded.
- The client uses the Trivial File Transfer Protocol[1] (TFTP) to download software into its memory and executes the software.

Administrators quickly realized that it would be beneficial to use BOOTP to get more configuration data and to configure systems that had disks and did not require the software download step.

For systems that did need TFTP software downloads, it often was convenient to use one server for BOOTP parameters and one or more separate servers for downloading software (as shown in Figure 11.2). For example, operating system software might best be obtained from a server with the same type of operating system as the client.

---

[1] See Chapter 14.

Figure 11.2
Using separate
servers for parame-
ters and software.

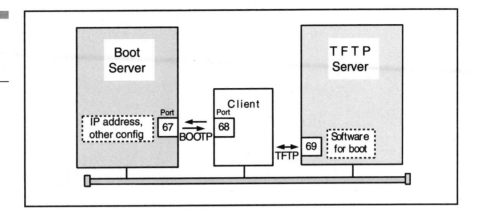

Evolution of BOOTP

BOOTP became very flexible:

- A client might have absolutely no information to start with, or the client may already have been partially configured.

- The client might be willing to accept information from any boot server, or it may wish to choose one specific server.

- The client might wish no software download, a default download, or a specific download file.

It did not take long for additional parameters—such as the subnet mask, addresses of default routers, addresses of Domain Name Servers, as well as other information—to be included in BOOTP configuration messages.

The parameter list grew and grew. Eventually, so many parameters were defined that it became quite possible that a response would not fit into a reasonably sized (unfragmented) UDP message. To solve this problem, overflow values could be entered into a configuration file that could be downloaded to the client via TFTP. A parameter that identified this file was added to the list. In fact, use of this file is rare. Most systems require only a few parameters.

Using BOOTP

In the sections that follow we take a brief look at:

■ What is involved in setting up a BOOTP server.

■ How a client interacts with a BOOTP server.

Assigning IP Addresses

A BOOTP server administrator configures IP addresses by manually creating a table that maps client hardware type/hardware address combinations to IP addresses. Sample hardware types include 1 for Ethernet and 6 for IEEE 802 networks.[2] MAC addresses are typical hardware addresses.

A tabulation could have a form such as:

Hardware Type	Hardware Address	IP Address
1	02 60 8C 12 14 AA	128.121.2.5
1	08 00 20 D3 20 14	128.121.2.19

Other implementations include another column identifying host nicknames in order to improve the readability of the table.

Most configuration parameters are easier for the administrator to deal with because they usually can be assigned to groups of computers. For example:

■ A single pair of Domain Name Server addresses might be entered for use by every computer in the network. We would say that the *scope* for the Domain Name Server address parameter is global.

■ A separate default router address could be defined for each subnet. We would say that the *scope* of a default router address is one specific subnet.

However, some parameters may apply to a single host. For example, an administrator could specify that the address of an X-Windows font server should be configured onto one specific system.

---

[2]Codes for hardware types were published in RFC 1700.

BOOTP Requests and Responses

As illustrated in Figure 11.2, BOOTP is a simple request/reply UDP application.

- The client transmits a *bootrequest* message from client port 68 to server port 67.
- The server responds with a *bootreply* message to client port 68.

A client that has no prior knowledge will send a request using an IP source address of 0.0.0.0 and a destination address of 255.255.255.255. A server on the client's LAN will hear the request. Since UDP is unreliable, the client will retransmit if no reply is received within a timeout period.

Several duplicate servers might be installed in order to assure server availability. in this case, several servers might reply, as shown in Figure 11.3. On its initial boot, a client usually accepts the first response that it receives.

BOOTP/DHCP Message Format

The same overall message format is used for *bootrequest* and *bootreply* messages. Some fields that will contain reply information are zeroed out in the request. Figure 11.4 shows the message format.

Figure 11.3
Receiving multiple responses.

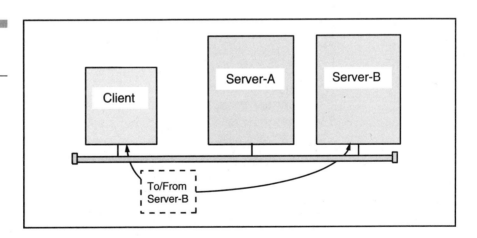

Figure 11.4
Bootrequest and
bootreply message
format.

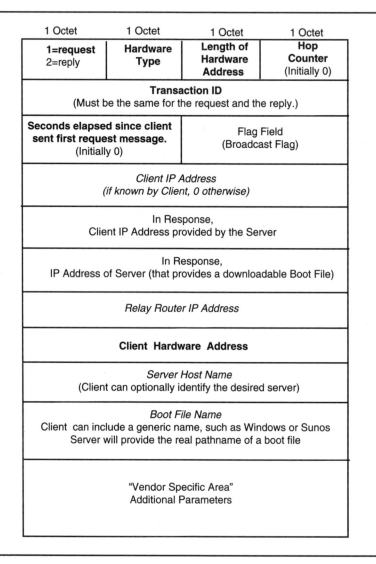

1 Octet	1 Octet	1 Octet	1 Octet
1=request **2=reply**	**Hardware** **Type**	**Length of** **Hardware** **Address**	**Hop** **Counter** (Initially 0)

Transaction ID
(Must be the same for the request and the reply.)

Seconds elapsed since client **sent first request message.** (Initially 0)	Flag Field (Broadcast Flag)

Client IP Address
(if known by Client, 0 otherwise)

In Response,
Client IP Address provided by the Server

In Response,
IP Address of Server (that provides a downloadable Boot File)

Relay Router IP Address

Client Hardware Address

Server Host Name
(Client can optionally identify the desired server)

Boot File Name
Client can include a generic name, such as Windows or Sunos
Server will provide the real pathname of a boot file

"Vendor Specific Area"
Additional Parameters

Fields that must be filled in for a *bootrequest* are shown in boldface.
Fields that the client may optionally specify in a request are shown in
italics. The message format was reused for DHCP messages. For
detailed encoding of messages and their parameters, see the documents
referenced at the end of the chapter.[3]

---

[3]Standards documents use special names for the fields. It may be useful to know that *ciaddr* is the term used for the Client's current IP Address (if any), *yiaddr* is the server-provided IP address, *siaddr* is the IP address of a boot file server, and *giaddr* is the relay router IP address.

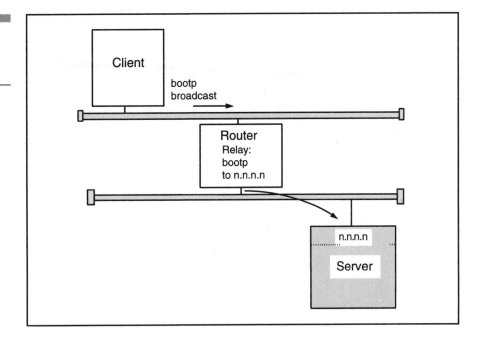

Figure 11.5
Relaying boot
requests to an
external server.

Using Relay Agents

It may be more convenient to use one or more centralized boot servers
instead of placing one on each LAN. But if a BOOTP client broadcasts a
request on its LAN, how can it reach a remote server? The answer is
that a helper system will relay the client's request (as shown in Figure
11.5).

A relay agent is a helper system that relays local BOOTP requests to
remote servers. Routers normally are used as relay agents (although the
specification allows for the use of hosts).

A router will be configured with the IP address(es) of one or more boot
servers to whom requests should be forwarded.[4] When a relay agent
receives a client request, it:

■ Checks the Relay Router IP Address field in the BOOTP request.
   If this is zero, the relay agent inserts the IP address of the inter-

---

[4]This is the best implementation, although the specification also allows a router to broadcast the request onto selected links, in order to search for a boot server when its IP
address is unknown. The *hops* field is included to prevent endless looping in this case.

face on which it received the request. (The BOOTP server will use this address to relay its reply back toward the client via the relay agent.)

■ The relay agent then sends the client request to one or more pre-configured server addresses. The agent will replace the IP header for the request with one containing a server destination address.

A simple scenario for a client that does not know its IP address is:

■ The client broadcasts a request (directed to server port 67).

■ A server receives the request.

■ The server uses the client's hardware type and hardware address as a key and looks up the IP address in the table.

■ If the client is local, the server broadcasts the response or encloses the response in a frame whose destination is the client's hardware address. The response is directed to client UDP port 68.

■ If the client is remote, the response is sent to port 67 at the IP address that has been filled into the Relay Router IP Address field by the relay agent. The relay agent then delivers the response to the client—using either a broadcast or the client's hardware address.

Booting Clients That Have IP Addresses

But suppose that a boot client has been preconfigured with an IP address or has stored an IP address that it was given in an earlier boot process. In this case the client may place that address into the Client IP Address field in the request.

Configuring Software Downloads

Recall that initially, the BOOTP model took the simple view that both the configuration data and the TFTP software download would be obtained from the same server. However, it is easy to separate the configuration service from the download service. The BOOTP configuration server simply returns the IP address of the TFTP server host, along with the pathname of the file to be downloaded.

But how does a BOOTP server select a TFTP server and download file? Software downloads might be dispersed across many TFTP servers. The BOOTP server can be configured with a table that maps system nicknames to the IP address of the TFTP server system that has the download file, and the pathname for that file. For example:

A BOOTP client sends an appropriate nickname to the server in the Boot File Name field. (DHCP provides a separate Class Identifier option field for this purpose instead.) The server looks up the nickname in the table, places the complete file pathname into the Boot File Name field, and writes the TFTP server's IP address into the Server IP Address field in the message.

A client sends a zeroed Boot File Name field if the client does not need a boot file or can accept preconfigured default values.

"Vendor Specific Area"

The *Vendor Specific Area* in the BOOTP message originally was included to carry miscellaneous information that system vendors might want to enclose. However, early in the use of BOOTP, it became clear that a lot of useful configuration data—such as the subnet mask and address of a default router—had been left out of the formal part of the message. The space in the Vendor Specific Area was used for the additional configuration parameters as well as optional vendor information. Many parameter subfields have been defined for this area. A special 4-byte code at the start of the area signals that standard parameters follow. This code is called a "magic cookie."

Sending the Response to an Addressless Client

The simplest way for a server to deliver its response back to a client is to:

1. Use an IP header with the newly assigned IP address as the destination address

2. Wrap the datagram in a frame addressed to the client's physical address

But some clients cannot receive an IP datagram with an explicit IP address unless they previously have been configured with that address. This is called the "chicken and egg" problem.

However, such a client will be able to receive a datagram with destination port 68 and IP broadcast address 255.255.255.255. BOOTP clients can signal their preference to receive a response via the broadcast IP address by setting the *broadcast flag* (located in the flag field) equal to 1 in their requests.

Seconds Elapsed

When a client sends its initial request for boot data, the *Seconds Elapsed* field is set to 0. If no response is received, the client times out, updates the seconds elapsed field, and tries again. The client uses randomized timeouts that increase until the average backoff reaches 60 seconds.

A relay uses the seconds value to give the client a chance to find a local server. After Seconds Elapsed reaches a preconfigured level, the relay will forward the request to one or more remote servers.

DHCP Features

The Dynamic Host Configuration Protocol extends BOOTP's capabilities significantly. The most important enhancements are:

- Easier administration
- Automated configuration
- Support for moves and changes
- Ability of the client to ask for specific parameter values
- New DHCP message types that support robust client/server interactions

BOOTP uses a very simple request/response interaction. DHCP requires a more complex exchange of messages. To achieve backward compatibility, the DHCP message format was based on the BOOTP message format. The intention was that all new DHCP servers would support both BOOTP clients and DHCP clients. However, some vendors have built DHCP products that do not support BOOTP clients.

Administration and Automated Configuration

DHCP is capable of greatly reducing the administrative effort required to configure systems. If desired, an administrator can simply identify a block of IP addresses that the DHCP server can allocate to LAN clients. A block of addresses is called a *scope*. A typical choice for a scope is a subnet.[5] It is an easy job for an administrator to enter other critical parameters such as the subnet mask, Domain Name Server addresses, and address of the default router for a LAN. The administrator also can enter additional parameters, as needed.

A DHCP client that requests boot information from the server can be assigned an IP address from the scope automatically. The client also is sent an appropriate set of parameters. DHCP's most important innovation is that addresses can be *leased* for a period of time instead of permanently assigned. This ensures that addresses that are no longer in use will return to the address pool without any administrative action. Leases are explained below.

A client that needs a fixed address or special parameters still can be configured individually, by entering the MAC address of its interface.

An important step in configuring a scope is to identify addresses that cannot be part of the pool because they already are in use, or are needed for new servers that will be configured manually.

DHCP simplifies an administrator's life, but one administrative chore that still is important is the backup of the server database—especially if there are any permanently assigned addresses.

DHCP Selection at a Client

Configuring a desktop client to use BOOTP or DHCP is very simple. The left side of Figure 11.6 shows how DHCP can be selected from a Windows 95 network configuration menu. Automatic configuration via a DHCP server is selected with a simple mouse click.[6] A very similar menu is available at NT systems.

The right side of Figure 11.6 shows a menu produced by the Windows 95 *winipcfg* command after the system has been configured by a DHCP server.

---

[5] A subnet may be split into two scopes so that some addresses can be controlled by a backup server. For example, a server on or near a LAN might hold 80 percent of the subnet's addresses while a backup has 20 percent.

[6] At the time of writing, Windows 95 and NT systems could use DHCP, but could not use BOOTP.

Figure 11.6
Setting up a Windows 95 desktop to
use DHCP.

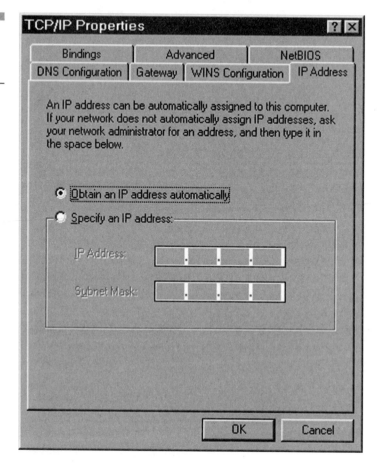

Figure 11.6
Setting up a Windows 95 desktop to
use DHCP.

DHCP Mechanisms

Assigning IP Addresses

There are, in fact, three types of address allocation supported by DHCP:

1. *Manual allocation:* An IP address that has been manually entered at the server is permanently assigned to the client with an identified MAC address.

2. *Automatic allocation:* An IP address is selected from the server's available pool and is permanently assigned to the client.

3. *Dynamic allocation:* An IP address is assigned to a client for a limited amount of time—or until it is given up by the client.

Figure 11.6
(Continued).

IP Configuration

Host Information

Host Name	DELL.mgt.com
DNS Servers	198.207.177.10
Node Type	Broadcast
NetBIOS Scope Id	
IP Routing Enabled ☐	WINS Proxy Enabled ☐
NetBIOS Resolution Uses DNS ☐	

Ethernet Adapter Information

ELNK3 Ethernet Adapter

Adapter Address	00-20-AF-3B-D4-50
IP Address	198.207.177.200
Subnet Mask	255.255.255.0
Default Gateway	198.207.177.5
DHCP Server	198.207.177.30
Primary WINS Server	
Secondary WINS Server	
Lease Obtained	Wed Jul 1 98 7:27:54 PM
Lease Expires	Wed Jul 1 98 7:37:54 PM

OK	Release	Renew	Release All	Renew All

Dynamic allocation is very useful in environments that have many moves and changes.

Leases

The way that the dynamic allocation works is that the server grants the client a *lease*, which identifies the period of time that the client may hold the address. The client can periodically renew the lease or let it expire. Expired IP addresses can be reused.

In order to renew a lease, a client has to identify the lease. When initially setting up a lease, the client can provide a DHCP Client Identifier value that will be used to name the client's lease in all future negotiations. Otherwise, the lease is indexed by the client's hardware type, hardware address, and assigned IP address. The association of a client index and all of the parameters assigned to the client is called a *binding*.

Moves and Changes

What happens when a user unplugs a computer, moves it to another building, and plugs it into a different subnet? A computer with a leased address must renew its lease every time it boots. When the user turns the computer on, the computer will communicate with a DHCP server and will not be able to renew its old lease. The computer will be assigned a new address that matches its new location, along with a subnet mask, default router, and any other parameters that are needed.

DHCP Message Format

In order to maintain compatibility with BOOTP, the overall DHCP message format is identical to the BOOTP format. However, the Vendor Specific Area of the message has been renamed—appropriately—the *Options field*. Also, several DHCP-specific options subfields have been added. For example:

- DHCP message type.
- Timers used for lease renewal.
- Parameter request list. A client can ask for parameters that it wants.
- A parameter that announces the maximum size message that the client can receive from the server.

Message Type Option

BOOTP clients use a very simple request/response message exchange. DHCP clients use a fairly complicated client/server dialogue involving several types of messages. The type for each message is identified in the DHCP Message Type option field. Types include:

1.	DHCPDISCOVER	The client sends a message to discover servers. The client can include a list of parameters that it would like to have.
2.	DHCPOFFER	One or more servers respond to the client and offer an IP address and parameter values.
3.	DHCPREQUEST	The client selects one server and sends a request message.
4.	DHCPDECLINE	Alternatively, the client refuses an offer because one or more parameters are invalid.
5.	DHCPACK	The server responds and provides parameters.
6.	DHCPNAK	A server refuses a request—for example, a client may have requested an IP address that already is in use. The client must start the whole process over again.
7.	DHCPRELEASE	The client no longer needs its IP address and releases it.
8.	DHCPINFORM	The client informs the server that it has a preconfigured IP address, and only wants other parameters.

Typical Initial Client/Server Message Scenario

The trace messages that follow show a typical initial DHCP client/server interaction. The trace information was gathered using a Windows NT client and server, and the NT Server Network Monitor program. In this dialog:

1. The client sends a DHCPDISCOVER broadcast aimed at finding one or more servers. The request includes a list of option (parameter) identifiers.

2. A server on the same LAN broadcasts a DHCPOFFER response. The response includes an IP address, subnet mask, lease expiration date, the identity of the server, and some configuration parameters for the client.

3. The client broadcasts a DHCPREQUEST with that server's identifier in the DHCP Server Identifier option field.

4. The server broadcasts parameters to the client in a DHCPACK message.

DHCPDISCOVER

System NTCLIENT sent the DHCP message below. Note the use of 0.0.0.0 as the source IP address. The broadcast message was sent from UDP port 68 to server port 67. The DHCP Options field includes:

- The DHCP message type.
- A client identifier which consists of the hardware type (Ethernet) and MAC address.
- A host name.
- A list of parameter identifiers.

Checking with Table 11.1, we can see that the client has requested the parameters:

1. Subnet mask.

15. Domain Name (such as *abc.com*).

3. Default router.

44. NetBIOS name server. (Relevant for Microsoft systems.)

46. NetBIOS node type. (Relevant for Microsoft systems.)

47. NetBIOS over TCP scope. (Relevant for Microsoft systems.)

6. Domain Name Servers.

The mysteriously named "magic cookie" field contains a code that indicates the type of data that follows. The cookie value X'63-82-53-63 introduces BOOTP/DHCP parameters.

```
Time  Src MAC Addr  Dst  MAC Addr  Protocol  Description  Src IPAddr
Dst IPAddr
95.836  NTCLIENT  *BROADCAST  DHCP  Discover  0.0.0.0  255.255.255.255
+ UDP: IP Multicast: Src Port:  BOOTP Client, (68); Dst Port: BOOTP
Server (67);
   DHCP: Discover            (xid=327E61CC)
       DHCP: Op Code         (op)     = 1 (0x1)
       DHCP: Hardware Type   (htype)  = 1 (0x1) 10Mb Ethernet
       DHCP: Hardware Address Length(hlen)    =6 (0x6)
       DHCP: Hops            (hops)   = 0 (0x0)
       DHCP: Transaction ID  (xid)    = 76565667 (0x4904CA3)
       DHCP: Seconds         (secs)   = 0 (0x0)
```

```
    DHCP: Flags                (flags)   = 0 (0x0)
        DHCP: 0..............        = No Broadcast
    DHCP: Client IP Address (ciaddr) = 0.0.0.0
    DHCP: Your IP Address    (yiaddr) = 0.0.0.0
    DHCP: Server IP Address (siaddr) = 0.0.0.0
    DHCP: Relay IP Address   (giaddr) = 0.0.0.0
    DHCP: Client Ethernet Address (chaddr)  =00A024A6EDE4
    DHCP: Server Host Name   (sname)  = <Blank>
    DHCP: Boot File Name     (file)   = <Blank>
    DHCP: Magic Cookie = [OK]
    DHCP: Option Field       (options)
        DHCP: DHCP Message Type      = DHCP Discover
        DHCP: Client-identifier      = (Type: 1) 00 a0 24 a6 ed e4
        DHCP: Host Name              = NTCLIENT
        DHCP: Parameter Request List = (Length: 7) 01 0f 03 2c 2e
        2f 06
        DHCP: End of this option field
```

DHCPOFFER

A DHCP server name COMPAQ responded with the broadcast message below, which was sent to client port 68. The server has offered the address 198.207.177.202 to the client in the field labeled "Your IP Address." The DHCP Option field includes the subnet mask, server address, domain name *mgt.com* (as a 0-terminated ASCII string), default router, and Domain Name Server address. The server did not return the NetBIOS parameter values that were requested because these were not configured at the server.

In addition, the client is notified that:

■ The lease time is 10 minutes.

■ The client should wait no more than 5 minutes before trying to renew its lease with this server.

■ If renewal has not succeeded when 8:45 minutes have elapsed, the client should try to contact any server.

These are unrealistically small values that were selected for testing purposes.

```
Time       Src MAC Addr   Dst MAC Addr   Protocol      Description
SrcIP      Addr    DstIP Addr
95.883     COMPAQ  *BROADCAST     DHCP      Offer  COMPAQ 255.255.255.255

+ UDP:  IP Multicast:  Src Port:  BOOTP Server, (67); Dst Port: BOOTP
Client (68);
  DHCP: Offer              (xid=327E61CC)
      DHCP: Op Code             (op)    =2 (0x2)
      DHCP: Hardware Type       (htype) =1 (0x1) 10Mb Ethernet
      DHCP: Hardware Address Length  (hlen) = 6 (0x6)
      DHCP: Hops                (hops)  = 0 (0x0)
```

TABLE 11.1

Parameters For
BOOTP And DHCP

Tag	Parameter	Description
1	Subnet Mask	For example, 255.255.255.0.
2	Time Offset	Offset in seconds, from UTC.
3	Router(s)	IP address for default router(s).
4	Time Server(s)	IP address for time server(s).
5	IEN 116 Name Server	(Obsolete)
6	Domain Name Server	Domain Name Server address(es).
7	Log Server(s)	Log server address(es).
8	Quote Serve	"Fortune Cookie" server address(es).
9	LPR Server	Printer server address(es).
10	Impress Print Server	Impress server address(es).
11	Resource Location Server	RLP server address(es).
12	Client Host Name	Hostname string.
13	Boot File Size	Number of 512-octet blocks in the boot file.
14	Merit Dump File	File to hold a core dump if the client crashes.
15	Domain Name	Domain name for client.
16	Swap Server	Swap disk server address.
17	Root Path	Pathname that contains the clientís root disk.
18	Extensions File	Pathname of a file with more BOOTP info.
19	Forwarding On/Off	Enable or disable IP forwarding.
20	Source Routing On/Off	Enable or disable source routing.
21	Policy Filter	Check source route against list of IP addresses and masks.
22	Maximum Datagram Reassembly Size	Largest datagram client should reassemble.
23	Default IP Time-To-Live	Default setting for TTL field.
24	Path MTU Timeout	Path MTU is discarded at timeout.
25	Path MTU Plateau Table	MTUs to try when router does not help.
26	Interface MTU	Biggest size that can be sent on the interface.
27	All subnets are local	All subnets of the network have the same MTU.
28	Broadcast Address	Broadcast address used on subnet.
29	Mask Discovery	Client should use ICMP subnet mask discovery.
30	Mask Supplier	Whether client should provide mask to others.

TABLE 11.1

Parameters For
BOOTP And DHCP
(Continued)

Tag	Parameter	Description
31	Router Discovery	Whether client should perform Router Discovery.
32	Router Request	Address to which the client should transmit router solicitation requests.
33	Static Routes	List of static routes for the client's routing cache.
34	Trailer Encapsulation	Whether to negotiate the (obsolete) use of trailers when using ARP.
35	ARP Cache Timeout	Timeout to flush the ARP table.
36	Ethernet Encapsulation	Ethernet Version 2 (DIX) or IEEE 802.3.
37	TCP Default TTL	TTL to be used when sending TCP segments.
38	TCP Keep-alive Time	Timeout for sending keep-alive messages.
39	Keep-alive Data	Include a "garbage" byte in keep-alive messages.
40	NIS Domain	NIS Domain name.
41	NIS Servers	NIS Server Addresses.
42	Network Time Protocol Server	NTP Server addresses.
43	Vendor Specific Information	Vendor is identified in the class-identifier option.
44	NetBIOS Name Servers	NetBIOS Name Server address(es).
45	NetBIOS over TCP/IP Datagram Distribution Server	Datagram Distribution Server address(es).
46	NetBIOS Node Type	NetBIOS over TCP/IP Node Type.
47	NetBIOS over TCP/IP Scope	Scope identifier.
48	X Window System Font Server	Font Server IP address(es).
49	X Window System Display Managers	Display Manager IP address(es).

```
DHCP: Transaction ID    (xid)   = 847143372 (0x327E61CC)
DHCP: Seconds           (secs)  = 0 (0x0)
DHCP: Flags             (flags) = 0 (0x0)
    DHCP: 0..............  = No Broadcast
DHCP: Client IP Address (ciaddr) = 0.0.0.0
DHCP: Your IP Address   (yiaddr) = 198.207.177.202
DHCP: Server IP Address (siaddr) = 0.0.0.0
DHCP: Relay IP Address  (giaddr) = 0.0.0.0
DHCP: Client Ethernet Address (chaddr) = 00A024A6EDE4
DHCP: Server Host Name  (sname)  = <Blank>
```

```
DHCP: Boot File Name      (file)   = <Blank>
DHCP: Magic Cookie = [OK]
DHCP: Option Field       (options)
    DHCP: DHCP Message Type        = DHCP Offer
    DHCP: Subnet Mask              = 255.255.255.0
    DHCP: Renewal Time Value (T1) = 0:05:00
    DHCP: Rebinding Time Value (T2) = 0:08:45
    DHCP: IP Address Lease Time    = 0:10:00
    DHCP: Server Identifier        = 198.207.177.30
    DHCP: Domain Name              = (Length: 8) 6d 67 74 2e 63
                                     6f 6d 00
    DHCP: Router                   = 198.207.177.5
    DHCP: Domain Name Server       = 198.207.177.10
    DHCP: End of this option field
```

DHCPREQUEST

The client responds immediately by broadcasting a request. The DHCP
options field contains the client's IP address, the server's IP address,
and the list of parameter types.

```
Time  Src MAC Addr                Dst MAC Addr        Protocol
Description       SrcIP           DstIP
95.883            NTCLIENT        *BROADCAST         DHCP    Request 0.0.0.0
255.255.255.255

+ UDP:  IP Multicast:  Src Port:  BOOTP Client, (68); Dst Port: BOOTP
Server (67); Length = 308 (0x134)
  DHCP: Request           (xid=7BA129D4)
      DHCP: Op Code            (op)    = 1 (0x1)
      DHCP: Hardware Type      (htype) = 1 (0x1) 10Mb Ethernet
      DHCP: Hardware Address Length (hlen) = 6 (0x6)
      DHCP: Hops               (hops)  = 0 (0x0)
      DHCP: Transaction ID     (xid)   = 2074159572 (0x7BA129D4)
      DHCP: Seconds            (secs)  = 0 (0x0)
      DHCP: Flags              (flags) = 0 (0x0)
          DHCP: 0.............. = No Broadcast
      DHCP: Client IP Address (ciaddr) = 0.0.0.0
      DHCP: Your IP Address    (yiaddr) = 0.0.0.0
      DHCP: Server IP Address (siaddr) = 0.0.0.0
      DHCP: Relay IP Address  (giaddr) = 0.0.0.0
      DHCP: Client Ethernet Address (chaddr) = 00A024A6EDE4
      DHCP: Server Host Name  (sname)  = <Blank>
      DHCP: Boot File Name     (file)  = <Blank>
      DHCP: Magic Cookie = [OK]
      DHCP: Option Field       (options)
          DHCP: DHCP Message Type       = DHCP Request
          DHCP: Client-identifier       = (Type: 1) 00 a0 24 a6 ed e4
          DHCP: Requested Address       = 198.207.177.202
          DHCP: Server Identifier       = 198.207.177.30
          DHCP: Host Name               = NTCLIENT
          DHCP: Parameter Request List  = (Length: 7) 01 0f 03 2c 2e
                                          2f 06
      DHCP: End of this option field
```

DHCPACK

The server completes the negotiation by sending a DHCPACK repeating some of the parameters. The client 's broadcast flag was 0, which means that the DHCPACK could have been sent using the client's MAC address and newly assigned IP address. However, the server has chosen to broadcast its response.

```
Time      Src MAC Addr    Dst MAC Addr    Protocol      Description
SrcIP     DstIP
95.946    COMPAQ *BROADCAST        DHCP    ACK     COMPAQ 255.255.255.255

+ UDP:  IP Multicast:  Src Port:  BOOTP Client, (68); Dst Port: BOOTP
Server (67); Length = 308 (0x134)
HCP: ACK  (xid=7BA129D4)
  DHCP: Op Code             (op)      = 2 (0x2)
      DHCP: Hardware Type        (htype)   = 1 (0x1) 10Mb Ethernet
      DHCP: Hardware Address Length (hlen)    =6 (0x6)
      DHCP: Hops              (hops)    = 0 (0x0)
      DHCP: Transaction ID      (xid)     = 2074159572 (0x7BA129D4)
      DHCP: Seconds           (secs)    = 0 (0x0)
      DHCP: Flags             (flags)   = 0 (0x0)
          DHCP: 0.............. = No Broadcast
      DHCP: Client IP Address (ciaddr) = 0.0.0.0
      DHCP: Your IP Address   (yiaddr) = 198.207.177.202
      DHCP: Server IP Address (siaddr) = 0.0.0.0
      DHCP: Relay IP Address  (giaddr) = 0.0.0.0
      DHCP: Client Ethernet Address (chaddr) = 00A024A6EDE4
      DHCP: Server Host Name  (sname)   = <Blank>
      DHCP: Boot File Name    (file)    = <Blank>
      DHCP: Magic Cookie = [OK]
      DHCP: Option Field      (options)
          DHCP: DHCP Message Type     = DHCP ACK
          DHCP: Renewal Time Value (T1) = 0:05:00
          DHCP: Rebinding Time Value (T2) = 0:08:45
      DHCP: IP Address Lease Time     = 0:10:00
      DHCP: Server Identifier         = 198.207.177.30
      DHCP: Subnet Mask               = 255.255.255.0
      DHCP: Domain Name               = (Length: 8) 6d 67 74 2e 63 6f
                                        6d 00
        DHCP: Router                  = 198.207.177.5
        DHCP: Domain Name Server      = 198.207.177.10
        DHCP: End of this option field
```

Watching for Duplicates

The appearance of duplicate IP addresses on a network causes many problems. There always is a possibility that an address that is part of the DHCP pool actually has been manually assigned to some system. Good DHCP client and server implementations check for a duplicate.

- The server should send one or more pings to an IP address before assigning it.

- The client should send an ARP request for the address before accepting it.

If the address is a duplicate, the client should be able to get a different address from the server. It is a good idea to check out a DHCP server product to make sure that it handles duplicates gracefully.

Renewing

Clients can keep their leases alive by means of a quick request response interaction:

- The client can send a DHCPREQUEST that includes its assigned IP address.

- The server that has stored the client's configuration will respond with DHCPACK if all is well.

- If the client's information is no longer valid (e.g., the user's workstation has been connected to a different LAN), servers respond with DHCPNAK, and the client must restart a full configuration procedure.

The request below was sent 5 minutes after the initial configuration. The client now knows the source and destination IP addresses, so there is no need to broadcast this request. The server responds with a DHCPACK similar to the one shown earlier.

```
Time      Src MAC Addr Dst MAC Addr Protocol Description SrcIP     DstIP
395.092 NTCLIENT      COMPAQ       DHCP      Request     NTCLIENT COMPAQ

+ UDP:  Src Port:  BOOTP Client, (68); Dst Port: BOOTP Server (67);
Length = 308 (0x134)
  DHCP: Request (xid=6D9403AA)
       DHCP: Op Code              (op)     = 1 (0x1)
       DHCP: Hardware Type        (htype)  = 1 (0x1) 10Mb Ethernet
       DHCP: Hardware Address Length (hlen) = 6 (0x6)
       DHCP: Hops                 (hops)   = 0 (0x0)
       DHCP: Transaction ID       (xid)    = 1838416810 (0x6D9403AA)
       DHCP: Seconds              (secs)   = 0 (0x0)
       DHCP: Flags                (flags)  = 0 (0x0)
           DHCP: 0.............. = No Broadcast
       DHCP: Client IP Address    (ciaddr) = 198.207.177.202
       DHCP: Your IP Address      (yiaddr) = 0.0.0.0
       DHCP: Server IP Address    (siaddr) = 0.0.0.0
       DHCP: Relay IP Address     (giaddr) = 0.0.0.0
       DHCP: Client Ethernet Address (chaddr) = 00A024A6EDE4
       DHCP: Server Host Name     (sname)  = <Blank>
```

```
DHCP: Boot File Name     (file)   = <Blank>
DHCP: Magic Cookie = [OK]
DHCP: Option Field       (options)
    DHCP: DHCP Message Type       = DHCP Request
    DHCP: Client-identifier       = (Type: 1) 00 a0 24 a6 ed e4
    DHCP: Host Name               = NTCLIENT
    DHCP: Parameter Request List  = (Length: 7) 01 0f 03 2c 2e 2f
                                     06
DHCP: End of this option field
```

BOOT Parameters

Table 11.1 contains a partial listing of the parameters that may be included in either BOOTP or DHCP messages in the options field. The parameters in Table 11.2 only may be used with DHCP.

TABLE 11.2

Parameters for DHCP

Tag	Parameter	Description
50	Requested IP Address	The client asks for a specific IP address.
51	IP Address Lease Time	Client's requested time or time granted by server.
52	Option Overload	*Server Host Name* or *Boot File Name* fields are carrying DHCP options in order to conserve space.
53	DHCP Message Type	For example, *DISCOVER, OFFER,* or *REQUEST.*
54	DHCP Server Identifier	Client identifies which server was accepted.
55	Parameter Request List	Parameters requested by client.
56	Message	Server sends error with DHCPNAK. Client sends error with DHCPDECLINE.
57	Maximum DHCP Message Size	Largest DHCP message that the client is willing to accept.
58	Renewal (T1) Time	Client should try to renew lease after this interval.
59	Rebinding (T2>T1) Time	If renewal fails, client should try to renew by contacting *any* server.
60	Class Identifier	Vendor code that describes the client. Some parameters can be returned based on vendor class.
61	Client Identifier	A unique identifier for the client. The server should use this to associate a client with its address binding.

Every option is identified by an 8-bit tag number. Except for option 0 and option 255, options have the format:

Tag   Length   Value

Option 0 is used for padding, and consists a single 0 tag byte. Option 255 marks the end of an option list, and consists of a single all-1s tag byte.

Tag numbers from 128 to 254 are reserved for site-specific options. The other numbers are used for standard options. To get a complete list of standard options, check the most recent list published by the Internet Assigned Numbers Authority.

Some of the values consist of one of more IP addresses. The IP addresses should appear in order of preference.

Other Automatic Configuration Methods

There have been a number of attempts to automate individual parts of the configuration process. A LAN-attached system can use Reverse ARP (RARP) to discover its IP address. The ICMP Address Mask request and reply can provide the subnet mask. But there is no particular benefit to using several separate protocols and messages to get information that can be obtained via a single BOOTP or DHCP response. These protocols only are used where there are old systems that still need them.

The ICMP router discovery mechanism does provide an advantage, since it provides continually updated information on available routers.

IP version 6 enables hosts to get the basic startup information that they need from a neighboring router. But DHCP servers also may be used with IPv6.

Recommended Reading

The references that follow were valid at the time of this writing:

- The BOOTP standard was defined in RFC 951.

- RFC 1542 clarifies and extends BOOTP, and includes a good description of relay agents.
- RFC 2131 describes the Dynamic Host Configuration Protocol.
- RFC 2132 contains detailed descriptions of BOOTP and DHCP parameters.

Domain
Name System

Introduction

An end user usually knows a host's name but not its address. But IP needs to know a host's address in order to communicate with the host. A user does not worry about this; the user types the name of a server host and the user's client application automatically looks up the address. But where does the application get the address?

For small, isolated networks, this problem sometimes is solved by maintaining a central name-to-address translation table called "hosts." Individual users on the network stay up to date by copying this table to their own disks periodically. For example, on Unix systems, the file is stored as */etc/hosts*. On Windows 95, the file is *C:\WINDOWS\HOSTS*, and on Windows NT server, the file is *C:\WINNT\System32\drivers\etc\hosts*.

A central table was used across the Internet in the early days of the TCP/IP. The Department of Defense Network Information Center (DOD NIC) maintained the master version of the Internet name-to-address translation table, and other systems retrieved a copy on a regular basis. As time went by, this method became burdensome and inefficient.

The Domain Name System (DNS) is a directory service that was set up to provide a better method of keeping track of Internet names and addresses. DNS databases provide automated name-to-address translation services. The system works well, and many organizations that are not connected to the Internet use DNS databases to track their own internal computer names.

DNS has been a great success, with the result that our client/server interactions rely on having a healthy Domain Name System. Unfortunately, the classic DNS directory system operates in a wide-open fashion, unprotected from a variety of possible cracker attacks. It is vital that we know that an authoritative server, not a cracker, has provided the information in a DNS response. The initial implementation of a secure version of the Domain Name System is under construction at the time of writing. The secure DNS mechanisms are described at the end of this chapter.

Structure of DNS

DNS is a *distributed* database. Using DNS, Internet names and addresses are distributed across servers spread around the world.[1] The organization that owns a Domain Name (such as *yale.edu*) is responsible for running and maintaining the name servers that translate between its own names and addresses. Local personnel enter node additions, deletions, and changes quickly and accurately at the domain's *primary server*. Because name-to-address translation is so important, the information is replicated at one or more *secondary servers*. The primary often is referred to as the master server, whereas the secondaries sometimes are called slave servers.

BIND Software

Many computer vendors provide free software that lets their systems function as name servers. Usually this software has been adapted from the *Berkeley Internet Domain* (BIND) package. Periodically, new versions of BIND are made available on the Internet.[2]

An organization can use this software to run a private Domain Name Service for its own internal use. If the organization wishes to connect to the Internet, it must set up at least two public name servers that will become part of the Internet Domain Name System.

Resolvers

A client program capable of looking up information in the Domain Name System is a standard part of TCP/IP and is called a *resolver*. In normal use, a resolver works quietly in the background, and users don't even notice it. For example, in the dialog below, a user requests a *telnet* connection to *elvis.vnet.net*. The user's *telnet* application calls on a local *resolver* subroutine[3] that looks up the IP address of that site:

```
> telnet elvis.vnet.net
Trying 166.82.1.5 ...
Connected to elvis.vnet.net.
```

---

[1]Later, we see that name servers also contain important mail routing information.

[2]BIND currently is maintained by a nonprofit organization called the Internet Software Consortium (*www.isc.org*). Academics and individual researchers can obtain the latest software at no cost. Vendors now pay a fee that helps to support the continued improvement of the software.

[3]For the Berkeley socket programming interface, the subroutine is called *gethostbyname*.

462

Chapter Twelve

When TCP/IP is installed at a host that will use Domain Name database lookups, the host's configuration information should include the IP addresses of two or more Domain Name Servers. Resolver programs need to know the addresses of Domain Name Servers that they can query.

The demonstration that follows was run at *katie,* a *telnet* server operated by *Vnet Internet Access.* Like most Unix systems, *katie* has a configuration file called */etc/resolv.conf,* which identifies the local domain name and the IP addresses of two Domain Name Servers for the domain.

```
> more /etc/resolv.conf
domain vnet.net
166.82.1.3
166.82.1.8
```

Desktop TCP/IP systems need Domain Name Server information too. The Microsoft Windows NT server menu shown in Figure 12.1 was obtained by choosing:

```
Start/Settings/Control Panel/Network/Protocols/TCP/IP
Protocols/Properties/DNS
```

IP addresses for the same DNS servers have been entered by clicking the Add button.

Looking Up Host Addresses

As we have seen earlier, many systems provide an interactive resolver program that enables a user to communicate directly to a Domain Name Server, sending queries and getting back responses. The dialog that follows uses the Unix *nslookup* resolver program[4]. In the dialog:

1. Immediately after the user types *nslookup,* the local default server identifies itself, displaying its name and address. In this case, the server's name is *char.vnet.net* and the server's address is 166.82.1.3.

2. The user types in the name of a host whose address is desired.

3. The request is sent to the server.

---

[4]There is a similar program on Windows NT systems.

Figure 12.1
Configuring DNS.

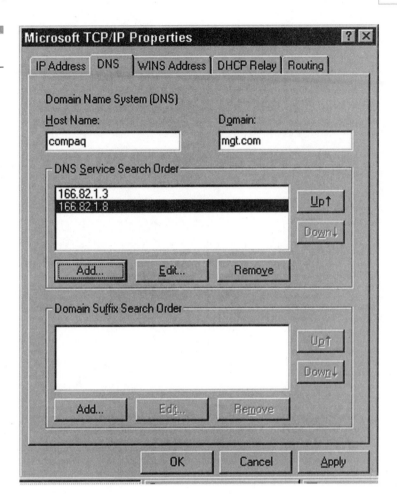

Figure 12.1
Configuring DNS.

4. After each query, the server (*char*) identifies itself and then provides the answer.

5. If the user has asked for local information, the server extracts the answer from its own database.

6. If the user has asked for information about an external host, the server first checks its *cache* of recent queries to see if the information is available, and if not, interacts with a remote authoritative server to get the answer.

7. When an answer comes back from the remote authoritative server, the answer is saved in the local server's disk cache for future reference and then is sent to the requesting user.

Each step in the dialog is explained by comments on the right. Note that a response retrieved from the server's cache is marked *non-authoritative*.

```
> nslookup
Default Server: char.vnet.net      The local server's name and
                                    address is displayed.

Address: 166.82.1.3

> elvis.vnet.net.                   User makes a query whose answer is in the
                                    local database.
Server: char.vnet.net              Server ID and address again.
Address: 166.82.1.3
Name: elvis.vnet.net               The name in the query.
Address: 166.82.1.5                The answer.

> www.ibm.com.                     User makes a query about an external host.
Server: char.vnet.net              Server ID and address again.
Address: 166.82.1.3

Name: www.ibm.com                  The name in the query.
Address: 204.146.18.33             The answer has been saved on char's disk and
                                   sent to the user.


> www.ibm.com.                     User repeats query about an external host.
Server: char.vnet.net              Server ID and address again.
Address: 166.82.1.3
Non-authoritative answer:          This came from the local cache.
Name: www.ibm.com                  The name in the query.
Address: 204.146.18.33             The answer.
```

Why does the server keep identifying itself? Recall that an organization will operate two or more servers because one of them might be very busy or even out of service (e.g., for maintenance). If the resolver cannot get an answer from the first system on the list, it tries the next. An administrator using *nslookup* can see immediately which server is answering a query.

Note that we have included a final period at the end of each queried name. Recall that "." is the name of the root. A complete domain name ends in a period.

Authoritative and Cached Responses

All DNS data is entered and updated at a *primary* name server. The data at a primary server is on its own hard disk. *Secondary* servers download their information from the primary.[5]

When a system sends a query to a Domain Name Server, the requester does not know or care whether it is talking to a primary or a secondary server. All of an organization's name servers—whether primary or secondary—are *authoritative* for its domain.

Recall that to cut down on traffic, your local server will *cache* (save) the answers on its own hard disk for a while. Any user who repeats a query that has been made recently gets the locally cached answer. How long will the information be cached? An answer's timeout period is configured by the primary server administrator and is included in the query result sent to the requester.

Address-to-Name Translations

The Domain Name System is versatile, and also enables you to perform address-to-name translations. The traditional way to do this looks a bit strange:

- Set the type of the query to be *ptr* (pointer).
- Write the address *backward,* followed by *.in-addr.arpa.*

For example:

```
> set type = ptr
> 5.1.82.166.in-addr.arpa.
Server:    char.vnet.net
Address:   166.82.1.3
```

---

[5]When there are many DNS servers distributed across a network, it may be convenient to set up a download hierarchy. One tier of secondaries can be configured to download their databases from the primary. Another tier downloads their databases from nearby secondaries that act as local masters. This reduces the processing load on the primary and the traffic load on wide-area links between the primary and remote secondaries.

```
5.1.82.166.in-addr.arpa name = elvis.vnet.net
82.166.in-addr.arpa      nameserver = ns.vnet.net
82.166.in-addr.arpa      nameserver = ns2.vnet.net
ns.vnet.net      internet address = 166.82.1.3
ns2.vnet.net     internet address = 166.82.1.8
```

This oddity makes sense when you know how global reverse lookups were designed. The organization that owns a network address is responsible for recording all of its address-to-name translations in the DNS database. This is done in tabulations that are separate from the name-to-address mappings.

The special *in-addr.arpa* domain subtree shown in Figure 12.2 was created to point to all of these address-to-name entries. When addresses are placed into the tree, it makes sense to put the first number at the top and work down. That way, all addresses of the form 128.*x.x.x* are under node 128.

If we read the labels in the tree using the same bottom-to-top convention that we used for names, the address appears backward—namely, *5.1.82.166.in-addr.arpa.*

The user interface for the most recent versions of *nslookup* hides this technicality, and lets you simply enter an address. The *nslookup* program automatically constructs the backward query just shown. However, note that the following response shows the traditional reversed order.

```
> set type = ptr
> 166.82.1.5
```

Figure 12.2
The *in-addr* domain subtree.

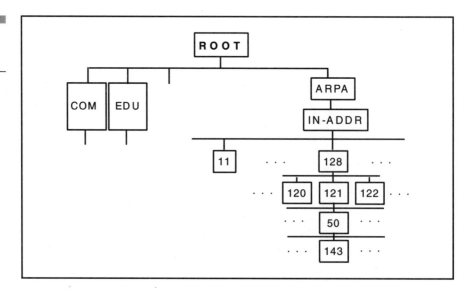

```
Server:    char.vnet.net
Address:   166.82.1.3

5.1.82.166.in-addr.arpa  name = elvis.vnet.net
82.166.in-addr.arpa      nameserver = ns.vnet.net
82.166.in-addr.arpa      nameserver = ns2.vnet.net
ns.vnet.net       internet address = 166.82.1.3
ns2.vnet.net      internet address = 166.82.1.8
```

There are even friendlier desktop versions of *nslookup,* like the one
shown in Figure 12.3, provided by Ashmount Research Ltd. Queries are
entered in a small box near the bottom of the window, and responses are
shown in the display area at the top. Note that both of the responses
include the names and addresses of name servers that contain authoritative information relating to the queries.

Local and Global Domain Name Servers

If you have a private TCP/IP network, you can use DNS software to create a primary name translation database and replicate it at convenient
points across your network. Your own name servers will answer all user
queries.

But if you connect your network to the Internet, you will need to supply at least a few public addresses to other Internet computers (such as
the address of your World Wide Web server and electronic mail server).
You (or an Internet Service Provider) will need to operate public Internet name servers that translate between your names and addresses.
How is this done? The key to making this work is that when an organization (e.g., *microsoft.com*) wishes to connect to the Internet, it registers
with an appropriate registration authority[6] and identifies the names and
addresses of at least two Domain Name Servers that it operates. The
registration authority adds this information to its database of Domain
Name Servers.

Currently, there is a single root database that contains the names and
addresses of Domain Name Servers for all names that end in *com, edu,*

---

[6]At the time of writing, the Network Solutions InterNIC was still the registration service
for the generic top level names *com, net, org,* and *edu.* See Appendix B for information
about other registries.

Figure 12.3
DNS queries.

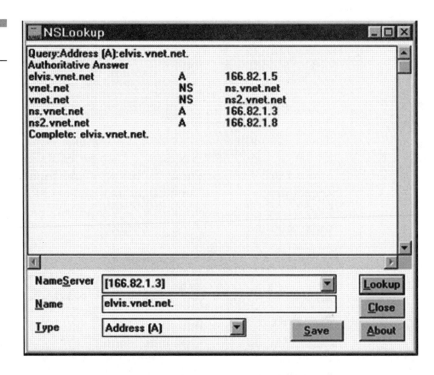

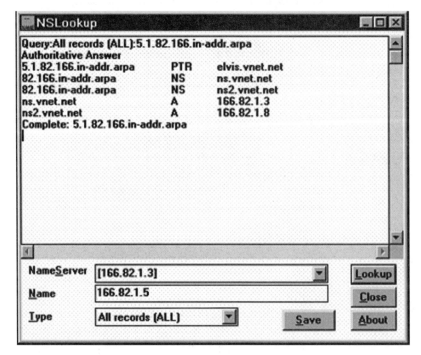

net, org, gov, and *mil.* This database also contains pointers to the data-bases for *int* and the various country codes. This root list is replicated at several *root servers* that play a key role in processing remote queries. For example, suppose that a name-to-address translation query for *www.microsoft.com* is sent to a local Domain Name Server (like *char.vnet.net*):

- The server notes that *www.microsoft.com* does not belong to the local domain.
- The server checks to see if the information is in its cache.
- If the name is not in the cache, the server sends a query to a root server.
- The root server returns the names and addresses of the Domain Name Servers that contain information for *microsoft.com.*

To see the current list of root servers, we run *nslookup* and set the type of query to be *ns.* If we enter "." (which stands for the root), the names and addresses of several root servers will be returned.

```
> nslookup
> set type = ns
> .

Server:    char.vnet.net
Address:   166.82.1.3

Non-authoritative answer:
(root) nameserver = B.ROOT-SERVERS.NET
(root) nameserver = C.ROOT-SERVERS.NET
(root) nameserver = D.ROOT-SERVERS.NET
(root) nameserver = E.ROOT-SERVERS.NET
(root) nameserver = I.ROOT-SERVERS.NET
(root) nameserver = F.ROOT-SERVERS.NET
(root) nameserver = G.ROOT-SERVERS.NET
(root) nameserver = J.ROOT-SERVERS.NET
(root) nameserver = K.ROOT-SERVERS.NET
(root) nameserver = L.ROOT-SERVERS.NET
(root) nameserver = M.ROOT-SERVERS.NET
(root) nameserver = A.ROOT-SERVERS.NET
(root) nameserver = H.ROOT-SERVERS.NET

Authoritative answers can be found from:
B.ROOT-SERVERS.NET    internet address = 128.9.0.107
C.ROOT-SERVERS.NET    internet address = 192.33.4.12
D.ROOT-SERVERS.NET    internet address = 128.8.10.90
E.ROOT-SERVERS.NET    internet address = 192.203.230.10
I.ROOT-SERVERS.NET    internet address = 192.36.148.17
F.ROOT-SERVERS.NET    internet address = 192.5.5.241
G.ROOT-SERVERS.NET    internet address = 192.112.36.4
J.ROOT-SERVERS.NET    internet address = 198.41.0.10
K.ROOT-SERVERS.NET    internet address = 193.0.14.129
```

```
L.ROOT-SERVERS.NET     internet address = 198.32.64.12
M.ROOT-SERVERS.NET     internet address = 202.12.27.33
A.ROOT-SERVERS.NET     internet address = 198.41.0.4
H.ROOT-SERVERS.NET     internet address = 128.63.2.53
```

As noted earlier, the root servers provide direct referrals to servers for the second-level domains (such as *microsoft.com* or *yale.edu*) under the generic names *com, edu, net, org,* and *gov.* For example, here is part of the information about *3com.com* taken directly from the root list file:

```
3COM.COM.    172800 NS   TMC.EDU.
TMC.EDU.     172800 A    128.249.1.1
3COM.COM.    172800 NS   XANTH.CS.ODU.EDU
TMC.EDU.     172800 A    128.82.4.1
```

Note that these name servers are not located on *3com*'s own network. Organizations often have name servers that are located at their Service Provider's network or on a university campus.

We can get all of an organization's name server information via *nslookup* by setting the type of query to *ns* (set type = ns):

```
> set type = ns
> 3com.com.
Server:     char.vnet.net
Address:    166.82.1.3

Non-authoritative answer:
3com.com    nameserver = TMC.EDU
3com.com    nameserver = XANTH.CS.ODU.EDU
3com.com    nameserver = NEWS.AERO.ORG
3com.com    nameserver = MAIL.AERO.ORG
3com.com    nameserver = FOUR11.3com.com
3com.com    nameserver = SEAWEED.THIRDCOAST.NET

Authoritative answers can be found from:
TMC.EDU internet address = 128.249.1.1
XANTH.CS.ODU.EDU   internet address = 128.82.4.1
NEWS.AERO.ORG   internet address = 130.221.16.4
MAIL.AERO.ORG   internet address = 130.221.16.2
FOUR11.3com.com   internet address = 129.213.128.98
SEAWEED.THIRDCOAST.NET   internet address = 209.116.84.10
```

Note that the responses came from *char*'s cache.

The entire Domain Name System administrative framework is currently under review, and the database structure might change. For example, the root database might contain only a list of root servers plus pointers to separate databases for *com, edu,* and so forth. The discussion in this chapter is based on the current database structure.

Delegating

Rather than have one registry try to maintain up-to-date lists of servers for organizations in Australia, Canada, or Switzerland, each country maintains its own registration service for computer names that end in its country code. The country's registration service operates country root servers that provide pointers to servers for organizations registered under that country.

When you look up names that end in a country code, the first step is to obtain a list of names and addresses of top-level servers for that country from the global *root* server. The *nslookup* dialog below shows the list of Canadian servers:

```
> ca.
Server:      char.vnet.net
Address:     166.82.1.3

Non-authoritative answer:
ca      nameserver = CLOUSO.RISQ.QC.ca
ca      nameserver = DNS2.UTCC.UTORONTO.ca
ca      nameserver = NS2.UUNET.ca
ca      nameserver = RELAY.CDNNET.ca
ca      nameserver = RS0.INTERNIC.NET

Authoritative answers can be found from:
CLOUSO.RISQ.QC.ca       internet address = 192.26.210.1
DNS2.UTCC.UTORONTO.ca   internet address = 128.100.102.201
NS2.UUNET.ca            internet address = 142.77.1.5
RELAY.CDNNET.ca         internet address = 192.73.5.1
RS0.INTERNIC.NET        internet address = 198.41.0.5
```

In fact, the Domain Name System is very flexible and allows a long chain of referrals. A country can use whatever subtree structure it wants for its naming tree. The root server for the country could point to a lower-level server that then might lead to a still lower-level server. In actual practice, referral chains are short and the authoritative server for a name is found in very few steps. Figure 12.4 illustrates the steps in resolving the name *www.titech.ac.jp:*

- First the root is consulted. It identifies servers for Japan.
- One of the root servers for Japan is queried. It identifies servers for the Titech University domain, *titech.ac.jp*.
- A Titech server provides the address of the host.

Note that the local server took responsibility for finding the answer for the client. This is because clients normally ask for *recursive* name resolution, meaning, "keep going until you get the result."

Figure 12.4
Resolving a name in
Japan.

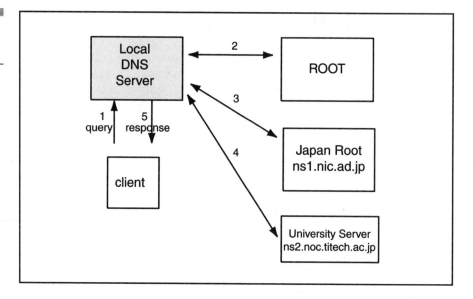

In contrast, the local server itself worked *nonrecursively* (*iteratively*). Each server that it queried returned a pointer for the next step. The local server then sent its next query directly to that database.

Keep in mind that a hierarchical structure can be used to handle name services inside a large private organization. The organization can set up an internal tree with a root of its own that points to private Domain Name Servers that are authoritative for parts of its own naming domain. (Of course, a prudent organization does not plug its private directory system into the Internet directory system where anyone could find out the names and addresses of its computers.)

Connecting Name Servers to the Internet

Connecting your own Domain Name Servers to the worldwide Internet database takes several steps:

1. Reserve a Domain Name

2. Register with an Internet Service Provider and obtain one or more blocks of public IP addresses.

3. Assign names and addresses to hosts that will be on the Internet.

4. Obtain the list of root servers that tie the worldwide service together.

5. Set up a primary Domain Name Server and at least one secondary. Copy the list of root servers to these computers. Install DNS software.

6. Test the servers.

7. Move to operational status.

8. Register the organization's Domain Name Servers with the appropriate registration service.

Many organizations outsource most of the work to their Internet Service Provider. However, it is very important to retain administrative control of your domain. Make sure that someone from your own organization is listed as the *Administrative Point of Contact* on any forms that are filed on behalf of your domain. See Appendix B for more information about registration.

DNS Data and Zones

What information does an Internet Domain Name Server need in order to do its job? It needs at least:

- A list of the worldwide *root* servers to find out where to send external queries. A file containing the current complete list can be copied from the registration service.

- A list of names and their corresponding addresses.

- A list of addresses and their corresponding names.

In today's implementations, Domain Name System information is simply typed into files called *zone files*. The data in the zone files then is loaded into the Domain Name System service. A *zone* is a subtree of the naming tree. A zone file contains information for the subtree.

- A list of names and their corresponding addresses is stored in a *forward* "zone file."

- A list of addresses and their corresponding names is stored in a *reverse* "zone file."

DNS Resource Record Entries

DNS data is stored as a series of entries called resource records (RR). A resource record contains:

```
[name]    [TTL]    [class]    Record-Type    Record-Data    [; comment]
```

For example:

```
3COM.COM.  172800   IN    NS  TMC.EDU.  ; a 3com name server record
```

- The Time-To-Live (TTL) indicates how long (in seconds) a record may be cached after it has been retrieved. In the example, the TTL is 48 hours. The TTL value is optional. If no value is entered, a default that has been established for the set of records containing this one is used.

- The *only* class currently in common use is "IN," for Internet. This often appears only once, in the first record, and is inherited by the rest of the records.

- There are many different record types, such as name server (NS), address (A), or mail exchanger (MX).

- The content in the record data field depends on the type. For example, for a name server type, the record data identifies a name server for the domain. For an address type, the content is (not surprisingly) an IP address.

The class and TTL often are omitted from a resource record.[7] Also, when there is a sequence of records with the same name, an administrator sometimes will omit the *name* column, allowing it to default to the last previously included values.

Earlier, when we sent a query that asked for 3com name servers, we received data corresponding to the records:

```
3COM.COM.  172800   IN   NS   TMC.EDU.   ; a 3com name server record
3COM.COM.  172800   IN   NS   XANTH.CS.ODU.EDU.
3COM.COM.  172800   IN   NS   NEWS.AERO.ORG.
3COM.COM.  172800   IN   NS   MAIL.AERO.ORG.
3COM.COM.  172800   IN   NS   FOUR11.3com.com.
3COM.COM.  172800   IN   NS   SEAWEED.THIRDCOAST.NET.
```

---

[7]Sometimes data is entered with the class and TTL fields included, and in reverse order. The TTL is numeric and hence cannot be confused with the class ("IN").

Related records like these, which have the same label, class, and type, are called a *resource record set.* It is a good idea to give all of the records in a set the same TTL. They always will be retrieved as a bunch, and it makes sense for them to age out as a bunch. Later, we see that secure DNS requires all of the records in a set to have the same TTL.

Resource Record Types

There are many different resource record types, and each is identified by a character or short acronym. Resource record types are listed in Table 12.1.

A Sample Name-to-Address File

The display that follows shows a zone file that translates names to addresses for a mythical *fishfood.com* domain. It also contains some other important information.

TABLE 12.1

Resource Record Types

Record Type	Description
SOA	Start Of Authority—identifies the domain or zone and sets a number of parameters.
NS	Maps a domain name to the name of a computer that is authoritative for the domain.
A	Maps the name of a system to its address. If a system (e.g., a router) has several addresses, then there will be a separate record for each.
CNAME	Maps an alias name to the true, *canonical name.*
MX	Mail Exchanger. Identifies the systems that relay mail into the organization.
TXT	Provides a way to add text comments to the database.
	For example, a *txt* record could map *abc.com* to the company's name, address, and telephone number.
WKS	Well Known Services. Can list the application services available at the host. Used sparingly, if at all.
HINFO	Host Information, such as computer type and model. Rarely used.
PTR	Maps an IP address to a system name. Used in address-to-name files.

```
;      fishfood.com file
FISHFOOD.COM.   IN  SOA  NS1.FISHFOOD.COM. postmaster.FISHFOOD.COM. (
        94101101 ; serial number
        86400 ; refresh after 24 hours
        7200 ; retry after 2 hours
        2592000 ; expire after 30 days
        172800 ; default TTL of 2 days
        )

FISHFOOD.COM.   IN  NS  NS1.FISHFOOD.COM.
FISHFOOD.COM.   IN  NS  NS2.FISHFOOD.COM.

NS1             IN  A        172.66.1.1
NS2             IN  A        172.66.7.1
;
MAIL-RELAY      IN  A        172.66.1.2
                IN  TXT      ftp on mail-relay
                IN  HINFO    SUN UNIX ;no reason to include this!
;
WWW             IN  A        172.66.1.5
FTP             IN  CNAME    MAIL-RELAY
;
FISHFOOD.COM.   IN  MX    1  MAIL-RELAY
*               IN  MX    1  MAIL-RELAY
WWW             IN  MX    1  MAIL-RELAY
;
;end of fishfood.com file
;
```

Name Completion

Recall that "." is the name of the root of the naming tree. Complete names in a zone file must end with a "." symbol. A name that does not end in "." is completed by adding the Domain Name for this zone, *fishfood.com*. Thus, in this file, *ns1* corresponds to *ns1.fishfood.com.* and *www* corresponds to *www.fishfood.com.*

The @ symbol has a special meaning in a zone file. Wherever it appears, it needs to be replaced with the name of the zone (in this case, *fishfood.com.*). That is the reason that the email address for the administrator had to be written as *postmaster.FISHFOOD.COM.* instead of *postmaster@FISHFOOD.COM.*

Comments

The file contains several comments. Comments are introduced by the ";" character.

The SOA Record

The first record of the file is the important Start of Authority (SOA) record.

```
FISHFOOD.COM.   IN  SOA  NS1.FISHFOOD.COM. postmaster.FISHFOOD.COM. (
                    94101101 ; serial number
                      86400 ; refresh after 24 hours
                       7200 ; retry after 2 hours
                    2592000 ; expire after 30 days
                     172800 ; default TTL of 2 days
                  )
```

The parentheses in the SOA record allow it to span several lines. Several timeout values, measured in seconds, are included in the record. Most of the SOA record contains marching orders for secondary servers. This SOA record indicates that:

- Server *ns1.fishfood.com* is primary for domain *fishfood.com*.
- Problems should be reported to *postmaster@fishfood.com* (you have to change the first dot to an @).

The first time that a secondary server connects to its primary, it will open a TCP session and copy this whole file to its disk. The secondary will obtain important configuration information from the next four items in the SOA record. The record shown previously indicates that each secondary should:

- Access the primary every 24 hours and read the SOA record.
- Check whether its current serial number is lower than the primary's. If it is, the primary has been updated, and the secondary needs to perform a *zone transfer*—that is, open a TCP session and obtain a fresh copy of the entire database.
- If the secondary cannot connect at the scheduled time, it should try again 2 hours later.
- If the secondary has not been able to contact the primary for 30 days, it should expire all of its data and stop answering queries.
- The time to live (TTL) is a default value for cache timeouts. Recall that timeout values are included in DNS responses.

The primary server's administrator chooses the values in the SOA record. They can be adjusted according to the usual frequency with which the Domain Name System database is updated.

Name Server (NS) Records

NS records identify the name servers for the domain. For example, the *fishfood.com* zone file shown earlier contains records that identify *nsl.fishfood.com* and *ns2.fishfood.com* as authoritative name servers for the *fishfood.com* zone. Many organizations create a single forward zone and enter all of their name-to-address data into that zone. They update the zone files at a primary server and set up one or more secondaries to improve reliability and response time.

However, a large organization may want to break its naming tree into subdomains and farm out responsibility for maintaining parts of the tree. For example, *fishfood.com* might define subdomains such as *chicago.fishfood.com* and *newyork.fishfood.com*. An administrator in Chicago or New York might set up a local primary server that holds the zone file for the local subdomain.

In this case, the parent "root" server for *fishfood.com* will contain records that identify the "child" name servers that are authoritative for the subdomains *chicago.fishfood.com* and *newyork.fishfood.com*. The parent also will have address records for these child name servers. The authoritative record for the address of a system with a name like *nls.chicago.fishfood.com* really belongs in the *chicago.fishfood.com* zone. However, a copy is needed in the parent zone file because that is the only way that the child zone server can be located. The copy of the address record is called a *glue* record.

Note that the administrator of the parent servers has to keep in touch with the administrators of child servers and update the child server names and addresses when changes occur.

Address Records

Address records simply map a name to an address. Thus, the address of *ns1.fishfood.com* is 172.66.1.1.

CNAME Records

Recall that you can assign alias nicknames to server hosts so users can guess their names. In the example, a file transfer service runs at the same machine that supports mail relay service. The canonical name (*CNAME*) record indicates that *ftp.fishfood.com*. is a nickname for *mail-*

relay.fishfood.com. and enables users to guess the name of the file transfer server.

Mail Exchanger Records

Mail Exchanger (MX) servers relay electronic mail to and from networks.[8] There are three MX records in the file that identify MX servers for *fishfood.com:*

```
fishfood.com.    IN MX 1 MAIL-RELAY
*                IN MX 1 MAIL-RELAY
WWW              IN MX 1 MAIL-RELAY
```

These actually indicate that:

- Mail addressed to *somebody@fishfood.com* should be sent to *mail-relay.fishfood.com.*
- The wild card (*) allows you to relay mail that has been addressed to specific hosts that are *not* listed in the DNS directory. Mail addressed to *somebody@anyhost.fishfood.com* would be passed to *mail-relay.fishfood.com.*
- Mail addressed to *somebody@www.fishfood.com* should be passed to *mail-relay.fishfood.com.*

It looks as if the wild card should take care of *www.fishfood.com,* so why do we need a separate statement? The rules say that the wild card can apply only to systems for which there are *no* other records in the DNS database.

The number that appears after the MX type identifier is called a *preference number* and is discussed in Chapter 16, which deals with electronic mail.

TXT and HINFO Records

TXT records have no real function, but they enable the administrator to embed some comments in the database.

HINFO records can be used to identify a system's hardware and operating system type. Since users are able to read this data via a program

---

[8]See Chapter 16, the email chapter.

such as *nslookup,* many administrators feel that HINFO records should *not* be included in the database; they help crackers to find systems for which some kind of vulnerability is known.

Address-to-Name Translations

Why would anyone want to do a reverse lookup and translate an address to a name? Some system programs invoke reverse lookups to improve the appearance of administrative displays. For example, the *netstat* display below shows all or part of host names instead of IP addresses:

```
> netstat -a
Local Address            Remote Address        Swind  Send-Q  Rwind  Recv-Q  State
katie.vnet.net.63733     home.durbs.co.za.80   8537   0       0      0       ESTABLISHED
katie.vnet.net.64159     u2.abs.net.6667       8192   0       9112   0       ESTABLISHED
katie.vnet.net.64226     fubar.bayou.com.3319  32736  0       8760   0       ESTABLISHED
katie.vnet.net.login     bosco.vnet.net.1023   32120  0       8760   0       ESTABLISHED
katie.vnet.net.telnet    res.labs.com.12516    61440  0       9216   0       ESTABLISHED
katie.vnet.net.telnet    erchg002.nt.com.2514  8192   0       9112   0       ESTABLISHED
```

Reverse lookups also are used by file transfer and World Wide Web servers, which create logs that record the names of systems that are using the service. *Some services refuse clients whose IP addresses do not correspond to some record in the Domain Name database.* In fact, some will perform a double lookup:

- Map the IP address to a name.
- Map the name to an IP address.

If the result does not match the incoming IP address, the client is discarded.

Reverse Zones

Recall that addresses have been placed into a special domain called *IN-ADDR.ARPA* and that since the tree must grow down from the most general part of the address to the least general, the order of the numbers in each address is reversed. For this reason, the subtree for network 172.66 is called 66.172.in-addr.arpa. The display below shows reverse lookup records.

The same name servers have been used for these entries as were used for the forward *fishfood.com zone*. Note that the entries are "backward." For example, the entry for 2.1 corresponds to address 172.66.1.2.

```
66.172.in-addr.arpa.IN  SOA  NS1.FISHFOOD.COM. postmaster.FISHFOOD.COM. (
                             94101101          ; serial
                             86400             ; refresh after 24 hours
                             7200              ; retry after 2 hours
                             2592000           ; expire after 30 days
                             172800            ; default TTL of 2 days
                             )
66.172.in-addr.arpa.IN  NS   NS1.FISHFOOD.COM.
66.172.in-addr.arpa.IN  NS   NS2.FISHFOOD.COM.
1.1              IN  PTR  NS1.FISHFOOD.COM.
1.7              IN  PTR  NS2.FISHFOOD.COM.
2.1              IN  PTR  MAIL-RELAY.FISHFOOD.COM.
5.1              IN  PTR  WWW.FISHFOOD.COM.
```

Designing a Name Server Database

If you have a small organization, you may need to create only a single forward name-to-address file and a single reverse address-to-name file for your DNS database. This may not be feasible if you have a large, geographically distributed organization.

There is a lot of choice in how you organize your data. The following sections describe the different ways that you can do this for your forward name-to-address zones.

Simple Zones

Recall that a name server database consists of a set of zones and a zone contains information for a subtree of the Domain Name System tree. For example, some simple zones are:

- A file containing all of the name-to-address information for *abc.com*.
- A file containing all of the address-to-name information for network 198.207.177.

Parent and Child Zones

A parent zone file contains pointers to name servers for child zones. For example, the Internet *root* is a zone that corresponds to the whole

Domain Name System tree. The *root* is the parent of the whole naming tree. Similarly, *ca* is a parent zone. The *ca* zone file contains pointers to all of the Canadian subzone servers.

An organization's zone file also can be a parent. Its primary content might be pointers to servers for various suborganizations. Or the file might contain both leaf entries and pointers to servers for subzones. For example, as shown in Figure 12.5, at Yale:

- The zone file for *yale.edu* contains many entries for individual computers within academic departments (such as art) that do not wish to maintain their own name servers.

- However, the Computer Science (cs) department wants to maintain its own database, and so the *yale.edu* file contains name server records that point to the computer science servers. The computer science servers will answer queries for names ending in *cs.yale.edu*.

The *yale.edu* zone is the parent of the *cs.yale.edu* zone. The management of the set of names ending in *cs.yale.edu* has been delegated to a different administrator.

Figure 12.5
Parent and child zones.

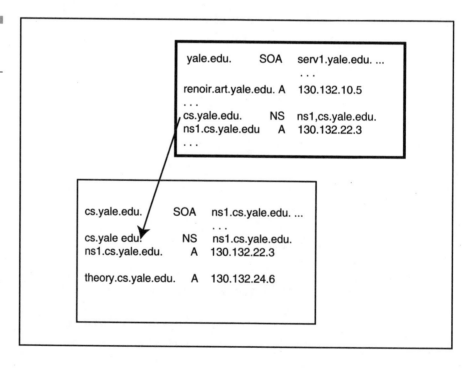

Note that in Figure 12.5, the first item in each zone file is a Start Of Authority (SOA) record. The top SOA record announces that this file contains data for names ending in *yale.edu*. Later in the file, we discover that names ending in *cs.yale.edu.* actually will be handled in a child zone file. The SOA record in the child zone announces that it is in charge of these names.

Glue

As we have seen, the top-level *yale.edu* server contains pointers to servers for delegated subtrees, such as *cs.yale.edu*. Each subtree zone contains the authoritative information for the subtree. There is one glitch that is necessary, but often causes headaches. The *yale.edu* zone must contain the names and addresses of the Domain Name Servers for each of its subzones. But the administrator of a subzone such as *cs.yale.edu* really is the person in control of the subzone servers. If that administrator changes the server addresses and does not tell the *yale.edu* administrator, then the computer science zone will disappear.

The address record in the *yale.edu* parent zone that points to the child server *nsl.cs.yale.edu* is called a *glue record*. Failure to keep glue records up to date is a common DNS problem.

Location of Domain Name Servers

Many organizations find it easier to run a single primary server in their internal network, even if they are partitioning data into several subzones. It is totally acceptable to use one server for multiple zones, if you want to. The data for each zone will be stored in a separate file. The appropriate administrator can update each file.

The secondary servers should be scattered around, so that a transmission or equipment failure in one LAN will not black out DNS service at other locations.

The Domain Name System was designed to be flexible. You have a lot of choice in the way that you set up your servers:

- A server can be configured to act as secondary for several zones, and can retrieve information about several zones from different primary servers.

- A server can act as primary for some zones and secondary for others.

More About Zone Transfers

A secondary server obtains its information from the primary server. The conventional way of doing this is via periodic examinations of the primary's SOA record followed by a complete zone transfer if the update number has changed. A secondary initiates a complete transfer by connecting to the primary via a TCP session and sending a request for complete transfer—this is called an *AXFR request*. For large, dynamically changing networks, this method is neither timely nor efficient. There are some additional DNS capabilities that solve the problem of keeping secondaries up-to-date:

- A primary (master) can send a notify message to secondary (slave) servers, letting them know that the database has changed.

- A secondary (slave) can request an incremental zone transfer (IXFR). The secondary includes its current update number in order to let the primary know its current status. The primary server's response contains a set of records to be deleted and a set of records to be added. (An existing record is changed by first deleting it and then adding the updated version.)

Secondaries may be at different update levels. To make incremental transfers work the primary has to keep a record of the changes since the last few update levels. But if a secondary server's update number is too stale, the primary can simply respond to an IXFR request with a complete zone transfer.

The Format of DNS Messages

DNS queries and responses often are sent as UDP messages, but a TCP session also can be used. When transmitted via UDP, the entire content (excluding UDP and IP headers) is limited to no more than 512 bytes. Queries usually are very short. However sometimes a response does not fit within the limit. In this case:

- A partial, truncated response is returned.

- A flag in the DNS header indicates that the message was truncated.

- The client opens a TCP session to the server and repeats its query.

The query and response messages exchanged between clients and DNS servers have a simple format. A server adds answers and other information to the original query and sends it back. The overall message format is shown in Figure 12.6.

Query Header

The same format is used for a query header and a response header, but several fields that are zeroed out when the query is sent are filled in when the response is sent back. The NT trace below shows the header for a query requesting the address of host *ftp.cert.org*. The query was sent to *char.vnet.net*.

```
(DNS: 0xD:Std Qry for ftp.cert.org. of type Host Addr on class INET
addr.)
     DNS: Query Identifier = 13 (0xD)
     DNS: DNS Flags = Query, OpCode - Std Qry, RD Bits Set, RCode -
No error
          DNS: 0............... = Query
          DNS: .0000.......... = Standard Query
          DNS: .....0......... = Server not authority for domain
          DNS: ......0........ = Message complete
          DNS: .......1....... = Recursive query desired
          DNS: ........0...... = No recursive queries
          DNS: .........000.... = Reserved
          DNS: ...........0000 = No error
     DNS: Question Entry Count = 1 (0x1)
     DNS: Answer Entry Count = 0 (0x0)
     DNS: Name Server Count = 0 (0x0)
     DNS: Additional Records Count = 0 (0x0)
```

Figure 12.6
Overall DNS message format.

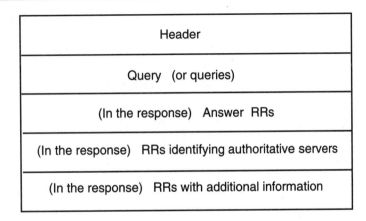

Header
Query   (or queries)
(In the response)   Answer RRs
(In the response)   RRs identifying authoritative servers
(In the response)   RRs with additional information

The fields that are relevant in queries are shown in bold print, and are:

- A 16-bit query identifier (13), which will enable the sender to match the response with the request.
- A "QR" flag with value 0 that indicates that this is a query.
- A 4-bit opcode. Its value here is 0, meaning that this is a "standard" query. A value of 1 means a "reverse" (address-to-name) query.
- An "RD" flag that indicates that the client desires the server, *char,* to act recursively—that is, keep going until it finds the answer.
- A 16-bit Question Entry Count of the number of queries that are included (equal to 1 in the example, which is usual).

Query Section

The query (question) section is very simple:

```
DNS: Question Section: ftp.cert.org. of type Host Addr on class
INET addr.
    DNS: Question Name: ftp.cert.org.
    DNS: Question Type = Host Address
    DNS: Question Class = Internet address class
```

A standard query contains:

- A domain name.
- A 16-bit code that represents a query type (address, mx, etc.). This example requests an address (which has code 1).
- A 16-bit code that defines the query class. The value here is 1, which is Internet class.[9]

Response Header

The unused fields get filled in for the response:

---

[9]The Domain Name System was designed to be able to perform name-to-address translation for any protocol, although up to this time its only use is with TCP/IP.

```
(DNS: 0xD:Std Qry Resp. for ftp.cert.org. of type Canonical name on
class INET addr.)
        DNS: Query Identifier = 13 (0xD)
        DNS: DNS Flags = Response, OpCode - Std Qry, AA RD RA Bits
             Set, RCode - No error
             DNS: 1............... = Response
             DNS: .0000.......... = Standard Query
             DNS: .....1......... = Server authority for domain
             DNS: ......0........ = Message complete
             DNS: .......1....... = Recursive query desired
             DNS: ........1...... = Recursive queries supported by
                                    server
             DNS: .........000.... = Reserved
             DNS: ...........0000 = No error
        DNS: Question Entry Count = 1 (0x1)
        DNS: Answer Entry Count = 2 (0x2)
        DNS: Name Server Count = 2 (0x2)
        DNS: Additional Records Count = 2 (0x2)
```

We see that:

- The answer was obtained from an authoritative server, not from *char*'s disk ("AA" flag = 1).

- The response message is complete ("TC" flag = 0). If the response is truncated, then the client will open a TCP connection, resend the query, and get the complete response.

- Recursion was desired ("RD" flag = 1).

- Recursion was available. *Char* was able to use recursion and get the answer ("RA" flag = 1).

- There was no error (response code = 0).

- There is 1 record in the question section. (This is a copy of the original query.)

- There are 2 records in the answer section.

- There are 2 records in the authority (name server) section.

- There are 2 records in the additional records section.

Query/Response Headers

To summarize, the fields that appear in a DNS query or response header are:

- Identifier. Used to match a response with its request.
- Flags
  Query or response

Standard or inverse lookup
In responses, whether authoritative
In responses, whether complete or truncated
Recursive or not
In responses, recursion available or not
In responses, error code.

■ Number of queries. In queries and responses.

■ Number of answers. In responses.

■ Number of authority records. In responses.

■ Number of additional records. In responses.

Other Response Sections

The rest of the response message is:

```
(DNS: Question Section: ftp.cert.org. of type Host Addr on class
    INET addr.)
        DNS: Question Name: ftp.cert.org.
        DNS: Question Type = Host Address
        DNS: Question Class = Internet address class
    DNS: Answer section: ftp.cert.org. of type Canonical name on
        class INET addr.
            (2 records present)
            DNS: Resource Record: ftp.cert.org. of type
                Canonical name on class INET addr.
            DNS: Resource Name: ftp.cert.org.
            DNS: Resource Type = Canonical name for alias
            DNS: Resource Class = Internet address class
            DNS: Time To Live = 3600 (0xE10)
            DNS: Resource Data Length = 14 (0xE)
            DNS: Owner primary name: ps2.cert.org.
        DNS: Resource Record: ps2.cert.org. of type Host Addr on
            class INET addr.
            DNS: Resource Name: ps2.cert.org.
            DNS: Resource Type = Host Address
            DNS: Resource Class = Internet address class
            DNS: Time To Live = 3600 (0xE10)
            DNS: Resource Data Length = 4 (0x4)
            DNS: IP address = 192.88.209.32
    DNS: Authority Section: cert.org. of type Auth. NS on class
        INET addr.
        2 records present)
        DNS: Resource Record: cert.org. of type Auth. NS on class
            INET addr.
            DNS: Resource Name: cert.org.
            DNS: Resource Type = Authoritative Name Server
            DNS: Resource Class = Internet address class
            DNS: Time To Live = 3600 (0xE10)
            DNS: Resource Data Length = 2 (0x2)
            DNS: Authoritative Name Server: cert.org.
```

```
          DNS: Resource Record: cert.org. of type Auth. NS on class
               INET addr.
          DNS: Resource Name: cert.org.
          DNS: Resource Type = Authoritative Name Server
          DNS: Resource Class = Internet address class
          DNS: Time To Live = 3600 (0xE10)
          DNS: Resource Data Length = 9 (0x9)
          DNS: Authoritative Name Server: tictac.cert.org.
   + DNS: Additional Records Section: cert.org. of type Host
        Addr on class INET addr.
             (2 records present)
DNS: Resource Record: cert.org. of type Host Addr on class INET
     addr.
          DNS: Resource Name: cert.org.
          DNS: Resource Type = Host Address
          DNS: Resource Class = Internet address class
          DNS: Time To Live = 3600 (0xE10)
          DNS: Resource Data Length = 4 (0x4)
          DNS: IP address = 192.88.209.5
     DNS: Resource Record: tictac.cert.org. of type Host Addr
          on class INET addr.
          DNS: Resource Name: tictac.cert.org.
          DNS: Resource Type = Host Address
          DNS: Resource Class = Internet address class
          DNS: Time To Live = 3600 (0xE10)
          DNS: Resource Data Length = 4 (0x4)
          DNS: IP address = 192.88.209.21
```

The answer, authority, and additional records sections all have the same structure. Each consists of a sequence of resource records. Each resource record contains the fields:

Name	For example, *tictac.cert.org*.
Type	The record type. For example, NS or A.
Class	IN for Internet.
Time-To-Live	Measured in seconds.
Length of the data field	Measured in bytes.
Data	For example, a name or IP address.

In the answer section, we discover that *ftp.cert.org* is a nickname. The first answer record contains the CNAME (canonical name) entry that identifies *ps2.cert.org* as the real name of the node. The second answer record contains the A entry that provides the IP address of the node.

The authority record section contains the names of the two name servers for domain *cert.org*. These are called *cert.org* and *tictac.cert.org*. The additional record section contains the address (A) records for the two name servers.

Note that every record has a Time-To-Live of 3600 seconds, so *char* will be allowed to cache the records for one hour. A query made 10 minutes later would return a nonauthoritative response with a decremented TTL. For example:

```
DNS: Resource Record: ps2.cert.org. of type Host Addr on class INET
    addr.
                DNS: Resource Name: ps2.cert.org.
                DNS: Resource Type = Host Address
                DNS: Resource Class = Internet address class
                DNS: Time To Live = 3000 (0xE10)
                DNS: Resource Data Length = 4 (0x4)
                DNS: IP address = 192.88.209.32
```

Transports

Recall that DNS queries and responses normally are transmitted via UDP, but TCP also is permitted. TCP is used for zone transfers.

Viewing Detailed Requests and Responses

Some implementations of the *nslookup* program enable you to view message exchanges in detail without using a monitor to trace the messages. Below, we run *nslookup* at a host at *katie* and turn on detailed debugging via the *set d2* command. The query asks for name-to-address translation for *www.utexas.edu,* and the response provides three addresses.

```
> nslookup
Server:   char.vnet.net
Address:  166.82.1.3

> set d2
> www.utexas.edu.
Server:   char.vnet.net
Address:  166.82.1.3

;; res_mkquery(0, www.utexas.edu, 1, 1)
_____

SendRequest(), len 32
    HEADER:
        opcode = QUERY, id = 33773, rcode = NOERROR
        header flags: query, want recursion
        questions = 1, answers = 0, authority records = 0,
          additional = 0
    QUESTIONS:
        www.utexas.edu, type = A, class = IN

_____
_____
```

```
Got answer (250 bytes):
    HEADER:
        opcode = QUERY, id = 33773, rcode = NOERROR
        header flags: response, auth. answer, want recursion,
            recursion avail.
        questions = 1, answers = 3, authority records = 4,
            additional = 4

    QUESTIONS:
        www.utexas.edu, type = A, class = IN
    ANSWERS:
    ->  www.utexas.edu
        type = A, class = IN, dlen = 4
        internet address = 128.83.40.16
        ttl = 600 (10 mins)
    ->  www.utexas.edu
        type = A, class = IN, dlen = 4
        internet address = 128.83.40.17
        ttl = 600 (10 mins)
    ->  www.utexas.edu
        type = A, class = IN, dlen = 4
        internet address = 128.83.40.15
        ttl = 600 (10 mins)
    AUTHORITY RECORDS:
    ->  utexas.edu
        type = NS, class = IN, dlen = 13
        nameserver = chisos.ots.utexas.edu
        ttl = 86400 (1 day)
    ->  utexas.edu
        type = NS, class = IN, dlen = 5
        nameserver = cs.utexas.edu
        ttl = 86400 (1 day)
    ->  utexas.edu
        type = NS, class = IN, dlen = 11
        nameserver = spica.cc.utexas.edu
        ttl = 86400 (1 day)
    ->  utexas.edu
        type = NS, class = IN, dlen = 19
        nameserver = cyclops.cso.uiuc.edu
        ttl = 86400 (1 day)
    ADDITIONAL RECORDS:
    ->  chisos.ots.utexas.edu
        type = A, class = IN, dlen = 4
        internet address = 128.83.185.39
        ttl = 86400 (1 day)
    ->  cs.utexas.edu
        type = A, class = IN, dlen = 4
        internet address = 128.83.139.9
        ttl = 86400 (1 day)
    ->  spica.cc.utexas.edu
        type = A, class = IN, dlen = 4
        internet address = 129.116.206.20
        ttl = 86400 (1 day)
    ->  cyclops.cso.uiuc.edu
        type = A, class = IN, dlen = 4
        internet address = 128.174.36.254
        ttl = 73455 (20 hours 24 mins 15 secs)
```

```
Name:    www.utexas.edu
Addresses:  128.83.40.16, 128.83.40.17, 128.83.40.15
```

Three different computers are acting as University of Texas World Wide Web servers and are sharing the client traffic between them. The client that originally sent the query will attempt to connect to the first address. (It may try the others if the first fails.) Many Domain Name Servers change the order of their answers in each response, so that traffic can be spread across the multiple hosts. A repeat of the query produced the following lines at the end of its output:

```
Name:    www.utexas.edu
Addresses:  128.83.40.17, 128.83.40.15, 128.83.40.16
```

Note that the order has been shifted.

Additional Record Types

One way to extend the usefulness of the Domain Name System is to define new record types. Over the years, a number of types have been proposed. Those that are useful are absorbed into the system; others never get beyond the experimentation stage.

There is a record type that is used at some locations. The Open Systems Interconnect (OSI) layer 3 Connectionless Network Protocol (CLNP) is implemented in part of the Internet. OSI uses Network Service Access Point (NSAP) addresses to route data to hosts. Since there is a need for name and address mappings for OSI hosts, name-to-address records with type NSAP have been defined for use in DNS databases. Address-to-name mappings are provided, as usual, via records of type PTR.

A new AAAA record type has been defined in order to translate names to IP version 6 addresses. Other recently defined types include KEY and SIG, which are needed in order to implement the secure version of DNS. They are described later in this chapter.

DNS Problems

The Domain Name System is a critical service. Incorrect database entries can make it impossible to reach application hosts. Since the database is distributed, and data is entered manually by many different administrators, it is easy to make mistakes. Typical problems include:

- Omitting a final period in a complete name.

- Missing NS records. Sometimes a new name server does not get listed everywhere that it needs to be listed (e.g., in a parent domain's database).

- The opposite problem—*lame delegations.* A lame delegation is an NS record for a name server that no longer exists. This can cause a *lot* of trouble.

- Failure to update *glue* records (which provide the addresses of name servers for child zones) when the name servers in the child zone change.

- Incorrect MX records that point to systems that do not act as Mail Exchangers for the domain.

- Forgetting that wild-card MX records do *not* apply to a system that already has an entry in the database. Separate MX records are needed for these systems.

- Alias names (CNAME records) that point to other alias records.

- Aliases that point to unknown host names.

- Forward name-to-address records without corresponding reverse address-to-name PTR records.

- PTR records without corresponding name-to-address records.

Fortunately, there are several free tools available that assist in DNS debugging. These are described in an RFC appropriately titled *Tools for DNS Debugging.*

Secure DNS

Using names like *www.weather.com* instead of addresses is one of the most useful features of TCP/IP. We depend on Domain Name Server directories to translate these names to addresses in both our private networks and the Internet. This dependency sometimes opens up opportunities for crackers. In Figure 12.7, cracker Joe has broken into a computer attached to a transit network. Joe watches DNS queries and fires off responses that misdirect users to the cracker's server. Cracker Jane has taken a more direct approach. She has found a weakness in the com-

Figure 12.7
Crackers disrupting
the Domain Name
System.

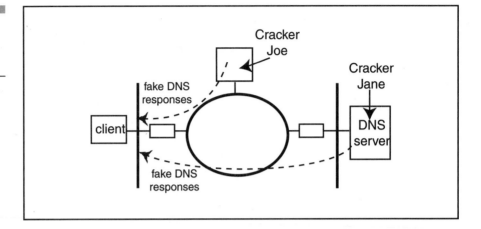

Figure 12.7
Crackers disrupting
the Domain Name
System.

pany's primary Domain Name Server and has changed some of the actual DNS records.

The integrity of any TCP/IP network depends on the integrity of DNS responses. However, until recently, there was no way to authenticate DNS information. This problem has been addressed by the *Domain Name System Security Extensions*.[10] These security extensions:

- Authenticate the validity of the set of records in a DNS response.

- Authenticate zone transfer downloads from a primary server to a secondary server.

- Can be used to ensure that a response corresponds to a specific request.

- Are backward compatible. An old, nonsecure requester will simply ignore the security information that is returned in a response.

Actually, the proposed standard includes capabilities that go far beyond the needs of the Domain Name Service. The DNS directory is enlarged so that it can hold authenticated public keys that are associated with individual hosts or users. It offers an infrastructure for IP Security, authentication of routing updates, secure logins, or secure electronic mail.

At the time of writing, secure Domain Name Servers were still at an experimental stage, and some of the details still needed to be hammered

---

[10]Initially published in RFC 2065, but currently undergoing revision.

out. In the remainder of this chapter we provide an overview of the secure DNS framework. We try to stick to the essentials, and hence deal only briefly with some of the options that are still under consideration.

Authentication and Digital Signatures

Chapter 3 explained how a digital signature protects the integrity of data and authenticates its source. DNS security is built on digital signatures. When a secure name server returns a set of resource records in response to a query, the server includes an authenticating digital signature. The receiver uses the signature to check the integrity of the set of records and verify the source of the records.

Figure 12.8 illustrates this procedure. A local client at *pc.xyz.com* has sent a query to its local name server. The query asks for the identity of the Mail Exchangers for domain *abc.com:*

Figure 12.8
An authenticated
DNS response.

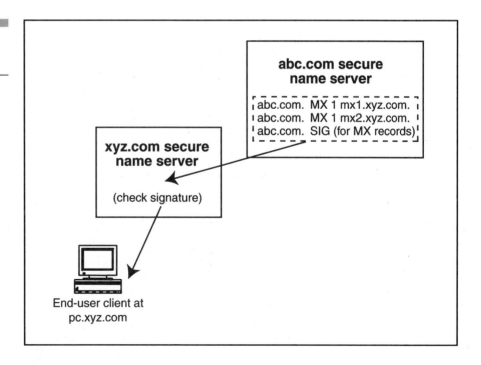

abc.com secure
name server

abc.com. MX 1 mx1.xyz.com.
abc.com. MX 1 mx2.xyz.com.
abc.com. SIG (for MX records)

xyz.com secure
name server

(check signature)

End-user client at
pc.xyz.com

- The local name server gets the address of a name server for *abc.com* (from the root database) and forwards the query to the *abc.com* name server.

- The *abc.com* name server sends back an answer that includes two Mail Exchanger records along with a signature record.

- The signature record contains a digital signature that authenticates the pair of Mail Exchanger records. The local name server for *xyz.com* checks the validity of the answer and then forwards the answer to the end-user client.

The software at most Domain Name Servers is updated on a regular basis so Domain Name Servers can be expected to migrate to secure operation in a timely manner. The software at client hosts is replaced far less often. It may take quite a long time before most client hosts can perform their own final verification of DNS records.

Creating and Checking Digital Signatures

Several digital signature algorithms have been defined. Currently, the ones that are most often used are MD5/RSA, signatures that use Diffie-Hellman keys, and United States Government Digital Signature Algorithm (DSA). For simplicity, the discussion below deals with MD5/RSA, which is widely used in commercial applications.

Recall (see Chapter 3) that to compute the MD5/RSA digital signature for a block of data:

- Compute the message digest of the data.

- Encrypt the message digest with a private key.

Figure 12.9 illustrates this procedure. The figure also shows how someone receiving the data uses a copy of the matching public key to check the signature on the data:

- Compute the message digest of the data.

- Decrypt the message digest in the signature using the public key.

- Compare the two message digest values to see whether they match.

Figure 12.9
Creating and check-
ing a digital
signature.

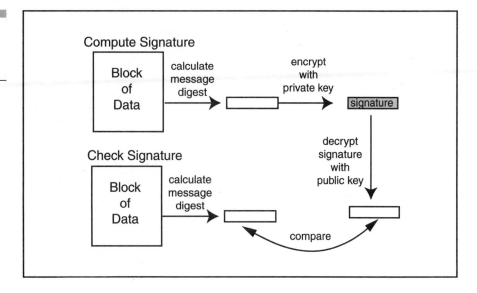

Figure 12.10
The public/private
key DNS framework.

The Secure DNS Framework

Let's examine what is needed in order to secure the Internet Domain
Name System. The implementation that is shown in Figure 12.10 conveys the ideas behind secure DNS.

■ It all starts with a public/private key pair that is generated for
the root of the entire Domain Name System. The root private
key is kept offline, in a secure repository.

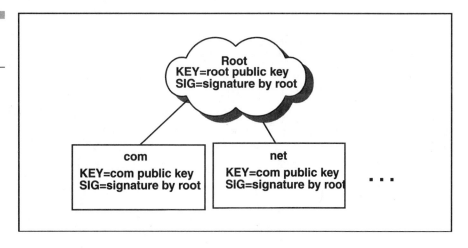

- The root public key is widely advertised. This public key is part of the standard configuration information for secure Domain Name Servers. It also is available for retrieval from the root database.

- Public/private key pairs are generated for each top-level domain (*com, net, org, edu,* etc.). The corresponding private keys are stored offline, in a secure repository.

- The top-level domain public keys are available for retrieval. They also are cached at name servers.

All trust is based on knowing the root public key. The root public key is self-signed using the root private key. The top-level public keys also are signed using the root private key.

Two new types of Domain Name System records have been defined to hold public keys and signatures—a KEY record type and a SIG record type.

The stage is now set. Suppose that the company with domain name *abc.com* wishes to operate its public name servers securely. To do this, the company must create a public/private signature key pair for the *abc.com* zone. The records in the *abc.com* zone file will be signed using the private key. Then new records will be added to the zone:

- A KEY record that contains the zone's public key.

- SIG records that contain signatures for the records in the zone. These signatures are created using the zone's private key.

The job is not quite done. We need to know that we can trust the zone's KEY record. To do this, the zone must be plugged into the overall security framework. Let's start over again:

- Mary Jones, the *abc.com* DNS administrator, adds the root public key and signature to the *abc.com* name server configuration data. She also stores the keys and signatures for *com* and the other generic top-level domains.

- Mary generates a public/private key pair for the *abc.com* zone. This is done at a carefully secured administrative computer that is not attached to the company network.

- Mary stores a copy of the private key in a vault.

- Mary creates a KEY DNS record. This record contains the zone's public key and some related information (such as the signature algorithm in use).

■ Mary submits the KEY record to her *com* key-signing registrar.
The registrar validates Mary's identity and role as the *abc.com*
administrator. Then the registrar signs Mary's KEY record using
the *com* private key. The registrar creates a SIG (signature)
record that contains this authenticating signature.

■ Optionally, the new KEY and SIG records are placed in the *com*
zone.

```
abc.com.   NS    (Name of abc.com name server)
abc.com.   KEY   (abc.com zone public key and related variables)
abc.com.   SIG   (key signature and related variables)
```

■ The registrar uses a secure method to deliver the KEY record
and its new SIG record back to Mary.

■ Mary adds the *abc.com* zone's KEY and SIG records to the
abc.com. zone database.

These records have the form:

```
abc.com.   KEY   (public key for the abc.com zone, and related vari-
                 ables)
abc.com.   SIG   (signature for the abc.com key, and related vari-
                 ables)
```

Keep in mind that this SIG record was created by the *com* administrator
and contains a signature that was created with the *com* private key.
There now is a chain of validation from the zone's public key all the way
up to the root. The chain of keys is illustrated in Figure 12.11.

Securing Zone Records

Once a zone has a signed public key, the corresponding private key will
be used to sign the records in the zone. Each signature is placed in a
SIG record that is added to the zone. However, a separate signature is
not created for each record. Instead, a signature is created for each *set* of
records. A set is made up of records with the same name and type. To
understand how this works, let's take a look at a DNS query and
response.

```
nslookup
> set type = mx
```

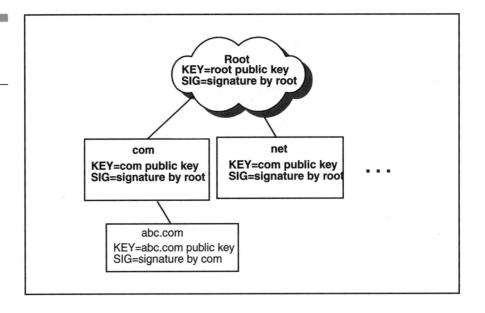

Figure 12.11
Adding a zone to
the security
infrastructure.

```
> cisco.com.
Server: char.vnet.net
Address:        166.82.1.3

cisco.com               preference = 10, mail exchanger = proxy2.cisco.com
cisco.com               preference = 10, mail exchanger = proxy3.cisco.com
cisco.com               preference = 10, mail exchanger = proxy1.cisco.com
cisco.com                nameserver = ns.cisco.com
cisco.com                nameserver = dennis.cisco.com
cisco.com                nameserver = ns1.barrnet.net
cisco.com                nameserver = noc.near.net
cisco.com                nameserver = ns.uu.net
cisco.com                nameserver = ns2.cisco.com
proxy2.cisco.com            internet address = 192.31.7.89
proxy3.cisco.com            internet address = 192.31.7.90
proxy1.cisco.com            internet address = 192.31.7.88
ns.cisco.com                internet address = 198.92.30.32
dennis.cisco.com            internet address = 171.69.2.132
ns1.barrnet.net             internet address = 131.119.245.5
noc.near.net                internet address = 192.52.71.21
ns.uu.net                   internet address = 137.39.1.3
ns2.cisco.com               internet address = 171.69.2.132
```

The first three records make up a set. They all have name *cisco.com* and
type MX. The source DNS records were:

```
(name)        (type)
cisco.com.    MX   10   proxy2.cisco.com.
cisco.com.    MX   10   proxy3.cisco.com.
cisco.com.    MX   10   proxy1.cisco.com.
```

The next six records also make up a set. They all have name *cisco.com* and type NS. The source DNS records were:

```
(name)      (type)
cisco.com.  NS    ns.cisco.com.
cisco.com.  NS    dennis.cisco.com.
cisco.com.  NS    ns1.barrnet.net.
cisco.com.  NS    noc.near.net.
cisco.com.  NS    ns.uu.net.
cisco.com.  NS    ns2.cisco.com.
```

A query response always includes all of the records in a set:

- When one MX record for a particular name is returned, all of the MX records for that name are returned.

- When one NS record for a particular name is returned, all of the NS records for that name are returned.

Therefore, it makes sense to create one signature for the set instead of many separate signatures. This reduces the number of SIG records in the DNS database and also reduces the size of secure responses, which contain SIG records. A secure DNS database includes a SIG record for each set:

```
cisco.com.  MX   10   proxy2.cisco.com.
cisco.com.  MX   10   proxy3.cisco.com.
cisco.com.  MX   10   proxy1.cisco.com.
cisco.com.  SIG      (signature for the 3 MX records)

cisco.com.  NS    ns.cisco.com.
cisco.com.  NS    dennis.cisco.com.
cisco.com.  NS    ns1.barrnet.net.
cisco.com.  NS    noc.near.net.
cisco.com.  NS    ns.uu.net.
cisco.com.  NS    ns2.cisco.com.
cisco.com.  SIG  (signature for the 6 NS records)
```

By the way, the last nine records in the response shown earlier do not make up a set. Each record has a different name and represents a one-record set. Therefore each of these records needs to have its own, separate signature. For example:

```
proxy2.cisco.com.  A     192.31.7.89
proxy2.cisco.com.  SIG   (signature for the proxy2 address record)
proxy3.cisco.com.  A     192.31.7.90
proxy3.cisco.com.  SIG   (signature for the proxy3 address record)
```

A signature record for a set of records is included in a response that includes the set.

Checking a Response

Now let's walk through the steps followed by the local *xyz.com* Domain Name Server when it looks up the Mail Exchanger for *abc.com:*

- The *xyz.com* server sends a query to the root server[11] requesting the addresses of Domain Name Servers for *abc.com*.
- The root server returns the addresses.[12]

The *xyz.com* server will retrieve the *abc.com* public key and its signature if it does not already have these records. At the time of retrieval, it validates the signature for the *abc.com* zone public key using the local copy of the *com* public key. Now the *abc.com* zone public key can be used to validate the signatures on the other records in the *abc.com* zone file.

- The *xyz.com* server sends an MX query to an *abc.com* name server.
- The response includes signature records for the MX and NS record sets. It includes signatures for as many of the address records as space allows.
- The *xyz.com* server uses the *abc.com* zone key to check the signatures.

Authenticating What Is Not There

What happens when you ask for the address of a nonexistent host? The two queries below show a typical response:

```
nslookup
> caa.vnet.net
***char.vnet.net can't find caa.vnet.net: Non-existent host/domain
```

The error message was not contained in the DNS response message. It was produced by the local name server. Here is an actual response message:

```
Got answer:
  HEADER
```

---

[11]If the database is split up, the query will be sent to a separate *com* database.

[12]It also can provide its copy of the zone public key and signature for the *abc.com* zone.

```
opcode = QUERY, id = 7620, rcode = NXDOMAIN
header flags: response, auth. answer, want recursion, recursion
  avail.
questions = 1, answers = 0, authority records = 1, additional = 0
QUESTIONS:
  caa.vnet.net, type = A, class = IN
AUTHORITY RECORDS:
-> vnet.net
    ttl = 21600 (6 hours)
    origin = ns.vnet.net
    mail addr = ns2.vnet.net
    serial = 9308102
    refresh = 10800 (3 hours)
    retry = 3600 (1 hour)
    expire = 1728000 (20 days)
    minimum ttl = 21600 (6 hours)
```

It is the "rcode = NXDOMAIN" statement in the header section of the preceding display that announces that the record does not exist. But this answer is not authenticated because headers are not signed—only records are signed. A cracker might try to disrupt communications by streaming "no such host" messages to your local name server. The secure DNS solution to this problem looks strange at first, but:

■ It was tailored to fit into the design used so far, which allows signatures to be precomputed and stored in a DNS zone.

■ Like the rest of the current design, it is backward compatible with nonsecure servers.

■ It works.

Software that implements secure DNS will:

■ Sort all of the records in a zone.

■ Automatically generate "NXT" records that mark the gaps between adjacent entries.

For example:

```
basket.isc.org.    A      192.1.2.3
basket.isc.org.    SIG    (signature for basket A record)

basket.isc.org.    NXT    clipper.isc.org. (types)
basket.isc.org.    SIG    (signature for the NXT record)

clipper.isc.org.   TXT    This host has a public FTP service.
clipper.isc.org.   SIG    (signature for clipper TXT record)
```

The NXT (nonexistence) record marks the gap between *basket* and *clipper*. If anyone asks for a name that falls into this gap (such as *cab.isc.org*), the NXT record and its signature are returned. This provides reliable evidence that the requested record is "nonexistent."

The "types" field in the NXT record is a bit map that flags all of the record types for clipper that are in the DNS zone. If the TXT record is the only record for *clipper,* a request for an A record for clipper would cause the NXT record and its signature to be returned. The bit map would show that there is no A record in the file.

What about nonexistent records that would be positioned after the last record? There is a wraparound NXT record:

```
apple.isc.org.    A       192.1.2.11
. . .
peaches.isc.org.  A       192.1.2.170
peaches.isc.org.  SIG     (signature for peaches A record)
peaches.isc.org.  NXT     apple.isc.org. (types)
peaches.isc.org.  SIG     (signature for the NXT record)
```

Other Keys and Signatures

The primary reason that keys and signatures have been defined for the Domain Name System is to strengthen and protect the system itself. The critically important private zone key is used to produce signatures associated with the records in a zone. The zone public key is used to check the signatures on records that are returned DNS responses. The zone public/private key pairs support the secure DNS infrastructure.

However, additional KEY and SIG records can be stored in a zone and used to promote general network and host security. A KEY record can hold a public key associated with:

- A host or an IP address
- A userid
- An electronic mail identifier

There is more than one use for a key associated with a host or IP address.

- A Domain Name Server host can use the *transaction security* feature to prove that its response corresponds to a specific request. The host uses a private key that it owns to compute a signature against a query concatenated with its response.

- A host or IP address key can be used for IP security.[13]
- A key associated with a userid can support login authentication. The name field of a userid key record has the form userid.host-domain-name. For example:

  j-smith.dbserver.abc.com   KEY   (parameters, public key)

- A key for an electronic mail identifier guarantees the owner's signature on an electronic mail message. It also enables people to encrypt mail that is sent to the owner so that only the key owner can read the mail. The format of an email key record is:

  jbrown@mailserver.abc.com   KEY   (parameters, public key)

Note that these additional keys are independent of the zone key that is used to sign record sets for DNS security. These keys can be administered and signed by entirely separate organizations.

Contents of KEY Records

A KEY record can hold a zone key or one of the additional types of keys. A KEY record has the form:

  name   TTL KEY   (parameters)

More specifically:

  name   TTL KEY   flags protocol algorithm public-key

The name identifies the "owner" of the public key. If this is a zone key, then the name of the owner is the name of the zone (e.g., *abc.com* or *isc.org*). If this is a host key, then the owner name is the name of the host. The display below shows a zone key obtained from a test DNS security site operated by Trusted Information Systems using the latest version of the *dig* domain name lookup utility:

```
netsec.tis.com.   14400   KEY   0x4101 3 1 (
        AQOalDCk4PPOFUGdKd7u2UgUcUVCokBUIUOPRODBA54eDzgGrukYVuwAD
        4fiClqoPuFpgZbTZPA29CQ3jK/6VbMj )
```

---

[13]See Chapter 24.

The parameters in a KEY record are described in the sections that follow.

Flags

The flags indicate whether the enclosed key is associated with the zone, a host, a userid, or an email identifier. There also are flags that can be used to indicate that there is no enclosed key for the named zone because the zone is not secure. (In this case, there would be no further parameters.) A flag in the previous example indicates that it is a zone key.

Protocol

The protocol parameter identifies how the key will be used. For example:

- DNS zone security
- IP Security
- Transport Layer Security
- Electronic mail security

The protocol value 3 in this sample record indicates that this key will be used for DNS security.

Algorithm

The algorithm field identifies the signature algorithm that has been selected. The algorithms that currently have been accepted are:

- RSA/MD5 (algorithm 1)
- Signature created using Diffie-Hellman keys (algorithm 2)
- Digital Signature Algorithm (algorithm 3)

The key in the example shown previously is compatible with the MD5/RSA algorithm.

Public Key

The actual format of the public key parameter depends on the algorithm that has been selected.[14] The RSA key in the example contains binary data. The binary bytes have been converted into a special "base64" encoding that looks like a string of text characters. See Chapter 16 for details of how this is done.

Contents of SIG Records

A signature:

- Is computed on a set of records with the same name and type.
- Is created by a signer that is identified by a parameter in the SIG record.
- Is created using the private key owned by the signer.
- Is checked using the public key owned by the signer.

The signatures attached to ordinary DNS records are created using the private key that is owned by the zone and are checked using the public key that is owned by the zone. A signature record has the form:

name   TTL SIG   (parameters)

More specifically:

name   TTL SIG   type-covered algorithm labels

expiration-time start-time key-tag signer's-name signature

Below we show the display format of the signature record for a zone key. The record was obtained from the test DNS security site. The display format omits some fields and converts others to a readable form. The binary signature has been represented in base64 encoding.

```
netsec.tis.com.   14400   SIG   KEY 1 (
     19980715131748 19980701131748 21939 netsec.tis.com.
     QLzelcAYv5VGwRgMu7ncv5xRXxnYsAE0JBBCzcbNYUCsVyfzDCznpcJfCK
        oDMeGGFqqBf0t3yRw0qFGMZSvrxA = = )
```

---

[14]Each "public key" actually is made up of several parameters, including a key length specification. Each of the various formats is described in a separate RFC document.

The signature parameters are discussed in the sections that follow. The sections do not follow the order just shown; the order has been selected to facilitate the explanations.

Type Covered

The type covered is the type of the resource record(s) covered by this signature—for example: A, NS, MX, and the like. The preceding example signs a KEY record.

Signature

The signature covers all records that:

- Have the specified type.
- Have the same name as the SIG record.

The signature is calculated on the block of data formed by concatenating parameters in the signature record with the set of records that are covered:

type-covered algorithm_signer's-name | record-1...record-n

Before computing the signature, each of these records has to be converted to a canonical format and the records must be sorted in ascending order by name. In addition, the Time-To-Live (TTL) parameter in each record must be restored to its original value. This is explained in the next section.

Original TTL

The signature for a record set is precomputed at the source Domain Name Server and stored there. All of the fields in each record, including the TTL, are used in the calculation.

But responses that are sent to a client often are constructed from records cached at a local name server. The fields in a cached record are identical to the original fields—except for the TTL. The TTL in a cached record is decremented until it reaches 0, when the record is discarded.

To illustrate this, the set of answers below shows the initial response to a query for *isc.org* name server records. The local server retrieved these from an authoritative server:

```
QUESTIONS:
        isc.org, type = NS, class = IN
    ANSWERS:
    -> isc.org
       nameserver = NS.UU.NET
       ttl = 172800 (2 days)
    -> isc.org
       nameserver = GW.HOME.VIX.COM
       ttl = 172800 (2 days)
    -> isc.org
       nameserver = UUCP-GW-1.PA.DEC.COM
       ttl = 172800 (2 days)
    -> isc.org
       nameserver = UUCP-GW-2.PA.DEC.COM
       ttl = 172800 (2 days)
```

A later query produces a result taken from the cache at the local server. These records contain decremented TTL values.

```
QUESTIONS:
        isc.org, type = NS, class = IN
    ANSWERS:
    -> isc.org
       nameserver = NS.UU.NET
       ttl = 163305 (1 day 21 hours 21 mins 45 secs)
    -> isc.org
       nameserver = GW.HOME.VIX.COM
       ttl = 163305 (1 day 21 hours 21 mins 45 secs)
    -> isc.org
       nameserver = UUCP-GW-1.PA.DEC.COM
       ttl = 163305 (1 day 21 hours 21 mins 45 secs)
    -> isc.org
       nameserver = UUCP-GW-2.PA.DEC.COM
       ttl = 163305 (1 day 21 hours 21 mins 45 secs)
```

If the cached set of records is sent to a secure client and the client checks the signature, the result will not tally because the TTL data has changed. Fortunately, the solution is simple. A copy of the original TTL is stored in the signature record for the set of records. The secure client replaces the TTLs in the records with the original TTL before checking the signature.[15]

Algorithm

The algorithm in the SIG is the same as the algorithm in the KEY record. It is the algorithm used to compute the signature. This is MD5/RSA in the SIG example shown earlier.

---

[15]To make this work, all of the records in a set stored in a secure zone are assigned the same TTL.

Labels

The labels parameter contains a count of the number of labels in the owner name for the signature record. For example, if the name for the record is *abc.com,* then labels = 2. The labels count is omitted from the display form of the record, since the full name appears in the first field.

Signature Inception and Expiration

These parameters state the start and end dates for the period of time that a signature is valid. A signature must not be trusted after the expiration date. The time is measured in seconds since January 1, 1970, Universal Time (formerly called Greenwich Mean Time).

The display form for the dates is YYYYMMDDHHMMSS. In the SIG example shown earlier, the expiration date, 19980715131748, is August 15, 1998 (1:17 PM). The start date, 19980701131748, was August 1, 1998 (1:17 PM).

Signer's Name

The signer's name ties the signature back to the public key that will be used to check the signature. This corresponds to the "owner" of the public key. (This is the name field for the corresponding KEY record.) For a key used to sign zone records, the signer's name is the domain name of the zone.

In the previous example, the signer's name is *netsec.tis.com.* This is a test zone, and the administrator has used the zone private key to create the zone signature. Normally, the *com* private key would be used.

Key Tag

Multiple keys might be associated with a given signer's name. The key tag is a small chunk of the public key that is the mate for the private key used to create the enclosed signature. The key tag is used to make a quick check that the public key that has been selected to validate this signature is the right one.

Transaction Signatures and Zone Transfers

A valid signature on a set of records shows that they are authentic, but it does not prove that they are the response to the client's original query or that they came from an expected source. The host uses a private key that it owns to compute a signature against a query concatenated with its response. The calculated signature is then placed at the end of the response. The host's signature is checked by looking up its public key.

A transaction signature also is a good way to authenticate a zone transfer between a primary and secondary Domain Name Server.

Request Signatures

DNS databases are open to anyone, and so client authentication is not an issue for normal database queries. However, authentication is essential for dynamic updates, which may become common in the future. A key associated with the client is used to create the signature.

Recommended Reading

There are many RFC documents that deal with the Domain Name System. We mention some important ones here.

RFC 1034 defines Domain Name concepts and facilities. RFC 1035 describes the implementation and protocol specification for the Domain Name System. It should be consulted if further details on the message formats are required.

RFC 1996 discusses prompt notification of zone changes, and RFC 1995 explains how incremental zone transfers are implemented.

RFC 1713 describes several tools available for DNS debugging. RFCs 1912, 1536, and 1537 describe common DNS configuration errors, implementation errors, and fixes. RFC 2182 is a Best Current Practices document on the *Selection and Operation of Secondary DNS Servers*. RFC 2181 presents some important clarifications of the DNS specification.

The book *DNS and BIND* by Albitz and Liu (O'Reilly & Associates) provides an excellent exposition of the Domain Name System.

At the time of writing, Domain Name System Security Extensions were published in RFC 2065. However, modifications to the original specification were in progress, and an updated RFC is in the works. Dynamic updates are described in RFC 2136 and Secure Domain Name System Dynamic Updates are discussed in RFC 2137.

Several related RFCs were in progress. These describe the calculation of digital signatures, various signature algorithms, and the storage of certificates and certificate revocation lists in DNS databases.

Up-to-date information on free and vendor implementations of secure DNS is available from the Internet Software Consortium at:

http://www.isc.org/

This site also has pointers to other useful DNS information. The BIND Operations Guide (BOG) from the Internet Software Consortium presents an excellent BIND tutorial.

CHAPTER 13

Telnet

Introduction

What use is a network that offers a rich collection of applications if users cannot login to different computers and use the applications? TCP gives us computer-to-computer connectivity, but there are other obstacles to overcome. For a long time it seemed as if every computer vendor was determined to market a totally proprietary environment. An application at a vendor's host could be accessed only by special terminals manufactured by that vendor.

The *telnet* (terminal networking) protocol overcomes vendor dissimilarities and lets a user connected to any host in a network login to any other host. *Telnet* terminal emulation was the first TCP/IP application. The *telnet* protocol also was designed to be a tool for general application-to-application communications. As organizations have moved away from legacy terminal-based applications, *telnet* increasingly has been used as a toolkit for building client/server applications. In fact, *telnet* underlies client/server interactions for file transfer, electronic mail, and the World Wide Web (WWW).

In this chapter, we explore *telnet*'s ability to help a user login to a remote application. We also find out what *telnet* offers the client/server application builder.

Using Telnet for Logins

Telnet provides emulation of various types of terminals, so you can access Unix computers, VAX/VMS systems, or IBM mainframes. Some implementations of *telnet* support special authentication procedures.

If you run *telnet* from a multiuser system, you probably will operate a simple text-based user interface. Using a text-based *telnet* client is very easy. You just type:

```
> telnet hostname
```

Often, IBM 3270 or 5250 emulation is packaged separately, and you access IBM hosts by typing:

```
> tn3270 hostname
```

```
> tn5250 hostname
```

Most people manage to use *telnet* successfully without knowing any more than this. Below, we show a login to a host called *tigger.jvnc.net* from a computer at Yale.

```
> telnet tigger.jvnc.net
Trying 128.121.50.145 ...
Connected to tigger.jvnc.net.
Escape character is '^]'.

SunOS UNIX (tigger.jvnc.net)

SunOS UNIX (pascal)

login: xxxxx
Password:
Last login: Wed Aug 23 19:24:02
TERM = vt100, PRINTER = lp
```

Desktop *telnet* products offer extra functionality, such as choosing the type of terminal to emulate from a list, saving all or part of a session in a log file, configuring your keyboard, or storing all of the information needed to access a frequently visited site. Some of these features are shown in Figure 13.1.

Figure 13.1
NetManage desktop *telnet* application.

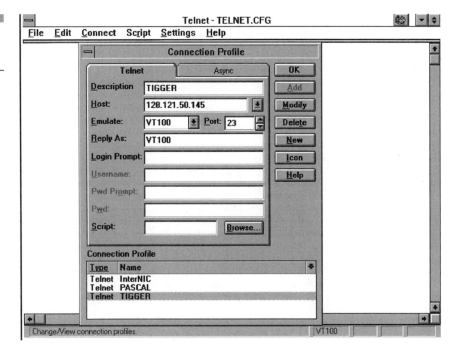

Telnetting to a Selected Port

Port 23 is the standard well-known port for *telnet* terminal access. When a client connects to port 23, the normal response is a prompt for a login ID and password.

But since *telnet* also was designed to support general application-to-application communications, it includes a magic carpet that can take a client to any port. For example, in the dialog below, we connect to an electronic mail server and pretend to be the email program at *katie:*

```
> telnet pop.vnet.net. 25
Trying 166.82.1.29...
Connected to pop.vnet.net.
Escape character is '^]'.
220 popserv.vnet.net ESMTP Sendmail 8.8.8/8.8.8; Thu, 18 Jun 1998
 08:32:20 -0400 (EDT)
HELO katie.vnet.net
250 popserv.vnet.net Hello sfeit@katie.vnet.net [166.82.1.7],
pleased to meet you quit
221 popserv.vnet.net closing connection
```

A cracker can have a direct conversation with many standard service programs that are built on top of *telnet*. This gives the cracker the opportunity to try out a grab bag full of tricks to try to break into the system and access its data. Old versions of the most popular electronic mail program, *sendmail,* were full of golden opportunities for crackers.

The ability to *telnet* to any port has proved to be a great convenience. It also has turned out to be a potential source of security problems, when crackers crash into a site via a poorly implemented program running openly at some port.

Telnet Terminal Emulation Model

As shown in Figure 13.2, a user at a real terminal interacts with the local *telnet* client program. The *telnet* client program has to accept keystrokes from the user's keyboard, interpret them, and display output on the user's screen in a manner that is consistent with the emulation in use.

The *telnet* client opens a TCP connection to the *telnet* server that is

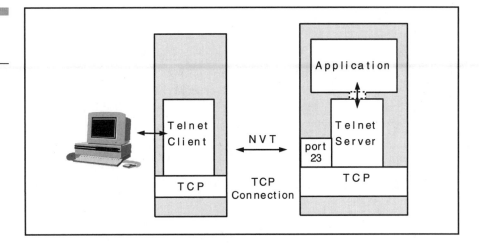

Figure 13.2
Telnet client and server.

accessed at well-known port 23. The *telnet* server interacts with applications and assists in emulating a native terminal.

Network Virtual Terminal

In order to get the session going, both sides initially exchange information using a very simple protocol called *Network Virtual Terminal,* or NVT.

The NVT protocol was modeled on an old-fashioned half-duplex keyboard and printer operating in line-at-a-time mode. NVT has well-defined characteristics:

- NVT data is made up of 7-bit USASCII characters padded to 8 bits via an initial 0 bit.
- Data is sent a line at a time.
- Each line ends with an ASCII Carriage Return <CR> Linefeed <LF> combination.
- Bytes with an initial (high-order) 1 bit are used for command codes.
- The protocol is "half-duplex." After sending a line, the client waits to receive data from the server. The server sends its data and then sends a *Go Ahead* command, indicating that the client can now send another line.

Common Terminal Types

Usually, the client and server stay in NVT mode for a very short time—just long enough to negotiate some type of terminal to be emulated, such as an ASCII VT100 or IBM 3270.

In the years since *telnet* was introduced, many terminal emulations have been added to the protocol.

ASCII Terminals

ASCII terminals are used with Unix and Digital Equipment Corporation VAX computers. ASCII terminals are characterized by:

- *Remote echoing* of each character. That is, each character is sent to the remote server host and then is sent back before it appears on the user's screen. (This is very hard on the network.)
- *Full-duplex transmission.* Characters flow in both directions simultaneously. The server will *not* need to send *Go Ahead* control codes.
- Support for *interactive* full-screen applications—with a lot of network overhead.
- A larger ASCII character set than NVT.

Basic ASCII terminal characteristics are defined in standards ANSI X3.64, ISO 6429, and ISO 2022. There have been many ASCII terminal products, each offering slightly different features (for example, ANSI, VT52, VT100, VT220, TVI950, TVI955, and WYSE50). The VT100 terminal type is frequently emulated for remote logins to Unix computers.

Configuring Keyboards

A PC or Macintosh keyboard is not identical to a VT100 or 3270 keyboard. A *telnet* product usually provides a way to configure individual keys—or control key combinations—to perform functions normally available on the keyboards of emulated systems. For example, one problem that arises with VT*XXX* terminals is that the command character used

Figure 13.3
Drag-and-drop key-
board mapping.

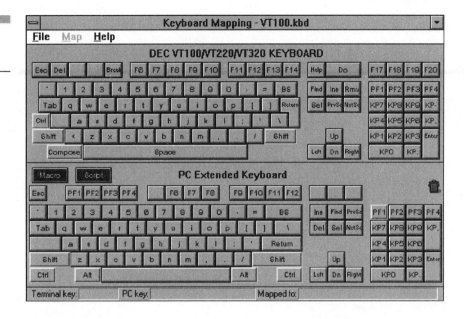

to erase a mistyped character is not standardized. Some terminals use
Backspace, while others use *Del.*

For Unix systems, you usually customize your terminal keyboard by
referencing entries in a configuration file called */etc/termcaps.* Dealing
with this file is challenging. The Microsoft Windows *telnet* client is a
bare-bones model that does not offer a lot of customization choices. The
Chameleon Windows *telnet* configuration screen shown in Figure 13.3 is
easy to use. It enables you to drag keys from the top keyboard and drop
them onto any convenient PC key. For example, if you wanted a PC's
Backspace key to send the *Del* code, you would just drag the VT100 *Del*
key onto the PC keyboard *Backspace* key.

IBM 3270 and 5250 Terminals

An IBM mainframe often needs to support hundreds or thousands of
interactive terminals. For many years, proprietary 3270 terminal sys-

tems have been used to access IBM mainframes. These terminals were optimized for data processing applications.

3270 terminals operate in *Block Mode,* which means that a user works with a screen of data at a time. When the user presses ENTER or some other function key, the information on the screen is sent to the host. The keyboard locks, and the host processes the data. The host then sends back one or more screens of data. When the host is finished, it unlocks the keyboard. 3270s are characterized by:

- EBCDIC 8-bit codes
- Half-duplex communication
- Block mode

IBM 5250 terminals, used to access AS/400 computers, also have these characteristics.

Options

Terminal emulation characteristics are established by exchanging commands that negotiate *telnet options.* Either side may ask its partner to *DO* a particular option, such as "echo individual characters." The partner can accept or refuse. Either side can volunteer that it *WILL* perform some option. Again, the partner can accept or refuse.

There are four request/response exchanges that will be seen during option negotiation:

DO (option code)	Ask partner to perform option.
WILL (option code)	Partner agrees. Option now holds.
DO (option code)	Ask partner to perform option.
WON'T (option code)	Partner refuses. Status unchanged.
WILL (option code)	Indicates desire to begin option.
DO (option code)	Partner gives permission. Option now holds.
WILL (option code)	Indicates desire to begin option.
DON'T (option code)	Partner refuses. Status unchanged.
WON'T (option code)	Confirms that status will be unchanged.

At connection start-up, a swarm of option requests bounce back and forth between the partners. Occasionally options also are exchanged in midsession. Some options signal the start of *subnegotiations* in which additional information is exchanged.

What happens if both sides refuse every option request? The session will stay in NVT mode.

Terminal Type Option

A very important option—*Terminal Type*—uses subnegotiation. A client that sends *WILL TERMINAL TYPE* wants to tell the server about the types of terminals that it can emulate. If the server is willing to see this information, it responds with *DO TERMINAL TYPE*.

Subsequently, in a subnegotiation, the server asks the client to identify one of the terminal types that it can emulate, and the client responds. The server can repeat the query until either the client provides a type that is acceptable to the server or the client's list of supported types is exhausted. Formal terminal type identifiers such as DEC-VT100, HP-2648, or IBM-3278-2 are defined in the *Assigned Numbers* RFC document.

Negotiating VT100 Options[1]

In the sample dialog below, we start up *telnet* and enter *toggle options* to cause *telnet* to show us its negotiations. Then *open* is used to start a login. The partners negotiate an ASCII VT100 emulation by selecting the following characteristics:

- The server will not send *Go Aheads* because the session will be full-duplex.
- A *Terminal Type* subnegotiation will be used to identify the specific ASCII terminal to be emulated.
- The server will *echo* the client's characters.

The partners also agree to negotiate about the window size ("NAWS"). Many other options are proposed and refused. We have italicized the successful options so that they are easy to pick out from the mass.

---

[1]The IANA publishes a summary of *telnet* options.

Neither side needs to wait for an answer to an option request before sending another request. A negotiator doesn't even have to respond to options in the same order that they were received. As a result, a series of negotiations sometimes needs to be untangled before it can be understood.

```
> telnet
telnet> toggle options
Will show option processing.
telnet> open float.vnet.net
Trying 166.82.1.14...
Connected to float.vnet.net.
Escape character is '^]'.
SENT DO SUPPRESS GO AHEAD
SENT WILL TERMINAL TYPE
SENT WILL NAWS
SENT WILL TSPEED
SENT WILL LFLOW
SENT WILL LINEMODE
SENT WILL NEW-ENVIRON
SENT DO STATUS
RCVD DO TERMINAL TYPE
RCVD DO NAWS
RCVD DO XDISPLOC
SENT WONT XDISPLOC
RCVD DO NEW-ENVIRON
RCVD DO OLD-ENVIRON
SENT WONT OLD-ENVIRON
RCVD WILL SUPPRESS GO AHEAD
RCVD DONT TSPEED
RCVD DONT LFLOW
RCVD DONT LINEMODE
RCVD WONT STATUS
RCVD DONT XDISPLOC
RCVD DONT OLD-ENVIRON
RCVD IAC SB TERMINAL-TYPE SEND
SENT IAC SB TERMINAL-TYPE IS "VT100"
RCVD IAC SB NEW-ENVIRON SEND
SENT IAC SB NEW-ENVIRON IS
```

```
RCVD WILL ECHO
SENT DO ECHO
RCVD DO ECHO
SENT WONT ECHO
RCVD DONT ECHO
login:
```

Negotiating 3270 Options

A similar exchange is used to set up a 3270 emulation. The dialogue below shows option negotiation for a 3270 login to an IBM VM host. The partners negotiate an IBM 3278 Model 2 emulation by selecting the following characteristics:

- A Terminal Type *subnegotiation* identifies the specific 3270 terminal to be emulated, a 3278 model 2.

- The client and server both request *END OF RECORD* options in order to set up the Block Mode environment used by 3270s.

- Both sides agree to use 8-bit BINARY data to represent 3270 data stream characters.

```
> tn3270

tn3270. toggle options
Will show option processing.

tn3270. open uoft.utoledo.edu
Trying...
Connected to uoft.utoledo.edu.
RCVD do TERMINAL TYPE (reply)
SENT will TERMINAL TYPE (don't reply)
Received suboption Terminal type - request to send.
Sent suboption Terminal type is IBM-3278-2.
RCVD do END OF RECORD (reply)
SENT will END OF RECORD (don't reply)
RCVD will END OF RECORD (reply)
SENT do END OF RECORD (reply)
RCVD do BINARY (reply)
SENT will BINARY (don't reply)
RCVD will BINARY (reply)
SENT do BINARY (reply)

RUNNING
```

Controlling a Text-Based Telnet Client

From time to time, you may want to interact with a text-based *telnet* client to set or display its parameters. You can find out about your own implementation by entering *telnet* and typing "?" or "help" to find out about your local commands.

```
> telnet
telnet> ?
Commands may be abbreviated. Commands are:

close           close current connection
logout          forcibly logout remote user and close the connection
display         display operating parameters
mode            try to enter line or character mode ('mode ?' for more)
open            connect to a site
quit            exit telnet
send            transmit special characters ('send ?' for more)
set             set operating parameters ('set ?' for more)
unset           unset operating parameters ('unset ?' for more)
status          print status information
toggle          toggle operating parameters ('toggle ?' for more)
slc             change state of special characters ('slc ?' for more)
z               suspend telnet
!               invoke a subshell
environ         change environment variables ('environ ?' for more)
?               print help information
```

Once you are within the *telnet* environment, the *open* command is used to connect to a remote host.

```
telnet> open plum.math.yale.edu
Trying 130.132.23.16 ...
Connected to plum.math.yale.edu.
Escape character is '^]'.

login: xxxxxxxx
Password: xxxxxxxx
Last login: Sat Dec 28 06:30:44 from golem.cs.yale.ed
Sun UNIX 4.2 Release 3.4 (Plum-EGP) #3: Tue Aug 2 10:25:24 EDT 988
**************************************************************************
*                                                                        *
*       Welcome to the Yale Mathematics Department's Fabulous            *
*                         ** Plum **                                     *
*                                                                        *
**************************************************************************
You have mail.
```

An Important Control Sequence

How can a user change an active session's characteristics or abort the session? One keyboard control sequence always is reserved to mean *escape to telnet command mode*. The default sequence usually is CONTROL and] (sometimes denoted by ^]). The user can redefine this escape sequence. Note the reminder that was printed in the previous dialog, three lines after the connection to *plum.math.yale.edu* was opened:

```
Escape character is '^]'.
```

At this point we will continue the dialog. After the escape sequence is entered, we get a *telnet* prompt and can look at the status of the current session:

```
^]
telnet> status
Connected to plum.math.yale.edu.
Operating in single character mode
Catching signals locally
Remote character echo
Escape character is '^]'.
```

After executing one command, we are returned to terminal emulation mode. To enter another control command, we have to enter another escape sequence. We will ask *telnet* to display its current attributes:

```
^]
telnet> display
will flush output when sending interrupt characters.
won't send interrupt characters in urgent mode.
won't skip reading of ˇ7E/.telnetrc file.
won't map carriage return on output.
will recognize certain control characters.
won't turn on socket level debugging.
won't print hexadecimal representation of network traffic.
won't print user readable output for "netdata".
will show option processing.
won't print hexadecimal representation of terminal traffic.

echo           [^E]
escape         [^]]
rlogin         [off]
tracefile      "(standard output)"
flushoutput    [^O]
interrupt      [^C]
quit           [^\]
eof            [^D]
erase          [^H]
kill           [^U]
lnext          [^V]
susp           [^Z]
reprint        [^R]
worderase      [^W]
start          [^Q]
stop           [^S]
forw1          [off]
forw2          [off]
ayt            [^T]

    DO ECHO
    DO SUPPRESS GO AHEAD
    WILL TERMINAL TYPE
    WILL NAWS
    WILL NEW-ENVIRON
```

NVT Features

In the sections that follow, we investigate the structure of *telnet* in more detail and get an idea of the features that *telnet* can offer a developer who is building a client/server application.

After option negotiation is complete, a particular terminal emulation might provide a rich repertoire of characters and graphic symbols for the interaction between a user and an application.

However, when *telnet* is used as a building block for client/server applications, often all of the interaction occurs in simple NVT mode. Therefore, let's take a look at the characteristics of a standard NVT session.

NVT Character Set

The bytes sent on an NVT session represent *USASCII* characters and *telnet* commands. There are 128 USASCII characters: 95 are printable letters, numbers, symbols, and punctuation marks; 33 are ASCII control characters (such as *horizontal tab*). USASCII was designed as a 7-bit code set. The USASCII characters are transmitted as bytes whose high-order bit is set to 0.

NVT "Printer"

During a basic NVT session, the *telnet* server sends characters and controls to the client's *NVT printer*—that is, the user's display. The NVT display is restricted to showing the 95 printable USASCII characters (corresponding to ASCII codes 32 through 126).

There is a small repertoire of ASCII control characters that the server can use to manipulate the client's display. These are shown in Table 13.1. In the table, the ASCII codes have been translated to decimal numbers.

NVT Telnet Client/Server Interaction

Recall that an NVT interaction is half-duplex, which means that at any time, either the *telnet* client or the *telnet* server is in charge:

■ After the *telnet* client has sent a line terminated by <CR> and <LF>, control switches to the server.

TABLE 13.1

NVT Printer
Controls

Description	ASCII Code
Null (for filler time)	0
Bell, to sound an audible signal	7
Backspace, to move one space left	8
Horizontal tab	9
Line Feed	10
Vertical tab	11
Form Feed (move to top of next "page")	12
Carriage return	13

- The server sends lines of output to the client. At the end of each line of output, the server uses <CR> and <LF> to move to the next line of the client's display.

- The *telnet* client accepts output from the server and can enter input again after receiving a *Go Ahead* control code sequence from the server.

Note that lines sent across the NVT *telnet* session end in <CR> <LF>, no matter what the client and server hosts may use as their local end-of-line characters. Each host translates its native end-of-line character(s) to and from the *telnet* end-of-line characters.

Telnet Commands

Before networks became commonplace, terminals were directly attached to computers. The keys that a user typed were immediately interpreted by the local computer's operating system.

There were some special control keys that caused the operating system to wake up and take notice. For example, an ASCII terminal user might hold down the CONTROL key and C at the same time (written ^C) to ask the operating system to kill the currently running application.

During a *telnet* session, control codes need to be translated to *telnet* commands and passed to the operating system at the *remote* end of a network connection. The *telnet* client program must therefore handle all of the raw keystrokes typed by the user, translate special control keys into *telnet* commands, and pass them to the *telnet* server.

Telnet commands are represented by an *Interpret As Command* (IAC) byte followed by one or more code bytes:

Interpret As Command is X'FF, or, in decimal, 255.

The *telnet* client sends command sequences to the server to support useful functions such as:

Break (BRK)	Send a break or attention signal to the remote application process.
Interrupt Process (IP)	Signal the remote operating system to stop the currently running remote application program (e.g., to stop a program that is in a loop).
Abort Output (AO)	Ask the server application not to send the rest of the output for the current operation.
Are You There? (AYT)	This means show evidence that the server is still running.
Erase Character (EC)	A user who makes a typing error while entering a line of data generally corrects it by using a *Backspace* or *del* key. When operating in ASCII character-at-a-time mode, the characters have already been sent to the remote application, so EC must be sent across the connection.
Erase Line (EL)	Asks the remote application to erase the current line.

Commands can be sent even after negotiation, when partners are no longer in basic NVT mode. But suppose that negotiation has enabled the partners to send binary data. How can a command sequence be recognized? The way that this is done is that whenever X'FF appears as *data,* it is doubled by the sender. The receiver corrects the doubling. When a receiver sees a single incoming X'FF (or an odd number of them), the receiver knows that a command is arriving.

It is easy to see how *telnet* commands could be useful to a client/server product developer. For example, the result of clicking a World Wide Web browser's STOP button might be to send an *Abort Output* command, to halt the downloading of a big image or a very long document.

By the way, it is easiest to understand *telnet*'s capabilities by thinking of an end user working at a client end and an application at the server end. But it is important to note that when using *telnet* as a development toolkit, commands can be sent in either direction.

Synch Signal

For some functions, such as *Interrupt Process,* just sticking a command into the data stream does not really do the trick. When a *real* terminal sends an interrupt, the host operating system sees it right away. The host would stop the currently running application promptly.

But *telnet* runs over a TCP session that delivers data *in order.* And normally, the remote *telnet* server processes all data that it receives *in order.* It might be quite a while before the *telnet* server sees an interrupt command that is buried in an incoming data stream.

The client wants to get the server's attention and tell the *telnet* server, "Throw away all of the characters that you have buffered *up to here* except for the commands." The client gets the server to do this by sending a special message called a *Synch signal.*

- The synch signal is sent in a TCP segment that is flagged as *Urgent Data.*
- The server will throw away everything except commands until it reaches a special command code called a *Data Mark* (DM).
- DM marks the spot where the server *stops* discarding data.

When the Synch signal segment arrives, the server extracts the NVT commands from the data stream and tosses away everything else—up to the Data Mark. The server executes the NVT commands. Normal processing resumes with data past the Data Mark.

Encoding Common Commands

Table 13.2 lists acronyms for some common commands along with the decimal values of their codes. Each would be preceded by 255 (X'FF), which is the IAC byte, when sent across the *telnet* connection.

Encoding Option Requests

Option requests are encoded with three bytes consisting of *IAC,* a request byte, and an option code. For example, the decimal representation of the sequence for *WILL TERMINAL TYPE* is:

IAC	WILL	TERMINAL TYPE
255	251	24

TABLE 13.2

Telnet Command
Codes

Acronym	Command	Code
EOF	End of File	236
SUSP	Suspend Current Process	237
ABORT	Abort Process	238
EOR	End of Record	239
NOP	No Operation	241
DM	Data Mark	242
BRK	Break	243
IP	Interrupt Process	244
AO	Abort Output	245
AYT	Are You There	246
EC	Erase Character	247
EL	Erase Line	248
GA	Go Ahead	249

This is one of the options that opens the door to subnegotiation. Subsequently, there could be a subnegotiation exchange:

```
SERVER
IAC     SB      TERMINAL TYPE       SEND    IAC             SE
255     250     24                  1       255             240


CLIENT
IAC     SB      TERMINAL TYPE       IS      DEC-VT220    IAC      SE
255     250     24                  0       DEC-VT220    255      240
```

Table 13.3 displays the decimal values for the negotiation and subnegotiation codes. It also includes the code numbers assigned to some frequently used options. Subnegotiation parameters and additional option numbers are defined in a variety of RFCs dealing with *telnet* options and are listed at the Internet Assigned Numbers Web site, *www.iana.org*.

More About Options

Many RFCs have been written detailing options that define special features. Some interesting options include:

TABLE 13.3

Negotiation and
Option Codes

Request	Code
Negotiation Codes	
WILL	251
WON'T	252
DO	253
DON'T	254
SB Start Subnegotiation	250
SE End Subnegotiation	240
Sample Option Codes	
Command Option	Code
Transmit Binary	0
Echo	1
Suppress Go Ahead	3
Status	5
Timing Mark	6
Output Line Width	8
Output Page Size	9
Extended ASCII	17
Data Entry Terminal	20
Terminal Type	24
End of Record	25
Window Size	31
Terminal Speed	32
Remote Flow Control	33
Linemode	34
Authentication	37
Encryption	38
Extended Options List	255

■ The ability to poll the partner for the current option settings. A status request and response are carried in a subnegotiation exchange.

■ Negotiating Window Size. The partners agree that the client can use a subnegotiation to inform the server of the height and width of the window that will be used for the *telnet* session. This feature is useful when a *telnet* session is run at a windowing station.

An implementation is not required to support all, or even most of, the defined options. Two of the options used for 3270 emulation have special features:

- *Transmit Binary.* Begin transmitting 8-bit binary data. Recall that IBM 3270 sessions are conducted in binary.
- *End of Record.* The partner receiving DO END-OF-RECORD will use a standard control code of IAC 239 to denote end of record in its data stream.

Even after entering binary mode, *telnet* commands can be sent to the partner by doubling *IAC* escape characters.

Telnet Benefits

From the point of view of users who want to access legacy applications via ASCII or IBM terminal emulations, the most important *telnet* feature is the ability to negotiate options and carry out emulations. But to application developers, a basic NVT *telnet* offers a sackful of client/server functions that would be difficult—and tedious—to reproduce. As we have seen, a basic NVT has the ability to:

- Find out if the peer application is alive
- Signal a break
- Request that the current remote process be interrupted
- Use a Synch signal to tell the peer to discard all data other than *telnet* commands
- Tell the partner to discard pending buffered output instead of sending it to you

Security Issues

Although switched LANs are becoming quite popular, there still are many broadcast-style LANs that are still in common use. Many organizations even use a broadcast-style Fiber Distributed Data Interface (FDDI) LAN as a backbone network.

It is very easy for a PC or Macintosh user to obtain software that turns a desktop system into a "snooper" that can eavesdrop on LAN traffic. Many Unix stations have the capability built in—it just has to be enabled by the station owner.

Traditionally, a user has "proven" its identity by sending a secret password to a host. But in a broadcast LAN environment, sending a userid and password in the clear across a network is almost as bad as yelling them in a crowded room. Somebody simply has to take the trouble to listen.

Just encrypting the password does not help. An eavesdropper can pick up the encrypted version of the password and send *that* in order to access your account. What is needed is a secure authentication mechanism. If the data that will be transmitted across the *telnet* session is confidential, then encryption also is needed.

Many security mechanisms are used with *telnet* today. For example:

- Kerberos authentication and encryption.
- S/KEY or OTP one-time passwords.
- Smart card one-time passwords.[2]
- SSL (using port 992).

Performance Issues

Telnet has some serious performance disadvantages. When emulating an ASCII terminal such as a VT100, *telnet* is very inefficient. Segments sent by the client often contain a single character or just a few characters. Each character must be echoed. A lot of overhead is consumed in order to transfer very little data.

The dialog that follows was taken from a trace of part of a *telnet* session. The user typed:

```
cat /etc/resolv.conf
```

To make the display easier to read, the lines corresponding to data sent from the client to the server are presented in bold font:

```
.AP..., len:  1,  seq:     13062785-13062785, ack:3840759217, src: 1046 dst:   23
.AP..., len:  1, seq:3840759217-3840759217, ack:  13062786, src:   23 dst: 1046
```

---

[2]A user carries a card that displays a password that changes whenever a given time interval elapses. The user enters the password, which is checked by a security server that tracks the time and the value for each user.

```
.AP..., len:  2, seq:     13062786-13062787, ack:3840759218, src: 1046 dst:   23
.AP..., len:  2, seq:3840759218-3840759219, ack:  13062788, src:   23 dst: 1046
.AP..., len:  1, seq:     13062788-13062788, ack:3840759220, src: 1046 dst:   23
.AP..., len:  1, seq:3840759220-3840759220, ack:  13062789, src:   23 dst: 1046
.AP..., len:  1, seq:     13062789-13062789, ack:3840759221, src: 1046 dst:   23
.AP..., len:  1, seq:3840759221-3840759221, ack:  13062790, src:   23 dst: 1046
.AP..., len:  1, seq:     13062790-13062790, ack:3840759222, src: 1046 dst:   23
.AP..., len:  1, seq:3840759222-3840759222, ack:  13062791, src:   23 dst: 1046
.AP..., len:  2, seq:     13062791-13062792, ack:3840759223, src: 1046 dst:   23
.AP..., len:  2, seq:3840759223-3840759224, ack:  13062793, src:   23 dst: 1046
.AP..., len:  1, seq:     13062793-13062793, ack:3840759225, src: 1046 dst:   23
.AP..., len:  1, seq:3840759225-3840759225, ack:  13062794, src:   23 dst: 1046
.A...., len:  0, seq:     13062794-13062794, ack:3840759226, src: 1046 dst:   23
.AP..., len:  1, seq:     13062794-13062794, ack:3840759226, src: 1046 dst:   23
.AP..., len:  1, seq:3840759226-3840759226, ack:  13062795, src:   23 dst: 1046
.AP..., len:  2, seq:     13062795-13062796, ack:3840759227, src: 1046 dst:   23
.AP..., len:  2, seq:3840759227-3840759228, ack:  13062797, src:   23 dst: 1046
.AP..., len:  1, seq:     13062797-13062797, ack:3840759229, src: 1046 dst:   23
.AP..., len:  1, seq:3840759229-3840759229, ack:  13062798, src:   23 dst: 1046
.AP..., len:  1, seq:     13062798-13062798, ack:3840759230, src: 1046 dst:   23
.AP..., len:  1, seq:3840759230-3840759230, ack:  13062799, src:   23 dst: 1046
.AP..., len:  1, seq:     13062799-13062799, ack:3840759231, src: 1046 dst:   23
.AP..., len:  1, seq:3840759231-3840759231, ack:  13062800, src:   23 dst: 1046
.AP..., len:  1, seq:     13062800-13062800, ack:3840759232, src: 1046 dst:   23
.AP..., len:  1, seq:3840759232-3840759232, ack:  13062801, src:   23 dst: 1046
.AP..., len:  1, seq:     13062801-13062801, ack:3840759233, src: 1046 dst:   23
.AP..., len:  1, seq:3840759233-3840759233, ack:  13062802, src:   23 dst: 1046
.AP..., len:  1, seq:     13062802-13062802, ack:3840759234, src: 1046 dst:   23
.AP..., len:  1, seq:3840759234-3840759234, ack:  13062803, src:   23 dst: 1046
.AP..., len:  1, seq:     13062803-13062803, ack:3840759235, src: 1046 dst:   23
.AP..., len:  1, seq:3840759235-3840759235, ack:  13062804, src:   23 dst: 1046
.AP..., len:  1, seq:     13062804-13062804, ack:3840759236, src: 1046 dst:   23
.AP..., len:  1, seq:3840759236-3840759236, ack:  13062805, src:   23 dst: 1046
.A...., len:  0, seq:     13062805-13062805, ack:3840759237, src: 1046 dst:   23
.AP..., len:  1, seq:     13062805-13062805, ack:3840759237, src: 1046 dst:   23
.AP..., len:  2, seq:3840759237-3840759238, ack:  13062806, src:   23 dst: 1046
.A...., len:  0, seq:     13062806-13062806, ack:3840759239, src: 1046 dst:   23
.AP..., len: 89, seq:3840759239-3840759327, ack:  13062806, src:   23 dst: 1046
.A...., len:  0, seq:     13062806-13062806, ack:3840759328, src: 1046 dst:   23
```

Note that every character sent by the client has to be echoed back by the server. It requires 39 datagrams for the client to finally get the characters in the request *cat /etc/resolv.conf* to the server, echoed back, and all acknowledged. The server then bundles the lines of the file into one datagram and shoots it back. This example illustrates the excruciating overhead imposed on a network by ASCII *telnet*.

Other Telnet Deficiencies

There are other disadvantages to legacy terminal-driven applications. Each interactive terminal application has a different user interface, with its own commands, control codes, and conventions. This means that users must be trained to use the application, and sometimes it takes a fairly long time to become proficient.

It is sometimes very difficult to rewrite an old application, but it often is pretty easy to hide a legacy application behind a Web server and present a browser-based user interface. Today, new applications routinely are built so that the user can access information via a browser client.

X Windows

Many applications have been designed for a standard X-terminal interface, rather than a proprietary terminal. The X Window System, designed and developed at the Massachusetts Institute of Technology, enables a user to run several concurrent applications in windows at the user's display. X Windows does not care where an application is located. Each application may in fact be running in a different computer on the network.

The X Window protocol provides a uniform way for applications to handle input and output to a display window. It is designed to be independent of hardware, operating system, and network type. Current implementations run over TCP/IP.

The protocol can run in a workstation or on a multiuser computer that controls bit-mapped displays. There are many dedicated X Window display products. X Window support is very widespread, and there are highly functional application development tools available. X Window development tools frequently are bundled with TCP/IP products.

There are some disadvantages to the use of X Windows. In order to draw the screen, a lot of data flows to the station—it is a heavy user of bandwidth.

There also are security problems associated with X Windows. It is not easy to prevent a process from masquerading as a legitimate data source.

Recommended Reading

RFC 854 defines the *telnet* protocol. Options defining different terminal types have been published in: RFC 1205 for 5250 emulation, RFC 1096 for X display location, RFC 1053 for the X.3 PAD option, RFC 1043 for data entry terminals, and RFC 1041 for 3270 regimes. The terminal-type option is explained in RFC 1091, and the window size option can be found in RFC 1073. RFC 1184 describes the *telnet* linemode option. RFCs 855 through 861 describe other frequently used emulation options. RFC 2355 defines some *telnet* 3270 enhancements that allow a terminal to request a specific Logical Unit name and also are helpful in emulating 3270 print devices.

File Transfer
Protocol

Introduction

In a networked environment, it is natural to wish to copy files between computer systems. Why isn't it always easy to do this? Computer vendors have devised hundreds of file systems. These differ in dozens of minor ways and in quite a few drastic major ways, too! This is not just a multivendor problem. Sometimes it is difficult to copy files between two different types of computers manufactured by the same vendor.

Among the problems that may be encountered when dealing with a multisystem environment are:

- Different conventions for naming files
- Different rules for traversing file directory systems
- File access restrictions
- Different ways to represent text and data within files

The designers of the TCP/IP protocol suite did not try to create a very complicated general solution to every file transfer problem. Instead, they produced a fairly basic but elegant *File Transfer Protocol* (FTP) that is serviceable and easy to use.

The File Transfer Protocol can be operated by interactive end users or by application programs. We confine the discussion here to the familiar interactive FTP end-user service that is universally available with TCP/IP implementations.

The user interface developed for the Berkeley Unix file transfer client has been ported to many types of multiuser computers. For example, Windows 95 and NT systems support this user interface (in a command window). In this chapter we see end-user dialogs based on that text-based interface, as well as some graphical desktop user interfaces.

The core file transfer functions enable users to copy files between systems, view directory listings, and perform housekeeping chores—such as renaming or deleting files. These functions are part of the standard TCP/IP protocol suite.

The *Trivial File Transfer Protocol* (TFTP), discussed at the end of this chapter, is a bare-bones file transfer protocol used for special situations such as downloading software to routers, bridges, or diskless workstations.

Public and Private FTP

Computer systems usually require a user to provide a login ID and a password before the user can view or manipulate files. However, there are times when it is useful to create a public file area. FTP accommodates both public information sharing and private file access by offering two kinds of services:

- Access to public files by means of "anonymous" logins
- Access to private files, which is restricted to users with system login identifiers and passwords

An Introductory Dialog

The dialog that follows demonstrates how a file may be copied from the public repository of documents at the Internet Assigned Numbers Authority (IANA).

Today, most people have desktop Graphical User Interfaces (GUIs) for file transfer, and one of these is shown later. However, the text interface gives a very good idea of how the protocol actually operates, so initially we connect to the IANA using a text-based client.[1]

The IANA file archive is public, so we enter the login identifier *ftp*. Traditionally, public systems were set up to accept login identifier *anonymous*. Now, most accept *ftp*, which is easier to type. Public file transfer servers expect you to enter your electronic mail identifier at the password prompt.

The *ftp>* prompt will be displayed whenever the local FTP application is waiting for user input. Lines that start with numbers contain messages from the remote file server.

`> ftp ftp.iana.org`	The user wants to connect to remote host *ftp.iana.org*.
`Connected to ftp.iana.org`	The local FTP client reports that it has connected successfully.

---

[1]The dialog was created at a Unix (SunOS) computer, but a Windows dialog would be virtually identical.

```
220- venera.isi.edu FTP
server
220- ...

220 ready.
```
This message comes directly from the remote system.

Note that *ftp.iana.org* is an alias for *venera.isi.edu.*

```
Name : ftp
```
The local FTP client prompts for a userid. The server will accept "ftp."

```
331 Guest login ok, send
your complete e-mail
address as password.
```
The local FTP client prompts for a password.

```
Password: ############
```
The polite response is our email identifier.

```
230 Guest login ok,
access restrictions
apply.
ftp>
```
The ftp> prompt means "What do you want to do next?"

```
ftp> cd in-notes
```
The user changes to remote directory in-notes.

```
250 CWD command success-
ful.
```
The cd command was sent to the server as the formal CWD (change working directory) command.

```
ftp> get rfc2231.txt
```
A second connection must be created to copy the file.

```
200 PORT command success-
ful.
```
The local FTP client has obtained a second port and has sent a PORT command to the server, telling the server to connect back to this port.

```
150 Opening ASCII mode
data connection for
rfc2231.txt (62578 bytes).
```
The data connection for the file transfer is opened.

```
226 Transfer complete.
```
The transfer is complete.

```
local: rfc2231.txt remote:
rfc2231.txt
```
A new local file has been created.

```
62578 bytes received in
8.5 seconds (7.2 Kbytes/s)
ftp> quit
```
Enough work for now.

```
221 Goodbye.
```

FTP allows us to write remote filenames exactly as users at the remote host would write them. When we copy a file to the local computer, we can assign it a local filename. If we do not assign a name, FTP will try to use the original name. Sometimes this is impossible because of local file naming rules. For example, a 30-character lowercase Unix name cannot be used at a DOS computer. If necessary, FTP will translate the remote filename to a format that is acceptable to the local host. Sometimes this will cause characters to be translated from lowercase to uppercase and names to be truncated.

The File Transfer Protocol has a distinctive style of operation. Whenever a file needs to be copied, a second connection is opened up and used to transfer the data. After the *get* command in the dialog, the local FTP client acquired a second port and told the server to open a connection to that port. We did not see this outgoing command, but we did see the response:

```
200 PORT command successful.
150 Opening ASCII mode data connection for rfc2231.txt (62578 bytes).
```

In Figure 14.1, we access another public archive using the *Chameleon* Windows-based file transfer client, which provides a Graphical User

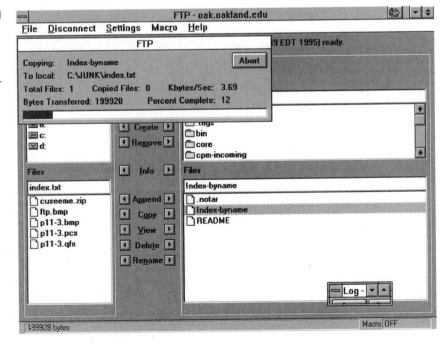

Figure 14.1
Accessing a file transfer archive with a *Chameleon* client.

Figure 14.2
Accessing a file trans-
fer archive using
Netscape.

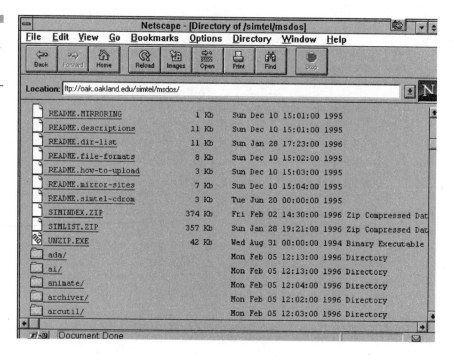

Interface. Files can be copied by dragging them from one window to another or by clicking a copy arrow. You have the option of entering a local filename in the box on the left, under the "Files" label.

The same site is accessed via the *Netscape* file transfer client in Figure 14.2. A file is copied by clicking on its name. A text file is displayed on the screen and can be saved by choosing *save* on the *file* menu. If a binary file is requested, a pop-up menu asks where it should be saved.

FTP Model

As we can see from the earlier dialog, a user interacts with a *local client* FTP process. The local client software conducts a formal conversation with the *remote server* FTP process across a *control connection* to port 21. When an end user enters a file transfer or file management command, the command is translated into one of the special acronyms used on the control connection. Figure 14.3 illustrates this model.

Under the covers, the control connection is just a simple NVT *telnet* session. The client sends commands to the server across the control con-

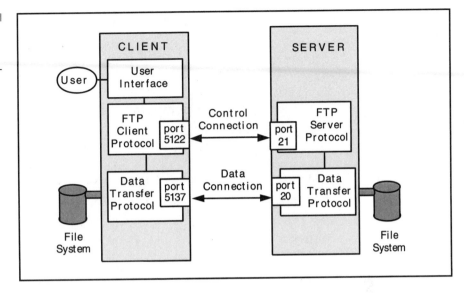

Figure 14.3
FTP control and data
connections.

nection, and the server sends responses back to the client across the control connection.

If the user requests a file transfer, a separate data connection is opened, and the file is copied across that connection. A data connection also is used to transmit directory listings. The server normally uses port 20 for its end of a data connection.

During the dialog in the previous section, the end user entered requests to change to a different directory and copy a file. These requests were translated to formal FTP commands and passed across the control connection to the remote FTP server. The file transfer took place over the separate data connection that was created for the purpose.

FTP Commands

What types of commands can be sent across the control connection? There are authentication commands that enable a user to identify the userid, password, and account to be used for a set of FTP activities. There are file transfer commands that enable a user to:

- Copy a single file between hosts
- Copy multiple files between hosts
- Append a local file to a remote file

- Copy a file and append a number to its name so that the name is unique[2]

There are file management commands that enable the user to:

- List the files in a directory
- Identify the current directory and change directories
- Create and remove directories
- Rename or delete files

There are control commands that enable the user to:

- Identify whether ASCII text, EBCDIC text, or binary data is to be transferred
- Establish whether the file is structured as a series of bytes or as a sequence of records
- Describe how the file will be transferred—for example, as a stream of bytes

The commands that are sent across the control connection are in the form of short, standard acronyms. For example, the *RETR* command is used to copy (retrieve) a file from a server to the client site.

FTP puts no restrictions on the kind of user interface that any vendor may provide and desktop systems provide ingenious and easy-to-use clients. Thus, typing "get," dragging an icon, or clicking a filename all could be translated to an *RETR* command.

The user interface generally includes additional commands that let the user customize the local environment, such as:

- Ask FTP to ring a bell at the end of a transfer.
- For a text-based user interface, ask FTP to print a hash symbol # for each 8K chunk of data transferred.
- Set up automatic translation of the case of letters in a filename or set up a table for automatically translating characters in the names of transferred files.

The complete set of functions supported by a particular host can be viewed using the FTP client's help facility. Consult your system's manuals for full information.

---

[2]For example, a daily log file could be retrieved and automatically called log.1, log.2, and so forth.

Using Commands in a Text-Based Dialog

Although most users prefer the Graphical User Interfaces available at their desktop systems, a text-based user interface reveals a lot about the inner workings of File Transfer Protocol. (It also offers many commands that are not visible in the GUI packages.)

The text-based Unix dialog below starts with a *help* display. There are a number of commands that have synonyms, such as *ls* or *dir* to ask for directory information, *put* or *send* to copy a file to a remote host, *get* or *recv* to copy a file from the remote host, and *bye* or *quit* to leave FTP.

Multiple files can be copied using *mget* or *mput* using "global wild card" naming. For example, *mget* a* retrieves a copy of every file whose name starts with the letter a. This will work if *globbing* is on; you turn global wild card naming on and off by typing *glob*.

```
> ftp
ftp> help
Commands may be abbreviated. Commands are:

!               cr          macdef      proxy       send
$               delete      mdelete     sendport    status
account         debug       mdir        put         struct
append          dir         mget        pwd         sunique
ascii           disconnect  mkdir       quit        tenex
bell            form        mls         quote       trace
binary          get         mode        recv        type
bye             glob        mput        remotehelp  user
case            hash        nmap        rename      verbose
cd              help        ntrans      reset       ?
cdup            lcd         open        rmdir
close           ls          prompt      runique
```

Here is the help listing for a Windows 95 client. All of the most commonly used commands are supported.

```
C:\WINDOWS> ftp
ftp> help
Commands may be abbreviated. Commands are:

!               delete      literal     prompt      send
?               debug       ls          put         status
append          dir         mdelete     pwd         trace
ascii           disconnect  mdir        quit        type
bell            get         mget        quote       user
binary          glob        mkdir       recv        verbose
bye             hash        mls         remotehelp
cd              help        mput        rename
close           lcd         open        rmdir
```

Going back to the Unix dialog, we turn debugging on in order to get some insight into how the protocol works:

- Lines starting with → show the messages that the local host sends across the control connection.

- Lines starting with a number show the messages sent from the remote server to report the outcome of a command.

```
ftp> debug
Debugging on (debug = 1).
ftp> open katie.vnet.net
Connected to katie.vnet.net.
220 katie FTP server (SunOS 5.6) ready.
```

A real userid and password are entered so private files can be accessed.

```
Name (katie.vnet.net:sfeit): sfeit
-> USER sfeit
331 Password required for sfeit.
Password: ###########
-> PASS 1234abcdef
230 User sfeit logged in.
```

The *status* command shows the current settings in effect for the FTP session. Many of these are explained later in this chapter. For now, note that the data *Type* is ASCII text. FTP often assumes by default that a client wants to transfer text files.

```
ftp> status
Connected to katie.vnet.net.
No proxy connection.
Mode: stream; Type: ascii; Form: non-print; Structure: file
Verbose: on; Bell: off; Prompting: on; Globbing: on
Store unique: off; Receive unique: off
Case: off; CR stripping: on
Ntrans: off
Nmap: off
Hash mark printing: off; Use of PORT cmds: on
```

Next, we request a directory listing. Directory listings can be long, so FTP sends directory listings on a data connection:

```
ftp> dir
```

FTP needs a port for the data transfer. The client sends a *PORT* command that identifies its IP address (4 bytes) and the new port (2 bytes) to be used for data transfer. The bytes are translated to decimal and separated by commas. The local IP address 128.36.4.22 is written as 128,36,4,22. Port 2613 is translated to 10,53.

```
-> PORT 128,36,4,22,10,163
200 PORT command successful.
```

The server will open a connection to this socket address. *LIST* is the formal message that asks for a detailed directory listing:

```
-> LIST
```

The server now opens the connection to the client's announced port:

```
150 ASCII data connection for /bin/ls (128.36.4.22,2613) (0 bytes).
total 4780
drwx--l---    5 sfeit     users          512 Jun 10 09:44 .
drwxr-xr-x 2017 root      other        33792 Mar 17 17:55 ..
-rwx------    1 sfeit     users         4797 Dec 17 1997 .cshrc
. . .
-rw-------    1 sfeit     users        12558 Dec 17 1997 netstat.man
. . .
226 ASCII Transfer complete.
1778 bytes received in 11 seconds (0.15 Kbytes/s)
```

After the directory listing has been transmitted, the server closes the data connection, which tells the client that the transaction is complete. Next, we get a file.

```
ftp> get netstat.man
```

The client identifies a new socket address for the file transfer. Note that this time, client port 2614 (10,54) is used.

```
-> PORT 128,36,4,22,10,54
200 PORT command successful.
-> RETR netstat.man
150 ASCII data connection for netstat.man (128.36.4.22,2614) (12558
bytes).
226 ASCII Transfer complete.
local: netstat.man remote: netstat.man
12954 bytes received in 13 seconds (1 Kbytes/s)
```

As soon as the file transfer is complete, the data connection is closed. Finally, we quit.

```
ftp> quit
-> QUIT
221 Goodbye.
```

Note that the scenario for the data connection was:

- The local client got a new port and used the control connection to tell the server FTP what the port number was.
- The FTP server connected to the client's new data port.
- The data was transferred.
- The connection was closed.

File Transfer Trace

The NT Server Monitor trace below shows a file transfer interaction. The client opens a control connection from port 1369 to well-known port 21. Some lines of the trace display the FTP control connection messages and responses in place of the corresponding TCP protocol data. (The monitor has been configured to show a trace of the highest-level protocol that is relevant.) After the client sends the command "RETR *testfile.txt*" the server opens a fresh data session from port 20 to client port 1370. The server closes the data session after the transfer has been completed. The client tells the server "quit" on the control connection, and the server shuts down that connection too.[3]

```
....S., len:    4, seq: 90197250-90197253, ack:        0, win: 8192, src: 1369 dst:   21
.A..S., len:    4, seq: 59377120-59377123, ack: 90197251, win: 8760, src:   21 dst: 1369
.A...., len:    0, seq: 90197251-90197251, ack: 59377121, win: 8760, src: 1369 dst:   21
Resp. to Port 1369, '220 compaq Microsoft FTP Service (Version 3.0).'
.A...., len:    0, seq: 90197251-90197251, ack: 59377170, win: 8711, src: 1369 dst:   21
Req. from Port 1369, 'USER ftp'
Resp. to Port 1369, '331 Anonymous access allowed, send identity (e-mai'
.A...., len:    0, seq: 90197261-90197261, ack: 59377242, win: 8639, src: 1369 dst:   21
Req. from Port 1369, 'PASS sfeit@mgt.com'
Resp. to Port 1369, '230 Anonymous user logged in.'
.A...., len:    0, seq: 90197281-90197281, ack: 59377273, win: 8608, src: 1369 dst:   21
```

[3]If you perform an NT Monitor capture between systems on a fast LAN, trace lines may appear in the wrong order. The Monitor timestamps messages to the nearest millisecond. Very closely spaced messages are viewed as concurrent and are reordered according to the contents of one of the output columns.

```
Req. from Port 1369, 'PORT 198,207,177,2,5,90'
Resp. to Port 1369, '200 PORT command successful.'
Req. from Port 1369, 'RETR testfile.txt'
....S., len:    4, seq: 59416294-59416297, ack:       0, win: 8192, src:   20 dst: 1370
.A..S., len:    4, seq: 90236200-90236203, ack: 59416295, win: 8760, src: 1370 dst:   20
Resp. to Port 1369, '150 Opening ASCII mode data connection for testfil'
.A...., len:    0, seq: 59416295-59416295, ack: 90236201, win: 8760, src:   20 dst: 1370
Data Transfer To Client, Port = 1370, size 1460
Data Transfer To Client, Port = 1370, size 605
.A...., len:    0, seq: 90236201-90236201, ack: 59418360, win: 8760, src: 1370 dst:   20
.A...F, len:    0, seq: 59418360-59418360, ack: 90236201, win: 8760, src:   20 dst: 1370
.A...., len:    0, seq: 90236201-90236201, ack: 59418361, win: 8760, src: 1370 dst:   20
.A...F, len:    0, seq: 90236201-90236201, ack: 59418361, win: 8760, src: 1370 dst:   20
.A...., len:    0, seq: 59418361-59418361, ack: 90236202, win: 8760, src:   20 dst: 1370
.A...., len:    0, seq: 90197325-90197325, ack: 59377373, win: 8508, src: 1369 dst:   21
Resp. to Port 1369, '226 Transfer complete.'
.A...., len:    0, seq: 90197325-90197325, ack: 59377397, win: 8484, src: 1369 dst:   21
Req. from Port 1369, 'QUIT'
Resp. to Port 1369, '221 '
.A...F, len:    0, seq: 59377403-59377403, ack: 90197331, win: 8680, src: 21 dst: 1369
.A...., len:    0, seq: 90197331-90197331, ack: 59377404, win: 8478, src: 1369 dst:   21
.A...F, len:    0, seq: 90197331-90197331, ack: 59377404, win: 8478, src: 1369 dst:   21
.A...., len:    0, seq: 59377404-59377404, ack: 90197332, win: 8680, src: 21 dst: 1369
```

Using PASV

An alternative scenario is possible. If the client sends a *PASV* command instead of a PORT command, the server will obtain a port number to be used for this connection and will send the port number back to the client across the control connection. The server then will listen for a data connection from the client. The server's port will be selected from the pool; it will not be a well-known port—and in particular, it will not be port 20.

Use of PASV is rare, but a number of GUI-based products enable an end user to configure this choice. The *PORT* command is the default and is the popular choice.

Aborting a Data Transfer

Sometime in your lifetime, you will request the transfer of a massively huge file and then realize that it was not the file that you wanted. A good implementation will enable a user to interrupt a transfer. For a text-based user interface, this usually is done by signaling interrupt via a combination such as CONTROL-C. A Graphical User Interface may provide an *Abort Transfer* button.

After being told to kill a transfer, the client application should instruct TCP to send a reset of the data connection to the server. Some FTP packages do not perform this function, forcing the user to wait and causing the receiver's disk to fill with unwanted data. You may want to test this feature before buying an FTP package.

Data Type, File Structure, and Transfer Mode

The two ends of a file transfer dialog need a common understanding of the format of the data that will be transferred. Is it text or binary? Is there any structuring of the data into records or blocks?

Three attributes are used to define the transfer format: *data type, file structure,* and *transmission mode.* In the PC, MAC, and Unix world, the only choice that ever comes up is the data type.

The values that can be assigned to these attributes are described in the sections that follow. The most common combination—and the one used for PCs, Macintoshes, and Unix systems—is:

- Either ASCII text or binary data is transferred.
- The file is unstructured and is viewed as a string of bytes.
- The mode of transfer is to send a file as a stream of bytes.

However, there are notable exceptions. Some hosts structure text files as a series of records. IBM hosts use EBCDIC encoding for their text files. And IBM hosts often prefer to exchange files with one another as a series of formatted blocks, rather than as a stream of bytes.

In the sections that follow, we describe the choices available for data type, file structure, and transfer mode.

Data Type

A file may contain ASCII text, EBCDIC text, or binary data.[4] A text file may contain ordinary text or text formatted for a printer. A print text file contains vertical format codes that are either:

- *Telnet* NVT vertical format controls (i.e., carriage return <CR>, line feed <LF>, new line <NL>, vertical tab <VT>, or form feed <FF>).
- ASA (FORTRAN) vertical format controls.

ASCII nonprint text is the default data type.

Transferring ASCII Text

Although ASCII text is a "standard," computers manage to use ASCII differently. The most frequently encountered problem is that computers use different codes to represent the end of a line. Unix systems use <LF>, PCs use <CR> <LF>, and Macintoshes use <CR>.

To prevent problems, the sending FTP converts a local ASCII text file to NVT format, and the receiver converts the NVT ASCII to its own local format. For example, if a text file is copied from a Unix system to a PC, all of the Unix end-of-line <LF> codes will be stored as <CR> <LF> at the PC.

Transferring EBCDIC Text

Hosts that support EBCDIC will provide a suitable user interface command that will cause the *TYPE E* command to be sent across the control connection. EBCDIC text characters are sent in their normal 8-bit form. Lines are terminated with the EBCDIC new line character.

Transferring Binary Data

It is easy to switch from default ASCII to binary image data. With a text-user interface, you just type the *binary* command. With a Graphical

---

[4]This is also called "image" data.

User Interface, you just click a button labeled "binary." The client will change the type by sending the formal *TYPE I* command across the control connection.

What happens if you forget to switch from ASCII to binary when copying a binary file? Good implementations of FTP will warn you that you are about to do something peculiar and give you a chance to change the setting.

Unfortunately, many implementations won't warn you, and automatically try to be "helpful." As we saw in the section on transferring ASCII text, if you are transferring data between different types of systems, FTP will process all binary bytes that look like end-of-line codes, stuffing in or removing bytes. A few really bad implementations start the transfer and crash in the middle.

For example, if you copy a binary PC program from a Unix host to your desktop and FTP thinks that this is a text transfer, FTP will stuff in a carriage return every time it sees a byte that looks like a line feed code.

File Structure

The two supported structures are:

- *File-structure,* which means no structure at all. The file is viewed as a sequence of bytes.

- *Record-structure,* which applies to a file made up of a sequence of records.

File-structure is the popular default for the protocol. The structure is changed to *Record* by sending the formal *STRU R* command across the control connection.

Transmission Mode

The transmission mode combined with the file structure determines how the data will be formatted for transfer. The three transmission modes are *stream, block,* and *compressed.*

- For stream mode and file-structure, the file is transmitted as a stream of bytes. FTP relies on TCP to provide data integrity, and no headers or delimiters are inserted into the data. The only way to signal that the end of the file has been reached is by a

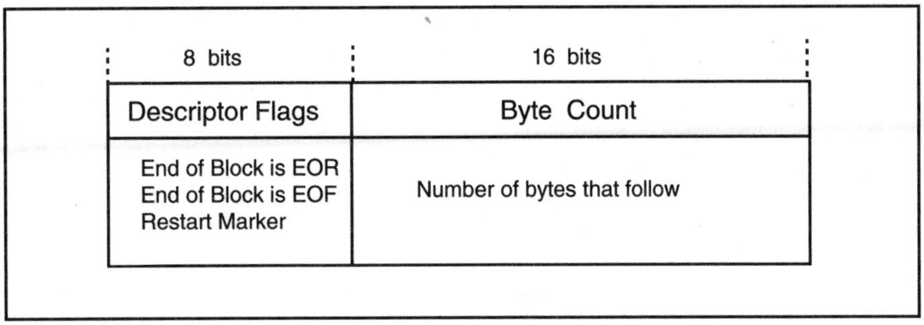

Figure 14.4
Header format used
for FTP block mode
transfers.

8 bits	16 bits
Descriptor Flags	Byte Count
End of Block is EOR End of Block is EOF Restart Marker	Number of bytes that follow

normal close of the data connection. This is the popular default.

- For stream mode and record-structure, each record is delimited by a 2-byte End Of Record (EOR) control code. Another 2-byte code is used to represent End Of File (EOF).[5]

- As you might guess, in block mode, a file is transmitted as a series of data blocks. Each block starts with a 3-byte header. The header has the format shown in Figure 14.4.

- Compressed mode is rarely supported because it provides only a very crude method of collapsing strings of repeated bytes. Normally, the user will call on one of the excellent compression programs that are available to compress a file prior to starting a transfer. The file would then be transferred as binary data.

A block may contain an entire record, or alternatively, a record can span several blocks. Note that the descriptor in the block header contains:

- An End Of Record flag that is used to identify record boundaries

- An End Of File flag that indicates whether the block is the last one in the file transfer

- A Restart Marker flag that indicates whether this block contains a text string that can be used to identify a restart point if the transfer fails at a later point

Stream mode is the one used for PCs, Macintosh computers, and Unix systems, and is the default. The mode is changed to block by sending the formal *MODE B* command across the control connection.

---

[5]EOR is X'FF 01 and EOF is X'FF 02. For the last record in a file, EOR and EOF can be represented as X'FF 03. If the file data includes an all-1s byte, it must be sent as X'FF FF.

An advantage of using record-structure or block mode is that the end of the file will be marked clearly so that a data connection could be held and reused for multiple transfers.

In the dialog shown earlier, the response to the status command included the statement:

```
Mode: stream; Type: ascii; Form: non-print; Structure: file
```

That is, the default setting for data transfer mode was stream, the data type was ASCII nonprint, and the organization of the file was file-structure, which really means unstructured.

FTP Protocol

There are several elements that make up the file transfer protocol, including:

- The command words and related parameters sent on the control connection
- The numeric codes returned in response to the commands
- The format of the data to be transferred

The set of FTP commands that can be sent over the control connection is summarized in the sections that follow. The set of commands has been growing steadily for years and has become quite large. However, hosts need not implement all of the commands listed below.

Sometimes a local user interface will not directly support a command that the user wants to send—and that actually is supported at the remote host. A good implementation will offer the *quote* command, which lets you enter the exact formal command that you want to send. Your input will be transmitted across the control connection, exactly as you entered it. Therefore, it can be helpful to know the formal commands and parameters.

Access Control Commands

The commands and parameters that define a user's access to a remote host's filestore are defined in Table 14.1.

TABLE 14.1

Commands Authorizing a User to Access a Filestore

Command	Definition	Parameter(s)
USER	Identify the user.	Userid.
PASS	Provide a password.	Password.
ACCT	Provide an account to be charged.	Account ID.
REIN	Reinitialize to start state.	None.
QUIT	Logout.	None.
ABORT	Abort the previous command and its associated data transfer.	None.

File Management Commands

The commands in Table 14.2 permit a user to execute typical directory positioning and file management functions at a remote host. The working directory is the one in which you are currently located.

TABLE 14.2

Directory Selection and File Management Commands

Command	Definition	Parameter(s)
CWD	Change to another server directory.	Directory name.
CDUP	Change to the parent directory.	None.
DELE	Delete a file.	Filename.
LIST	List information about files.	Directory name, list of files, or else none to get information about the working directory.
MKD	Make a directory.	Directory name.
NLST	List the files in a directory.	Directory name or none for the working directory.
PWD	Print the name of working directory.	None.
RMD	Remove a directory.	Directory name.
RNFR	Identify a file to be renamed.	Filename.
RNTO	Rename the file.	Filename.
SMNT	Mount a different file system.	Identifier.

TABLE 14.3

Commands That
Define the Type,
Structure, and
Mode

Command	Definition	Parameter(s)
TYPE	Identify the data type and optionally, the print format (if any) for the transfer.	A (ASCII), E (EBCDIC), I (binary Image). N (Nonprint), T (Telnet), C (ASA).
STRU	Organization of the file.	F (File) or R (Record).
MODE	Transmission format.	S (Stream), B (Block), C (Compressed).

Commands That Set Data Formats

The commands in Table 14.3 are used to establish the combination of data format, file structure, and transmission mode that will be used when copying files.

File Transfer Commands

The commands in Table 14.4 set up data connections, copy files, and support restart recovery.

TABLE 14.4

Commands That
Support File
Transfer

Command	Definition	Parameter(s)
ALLO	Allocate (reserve) enough storage for data that follows.	Integer number of bytes.
APPE	Append a local file to a remote file.	Filenames.
PASV	Identify a network address and port that will be used for a data connection to be initiated by the client.	IP Address and Port number.
PORT	Identify a network address and port to be used for a data connection to be initiated by the server.	IP Address and Port number.
REST	Identify a restart marker (to be followed by the transfer command to be restarted).	Marker value.
RETR	Retrieve or get a file.	Filename(s).
STOR	Store or put a file.	Filename(s).
STOU	Store unique: create a version of a file with a unique name.	Filename.

	Command	Definition	Parameter(s)
TABLE 14.5 Miscellaneous User Information Commands	HELP	Return information about the server implementation.	None.
	NOOP	Asks server to return an "OK" reply.	None.
	SITE	Used for server-specific subcommands that are not part of the standard, but may be needed at the server's site.	None.
	SYST	Asks the server to identify its operating system.	None.
	STAT	Requests parameter information and connection status.	None.

Miscellaneous Commands

The final set of commands in Table 14.5 provides helpful information to an end user.

Site Command

Many Unix file transfer servers use file transfer server software developed at Washington University in St. Louis, called WU-FTP. This implementation accepts a *SITE* command that can be used to execute a variety of special-purpose programs at the file transfer server. For example, users can first gain access with userid *ftp* and then can use the *SITE* command to provide a group login ID and password. The group login ID authorizes the user to access more files than an ordinary anonymous user can.

Error Recovery and Restart

Many organizations have a need to transfer very large files. Suppose that a system that is executing the transfer of a very large file fails. The FTP restart service was designed to solve this problem. Implementation of the restart service is optional. Unfortunately, at the time of this writing, few if any TCP/IP products include this service. However, we take an optimistic view of the future and describe it here.

If block mode transfer is used and the restart service is supported, the sending FTP can transmit blocks containing restart markers at convenient points of the data transfer. Each marker is a printable text string. For example, successive markers could be 1, 2, 3, and so on. Whenever the receiver gets a marker, the receiver writes the file data onto nonvolatile storage and keeps track of the marker's position in the data.

If the client is the receiving system, the end user is notified of each marker as soon as the data has been stored. If the remote server is the receiving system, a message is sent back to the client on the control connection indicating that data up to the marker has been safe-stored.

After a system failure, the user can invoke a restart command with a marker value as its argument. This is followed by the command that was being executed (get or put) when the system failed.

Reply Codes

Each command in a dialog is answered with a reply code and message. For example:

```
ftp> get netstat.man

->  PORT 128,36,4,22,10,54
200 PORT command successful.
->  RETR netstat.man
150 ASCII data connection for netstat.man (128.36.4.22,2614) (12558
bytes).
226 ASCII Transfer complete.
```

Reply codes consist of three digits. Each has a specific purpose:

- Codes in the 200s indicate successful completion of a command.
- Codes in the 100s indicate that an action is being started.
- Codes in the 300s indicate that an intermediate point has been reached successfully.
- Codes in the 400s signal transient errors.
- Codes in the 500s are really bad news and announce a permanent error.

The second and third digits of a reply code classify the reply more precisely.

Security Issues

Checking the Client's Host Name

Sometimes users are mysteriously refused access to an anonymous file archive. If it happens only occasionally, the cause is that the server is just busy. If it happens all of the time, you may have a Domain Name problem.

Some file transfer servers will not accept a client from any system that is not listed in the Domain Name System. The FTP server will perform a reverse lookup on each incoming IP address. If it is not in the DNS database, access is refused. The only solution is to contact your DNS administrator and arrange to have your computer listed. Some servers do a *double lookup*. They translate a client address to a name and then translate that name to an address and compare the result with the original address. This means that a wild-card DNS entry is not sufficient.

PASV Versus PORT

Organizations protect their networks by configuring a firewall system that applies filtering criteria to datagrams and discards any traffic that has not been specifically enabled. Often, a simple filtering firewall allows users on a LAN to initiate connections to external locations but rejects all incoming connection attempts.

The FTP specification defines the *PORT* command as the default way to set up a data connection. As a result, many implementations were built for which this was the only way to set up a data connection. But use of *PORT* requires an external file server to open a connection *to* the client, which normally will be forbidden by a firewall.

Use of *PASV*, which enables the client to open a data connection to the server, will not help unless the filtering router is willing to allow internal clients to open connections to random non-well-known external ports. This is not considered a good security practice.

The best solution is to use a smart stateful firewall or proxy firewall, which watches the PORT negotiation and can open up access to an appropriate incoming data transfer connection.

Configuring a Client to Use a Proxy Firewall

Most desktop file transfer clients are easy to configure to access external servers via a proxy firewall. The first step is to define a default proxy firewall by entering:

- The name or IP address of the firewall
- A userid and password to gain access to the firewall
- The port at which file transfer clients will access the firewall
- Additional information, depending on how the firewall has been implemented

The proxy firewall administrator chooses the port to which clients will connect. Sometimes a well-known port can be used, but often a non-well-known port is selected. Many administrators choose 2100, which is easy to remember since the FTP port is 21. Why isn't port 21 used to access the proxy firewall? Keep in mind that the proxy provides a security service, not a file transfer service. When a client connects to port 21, it should be talking directly to a file transfer server.

The left side of Figure 14.5 illustrates a client's default firewall configuration screen. Once the configuration data is entered, the end user operates the file transfer application in the normal way. The right side of Figure 14.5 shows how a user can choose when to use the proxy firewall. A user who wishes to access an external file transfer server simply clicks a check box to indicate that this connection should be passed to the proxy. The user can skip the proxy when connecting to an internal file transfer system.

Performance Issues

The efficiency of file transfer operations depends on a number of factors:

- Host file system and disk efficiency
- Processing required to reformat data
- Underlying TCP service
- Receive buffer memory

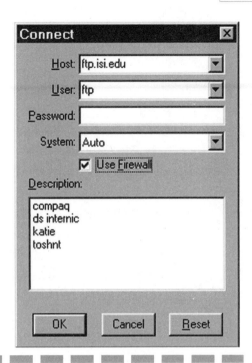

Figure 14.5 Configuring a firewall and choosing when to use it.

Note that a brief throughput report usually is printed at the end of a file transfer:

```
226 Transfer complete
local: rfc1261 remote: rfc1261
4488 bytes sent in 0.037 seconds (118.5 Kbytes/s)
```

A bulk transfer can be initiated in order to obtain a rough measure of TCP and FTP performance.

Trivial File Transfer Protocol

There are file copying situations that require a very simple level of functionality. For example, an initial download of software and configuration files to a router, hub, or diskless workstation that is booting is best carried out using a very simple protocol.

The Trivial File Transfer Protocol (TFTP) has proved to be very useful for basic file copying between computers. TFTP transfers data via UDP datagrams.[6] Very little communications software—only IP and UDP—needs to be running in a system that participates in a TFTP download. TFTP has proved to be very useful for initializing network devices such as routers, bridges, and hubs.

The Trivial File Transfer Protocol:

- Sends uniformly sized blocks of data (except for the last)
- Prefixes each data block with a simple 4-octet header
- Numbers the blocks starting with 1
- Supports ASCII or binary octet transfers
- Can be used to read or write a remote file
- Has no provision for authentication

One partner in a TFTP interaction sends numbered, uniformly sized blocks of data, and the other partner acknowledges (ACKs) the data as it arrives. The sender must wait for an ACK of a block before sending the next block. If no ACK arrives within a timeout period, the current block is resent. Similarly, if the receiver does not get any data during a timeout period, an ACK is retransmitted.

The default block size is 512. This can be changed by means of a negotiation in the initial message exchange.

TFTP Protocol

A TFTP transaction starts with a *Read Request* or a *Write Request*. The TFTP client starts off by obtaining a port and then sends the Read Request or Write Request message to port 69 at the server. The server then will identify a different server port, which it will use for the remainder of the file transfer. The server directs its messages to the client's port. Data transfer proceeds with an exchange of data blocks and ACKs.

---

[6]TFTP could be run on top of a packet delivery service for another protocol family.

By default, all blocks except for the last must contain a full block (e.g., 512 bytes) of data, and this is how End-Of-File is signaled. If the file's length is a multiple of the block size, the final block consists of a header and no data. Data blocks are numbered, starting with 1. Each ACK contains the block number of the data that it is acknowledging.

A client can add options to the end of a read or write request. The server responds with an option ACK message that indicates which (if any) options are acceptable. Current options include:

- A blocksize other than 512. For example, a size of 1468 will fit into an Ethernet datagram of size 1500 (after subtracting a 20-byte IP header, 8-byte UDP header, and 4-byte TFTP header.

- A retransmission timeout value.

- Transfer size. A size of 0 is sent in a read request, and the server provides the file size in its response. The client can abort the session if the file is too big. The size of a file to be sent can be included in a write request.

TFTP Messages

There are six types of messages:

1. Read Request (RRQ)

2. Write Request (WRQ)

3. Data (DATA)

4. Acknowledgment (ACK)

5. Error (ACK)

6. Option Acknowledgment (OACK)

Error messages signal conditions such as "file not found" or "no space to write file on disk."

Each TFTP header starts with an operation code identifying its message type. The message formats are displayed in Figure 14.6.

Note that the lengths of Read Requests and Write Requests vary, depending on the length of the filename, mode, and option fields, each of which contains an ASCII text string terminated by a 0 byte. The mode field contains "netascii" or "octet."[7]

---

[7]There was a mode called "mail" that also was defined in the original TFTP RFC.

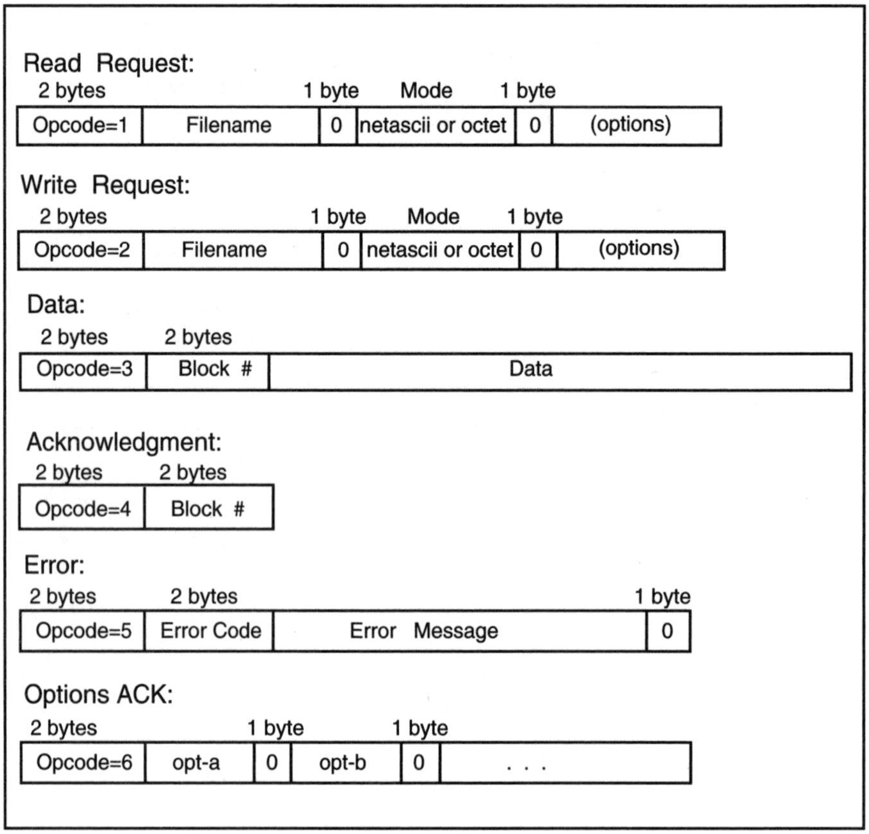

Figure 14.6
Formats for TFTP
messages.

Read Request:

2 bytes		1 byte	Mode	1 byte	
Opcode=1	Filename	0	netascii or octet	0	(options)

Write Request:

2 bytes		1 byte	Mode	1 byte	
Opcode=2	Filename	0	netascii or octet	0	(options)

Data:

2 bytes	2 bytes	
Opcode=3	Block #	Data

Acknowledgment:

2 bytes	2 bytes
Opcode=4	Block #

Error:

2 bytes	2 bytes		1 byte
Opcode=5	Error Code	Error Message	0

Options ACK:

2 bytes	1 byte		1 byte		
Opcode=6	opt-a	0	opt-b	0	. . .

TFTP Scenario

The protocol can be illustrated by means of a simple scenario. Figure 14.7 illustrates how a TFTP originator reads a remote file (without using options). After the responder sends a block to the reader, the responder will wait until an ACK for the block arrives before sending the next block.

Recommended Reading

RFC 959 defines the File Transfer Protocol, and RFC 1350 describes the Trivial File Transfer Protocol. RFCs 2347, 2348, and 2349 discuss TFTP options.

Figure 14.7
Using TFTP to read a
remote file.

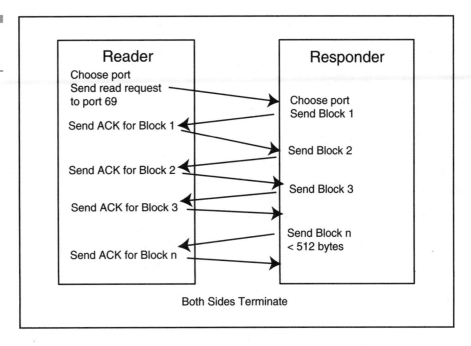

RPC and NFS

Introduction

The computer environment has changed over the past few years. Instead of dumb terminals tied to a central computer, we have intelligent desktop stations, one or more servers, and local area networks (LANs).

Users have been drawn to the convenience, availability, and control that comes with a personal system. But they also need to access common information and share printers. And someone still must be responsible for configuration, maintenance, and backup chores. As a result, today's systems managers coordinate software updates, supervise resources, schedule backups, and configure network parameters for large numbers of computers.

Over a period of years, many organizations turned to a network operating system for resource sharing and central management. More recently, client/server computing has elevated network interactions to the application layer.

Purpose of the Network File System

Sun Microsystems introduced its *Network File System* (NFS) to support resource-sharing services for Unix workstation LANs. NFS makes remote file directories appear to be part of the local directory system—end users and programs access remote files exactly as if they were on a directly attached disk. NFS offers many benefits.

For example, a single copy of software or of important data can be kept at a server and shared by all users. Updates can be installed at the server rather than at multiple computers across the network. Figure 15.1 shows a LAN with one central server that provides NFS services.

WebNFS

WebNFS is a new version of the protocol that enables Web browsers and Java applets to access NFS servers and also makes it easy to access Internet NFS servers through corporate firewalls. WebNFS allows

Figure 15.1
NFS server on a LAN.

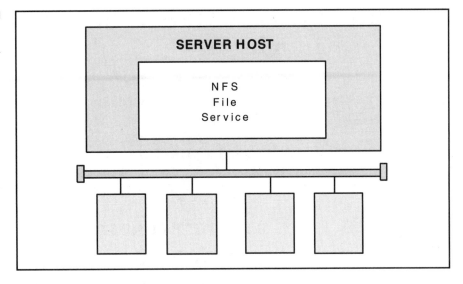

clients to access an NFS server without the usual administrative pre-configuration and extensive protocol setup procedures that characterize classic NFS file access.

Relationship Between NFS, RPC, and XDR

NFS was built on top of a *Remote Procedure Call* (RPC) framework that was designed from the start to support general client/server application development. In this chapter, we outline NFS services and describe the *Open Network Computing* (ONC) *Remote Procedure Call* architecture.

The *eXternal Data Representation* (XDR) standard is an important part of the RPC architecture. XDR includes a datatype definition language and a method of encoding datatypes in a standard format. This enables data to be exchanged between different types of computers, such as Unix hosts, PCs, Macintoshes, Digital Equipment Corporation VAX VMS systems, and IBM mainframes.

RPC and NFS As Internet Standards

Sun Microsystems published RFCs describing Remote Procedure Calls in 1988 and NFS in 1989. In 1995, Sun turned over the Open Network Computing Remote Procedure Call and its supporting protocols to the Internet Engineering Task Force (IETF). From that point on, updates were to be submitted to the Internet standards process. Sun turned NFS over to the IETF standards process in 1998.

DCE and Microsoft

Although the Sun RPC is an IETF proposed standard, it is not the only Remote Procedure Call protocol on the market. A different Remote Procedure Call protocol was developed by the Open Software Foundation (OSF), a Consortium of computer vendors. This RPC was at the core of their Distributed Computing Environment (DCE) protocol suite. Eventually, the Open Group consortium (*www.opengroup.org*) assumed responsibility for DCE.

Several vendors provide implementations of the Open Group DCE suite and have developed applications built on top of DCE. Microsoft built many NT Server functions on top of its own implementation of Remote Procedure Calls. This implementation is modeled on the DCE Remote Procedure Call.

RPC and NFS Implementations

RPC and NFS have been implemented by most Unix vendors and also have been ported to many proprietary operating systems. For example, IBM VM, IBM MVS, and DEC VAX VMS systems can act as NFS file servers. Several vendors have written NFS server code for Windows 95 and NT platforms. An RPC programming library often is bundled with an NFS server.

An extension to Novell's NetWare supports NFS along with NetWare file and print services. Any client that can speak either of these protocols can access the server. In particular, DOS, Macintosh, and Unix clients are supported.

Remote Procedure Call Model

Open Network Computing client/server applications are built on top of Remote Procedure Calls. A Remote Procedure Call is modeled on an ordinary subroutine call. For example, in the C programming language, an ordinary subroutine procedure call commonly has the form:

```
return-code = procedure-name(input_parameters, output_parameters)
```

Input values are stored in the input parameters before the procedure is invoked. If the procedure executes correctly, results are stored in the output parameters. On completion, the return-code indicates whether the procedure completed successfully.

A Remote Procedure Call is similar. The local system sends a call request to a remote server. The request identifies the procedure and includes values for the input parameters. The remote server executes the procedure. When its work is complete, the remote server replies, indicating whether the procedure succeeded. If the procedure completed successfully, the response contains the procedure's output parameters. Figure 15.2 illustrates the exchange of request and reply messages. The Remote Procedure Call protocol defines the mechanisms that make this happen.

Figure 15.2
An RPC interaction.

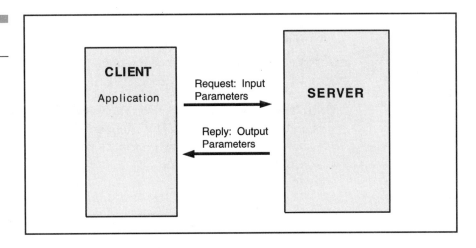

Figure 15.3
A client application
accessing a remote
procedure.

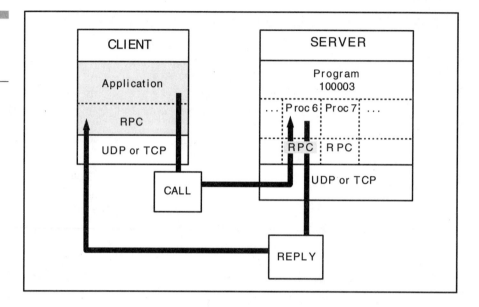

RPC Programs and Procedures

The components of the RPC framework are easy to understand (see
Figure 15.3):

- An RPC service is implemented by one or more *programs* that
  run at a server. For example, there are separate programs for
  file access and file locking services.

- Each program can execute several *procedures*. The idea is that a
  procedure should perform one simple well-defined function. For
  example, there are separate NFS procedures that read, write,
  rename, and delete files.

- Each program is assigned a numeric identifier.

- Each procedure in a program is assigned a numeric identifier.

Up to the time of writing, Sun Microsystems still administered the
assignment of unique program numbers.[1] Number assignment ranges
are shown in Table 15.1. The program's designers assign numeric IDs to
a program's procedures. For example, *read* is NFS procedure 6 and
rename is NFS procedure 11.

---

[1]The Internet Assigned Numbers Authority might have this job in the future.

TABLE 15.1

RPC Number
Assignments

Number	Description
0-1fffffff	Defined by Sun (rpc@sun.com).
20000000-3fffffff	Numbers used only within one site.
40000000-5fffffff	For applications that generate program numbers dynamically.
60000000-7fffffff	Reserved.
80000000-9fffffff	Reserved.
a0000000-bfffffff	Reserved.
c0000000-dfffffff	Reserved.
e0000000-ffffffff	Reserved.

A client RPC request identifies the program and procedure to be run. For example, to read a file, the RPC request will ask for program 100003 (*NFS*) and procedure 6 (*read*). Figure 15.3 shows a client application accessing remote procedure 6 within program 100003.

Experience shows that over time, programs change. The procedures are refined and more procedures are added. For this reason, an RPC call must identify a program's version. It is not unusual for multiple versions of an RPC program to be running at a server host.

A Remote Procedure Call is sent from a client to a server in a formatted message. RPC does not care what transport protocol is used to carry its messages. In the TCP/IP world, RPC runs over both the UDP and TCP, but it could be implemented over other transports.

Although we usually think of a client interacting with a unique server, RPC requests may also be multicast or broadcast.

Typical RPC Programs

NFS is the best-known RPC program. The related *mount* program that enables a client to glue a remote directory into a local directory system also is implemented as an RPC program. There are *lock manager* and *status* programs that provide a crude locking apparatus when users want to update shared files at an NFS server.

Spray is an example of a very simple RPC program. A *spray* client sends a batch of messages to a remote system and gets a report on the result. The following command sends 100 datagrams to host *plum:*

```
> spray -c 100 plum
sending 100 packets of lnth 86 to plum …
in 10.1 seconds elapsed time,
29 packets (29.00%) dropped by plum
Sent: 9 packets/sec, 851 bytes/sec
Rcvd: 7 packets/sec, 604 bytes/sec
```

The *rusers* program finds out who is logged on at either a selected list of hosts or at all hosts on the local network. An *rusers* client broadcasts its RPC call on the LAN. Responses contain a hostname and the host's logged-in users.

```
> rusers
zonker.num.cs.yale.edu leonard jones harris
mark.num.cs.yale.edu davis    sherman
duke.num.cs.yale.edu burry    victor
. . .
```

Dealing With Duplicate RPC Requests

When an RPC service is based on TCP, requests and responses will be delivered reliably. TCP takes care of ensuring that nothing gets lost in transmission.

If the service is based on UDP, the client and server must provide their own timeout, retransmission, and duplicate detection strategies. These will vary, depending on the needs of the application. The application developer can adopt either of the following client strategies:

- If no response is received within a timeout, just return an error message to the end user. Let the end user try the service again.

- If no response is received within a timeout, resend the request. Repeat until a reply is received or a maximum retransmission limit is reached.

If the client resends, the application developer must provide the server with a strategy to deal with duplicates. The server might:

- Keep no record of what was done in the past. If a request arrives, execute its procedure, even though it may be a duplicate. Note that there are procedures—such as reading a particular set of bytes from a file—for which this would be a harmless way to proceed. Of course, the client may end up receiving duplicate replies but can discard duplicates by keeping track of recently completed transactions.

■ Keep a copy of the replies that have been received during the past few minutes. If a request with a duplicate transaction identifier arrives from a client and the server already has performed the procedure and sent back a response, the server could send back a copy of the original response. If the server currently is performing the procedure, it can discard the duplicate request.

Keep in mind that each client/server application can incorporate whichever strategies fit it best.

RPC Portmapper

Many client/server programs have been written, and more are being produced all of the time. The supply of well-known ports is limited—how will clients be able to identify the growing family of services?

Role of the Portmapper

The RPC architecture introduced a method for dynamically discovering the port at which a service can be accessed. At each server host, a special RPC program, called the *portmapper* (or, in newer versions, *rpcbind*), acts as a clearinghouse for information about the ports that *other* RPC programs use. In the remainder of this discussion, we refer to the *portmapper*, but *rpcbind* performs the same functions.

The *portmapper* maintains a list of:

■ The local active RPC programs

■ The programs' version numbers

■ Transport protocol or protocol

■ Ports at which the programs are operating

The *portmapper* program is started when an RPC server computer initializes. As shown in Figure 15.4, when an RPC program starts up, it gets an unused port from the operating system and then tells the *portmapper* that it is ready to go to work; that is, it registers its port, program number, and version with the *portmapper*.

Figure 15.4
Finding service ports
via the portmapper.

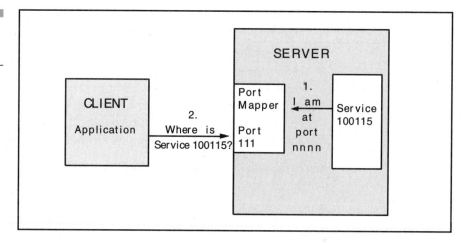

The *portmapper* (or *rpcbind*) listens at well-known port 111. When a client wants to access an RPC service, the client sends an RPC message to the *portmapper* at port 111. The message contains the service's program number, version, and transport protocol (UDP or TCP). The *portmapper* responds, giving the current port for the service.

The *portmapper* also enables some RPC services to be based on broadcast. In this case, a client broadcasts an RPC request on a link. For example, a broadcast *rusers* RPC call asks every machine on a LAN to report its logged-on users.

But note that the *rusers* program at each host could be operating out of a different port. What port number should a client put into the request message that it broadcasts?

The answer is that the client wraps its request inside a special *indirect request* call to the *portmapper* and sends the request to port 111. The *portmapper* relays the request to the service and then relays the response back to the client. The port number for the service is added to the response so that future (individual) calls can be sent directly.

Portmapper Procedures

The procedures executed by a *portmapper* program are listed in Table 15.2.

TABLE 15.2

Portmapper
Procedures

Procedure	Description
PMAPPROC_NULL	Returns a response that shows that the portmapper is active.
PMAPPROC_SET	Used by a service to register (i.e., add a local program, version, protocol, and port number to the list of active servers).
PMAPPROC_UNSET	Used by a service to unregister (i.e., remove a local program from the list of active servers.)
PMAPPROC_GETPORT	Used by a client to find out a server's port number. Input includes a specific program number, version, and transport protocol (UDP or TCP).
PMAPPROC_DUMP	Returns a list of all local RPC programs, their versions, their communications protocols, and their ports. (Used by *rpcinfo -p*.)
PMAPPROC_CALLIT	Relays an incoming client's indirect request to a local RPC program. Returns the result if the procedure completes successfully. It also returns the program's port number. Intended for use with broadcast requests.

Viewing Portmapper RPC Services

The Unix *rpcinfo* command displays useful information about RPC programs by sending RPC queries to a *portmapper*. Other operating systems that support RPC clients provide similar commands.

The *rpcinfo -p* display that follows asks the *portmapper* at host *bulldog.cs.yale.edu* for a list of the Remote Procedure Call programs that are running at that host. (That is, it sends a request to the *portmapper*'s *PMAPPROC_DUMP procedure.*)

The output includes the program number, version, transport protocol, port, and identifier for each program at the server. We see that the *portmapper* itself is listed first:

```
> rpcinfo -p bulldog.cs.yale.edu:
program    vers    proto    port
100000     2       tcp      111      portmapper
100000     2       udp      111      portmapper
100029     1       udp      657      keyserv
100005     1       udp      746      mountd
100005     2       udp      746      mountd
100005     1       tcp      749      mountd
100003     2       udp      2049     nfs
100005     2       tcp      749      mountd
100026     1       udp      761      bootparam
```

```
100024      1      udp      764      status
100024      1      tcp      766      status
100021      1      tcp      767      nlockmgr
100021      1      udp      1033     nlockmgr
100021      3      tcp      771      nlockmgr
100021      3      udp      1034     nlockmgr
100020      1      udp      1035     llockmgr
100020      1      tcp      776      llockmgr
100021      2      tcp      779      nlockmgr
100021      2      udp      1036     nlockmgr
100011      1      udp      1070     rquotad
100001      2      udp      1111     rstatd
100001      3      udp      1111     rstatd
100001      4      udp      1111     rstatd
100002      1      udp      1124     rusersd
100002      2      udp      1124     rusersd
100012      1      udp      1127     sprayd
100008      1      udp      1132     walld
```

Note that we have used a Remote Procedure Call application to find out about the activities of other Remote Procedure Call applications.

The *rpcinfo -b* command broadcasts on the network, asking for all servers running a specific program and version. Below, we ask who is running version 1 of *spray. Spray* is program number 100012.

```
> rpcinfo -b 100012 1
128.36.12.1 casper.na.cs.yale.edu
128.36.12.28 tesla.math.yale.edu
128.36.12.6 bink.na.cs.yale.edu
  . . .
```

Every RPC program includes a null procedure, number 0, which does nothing but return an "I am alive" response. The following *rpcinfo -u* command sends a message to the null procedure of the *spray* program at *bulldog.cs.yale.edu:*

```
> rpcinfo -u bulldog.cs.yale.edu 100012
program 100012 version 1 ready and waiting
```

Rpcbind

Recall that recent versions of RPC have replaced the *portmapper* program with a program called *rpcbind.* The original *portmapper* was tied to UDP and TCP. *Rpcbind* is independent of the transport that is used. It returns an ASCII string containing address information. This transport-independent information is called the *universal address format.*

Role of Rpcbind

Rpcbind operates on exactly the same principles as the *portmapper.* When an RPC program initializes, it obtains one or more dynamically assigned transport addresses. It registers these addresses with the *rpcbind* program, which makes the addresses available to clients.

As before, a client query contains a program number and version number. But an *rpcbind* response contains the universal address, which might provide information for NetWare SPX/IPX, SNA, DECnet, or AppleTalk, rather than TCP or UDP. The type of transport address that is provided in the response depends on the transport that was used for the query.

Just like the *portmapper, rpcbind* is accessed at well-known port 111 for UDP or TCP. Appropriate predefined access locations must be used for other communications protocols.

Like the *portmapper, rpcbind* supports broadcast RPC services. Broadcasts are directed at the well-known transport access point for the *rpcbind* service—for example, port 111 for UDP or TCP. Each *rpcbind* program that hears the broadcast calls the desired local service program on behalf of the client, gets the response, and forwards it to the client. Version 4 of RPC enables clients to get the same kind of indirect service via *rpcbind* when a query is unicast, rather than broadcast.

Rpcbind Procedures

Rpcbind version 4 procedures are listed in Table 15.3.

RPC Messages

An RPC client sends a call message to a server and gets back a corresponding reply message. What should these messages contain so that the client and server understand each other?

A transaction identifier is needed to match a reply with its call. The client's call must identify the program and procedure that it wants to run. The client may need some way to identify itself via credentials that prove its right to invoke the service. Finally, the client's call will carry input parameters. For example, an NFS *read* call identifies the file to be accessed and the number of bytes to be read.

TABLE 15.3

Rpcbind
Procedures

Procedure	Description
RPCBPROC_SET	Used by a service to register a program with a local RPCBIND.
RPCBPROC_UNSET	Used by a service to unregister a local program.
RPCBPROC_GETADDR	Returns a program's universal address to a client.
RPCBPROC_GETVERSADDR	Includes a desired version number in a universal address request.
RPCBPROC_GETADDRLISTMO	Provides a list of addresses for a program. The client then may choose from several available transports.
RPCBPROC_DUMP	Lists all entries in RPCBIND's database. (i.e., provides information for an *rpcinfo* display.)
RPCBPROC_BCAST	Supports broadcast requests—RPCBIND passes the request to a local program.
RPCBPROC_INDIRECT	Supports indirect requests that are unicast—RPCBIND passes the request to a local program, and sends the result or an error indication back.
RPCBPROC_GETTIME	Returns the local time at the server measured in seconds since midnight of the first day of January, 1970.
RPCBPROC_UADDR2TADDR	Converts universal addresses to transport specific addresses.
RPCBPROC_TADDR2UADDR	Converts transport specific addresses to universal addresses.
RPCBPROC_GETSTAT	Provides statistics on the number and kind of requests that have been received.

In addition to reporting the results of successful calls, the server must let the client know when its requests are rejected and why. A call may be rejected for reasons such as mismatched versions or a client authentication failure. The server needs to report errors caused by a bad parameter or a failure such as "unable to find file."

Figure 15.5 illustrates a client interacting with a server program. The client sends a call. When the requested procedure completes, the server program returns a reply. As shown in Figure 15.5, a request includes:

■ A Transaction identifier

■ The current RPC version number

Figure 15.5
Remote Procedure
Call messages.

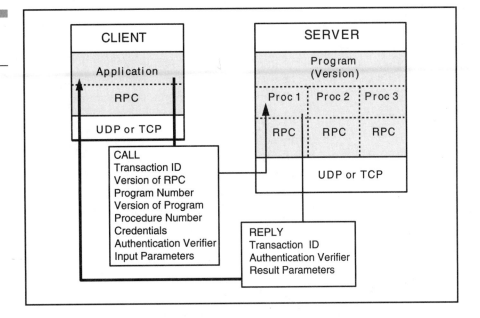

- The program number
- The program version
- The procedure number
- Authentication credentials
- An authentication verifier
- Input parameters

If the procedure is executed successfully, the reply contains the results. If there was a problem, the reply will contain information that describes the error.

RPC Authentication

Some services do not need any security protection. An RPC service that tells users the time of day at a server can safely be left open to the public. However, a client that wishes to access private data needs to provide some authentication information. In some cases, it also is important to have a server authenticate itself. You might not want to store a private file at a server without some assurance that the server's identity was valid. Thus, there are times when some kind of authentication information must be included in both requests and responses.

In a call message, RPC authentication information is carried in two fields:

- The *credentials* field contains identification information.

- The *verifier* field contains additional information and validates the identity. For example, the verifier could contain an encrypted password and timestamp.

There is no single standard for authentication. It is left to each program's designer to decide what is needed for that program. However, there is an ongoing effort to provide standards in this area.

Currently, each method of authentication is called a *flavor*. The flavor used in a credentials or verifier field is identified by an integer flavor value at the start of the field. New authentication flavor values can be registered in the same way that new programs are registered. The credentials and verifier fields each start with a flavor number.

Null Authentication

Null authentication is just what it sounds like. No information is provided—the call message's credentials and verifier and the reply's verifier all contain a 0 flavor number, meaning that no more information is included.

System Authentication

System authentication provides information modeled on Unix user information. The System credentials include:

stamp	An arbitrary ID generated by the calling computer
machinename	Name of the caller's machine
uid	The caller's effective user ID number
gid	The caller's effective group ID number
gids	A list of groups that the caller belongs to

The caller's verifier field is null. The verifier returned by the server may be null or may have a flavor of "short," which means that a system-specific byte string has been returned. In some implementations, the caller will use this byte string as credentials in subsequent messages, instead of providing the user and group information.

Note that this method does not provide any security. The next two methods use encryption to protect authentication information. However, there is a trade-off between providing secure RPC services and achieving satisfactory performance. Encryption of even a single field can inflict a substantial overhead burden on a high-performance service such as NFS.

DES Authentication

The *Data Encryption Standard* (DES) is a symmetric encryption algorithm. DES is a Federal Information Processing Standard (FIPS) that was created by IBM and selected to be a government standard by the United States National Institute of Standards and Technology (NIST).

RPC DES authentication is based on a mixture of asymmetric public and private keys and symmetric DES encryption:

■ A username is associated with a public key.

■ The server encrypts a DES session key with the public key and sends it to the user's client process.

■ The DES session key is used to encrypt client and server authentication information.

Kerberos Authentication

Kerberos authentication is based on the use of a Kerberos security server at which user and server keys (based on passwords) are stored. Kerberos authenticates an RPC service by:

■ Using the secret client and server keys that are registered at the Kerberos security server to distribute a DES session key to the client and server.

■ Using the DES session key to encrypt client and server authentication information.

Sample Version 2 RPC Messages

Figure 15.6 shows a Network General *Sniffer* network monitor display of the UDP header and RPC fields for an NFS call message that requests file attributes. The data link and IP headers have been omitted from the display.

Figure 15.6 Format of an RPC message carrying an NFS request.

```
UDP:   --- UDP Header ---
UDP:
UDP:   Source port = 1023 (Sun RPC)
UDP:   Destination port = 2049
UDP:   Length = 124
UDP:   No checksum
UDP:
RPC:   --- SUN RPC header ---
RPC:
RPC:   Transaction id = 641815012
RPC:   Type = 0 (Call)
RPC:   RPC version = 2
RPC:   Program = 100003 (NFS), version = 2
RPC:   Procedure = 4 (Look up file name)
RPC:   Credentials: authorization flavor = 1 (Unix)
RPC:   len = 32, stamp = 642455371
RPD:   machine = atlantis
RPC:   uid = 0, gid = 1
RPC:   1 other group id(s):
RPC:   gid 1
RPC:   Verifier: authorization flavor = 0 (Null)
RPC:   [Verifier: 0 byte(s) of authorization data]
RPC:
RPC:   [Normal end of "SUN RPC header".]
RPC:
NFS:   --- SUN NFS ---
NFS:
NFS: [Params for Proc = 4 (Look up file name) follow]
NFS:   File handle = 0000070A00000001000A0000000091E3
NFS:                 5E707D6A000A0000000044C018F294BE
NFS:   File name = README
NFS:
NFS:   [Normal end of "SUN NFS".]
NFS:
```

Note that a call is an RPC message of *type 0*. The reply will have *type 1*. The RPC protocol is periodically updated, and so the RPC protocol version is stated. In this call, the version is 2.

In the example, the caller uses *Unix credentials,* which identify its machine and include an effective Unix userid and groupid. One additional groupid is included. The *stamp* is an arbitrary identifier created by the caller. The *verifier* field has flavor 0 and so provides no further information. NFS often is implemented with sketchy authentication because fuller protection would slow down performance.

The parameters for program 100003 (NFS) and procedure 4 (look up filename) appear next in the message. The parameters are a *file handle* and a filename.

A *file handle*[2] is a special identifier associated with a directory or file at a server. We are interested in a file named *README* located in the directory identified by the file handle.

The fields in the call message are encoded using simple XDR format rules that are discussed in the next section.

We can get a feeling for the way that XDR works by looking at some of the hexadecimal encodings that appear in the call message:

Type = 0 is encoded (in hex) as:

```
00 00 00 00
```

RPC version = 2 is encoded as:

```
00 00 00 02
```

Machine = atlantis is encoded as:

```
(length of string = 8)    a    t    l    a    n    t    i    s
    00 00 00 08           61   74   6C   61   6E   74   69   73
```

The reply shown in Figure 15.7 has a matching transaction identifier. Null authentication information is included. The call has been accepted and has completed successfully.

The reply contains a lot of useful information about file *README:*

- Its *file handle* identifier is returned. Any further operations on this file will refer to the file using this file handle.

- Its *mode* describes the type of file and indicates who may access the file (owner, group, or world). The mode also declares whether users can read or write the file. If the file is application software, the mode shows whether users can execute the application.

- Additional file attributes are included, such as the file size, last time accessed, and last time updated. We would expect these attributes to be maintained in just about any file system.

XDR

When heterogeneous machines want to operate in a client/server environment, how can they understand one another's data? For example, an

---

[2]A version 2 file handle is a 32-byte fixed length string. A version 3 file handle is a variable-length string at most 64 bytes in length.

Figure 15.7
Format of an RPC
message carrying an
NFS reply.

```
RPC:   --- SUN RPC header ---
RPC:
RPC:   Transaction id = 641815012
RPC:   Type = 1 (Reply)
RPC:   Status = 0 (Accepted)
RPC:   Verifier: authorization flavor = 0 (Null)
RPC:   [Verifier: 0 byte(s) of authorization data]
RPC:   Accept status = 0 (Success)
RPC:
RPC:   [Normal end of "SUN RPC header".]
RPC:
NFS:   --- SUN NFS ---
NFS:
NFS:   Proc = 4 (Look up file name)
NFS:   Status = 0 (OK)
NFS:   File handle = 0000070A00000001000A000000005AC9
NFS:               3298621C000A0000000044C018F294BE
NFS:   File type = 1 (Regular file)
NFS:   Mode = 0100644
NFS:    Type = Regular file
NFS:    Owner's permissions = rw-
NFS:    Group's permissions = r-
NFS:    Others; permissions = r-
NFS:   Link count = 1, UID = 303, GID = 1
NFS:   File size = 130, Block size = 8192,
          No. of blocks = 2
NFS:   File system id = 1802, File id = 23241
NFS:   Access time       = 23-Oct-95 16:35:01 GMT
NFS:   Modification time = 20-Oct-95 12:10:43 GMT
NFS:   Inode change time = 20-Oct-95 12:10:43 GMT
NFS:
NFS:   [Normal end of "SUN NFS".]
NFS:
```

NFS client may want to ask a server to read 1000 bytes of data from some position in a file. How are the parameters of that request encoded? Typical parameters include file or directory names, file attributes such as file size, and integers specifying a number of bytes or position in a file.

All of the parameters in Sun RPC messages are *defined* and *encoded* using XDR, the *eXternal Data Representation* protocol. Specifically:

■ The XDR data description language is used to define the datatypes that appear in calls and replies.

■ The XDR encoding rules are applied to these definitions to format the data for transmission.

A large part of the RPC programming library consists of calls that translate datatypes to and from the XDR network format.

XDR Data Description Language

XDR definitions are similar to programming language datatypes, and they are quite easy to understand. There are a number of basic XDR datatypes such as unsigned and signed integers, enumerated integers, ASCII strings, booleans, and floating point numbers. The *opaque* datatype is used to carry general byte strings. Encrypted information can appear in an opaque field. More complicated array, structure, and union datatypes are built from the basic datatypes.

An enumerated integer type assigns a meaning to each number on a short list of integers. A simple example of an enumerated integer datatype is the message type (*msg_type*), which identifies whether a message is a call or a reply:

```
enum msg_type {
  CALL = 0,
  REPLY = 1
  };
```

Only one of the enumerated values, 0 or 1, may appear in this field. Entering any other integer into the field would be an error.

The structure that defines the body of an RPC call message is:

```
struct call_body {
   unsigned int rpcvers;     /* The version must be equal to two  */
   unsigned int prog;        /* This is the program number        */
   unsigned int vers;        /* This is the program version       */
   unsigned int proc;        /* This is the specific procedure    */
   opaque_auth cred;         /* Credentials, e.g., userid         */
   opaque_auth verf;         /* Verifier for the credentials      */
                             /* This might be an encrypted field  */
   /* procedure specific parameters start here                    */
};
```

XDR Encoding

Call and reply messages for a given version of a program and procedure are designed to have a fixed format. You know what kind of data will be in a field by its position in the message. The length of every field must be a multiple of 4 bytes.

There are many parameters represented by unsigned integers, which occupy 4 bytes. For example, *Procedure = 5* is represented by:

```
00 00 00 05
```

ASCII strings are encoded as a 4-byte integer that contains the string length followed by the ASCII characters and padded so that the field's length is a multiple of 4. For example, the string *README* appears as:

```
(string length = 6)      R     E     A     D     M     E     (pad)
  00  00  00  06        52    45    41    44    4D    45     00  00
```

The OSI *Abstract Syntax Notation 1* (ASN.1) data definition standard and *Basic Encoding Rules* (BER) encoding standard provide an alternative method for defining and encoding data. ASN.1 and BER are used by some TCP/IP applications—most notably, the Simple Network Management Protocol (SNMP).

The standard BER encoding precedes the data contents of a field with an identifier and length for the field. ASN.1 and BER are discussed in Chapter 20. The advantage of XDR is that data is encoded with far fewer bytes. The disadvantage of XDR is that each field must be in a predetermined position.

RPC and XDR Programming Interface

RPC client/server applications are developed using a library of subroutines that create, send, and receive RPC messages. Other library routines are used to convert between the local data representation of message parameters and their XDR format. A typical RPC subroutine is:

```
int callrpc (host, prognum, versnum, procnum, inproc, inparams,
outproc, outparams)
```

The *host* parameter identifies the server computer, *prognum* identifies the program, and *procnum* is the procedure to be executed. The input parameters to be sent in the call message are in structure *inparams*. The *inproc* routine will convert the input parameters to XDR format. When the reply arrives, the *outproc* routine will convert the XDR reply parameters to a local format and store them in structure *outparams*.

NFS Model

The Network File System is a file server architecture that is portable across different hardware, operating systems, transport protocols, and network technologies. However, it was designed with the Unix file system in mind.

A client host prepares to use NFS by *mounting* a remote directory subtree into its own file system. A client accomplishes this by sending an RPC request to the *mount* program at the server.

An end user or application is not aware of NFS. When a call is made to perform a file operation (such as open, read, write, copy, rename, delete, etc.) and the file happens to be located at a remote computer, the operating system redirects the request to NFS. The request is transmitted in a Remote Procedure Call request message. The input and output parameters are encoded using XDR.

Figure 15.8 shows the components that support NFS calls. NFS originally was implemented as a LAN file server application and ran over a UDP transport to keep overhead low. There are current implementations over TCP that run just as efficiently, and TCP is becoming the preferred protocol. Use of TCP is essential when communicating across a wide area network, where retransmission timeout calculations and congestion recovery are needed.

Typically multiple NFS service processes run in parallel at a server so that many clients can be handled concurrently.

Figure 15.8
Components supporting NFS.

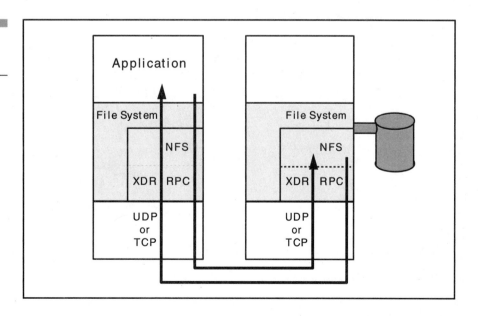

NFS File Pathnames

NFS works best for clients and servers that have a Unix-like file structure. Unix files are stored in a hierarchical tree of directories.[3] A Unix file is accessed as a sequential stream of bytes.

Unix directories and files are identified by pathnames that are formed by listing the names along the path from the root, separating the names by a slash (/). For example, *letc/hosts* and *lusr/john/abc* are pathnames.

The syntax used to write pathnames on non-Unix systems can be different. For example, *E:\WP\LETTER.DOC* is a DOS pathname. NFS assumes that every file can be identified by a pathname.

NFS File Pathnames and the Unix File System

Pieces of a Unix directory system can reside on different hard disks. For example, files and subdirectories under *letc* may be on one physical disk, while *lvar* and all of its subdirectories are on another. The Unix *mount* command is used to glue a piece such as *lvar* into the overall directory tree. A typical Unix *mount* command to do this is:

```
mount /dev/xy0b /var
```

The files on the physical device *xy0b* are identified with the files in directory *lvar*.

In designing NFS, it was natural to simply extend the *mount* command so remote subtrees also could be glued into a computer's directory tree. For example, suppose a network administrator wants the user files for host *tiger* to be physically located at computer *bighost,* where they will safely be backed up every night. The administrator creates directories for the user's files at *bighost,* say under *lusers*. From *tiger,* the administrator issues the command:

```
mount -t nfs bighost:/users /usr
```

Server directory *lusers* and all of its subdirectories are logically glued on top of *tiger*'s directory *lusr*. To end users, *tiger*'s directory system appears

---

[3]There have been successful implementations for servers without a hierarchical directory tree.

Figure 15.9
Mounting a remote directory.

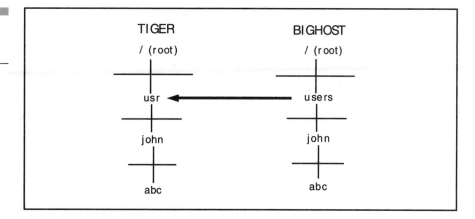

as shown in the left half of Figure 15.9. However, the file */usr/john/abc* actually is stored in */users/john/abc* at server *bighost*.

Another way of putting this is that whenever a local user asks for a file that is in a tree under */usr*, the operating system knows that the file really is at *bighost* under */users*.

Whereas Unix directory systems form a single tree, DOS directory systems have multiple trees (a forest?) rooted at devices A:, B:, C:, and so on. DOS computers glue a remote NFS directory onto a device such as E:.

Many other operating systems have hierarchical directories. Those that do not are mapped onto this model by incorporating restrictions on the depth of the tree that can be attached and on the directory and file-name syntax.

Mount Protocol

Mount, which is used to glue a remote directory into the local file system, is RPC program number 100005, and its port is advertised by the *portmapper. Mount* runs over both UDP and TCP.

Before a computer can mount a directory from a server, the server must be configured to *export* the directory. The way that this is typically done is that an administrator edits a file that lists the server directories to be exported, the hosts allowed to access them, and the access restrictions to be imposed. For example, a Unix */etc/exports* configuration might have the form:

```
/ma       -ro
/bin      -ro,access = tiger:lion
/users    -rw,access = tiger
```

The first directory is accessed read-only (ro), and is accessible from any host. Hosts *tiger* and *lion* can read the second directory. Host *tiger* has read-write access to the third directory.

A server can export only its own directories. It cannot export a directory that it has mounted from another NFS server. A client system can mount directories from as many servers as it likes. Of course, a directory can be mounted only if the server's export restrictions make the directory available to the client.

The client needs to identify all of the remote servers and directories that it wants to mount. Typically, this is done by a sequence of *mount* commands that is automatically executed at system start-up. Sometimes client *mount* command information is read out of a configuration file.

There are many optional parameters for a *mount* command. The most important select:

- Whether the directory should be mounted read-only or read-write.

- Whether to periodically retry failed mounts in the background and what limit to set on the number of retries.

- Whether a user can interrupt an NFS RPC call that is taking a very long time to complete.

- Whether to use a version of NFS that is based on secure Remote Procedure Calls.

A *mount* command causes an *Add Mount Entry* RPC message to be sent to the server. *In the response message, the mount protocol returns the file handle that the client will use to identify that directory in all future calls.* Recall that a file handle is a string that has meaning for the server system and identifies a corresponding directory or file. For example, when we mount */users* as local directory */usr*, the response to the *mount* request contains a file handle for directory */users*.

Mount Procedures

The procedures supported by a *mount* server program are listed in Table 15.4.

TABLE 15.4

Mount Procedures

Procedure	Description
0	*Null:* Respond showing the program is active.
1	*Add Mount Entry:* An entry for the client host is added to the mount list, and a file handle for the mounted directory is returned.
2	*Return Mount Entries:* Reports to the client on the currently mounted pathnames.
3	*Remove Mount Entry:* Removes the mount of a specified directory.
4	*Remove All Mount Entries:* Removes all of the client's mounts.
5	*Return Export List:* Returns a list consisting of directories and the hosts allowed to access each directory.

Statelessness And Idempotents

The spirit of NFS is that the server should be as *stateless* as possible. What this means is that an NFS server should have a minimum of client information to remember so that recovery from a client or server crash is painless and simple. Similarly, loss of a session when using TCP should not harm the relationship between a client and a server; the client should be able to set up a fresh session and continue its work.

A client knows that the NFS server has completed all of the work for a request when a reply is received. But NFS often runs on top of UDP, and UDP is unreliable. What should be done if no reply arrives? NFS repeats requests after a timeout period.

However, it is possible that the original request actually got through to the server but the reply was lost. For this reason, NFS servers usually are not perfectly stateless. They cache some recent replies so duplicate requests can be handled correctly.

Which replies should be kept? Some operations—such as a *read* or *lookup*—are *idempotent*. This means that they can be executed more than once and still return the same result. Others, such as *remove file* or *create directory,* are not idempotent. If the original result was lost, a second execution will return a misleading error message. Caching the results of nonidempotent operations enables NFS to send the appropriate reply to a retransmitted request.

NFS Protocol

The most current NFS version is 3, but many version 2 implementations can be expected to persist for quite a long time. The NFS server program number is 100003. By convention, an NFS server grabs port 2049 when it initializes.

More About File Handles

Recall that when a client mounts a directory, the *mount* protocol returns a file handle that identifies that directory in all future calls. The directory that is mounted may have subdirectories, and these may have subdirectories. A file's pathname can be nested several levels deep. For example, before a user at the client can update the file:

```
/usr/john/book/chapter3
```

it is necessary to obtain the file handle of the corresponding file, */users/john/book/chapter3,* from the server. The way that NFS does this is to look up one pathname at a time. For our example, the NFS client would:

- Send a lookup call to the server that includes the file handle for */users* and pathname component *john.* The reply contains a handle for */users/john.*

- Send a lookup call to the server that includes the file handle for */users/john* and pathname component *book.* The server returns a file handle for */users/john/book.*

- Send a lookup call to the server that includes the handle for */users/john/book* and filename *chapter3.* The reply contains the file handle that we want.

The result of this long-winded approach to getting to a file handle that we want is that NFS clients issue lots of lookup calls.

NFS Procedures

There are NFS procedures that let a client access, read, and write files. The client can find out about the organization and capacity of the remote file system and can ask to see the attributes of individual files.

The client can delete or rename files. Some of the procedures deal with features provided specifically by the Unix file system, such as linking an alias name to a file. The NFS procedures for versions 2 and 3 are described briefly in Table 15.5.

TABLE 15.5

NFS Version 2 and Version 3 Procedures

Procedure	Version 2	Version 3
0	Null procedure for testing.	Null procedure for testing.
1	Get file attributes.	Get file attributes.
2	Set file attributes.	Set file attributes.
3	Obsolete operation.	Look up a file name.That is, given the file handle for a directory and the name of a subdirectory or file, return the file handle for the sub-directory or file.
4	Look up a file name.	Check access permission.
5	Read information associated with a symbolic link.	Read information associated with a symbolic link.
6	Read data from a file.	Read data from a file.
7	Not used.	Write data to a file. The call can indicate whether the write can be to cache, or whether it must be committed to stable storage before a reply can be sent.
8	Write data to a file.	Create a file.
9	Create a file.	Create a directory.
10	Remove a file.	Create a symbolic link.
11	Rename a file.	Create a node (i.e., a special device).
12	Create a link to a file.	Remove (delete) a file.
13	Create a symbolic link.	Remove a directory.
14	Create a directory.	Rename a file or directory.
15	Remove a directory.	Create a link to an object.
16	Read filenames and fileids from a directory.	Read filenames and fileids from a directory.
17	Get file system information such as the block size and number of free blocks.	Read filenames, fileids, attributes, and handles from a directory.

TABLE 15.5

NFS Version 2
and Version 3
Procedures
(Continued)

Procedure	Version 2	Version 3
18		Get dynamic file system information such as the total size and amount of free space.
19		Get static file system information such as the maximum sizes for read and write requests.
20		Retrieve POSIX information, such as attributes and the maximum length of a filename.
21		Commit—forces data that previously was written to memory cache to be written to stable storage.

Special NFS Utilities

Ideally, NFS should be transparent to a user. Server files are opened, read, written, and closed as if they are local. Ordinary local commands are used to copy, rename, or delete server files.

When the client and server have the same operating system, this is straightforward. Sometimes a few special additional commands make NFS work better when the client and server file conventions are very different. An example may help to clarify this.

When a DOS client uses a Unix system as a file server, files that are created and named by the DOS client will conform to DOS conventions and will be a natural part of the client's file system.

If the DOS client wants to read a text file created by a Unix user, there are some problems. First of all, DOS names consist of up to eight characters optionally followed by a dot and up to three more characters. When a DOS user types a filename, all letters are converted to uppercase. For example, COMMAND.COM is a DOS filename. Unix names can be much longer and can contain a mixture of upper- and lowercase letters. For example, *aLongerName.More* is a valid Unix filename.

How can a DOS user access the Unix file? Vendors usually perform automatic name translation and also include a utility that enables users to view the native filename.

There is one other hurdle to get over. Lines in a DOS text file end with carriage return (CR) and line feed (LF) characters while lines in a Unix text file end with LF. Some vendors perform automatic translation, while others provide utilities that enable a user to convert a text file to the local format.

File Locking

There are some files that must be accessed by several users. For example, many application processes may need to read a configuration file. A user who needs to update a shared file will want to obtain exclusive access to the file—that is, lock the file—during the update activity.

File locking in an NFS environment is handled by two RPC services: the *lock manager* and the *status* program. The *lock manager* handles client requests for file locks. A server's *status* monitor tries to keep track of which client hosts currently hold locks. If a server crashes, it will send notification to the status monitors at registered client hosts, asking them to resubmit their lock requests.

NFS Implementation Issues

A program may repeatedly ask its operating system to read or write a few bytes of data. Accessing a hard disk frequently for small amounts of data is not efficient. Normally, operating systems read in entire blocks of data ahead of time and respond to read calls using data stored in memory. Similarly, writes are saved in memory and periodically written to disk.

Frequent accesses to a remote NFS server for small amounts of data are even more inefficient than local disk accesses. Client NFS implementations perform read-aheads of blocks of data. Eight kilobytes was the maximum read or write request for version 2 of NFS. Version 3 removes this maximum and enables the client and server to negotiate a maximum size. In fact, a client could issue a read request that downloaded an entire file. This reduces overhead and enables the client and server to work a lot more efficiently across very high-speed links or across paths that have a big delay.

An NFS server improves its performance by keeping directory and file attribute information in memory and by reading ahead to anticipate client calls. Version 3 supports writes to memory cache, which can be forced onto permanent media by calling a *commit* procedure.

WebNFS Alternative

NFS was designed for long-term relationships between clients and servers. Recall that before a client can read a file located at an NFS server, it must:

■ Contact the server's portmapper and obtain the *mount* program's port number. The mount protocol gives the client an essential piece of information—a filehandle that is used to identify the mounted director in future transactions.

■ Consult an internal configuration file and mount the desired directories.

■ Contact the server's portmapper and obtain NSF's port number (although 2049 would be a good guess).

■ Make separate lookup calls for each component in a pathname, obtaining a filehandle for each.

WebNFS leapfrogs this entire procedure in order to support ad hoc file access. WebNFS also makes it feasible to use NFS on the Internet. Both version 2 and version 3 NFS servers can be outfitted to act as WebNFS servers. The changes that make this possible are:

■ The *mount* protocol is not needed because the client will use a special public filehandle as the initial filehandle. (An all 0s filehandle is used with a version 2 NFS server. A zero length filehandle is used for version 3 NFS server.)

■ A WebNFS server will operate out of a stable, selected port—by default, 2049. If for some reason a different port has been configured, the client can request access at that port. The client does not have to consult the portmapper.

■ The client can submit a file's entire pathname and get the filehandle in one step. (This is called multicomponent lookup.)

A WebNFS server can be used much like a public file transfer server. The server could make a selected directory accessible to anyone. WebNFS also can be used for authenticated private file access. There are some important differences between using a WebNFS server and a file transfer server:

■ After connecting to a WebNFS server, a whole new directory tree appears to be connected to your system. You can navigate this tree and access files of interest.

- When you connect to a file transfer or *http* server, each request asks for an entire file. With WebNFS, you can browse through a file. Blocks of data are acquired as needed.

- If you lose your connection along the way, you can reconnect and continue where you left off. This is especially valuable if you are doing a download of a big file.

The WebNFS modifications make it perfectly feasible to access an NFS server through a firewall.

WebNFS URL

As its name suggests, WebNFS can be used with browsers. The WebNFS URL has the form:

nfs://hostname:port/filename

If the port is omitted, it defaults to 2049.

Monitoring NFS

The Unix *nfsstat* command results in a report on NFS activities. Similar commands are available at other operating systems. In the example shown below, the local system is acting as both a server and as a client. There is very little server activity reported. However, the system's users are making a large number of client calls.

The display shows the number of users of each type of call over the monitoring period. Note the large number of *lookups*. Recall that these calls are used to walk down a file's pathname one step at a time in order to obtain the filehandle.

```
> nfsstat
Server rpc:
calls      badcalls    nullrecv   badlen   xdrcall
25162314   0           0          0        0

Server nfs:
calls      badcalls
25162314   491

null       getattr      setattr     root  lookup        readlink
478 0%     9689121 38%  380591 1%   0 0%  5596396 22%   5992775 23%
read
1009813  4%
```

wrcache	write	create	remove	rename	link	symlink
0 0%	1146142 4%	627381 2%	66180 0%	13089 0%	6042 0%	265 0%
mkdir	rmdir	readdir	fsstat			
1718 0%	66 0%	626437 2%	5820 0%			

Client rpc:

calls	badcalls	retrans	badxid	timeout	wait	newcred	timers
3931394	2069	0 42	2037	0	0	1697	

Client nfs:

calls	badcalls	nclget	nclsleep		
3929178	32	3929357 0			
null	getattr	setattr	root	lookup	readlink
0 0%	2221718 56%	6689 0% 0	0%	1423702	36% 93498 2%
read	wrcache	write	create	remove	rename
54110 1%	0 0%	19501 0%	7362 0%	6493 0%	158 0%
link	symlink	mkdir	rmdir	readdir	fsstat
5 0%	0 0%	28 0%	12 0%	95804 2%	98 0%

Recommended Reading

At the time of this writing, the *portmapper* and *RPCBIND* were defined
in RFC 1833, Remote Procedure Call Protocol version 2 in RFC 1831,
and XDR in RFC 1832.

Version 2 of NFS was described in RFC 1094, and version 3 was
described in RFC 1813. A very complete specification of version 2 of NFS
can be found in *X/Open CAE Specification: Protocols for X/Open Internetworking: XNFS,* published by the X/Open Company, Ltd.

RFC 2055 presents the WebNFS Server Specification and RFC 2054
contains the WebNFS Client Specification. RFC 2224 describes the NFS
URL scheme.

Electronic Mail
and MIME

Introduction

Of all of the TCP/IP applications, electronic mail engages the largest number of people. When an organization offers good access to mail, usage grows explosively. Mail attracts users who never dreamed that they would use a computer.

Electronic mail is a convenient way to reach people and is easy to use. The dialog below shows a very simple interaction with a bare-bones Unix mail program. The program prompts for the Subject: and the user signals the end of the message by typing a period as the only character on a line.

```
> mail fred
Subject: New Materials
The manuals have arrived.
Let's discuss them next week.
.
```

There are mail programs that are far more elegant, with full-screen user interfaces and point-and-click options. For example, Figure 16.1 shows the user interface for the *NetManage Zmail Pro* Windows 95 and NT

Figure 16.1
A NetManage ZMail Pro user interface.

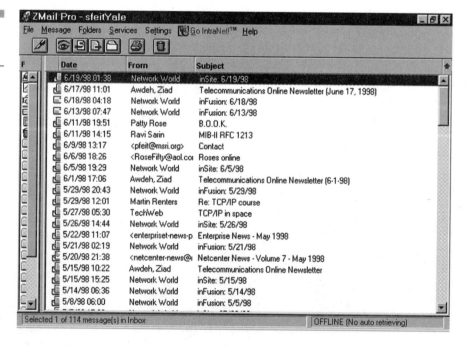

Figure 16.2
A Macintosh Eudora
user interface.

In				
gberg	2:03 PM 5/10/96 -	2	Shah/HP-UX SYSTEM AND ADMINISTRATION
Feit	1:56 PM 5/15/96 -	1	Chapter 24 figures 5-9
interramp	2:52 AM 5/26/96 -	4	Estimated Bill for Service
Feit	8:52 AM 5/28/96 -	6	TCP/IP figures
Feit	8:57 AM 5/28/96 -	2	More TCP/IP figures

You have new mail.

OK

electronic mail client, and Figure 16.2 shows the Macintosh *Eudora* electronic mail program.

The formal name for an electronic mail client is a *User Agent* (UA). An email client is expected to perform several chores, such as:

- Display information about incoming mail messages that are waiting in a user's mailbox
- Save incoming or outgoing messages in folders or local files
- Provide a good editor for entering message text

An individual's choice of email client user interface always has been viewed as a matter of personal taste and not subject to standardization. The important thing is that the end result always is the same—mail items are sent and delivered.

Let's return to our original mail transaction. It all looks very easy, but there is a lot of muscle hiding behind the scenes. As it happens, "fred" is a *nickname* or *alias* that I have defined in my private address book. When my email client looks it up, it discovers that the real recipient identifier is *fred@microsoft.com*.

This identifier has a format that is typical for Internet mail. However, vendors of proprietary electronic mail software and public mail service providers have expressed a lot of individuality in designing their own recipient formats. There are *mail gateways* that are kept very busy converting between these formats.

How is mail delivered? In earlier times, mail was transferred across a direct TCP connection between a source host and recipient host. But today, mail is likely to be relayed via one or more intermediate hosts. We have a lot more to say about relaying later.

Internet Mail Protocols

Mail is heavily used, and many Internet protocols have evolved to meet the requirements of electronic mail users. Figure 16.3 illustrates the Internet mail protocols.

The *Simple Mail Transfer Protocol* (SMTP) is the classic Internet standard for moving mail between computers. SMTP was designed to carry simple text notes and was implemented on top of a Network Virtual Terminal (NVT) *telnet* session. A series of more recent standards define *Extensions to SMTP* (ESMTP) that update SMTP. An ESMTP session can carry any type of information efficiently.

When mail arrives, an email client needs to understand message elements such as the sender's identifier, date sent, subject, and the information part of the message. The venerable *Standard for the Format of*

Figure 16.3
Internet mail protocols.

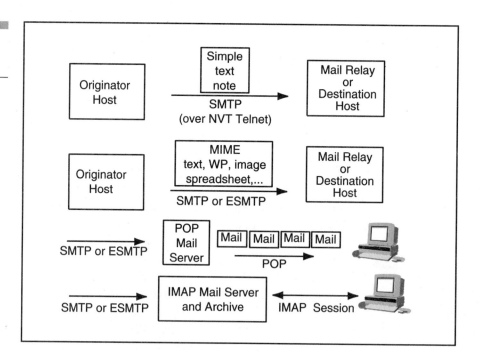

ARPA *Internet Text Messages* provides the durable format for simple Internet US-ASCII text-mail messages.

New, multipart message bodies are described in *Multipurpose Internet Mail Extensions* (MIME) standards. Many different types of information can be delivered, such as documents created by word processors, Macintosh Binhex files, images, videos, encoded sounds, spreadsheets, executable code, or whatever. MIME has been updated with support for international character sets. New MIME types are defined as needed and are registered with the Internet Assigned Numbers Authority.

Another set of standards was designed to fit the way that many people work today. The *Post Office Protocol* (POP) enables a desktop client to download mail from a mail server. An alternative choice, the *Internet Message Access Protocol* (IMAP), enables a user to read, copy, or delete messages that are stored at a server, but the server is the authoritative repository for messages. This is helpful for users who want to take advantage of administrative services (such as daily backup), save desktop disk space, or access their mail when they are traveling. Mail is delivered to a server via SMTP or ESMTP.

Some organizations relay mail by means of the OSI X.400 protocols, which is discussed briefly later in this chapter.

Model for Mail Transmission

Figure 16.4 shows the elements of a mail system. Mail is prepared with the help of an email client application. The email client typically queues mail to a separate application, called a *Message Transfer Agent* (MTA), which is responsible for setting up communications with remote hosts and transmitting the mail. *Message Transfer Agent* is a term used in the X.400 message system standards, but the term describes a component that is valid for TCP/IP mail as well.

The mail may be sent directly between the source and destination MTAs or relayed via intermediate MTAs. When a mail item is relayed, the entire message is transmitted to an intermediate host, where it is stored until it can be forwarded at a convenient time. Mail systems that use relaying are called *store-and-forward* systems.

At the recipient host, mail is placed on an incoming queue and later is moved to a user's *mailbox* storage area. When a recipient user invokes an email client program, the client usually displays a summary of the incoming mail that is waiting in the mailbox.

Figure 16.4
Components of an
electronic mail
system.

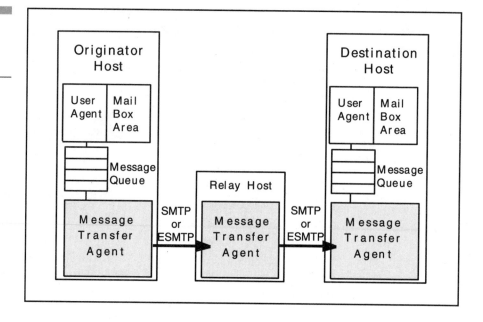

Sendmail MTA

For many years the Unix *sendmail* program has been the dominant
SMTP Message Transfer Agent. The Sendmail Consortium is a worldwide team of volunteers that has maintained the free *sendmail* package
for several years. (See *www.sendmail.org.*) *Sendmail's* original developer, Eric Allman, continues to lead the evolution of *sendmail,* and is Chief
technical Officer of Sendmail, Inc., which provides both freeware and
commercial versions of the package. *Sendmail* is a very big program
with a lot of useful features.

Relaying Mail

Why would a Message Transfer Agent ever want to relay mail rather
than connect directly to the recipient host? When a host uses a direct
connection, it can be sure that mail has reached its destination. Relayed
mail uses intermediate storage resources and requires multiple connections. To relay mail, we have to design a store-and-forward mail relaying
road map, and if we do not do a good job, mail will wander around in an
inefficient manner.

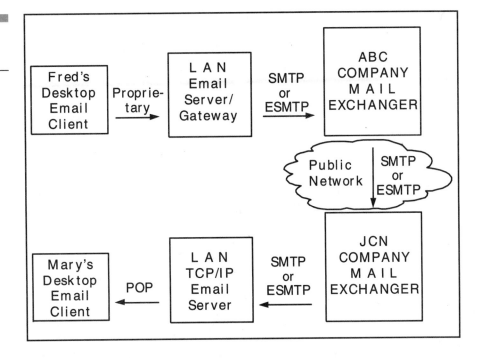

Figure 16.5
Relaying electronic
mail. ·

A Mail Relay Scenario

In order to see why store-and-forward is so prevalent, let's walk through the scenario that is illustrated in Figure 16.5. Fred, who works for ABC Industries, is sending a mail item to Mary, who works for JCN Computers. Fred's computer is a LAN workstation that is powered down much of the time. The workstation sends and receives mail via a relay server on the LAN.

Both ABC Industries and JCN Computers are very security-minded. They allow mail to be exchanged with the outside world only via designated *Mail Exchanger* relay hosts. Each company is attached to the outside world by a router that blocks all traffic except for connections to the mail port (25) at the company's Mail Exchanger.

A proprietary LAN electronic mail product is used on Fred's LAN. TCP/IP electronic mail protocols are used at Mary's site.

As Figure 16.5 shows, mail is transferred from Fred's desktop to a LAN server using a proprietary mail protocol. The LAN server has gateway software that translates between the proprietary mail format and Internet message format. Then the mail is forwarded to ABC's Mail Exchanger. From there, it is transmitted across the Internet to JCN's

Mail Exchanger. It is relayed again to Mary's LAN electronic mail server, where it will be stored until Mary connects and picks up her mail via the Post Office Protocol.

This scenario illustrates that relaying offers a number of benefits:

- PCs and workstations can depend on a LAN server system to forward outgoing mail and hold their incoming electronic mail for them.

- A company's employees can use electronic mail but still maintain security by funneling mail through a Mail Exchanger.

- Cost savings can be realized by batching mail from a relay at favorable times.

- A mail relay can perform mail format translations.

In the sections that follow, we take a closer look at the mechanisms that have evolved within the TCP/IP protocol family to support an expanding electronic mail universe.

Mail Recipient Identifiers and Mail Exchangers

Internet mail recipients are identified by names following the general pattern:

name-part@domain-name

We shall see that this format is quite flexible. For many years, the prevalent format for Internet-style names was:

userid@hostname

For example:

smithm@sales.chicago.jcn.com.

Today, far more convenient formats are used, such as:

firstname-lastname@mail-domain-name or *firstname.lastname@mail-domain-name*

For example:

Mary-Smith@jcn.com or *Mary.Smith@jcn.com*

In this identifier, *Mary-Smith* is not a userid, and *jcn.com* is not the name of a computer—it is a nickname (formally called a *logical name*) assigned to a Mail Exchanger. So how does this mail get delivered? The mail relaying architecture depends on the Domain Name System. The way that it works is:

- One or more computers are selected to act as Mail Exchangers for an organization.

- A logical name—usually the organization's Domain Name—is selected for the Mail Exchanger, and a Mail Exchanger (MX) entry is added to the DNS database.

- A Message Transfer Agent program looks up the mail-domain-name part of the recipient identifier in the DNS, retrieves the real name and address of a Mail Exchanger, and relays the mail to the Mail Exchanger.

A demonstration will make this clearer. Below, we start the *nslookup* program and ask for the identity of Sun's Mail Exchanger. We discover that actually there are seven. It is a good idea to run multiple mail servers to ensure availability of the service for a large company like Sun Microsystems.

Note the *preference* numbers (5, 10, 15, 20, 40, 50, and 60). The server with the lowest is most preferred and will be tried first. The actual preference numbers used do not matter, only their relative size does.

```
> nslookup
> sun.com.
Server:    char.vnet.net
Address:    166.82.1.3

sun.com preference = 10, mail exchanger = saturn.sun.com
sun.com preference = 15, mail exchanger = mercury.sun.com
sun.com preference = 20, mail exchanger = venus.sun.com
sun.com preference = 40, mail exchanger = mars.sun.com
sun.com preference = 50, mail exchanger = dollar.usec.sun.com
sun.com preference = 60, mail exchanger = franc.usec.sun.com
sun.com preference = 5, mail exchanger = earth.sun.com
sun.com nameserver = admii.arl.mil
sun.com nameserver = ns1.barrnet.net
sun.com nameserver = vgr.arl.mil
sun.com nameserver = ns.sun.com
saturn.sun.com     internet address = 192.9.25.2
mercury.sun.com    internet address = 192.9.25.1
venus.sun.com      internet address = 192.9.25.5
mars.sun.com       internet address = 192.9.22.1
dollar.usec.sun.com    internet address = 192.9.51.3
franc.usec.sun.com     internet address = 192.9.51.4
earth.sun.com      internet address = 192.9.25.3
admii.arl.mil      internet address = 128.63.31.4
```

```
admii.arl.mil      internet address = 128.63.5.4
ns1.barrnet.net    internet address = 131.119.245.5
vgr.arl.mil        internet address = 128.63.16.6
vgr.arl.mil        internet address = 128.63.2.6
ns.sun.com         internet address = 192.9.9.3
```

The next demonstration shows how some organizations build in an extra layer of security. Note that there are three Mail Exchangers, but two of them actually belong to the UUNET Service provider:

```
> clarinet.com.
Server:   DEPT-GW.cs.YALE.EDU
Address:     128.36.0.36

clarinet.com preference = 10,     mail exchanger = looking.clarinet.com
clarinet.com preference = 100,    mail exchanger = relay1.uu.net
clarinet.com preference = 100,    mail exchanger = relay2.uu.net
looking.clarinet.com   inet address = 192.54.253.1
relay1.uu.net    inet address = 192.48.96.5
relay2.uu.net    inet address = 192.48.96.7
>
```

Clarinet could set up its network so that incoming mail would first be funneled through one of the UUNET Mail Exchangers and then would be relayed to *looking.clarinet.com*.

Figure 16.6 shows how this is done. A filtering router has been set up to refuse connections from all systems except for the UUNET service provider's Mail Exchangers. An external system will try to connect to the most preferred site, *looking.clarinet.com*. But in step 1, the filtering router prevents the connection from going through. Therefore, one of the

Figure 16.6
Forcing mail along a path.

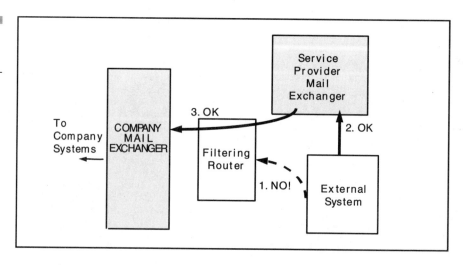

less preferred sites is tried, and the mail is forwarded to *relay1* or *relay2*. The UUNET system now can forward the mail to Clarinet's Mail Exchanger.

When mail reaches a company's Mail Exchanger, the name-part will be looked up in an alias file and converted to a userid and host name— or whatever type of mail identifier is used in the destination network. Thus, a Mail Exchanger also can act as a gateway to non-Internet-style mail services.

There is one more problem to be solved in order to route mail through a Mail Exchanger. Suppose that users at host *sales.clarinet.com* had mail identifiers of the form *username@sales.clarinet.com*. What would happen to mail with an address like *jonesj@sales.clarinet.com?* A few more entries in the Clarinet DNS database take care of this problem:

```
*.clarinet.com.    IN    MX    10     looking.clarinet.com.
*.clarinet.com.    IN    MX    100    relay1.uu.net
*.clarinet.com.    IN    MX    100    relay2.uu.net
```

These "wild card" entries direct mail that is addressed to the old-style *userid@hostname* to the Mail Exchangers.

Organizations are replacing their old *userid@hostname* identifiers with the more up-to-date name formats (like *Mary-Smith@jcn.net*), which do not reveal userids to outsiders. In addition to improving the security of a network, these names also permit users to acquire new userids or move to different computers without changing their mail identifiers.

Simple Mail Transfer Protocol

The Simple Mail Transfer Protocol (SMTP) defines a straightforward way to move mail between hosts. There are two roles in the SMTP protocol: sender and receiver. The sender acts as client and establishes a TCP connection with the receiver, which acts as server. The well-known port used for a receiver is 25. Even when the sender is a mail service program (a "Message Transfer Agent"), the sender acts as client and uses a temporary port from the pool.

During an SMTP session the sender and receiver exchange a sequence of commands and responses. First, the receiver announces its host name. Then the sender:

■ Announces its host name

- Identifies the message originator
- Identifies one or more recipients
- Transmits the mail data
- Transmits a line containing a period followed by <CR> <LF> which indicates that the item is complete

Note that an item can be delivered to several recipients at a host via one transaction because multiple recipients can be identified before the message data is sent. At the end of a transaction, the sender can:

- Start another transaction
- Quit and close the connection[1]

Mail Dialog

In the dialog that follows, a client uses SMTP to transfer a message to a mail server named *popserv.vnet.net.*. The message will be forwarded to a VNET Mail Exchanger and then will be delivered to the system that acts as a Yale Mail Exchanger and POP server.

```
Trying 166.82.1.29...
Connected to popserv.vnet.net.
Escape character is '^]'.
220 popserv.vnet.net ESMTP Sendmail 8.8.8/8.8.8; Sun, 21 Jun 1998
10:39:13 -0400
    (EDT)
HELO katie.vnet.net
250 popserv.vnet.net Hello sfeit@katie.vnet.net [166.82.1.7],
pleased to meet you
MAIL FROM: <sfeit@vnet.net>
250 <sfeit@vnet.net>... Sender ok
RCPT TO: <feit-sidnie@math.yale.edu>
250 <feit-sidnie@math.yale.edu>... Recipient ok
DATA
354 Enter mail, end with "." on a line by itself
Date: Sun, 21 Jun 1998 10:39:59 -0400 (EDT)
Subject: It's OK to talk to yourself!!!
To: feit-sidnie@MATH.YALE.EDU
Message-Id: <199806211439.KAA12659@katie.vnet.net>

Hi there.
See you soon.
    .
```

---

[1]The standard includes a *TURN* command that enables the sender to reverse roles so it becomes the receiver. However, this is rarely (if ever) implemented.

```
250 KAA12659 Message accepted for delivery
QUIT
221 popserv.vnet.net closing connection
Connection closed by foreign host.
```

To transmit, the client opens a connection to port 25 at the receiver. Then the receiver starts the dialog by announcing its domain name. During the dialog, the client:

- Identifies itself.
- Sends the email identifier of the originator.
- Sends the email identifier of the recipient.
- Sends a DATA command.
- Provides message headers.
- Sends an empty line followed by the message text.
- Terminates the message with a line consisting of a period (followed by <CR> <LF>).

The command/reply model that we have seen in the File Transfer Protocol (FTP) also applies here, and the encoding of the reply messages is similar. All messages from the remote electronic mail server start with a reply number.

Note that electronic mail identifiers are enclosed in angle brackets in the MAIL FROM: and RCPT TO: commands (e.g., *<sfeit@vnet.net>*). Host names are not case sensitive and may appear in upper- and lowercase. However, a username may be case-sensitive, depending on the user naming conventions in use by the electronic mail system.

Note that the end of the message is signaled by a period on a line by itself. If a user actually wants to send a line containing a single period as part of a message, an additional period is inserted by the sending SMTP and deleted by the receiving SMTP.

Timestamps and Message ID

When you receive mail, you might want to know what time it was sent and when it arrived at your computer. SMTP adds this information to your message. SMTP also keeps track of all of the hosts that relayed the message and the time that each received the message.

When a message is passed to an SMTP Message Transfer Agent, the agent inserts a timestamp at the top of the message. Each time that an item is relayed, another timestamp is added at the top. Each timestamp shows:

- The identity of the host that sent the message
- The identity of the host that received the message
- The date and time that the message was received

The timestamps in the message header provide invaluable debugging information when there are mail delivery problems. For example, they might reveal that an item was stalled at some intermediate host for a day or two.

Timestamp formats vary, and different vendors include diverse information. Newer implementations provide timestamps that report the local time, followed by the offset from *Universal Time* (formerly called Greenwich Mean Time). This offset is in the form of + or − the number of hours in the offset.

Computer clocks are sometimes inaccurately set, so some timestamp sequences don't seem to make very good sense. (For example, occasionally messages appear to arrive before they were sent.) Since network administrators usually are the only people who need to pay close attention to timestamps, the anomalies are tolerated.

When the mail arrives at its final destination, the recipient email client optionally may insert an extra line or two at the top that contains whatever summary information it wants to add.

In the previous section, we showed a mail transmission dialog. Let's examine the format of the message after a client picked it up from the Mail Exchanger/POP server:

```
From smap Sun Jun 21 10:34:04 1998
Received: by PLUM.MATH.YALE.EDU; Sun, 21 Jun 1998 10:34:03 -0400
Received: from elvis.vnet.net(166.82.1.5) by PLUM.MATH.YALE.EDU via
smap (V1.3)
id sma020142; Sun Jun 21 10:33:35 1998
Received: from popserv.vnet.net (popserv.vnet.net [166.82.1.29])
by elvis.vnet.net (8.8.8/8.8.4) with ESMTP
id KAA09915 for <feit-sidnie@math.yale.edu>; Sun, 21 Jun 1998
10:40:39 -0400 (EDT)
From: SFEIT <sfeit@vnet.net>
Received: from katie.vnet.net (sfeit@katie.vnet.net [166.82.1.7])
by popserv.vnet.net (8.8.8/8.8.8) with SMTP id KAA12659
for <feit-sidnie@math.yale.edu>; Sun, 21 Jun 1998 10:39:59 -0400
(EDT)
Date: Sun, 21 Jun 1998 10:39:59 -0400 (EDT)
Subject: It's OK to talk to yourself!!!
To: feit-sidnie@MATH.YALE.EDU
Message-Id: <199806211439.KAA12659@katie.vnet.net>
```

```
Hi there.
See you soon.
```

The timestamps reported in the "Received:" fields must be read from bottom to top. The message first went from *katie.vnet.net* to *popserv.vnet.net*. Next, the message was forwarded to *elvis.vnet.net,* and then it was sent on to the destination server, *plum.math.yale.edu.* This message was submitted at 10:39:59 and was received by *plum* at 10:34:03! Email service can be very efficient—but not that efficient! This is just a case of clocks out of synchronization. Note the offset -0400 showing that Eastern Daylight Time is four hours earlier than Universal Time.

The first and third lines indicate that the message has been received using a program called SMAP. SMAP is a very simple program that does nothing but accept incoming mail and pass it to *sendmail. Sendmail* is popular because of its powerful functionality, but is so big and complicated that it is difficult to be sure that it is 100 percent secure. *Plum* is protecting itself by using the simple SMAP program to receive its mail.

Bounced Mail

Occasionally, it will be impossible to deliver mail to its destination. Most often, this is because the originator has provided an incorrect recipient identifier. Mail that cannot be delivered is sent back to the originator and is called *bounced* mail.

SMTP Commands

The mail dialog presented earlier contained the most frequently used SMTP commands. The complete set of SMTP commands is described in Table 16.1.

A command is transmitted as a four-character mnemonic. Many commands are followed by a parameter. A session between SMTP partners employs *telnet* NVT conventions such as sending using ASCII characters and ending a line with carriage return and line feed.

There is a 1000-character limit on the size of a line (including <CR>

TABLE 16.1

SMTP/ESMTP Commands

Command	Description
HELO	Identifies the sender to the receiver.
EHLO	Identifies the sender to the receiver and announces extended capability.
MAIL FROM	Starts a mail transaction and identifies the mail originator.
RCPT TO	Identifies an individual recipient. The command is repeated in order to identify multiple recipients. If possible, the receiver checks the validity of the recipient name and indicates the result in the reply message. A relay host can't check the recipient name and always responds with "OK.". If it later turns out that some recipient was not valid, a brief mail item reporting the error will be sent back to the originator.
DATA	The sender is ready to transmit a series of lines of text terminated with <CR> <LF>. The maximum length of a line, including <CR> <LF>, is 1000 characters. The SMTP rules require an implementation to be able to send and receive messages that are up to 64 kilobytes in length. Today, many messages are larger than this.
RSET	Abort the current mail transaction, clearing out all originator and recipient information.
NOOP	Asks the partner to send a positive reply.
QUIT	Asks the partner to send a positive reply and close the connection.
VRFY	Asks the receiver to confirm that a name identifies a valid recipient.
EXPN	Asks the receiver to confirm that a name identifies a mailing list and, if so, to return the membership of that list. This command is purely informational, and will not add to the current list of recipients.
HELP	Asks the partner for information about its implementation, such as the list of commands that are supported.
Defined, But Rarely Implemented or Used	
TURN	Asks the partner to switch roles and become the sender. The partner is allowed to refuse.
SEND	If the recipient is logged in, deliver a mail item directly to the recipient's terminal.
SOML	Send or Mail—if the recipient is logged in, deliver direct to the terminal. Otherwise, deliver as mail.
SAML	Send and Mail—deliver to the recipient's mailbox. If the user is logged in, also deliver to the terminal.

<LF>). If you cut and paste text from a word processing document into an email editor, you might accidentally create a line that is too large. The result will be a message that mysteriously cannot be transmitted.

Reply Codes

The SMTP reply codes look a lot like the FTP reply codes. The codes are made up of three digits. The first digit indicates the status of the command:

1yz   Positive Preliminary reply (currently not used in SMTP).

2yz   Positive Completion reply.

3yz   Positive Intermediate reply.

4yz   Transient Negative reply ("try again").

5yz   Permanent Negative reply.

The second digit classifies the reply:

x0z   In reply to a problem, this indicates a syntax error or unknown command.

x1z   Reply to information request such as help.

x2z   Reply referring to the connection.

x3z   Unspecified as yet.

x4z   Unspecified as yet.

x5z   Reply that indicates the status of the receiver mail system.

The meaning of the third digit varies depending on the command and the first two digits.

More About the Internet Message Format

The standard for the format of Internet text messages, defined in RFC 822, is straightforward. It consists of the following, in the order listed:

- A set of header fields (most of which are optional)
- A blank line
- The text or *body* of the message

A header field has the form:

Field-name: Field-contents

Field names and contents are expressed using ASCII characters. There are many header fields. A representative sample includes:

```
Received
Date
From
To
cc
bcc (blind cc)
Message-Id
Reply-To
Sender (if not the message creator)
In-Reply-To
References (to earlier Message IDs)
Keywords
Subject
Comments
Encrypted
```

We expect every message header to include *Date, From,* and *To* fields. *Received* fields are constructed using the timestamp information gathered as mail is transferred between Message Transfer Agents. Most mail software can create a message identifier that is included in the message. For example:

```
Message-Id: <199806211439.KAA12659@katie.vnet.net>
```

The Message-Id is designed to be unique across the network. To achieve this, it usually includes the originating host's name, along with a unique alphanumeric identifier. Note that the preceding identifier contains the date (1998 06 21), the time (11439), and an additional string that ensures that the ID is unique for that host and time.

Resent fields are added if a message is forwarded. Examples are *Resent-To, Resent-From, Resent-cc, Resent-bcc, Resent-Date, Resent-Sender, Resent-Message-Id,* and *Resent-Reply-To.*

The blank line that follows the headers is important. It tells the email client that the introductory header information is complete and that the actual message follows.

Mail Extensions and MIME

The simplicity of SMTP and the mail format made Internet mail easy to implement and led to widespread use. However, users grew impatient with its limitation to simple text messages. It was clear that SMTP needed an overhaul, but how could this be done without disturbing the installed base of mail applications?

A very practical approach was taken. New MIME clients would be implemented with the ability to create and receive multipart messages containing many useful types of information. These messages could be exchanged:

- Efficiently, via new Extended SMTP Message Transfer Agents.

- Less efficiently, via the old standard SMTP. Before passing a nontext body part to an old SMTP agent, a MIME sender will convert the item so that it "looks" like ordinary NVT text.

Figure 16.7 shows how the architecture works.

Extended MTA

An Extended Message Transfer Agent needs to support one additional command. It sends an *EHLO* greeting instead of HELO. If the reply is positive, the partner also is an Extended MTA. If the reply is an error message, the MTA can revert to SMTP and send a HELO command.

Although the need to support MIME was the motive for extending the MTA, more services can be added at any time by defining new keywords for EHLO. For example, message sizes have been growing, and there is

Figure 16.7
Delivering MIME
messages.

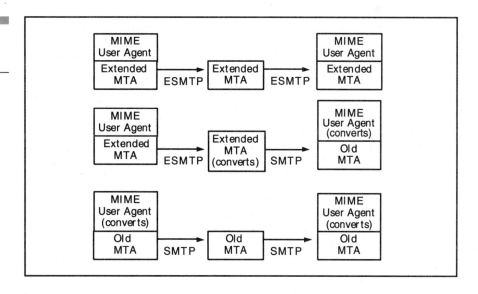

a new option that enables the sender to declare the size of a message before transmitting it. The receiver can indicate whether it is willing to accept a message of that size. The receiver also can declare the biggest size that it is willing to accept.

Official extensions are registered with the Internet Assigned Numbers Authority. Some software is available that includes new, experimental extensions. These are assigned temporary names starting with X.

Extended SMTP Dialog

Text in classic Internet mail messages used *telnet* NVT ASCII 7-bit characters (with eighth bit set to 0). MIME messages can contain 8-bit characters. The sample below illustrates how an Extended MTA sets up a transaction that will send a MIME message containing 8-bit characters.

- The receiver announces its extended capabilities, including 8BITMIME.

- The MAIL FROM command includes a BODY = 8BITMIME parameter.

```
Trying 205.217.47.98...
Connected to knecht.sendmail.org.
Escape character is '^]'.
220 knecht.Sendmail.ORG ESMTP Sendmail 8.9.0/8.9.0; Sun, 21 Jun 998
05:16:19 -0
700 (PDT)
EHLO katie.vnet.net
250-knecht.Sendmail.ORG Hello sfeit@katie.vnet.net [166.82.1.7],
pleased to meet
    you
250-8BITMIME
250-SIZE
250-DSN
250-ONEX
250-ETRN
250-XUSR
250 HELP
MAIL FROM:feit-sidnie@math.yale.edu. BODY = 8BITMIME
250 feit-sidnie@math.yale.edu.... Sender ok
RCPT TO: Mary-Smith@jcn.com.
250 Mary-Smith@jcn.com.... Recipient ok
DATA
354 Send 8BITMIME message, ending in CRLF.CRLF.
...
.
250 OK
QUIT
250 Goodbye
```

Format of MIME Messages

A MIME message contains a set of headers and one or more *body parts*. An ordinary Internet mail message starts with headers such as *From:*, *To:*, and *Date:*. A MIME message contains additional introductory headers that describe the overall structure and content of the message.

If there are multiple parts, one of the introductory headers defines a string that will be used to mark the *boundaries* between parts. Furthermore, after the boundary string that introduces a part, there will be additional headers that describe the body part that follows.

MIME Content-Type Headers

There are many different types of information that can be carried in a message. The overall structure of the message and the type of information in each part are announced by *Content-Type* headers. Sample headers include:

```
Content-Type: MULTIPART/MIXED; BOUNDARY = "xxxxxxxxx"
Content-Type: TEXT/PLAIN; charset = US-ASCII
Content-Type: image/gif
Content-Type: audio/basic
```

In general, a Content-Type header has the form:

Content-Type: *type/subtype; param = value; param = value;...*

Content-Types, subtypes, and parameter names are case-insensitive. They can be written in upper-, lower-, or mixed case. However, parameter *values* may be case-sensitive.

Note that although MIME headers are written as English phrases, a *charset = parameter* statement can announce a part that is coded in ISO-8859-1 or in Japanese, Cyrillic, Hebrew, or Arabic.

Importance of MIME Headers

Electronic mail is not the only application that relies on MIME. MIME headers also are used in the World Wide Web hypertext transfer protocol. They enable browsers to describe the types of data that they can process, and servers to describe the types of data that they are delivering.

A Sample MIME Message

The sample message that follows has multiple parts—it contains a text message and an attached Microsoft WORD file that has been translated to a special "base64" encoding that looks like a string of text characters.

The first Content-Type header:

```
Content-Type: multipart/mixed;
    boundary = "---- = _NextPart_000_01BD9882.0A642E70"
```

indicates that this is a multipart message. The boundary parameter defines the delimiter that will mark the beginning and end of each part. The source client program selected the delimiter. The actual boundary line that is used will consist of two hyphens (--) followed by the boundary string.

MIME headers and boundary lines are displayed below in bold print so that they will stand out. Each part of the message is introduced by a set of headers that describe the content of the part.

Content-Type: multipart/mixed;
    boundary = "---- = _NextPart_000_01BD9882.0A642E70"

This message is in MIME format.

------ = _NextPart_000_01BD9882.0A642E70
Content-Type: text/plain

Here is the chapter that you requested. It is in WORD format.

JOE RIVELLESE
Electronic Art Supervisor
McGraw-Hill Companies
11 West 19th Street, 4th Floor
New York, NY 10011
USA

------ = _NextPart_000_01BD9882.0A642E70
Content-Type: application/applefile;
    name = "ch11.doc"
Content-Transfer-Encoding: base64
Content-Disposition: attachment;
    filename = "ch11.doc"

. . .
biB3aXRoC0JPT1RQIGFuZCBESENQDTExLjFJTlRST0RVQ1RJT04NT25lIG9mIHRoZ
    SBtb3N0IHJl
bWFya2FibGUgY2hhbmdlcyBpbiB0aGUgdXNlIG9mIGNvbXB1dGVycyBpbiByZWNl
    bnQgeWVhcnMg
. . .
BDgFoAQ4AAAC0EIAgAEAAQABAAAAAAAAAAA =
------ = _NextPart_000_01BD9882.0A642E70-

MIME Content Types

There are seven standard top-level media types. Five of these are "discrete" types and two are "composite" types. The discrete types include:

Text
Image
Audio
Video
Application

There are many subtypes of each of these top-level types, such as text/html, image/gif, or video/mpeg.

The two composite types are:

■ Multipart. Consists of multiple components, each with an independent data type. The multipart message in the previous section contained two text parts and a Microsoft WORD document.

■ Message. An enclosed message, such as a forwarded email message.

Table 16.2 shows a sampling of content types and subtypes. As might be expected, the complete list is available at the Internet Assigned Numbers Authority Web site.

MIME Encoding Methods

How should the various types of contents of a MIME message be encoded for transmission? Wisely, the method of encoding can vary according to the capabilities of the sender, receiver, and Message Transfer Agents.

■ Binary data included in a mail message can be translated to look like text, if the message needs to be relayed using SMTP.

■ An efficient encoding can be used when ESMTP is available.

Encoding methods are listed in Table 16.3. If an encoding method other than ordinary NVT USASCII is used, it is announced in a Content-Transfer-Encoding header. For example:

```
Content-Transfer-Encoding: base64
Content-Transfer-Encoding: Quoted-printable
```

TABLE 16.2

MIME Content
Types and
Subtypes

Type	Subtype	Description
multipart	mixed alternative digest parallel appledouble header-set form-data report voice-message signed encrypted	A user can choose from several renditions. Each part is itself a message. Parts that go together, such as video and sound.
message	rfc822 partial external-body news http delivery-status	An encapsulated message. Classic email message. Part of a message. Points to a remote document. Contains Usenet news format.
text	plain richtext tab-separated- values html sgml	A standard mail text message.
image	jpeg gif ief tiff g3fax png	Joint Photographic Experts Group. Graphics Interchange Format. Image exchange format. Tag image file format. Portable network graphic.
audio	basic 32kadpcm vnd.qcelp	
video	mpeg quicktime vnd.vivo	
application	octet- stream postscript rtf pdf zip macwriteii msword remote-printing	Uninterpreted binary or formatted data. Formatted for Postscript display of printing. Rich text format. Portable Document Format. Compressed.

TABLE 16.2

MIME Content
Types and
Subtypes
(*Continued*)

Type	Subtype	Description
	EDI-X12	Electronic Data Interchange (US).
	EDIFACT	Electronic Data interchange (International).
	dec-dx	DEC document format.
	dca-rft	IBM Document Content Architecture.
	activemessage	
	applefile	
	mac-binhex40	Mac file converted for transfer.
	news-message-id	
	news-transmission	
	wordperfect5.1	
	mathematica	
	pgp-encrypted	
	pgp-sugnature	
	pgp-keys	
	andrew-inset	
	slate	
	set-payment	
	set-registration	
	sgml	
	wita	
	vnd.lotus-wordpro	
	vnd.lotus-1-2-3	
	vnd.lotus-organizer	
	vnd.ms-excel	
	vnd.powerbuilder-6	

TABLE 16.3

Encoding Methods

Method	Description
7bit	Ordinary NVT US-ASCII lines of text.
quoted-printable	Content is mostly ASCII text, but a few special characters need to be included. Each of these characters are mapped to special sequences of text characters.
base64	The entire content is mapped to a representation that looks like ordinary characters.
8bit	The message is still organized as a sequence of lines ending in <CR> <LF> and at most 1000 characters long. However, 8-bit characters can be included.
binary	True binary data.
x-*token-name*	Any experimental encoding must be given a name starting with "x."

Quoted-Printable Encoding Method

The quoted-printable encoding method is used for messages that contain a few characters that do not belong to the basic ASCII set. These characters are mapped to special sequences, while the bulk of the item remains in its natural form. The encoding has the form:

= *hex code for character*

For example, a form feed, which is X' 0C, would be coded as = 0C.

Base64 Encoding Method

Base64 encoding converts binary data to textual characters. The result of the conversion is that the total number of bytes increases by 33 percent.

The way that it works is that the byte stream is organized into sets of three 8-bit bytes. For example:

```
10001000 00110011 11110001
```

To convert, we first break this into four 6-bit groups:

```
100010 000011 001111 110001
```

We then interpret each group as a number:

```
34 3 15 49
```

And finally, we replace each number by the corresponding character from Table 16.4.

If the total number of bytes is not a multiple of 3, there will be 1 or 2 bytes at the end. The "leftover" is padded with zero bits and encoded. One byte is then translated to two characters followed by = = , while two bytes are translated to three characters followed by =.

Post Office Protocol

The Post Office Protocol (POP) is used to transfer mail from a mail server to a desktop station or a laptop portable.

The POP specification defines some extra features, such as the ability to view a listing of incoming mail items and their sizes and selectively

TABLE 16.4

Base64 Encoding

Value	Code	Value	Code	Value	Code	Value	Code
0	A	17	R	34	I	51	z
1	B	18	S	35	j	52	0
2	C	19	T	36	k	53	1
3	D	20	U	37	l	54	2
4	E	21	V	38	m	55	3
5	F	22	W	39	n	56	4
6	G	23	X	40	o	57	5
7	H	24	Y	41	p	58	6
8	I	25	Z	42	q	59	7
9	J	26	a	43	r	60	8
10	K	27	b	44	s	61	9
11	L	28	c	45	t	62	+
12	M	29	d	46	u	63	/
13	N	30	e	47	v		
14	O	31	f	48	w		
15	P	32	g	49	x		
16	Q	33	h	50	y		

retrieve and delete mail items. However, implementations usually simply download all waiting mail. The user may have the option either to leave copies of all mail at the server or else to delete items from the server after they have been downloaded.

A desktop system uses POP to download its mail and SMTP or ESMTP to send its mail. In most cases, the download server for incoming mail will be the same as the outgoing gateway for outgoing mail, as shown in Figure 16.8. However, your client application may allow you to use different systems as your POP server and outgoing gateway, if you want to.

In the dialog below, a client picks up a mail item from a POP server. The client program connects to the POP server port, 110. Messages from the server start with a "+" symbol rather than a status number, unlike most of the other protocols that we have viewed.

Figure 16.8
A combined POP
server and Mail Gate-
way system.

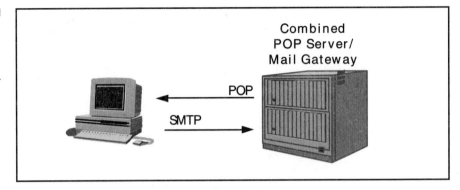

Figure 16.8
A combined POP
server and Mail Gate-
way system.

After the client sends a username and password, the server
announces that it has one message. The client sends a STAT (status)
command that retrieves the same information, but this time it is presented in a formatted manner. The client retrieves the message, deletes
the server's version, and quits.

```
+OK plum.math.yale.edu POP server ready
(Comments to: PostMaster@plum.math.yale.edu)
USER sfeit
+OK password required for sfeit
PASS xxxxxxxx
+OK maildrop has 1 message (4107 octets)
STAT
+OK 1 4107
RETR 1
+OK 4107 octets
From smap Fri Jul 3 00:29:20 1998
Received: by PLUM.MATH.YALE.EDU; Fri, 3 Jul 1998 00:29:20 -0400
Received: from bigsale.xxx.com(206.34.172.8) by PLUM.MATH.Y ALE.EDU
via smap (V1.3)
.id sma004233; Fri Jul 3 00:29:05 1998
Received: (from bigsale@localhost)
.by bigsale.xxx.com
. . .
Subject: BIDS START AT $1.00!!!
. . .
DELE 1
+OK message 1 deleted (4107 octets)
QUIT
```

Other Mail Applications

There are many Internet *mailing lists* that enable participants to
exchange questions and answers and receive the latest news for a specific topic—such as vacation spots, new CD-ROMs, or computer security
problems.

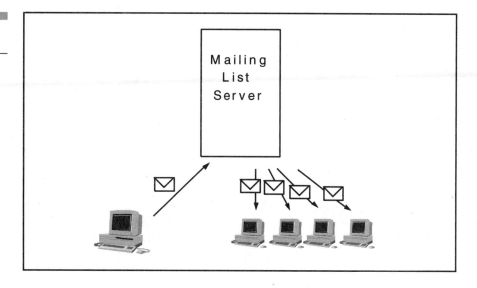

Figure 16.9
A mailing list server.

Users join a list by sending a request to an advertised mailbox that has been created for subscription (and unsubscription) requests (such as *subscribe-art@artschool.edu*). A second mailbox (such as *art@artschool.edu*) is used for the real work of the mailing list. Messages sent to the second mailbox are relayed to all subscribers, as shown in Figure 16.9. Free mailing list software, including a very popular program called *Majordomo,* is available for many platforms.

Performance

Message Transfer Agent services use memory, disk, processing, and transmission bandwidth resources. A mail service is enormously useful, and traffic can be expected to build steadily.

Messages must be saved while they await transmission or relay. Mail must be kept at a destination server until users login and access their mailboxes. It can be hard to predict the amount of storage that will be consumed in supporting a mail application.

Since mail handling is automated, items could conceivably sit in a Message Transfer Agent's queue forever. It is important for an administrator to define timeouts for every mail activity, to prevent black holes from swallowing up computer resources.

Security

Sendmail Problems

Recall that the most commonly used message transfer program is an application called *sendmail*. *Sendmail* is a big, complicated program that performs many functions, including translation of email alias names and expansion of mailing lists. Some security specialists feel that the bigger a program is, the more likely it is to contain bugs. Since *sendmail* speaks SMTP, which runs on top of NVT *telnet,* it is easy for hackers to connect to *sendmail* at port 25 and try to break into a computer by searching for weaknesses in *sendmail*.

One solution is to hide *sendmail* behind a very simple program that receives incoming mail.[2] The program then passes the mail to *sendmail,* which performs more complicated functions such as translating header formats and routing messages.

Secure Mail Transmission

Sometimes crackers are able to eavesdrop on mail transmissions after breaking into a computer on a remote network. Internal personnel who want to read passing email can do so easily on a broadcast-style LAN by installing monitoring software and configuring their LAN interface card to operate in "promiscuous" mode. However, there is a solution. Recall (see Chapter 9) that secure an SSL-capable mail client can open a secure (E)SMTP session to an SSL-capable mail server by connecting to port 465. Clients and servers that can transfer mail via SSL are available today.

Secure Electronic Mail

It is fairly easy to forge electronic mail. Using a secure session does not solve this problem. It also does not protect mail from the prying eyes of crackers who have invaded a mail server. The source of an email message needs to be authenticated, and any sensitive content should be

---

[2]A small program called *SMAP* that was created by Trusted Information Systems often is used.

encrypted. Fortunately, the methods described in Chapter 3 have been applied to electronic mail, and products are available that authenticate and encrypt mail.

Two competing formats have been presented for secure MIME messages:

- MIME Security with Pretty Good Privacy (PGP)
- S/MIME Message Specification

Both protect mail by means of message digests, public keys, and symmetric session keys. Public keys are reliably associated with their owners via a hierarchy of digital certificates whose format is defined by the X.509 standard.

Messaging via X.400

In this section, we present a brief description of the X.400 messaging system. X.400 has not been a big commercial success, but its naming conventions have been influential. X.400 also sparked the effort to develop directory services.

The International Telegraph and Telephone Consultative Committee (CCITT) produced the X.400 standards.[3] The X.400 standards subsequently were adopted by the International Standards Organization (ISO). Some of the characteristics of X.400 are:

- Definition of a general store-and-forward service that can be used for electronic mail (which they call *interpersonal messaging*) as well as for other applications.
- Global, international scope for message delivery and support for international alphabets.
- The ability to send information types besides text, such as binary, image, or digitized voice.
- If the sender wishes, notification of delivery to a recipient system and detailed nondelivery notices. There is an optional feature that can signal that the recipient end user has received the mail.

---

[3]Now called the International Telecommunications Union Telecommunication Standardization Sector or ITU-T.

- Support for mail priority.
- The ability to convert a message to a different medium—for example, deliver via fax or convert to hardcopy and use postal delivery.
- Definition of "user-friendly" identifiers for originators and recipients.
- Use of a formal envelope that contains fields that can be used to trace messages and gather other mail management information.

X.400 primarily defined a standard for the exchange of mail between national administrations. It acted as a gateway standard. X.400 has won support in Europe and was mandated for use by some U.S. government agencies.

However, X.400's star appears to be fading. The Internet mail standards are the ones that are alive and evolving, transporting every type of data, carrying EDI business documents, and offering powerful authentication and encryption capabilities.

Sample X.400 Message

Unlike the early Internet standards, X.400 did not rely on 7-bit ASCII and NVT conventions. Fields are formatted using the ISO Basic Encoding Rules (BERs) that are described in Chapter 20. This encoding introduces each field with a hex identifier code and length value. This gave X.400 an international applicability that was missing from earlier Internet email implementations. Figure 16.10 shows an outline for a sample message that illustrates general features of the X.400 format.

Naming X.400 Recipients

How do you identify people when you refer to them in conversation? You might say "Mary Jones, who is a Technical Consultant at the Milwaukee unit of MCI Telecommunications Corporation." Or you might say "Jacques Brun, who lives at 10 Rue Centrale in Paris, France." The drafters of X.400 wanted to define a universal naming system that would correspond to the natural way that people are identified.

An X.400 originator or recipient name is a list of attributes. The standard defines many optional attributes that may be used in various combinations. The most useful attributes for a business recipient are:

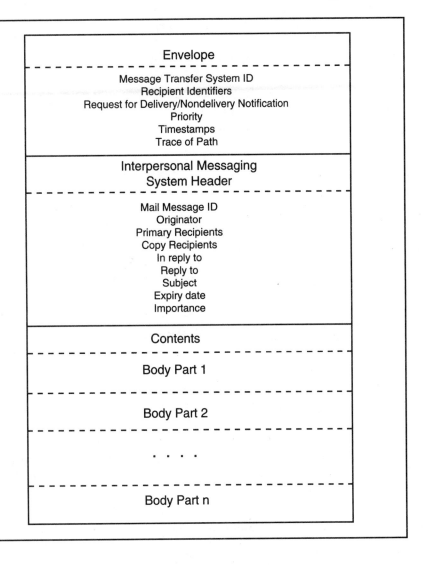

Figure 16.10
Format of an X.400
Interpersonal
Message.

- Country name
- Administration domain name
- Personal name (e.g., John H. Jones III)
- Organization name
- Organizational unit names
- Private domain name
- Domain-defined attributes

Private domains include facilities such as commercial electronic mail services and corporate electronic mail systems based on proprietary mail products. Domain-defined attributes allow names used by existing mail systems to be embedded in an X.400 identifier. This is an important feature. It allows an X.400 gateway to switch mail between proprietary mail systems as well as between a proprietary system and an X.400-compliant system.

Interworking Between X.400 and Internet Mail

Since both X.400 and Internet mail are store-and-forward services, mail can be passed between these services by means of mail gateways. Several RFCs have been written that deal with mapping between the Internet message format and X.400 message format.

X.500 Directory

Producing the correct identifier for an X.400 recipient can be difficult. The naming attributes that are selected vary from user to user. When X.400 was completed, it was realized immediately that a directory service was needed if X.400 was to succeed. The X.500 recommendations defined directory services and protocols intended to solve the problem by enabling users to look up recipients in a directory.

The designers of the X.500 directory realized that directory services had the potential to do far more than email recipient lookups. The standard is very broad in scope. The X.500 directory is a distributed database that can include information such as:

- Names of people
- Postal addresses
- User identifiers for X.400 mail
- Internet-style mail identifiers
- Telex and fax numbers
- Telephone numbers
- Names and locations of printers
- Names and locations of applications
- Names and locations of data

X.500 Directory Model

X.500 directory information is distributed across a community of databases controlled by *Directory Service Agents* (DSAs). Users access directory information by means of a *Directory User Agent* (DUA). A DUA provides the user interface for interactive queries and updates and passes user requests to a DSA.

The X.500 standards define a complex formal protocol that governs the interaction between a DUA and a DSA. There also is a DSA-to-DSA protocol that enables DSAs to relay user queries or download copies of parts of the Directory Information Base.

The X.500 standards include a method of validating the authenticity of a directory entry. An encrypted certificate from a trusted source validates an entry. The format of a certificate is defined in standard X.509.

Fate of X.500

Although there are a few X.500 directory products on the market at the current time, X.500 turned out to be difficult and expensive to implement. The DUA-to-DSA protocol was complicated and the DSA-to-DSA protocol was more complicated.

The *Lightweight Directory Access Protocol* (LDAP) was designed as a simpler client interface to an X.500 directory. Then everyone got very smart and realized that it really did not matter how the directory itself was designed internally, as long as you had this nice, simple interface to it. We describe LDAP in Chapter 19.

Recommended Reading

RFC 821 defines the Simple Mail Transfer Protocol, and RFC 822 describes the format of Internet messages. RFC 1939 describes the Post Office Protocol used to transfer mail between desktop workstations and a mail server.

RFCs 2045 to 2049 describe MIME. RFC 2045 defines the format of message bodies and RFC 2046 discusses media types. RFC 2047 defines extensions for non-ASCII text. MIME types are published by the Internet Assigned Numbers Authority and RFC 2048 explains the IANA registration procedures. RFC 2049 discusses implementation conformance criteria.

RFC 2197 describes an ESMTP extension that enables an SMTP client to batch email commands to an SMTP server. The SMTP Service Extension framework is described in RFC 1869.

X.400 was initially published as part of the 1984 CCITT recommendations and was updated in the 1988 recommendations. ISO published its version of X.400 in ISO 10021, which is made up of several parts. X.500 was a 1988 CCITT recommendation and has been updated repeatedly since that time.

See Chapter 19 for more information about LDAP.

Network News

Introduction

Every day, up-to-date information on science, technology, computers, economics, travel, sports, music, education, and more is contributed to the Internet *Usenet News*. A *news group* is like a bulletin-board service. News is made available in the form of *articles* that are *posted* (sent) to the group.

Currently, there are thousands of public and private news groups, and many provide information not easily found elsewhere. Often, postings consist of questions and answers relating to a specific topic. Sometimes the flow of information is one way: an individual or organization uses the news group as a way of publishing information.

Each news group is maintained by an administrator at a primary news server. If the news group is private, the news might reside exclusively at that server and users would retrieve news items from that server. However, postings for a public Usenet News group are propagated from its primary news server to hundreds of other news servers all over the world.

The news application has proved to be useful beyond its original Internet bulletin-board role. News software has spawned a new publishing business. Publishers feed regular news stories from wire services, such as AP, UPI, and Reuters, to subscribing sites using the Internet news protocol.

There are many excellent and easy-to-use desktop news clients. In this chapter, we take a behind-the-scenes look at some of the underlying client/server interactions.

Internet News Servers

Like many other Internet servers, the InterNetNews (INN) package was written for Unix computers. Like BIND, INN currently is maintained and distributed by the Internet Software Consortium.

Hierarchy of Internet News Groups

Thousands of Internet news groups have been created. Each group is assigned a name that indicates its purpose. The names are arranged in a tree. Figure 17.1 shows part of the tree structure.

Figure 17.1
News group
hierarchy.

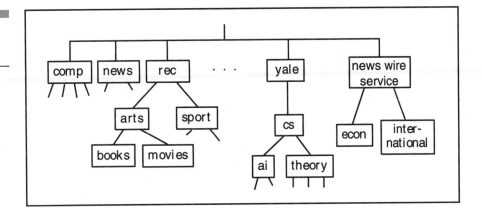

Unlike the other hierarchical names that we have met so far in this book, these names are read from top to bottom. For example:

rec.sport.basketball.college

News Agents

Just as there are User Agent programs that enable end users to send and receive mail, there are programs—which we will call *news agents*—that enable users to subscribe to news groups, read news articles, and *post* their own articles to groups.

News Model

A news client process interacts with a network news server via the *Network News Transfer Protocol* (NNTP). A client process can reside in an end user's news agent or in a peer news server. NNTP enables:

- A news server to obtain news from another news server
- A news agent to obtain news from a news server
- A news agent to post a new article to a news server

Figure 17.2 shows a news agent retrieving news from a server via NNTP and servers exchanging news via NNTP.

Figure 17.2
Requesting and
transmitting news.

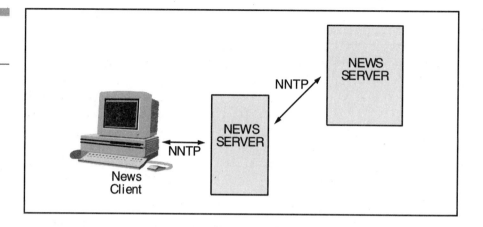

NNTP Scenario

Like the Simple Mail Transport Protocol (SMTP) NNTP runs over a *telnet* Network Virtual Terminal (NVT) session. A client transmits formal commands and the server sends responses. A command or response line is terminated with <CR> <LF>. A command line contains at most 512 characters (including <CR> <LF>). Each response begins with a status line that starts with a number. Any number of lines of text can follow the status line. The last line of a response consists of a period on a line by itself (that is, period <CR> <LF>).[1]

The dialog below shows a news transfer interaction. In the dialog, the client:

- Connects to the server
- Asks what news commands are supported by the server
- Requests a list of news groups that have been created since June 6, 1998
- Accesses a news group called *news.answers*
- Reads an article in *news.answers*

The server identifies itself and indicates that it accepts articles posted by users:

```
200 news.ycc.yale.edu InterNetNews NNRP server
INN 1.7 16-Oct-1997 ready (posting ok).
```

---

[1]Doubling the period represents a line of content that consists of a period.

The client sends a help message. The server displays the commands that it supports.

```
help
100 Legal commands
  authinfo user Name|pass Password|generic <prog> <args>
  article [MessageID|Number]
  body [MessageID|Number]
  date
  group newsgroup
  head [MessageID|Number]
  help
  ihave
  last
  list [active|active.times|newsgroups|distributions|distrib.pats|
  overview.fmt|subscriptions]
  listgroup newsgroup
  mode reader
  newgroups yymmdd hhmmss ["GMT"] [<distributions>]
  newnews newsgroups yymmdd hhmmss ["GMT"] [<distributions>]
  next
  post
  slave
  stat [MessageID|Number]
  xgtitle [group_pattern]
  xhdr header [range|MessageID]
  xover [range]
  xpat header range|MessageID pat [morepat...]
  xpath MessageID
Report problems to <news@news.ycc.yale.edu>
```

The *list* command would produce a huge list of all of the news groups available at this server. The following *newgroups* command requests a list of new groups that have been created since June 6, 1998 (at 1 A.M.). The symbols (such as " 6 1 y") following a news group name represent the last article in the group, the first article, and whether posting to the group is allowed (y or n).

```
newgroups 980620 010000
231 New newsgroups follow.
alt.picture-framing 6 1 y
 . . .
alt.real-estate.commercial.nh 10 1 y
 .
```

Frequently Asked Questions (FAQ) documents on many topics are published in *news.answers*. The following command positions the client in this group. The response includes the status code (211), the number of current articles that are available (626), the first article number (108901), and the last article number (110374). The range of article numbers is bigger than the number of stored articles, which means that only some of the numbers have a matching article.

```
group news.answers
211 626 108901 110374 news.answers
```

Below, we move to article number 110300 and view its message identifier:

```
stat 110300
223 110300 <music/performing/welcome_898426988@rtfm.mit.edu> status
```

The article header contains more information:

```
head
221 110300 <music/performing/welcome_898426988@rtfm.mit.edu> head
Path: news.ycc.yale.edu!news-
out.internetmci.com!newsfeed.internetmci.com!209.6.
107.173!newsfeed.xcom.net!cam-news-
hub1.bbnplanet.com!news.bbnplanet.com!bloom-b
eacon.mit.edu!senator-bedfellow.mit.edu!faqserv
From: Sandy Nicholson <s.nicholson.remove.these@four.words.ed.ac.uk>
Newsgroups: rec.music.classical.performing,rec.answers,news.answers
Subject: Welcome to rec.music.classical.performing!
Supersedes: <music/performing/welcome_897134136@rtfm.mit.edu>
Followup-To: poster
Date: 21 Jun 1998 11:03:16 GMT
Organization: Dept of Mathematics and Statistics, Edinburgh University,
Scotland
Lines: 43
Approved: news-answers-request@MIT.Edu
Expires: 19 Jul 1998 11:03:08 GMT
Message-ID: <music/performing/welcome_898426988@rtfm.mit.edu>
NNTP-Posting-Host: penguin-lust.mit.edu
Summary: An introduction to the newsgroup rec.music.classical.performing,
         differentiating it from related newsgroups in the rec.music
         hierarchy. People intending to post to the newsgroup are strongly
         advised to read this article and the FAQ prior to doing so. . . .
         .
```

The body command produces the content of the current article. Both the header and body could have been viewed with the single command *article 110300*.

```
body
222 110300 <music/performing/welcome_898426988@rtfm.mit.edu> body
Archive-name: music/performing/welcome
Last-modified: 20 November 1996
Version: 0.2

            Welcome to rec.music.classical.performing!

This is a fortnightly posting aimed at introducing new readers to
rec.music.classical.performing. . . .
         .
```

The session is ended with the *quit* command.

```
quit
205
Connection closed by foreign host.
```

Using Desktop News Agents

A desktop news agent makes it easy to:

- View the list of available news groups.
- "Subscribe" to groups. Your desktop news agent automatically will present new article headlines, and track which articles you already have read.
- Browse news headlines.
- Read or save news stories.

Let's take a look at how a news dialog would look with a desktop news agent. News agents are bundled with Netscape and Microsoft browsers. Figure 17.3 shows a NetManage *Chameleon* news display. A list of new news groups can be requested by clicking a menu selection.

Figure 17.3
News group menu options.

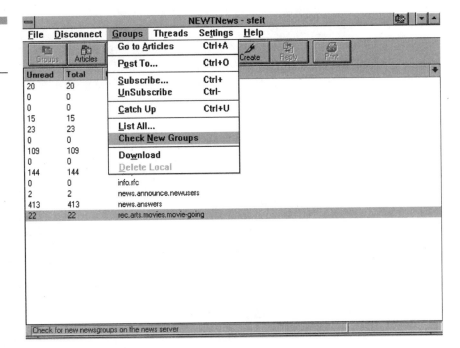

Figure 17.4
Overview of sub-
scribed groups.

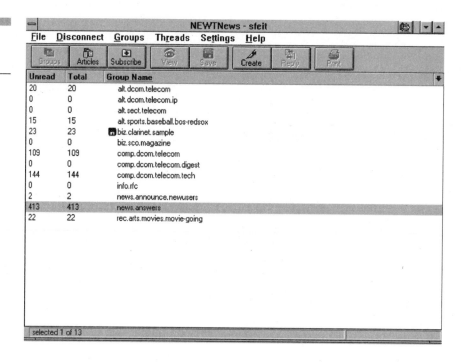

Figure 17.4 shows that the desktop news agent keeps track of a set of news groups selected (*subscribed to*) by the user.

A list of unread articles in the popular group *news.answers* is requested by double-clicking on the *news.answers* line. The result is shown in Figure 17.5. An article is displayed in Figure 17.6. The article's long header need not be viewed unless the user wishes to see it.

NNTP Protocol

NNTP Commands

To access news articles, a client process connects to port 119 at a news server. The client sends a series of commands and receives responses. Commands are not case sensitive.

There are commands that enable the requester to:

- List all groups
- Choose a group
- Select specific articles

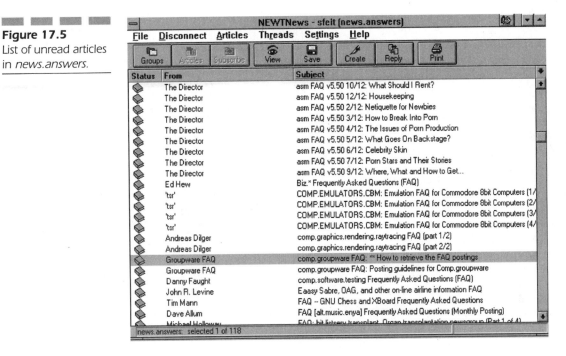

Figure 17.5
List of unread articles
in *news.answers.*

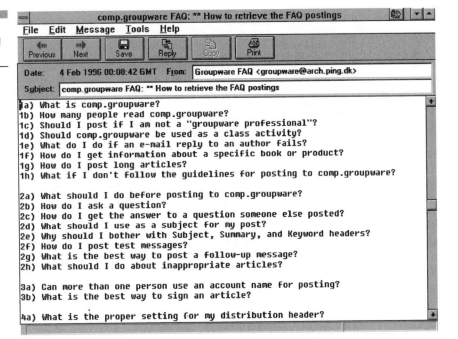

Figure 17.6
Display of a selected
article.

TABLE 17.1

NNTP Commands
and Parameters

Command	Parameter(s)	Definition
article	"<Messageid>" or message number or none.	Retrieve the article identified by the id or number, or get the current article.
body		Retrieve the current article's body.
group	Groupname.	Move to the selected news group.
head		Displays the current article's header.
help		Asks for a list of commands supported by the server.
ihave	<Messageid>.	A server tells another server that it has an article. The other server can request a copy if it wishes.
last		The current article pointer is moved back one article in the current group.
list		Requests a list of newsgroups and the range of articles that are available.
newgroups	Date, time, and optionally, <distribution>.	Requests a list of newsgroups (optionally, within a category) created since the given date and time.
newnews	Newsgroups, date, time, and optionally, <distribution>.	Requests a list of new articles for the groups since the given date and time.
next		The current article pointer is moved forward one article in the current group.
post		Send a new article to the news group.
quit		
slave		Indicates that the requester is a mail server rather than an individual client.
stat	Message number.	Selects an article.

A *current article pointer* at the server keeps track of the requester's position. The commands are summarized in Table 17.1.

The optional *distributions* parameter enables the user to select a list of top-level categories, such as *comp* or *news*. The list must be enclosed in angle brackets, and items must be separated by commas. For example, below we ask for a list of new news groups under *sci*.

```
newgroups 980601 010000 <sci>
231 New newsgroups follow.
```

```
sci.physics.cond-matter 552 1 y
sci.techniques.mass-spec 279 1 m
sci.psychology.consciousness 164 1 m
. . .
```

NNTP Status Codes

The dialog displayed in the "NNTP Scenario" section showed that each response from an NNTP server starts with a numeric status code. This is the same convention that was used for SMTP and FTP servers. The codes are:

1xx	Informative message
2xx	Command successful
3xx	Command successful so far; send the rest of it
4xx	Command was correct but couldn't be performed for some reason
5xx	Command unimplemented or incorrect or a serious program error occurred

As before, the second digit in the code provides more specific information about the response:

x0x	Connection, setup, and miscellaneous messages
x1x	News group selection
x2x	Article selection
x3x	Distribution functions
x4x	Posting
x8x	Nonstandard extensions
x9x	Debugging output

Differences Between News and Mailing Lists

A news application is more efficient than a mailing list in several ways. News is stored at centralized servers that can be accessed by many users. Many users can read news out of a single shared database.

Mailing list distributions can clutter up your mailbox with extraneous information, making it difficult to weed out the really important mail. In contrast, you access news at your own convenience, and sophisticated news screening capabilities are being built into news agents, making them even more convenient to use.

You do not have to subscribe to a news group in order to read its news or post to it. In fact, subscription is just a news agent function that is used to help you track what groups you wish to follow and which items you already have read.

There are many mailing lists that automatically feed their items to a news group.

Recommended Reading

The Network News Transfer Protocol is defined in RFC 977. Information about the current implementation of the InterNetNews package is available at the Internet Software Consortium's Web site (*www.isc.org*).

The World Wide Web

Introduction

In this chapter, we present an overview of the components that make up the World Wide Web environment. Use of Web servers and browsers has grown explosively, and the protocols and technology have advanced rapidly.

Background

Hypertext

Hypertext is an idea that has been around for several years. The basic idea is that:

- An underlined phrase in a document is associated with a pointer to another document.
- A user can *link* to the other document by clicking on the phrase.

Users of Microsoft Windows or Macintosh help screens depend on Hypertext routinely, although the users might not ever have heard of the term. For example, suppose that we are presented with a help menu like:

Files
Copying
Finding
Saving

It is intuitively clear that we will get more information on an underlined topic by clicking on that topic. In this example, phrases that provide hypertext links to other documents are underlined. Other user interfaces might present links in a different color or that are highlighted.

Hypermedia

This idea has been extended to *Hypermedia*—an underlined phrase may point to a picture, a sound file, a film clip, or some other type of binary data. Or a picture may contain clickable elements that point to documents, pictures, sound data, or a film clip. This kind of display is commonplace on CD-ROMs.

Hypermedia and the WWW

The use of Hypermedia is extended to *networked* information via the *World Wide Web* (WWW). An underlined phrase can point to a local item—or to an item that actually is stored at a remote computer. This simple idea led to the attractive user interfaces that make it easy to navigate the Internet.

Where the WWW Came From

The idea for the World Wide Web came out of the physics research community. It was the brainchild of Tim Berners-Lee at CERN, the European Laboratory for Particle Physics, located in Switzerland. Tim Berners-Lee wrote the software for the first Web server and client.

The World Wide Web is so pervasive that many people call the Internet "the Web." The Internet is made up of all of the networked computers that can communicate with one another across the interlocked set of Internet Service Providers. The World Wide Web started out as one Internet application among many, but grew into a software infrastructure for distributed computing.

WWW Browsers

The Web was given a tremendous boost by Marc Andreessen, who conceived the powerful *Mosaic* WWW client in 1992, when he was an undergraduate student at the University of Illinois and a staff member at the university's National Center for Supercomputing Applications (NCSA). Mosaic was the first Internet *browser.* Today, almost everyone is familiar with Netscape's Communicator browser or Microsoft's Internet Explorer. A browser can access data from multiple sources including hypertext servers, file transfer sites, news servers, and electronic mail servers.

As illustrated in Figure 18.1, a browser can run the multiple protocols required to reach information.

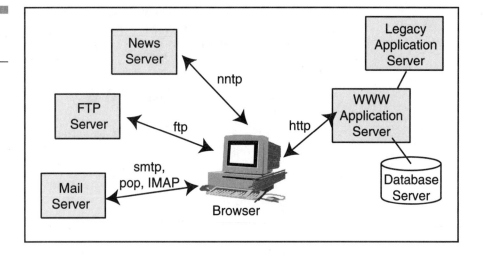

Figure 18.1
A browser running
multiple protocols.

From Static to Active

Early Web content was static. A user selected a page to be viewed and the content of the page was downloaded to the user's desktop. Then forms were introduced. After entering data into a form, the user would press a *submit* button. This caused the entered data to be sent to a Web server along with the name of a program that should process the data.

Server programs that accessed a backend database became commonplace. Then vendors and end users wrote Web programs that provided a Web front end for legacy systems. Data extracted from a legacy environment was presented in the form of hypertext pages.

The desktop became a full partner to the server with the introduction of JavaScript, Java code, and ActiveX. Program elements downloaded from the server were executed at the desktop. At the same time, Web servers became capable of delivering content that was dynamically generated from backend databases or applications, and was tailored differently for various classes of users. For example, a business would provide different views of information—or customized product and price lists—based on a customer's profile.

Web servers were integrated into sophisticated application servers that supported reliable business transaction processing. These servers had an internal object-oriented architecture, supported substantial throughput rates, and offered high availability.

Where WWW Is Going

Currently, Tim Berners-Lee is director of the World Wide Web Consortium (also called W3C) located in Cambridge, Massachusetts. The consortium designs, develops, and perfects new Web technologies at a breakneck pace. The marketplace has adopted these technologies as quickly as it could. The list below includes just a few of the technologies for which W3C is responsible. Each of these is evolving rapidly:

- *Hypertext Markup Language (HTML).* A set of descriptive tags that describe how a document should be displayed.

- *Hypertext Transfer Protocol (HTTP).* The protocol that defines the interaction between a Web client and a Web server.

- *Cascading Style Sheets.* A method of defining fonts, colors, and spacing that can be used to give a set of Web documents a consistent design.

- *Extensible Markup Language (XML).* XML makes it possible to define and describe new types of document formats. Among other things, XML is being used to move data between databases in a vendor-neutral format.

- *Document Object Model (DOM).* A standard interface that will enable programs and scripts to dynamically access and update the content, structure, and style of documents. The Document Object Model provides a standard set of objects for representing HTML and XML documents.

Uniform Resource Locators

Tim Berners-Lee introduced a very important unifying concept. A Web information resource is identified by a *Uniform Resource Locator* (sometimes called Universal Resource Locator), or *URL*. The URL:

- Names the item
- Tells where it is
- Indicates the protocol to be used to get it

URLs are a special case of *Universal Resource Identifiers* (URIs). URI syntax provides a general way of expressing the names of information resources.

Hypertext URL

If you give a Web browser the URL for a hypertext document, the browser will go out and get the document using a protocol called the *Hypertext Transfer Protocol,* or *HTTP.* A hypertext URL has the form:

http://system-name/filename

For example:

http://www.ibm.com/index.html

If we provide just:

http://system-name/

the Web server will return its default *home page,* which often is called *home.html* or *index.html.* The most general HTTP URL is:

http://system-name:port/path?searchpart-or-data

A Web server can be set up to run at a port other than well-known port 80. It then can be accessed by including its port number in a URL. A host could be identified by its IP address rather than its domain name.[1] URLs easily extend to other protocols.[2]

File Transfer URL

We plug into file transfer with a URL such as:

ftp://ftp.vnet.net/

which connects to a default directory, or identify a specific file with:

ftp://ftp.vnet.net/pub/README

To FTP to a site where you must enter a userid and password, use:

ftp://username:password@system-name/

[1]It is better practice to use a Web host's name than an address because a Web server's name often maps to several rotating addresses. In addition, the addresses used for Web servers change fairly often.

[2]URLs were defined for the *gopher* and *wais* protocols, which have fallen out of use. A *prospero* URL was defined for access to a special type of directory.

File URL

The file URL simply identifies an accessible file at some host. When we access a file with a URL such as:

```
file://katie.vnet.net/ets/services
```

Note that a protocol is not identified. The file URL provided a format that could be tied to different proprietary access protocols defined by vendors. This has not proven to be useful. The main use for a file URL is to retrieve a file at the client's own computer.

Telnet URL

We can tie into *telnet,* for example, with

telnet://openhost.abc.com/

More generally, the URL is:

telnet://username:password@system-name/

The common implementation is to configure a browser with a pointer to a separate, favorite desktop *telnet* client program.

News URL

The URL for a news group has the form *news:newsgroup-name,* for example:

news:rec.airplane

The news server is not identified in the URL. Instead, the user's news server name (or address) is entered into a browser's configuration information.

Mail URL

There even is a URL for sending electronic mail:

mailto:user@mail-location

As was the case for news, the name or address of a mail gateway is entered into a browser's configuration information.

LDAP URL

A Lightweight Directory Access Protocol (LDAP) URL is used to access a directory service that has an LDAP interface. The LDAP URL that follows accesses an X.500 directory at the University of Michigan and looks for entries for people named "Davis."

ldap://ldap.itd.umich.edu:389/o = University%20of%20Michigan,c = us??sub?(cn = Davis)

The LDAP URL format is complicated, but is explained in Chapter 19.

General URL Format

To summarize, note that:

- A URL starts with the access protocol to be used.
- For applications other than news and electronic mail, this is followed by the delimiter ://.
- Next, the name (or address) of the server host is indicated. Optionally, an access port may be included.
- Finally, the resource to be accessed is identified—or else a default file is retrieved.

Recall that in the case of news and electronic mail, the location of a preferred news server and mail gateway is part of the browser's configuration information. Only the : part of the delimiter is used, and no host server is identified in the URL.

Special Characters

Sometimes a resource identifier contains a space or some other character—such as a slash or a colon—that normally is used as a delimiter or special character in a URL. For example, Macintosh and Windows 95 filenames can contain spaces and other unusual characters.

Special characters are identified as belonging to the actual resource name by mapping them to strings that start with a % symbol. Table 18.1 shows the mappings.

TABLE 18.1

Mappings of Spe-
cial URL Characters

Special Character	Mapped Representation
space	%20
/	%2F
#	%23
=	%3D
;	%3B
?	%3F
:	%3A
~	%7E

An Introduction to HTML

WWW documents containing hypertext links are written using *Hyper-text Markup Language,* or *HTML.* Hypertext files usually have names of the form:

> *filename.html* or *filename.htm*

The Hypertext Markup Language was defined using the *Standard Generalized Markup Language* (SGML). SGML is a system that is used to create markup languages. Each markup language is used to format one class of documents.

HTML is a markup language for Web documents. An author places HTML *tags* into a document to identify elements such as its title, section headings, paragraph boundaries, bulleted lists, figures, and so forth.

HTML is platform-independent, enabling hypertext documents to be viewed by client devices ranging from dumb text terminals to sophisticated workstations. Clients can display documents on a screen of any size and can use locally selected fonts.

We learn some HTML basics in the next sections. HTML started out small and simple but has grown into a large language, and this book would have to be devoted exclusively to HTML to cover all of it. Our goal in this chapter is simply to give the reader a feeling for the way that Web pages are constructed, and an understanding of the capabilities of today's HTML. The comments are based on HTML version 4.0.

Eventually, instead of expanding HTML from version to version, HTML will be rewritten as a set of XML modules. Then new features can be added by tacking on extra modules as they are needed.

Spirit of HTML 4.0

The character of HTML 4.0 is very familiar to authors. When we send a text manuscript to a publisher, we mark it up, indicating where paragraphs begin and end, where tables should be inserted, the location of block quotes, and so forth. It is up to the publisher to decide how these should be rendered. Should the first line of a paragraph be indented or should a blank line be placed between paragraphs? Should a block quote be indented on one side or both, and should it be displayed in a different font? The author is sometimes pleasantly surprised—and sometimes horrified—by the final result.

A markup system has the benefit that every time a particular element appears, the same rules will be used to display it. Web authors are fortunate because they can be their own publishers. After marking up a document, they can get the consistent rendition that they want by defining it in a separate style sheet.[3] Alternatively, style instructions can be included within a document.

Writing Hypertext Markup Language

An HTML author defines document elements such as:

- Document title
- Section headers
- Paragraph definition
- Quotations
- Links via URLs

---

[3]Cascading Style Sheets are a W3 contribution. There are other types of style sheets that may be used.

- Lists
- Data entry forms
- Scripts to be executed at the desktop
- Clickable maps
- Tables and formulas
- Pointers to in-line images
- Pointers to applets to be executed at the desktop

Tags included in an HTML document state what each element is. For example, the tag <TITLE> introduces the document's title.

You could write a hypertext document using an ordinary text editor. Popular word processor programs provide add-ons that automate the creation of tags and let you work in "What-You-See-Is-What-You-Get" mode. But today, the normal procedure is to use one of the state-of-the-art Web page design products.

A basic understanding of how HTML works can be helpful in learning how to use a design tool effectively. Also, new capabilities tend to out-strip releases of the tools, and therefore some information may still have to be entered manually.

HTML Tags

Tags consist of element names and attribute parameters enclosed in angle brackets (<...>). We describe a few commonly used tags in the sections that follow. Tags are not case-sensitive, but for consistency, we will write all tags in uppercase.

Almost all tags come in pairs, showing where an element begins and where it ends. The closing tag name mirrors the opening tag name but is enclosed by </...>. For example:

<TITLE>Welcome To The Web</TITLE>

Overall Format

A few tags are used to delimit the beginning and end of an HTML docu-ment and divide it into a head and body. This is illustrated in the exam-ple that follows:

```
<!DOCTYPE HTML PUBLIC "-//W3C//        Declares the document type
DTD HTML 4.0//EN"                      and language.

"http://www.w3.org/TR/REC-html40/
strict.dtd">

<HTML>                                 Start of hypertext doc.

<HEAD.>                                Start of header items.

<!--Last Modified on                   A comment.
October 21, 1995-->

<BASE HREF 5 "http://www.abc.com/      A base allows short names to
index.html">                           be used for linked items.

<TITLE>Welcome to the Web</TITLE>      The title usually is displayed at
                                       the top of the client's screen.

</HEAD>                                End of header items.

<BODY>                                 Start of document body.

...

</BODY>                                End of document body.

</HTML>                                End of hypertext.
```

Base URL

A document usually includes pointers to colocated files that contain images, sound, or other display text. The BASE statement in the preceding example puts a stake in the ground. It identifies the base document and allows other file names to be shortened because their location is relative to the location of the base document.[4] For example, a pointer to "gifs/banner.gif" identifies a file at "http://www.abc.com/gifs/banner.gif/."

Pointers also can identify a location within the current document. For example "#Chapter 3" points to a location in the current document that contains a tag with the identifier "Chapter3."

HTML Headers

Chapters, sections, and subsections of a document are introduced by header elements. Six levels of headers are available for use.

---

[4]If no base is defined, the current document is assumed to be the base.

<H1>This is a level 1 header—which is a major header.</H1>

<H2>A level 2 header might be used for sections.</H2>

<H3>You also can insert level 3, 4, 5, or 6 headers.</H3>

Each header displayed with a different format. For example, level 1 headers usually are presented in large, boldface type. A style sheet can be used to specify the color, size, rendition (e.g., bold or italicized), and spacing for each header.

Paragraphs and Breaks

An author must identify paragraph boundaries. Otherwise, all text will just be run together when it is displayed. A client program will collapse multiple spaces and multiple blank lines into a single space unless told to do otherwise.

Paragraphs can be delimited by placing a <P> tag at the start of each new paragraph:

```
<P>This is a paragraph.
<P>This is another paragraph.
```

To be formally correct, a pair of tags should be used to show where a paragraph begins and ends:

```
<P>This is a paragraph.</P>
```

By default, most browsers insert a blank line between paragraphs, although this could be overridden with a style sheet. If you do not want to start a new paragraph but want to move to the next line, use a break:

```
Roses are red.<BR>
Violets are blue.<BR>
```

Lists

Numbered, bulleted (unordered), and definition lists can be defined. The tag at the start of the list identifies its type. For example:

```
<UL>
<LI>The first list item.
<LI>The second list item.
</UL>
```

Once again, a style sheet can be used to set fonts, size, and spacing.

Special Blocks of Text

Sometimes, you will have text that already is laid out exactly the way you want it. A preformatted (<PRE>) tag tells the browser to preserve white space and not wrap text:

```
<PRE>
    This text will be displayed
    just as it is written-    including blank spaces.
</PRE>
```

A block quote is a long quoted block of text. A style sheet might cause it to be indented.

```
<BLOCKQUOTE>
    This is a block quote.
    It will probably be indented when displayed to the user.
</BLOCKQUOTE>
```

Quote tags (<Q>...</Q>) delimit a short, in-line quote.

Formatting Text and Text Phrases

Leafing through a book, you will see many different presentations for text. Some will be emphasized with italics or bolding. Special fonts may be used to display a computer program or computer output. The markup elements defined in HTML 4.0 include:

EM	Emphasize
STRONG	Emphasize strongly
DFN	Defines a term
CODE	Computer code
SAMP	Sample output
KBD	Text to be entered by the user
VAR	A variable or program argument
CITE	A citation or a reference to other sources
ABBR	Indicates an abbreviation
ACRONYM	Indicates an acronym

SUB	Subscripted text
SUP	Superscripted text

Tables

Tables with any number of rows and columns can be defined. The author can control borders, column widths, cell margins, alignment (left, right, or centered content), and background color.

Links

When a user clicks on a link, a new document is loaded. To embed a link in a document you need to:

- Use start and end link tags
- Provide the URL parameter that identifies the linked document
- Provide a clickable label that will be displayed and underlined

A sample link is shown below. The *A* is the name of the tag and is called an *anchor*. The *HREF* parameter identifies the item to be linked. The text before the </A> delimiter becomes the clickable label for the link:

```
<A HREF = "http://www.abc.com/wwwdocs/showme.html">Click here to
see something good</A>
```

You don't always have to write a complete URL for a linked item. Suppose that document *showme.html* contains a link to a file named *more.html* in the same directory. Then the following relative pathname would work:

```
<A HREF = "more.html" > more here </A>
```

As we saw earlier, you also can use a relative pathname for documents in a subdirectory of the current directory.

Links to Local Documents

You can reference a document in your local host from your browser. For example, here is a link to a local Windows document:

```
<A HREF = "file:///c:\webdocs\home.htm">My Home Document</A>
```

You do not use the hypertext transfer protocol to retrieve a local file. Note that the host name is null—no host is listed between the slashes (////).

You can jump to a location within the current document. First, mark the spot. This is done by inserting an anchor tag at the location and using a NAME parameter:

```
<A NAME = "Section3"> 3. Airplanes </A>
```

Then you can refer to that location by prefacing the name with a pound sign:

```
See <A HREF = "#Section3">section three</A> for more information.
```

When a user clicks on the underlined phrase (section three), the client will jump to the marked location.

Alternatively, instead of creating a separate anchor tag, you can add an ID parameter to an existing tag for an item. Here, for example, we add an ID parameter to an H2 tag:

```
<H2 ID = "Section3">3. Airplanes</H2>
```

The inclusion of LINK statements in the HEAD section of a document is an interesting feature. These are used to define the overall structure of a document and provide pointers that a client could use in order to aid navigation:

```
<LINK rel = "Index"  href = "index.html">
<LINK rel = "Next"   href = "Chapter6.html">
<LINK rel = "Prev"   href = "Chapter4.html">
```

A link statement also is used to point to an external style sheet for the document.

Images, Applets, and Frames

Earlier versions of HTML defined tags that identified images, applets, and frames to be used with the current page. For example, an in-line image was defined by a statement such as:

```
<IMG SRC = "http://www.abc.com/wwwdocs/ourlogo.gif">
```

In HTML 4.0, a preferred OBJECT tag is introduced for images, Java or ActiveX applets, frames, and other items that will be added. For example:

```
<OBJECT data = "http://www.abc.com/wwwdocs/ourlogo.gif" type =
"image/gif">
<OBJECT classid = "java:program.start">
```

More About Images

Graphics Interchange Format (GIF) files often are used to hold images for a WWW page. *Portable Network Graphics* (PNG) is a standard for compressed bitmapped image files. Another popular type is a *Joint Photographic Experts Group* (JPEG) compressed picture. JPEG was designed for photographic images but sometimes is used for other types of pictures.

A browser that cannot display images will display an IMG element as a framed blank space unless it contains an ALT parameter. For example:

```
<IMG SRC = "bigpic.jpeg" ALT = "Washington's Monument">
```

A browser that could not display images would display the string "Washington's Monument" instead of the picture.

The *title attribute* is one of several additions to HTML to support accessibility for people with disabilities. A client program could be configured to speak the information in title attributes.

```
<IMG SRC = "bigpic.jpeg" title = "jpeg image of Washinton's Monument">
```

Forms

Forms enable a user to enter data and pass it back to a server. There are tags that identify several types of input fields that can be placed in a form:

- Text. For textual data entry.
- Password. Like text, but the data that is entered is not displayed on the screen.
- Drop down selection boxes.
- Check box.

- Radio button.
- Push button.
- File. Name of a file to be sent to a server.
- Reset button. Clears the fields of data.
- Plain or image submit button. The form data is transmitted when a user clicks the submit button.

The FORM tag contains an *action* statement that indicates which of the following should happen when the user clicks *submit:*

- A *mailto* URL causes the form data to be mailed to an indicated recipient.
- An *http* URL identifies the Web server to which the data will be sent, and includes the pathname of a program that will be run when the data arrives.

For example:

```
<FORM action = "http://www.abc.com/cgi/custinfo" method = get>
    <P>
    <LABEL for = "firstname">First name: </LABEL>
            <INPUT type = "text" id = "firstname"><BR>
    <LABEL for = "lastname">Last name: </LABEL>
            <INPUT type = "text" id = "lastname"><BR>
    <INPUT type = "radio" name = "sex" value = "M"> Male<BR>
    <INPUT type = "radio" name = "sex" value = "F"> Female<BR>
    <INPUT type = "submit" value = "SUBMIT">
    </P>
</FORM>
```

Before being sent to the Web server, the data that has been entered is put into a long string that consists of name = value statements separated by ampersand signs.[5] For example:

```
firstname = Jane&lastname = Jones&sex = F
```

There actually are two methods of passing form data to the Web server. The default, or GET, method places a question mark at the end of the action URL and then adds on the string of data. The second method of sending data up to the Web server is called POST. In this case, the string is not placed at the end of the URL. The string is put into the body of a message that is sent to the action URL.

---

[5]If a text string includes white spaces, they are converted to + symbols.

Common Gateway Interface

When input data arrives at a Web server, we want the Web server to start a program and pass the data to that program. This means that someone must write a program that takes this data and performs a search, queries a database, updates a database, or carries out some other function.

Many different vendors build Web servers and applications and so standard Web server programming interfaces are needed. The *Common Gateway Interface* (CGI) was the first industry standard Web Application Programming Interface (API), and still is the one that is most frequently used. CGI provides some very simple conventions for passing input data to the program identified in a Submit URL. A CGI program can be written in just about any language.

It is common practice to gather all of the Web server programs into one directory. Frequently the name */cgi* or */cgi-bin* is used for this directory.

Newer Web application servers use more sophisticated programming interfaces. Server programs are preloaded into threads and have a runtime environment that is separate from the Web server. A problem in a program does not affect the Web server, and the environment provides automatic cleanup and restart of the programs.

Scripts

A *script* is a program written in a scripting language such as JavaScript, Tcl, or VBScript. Some script programs are designed to run at a Web server. Others are used to create pages dynamically at the client's desktop.

A client script can make desktop pages "active"—which means that small programs are run in response to user actions. One or more scripts may be included in a page or referenced through URLs in the page.

- Some scripts are executed once, when the page is loaded.
- Some scripts are tied to an event such as entering or leaving a form field, passing a mouse over an area, or clicking a button. This type of script is triggered every time the event happens.

If you look at the HTML source of a page, you may see a script that is buried in a comment. This is done so that older browsers that do not support scripts can jump over them; newer browsers will search the comments for scripts.

Viewing HTML Sources

A good way to learn HTML is to peek at the source of the documents that you retrieve. Usually, your browser will let you do this—or you can save the document to disk and then read it with an ordinary text editor.

XML

HTML has become the most popular networked presentation language, and will continue to flourish. This markup language was so useful that it inspired the design of a higher-level language, XML. XML makes it easy to create new "designer" markup languages with tags that fit the needs of specific applications. Health organizations, insurance organizations, and other professional groups are taking advantage of XML to create portable data formats.

HTTP Architecture

The hypertext transfer protocol is at the heart of Web client/server interactions. HTTP started out as a very simple protocol. It has become more complex as new functionality has been added. It is easiest to understand HTTP if we start with a brief discussion of the original protocol.

Classic HTTP

The original design for hypertext retrieval was simple. As shown in Figure 18.2, a client connects to a WWW server and requests an item via a command such as:

```
GET /index.html HTTP/1.0
```

The server sends the items and terminates the session. The browser displays the item to the user. Then the user can think and choose the next step. In the early days of the Web, plain text documents containing links to other documents were the state of the art. The user would read a document and choose a link to another document.

However, even the original HTTP design allowed for more than plain

Figure 18.2
A browser retrieving
an item from a
WWW server.

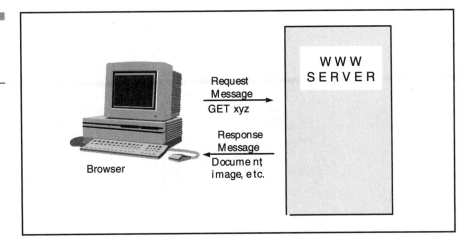

text. An author could indicate where images should be displayed on a Web page, or identify a sound file that would provide background music to be played. How did this work?

A Web page is a hypertext document along with whatever images, animations, sounds, and scripts that may accompany it. A page may consist of a single screen or may scroll down through many screens. The way that a classic (HTTP 0.9) user retrieved a page was:

- The user selected an *http* URL that identified a server and an HTML file.
- The browser opened a TCP session to Web server port 80[6] and requested the file.
- The server sent the file to the browser.
- The server indicated that the transfer was complete by closing the TCP session.

As the browser received the HTML file, whenever it came to a tag that pointed to an in-line image or sound file, the browser opened a new TCP session and requested the image or sound file. The server returned the requested item and closed the TCP session to indicate end-of-file.

---

[6]Other ports can be used, and sometimes are. The desired port number is included in the URL.

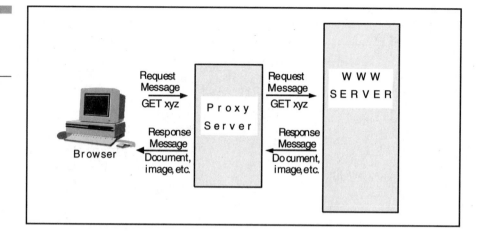

Proxy Server

The business world quickly discovered that there was a great benefit in giving employees access to Internet World Wide Web servers. This had to be done without opening up a corporate network to security exposures. The use of a proxy WWW server is a popular solution.

To use a proxy, a client browser is configured to forward requests to the proxy server. The proxy interacts with the actual server and relays results back to the client. Figure 18.3 shows a client accessing a WWW server via a proxy.

A proxy server offers more than security. It can cache Web pages so that many requests can be answered immediately from the local proxy server.

When a proxy is used, the client must include a complete URL in a request—the proxy has to be told exactly what the client has asked for and where it is. For example, a request to a proxy might look like:

```
GET http://www.abc.com/WWWdocs/index.html HTTP/1.1
```

or

```
GET http://www.abc.com/ HTTP/1.1
```

Flaws in Classic HTTP

Web traffic ramped up quickly and the Web became serious business. Companies employed staffs of graphic designers to create attractive pages.[7] A

---

[7]These were—and still are—often unnecessarily elaborate, killing performance at the server.

separate TCP session was used to retrieve each graphic element. Designers loved to create graphics—even replacing individual words with graphics. With 20 or 30 separate sessions required to download a page:

- Listen queues filled up, locking users out.
- Communications overhead mushroomed.
- Since the server initiated each session close, the server was left in TIME-WAIT state and the server's memory was clogged with old session control blocks.

There also were some difficult structural problems. Many clients were separated from Web servers by a string of proxy servers. Also, sometimes clients communicate with a server that is acting as a gateway to another server (such as a database, news, or email server). Formal rules for the interactions between all of these participants had never been defined, leading to many problems that were hard to diagnose.

Faced with customer problems that had to be solved, vendors introduced a number of solutions (such as persistent connections) incrementally. These and other changes were cleaned up and wrapped into HTTP 1.1. The sections that follow are based on HTTP 1.1. Two major features of HTTP 1.1 are worth noting:

- Persistent connections are the default.
- On a persistent connection, a client can send multiple requests to the server without waiting for each response. The server will return the responses in order.

HTTP Methods

In keeping with object-oriented language, the term *method* is used in HTTP documents instead of *command* or *function*. A client can request the following HTTP 1.1 methods:

GET

HEAD

POST

PUT

DELETE

TRACE

CONNECT

OPTIONS

Some of these are well established, wheres others are in the formative stage. They are described below.

GET

GET requests a resource. It also can be used to upload form data that has been concatenated to a URL.[8]

HEAD

A HEAD request looks very much like a GET, except the server should return only the HTTP headers, not the item.

POST

POST is used to send a block of data to the server. This might be form data or some other application-specific information. The URL identifies a function that will process the block of data.

PUT

PUT is another upload function. It asks the server to store the enclosed body as the resource (file) named in the URL.

DELETE

DELETE asks the server to delete the resource named in the URL.

---

[8]This is very insecure, since this URL may be viewed—and cached by proxies and gateways along the way.

TRACE

It can be hard to debug a faulty Web client/server interaction that is handled via a chain of gateways and proxies. The TRACE command asks the final recipient of the client's message to reflect a message back to the client. The message consists of a set of headers.

TRACE can be made to behave like a *traceroute* by sending successive messages with 1, 2, 3,...in a *Max-Forwards* header. The system that receives Max-Forwards of 0 must reflect the message back.

CONNECT

This method is reserved for use with Secure Sockets Layer tunneling.[9]

OPTIONS

An OPTIONS method conveys a request for information about the communication options available on the chain consisting of proxies, gateways, and the server identified by a Request-URI. The response contains headers that disclose server features applicable to the resource.

Dynamic Pages and Chunked Encoding

Persistent sessions and pages that are dynamically generated at the server by programs that access backend databases and legacy applications are great strides forward. However, they don't get along with each other unless something special is done. To use a persistent session, a client has to know when an entire response item has been received. Normally, the item's length is announced in a server header at the start of the item. But if the item is being created on the fly and streamed out, the server will not know the size ahead of time.

---

[9]At the time of writing, this usage was still under study.

The solution is called "chunked encoding." The body of a message is transferred as a series of chunks. Each has its own size indicator. The chunked encoding is ended by a chunk of size 0, followed by an optional trailer that contains wrap-up information. The trailer information consists of a set of HTTP headers—which seems an odd way to describe the contents of a *trailer.*

HTTP Headers

The first big improvement to the hypertext transfer protocol was the introduction of a set of header fields that a client uses to describe its capabilities and its request, and a server uses to describe its response. In designing headers, Web designers did not take time out to reinvent the wheel. Header formats and datatypes were borrowed from classic electronic mail and MIME standards.

The following display shows a request sent by a Microsoft Internet Explorer client:

```
GET / HTTP/1.1
Accept: image/gif, image/x-xbitmap, image/jpeg, image/pjpeg,
   application/msword, application/vnd.ms-powerpoint, */*
Accept-Language: en-us
Accept-Encoding: gzip, deflate
Range: bytes = 7015-
Unless-Modified-Since: Fri, 12 Jun 1998 19:37:10 GMT
If-Range: "0f78d7d3996bd1:35746"
User-Agent: Mozilla/4.0 (compatible; MSIE 4.0; Windows NT)
Host: www.microsoft.com
Connection: Keep-Alive
```

As is the case for classic Internet email and MIME email headers, a message consists of a set of headers followed by an empty line, optionally followed by body contents. The preceding client request ends with an empty line.[10] A GET message never includes a message body. A client POST request message contains a block of data to be uploaded and would contain a message body.

The "GET /" request above asks for the default "home page" at the server. The client indicates that it understands HTTP 1.1. A series of headers in MIME format follows. These are discussed in the sections that follow.

---

[10]In other words, the request ends with <CR> <LF> <CR> <LF>.

Accept Headers

The client's accept headers indicate:

- The client is willing and able to receive a variety of image datatypes, Microsoft World documents, and PowerPoint presentations.
- The user's language is English.
- The client is willing to receive information that has been compressed using *gzip* or *deflate* (the method used to create *zip* archives).

An accept field can include alternative choices. For example the preceding Accept-Encoding field indicates that either *gzip* or *deflate* compression is all right. A client can assign a quality (preference) number to each choice, such as gzip;q = 1.5. The highest number is the most preferred.

Range, If-Range, and Unless-Modified-Since Headers

In this example, the client already has part of an item cached on disk. The client asks for the remaining part, from byte 7015 to the end—unless the item has been changed. The If-Range header contains a unique tag that the server sent down with the original item, which has been cached. If the tag at the server still is the same, then the server will send the requested byte range. If the item has changed, the tag will not match, and the server will send the entire item. For good measure, Microsoft's browser has included an Unless-Modified-Since header, which is nonstandard.

In general, a client can ask for parts of an item by means of a range statement.

User-Agent Header

The client identifies the browser product and version in the User-Agent header. Client capabilities diverged during the browser wars, and servers that wanted to exploit the latest and greatest features of each client had to send different responses to Microsoft and Netscape clients.

Host Header

The Host header identifies the server that was named in the request URL. Without this field, the server would not get to see the host name. The client sent the host name in the URL to a Domain Name Server in order to translate it to an address. The client then requested a connection to that address. Until the host field was added, Web servers never saw the host name that was used in the URL.[11]

Why should it care—doesn't the server know its own name? The problem is that many Web servers have a lot of names and addresses. It is very common for Web sites to be outsourced to a service provider. Unless a company's Web service is very big and very busy, the provider will load it onto a computer shared with a lot of other companies. A separate disk directory contains each company's Web pages. Before the Host header was introduced, a trick had to be used to sort through incoming requests and construct a response from the correct directory:

- The server's network interface card was given several IP addresses—one for each company.

- A Domain Name Server lookup for *www.abc.com* or *www.def.com* would produce the appropriate address.

- The directory containing a company's Web files was tied into a specific address. The destination IP address of an incoming request was used to choose the correct directory.

This practice burns up masses of IP addresses. Unfortunately, there still are many clients that do not send a Host header, so this way of doing things may persist for a while.

Connection Header

The use of this header in the earlier example mixes HTTP 1.0 with 1.1. The header indicates that the server should not close the session after delivering its data. The session should be kept alive and reused for more requests and responses. In HTTP 1.1, persistent connections are the default.

---

[11]However, recall that an intermediate proxy server is sent the complete URL.

Server Response

The response below came from a Microsoft Internet Information Server.

```
HTTP/1.1 200 OK
Server: Microsoft-IIS/4.0
Content-Location: http://www.microsoft.com/Default.htm
Date: Wed, 01 Jul 1998 23:48:34 GMT
Content-Type: text/html
Accept-Ranges: bytes
Last-Modified: Wed, 01 Jul 1998 18:07:32 GMT
ETag: "08add1d1ba5bd1:61fd"
Content-Length: 16279

<HTML>
<HEAD>
<TITLE>Microsoft Corporation Home Page; Welcome to
Microsoft</TITLE>
  . . .
```

In the initial status line, the server indicates that it speaks HTTP 1.1. The "200 OK" statement is a numbered status response much like the ones we saw earlier for file transfer and electronic mail.

Server Header

The server provides product information, just as the client did.

Content-Location Header

The server provides the complete URL for the item that will be downloaded.

Content-Type Header

A typical MIME Content-Type header announces that this is an item of type text and subtype html.

Accept-Ranges Header

The server is willing to accept requests that ask for parts of resources by specifying one or more ranges of bytes.

Last-Modified Header

A client caches a downloaded page in a local disk area along with the date on which the page was retrieved. This date is used in a request if the user asks for the same page at a later time. The client's request has a timestamp of Fri, 12 Jun 1998 19:37:10 GMT and the last-modified time is Wed, 01 Jul 1998 18:07:32 GMT, so the page has been changed since it was cached.

ETag Header

The fact that the resource has been modified also shows up in the ETag (Entity Tag) header. The client's cached value was "0f78d7d3996bd1:35746" and the server's current value is "08add1d1ba5bd1:61fd."

Content-Length Header

This is a very important header. Since the server can announce how long the content will be, the server does not have to close the session in order to signal end-of-file. Hence the session can be persistent. The length that is reported is the length of the message body.

Since the document in the request has changed, the server has included the entire updated version in a body that is 16,279 bytes in length.

Message Headers

Tables 18.2 through 18.5 provide brief definitions of the headers that can accompany a request or a response. The set of headers continues to expand, and experimental extension headers can be defined at any time.

- *General* headers appear first in a message and may be found in requests or responses. These are listed in Table 18.2.

TABLE 18.2

HTTP General
Headers

General Headers	Description
Cache-Control	Contains instructions that control cache usage. For example, a client might insist that proxies along the way get a fresh version of the item. A server might mark a returned item as public, private (for one user), or indicate that it must not be cached.
Connection	Can indicate whether a connection should be persistent (keep-alive) or closed as soon as the response has been sent. Also provides a way for a client or server to pass some information to an adjacent proxy.
Date	The date and time at which the message originated.
Pragma	A catch-all for implementation specific directives.
Transfer-Encoding	A client states which encodings are acceptable. A server announces which encoding was used.
Upgrade	The client indicates that it can support a different (e.g., higher version number) protocol than the one that it announced. The server can ignore this or can make a "Switching Protocols" response.
Trailer	Identifies header fields that are present in the trailer of a message encoded with chunked transfer-coding.
Via	Like the "Received" field in an email header. In a request, it tracks the gateways and proxies on the path from the client to the server. In a response, it tracks the gateways and proxies on the path from the server to the client.

■ Next are headers specific to either requests (Table 18.3) or responses (Table 18.4).

■ Finally, *entity* headers appear last and provide detailed information about the body of a message. These are listed in Table 18.5.

Keep in mind that a POST request transfers body information—such as the information from a data entry form—from a client to a server. A PUT also includes body data. Therefore entity headers can appear in requests as well as responses.

TABLE 18.3

HTTP Request
Headers

Request Headers	Description
Accept	Media types that are acceptable for the response.
Accept-Charset	Character sets that are acceptable for the response.
Accept-Encoding	Can indicate whether various types of compression are acceptable.
Accept-Language	For example, U.S. English or Swedish.
Authorization	Contains authentication credentials.
Expect	Describes server behaviors that are required by the client. For example, the client may indicate that it wants to upload a file, and may check with the server to find out whether the server would allow this.
From	Email address of the user.
Host	The host name and port number, taken from the requesting URL.
If-Modified-Since	Contains a date and time. The resource will be returned only if it was modified since that date and time.
If-Match	Contains one or more tags for cached items. The server should not perform the request unless the server's tag for the resource matches one of these tags. Useful to prevent the client from using PUT to update a file at the server that already has been changed by somebody else.
If-None-Match	Contains a list of tags. The client only wants a resource if its tag does not match any of these tags taken from the cache.
If-Range	If the item has not changed, the client requests some specific byte ranges. If the item has changed, the server should send the entire item.
If-Unmodified-Since	If the requested item has been modified since the time specified in this header, then the server should not fulfill the request and should return an error code.
Max-Forwards	Decremented by each proxy or gateway that forwards the request. If the received value is 0, that system must respond.
Proxy-Authorization	Contains credentials that authenticate the client to a proxy.
Range	The client can ask for specific byte ranges in the item instead of the whole item.
Referer	The URI of the resource from which the current request URI was obtained.
TE	Indicates the transfer encodings (e.g., types of compression) that are acceptable in the response.
User-Agent	Identifies the client product.

TABLE 18.4

HTTP Response
Headers

Response Headers	Description
Accept-Ranges	An HTTP 1.1 client can make a range request that asks for part(s) of an item to be returned. The server can use this field to indicate that it accepts or rejects the request.
Age	A proxy indicates the number of seconds since a cached value was generated or revalidated by the originating server.
ETag	A unique tag for an item returned by a server.
Location	Redirects the client to a new URL to be used to complete the request.
Proxy-Authenticate	A client that requests a resource from a proxy that requires authentication will receive a Proxy Authentication Required error response that includes a Proxy-Authenticate field. The field contains a challenge that indicates the authentication scheme and parameters applicable for this Request-URI.
Retry-After	Used with a Service Unavailable error response to indicate how long the service is expected to be unavailable to the client.
Server	Describes the server product.
Vary	A document may have several forms (e.g., by language choice). A picture may have alternate forms (e.g., png or jpeg). HTTP 1.1 supports content negotiation that enables a client to choose a preferred representation.
Warning	Adds additional information that explains a status code.
WWW-Authenticate	Included with a response that indicates that authentication is required. It includes a challenge string and identifies the authentication scheme that is in use.

Status Codes

Status codes are used much as they are in electronic mail and file transfer. General code assignments are:

1xx   Informational. For example, request received, continuing process.

2xx   Success. The action was successfully received, understood, and accepted

3xx   Redirection. Further action must be taken in order to complete the request

4xx   Client Error. The request contains bad syntax or cannot be fulfilled

5xx   Server Error. The server failed to fulfill an apparently valid request

More detailed information is provided by the specific codes.

TABLE 18.5

HTTP Entity
Headers

Entity Headers	Description
Allow	Lists methods supported for the request resource, such as GET, HEAD, PUT.
Content-Encoding	Indicates how the content has been transformed, for example by being compressed by gzip.
Content-Language	Indicates the language or languages in which the content is presented.
Content-Length	Size in bytes.
Content-Location	Indicates a URL different from the one in the request from which the item can be retrieved. For example, the location of items may have changed.
Content-MD5	Contains the MD5 message digest of the body content.
Content-Range	The message body contains part of an item. The header indicates the range of bytes relative to the original item.
Content-Type	Media type of the body.
Expires	The date and time after which the response should be considered stale.
Last-Modified	Date and time indicating when the resource was last modified.

Recommended Reading

RFC 1738 contains descriptions of URLs. RFC 1630 is a technical description of Universal Resource Identifiers.

The HTTP 1.1 specification was published as RFC 2068. The most recent update can be obtained from the World Wide Web Consortium (*http://www.w3.org/*). Information about the latest version of HTML and other Web-related projects can be found at this site.

Directories and the Lightweight Directory Access Protocol

Introduction

In this chapter we talk about directory systems and a protocol that enables clients to search and update directories. A detailed discussion of directory architecture and protocols could easily fill a big thick volume on its own. Our goal is to present some key concepts and promote a good general understanding of the topic.

Just as there are many different applications that can be based on relational databases, there are diverse applications that can be based on directory databases. But what characterizes a directory database—in contrast to other database systems? Ordinary telephone books are a good starting point for understanding what directory databases are all about.

Telephone Directories

The telephone book that sits on a table next to your telephone is a typical directory. Its white pages section lists the names, telephone numbers, and addresses of people within your locality. It is organized alphabetically by name. The yellow pages section lists names, telephone numbers, addresses, and additional information about businesses. It is organized by type of business, such as Automobile Repair or Pharmacies.

Even though we usually deal with telephone directories in paper form, the telephone directory system is implemented as a computer database. In fact, it is a distributed computer database whose structure is shown in Figure 19.1. To get conventional white pages directory assistance for a locality in the United States, you need to look up the appropriate area code, dial (area code)-555-1212 and ask an operator to enter your query into the remote directory database.

It probably will take only a few years for paper telephone directories and manual lookups to become obsolete. In France, telephone owners already get directory assistance from an online database using computers that are integrated with their telephones. Around the world, Internet users access telephone number, email, and business yellow pages information at *http://www.four11.com/* and other directory sites.

One characteristic that directory databases have in common is that they have a hierarchical structure. The telephone white pages directory system is organized by country, area, city, and name.

Figure 19.1
The world's distributed telephone directory.

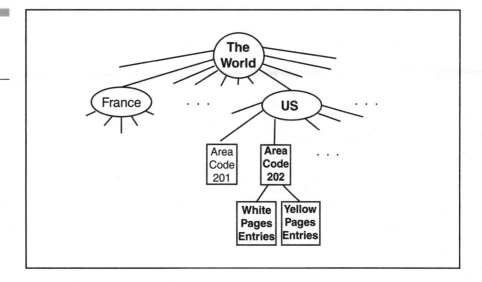

Organizational Directories

It is becoming more and more common for applications to be distributed across internal and external servers. Users connect to Web servers, update databases, perform business transactions, and exchange electronic mail with peers who may be scattered around the world. A directory service that helps users to locate network servers and find email addresses would be a great convenience.

But there is another directory service that can offer even more compelling value to network and system administrators—a user directory. User rights and privileges need to be established for each network server that is accessed, and more servers are added every day. In a distributed computing environment, network administration can quickly mushroom out of control. The ability to simplify and centralize user administration is the appeal of directory service applications such as NetWare's NDS, Netscape's Directory Server, and Microsoft's Active Directory.

Users benefit as much as administrators because a directory can be the basis of a "single sign-on" system. With the help of a directory, a single username and password or public key certificate can be the basis for authenticating the user to every server on the network. User privileges can be stored in the directory, which becomes a participant in each sign-on process.

Definition of a standard SQL command interface helped to win acceptance for relational databases. A standard client/server protocol is the key to widespread acceptance of directory products. Fortunately, the IETF Lightweight Directory Access Protocol (LDAP) can do the job. This chapter describes features of version 3 of LDAP.

A Word of Warning

Directory database vendors have given strong support to LDAP, which provides a standardized access method and good directory search and update operations. However, the extensible Markup Language (XML) is a contender that is just warming up. New mechanisms based on XML may undercut the use of LDAP some time in the future.

LDAP Background

LDAP is hard to understand if you do not know its history. In 1984, the CCITT (now called ITU-T) published its X.400 electronic mail specifications. X.400 was immediately adopted into the International Standards Organization Open Systems Interconnect protocol family. There was a lot of excitement about the X.400 specifications at the time. It was believed that X.400 would be deployed quickly and would become the basis for the worldwide exchange of electronic mail.

However, even the most enthusiastic X.400 supporters admitted that there was a problem. If Jane Jones in Michigan wanted to send email to Harry Wu in Hong Kong, how could she find his electronic mail address? Obviously, a directory system was needed. Committees went to work and in 1988 an initial version of the X.500 directory standard was published. Work on extending and refining X.500 has continued into the 1990s.

The X.500 directory designers thought big. They wanted a global international directory system that could hold many different types of information. Like the Domain Name System, the public X.500 directory would be implemented in chunks, with each organization responsible for its own data. But an X.500 directory is very different from the Domain Name System. Table 19.1 compares characteristics of the Domain Name System with X.500.

TABLE 19.1

Characteristics of
the Domain Name
System and X.500

Domain Name System	X.500
The Domain Name System application is the basis of a global, distributed service.	X.500 is the basis of a global, distributed service.
A private Domain Name Server can be used internally to a company, to hold purely local information.	A private X.500 server can be used internally to a company, to hold purely local information.
The Domain Name System was designed to work invisibly, behind the scenes.	Both end users and applications interact with an X.500 directory.
The Domain Name system contains simple information, such as name and address translations.	An X.500 directory can hold a rich variety of information.
The Domain Name System provides a simple lookup service.	An X.500 directory supports very general searches that can return long lists of entries.
The information is quite stable and it is fairly easy for an administrator to keep it up-to-date.	It will be difficult for an administrator to keep track of some directory information—such as job titles, telephone numbers, and addresses. Some updates need to be done by end users.

In spite of a number of pilot implementations and adoption by a handful of customers, X.400 and X.500 did not gain commercial success. They were too complicated, expensive, and hard to operate. The end-user interfaces were poor. The Directory Access Protocol (DAP) designed for directory client/server interactions was big, unwieldy, and costly to implement.[1] Although some universities and a few research labs implemented X.500, the vision of a true global directory was not realized.

In 1993, Wengyik Yeong, Tim Howes, and Steve Kille reawakened interest in directory technology by designing the Lightweight Directory Access Protocol (LDAP).[2] Their original goal when they created LDAP was to provide a simpler way to access a global X.500 directory that would enable Internet users to look up information about organizations and people. However, LDAP could do a lot more.

---

[1] DAP was supposed to run on top of the OSI protocol stack. Its messages included complicated nested data structures encoded in Abstract Syntax Notation 1 (ASN.1). Just the job of parsing the messages slowed processing to a crawl.

[2] Their initial design was described in RFC 1487.

Figure 19.2
LDAP clients interacting with multiple LDAP servers.

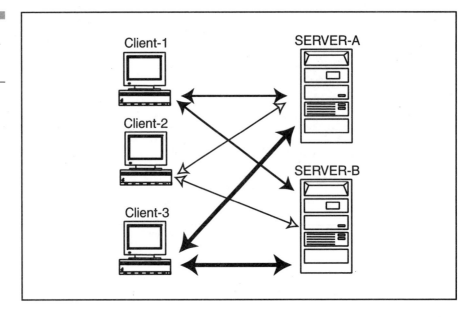

Figure 19.2
LDAP clients interacting with multiple LDAP servers.

Client-1

Client-2

Client-3

SERVER-A

SERVER-B

LDAP for General Directories

It did not take long for the full potential of LDAP to be appreciated. LDAP does what the best Internet standards do. By implementing a standard LDAP interface, a directory vendor can open up its product to any compatible client.[3] This, in turn, stimulates desktop vendors to build client software and middleware developers to offer Web gateways and general application gateways to directory services.

This produces an ideal result. Directory server vendors have built an array of different products that compete by offering desirable functions and features. Directory client vendors will offer competing products that can connect users to many different storehouses of information.

Figure 19.2 illustrates this many-to-many relationship. A large number of vendors now offer LDAP-accessible directory servers and/or LDAP clients. To cite just a few: NetWare Directory Services (NDS); Netscape Directory Service[4] and Netscape Communicator; Microsoft Exchange

---

[3]The LDAP developers provided a programming library and a set of simple API calls that made it fairly easy for vendors to offer the standard LDAP interface.

[4]Netscape designed their directory as a "native" LDAP directory. Its whole structure is aligned with LDAP.

Server, Microsoft Active Directory Server, and Microsoft Internet Explorer; the IBM DSSeries LDAP Directory; and Siemens Nixdorf DIR.D and DIR.X.[5] There is a list of pointers to implementations at:

http://www.critical-angle.com/ldapworld/

Introduction to X.500 Directories

Although LDAP now is targeted for general directory access, it was designed for the X.500 world and some understanding of the X.500 directory is needed in order to master LDAP. Since most directory vendors have incorporated X.500 concepts, terminology, and structures into their products, learning basic information about X.500 is useful in its own right.

The University of Michigan is an important center for both X.500 and LDAP design and development. There is a big campus directory that is heavily used by the university community. This campus directory has pointers to other X.500 directories.

An X.500 directory is organized as a tree of entries. Figure 19.3 shows the part of a global directory tree that includes the University of Michigan directory information.

Directory Entries

Every node in the tree corresponds to an entry that contains some information. In the part of the global tree shown in Figure 19.3, there are entries that describe countries (for example, c = US), organizations (for example, o = University of Michigan), and organizational units (for example, ou = people or ou = Students). The organizational units shown in Figure 19.3 have been designed to partition the information in the University of Michigan subtree into manageable chunks.

---

[5]One reason that LDAP is a lot easier to implement than DAP is that LDAP encodes most information as simple flat strings, while DAP uses complicated, nested encodings.

Figure 19.3
The global X.500 directory tree.

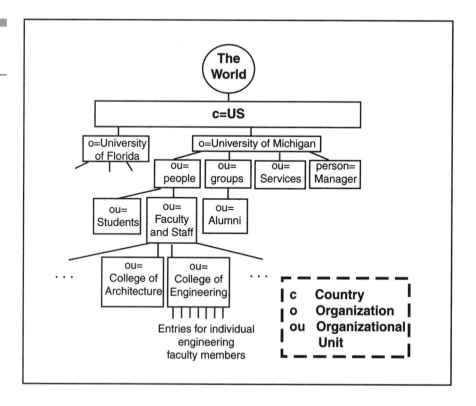

An entry is said to be *subordinate* to the entry directly above it. For example, in Figure 19.3, ou = People is subordinate to o = University of Michigan. The *immediate superior* of an entry is the one directly above it. Thus ou = Faculty and Staff is the immediate superior of ou = College of Engineering.

The University of Michigan has implemented a handy Web gateway that enables users to browse and search its server and other directory servers in the global tree.[6] The gateway software has been installed at several other locations.[7]

[6]Web500gw was wriitten by Frank Richter at the Technical University of chemnitz-Zwickau, Germany. the Code was based on the Gopher-X.500 gateway (go500gw) implementation created by Tim Howes at the University of Michigan.

[7]See, for example, *http://ldap.utexas.edu:8888/* or *http://whitepages.rutgers.edu:8888/*.

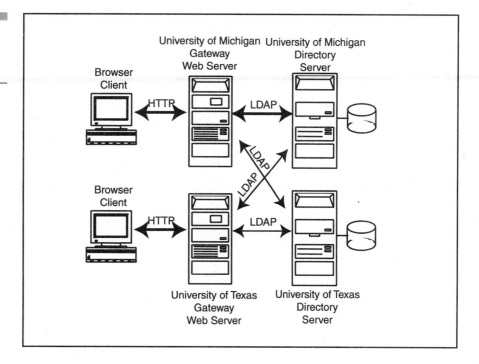

Figure 19.4
Web gateways that
pass LDAP requests
to directory servers.

The entries that are shown in this section were obtained using the University of Michigan Web gateway at:

http://web500gw.itd.umich.edu:8888/

To use the gateway, a client browser connects to the Web gateway. The user selects entries by clicking on links or filling out a search form. Figure 19.4 illustrates how a Web gateway transforms data that has been sent to a Web server into an LDAP request that is passed to a local or remote directory server.

Figure 19.5 shows part of a Netscape display of the Web page presented by the University of Michigan gateway. The page contains a link to the United States entry and a very long list of links down to directories at various organizations within the United States.

From this page, you can click on **The World** to go to the top of the tree, click on one of the organizations in the list to go down the tree, or click on **United States of America** to view the US entry.

Figure 19.5
University of Michigan Web gateway to X.500.

Figure 19.5
University of Michigan Web gateway to X.500.

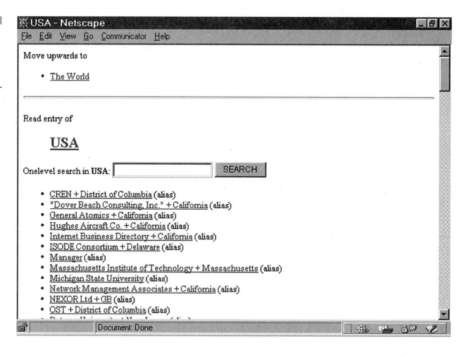

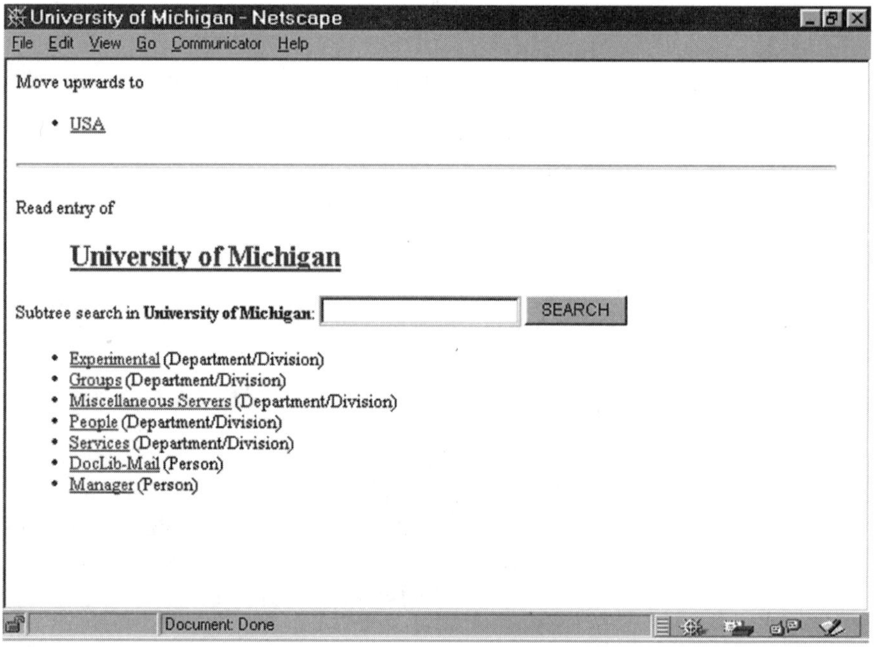

Figure 19.6
Search menu for the University of Michigan X.500 directory.

Attributes and Their Values

The Web page for the United States of America entry displays the information:

c
> US

description
> We the People of the United States.
> Sipapuni (Honoring Native Americans) "Place of Emergence"

associatedDomain
> us
> org
> net
> mil
> gov
> edu
> com
> bitnet

co
> USA
> US
> United States of America

e-mail
> None registered in this service

The entry consists of a set of *attributes*. Each attribute has a type, such as "description," and a value. Some attributes are allowed to have several values. For example, in the preceding entry there are two values for description and there are eight values for "associatedDomain."

After returning to the list of organizations, we can select the link to University of Michigan and view the menu shown in Figure 19.6.

The attributes for the University of Michigan entry are shown below:

Locality
> Ann Arbor, Michigan

State
> Michigan

Street Address
> 535 West William St.

Organization
> University of Michigan

        UMICH
        UM
        U-M
        U of M
Description
        The University of Michigan at Ann Arbor
Postal Address
        University of Michigan
        535 W. William St.
        Ann Arbor, MI 48109
        US
Postal Code
        48109
Telephone Number
        +1 313 764-1817
Internet-Domain
        umich.edu

We can go back to the search menu and browse our way down the tree
(see Figure 19.3) through people, faculty and staff, and College of Engineering until we reach directory entries for individual engineering faculty members, such as the one displayed below:[8]

cn
        Joseph B Davis
title
        Professor, Electrical Engr & Computer Sci
postalAddress
        Elec Engr & Comp Science
        9999X EECS
        9999
telephoneNumber
        +1 313 999-9999
uid
        jdavis
mail
        jdavis@eecs.umich.edu
homePhone
        +1 313 999-9999

---

[8]The actual information is fictional, but the attributes are the same as those in real
entries.

homePostalAddress
9999 Elm Avenue
Ann Arbor MI
48101
labeledURL
Home Page for Joseph Davis

Distinguished Names

Every entry in a directory tree has a name label that is called a *Relative Distinguished Name*. For example, the Relative Distinguished Name for the University of Michigan directory entry is:

o=University of Michigan

The relative distinguished name is composed of one or more selected attributes from the entry. Most often, it is a single attribute.

Every entry has a unique *Distinguished Name* that is formed by concatenating the Relative Distinguished Names along the path from the entry to the top of the tree. For example, the complete Distinguished Name for Joseph B. Davis is:

cn=Joseph B Davis, ou=College of Engineering, ou=Faculty and Staff, ou=People, o=The University of Michigan, c=United States of America

A complete distinguished name pinpoints an entry's position in the directory tree and identifies it uniquely. Anyone who knows that Joseph Davis is on the engineering faculty can easily follow the labels down to his entry.

Aliases

Each item in a directory has a unique distinguished name, but sometimes a real-world entity has a popular nickname. Aliases are used to provide alternate nicknames. An alias is a placeholder entry that contains the name of the real entry. Aliases provide a very convenient way to handle moves and changes. For example, if Professor Davis transferred to the School of Engineering in Dearborn, then his Distinguished Name would change to:

cn=Joseph B Davis, ou=School of Engineering-Dearborn, ou=Faculty and Staff, ou=People, o=University of Michigan, c=United States of America

It would be convenient to keep an alias pointer at Professor Davis's old name to direct people who were unaware of the change to the new location. A user who accessed the entry for the old Distinguished Name would find the alias.

Aliases are helpful to people who are performing searches. Before performing a search, a user can set an option so that when an alias matches the search criteria, the alias pointer will be followed automatically and the new entry will be returned. This process is called "dereferencing" aliases.[9]

We finally are ready to take a look at LDAP.

LDAP Operations

LDAP enables a client to send requests to a directory and receive responses. There are several different types of requests. The central purpose of a directory service is to enable people or programs to search for information. Thus the *search* request is the most important LDAP operation. There also is a simple *compare* operation that is used to check whether the value of an attribute in an entry matches a given value.

Sometimes a search or compare operation will grind away for a very long time or a search will start to return voluminous data. Fortunately, a user can request that an operation be *abandoned* (cancelled).

It may be difficult—or even impossible—for an administrator to keep track of entry details such as job titles, telephone numbers, addresses, or the location of personal Web pages. The solution is to permit authenticated users to update some of their own entry information using a *modify* request.

Some database maintenance tasks need to be performed by an administrator. An administrator can *delete* a leaf entry, *add* a new entry, *modify the Distinguished Name* of an entry, or move an entire directory subtree.

---

[9]Aliases can be set up for entries that have subordinates, as well as entries that are "leaves," that is, are located at the bottom of the tree.

Users or administrators should not be allowed to update a directory without authenticating themselves. *Bind* requests and responses implement authentication procedures. Whereas bind is used at the start of a session, an *unbind* request terminates the session.

Finally, version 3 of LDAP includes an extended request message that enables additional standard or private operations to be defined and used. An extended request message starts with a field that contains an identifier for the new operation.

To summarize, the standard LDAP operations include:

- Bind
- Unbind
- Search
- Compare
- Abandon
- Modify
- Delete
- Add
- Modify Distinguished Name

The operations are described in the sections that follow.

Bind

Authentication is needed to protect sensitive information or to limit directory update privileges. A bind enables a client to "login" to a directory by exchanging authentication information with a directory server at the start of a session.

Some directories are set up to permit clients to connect and request information without performing a bind. Some require a bind request to be sent at the start of the session, but will accept a bind that contains no authentication data. Normally, there will be some body of public information that can safely be made available to unauthenticated users. However, many directories are set up so that even casual access requires each user to provide a username and password. Note that the username normally is the Distinguished Name of an entry that has been created for the user in the directory being accessed.

A challenge handshake may be sufficient to authenticate end users that wish to update information in their own entries. A stronger method based on public keys would be appropriate for directory administrators.

At the time of writing, no specific authentication method has been mandated. The initial bind request and response negotiate an authentication method and also can carry some authentication data. A series of bind requests and responses sometimes are needed in order to complete an authentication process (such as a challenge handshake). The client's initial bind request:

- Identifies the version of LDAP that the client is using
- Includes an LDAP Distinguished Name that identifies the user. (Sometimes a null value is accepted.)
- Identifies the authentication mechanism that is to be used.
- May include a parameter that is used to start the authentication procedure.

The LDAP version 3 standard recommends use of a registered Simple Authentication and Security Layer (SASL) method for authentication. However, some current implementations secure LDAP by means of SSL,[10] versions of Kerberos that are not registered SASL methods, or by proprietary algorithms.

Unbind

A client sends an unbind request to end a session. The server does not need to respond. It simply closes the communications session.

Search Request

Searching is the most important—and the most complex—LDAP operation. A client's search request identifies:

- The Distinguished Name of an object that will act as the "base" entry for the search.
- The scope to be searched, which can be:
  The single base entry
  All entries immediately below the base entry
  An entire subtree below the base entry

---

[10]SSL had not yet been registered at the time of writing.

- A search filter. A filter lists criteria used to select entries. Search criteria can be combined using AND, OR, and NOT. Criteria that can be used include:
  A particular attribute is present.
  A specified string matches a value.
  A specified string is a substring of a value.
  A specified string approximately matches (used for special functions such as "sounds like").
  A specified integer is equal to (or less than, greater than) a value.
- The list of the attributes to be returned from each entry that matches the search filter. A list that is empty or consists of the "*" string asks the server to return all attributes that the client is allowed to see.
- Limits on the amount of data to be returned:
  Maximum number of entries to be returned.
  Maximum time allowed for the search.
  Whether to return a skeleton list of types instead of types and their values.

Search Response

A client sends a search request to the server and the server sends back one or more search response messages. Responses can include:

- *Search Result Entries.* Each entry that matches the search criteria is packaged in a separate response message.
- *Search Result References.* These are URLs that point to other directories that may have matching entries. For example, a user may be searching a complete subtree, and entries for part of that subtree may be located at a different server.
- A *final Search Result Done result report.* This is a message that indicates whether the search was successful. If there was a problem, the message reports what error occurred.

Compare

An LDAP compare is very simple. A compare request identifies:

- The Distinguished Name of an entry.

- An attribute type to be examined.
- The attribute value to be matched.

The result of the compare is returned in a compare response. The response states whether the comparison was true or false—or reports that there was a problem that prevented the comparison from being made. For example, there might not be an attribute of the requested type in the entry, or access to the data may require a higher level of authentication.

What is the difference between a compare and a search whose scope is a single entry? If there was a match, the search would return either the whole entry or a set of requested attributes along with a result report, whereas a compare would just return the result report. Compare may seem weak, but there are times when it is needed. For example, it may be legal to compare a given string with a stored password value, but reading the password would not be allowed.

Abandon

A client uses an abandon request to ask the server to abandon an earlier request. A client might use this when a server was returning a very large amount of information, or when an operation was taking a long time to complete. There is no response to an abandon request.

Modify

A modify request:

- Identifies the Distinguished Name of the entry to be modified.
- Contains a list of add/create, delete, and replace operations to be performed on attribute values in the entry.

The modifications must be performed in their listed order, and the update must be atomic—that is, either all updates succeed or all must be rolled back to the former values. The response to the modify request indicates whether it succeeded or failed. The specific modifications that can be made are:

- Add values to an existing attribute, or create a new attribute with given value(s).

■ Delete values from an existing attribute, and remove the attribute if all of its values have been deleted.

■ Replace all values of a given attribute with new values. Create the attribute if it does not already exist, or delete it if the replace provides no value for the attribute.

Add

An administrator uses an add request to add an entire new entry to a directory. The request:

■ Identifies the Distinguished Name for the new entry.

■ Provides a list of attribute types and values for the entry.

The add response indicates whether the add succeeded or failed. An administrator uses add requests to create and enlarge the tree structure of an organization's directory.

Delete

An administrator uses a delete request to delete a single "leaf" entry from the directory. A leaf entry is at the bottom of a tree. A delete request contains:

■ The Distinguished Name of the entry to be deleted.

The delete response indicates whether the delete succeeded or failed.

Modify DN

An administrator can perform two functions using modify Distinguished Name requests:

■ Change the leftmost name component of an entry. The entry is allowed to have subordinates.

■ Change the leftmost name component of an entry and move the subtree consisting of this entry and its subordinates to a new location in the directory tree.

The modify DN parameters include:

- The Distinguished Name of the entry.
- The new Relative Distinguished Name for the leftmost component.
- A parameter that indicates whether the old Relative Distinguished Name value (or values) should be retained in the entry. An old value can be kept as a name that is not the Relative Distinguished Name.
- If the entry is to be moved, the Distinguished Name of the new immediate superior entry is included in the request.

The modify DN response indicates whether the modify DN succeeded or failed.

Unsolicited Notification

The unsolicited notification is a special message. A server sends an unsolicited notification to a client in order to report some type of problem—for example, that the server is about to close the connection due to an error condition. There is no response.

LDAP Sessions

LDAP messages usually are sent over a reliable connection-oriented transport.[11] TCP is the transport most commonly used.

A common scenario (shown in Figure 19.7) is that a TCP client connects to well-known port 389 and sends one or more search requests to the directory. Note that the client uses an unbind request to terminate the session.

If the client wishes to access sensitive data or perform updates, an authentication step will be needed. Recall that a bind request is used to perform authentication.[12] Several bind requests and responses may be needed in order to complete the authentication. Figure 19.8 illustrates an interaction that requires bind.

---

[11]A connectionless version of the protocol was described in RFC 1798.

[12]In version 2 of LDAP, a bind always was required. If no authentication actually was needed, the bind parameters were set to null values.

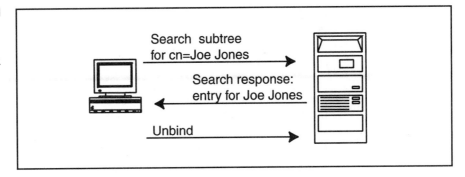

Figure 19.7
Sending a search request to a directory.

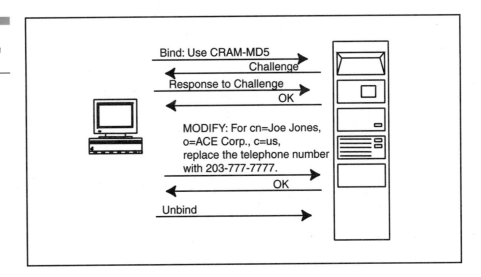

Figure 19.8
Authenticating via a bind request.

Alternatively, an LDAP session can be protected by authentication and encryption by using SSL (or TLS). Well-known port 636 has been set aside for this purpose.

Searching Using URLs

In examples shown earlier in this chapter we retrieved information from a directory via a Web gateway. This gateway enables a user to browse or search a directory by clicking on links or filling in a simple search box. Figure 19.4 showed how a user interacts with a Web gateway that translates the user input into directory queries. Alternatively, a desktop client could be used to interact directly with LDAP directories, as was shown in Figure 19.2.

It seems fairly natural to integrate a desktop LDAP client with a browser. LDAP URLs have been defined in order to promote the integration of LDAP clients into browsers. Browsers that can interpret these URLs enable users to search a directory by typing a URL or by filling out a form whose input is translated into an LDAP URL at the desktop. Netscape Communicator includes an LDAP client that can perform sophisticated searches when a user types in a URL. You can use this client to get some hands-on experience with LDAP.

LDAP URLs have a tortured syntax that gets complicated fast. However, a few query examples may help you to form your own requests. In the examples that follow, we are going to go straight into the directory at the University of Michigan located at host *ldap.itd.umich.edu* and operating at the well-known port for LDAP, which is 389.

First, we will retrieve the entry for the university by entering its Distinguished Name. However, we have to be a little careful. Recall (see Chapter 18) that each space character in a URL must be replaced by %20. This makes the Distinguished Name look a little messy.

ldap://ldap.itd.umich.edu/o=University%20of%20Michigan,c=us

Any entry can be retrieved by typing its Distinguished Name. For example, to get the entry for Joseph B. Davis:

ldap://ldap.itd.umich.edu/cn=Joseph%20B%20Davis,
    ou=College%20of%20Engineering,ou=Faculty%20and%20Staff,
    ou=People,o=University%20of%20Michigan,c=us

If we just wanted to retrieve the telephone number of the university instead of getting its complete entry, we would add a "?" character and the name of the attribute.

ldap://ldap.itd.umich.edu/o=University%20of%20Michigan,c=us?tele-
    phoneNumber

Let's go back to the entry for Joseph Davis. It is not too likely that we would know his entire Distinguished Name. However, it is easy to search the whole university directory. We will provide a "base" Distinguished Name (o=University of Michigan, c=us) and request a search of the whole subtree (sub) under that base.

ldap://ldap.itd.umich.edu/o=University%20of%20Michigan,c=
us??sub?(cn=*Davis)

LDAP URL Syntax

This is starting to look pretty complicated, so we'd better take a look at the structure of these URLs. There are four elements that can be included:[13]

1. Base Distinguished Name

2. Attributes that we wish to see

3. Scope of the search

4. Search filter

Note that:

- Elements that are present must appear in the listed order.
- The elements are separated by "?" characters.
- The only required element is the base Distinguished Name.
- If specific attributes are not mentioned, then all attributes are returned.
- Choices for the scope are "base" for the single entry corresponding to the base Distinguished Name, "sub" for the complete subtree under the base Distinguished Name, and "one" for a one-level search under the name. If the scope is omitted, then the scope defaults to "base."
- A search filter places constraints on the search. If it is omitted, then there are no constraints.

Now we are ready to analyze:

ldap://ldap.itd.umich.edu/o=University%20of%20Michigan,c=
us??sub?(cn=*Davis)

---

[13]A fifth item, Extensions, has been defined as a placeholder for future extensions.

Base

The base Distinguished Name is University%20of%20Michigan, c=us.

Attributes

The "??" string indicates that the attributes field is empty, which means that we want all of the attributes in the entry.

Scope

"Sub" indicates that we want to search the subtree under the base.

Search Filter

The last item in the example is its search filter. Only entries containing a cn (common name) attribute whose value ends in "Davis" (*Davis) should be returned. Filter items always are enclosed in parentheses. Because of the parentheses, we do not need to translate the spaces to %20 because the URL cannot end until all parentheses are paired off.

The university community is very large. It is likely that several entries will be returned. You can narrow the search by providing more information. For example, you might know that Davis's title has the word "Electrical" in it.

We will make the filter more precise. The filter below says that the common name ends with Davis and that his title contains the string "Electrical." The & (and) symbol at the beginning of the filter is applied to the sequence of parenthesized statements that follow. Note the use of the * wild card to denote any string of characters:

(&(cn=*Davis)(title=*Electrical*))

Here is the complete URL:

ldap://ldap.itd.umich.edu/o=University%20of%20Michigan,c=us?? sub?(&(cn=*Davis)(title=*Electrical*))

If all that we wanted was Professor Davis's telephone number and electronic mail addresses, we would ask for just those attributes from the entry:

ldap://ldap.itd.umich.edu/o=University%20of%20Michigan,c=us?
telephoneNumber,mail?sub?(&(cn=*Davis)(title=*Electrical*))

There is a lot more that can be done with filters. In addition to simple equalities such as (cn=*Davis), you could specify:

greater   ">=" (for text, this could be a lexicographic comparison)

less   "<="

approx   "~=" (used, for example, to mean "it sounds like")

And (&), or (|), and not (!) phrases can be combined using parentheses appropriately. For example, A and (B or C) and not D would be:

(&(A)(|(B)(C))(!D))

LDAP Message Format

All of the options shown previously have a place in the LDAP message format. The format is defined using a popular standard message definition language called Abstract Syntax Notation 1 (ASN.1). ASN.1 definitions look rather like computer data structure definitions, and are a little friendlier than the message definitions that we have seen in some earlier chapters, which were expressed in bits and bytes. There is a set of Basic Encoding Rules (BER) that specify how an ASN.1 structure should be expressed as a byte stream. Since this conversion is done automatically by a computer program, we do not have to worry about the details of the message layout. ASN.1 lets us concentrate on its content.[14]

Each LDAP message starts with a message identifier. This allows a response to be matched with its request. Every operation has been assigned a different numeric identifier—for example, 0 for a bind request and 3 for a search request.

The ASN.1 definition of a search request operation follows. Some values in the request are represented by numbers. For example, the definition indicates that scope = wholeSubtree should be encoded as the value

---

[14]See Chapter 20 for more information about Abstract Syntax Notation 1 and the Basic Encoding Rules.

2. Parts of the message contain a choice of variables and each choice is tagged with a number. For example, under filter, an equalityMatch string will be tagged with a 3.

```
SearchRequest ::= [APPLICATION 3] SEQUENCE {
          baseObject      LDAPDN,
          scope           ENUMERATED {
                  baseObject          (0),
                  singleLevel         (1),
                  wholeSubtree        (2) },
          derefAliases    ENUMERATED {
                  neverDerefAliases       (0),
                  derefInSearching        (1),
                  derefFindingBaseObj     (2),
                  derefAlways             (3) },
          sizeLimit       INTEGER (0 .. maxInt),
          timeLimit       INTEGER (0 .. maxInt),
          typesOnly       BOOLEAN,
          filter          Filter,
          attributes      AttributeDescriptionList }
Filter ::= CHOICE {
          and             [0] SET OF Filter,
          or              [1] SET OF Filter,
          not             [2] Filter,
          equalityMatch   [3] AttributeValueAssertion,
          substrings      [4] SubstringFilter,
          greaterOrEqual  [5] AttributeValueAssertion,
          lessOrEqual     [6] AttributeValueAssertion,
          present         [7] AttributeDescription,
          approxMatch     [8] AttributeValueAssertion,
          extensibleMatch [9] MatchingRuleAssertion }
SubstringFilter ::= SEQUENCE {
          type            AttributeDescription,
          -- at least one must be present
          substrings      SEQUENCE OF CHOICE {
                  initial [0] LDAPString,
                  any     [1] LDAPString,
                  final   [2] LDAPString } }
MatchingRuleAssertion ::= SEQUENCE {
          type            [2] AttributeDescription OPTIONAL,
          matchValue      [3] AssertionValue,
          dnAttributes    [4] BOOLEAN DEFAULT FALSE }
```

We make no attempt to explain every detail here, but a few comments may be helpful.

derefAliases

This indicates how aliases are to be handled. Recall that "dereference aliases" means that if an alias satisfies the search criteria, then the search operation should follow the alias pointer and return the actual entry.

typesOnly

Setting this flag to true indicates that only the names of the attributes in an entry should be retrieved. The values of the attributes will be omitted. For example, the result of a typesOnly search might be "The entry xxx which matches the search contains a common name, an organizational, unit, a telephone number" and so forth.

MatchingRuleAssertion

This provides a way to add on new rules used to match search criteria. For example, you might wish to match up pictorial icons that are used to classify images.

There are a few more concepts that need to be understood in order to implement a directory. The sections that follow describe some behind-the-scenes directory structure.

Object Classes

The list of attributes that describe an organization is different from the list of attributes that describe a person. For example, the University of Michigan entry has locality and Internet-Domain attributes, which are not found in a person's entry. The entry for Joseph B. Davis has title and uid attributes, which are not found in an organization's entry. On the other hand, these entries do have some attributes in common, such as address and telephoneNumber.

Directories are supposed to be flexible. An organization can define any kinds of entries it wants and can choose whatever attributes it wants to put into each kind of entry. However, clumps of attributes tend to show up together again and again, and it is convenient to group them together. An *Object Class* is a named group of required and optional attributes.

Object Classes also serve a second purpose. Certain selected Object Classes give a directory its hierarchical structure. For example, for the global directory in Figure 19.3, an organization Object Class has a parent-child relationship with an organizationalUnit Object Class.

TABLE 19.2

Frequently Used
Object Classes

Object Class (Type of Entry)	Comment
country	
locality	This might be a state, county, or other regional identifier.
organization	
organizationalUnit	Part of an organization, such as a division or department.
person	This class includes just a few attributes.
residentialPerson	The attributes in this class provide information needed to deliver information to a person.
organizationalPerson	This class includes delivery information, but also includes a job title and an organizational unit.
organizationalRole	Some sample roles are President of a company or Electronic Mail Administrator.
groupOfNames	This lists the Distinguished Names of members of a group.
groupOfUniqueNames	Each member of this type of group has been assigned a unique identifier, ensuring that each name in the group will be unique.
applicationProcess	
device	
alias	An entry that provides an alternative name. For example, a yellow pages directory might contain an entry for the American Automobile Association. An alias "AAA" entry could contain a pointer to the organization's real entry.
dSA	Identifies a Directory System Agent, which is an X.500 directory server.
dmd	An entry that provides information about the Directory Management Domain.

Standard Object Classes

A set of standard Object Classes was defined for the global X.500 directory project. These standard classes can be used as a starter set when defining your own directory database. Table 19.2 lists frequently used Object Classes that have been defined in X.500 standards and in RFC documents.[15] There are a few more standard classes, but a huge number of other Object Classes have been defined by directory vendors and by end-user organizations.

---

[15]A summary may be found in RFC 2256.

Creating/Choosing Directory Object Classes

When designing a directory, you list the attributes that you will need for each kind of entry. Then you define Object Classes (or borrow standard ones) that contain groups of these attributes. Where possible, you define groups that can be reused for multiple kinds of entries. When you finish, you should be able to summarize the attributes in any entry by means of a short list of Object Classes.

Attributes for Standard Object Classes

Table 19.3 lists attributes for each of the classes in Table 19.2. If we check Table 19.3, we see that an entry that contains attributes from Object Class country must contain a c attribute that provides the country's name as a two-letter ISO 3166 country code (c=US). The entry optionally may include a description of the country and a search guide that indicates how search matches will work (for example, whether the case of characters in a text string should be ignored).

The meaning of many of the attributes—such as userPassword or postalCode—is clear from their names. Others are not so obvious, and Table 19.4 provides definitions for attributes that may need some further description. The attributes in the tables are just a core set described in standards documents. Many more attributes have been defined. For example, earlier, we saw that the entry information for the United States of America included an attribute named co whose values were user-friendly names for the country. The entry information for the University of Michigan included an attribute named internetDomain whose value was *umich.edu*.

Both the NetWare and Netscape directory products include dozens of additional attributes, and enable an administrator to add even more locally defined attributes.[16]

---

[16]Netscape has included useful attributes such as pager for a pager phone number, photo for a picture, and drink, which describes a person's favorite drink.

TABLE 19.3

Attributes for Frequently Used Object Classes

Object Class (Type of Entry)	Required Attributes	Optional Attributes
country	c	enhancedSearchGuide, description
locality		street, seeAlso, enhancedSearchGuide, st, l, description
organization	o	userPassword, enhancedSearchGuide, seeAlso, businessCategory, x121Address, registeredAddress, destinationIndicator, preferredDeliveryMethod, telexNumber, teletexTerminalIdentifier, telephoneNumber, internationaliSDN Number, facsimileTelephoneNumber, street, postOfficeBox, postalCode, postalAddress, physicalDeliveryOfficeName, st, l, description
organizationalUnit	ou	userPassword, enhancedSearchGuide, seeAlso, businessCategory, x121Address, registeredAddress, destinationIndicator, preferredDeliveryMethod, telexNumber, teletexTerminalIdentifier, telephoneNumber, internationaliSDN Number, facsimileTelephoneNumber, street, postOfficeBox, postalCode, postalAddress, physicalDeliveryOfficeName, st, l, description
person	cn, sn	userPassword, telephoneNumber, seeAlso, description
residentialPerson	l	businessCategory, x121Address, registeredAddress, destinationIndicator, preferredDeliveryMethod, telexNumber, teletexTerminalIdentifier, telephoneNumber, internationaliSDN Number, facsimileTelephoneNumber, preferredDeliveryMethod, street, postOfficeBox, postalCode, postalAddress, physicalDeliveryOfficeName, st, l
organizational Person		title, x121Address, registeredAddress, destinationIndicator, preferredDeliveryMethod, telexNumber, teletexTerminalIdentifier, telephoneNumber, internationaliSDNNumber, facsimileTelephoneNumber, street, postOfficeBox, postalCode, postalAddress, physicalDeliveryOfficeName, ou, st, l
organizationalRole	cn	x121Address, registeredAddress, destinationIndicator, preferredDeliveryMethod, telexNumber, teletexTerminalIdentifier, telephoneNumber, internationaliSDNNumber, facsimileTelephoneNumber, seeAlso, roleOccupant, preferredDeliveryMethod, street, postOfficeBox, postalCode, postalAddress, physicalDeliveryOfficeName, ou, st, l, description

TABLE 19.3

Attributes for
Frequently Used
Object Classes
(Continued)

Object Class (Type of Entry)	Required Attributes	Optional Attributes
groupOfNames	member, cn	businessCategory, seeAlso, owner, ou, o, description
groupOfUnique Names	unique Member, cn	businessCategory, seeAlso, owner, ou, o, description
applicationProcess	cn	seeAlso, ou, l, description
device	cn	serialNumber, seeAlso, owner, ou, o, l, description
alias	aliased Object Name	
dSA (Directory ServerAgent)	presentation Address, cn	supportedApplicationContext, seeAlso, ou, o, l, description, knowledgeInformation
dmd(Directory Management Domain)	dmdName	userPassword, searchGuide, seeAlso, business Category, x121Address, registeredAddress, destinationIndicator, preferredDeliveryMethod, telexNumber, teletexTerminalIdentifier, tele-phoneNumber, internationaliSDNNumber, fac-simileTelephoneNumber, street, postOfficeBox, postalCode, postalAddress, physicalDeliveryOff-iceName, st, l, description

TABLE 19.4

Attribute
Definitions

Attribute	Comment
c	Country name. A two-letter ISO 3166 country code.
st	The full name of a state or province.
o	Name of an organization.
ou	Name of an organizational unit.
businessCategory	Describes the kind of business performed by an organiza-tion.
cn	Common name, such as the complete name of a person.
givenName	"First" name (not middle or surname).
initials	The initials of some or all of an individuals names, but not the surname(s).

TABLE 19.4

Attribute	Comment
sn	Surname (family name) of a person.
generationQualifier	As in "John Jones IIIrd."
title	A person's organizational title, such as "President."
roleOccupant	Distinguished Name of the role occupant.
member	Distinguished Name of a member of a group.
uniqueMember	A Distinguished Name followed by a unique identifier.
owner	Distinguished Name of the owner.
seeAlso	The Distinguished Name of an entry that contains related information.
l	Locality, such as a city or county.
street	Street address, for example, for package delivery.
houseIdentifier	Used to identify a building within a location.
preferredDeliveryMethod	For example, electronic mail (mhs) or fax (g3fax).
registeredAddress	A postal address suitable for reception of telegrams or expedited documents, where it is necessary to have the recipient accept delivery.
x121Address	Used for X.25 calls.
destinationIndicator	Used for telegram delivery service.
description	A human-readable description of an object.
serialNumber	Serial number of a device.
dnQualifier	Information to add to the relative distinguished name of entries so that there will not be name conflicts between data from different sources that is to be merged.
enhancedSearchGuide	Provides guidance on how to perform value matching for searches. For example, the guide may state that case is irrelevant when matching text, or that it suffices to match a search term with a substring of a value.
aliasedObjectName	The real name of an entry that has an alias name.
dmdName	Directory Management Domain name; the name of the administrative authority that operates the directory.

Schema

The set of Object Classes and attributes that you decide to use in your directory defines your *schema*. Suppose that you discover that you have left something important out of your schema. Many directory products allow you to add new Object Classes to your schema without even stopping the directory.

Directory Structure

If you plan to build a directory for your organization, you will need to decide on an overall structure. Figure 19.9 shows a simple structure for a small company with only a single location.

Figure 19.10 shows a more complicated example for a company with divisions in Chicago, New York City, and Dayton. There are sales offices in Chicago and New York, whereas manufacturing and accounting are centered at the headquarters in Dayton, Ohio. The company plans to open sales offices in additional locations.

Directory structure rules describe:

- What Object Classes will be used.
- Parent/child relationships between structural Object Classes.

The rules for Figure 19.10 might be:

1. Entries whose Object Class is locality may be placed under organization.

Figure 19.9
A simple directory structure for a small company.

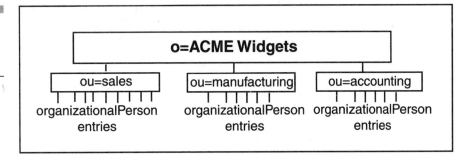

Figure 19.10
A directory structure
for a more complex
organization.

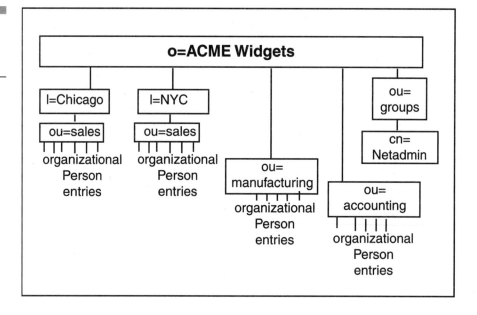

2. Entries whose Object Class is organizationalUnit may be placed under organization or locality.

3. Entries whose Object Class is organizationalPerson may be placed under organizationalUnit.

Note that the directory designer decided to include locality classes in the tree for the sales office locations, but attached manufacturing and accounting to the organization node. This might turn out to be a mistake. The directory tree will need to be reorganized if an additional manufacturing facility is opened up at a remote location. A conventional structure based on organizational units and localities works well for stable institutions (like universities). For volatile companies that reorganize themselves frequently, it may be better to use a flat directory organized by people and groups.

Object Class Hierarchy

A close look at the attributes for organizationalPerson in Table 19.3 shows that they do not include a couple of attributes that one would

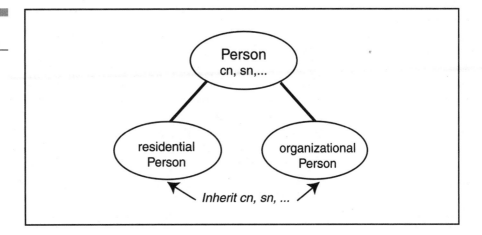

Figure 19.11
Inheriting attributes.

expect to see—for example, common name (cn), surname (sn), and user-Password. In fact, these *are* attributes of organizationalPerson; they are *inherited* from person. This is another shortcut that allows you to create an Object Class like person, and then define subclasses of person that inherit all of the attributes in person.[17] The inheritance relationship is illustrated in Figure 19.11.

Not all implementations support this inheritance shortcut. Some require you to list all of the required and optional attributes for each Object Class.

Structural and Auxiliary Object Classes

Every entry has a *structural* Object Class such as country, organization, or person. Additional attributes for an entry are defined in *auxiliary* Object Classes. An entry contains a special attribute (often hidden) that identifies its structural Object Class and lists all of its auxiliary Object

---

[17]For some strange reason, the defining RFC lists telephoneNumber for both person and organizationalPerson.

Classes. To make a confusing situation just a little more confusing, the name of this special attribute is objectClass. An example may shed some light on this.

The objectClass attribute was not displayed with the University of Michigan attributes that were displayed earlier. However, the original Web page that displayed these attributes contained a link labeled "See all attributes." The following shows the display for the objectClass attribute that appears:

Object Classes
    top
    organization (structural)
    domainRelatedObject
    quipuObject
    quipuNonLeafObject

We see that this entry contains attributes from five different Object Classes. The structural Object Class of this entry is organization. Auxiliary Object Classes include domainRelatedObject, quipuObject, and quipuNonLeafObject.[18]

The Object Class top is special. It contains exactly one attribute, the objectClass attribute. Since every class is a subclass of top, its objectClass attribute always is inherited, which is just another way of saying that all entries must contain an attribute that lists their Object Classes. (If this makes you dizzy, lie down.)

Administrative Attributes

Several more University of Michigan attributes appeared in the complete display, including:

Last Modified
    Wednesday, 06-Jan-93 18:28:00 GMT
Modified By
    manager

These are operational attributes that are useful for directory administration. Table 19.5 describes a set of operational attributes.

---

[18]Quipu is the name of an early implementation of the X.500 directory specification.

	Attribute	Description
TABLE 19.5 *Standard Operational Attributes*	creatorsName	Distinguished Name of the user who added the entry to the directory.
	createTimestamp	Time at which the entry was added to the directory.
	modifiersName	Distinguished Name of the user who last modified the entry.
	modifyTimestamp	Time of last modification.
	subschemaSubentry	Distinguished Name of the subschema entry or subentry in which this server specifies the attribute structure for the entry.

Authentication

Authentication is the process of validating a user's identity. Directory administrators need to be authenticated, as do end users who wish to access restricted information or update their own entries.

At the current time, no standard authentication method has been established for directories. Many different methods are in use today including:

- Userid (or Distinguished Name) and password sent in the clear.
- Userid (or Distinguished Name) sent in the clear followed by a challenge handshake.
- Some version of Kerberos.
- SSL.
- Guillou-Quisquater (GQ) zero-knowledge proof of identity signature scheme (used by NetWare Directory Service).

One or more bind requests and responses are used to execute an authentication process. If an SSL session to port 636 were used, then bind requests would not be needed, since the SSL security procedures would kick in automatically.

For some directory operations, simply validating identities at session start-up time is not enough. Authentication can be strengthened by attaching a digital signature to every request and response. In order to use digital signatures or SSL reliably, public key Certificates, Certificate Authorities (CAs), and Certificate Revocation Lists need to be integrated into a directory. Specifically, additional attributes and Object Classes are defined so that:

- Public key certificates may be stored in user entries.
- The directory may include an entry for the CA, and this entry would contain the CA's certificate.
- Certificate Revocation Lists may be stored in the directory.

Table 19.6 lists Object Classes that are used for security, and Table 19.7 describes a set of security attributes. The first two Object Classes are auxiliary classes that can be added to user entries (e.g., those that have structural class person or organizationalPerson). The strongAuthenticationUser class adds a certificate to an entry. The userSecurityInformation class attributes list the encryption and message digest algorithms that are supported.

The certificationAuthority auxiliary class adds the CA's certificate and revocation lists to a suitable entry. Alternatively, a separate entry of class cRLDistributionPoint could be used to hold revocation lists.

Cross-Certification

The crossCertificatePair attribute enables one CA to validate certificates issued by a different CA. For example, suppose Company A and Company B decide to cooperate on a project. Both companies use public keys and each has an internal CA that has signed its keys. How can these directories cooperate?

TABLE 19.6

Security Object Classes

Object Class (Type of Entry)	Required Attributes	Optional Attributes
strongAuthentication User (Auxiliary)	userCertificate	
userSecurityInformation (Auxiliary)		supportedAlgorithms
certificationAuthority (Auxiliary)	authorityRevocationList, certificateRevocationList, cACertificate	crossCertificatePair
certificationAuthority-V2 (Auxiliary)		deltaRevocationList
cRLDistributionPoint	cn	certificateRevocationList, authorityRevocationList, deltaRevocationList

TABLE 19.7

Security Attributes

Attribute	Comment
userPassword	Already included in earlier tables.
supportedAlgorithms	Algorithms for public keys, message digests, and symmetric encryption.
userCertificate	A public key certificate for a user.
cACertificate	Certificate for an accepted Certificate Authority.
authorityRevocationList	A timestamped list of all revoked certificates of other CAs that have been certified by this CA.
certificateRevocationList	A timestamped list of all certificates issued by this CA that have been revoked.
deltaRevocationList	A timestamped list containing certificates revoked since a given time.
crossCertificatePair	A pair of CA certificates, each signed by the partner CA.

- The CA for company A signs the certificate for Company B.
- The CA for company B signs the certificate for Company A.
- The two signed certificates form a *cross certificate pair*, which is stored in the entry for each local Certificate Authority.

If Jane Jones from Company A needs to be assigned an entry in the directory for Company B, her entry can contain her Company A certified public key. During authentication, the cross-certificate for Company A, which has been signed by the CA for Company B, is used to validate her identity.

Managing security information is the main function of some directories. Applications consult a security directory to check whether certificates presented by users are still valid.

Access Control Overview

Authentication tells you who a user is. Access control establishes exactly what information users can read or update. Directory access control has some traits in common with file access control.

File System Access Control	Directory System Access Control
An administrator can define privileges for a single file or directory, or for a directory and the tree of subdirectories under it.	An administrator can define privileges for a single entry or for an entry and the tree of subentries under it.
An administrator can control the right to read, write, or execute files, or view the tree structures of parts of the file system.	An administrator can control the right to read, write, or search entries, or view the tree structures of parts of the directory.

However, directory access control is a lot more granular than file system access control; selected attributes for a single entry, a tree of entries, or entries that satisfy a search filter can be blocked out or made visible.

Access Control Example

Every implementation performs access control a little differently. In order to get a sense of how access control information is added to a directory, let's take a brief look at the Netscape Directory Server access control scheme. By default, all users are denied access to a Netscape directory. Specific access permissions are then explicitly granted by writing access control information statements.[19] The statements that follow give a flavor of the types of permissions that might be set up:

- Allow anyone (including unauthenticated users) to search the directory and read common names, surnames, telephone numbers, and electronic mail addresses.

- Allow anyone who has been authenticated by a challenge handshake to search the directory and read any information except passwords.

- Allow a user who has been authenticated by a challenge password to modify the information in the user's own entry. However, this may be done only between 9 A.M. and 5 P.M. on Monday through Friday.

- Allow members of the network administration group who have been authenticated using public keys and certificates to modify

---

[19]Statements that deny access also can be written. Sometimes this will be done to place some restriction on another statement that opened up access.

information in any entry, and add, delete, and move entries. However, this may be done only if they access the directory from within the company's own network.

Access control information statements are stored in database entries. Netscape has defined an access control information (aci) attribute and has made it an optional attribute that is included in every Object Class. This means that access control information statements can be stored at any convenient point in the directory. Usually they are stored in organization, organizationalUnit, organizationalPerson, groupOfNames, or groupOfUniqueNames entries.

One way to set up access control is to:

- Place rules that apply to the whole organization in the organization entry.
- Place rules that apply to an organizational unit in its entry.
- Group users by privilege level, and store group permissions in the entry for the group.

Access Control Permissions

As the examples in the previous section illustrate, an access control information statement identifies:

- The scope of the data that the statement covers.
- Which operations on the data are to be allowed (or denied).
- The users or groups of users that are covered by the statement.
- The type of authentication required before a user is permitted to access the data.
- The time of day and day of the week.
- Permitted network addresses, subnet addresses, IP addresses, or domain names from which a user may operate.

Scope

The scope of the data covered by the access control instruction may be:

- The whole directory
- A specific entry

- A subtree
- Subtree entries that match a search filter

Access might be limited to a particular set of attributes within the scope. For example, one instruction might grant permission so that anyone can read telephone numbers and email addresses from any entry in a directory.

Netscape Operations for the Scope

Netscape operations include:

- Search the indicated scope. The attributes that can be used for searching may have been limited when the scope was described.
- Read data from an entry. There may be limits on the attributes that can be read from an entry located during a search.
- Write data. A user may change or add attribute values, or add and delete attributes.
- Compare.
- Selfwrite. That enables users to join a group or remove themselves from a group.
- Add entries.
- Delete entries.

Summary

This has been a complicated chapter, so it may help to review some of the main points.

- A directory is made up of a set of entries arranged in a tree structure.
- Each entry contains a set of attributes.
- Each attribute has a type and one or more values.
- Directory access control privileges can be controlled using an access control information attribute.
- Attributes are grouped into sets called Object Classes.

The Lightweight Directory Access Protocol provides a standard client/server interface to directories. LDAP enables users to search a directory. If appropriate, users may be allowed to update some of the attributes in their own entries. LDAP enables administrators to add, modify, and delete entries. The LDAP bind operation can be used to support a variety of authentication methods.

Recommended Reading

See RFC 2251 for more details about the Light Directory Access Protocol. RFCs 2252-2256 contain additional information, such as the LDAP URL format, attribute syntax, and directory schema.

Simple Network
Management Protocol

Introduction

Network management has been a slow runner, lagging far behind other network facilities. Very large TCP/IP networks have operated and functioned quite well, but administration and management of these networks has been a labor-intensive task, requiring experienced personnel with a high level of technical skill.

This especially has been the case for the Internet, with its ever-expanding size and complexity. In the late 1980s, the Internet Architecture Board (IAB), which is charged with setting technical policy for the Internet, concluded that there was a critical need to define a network management framework and set of protocol standards and to turn these into working tools as quickly as possible.

Although quite a lot of work had been carried out by OSI committees responsible for producing network management standards, there was no prospect for quickly translating their draft documents into tools that would fit TCP/IP management needs.

An Internet working group created the Simple Network Management Protocol (SNMP) to meet immediate TCP/IP needs. SNMP's architecture was designed with OSI's model in mind. It was believed that the OSI network management standards—Common Management Information Services/Common Management Information Protocol (CMIS/CMIP)—would be the long-term solution. However, within a few months, it was clear that SNMP needed to evolve independently and be shaped by the experience of implementers and the needs of network managers.

Results of IAB Adoption of SNMP

The initial SNMP specifications established a starting point. The IAB expected that changes and enhancements would evolve rapidly. As stated in RFC 1052, IAB Recommendations for the Development of Internet Network Management Standards:

> We will learn what [Inter]Network Management is by doing it.
> (a) in as large a scale as is possible
> (b) with as much diversity of implementation as possible
> (c) over as wide a range of protocol layers as possible
> (d) with as much administrative diversity as we can stand.

The results of the IAB policy have exceeded their expectations. Since the time that the SNMP specifications and sample source code were made available on the Internet, the protocol has been incorporated into thousands of products ranging from complex mainframe hosts to the simplest communications devices. The scope of SNMP has steadily been enlarged and strengthened.

Vendors have been able to create network management stations that use a well-defined protocol to communicate with a vast array of different devices. A thriving market was created in which vendors competed to enhance their management stations with features such as graphical user interfaces (GUIs), history databases, and report generation capabilities. The continuing production of a stream of RFCs devoted to network management is evidence of the dynamic expansion of the scope of the protocol.

Version 2 of SNMP was published early in 1996 and added some useful features to SNMP. Version 3, published in 1998, expanded the SNMP model and included much-desired security functionality.

SNMP MODEL

Logical Database

SNMP was designed with a database model. Every network system contains configuration, status, error, and performance information that network administrators would like to access. This information is viewed as being stored in a *logical database* at the system.

Agents

In order to make the information accessible a managed system must contain a software component called an *agent*. The agent responds to queries, performs updates, and reports problems. One or more *management stations* send query and update requests to agents and receive responses and problem messages.

Managers

As shown in Figure 20.1, a management station contains *manager* software that sends and receives SNMP messages and has a variety of *man-*

Figure 20.1
The SNMP model.

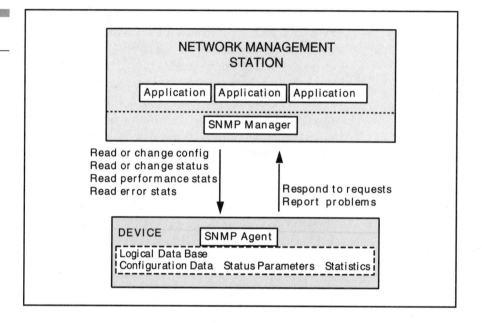

agement applications that communicate with network systems via the manager.

Management Information Base

The *Management Information Base* (MIB) is the logical description of all network management data. There are many RFC documents that describe MIB variables. Each document describes a MIB *Module,* which is a set of related variables. There also are additional MIB Modules written by vendors. Vendor MIB documents define product-specific variables.

A MIB variable definition does not deal with how the variable is stored; it includes:

- A definition of what a variable is
- A description of how its value is determined or measured
- A name to be used when reading or updating the variable's database value

Although the network management MIB formally is a set of definitions, it is convenient to call the specific data that is stored at a device its *MIB database*—or simply, its *MIB*. A typical MIB database contains:

- System and status information
- Performance statistics
- Configuration parameters

A system's MIB contains only those variables that make sense for the system. For example, a simple LAN bridge does not need variables that count TCP statistics.

Context

Many systems contain multiple devices that need to be managed. For example, a network switching device might include a switched Ethernet LAN, a switched Token-Ring LAN, and a WAN interface, and a single agent might be used to perform all SNMP functions for the device.

- Some variables, such as collision counts, make sense only for an Ethernet.
- Some variables, such as traffic counts, make sense for all of the technologies, but need to be broken out separately for each type of traffic.
- Some variables, such as a system identifier and the contact person for the system, are unique to the overall system.

The concept of a context makes sense of this jumble. A context is just some selected set of variables. The variables for Ethernet, Token-Ring, and WAN line each form a separate context. When a request message arrives, it must be handled within one context.

This is not hard to implement. In SNMP version 3, each context is assigned a name (the *contextName*). An SNMP message includes the name of the relevant context. Note that it is perfectly all right for a variable such as the system identifier to belong to all three contexts.

Roles of Managers and Agents

A network management application provides the user interface that enables an operator to invoke network management functions, view the status of components, and analyze data that has been extracted from network nodes.

A manager *supervises* a system by asking the system's agent to send back data values that are in its MIB database. Typical values in a MIB include the types of physical network interfaces that the system has and traffic counts for each interface.

A manager *controls* a system by asking its agent to update MIB status or configuration parameters. A parameter change can be tied to an action. For example, a network interface can be disabled by setting a status variable to *down*.

New supervision and control functions are defined by adding new variables to the MIB database.

An ever-increasing range of devices can be monitored from today's management stations. There are management station products that run on platforms ranging from PCs to mainframes. Some sections that follow include screens from an *HP OpenView for Windows Workgroup Node Manager,* which runs on a Windows 95 or NT PC.

Nature of Management Information

The definition of management *variables* was completely separated from the specification of the *protocol* used between managers and agents. This is an important feature of the management architecture.

The definition of variables is delegated to committees of experts for

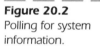

Figure 20.2
Polling for system
information.

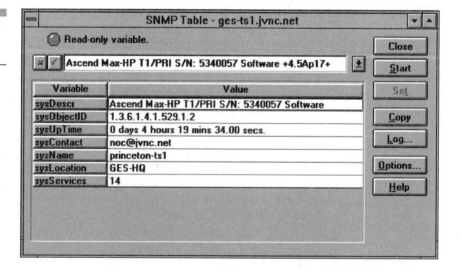

each technology. Separate groups have designed MIBs for bridges, hosts, telephony interfaces, and so on.

The first MIB document focused on information that would be useful in managing a TCP/IP network. It included data such as:

- What kind of system is this?
- What is its name and location?
- What types of network interfaces does the system have?
- How many frames, datagrams, and TCP segments has it sent and received?

For example, Figure 20.2 shows system information retrieved from a router using HP *OpenView*.

Structure of Management Information

A framework for defining network management variables needs to include:

- *An administrative structure.* The work of defining MIB variables for different types of network components is delegated to experts in the field. An administrative structure is needed to describe and track the partitioning of the work and delegation of authority.

- *An information structure.* Network information will not remain static. Information must be structured so that it is easy to extend or revise old technologies and add new ones.

- *A naming structure.* There will be hundreds of variables that will be defined for network management. We need a consistent method of defining, describing, and naming these variables.

A tree-structured framework meets all three requirements. The framework is called the *Structure of Management Information,* or *SMI.*

SMI Tree

Recall that initially, SNMP was supposed to be a temporary stopgap until ISO management standards were ready for use. The administra-

Figure 20.3
The SMI administra-
tive/naming tree.

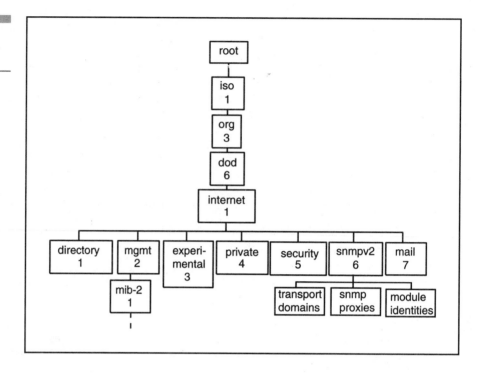

tive/naming tree, shown in Figure 20.3, reflects the initial effort to fit
into the ISO world.

The higher nodes in the tree were supposed to represent the administrative authorities responsible for the lower parts of the tree, as shown
in Table 20.1. The tree is administratively very out of date. There no
longer is an effort to coordinate SNMP standards with ISO. The Department of Defense (dod) no longer runs the Internet.

TABLE 20.1

Nodes in the SMI
Tree

Label	Description
iso (1)	International Standards Organization
org (3)	National and international organizations
dod (6)	Department of Defense
internet (1)	Internet Architecture Board

However, the tree still serves its primary function of defining MIB variable names. The tree is immensely useful. Whenever a new technology is added to the network management environment, a committee is created and is assigned a new branch in the tree. The committee then creates whatever variables are needed within its own subtree.

Object Identifier Names

Figure 20.4 focuses on the important parts of the tree. The tree is used to assign names called *OBJECT IDENTIFIER*s to management variables.

OBJECT IDENTIFIERs are formed by starting at the top of the tree and concatenating the numeric identifiers for each node. Each node also is assigned a text label, intended to help users and designers to understand what the variable is. For example:

OBJECT IDENTIFIER   **1 . 3 . 6 . 1 . 2 . 1 . 1 . 1**

Text Name   **iso.org.dod.internet.mgmt.mib-2.system.sysDescr**

Figure 20.4
Naming tree for MIB objects.

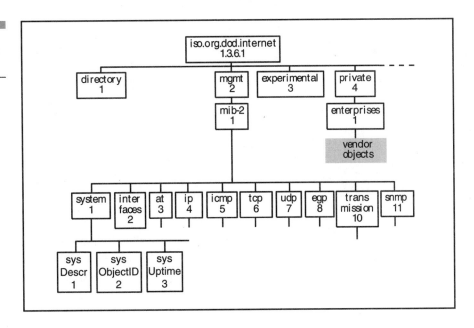

Identifying MIB Database Values

In order to identify an actual value at a device, a "which one" index is added at the end of the variable's OBJECT IDENTIFIER. For example, information about all of a device's interfaces is stored in a table. The OBJECT IDENTIFIER for the *ifType* table variable is 1.3.6.1.2.1.2.2.1.3. If we want to identify the *ifType* for the fourth interface on a router, its ID is:

1 . 3 . 6 . 1 . 2 . 1 . 2 . 2 . 1 . 3 . *4*

The convention of adding an index at the end is extended to one-of-a-kind variables, such as *sysDescr* or *sysUpTime*. A 0 is added at the end of one-of-a-kind variables. For example, the full identifier for a *sysDescr* variable is 1.3.6.1.2.1.1.1.*0*.

Lexicographic Order

The variables in a device's MIB are ordered *lexicographically* (like a dictionary). To compare two values:

1 . 3 . 6 . 1 . 2 . 1 . 2 . 2 . 1 . **19** . 3
1 . 3 . 6 . 1 . 2 . 1 . 2 . 2 . 1 . **21** . 2

- Start at the left.
- Compare until you find the first value that is different.
- The item with the bigger number in this position is the bigger item.

The second item above is bigger. What about the next example?

1 . 3 . 6 . 1 . 2 . 1 . 2 . 2 . 1
1 . 3 . 6 . 1 . 2 . 1 . 2 . 2 . 1 . 21 . 2

For this kind of tie, the longer identifier is bigger.

By the way, when traversing a table in lexicographic order, you would march all the way down one column and then jump to the top of the next column, as shown in Figure 20.5.

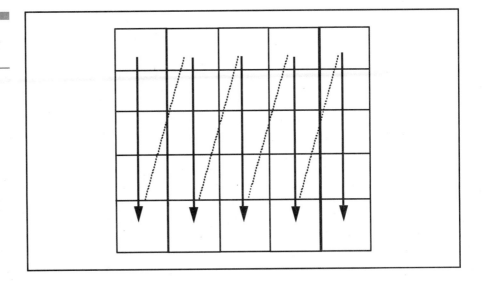

Figure 20.5
Lexicographic order
in a table.

Important MIB Modules

Dozens of MIB modules have been written, covering everything from RS-232 interfaces to electronic mail servers. We describe a few of the most important ones in the sections that follow.

MIB-II

The groups of variables shown in Figure 20.4 (*system, interfaces,* etc.) were defined in the first MIB document, which described variables relating to TCP/IP networking. After some testing and experience, the module was updated and called *MIB-II*. MIB-II provided the basic variable definitions for version 1 SNMP implementations. An update that includes some additional variables and a few modifications was published for version 2 of SNMP.

Transmission Modules

Many modules that describe variables relating to local and wide area technologies have been written. Some of the subtrees that have been

Figure 20.6
Transmission MIB
modules.

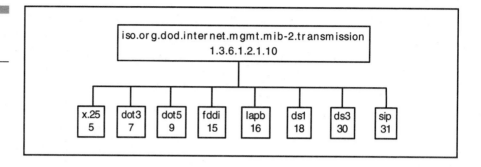

created under the *transmission* node are shown in Figure 20.6. See the
Internet Assigned Numbers Authority Web site for a complete list.

RMON MIB

A network *monitor* or *probe* is a device that passively watches link traffic
continuously. A monitor can be configured to gather data about the traffic,
revealing usage patterns and providing network performance statistics.

Monitors can be *configured* to watch for and report individual errors.
They can track numerous variables. They can report on which hosts are
most active, and create a matrix of client/server sessions. Most significantly, they can be configured with thresholds that are used to spot
problems before they become critical. Best of all, monitors work silently.
They do not add to the traffic load on their networks.

The *Remote Network Monitoring MIB* (RMON MIB) integrates the valuable information collected by monitors into the SNMP framework. This
gives a significant boost to the power of SNMP management stations.

A remote monitor can independently collect local data, carry out diag-
nostics, and detect alarm situations. Since problems will be reported as
they arise, a network management station can cut back on the frequency of its requests to read MIB data from individual devices. It could perform most of its oversight tasks by interacting with monitors, and only
communicate with an individual device when it has been diagnosed as
having a problem.

The nine data groups defined for the original RMON-1 MIB are
shown in Table 20.2. The original RMON-1 MIB collected information
about network activity at the link level. RMON-2 expanded the monitoring functionality to higher layers, including applications. Table 20.3
describes the RMON-2 groups.

TABLE 20.2

Groups of RMON-1
MIB Variables

Group	Description
statistics	Statistics specific to a given type of interface, such as Ethernet (collisions, jabbers) or Token-Ring (beacons, lost tokens).
history	Compiles statistics for a configured polling interval.
alarm	Generates an event if values for an interval exceed a configured threshold.
host	Reports hosts that have been detected by the monitor as well as related statistics, such as how many frames each sent.
hostTopN	Reports statistics for the hosts that top a list sorted on values for a selected performance or error statistic.
matrix	Reports statistics for conversations between pairs of MAC addresses.
filter	Defines criteria for selecting a particular set of frames for closer examination.
packet capture	Allows frames that match filter criteria to be captured.
event	Controls the generation and notification of events. An event may be caused by a local occurrence such as exceeding a threshold. An event can trigger a local activity such as writing a message to a log or initiating packet capture, or cause a trap message to be sent to a management station.

TABLE 20.3

Groups of RMON-2
MIB Variables

Group	Description
protocol directory	Lists the protocol types that the monitor is able to decode and count.
protocol distribution	Counts of bytes and packets for selected protocol types.
address mapping	Tabulates MAC address to network address translations discovered on each interface.
network layer host	Counts the sent and received bytes and packets for each network address. This is done for each selected network-layer protocol.
network layer matrix	Counts bytes and packets exchanged between pairs of network addresses. "Top N" entries can be selected based on some variable value.
application layer host	Counts the sent and received bytes and packets for a selected host and protocol.
application layer matrix	Counts bytes and packets exchanged between pairs of network addresses for a selected protocol. "Top N" entries can be selected based on some variable value.
user history	Collects statistics for specified variables for some number of time intervals. This provides data similar to periodic polling data, but without the message overhead.
probe configuration	Includes variables that describe probe characteristics and capabilities or control miscellaneous operating parameters.

Figure 20.7

Part of the Cabletron MIB.

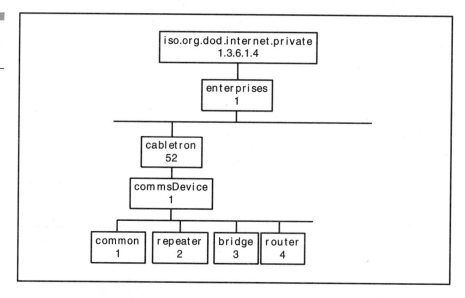

How Vendor MIBs Fit In

From the beginning, there was room in the object tree for vendor[1] MIB objects. To obtain a branch in the tree, a vendor simply registers with the Internet Assigned Numbers Authority (IANA).

Figure 20.7 shows part of the Cabletron MIB. Cabletron has been assigned OBJECT IDENTIFIER

1 . 3 . 6 . 1 . 4 . 1 . 52.

SNMP Message Protocols

Now let's look at the message protocol that enables managers to communicate with agents. There were a few principles that guided the design of SNMP:

■ Choose a very undemanding preferred transport but do not make the choice of transport an absolute—leave the choice open so that SNMP can be used on non-TCP/IP networks.

■ Use a very small number of message types.

---

[1]"Enterprises," such as companies, organizations, or government agencies, also can obtain tree identifiers and define their own MIB variables.

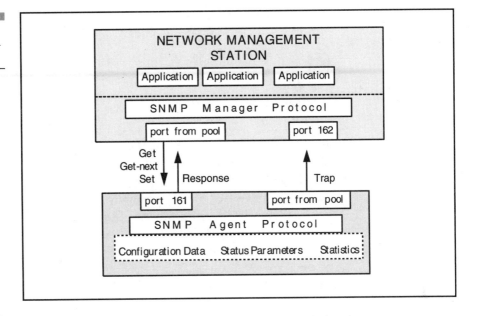

Figure 20.8
SNMP version 1 message types.

SNMP Version 1 Message Types

Managers and agents communicate with each other by sending SNMP messages. We examine the version 1 messages, because many current implementations still are based on version 1. As shown in Figure 20.8, there were only five message types for version 1 of SNMP:

get-request	Requests one or more values from a managed system's MIB.
get-next-request	Enables the manager to retrieve values sequentially; used to read through the rows of a table or to "walk" through an entire MIB.
set-request	Enables the manager to update variables.
get-response	Returns the results of a *get, get-next,* or *set* request operation (just called a *response* in version 2).
trap	Enables an agent to report important events or problems.

Limiting exchanges to these five message types kept the implementation simple, while still providing for plenty of functionality.

Typically, network administrators configure a management station to read statistics at regular periods—such as every 15 minutes. These values can be saved and analyzed in order to discover normal baseline behavior, detect peak hour bottlenecks, and spot unusual activities.

A *trap* is used to report general events such as:

- Reinitializing self
- Local-link failure
- Link functioning again

MIB standards committees have defined additional trap messages for specific communications technologies. In addition, vendors define traps that deliver critical problem information that relates to their products.

It is part of the SNMP philosophy that the number of *trap* messages that are transmitted should be kept relatively small. Network managers are familiar with the phenomenon that when one thing goes wrong, a lot of other problems get triggered. A flood of problem messages can clog the network, slowing down recovery procedures.

Transports

UDP was selected as the preferred transport because it is simple and can be implemented with very little code. It also is the choice most likely to work, even when a device is stressed or damaged. However, other transports can be used. For example, SNMP can be run over IPX in the NetWare environment.

When UDP is used, each SNMP message is enclosed within a single UDP datagram and is delivered via IP. As shown in Figure 20.8, requests are sent from any convenient UDP port to port 161. *Responses* are sent back to the requesting port. *Traps* are sent from any convenient UDP port to port 162.

Every version 1 implementation must be able to handle messages of at least 484 bytes.

SNMP Message Formats

An SNMP version 1 message consists of some introductory "wrapper" material followed by a message Protocol Data Unit, which is one of the five types, *get-request, get-next-request, get-response, set-request,* or *trap.* The version 1 introductory material also is used with version 2 and includes the:

Protocol version	0 for version 1 and 1 for version 2
Community name	Used like a password

An agent is configured to restrict what information can be accessed, and whether it can be read or written, based on the community name, which is used like a password. Agents also are configured with the IP addresses of the management stations that are permitted to read or write MIB information.

Unfortunately, LAN eavesdroppers can read the community name in a message, and IP source addresses can be forged. One solution is to access important devices, such as routers, via a separate, secured communications link when performing updates to a system's configuration or status.

Another solution is to use a Web interface to configure intelligent systems, such as routers, smart switches, and hosts. It has become routine for vendors to include a small Web server in their smart systems, and use a browser and Secure Sockets Layer (SSL) security to configure and administer the system.

Format of Version 1 *Gets, Sets,* and *Responses*

The main information content in all of these messages is the same. It consists of a list:

Variable name	Value[2]
Variable name	Value
...	...

OBJECT IDENTIFIERs are used as variable names. In a *get* or *get-next*, the value field is a null place holder. The agent just has to fill in the missing values.

A complete version 1 *get-request, get-next-request, set-request,* or *response* Protocol Data Unit consists of:

A request-id	Used to correlate requests with responses.
An error-status field	0 in requests. A non-0 value in a response means something went wrong.

---

[2]The pairing of a variable name and a value is formally called a *variable binding.*

An error-index field	0 in requests. In responses, it indicates which variable caused the problem.
List of object identifiers and values	In a *get* or *get-next,* the values are null. In a *set* or a *response,* the values are filled in.

Get Request and Response

The display below shows a Network General *Sniffer* analysis of a *get-request*. Note that SNMP version 1 messages have a Version field whose value is 0. The request includes a list of five variables whose values are desired. A "null" placeholder is included after each variable identifier.

```
SNMP: Version = 0
SNMP: Community = public
SNMP: Command = Get request
SNMP: Request ID = 112
SNMP: Error status = 0 (No error)
SNMP: Error index = 0
SNMP:
SNMP: Object = {1.3.6.1.2.1.1.3.0} (sysUpTime.0)
SNMP: Value  = NULL
SNMP:
SNMP: Object = {1.3.6.1.2.1.5.1.0} (icmpInMsgs.0)
SNMP: Value  = NULL
SNMP:
SNMP: Object = {1.3.6.1.2.1.5.2.0} (icmpInErrors.0)
SNMP: Value  = NULL
SNMP:
SNMP: Object = {1.3.6.1.2.1.5.3.0} (icmpInDestUnreachs.0)
SNMP: Value  = NULL
SNMP:
SNMP: Object = {1.3.6.1.2.1.5.4.0} (icmpInTimeExcds.0)
SNMP: Value  = NULL
```

To create a response, the agent just has to "fill in the blanks" and replace the nulls with actual values.

```
SNMP: Version = 0
SNMP: Community = public
SNMP: Command = Get response
SNMP: Request ID = 112
SNMP: Error status = 0 (No error)
SNMP: Error index = 0
SNMP:
SNMP: Object = {1.3.6.1.2.1.1.3.0} (sysUpTime.0)
SNMP: Value  = 1037388 hundredths of a second
SNMP:
SNMP: Object = {1.3.6.1.2.1.5.1.0} (icmpInMsgs.0)
SNMP: Value  = 1 messages
```

```
SNMP:
SNMP: Object = {1.3.6.1.2.1.5.2.0} (icmpInErrors.0)
SNMP: Value  = 0 messages
SNMP:
SNMP: Object = {1.3.6.1.2.1.5.3.0} (icmpInDestUnreachs.0)
SNMP: Value  = 0 messages
SNMP:
SNMP: Object = {1.3.6.1.2.1.5.4.0} (icmpInTimeExcds.0)
SNMP: Value  = 0 messages
```

Get-Next Request and Response

A *get-next* works differently. When you send an OBJECT IDENTIFIER, the *next* OBJECT IDENTIFIER and matching value are returned. For example, if you sent a *get-next* request with:

```
SNMP: Object = {1.3.6.1.2.1.5.1.0} (icmpInMsgs.0)
SNMP: Value  = NULL
```

The response would be the name and value for the next variable:

```
SNMP: Object = {1.3.6.1.2.1.5.2.0} (icmpInErrors.0)
SNMP: Value  = 0 messages
```

This enables you to "walk" through a MIB or move from row to row of a table.

Set Request

A *set* request writes data into an agent's database. The message format is very simple—it looks just like a *get-request,* except that the actual update values are filled in. The request below sets *ipForwarding* to 2 which means that the system is not allowed to route datagrams. The default Time-To-Live for datagrams sent from this system is set to 70 hops.

```
SNMP: Version = 0
SNMP: Community = xyz
SNMP: Command = Set request
SNMP: Request ID = 0
SNMP: Error status = 0 (No error)
SNMP: Error index = 0
SNMP:
SNMP: Object = {1.3.6.1.2.1.4.1.0}      (ipForwarding.0)
SNMP: Value  = 2
SNMP: Object = {1.3.6.1.2.1.4.2.0}      (ipDefaultTTL.0)
SNMP: Value  = 70
```

All updates must succeed or else the whole request will fail. This makes sense because there often will be several variables that ought to be changed together or not at all. This all-or-nothing rule for *sets* is kept in version 2.

The response to a *set* looks just like the request, except that the error-status and error-index fields will be given nonzero values if there was a problem.

Trap Messages

An agent uses *trap* messages to report serious problems to a manager. Very few traps were defined in the SNMP standard. The definition of additional traps is left to technology standards committees and vendors—with a warning to keep the number down. When the network is stressed, you do not want to get dozens of messages from every device on the network, complaining about its problems.

Version 1 traps were slightly more complicated than they needed to be. Version 2 got it right. Let's look at the version 1 *trap* message first. There is a field called *generic trap* whose value identifies the type of trap as one of the following:

coldStart(0)	The sender is reinitializing, and its configuration may change.
warmStart(1)	The sender is reinitializing, but its configuration will not change.
linkDown(2)	An adjacent link has failed.
linkUp(3)	An adjacent link has come up.
authentication Failure(4)	Someone has sent the agent a request that was not properly authenticated (i.e., the message had an inappropriate community name).
egpNeighbor Loss(5)	An Exterior Gateway Protocol neighbor is down.
enterprise Specific(6)	Other. This is a trap defined by a standards committee, a vendor, or some other enterprise.

The display below shows a very simple version 1 *trap* message that reports a cold start.

- The *enterprise* field indicates that this trap was sent by a system running FTP Software's TCP/IP product.

- Since the *generic trap* value is 0, this message reports a cold start.

- The *time ticks* field contains the *sysUpTime,* which is 0 because this system just made a cold start initialization.

```
SNMP: Version = 0
SNMP: Community = public
SNMP: Command = Trap
SNMP: Enterprise = {1.3.6.1.4.1.121.1.1}
SNMP: Network address = [198.207.177.10]
SNMP: Generic trap = 0 (Cold start)
SNMP: Specific trap = 0
SNMP: Time ticks = 0
```

Any version 1 trap that was defined by a MIB committee or vendors will have *generic trap* = 6. In this case, the *enterprise* field combined with the *specific trap* field tells you what the trap is all about.

If this seems too complicated, you are right. Traps are simplified in version 2.

Version 1 Problems and Version 2 Corrections

There were some features of SNMP version 1 that were irritating:

- If just one variable in a *get* or *get-next* request was not in the agent's database, the entire operation failed.
- If a *request* asked for several variables, and the agent could not fit the entire answer into the biggest message that it was able to send, the entire operation failed.
- *Traps* performed a simple function but were hard to describe.

Version 2 solved these problems. An agent can put an error code into the *value* field for a variable that cannot be retrieved. There is a *get-bulk* request that asks the agent to return as much of the requested information as it can. And *trap* messages are given the same simple format as all of the other messages.

Version 2 also expanded the list of error codes that are supported, which gives managers a better idea of what has gone wrong when a request fails.

Version 2 Get-Bulk Message

A *get-bulk* message says "Here is what I want. Give me as much of it as you can." Like *get-next, get-bulk* asks for variables whose OBJECT

IDENTIFIERs follow the OBJECT IDENTIFIERs in the request. However, a simple trick allows you to ask for a variable directly by omitting the "which one" number at the end of an identifier. For example, a normal *get* asks for the system description (*sysDescr*) via *OBJECT IDENTIFIER 1.3.6.1.2.1.1.1.0. A get-bulk* obtains the system description by asking for 1.3.6.1.2.1.1.1. This works because the response is the value of the "next" variable, which is defined to be the completed string, 1.3.6.1.2.1.1.1.0.

If you omit the final "which one" number from the OBJECT IDENTIFIERS of the variables in a table, *get-bulk* will start retrieving values at row one of the table.

A *get-bulk* request has parameters that indicate:

■ The number of initial stand-alone (nonrepeater) variables requested

■ For the remaining (repeater) variables, the number of repeats requested

For example, you might ask for the two nonrepeater stand-alone variables:

sysDescr

sysUpTime

and then ask for 10 rows of the table variables: *ifIndex, ifDescr, ifType, ifMTU,* and *ifSpeed.* In this case:

■ There would be seven variables in the variable list.

■ Nonrepeaters = 2.

■ Max-repetitions = 10.

The response will pack in as much of the requested information as it can. If it can't hold everything, it is easy for an application to send another *get-bulk* to ask for more.

Since the error-status and error-index fields really serve no function in requests, they are commandeered in the *get-bulk* request to hold the *nonrepeaters* and *max-repetitions* parameters. This means that the basic message format does not have to be changed at all to accommodate *get-bulk.*

Version 2 Traps

In version 2, a *trap* has the same format as a response. It starts with the standard header information, followed by a variable list:

```
OBJECT IDENTIFIER      Value
  . . .                 . . .
  . . .                 . . .
```

The *sysUpTime* and a unique trap identifier are moved to the head of the variable list. Additional variables that shed light on the problem can be included.

Version 2 Inform Messages

Version 2 also added the idea of *inform* messages, which simply are acknowledged *traps*. These are very handy for manager-to-manager or monitor-to-manager communications, in situations where the sender really wants to know that the destination manager received the message. An ordinary response message is used as the acknowledgment.

Other Version 2 Enhancements

How precisely does the implementation of a module have to match its MIB definition in order for a vendor to claim compliance? And how can a vendor declare departures from the specification that may have been necessary because of some product limitation?

Version 2 provides the mechanisms for expressing:

- *Compliance statements:*   The actual minimum requirements for a module
- *Capability statements:*   Vendor-provided statements that describe the actual capabilities of an agent

These statements enable a customer to look further than the claim "we support SNMP" when evaluating a product.

Reading MIB Documents

The documents that define MIB variables contain a lot of extremely useful information. They describe exactly how each variable is defined and measured. Often there is extensive additional material that describes the technology, error conditions, and typical configurations.

In the sections that follow, we discuss some concepts that should be helpful in reading MIBs.

Managed Objects

Up to this point, we have used the informal term, *MIB variable*. But MIB standards actually define *Managed Objects*. A variable just has a name and a value, but the definition of a Managed Object includes:

- A name—the OBJECT IDENTIFIER
- A set of attributes, including:
  1. A datatype
  2. A description providing implementation details
  3. Status information
- A list of operations that can be performed on the object

Let's look at a typical MIB definition:[3]

```
sysDescr OBJECT-TYPE
    SYNTAX       DisplayString (SIZE (0..255))
    MAX-ACCESS   read-only
    STATUS       current
    DESCRIPTION
            "A textual description of the entity. This value should
            include the full name and version identification of the
            system's hardware type, software operating-system, and
            networking software."
    ::= { system 1 }
```

The definition starts with the text label for the node, *sysDescr.* It ends with { *system 1* }, which means "put this node under *system* and assign the number 1 to the node." This allows us to construct the complete OBJECT IDENTIFIER, which is:

1.3.6.1.2.1.1.1

The rest of the definition consists of a series of *clauses*—SYNTAX, MAX-ACCESS, STATUS, and DESCRIPTION.

In this case, the *SYNTAX* (datatype) is a display string, that is, a string of printable characters, at most 255 characters in length.

The *MAX-ACCESS* identifies the operation(s) that may be performed. In this case, the MAX-ACCESS is read-only, so a manager may only read the value.

---

[3]This is the version 2 definition format.

In early MIB documents, the *STATUS* could be *mandatory, optional, obsolete,* or *deprecated.* However, values of mandatory and optional were not useful. Newer MIBs do not include variables unimportant enough to be labeled optional. STATUS now is used to indicate whether a variable is *current, deprecated* (on the way out), or *obsolete.*

Abstract Syntax Notation 1

MIB definitions like the one shown previously are written in Abstract Syntax Notation 1 (ASN.1), the ISO message description language that was used to define the LDAP messages in Chapter 19. The Basic Encoding Rules (BER) mentioned in Chapter 19 also define the transmission format for values defined using ASN.1.

A management station learns MIB variables by *compiling* ASN.1 MIB definitions. Good management stations allow you to compile as many MIBs as you need.

A management station then is ready to send and receive SNMP messages that include any of the compiled variables. A well-designed station also can display variable descriptions. Figure 20.9 shows how HP *OpenView* displays the DESCRIPTION clause in the *sysDescr* definition.

Figure 20.9
Manager display of a variable's description.

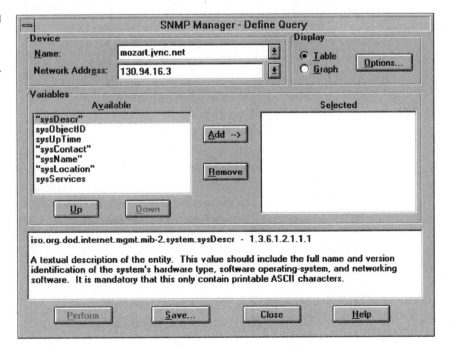

MIB Datatypes

One reason that SNMP has been implemented widely is that the designers stuck to a "Keep It Simple" rule:

- All MIB data consists of simple scalar variables, although parts of a MIB may be *logically* organized into a table.
- Only a few datatypes—such as integers and octet strings—were used to express the values of MIB variables.

In fact, the underlying datatypes are INTEGER, OCTET STRING, and OBJECT IDENTIFIER.

Integers

Integers are used in two ways:

- To state "how many" of some item
- To enumerate a list of possibilities, such as 1 = up, 2 = down, 3 = testing

The definitions that follow illustrate the use of these datatypes. Note that in the first definition, the SYNTAX statement restricts the range of values.

```
tcpConnLocalPort OBJECT-TYPE
    SYNTAX      INTEGER (0..65535)
    MAX-ACCESS  read-only
    STATUS      current
    DESCRIPTION
            "The local port number for this TCP connection."
    ::= { tcpConnEntry 3 }

ifAdminStatus OBJECT-TYPE
    SYNTAX  INTEGER {
                up(1),      -- ready to pass packets
                down(2),
                testing(3) -- in some test mode
            }
    MAX-ACCESS  read-write
    STATUS      current
    DESCRIPTION
            "The desired state of the interface. The testing(3)
            state indicates that no operational packets can be
            passed. When a managed system initializes, all
            interfaces start with ifAdminStatus in the down(2)
            state. As a result of either explicit management
            action or per configuration information retained by
```

```
                              the managed system, ifAdminStatus is then changed to
                              either the up(1) or testing(3) states (or remains in
                              the down(2) state)."
                  :: = { ifEntry 7 }
```

Counters

A *counter* is a nonnegative integer that increases to a maximum value and then wraps around. Specifically, a 32-bit counter can increase to $2^{32} - 1$ (4,294,967,295) and then wraps around to 0. Version 2 adds a 64-bit counter that can increase to 18,446,744,073,709,551,615 before wrapping.

A single counter value has no intrinsic value. Counters are polled, and their current values are compared with their previous values. *Differences* in the readings are what matter. An example of a counter variable is:

```
ifInOctets OBJECT-TYPE
        SYNTAX        Counter32
        MAX-ACCESS    read-only
        STATUS        current
        DESCRIPTION
              "The total number of octets received on the interface,
              including framing characters.

              Discontinuities in the value of this counter can occur
              at re-initialization of the management system, and at
              other times as indicated by the value of
              ifCounterDiscontinuityTime."
        :: =  { ifEntry 10 }
```

Gauges

A *gauge* is an integer that behaves in quite a different manner. Gauge values go up and down. Gauges are used for quantities such as queue lengths. Sometimes the value builds up and sometimes it decreases.

A 32-bit gauge can increase to $2^{32} - 1$ (4,294,967,295). If the quantity that it is measuring goes higher than this, the gauge just has to "latch" at the maximum until the value comes down again, as shown in Figure 20.10. An example of a gauge variable is:

```
ifOutQLen OBJECT-TYPE
        SYNTAX        Gauge32
        MAX-ACCESS    read-only
        STATUS        deprecated
        DESCRIPTION
              "The length of the output packet queue (in packets)."
        :: =  { ifEntry 21 }
```

Figure 20.10
Behavior of gauge
values.

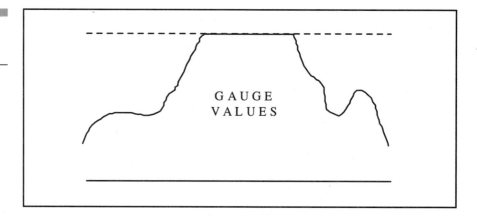

Note that this definition is "deprecated," which means that its use is on the way out.

TimeTicks

Time intervals are measured in *TimeTicks,* which measure time in hundredths of a second. A TimeTick value is a nonnegative integer ranging from 1 to $2^{32} - 1$ (4,294,967,295). It takes over 497 days to exhaust a TimeTick counter.

The *sysUptime,* which measures the time elapsed since the agent software initialized, is the most frequently used TimeTick variable.

```
sysUpTime OBJECT-TYPE
    SYNTAX      TimeTicks
    MAX-ACCESS  read-only
    STATUS      current
    DESCRIPTION
        "The time (in hundredths of a second) since the network
        management portion of the system was last re-initialized."
    ::= { system 3 }
```

OCTET STRINGs

An OCTET STRING is just a sequence of bytes. Just about anything can be represented by an OCTET STRING.

Textual Conventions

Rather than define a lot more datatypes, *Textual Conventions* are used in MIB definitions to indicate what kind of information is packaged in an OCTET STRING value and how the information should be displayed to users.

A type that is defined using a Textual Convention is encoded for transmission as a plain OCTET STRING. However, its actual meaning is determined from the Textual Convention definition. There is a MIB template that is used to define Textual Conventions. Here is the definition of *MacAddress:*

```
MacAddress :: = TEXTUAL-CONVENTION
    DISPLAY-HINT  "1x:"
    STATUS        current
    DESCRIPTION
         "Represents an 802 MAC address represented in the
         `canonical' order defined by IEEE 802.1a, i.e., as if it
         were transmitted least significant bit first, even though
         802.5 (in contrast to other 802.x protocols) requires MAC
         addresses to be transmitted most significant bit first."
    SYNTAXOCTET   STRING (SIZE (6))
```

Keep in mind that in a message, a value always is introduced by an OBJECT IDENTIFIER. A management station application could use the MIB definition that corresponds to that identifier and the Textual Convention definition to decide how to display, store, and use an OCTET STRING value.

BER Encoding of Datatypes

Along with the ASN.1 datatype definition language, ISO defined a set of *Basic Encoding Rules (BERs)* that can be used to encode data values for transmission. The BER encoding for a data value has the form:

[*identifier*] [*length (of contents)*] [*contents*]

For example, the identifier X'02 is used for an INTEGER, X'04 is used for an OCTET STRING, and X'06 is used for an OBJECT IDENTIFIER.

An entire SNMP message actually is a sequence of ASN.1 values, and each message is entirely encoded using BER.[4]

SNMP Version 3

The most important piece of work that was left undone in the version 2 update of SNMP was the provision of authentication and encryption standards so that devices could safely be configured remotely. Version 3 adds significant security capability to SNMP:

- Messages can be authenticated.
- Messages can be encrypted.
- Data can be protected by access control mechanisms.

Version 3 recognizes that there are three major SNMP roles:

- *Manager:* A manager sends requests and receives responses and notification messages.
- *Agent:* An agent responds to requests and sends notification messages.
- *Midlevel Manager:* A midlevel manager acts as a manager for some agents. A midlevel manager plays an agent role with respect to higher-level managers, responding to their requests and sending notification messages.

Proxies

There also is a fourth minor role. A proxy SNMP entity acts as a message relay point. The proxy forwards messages between managers and agents or managers and managers.

The concept of a proxy was introduced in the initial version of SNMP. A version 1 proxy was a go-between that could receive requests from a management station, extract and process information from local computers—possibly using a proprietary management protocol, and then

---

[4]BER optionally allows composite datatypes to have a code meaning "indefinite" in the length field. This means that the total length has to be computed by adding up the lengths of all of the parts. Indefinite lengths are not used when encoding SNMP messages.

return SNMP responses to the original requestor. Version 2 of SNMP shrank the role of proxies; they were to be used to relay information between version 1 and version 2 environments. In version 3, a proxy is just an application that relays SNMP requests and responses between sources and destinations.

Version 3 Model

Version 3 introduces a new architectural model for SNMP (shown in Figure 20.11). The new architecture recognizes that there is a lot of functionality that managers, agents, midlevel managers, and proxies all share in common. This became especially evident when authentication and encryption functions were added to SNMP; all parties need the ability to:

- Create messages that contain authentication information, and validate incoming authenticated messages.
- Create messages that contain encrypted data, and decrypt incoming encrypted messages.

Figure 20.11
The SNMP version 3 model.

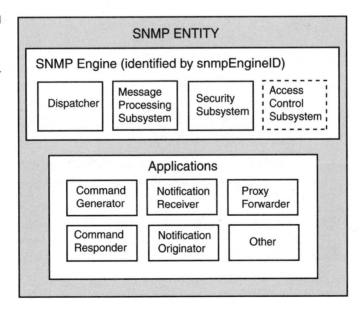

The common components of any SNMP entity are:

- Dispatcher
- Message Processing Subsystem
- Security Subsystem

A fourth basic component is built into agents:

- Access Control Subsystem

An "SNMP engine" is made up of these components. An SNMP entity is created by adding "application components" to the engine. For example, add a command generator and notification receiver to the common components, and you have a manager. Alternatively, include access control and add a command responder and a notification generator, and you have an agent. Combine all of these pieces, and you have a midlevel manager. A vendor might want to build a device that participates in SNMP only by sending trap notifications. Another vendor might want to build a system that only receives and reports notifications. With the Tinkertoy approach, any level of functionality can be created.

The version 3 model opens up SNMP in important ways. Old applications can be modified and improved. New applications can be added. Methods for providing security and access control can be improved, or new methods can be added.

Version 3 Message Processing Subsystem

The message processing subsystem:

- Formats outgoing messages, interacting with the security subsystem as needed to include authentication information or encrypt the contents.
- Extracts data from incoming messages, interacting with the security subsystem as needed to check authentication information or decrypt the contents.

Inevitably, having multiple incompatible versions of a protocol means that real-world engines will support multiple versions. A message processing subsystem can include separate modules for handling version 1, 2, and 3 messages.

Figure 20.12
Relationship of the
dispatcher to other
components.

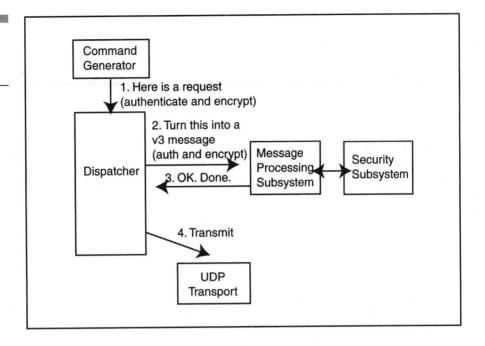

Version 3 Dispatcher

The dispatcher is the engine's coordinator and is at the center of all message-processing activities. For example (as shown in Figure 20.12), a command generator passes a request to the dispatcher. The dispatcher passes the request data to the appropriate message-processing module that formats the message and returns the result to the dispatcher. The dispatcher selects a transport and transmits the message onto the network.

The dispatcher coordinates all of the functions performed on incoming messages in a similar manner.

Version 3 Application Components

As we have seen, in the version 3 model, the functions performed by an SNMP entity are split among several "applications." Applications play the roles of command generators, command responders, notification originators, notification receivers, and proxy forwarders.

- A command generator application initiates SNMP Get, GetNext, GetBulk, and/or Set requests, and processes the responses to these requests.

- A command responder receives and answers SNMP get, get-next, get-bulk, and/or set requests.

- A notification originator monitors a system for events or conditions and generates Trap and/or Inform messages. These are sent to notification receivers at preconfigured management systems.

- A notification receiver listens for notification messages and generates an acknowledging response message when it receives an Inform PDU.

- A proxy forwarder is an optional application that acts as a go-between, forwarding SNMP messages. Much early confusion about the role of a proxy is solved by making it an application.

Opening Up SNMP

Version 3 opens up SNMP to experimentation with new features and alternative ways of implementing network management functionality by establishing an architecture that can live with diversity.

The ability to install new message-handling applications at a node is an important architectural idea. Each application registers with the Dispatcher and identifies the types of messages that it will process.

Security

It was hoped that version 2 of SNMP would provide security services. The "right" way to implement security was a contentious issue and was not resolved. As a result, security capabilities were not added to the version 2 standard.

One reason that is was so hard to add security to network management is that it is impossible to be sure that any single security scheme will work forever. Version 3 works around the problem by allowing for the existence of multiple security models and mechanisms.

The new SNMPv3 message header data contains a parameter that identifies the security model that was used by the sender. Of course, the receiver must be able to use the same security model to process the message.

Security Goals

The primary security goals of SNMP version 3 are the ability to:

- Verify that an SNMP message has not been modified in transit.
- Authenticate the identity of the user who initiated the generation of the message.
- Detect that a message is old and stale (and protect against replay).
- Encrypt contents when needed.

An organization can choose the level of security that it needs for various management functions. An SNMP message may be sent:

- Without authentication or privacy
- With authentication alone
- With both authentication and privacy

There is one simple security rule that does not require any complicated mechanisms; responses that do not match any outstanding request are dropped immediately.

User-Based Security Model

The first security model that has been proposed is called the *User-Based Security Model*. This model enables network administrators to interact securely with a large number of devices after entering a username and one or two passwords.

The current version of user-based security uses message digests for authentication (HMAC-MD5-96 or HMAC-SHA-96). Recall that these are implemented by combining a secret authentication key with message data and then computing a message digest on the result. Symmetric encryption (CBC-DES) is used for privacy.

These specific mechanisms are "drop-in" modules and can be replaced or supplemented with other methods in the future. However, starting out with specific security protocols enables implementations to inter-work with one another.

Local Keys

User-based security controls access to network devices by means of administrator usernames and simple passwords. One password is used for an authentication key. If encryption is needed, a second password is used for an encryption key.

However, a single administrator may manage hundreds or thousands of network devices. Storage of the same passwords at every managed system is very bad security practice. Fortunately, a simple and inge-nious solution called "local keys" has been devised. A user's authentica-tion or encryption password is turned into a different key for each device. To make this work, every SNMP engine is required to have a unique snmpEngineID. After an engine ID has been assigned, a local key can be computed:

- First, a user password is mapped to an intermediate key by means of an algorithm that scrambles its bits via repeated appli-cation of a message digest function.[5]

- The local key is computed by combining the intermediate key with the snmpEngineID and then computing a message digest on the result.

The engine identifiers can be stored at a management station, which then can turn a user password into dozens, hundreds, or thousands of different keys to be used to access systems on the network. When a sys-tem initially is set up, it needs to be manually configured with one user-name and a pair of local keys.[6] Subsequently, encrypted *set* messages can be used to add new usernames and keys, or to change a key after the corresponding password has been updated.

---

[5]The exact algorithm is described in RFC 2274.

[6]The same key could be used for authentication and encryption, but separate keys are safer.

Access Control

The purpose of access control is to restrict:

- Who can access management data
- Which data can be accessed
- What can be done with the data (read it, update it, include it in notification messages)
- The security level required for the access

The current access control model is called *view-based* control.[7] A look at computer access control lists may help us to understand the view-based control model. Computer access control lists are a popular way to control access to computer data:

- Groups of users are defined.
- A group will have read access to certain files and write or execute access to others.

Security-conscious administrators add controls that restrict access depending on whether a user has provided weak authentication, strong authentication, or is communicating via an authenticated, encrypted session.

When protecting a computer file system, access control often is applied to a set of directory trees. SNMP access control is applied to a *MIB view,* which consists of one or more MIB subtrees. Choosing a set of subtrees (such as *system, interface, transmission,* and *IP*) is not so different from choosing a set of file directories.

However, SNMP access control is a little different from computer access control. When an agent receives a request from a username—or needs to send a notification on behalf of a configured username—the agent wants to find out the privileges for that username right away. SNMP access rights are configured according to:

- The context (which is identified in the request message)
- Group membership (a group is a list of usernames)[8]

---

[7]Recall that other models can be introduced at any time.

[8]Since we cannot assume that the user-based security model will always be the only one that is used, the definition of a group actually has been broadened so that it is a set of *<securityModel, securityName>* pairings.

- Security level (unauthenticated, authenticated, or authenticated and encrypted)

Each combination of the above is assigned a read-view, write-view, and notify-view. Now the agent's job is easy. The agent:

- Extracts the context name and the username from a request
- Looks up the group memberships for the username
- Checks the message security level that is required

The agent retrieves the corresponding view information and can quickly determine which variables can be read, written, or placed in notifications.

Security Message Formats

Overall Message Formats

The new format that has been proposed for SNMPv3 messages is shown below:

```
SNMPv3Message ::= SEQUENCE {
        msgVersion INTEGER { snmpv3 (3) },
        msgGlobalData HeaderData, — administrative parameters
        msgSecurityParameters OCTET STRING,
        msgData ScopedPduData
    }
```

The sections that follow describe the components of the message.

Global Header Data

The global header data component is defined as:

```
HeaderData : := SEQUENCE {
        msgID       INTEGER (0..2147483647),
        msgMaxSize INTEGER (484..2147483647),

        msgFlags   OCTET STRING (SIZE(1)),
            -- .... ...1   authFlag
            -- .... ..1.   privFlag
            -- .... .1..   reportableFlag
            --             Please observe:
            -- .... ..00   is OK, means noAuthNoPriv
```

```
-- .... ..01    is OK, means authNoPriv
-- .... ..10    reserved, must NOT be used.
-- .... ..11    is OK, means authPriv

msgSecurityModel INTEGER (0..2147483647)- Security Model to be used
    }
```

The *msgMaxSize* field announces the biggest incoming message size that this sender can accept. The preceding *msgSecurityModel* field identifies the security model used by the sender. The message needs to be processed using this model.

Message Data

The message data is either a cleartext "scoped protocol data unit" or an encrypted unit. A cleartext message has the form:

```
ScopedPDU :: = SEQUENCE {
        contextEngineID   OCTET STRING,
        contextName       OCTET STRING,
        data              ANY - e.g., PDUs as defined in RFC1905
    }
```

Recall that the context name identifies a set of variable values that may correspond to a specific device, to an application, or to any other object that makes sense to network management administrators.

Security Parameters and the Authoritative Partner

The security parameters that are included in messages when the User Security Model is implemented are:

```
UsmSecurityParameters :: =
        SEQUENCE {
        -- global User-based security parameters
          msgAuthoritativeEngineID    OCTET STRING,
          msgAuthoritativeEngineBoots   INTEGER (0..2147483647),
          msgAuthoritativeEngineTime    INTEGER (0..2147483647),
          msgUserName OCTET STRING      (SIZE(1..32)),
        -- authentication protocol specific parameters
          msgAuthenticationParameters   OCTET STRING,
        -- privacy protocol specific parameters
          msgPrivacyParameters          OCTET STRING
    }
```

Note the use of the term "authoritative" in the first three parameters. One of the partners in a message transfer is authoritative:

- For a request/response interaction, the receiver of the request (who also is the sender of the response) is authoritative.

- The sender of a message that does not require a response (SNMPv2-Trap or Report) is authoritative.

Two time values (*msgAuthoritativeEngineBoots* and *msgAuthoritativeEngineTime*) are included in an authenticated message. These values are used to detect replayed messages. The time values in an authenticated message have to be close to the authoritative partner's current time values.

The *msgUserName* parameter is important. A request is made on behalf of an identified username. The secret keys used for authentication and encryption are part of the user information stored at the sending and receiving system.

The content of the authentication and privacy parameters fields identifies the security mechanisms that are used, and includes other values that depend on the specific mechanisms. Currently, message digests are used for authentication, and so the message digest computed on the message and the secret key would be included.

Checking the Timeliness of V3 Messages

It only makes sense to check the timeliness for authenticated messages. Timestamps can be forged in nonauthenticated messages, but it is not possible to change the timestamp in an authenticated message without detection.

The two time parameters introduced in the previous section are used to check whether a message is stale.

- *snmpEngineBoots:* The number of times that the SNMP engine has reinitialized itself since its initial configuration.

- *snmpEngineTime:* The number of seconds since the SNMP engine last incremented *snmpEngineBoots*.

We are interested in the time at only one side of a message transfer—the "authoritative" side. The nonauthoritative partner has to find out the authoritative partner's time setting, and occasionally resynchronize with it.

The time at the authoritative partner can be discovered and synchronized by sending an authenticated message with the time parameter fields set to 0. The response will report the current time values.

Thereafter, to be valid, the time in a message must be within 150 seconds (plus or minus) of the authoritative partner's time.

Recommended Reading

There is a long and growing list of RFCs dealing with SNMP and MIBs. The RFC archive should be consulted for the most recent versions of these documents.

CHAPTER 21

The Socket
Programming
Interface

Introduction

Communications standards define all of the rules needed to exchange data across a network. However, until recently, the need to standardize Application Programming Interfaces (APIs) for communication has been ignored. How can a programmer write a client/server application if the programs are completely different on every computer?

Berkeley Programming Interface

Fortunately, most TCP/IP implementations offer a programming interface that follows a single model, the *socket programming interface*. The socket programming interface was first introduced with the 1982 4.1c Berkeley Software Distribution (BSD) version of the Unix operating system. A number of improvements have been incorporated into the original interface over time.

The socket programming interface was designed for use with several communications protocols, not for TCP/IP alone.

Another important addition to the socket family was the Windows Socket programming interface, or WinSock. It has enabled TCP/IP applications to run on Windows 3.X, Windows 95, and Windows NT systems.

The socket interface is a de facto standard because it is almost universally available and is in widespread use. This chapter is intended to provide a general understanding of how the socket interface works. There will be minor differences in the APIs offered on various computers, due to the way that each vendor has implemented communications services within its operating system. The manual for the appropriate system should be consulted for programming details.

Unix Orientation

The original socket interface was written for a Unix operating system. The Unix architecture provides a framework in which standard file, terminal, and communications I/O all operate in a similar fashion. Operations are performed on a file by means of calls such as:

```
descriptor = open(filename, readwritemode)
read(descriptor, buffer, length)
write(descriptor, buffer, length)
close(descriptor)
```

When a program opens a file, the call creates an area in memory called a *file control block*. Information about the file, such as its name, attributes, and location, are stored in the file control block.

The call returns a small integer called a *file descriptor*. The program uses this descriptor to identify the file in any subsequent operations. As the user reads from or writes to the file, a pointer in the file descriptor keeps track of the current location in the file.

A very similar framework is used for TCP/IP socket communications. The primary difference between the socket programming interface and the Unix file I/O interface is that a couple of preliminary calls are required in order to assemble all of the information that is needed to carry out communications. Apart from the extra work at setup time, ordinary read and write calls can be used to receive and send data across a network.

Socket Services

The socket programming interface provides three TCP/IP services. It can be used for TCP *stream* communication, UDP *datagram* communication, and *raw* datagram submission to the IP layer. Figure 21.1 illustrates these services.

Recall that the socket API was not designed for use exclusively with TCP/IP. The original idea was that the same interface could also be used for other communications protocol families, such as Xerox Network Systems (XNS).

Figure 21.1
Socket Application Programming Interfaces.

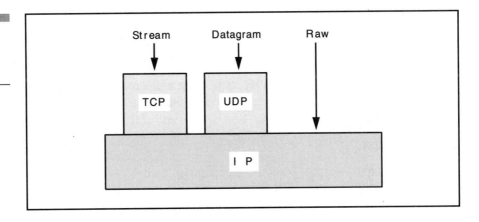

The result can be slightly confusing. For example, we shall see later that some socket calls contain optional parameters that are not relevant for TCP/IP communications—they are needed for some other protocol. Also, occasionally a programmer will be required to spell out the length of a fixed quantity such as a version 4 IP address. The reason for this is that although it is obvious that a version 4 IP address contains 4 bytes, the programming interface can be used for other protocols with different address lengths.

Blocking and Nonblocking Calls

When a program reads data from a network connection, it is hard to predict how long it will take before some data arrives and the call can complete. One issue that a programmer must decide is whether to wait for the outcome of a read or return immediately and get the data either by checking a status variable periodically or by responding to an interrupt.

- Calls that wait are called blocking, or synchronous.
- Calls that return right away are called nonblocking, or asynchronous.

Are socket programming interfaces blocking or nonblocking? The answer is Yes. The programmer usually can take control of how the calls will behave.

Socket Call

The *socket* call prepares for communication by creating a *Transmission Control Block* (TCB). Some manuals call this process "creating a socket." The *socket* call returns a small integer called a *socket descriptor* that is used to identify the communication in any subsequent operations.

There are many parameters that can be included in a TCB. We list a few to give an idea of the type of information that is included in the TCB for a TCP session:

- Local IP address
- Local port
- Protocol (e.g., TCP or UDP)

- Remote IP address
- Remote port
- Send buffer size
- Receive buffer size
- Current TCP state
- Smoothed round-trip time
- Smoothed round-trip deviation
- Current retransmission timeout value
- Number of retransmissions that have been sent
- Current send window size
- Maximum send segment size
- Sequence number of last byte that was ACKed
- Maximum receive segment size
- Sequence number of next byte to be sent
- Enable or disable tracing

TCP Socket Programming

In this section, we examine the socket programming calls that are used to interface with TCP. For simplicity, we will omit the I/O parameters for the calls at this stage and will concentrate on their major functions and their relation to one another. The details will be provided later.

TCP Server Model

A typical scenario for a TCP server is that there is a master process that spends most of its time listening for clients. When a client connects, usually the server creates a new "child" process that will do the actual work for the client. The server passes the client over to the new child process and then goes back to listening.

Sometimes clients arrive faster than the master process can get to them. What should be done with them? The standard mechanism is that when the master starts up, it tells TCP to create a queue that can hold a certain number of connection requests. Clients that can't be served immediately are put on the queue and served in turn. Suppose that the queue fills up and another client arrives? The new client's connection request will not be accepted.

TCP Server Passive Open

A server gets ready to communicate and then waits passively for clients. To get ready, the server makes a series of calls:

socket( )   The server identifies the type of communication (TCP in this case). The local system creates an appropriate TCB data structure for the communication and returns a *socket descriptor.*

bind( )   The server establishes the local IP address and port that it wants to use. Recall that a host may have multiple IP addresses. The server may specify one IP address or else indicate that it is willing to accept connections arriving at any local IP address. The server may ask for a specific port or else let the bind call obtain a free port that it can use.

listen( )   The server sets the length of the client queue.

accept( )   The server is ready to accept client connections. If the queue is not empty, the first client connection request is accepted. The *accept*() call creates a *new TCB* that will be used for this client's connection and returns a *new descriptor* to the server.

Usually a synchronous form of *accept* is used so that if the queue is empty, *accept*() will wait for the next client to show up before returning.

TCP Client Active Open

A client actively requests a connection via two calls:

socket( )   The client identifies the type of communication (TCP in this case). The local system creates an appropriate TCB data structure for the communication and returns a local socket descriptor.

connect( )   The client identifies a server's IP address and port. TCP will attempt to establish a connection with the server.

If the client wishes to specify exactly which local port it wants to use, the client must call *bind*() before calling *connect*(). If the port is available, the *bind* will assign it to the client.

If the client does not call *bind*() to ask for a port, the *connect* call will assign an unused port to the client. The port number will be entered into the TCB.

Other Calls

The remaining calls are used in exactly the same way by both the client and the server. Data can be transmitted and received using ordinary *write* and *read* calls. The connection can be terminated by calling *close*. There also are *send* and *recv* calls that are specific to communications. They support sending and receiving urgent data as well as ordinary data:

send()   Writes a buffer of data to the socket. Alternatively, *write*() may be used.

sendv()   Passes a sequence of buffers to the socket. Alternatively, *writev*() may be used.

recv()   Receives a buffer of data from a socket. Alternatively, *read*() may be used.

recvmsg()   Receives a sequence of buffers from a socket. Alternatively, *readv*() may be used.

Sometimes a program needs information that is stored in the TCB:

getsockopt() Reads selected information out of the TCB. Optionally, a system may provide additional I/O system calls that can be used to read various parts of the TCB.

Later, when we examine the input parameters for the opening calls, sends, and receives, we shall see that very few parameters are included in these calls. The reason is that a set of default values normally are used for most TCB parameters. For example, default values are preset for important environment information such as the receive buffer size, whether event logging is enabled, and the use of blocking or nonblocking processing for calls such as *recv*. Some defaults can be changed by using the functions:

setsockopt() Sets a number of TCB parameters such as input and output buffer sizes, use of logging, whether urgent data should be received in the normal sequence order, and whether a close should block until all outstanding data has been safely sent.

iocntl() or *fcntl*() Sets socket I/O to blocking or nonblocking.

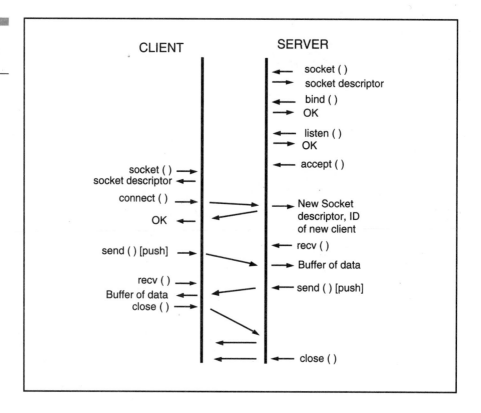

Figure 21.2 shows the sequence of calls in a typical TCP session. *Socket*(), *bind*(), and *listen*() calls complete quickly and return immediately.

The *accept*(), *send*(), and *recv*() calls shown are assumed to be blocking,[1] which is their normal default. *Write*() and *read*() could have been used instead of *send*() and *recv*().

A TCP Server Program

Now we are ready to take a close look at a sample server program. The server is designed to run forever. The server will:

1. Call *socket* to create a master TCB and return an integer socket descriptor that will identify this TCB in future calls.

---

[1]A *send* call blocks when the TCP send buffer already is full.

2. Enter the server's local socket address information into a program data structure.

3. Call *bind,* which will copy the local socket address into the TCB.

4. Set up a queue that can hold up to five clients.

The remaining steps are repeated over and over:

5. Wait for clients. When a client arrives, create a new TCB for the client. The new TCB is constructed by making a copy of the master TCB and writing the client's socket address and other client parameters into the new TCB.

6. Create a child process to serve the client. The child will inherit the new TCB and handle all further communication with the client. The child will wait for a message from the client, write the message, and exit.

Each step in the program is explained in the section that follows.

```
/*  tcpserv.c
 *  To run the program, enter "tcpserv".
 */
/* First we include a bunch of standard header files.
 */
#include <sys/types.h>
#include <sys/socket.h>
#include <stdio.h>
#include <netinet/in.h>
#include <netdb.h>
#include <errno.h>

main()
{
int sockMain, sockClient, length, child;
struct sockaddr_in servAddr;

/*   1. Create the master transmission control block.
 */
if ( (sockMain = socket(AF_INET, SOCK_STREAM, 0))<0)
   {perror("Server cannot open main socket.");
exit(1);
   |
/*   2. Create a data structure to hold the local IP address
 *       and port that we will use. We are willing to accept
 *       clients connecting to any local IP address (INADDR_ANY).
 *       Since this server will not use a well-known port,
 *       set the port = 0. The bind call will assign a port to the
 *       server and write the port into the TCB.
 */
bzero( (char *) &servAddr, sizeof(servAddr));
servAddr.sin_family = AF_INET;
servAddr.sin_addr.s_addr = htonl(INADDR_ANY);
servAddr.sin_port = 0;
```

```
/*    3. Call bind. Bind will pick a port number and write it
 *     into the TCB.
 */
if ( bind(sockMain, &servAddr, sizeof(servAddr)) )
   { perror("Server's bind failed.");
     exit(1);
   }
/* We want to look at the port number. We use the
 * getsockname() function to copy the port into servAddr.
 */
length = sizeof(servAddr);
if ( getsockname(sockMain, &servAddr, &length) )
   { perror("getsockname call failed.");
     exit(1);
   }
printf("SERVER: Port number is %d\n", ntohs(servAddr.sin_port) );
/*    4. Set up a queue that can hold up to five clients.
 */
listen(sockMain,5);
/*    5. Wait for an incoming client. Accept will return
 * a NEW socket descriptor that will be used for this client.
 */
for ( ; ; ) {
if ( (sockClient = accept(sockMain, 0, 0))<0)
   { perror("Bad client socket.");
     exit(1);
   }
/*    6. Create a child process to handle the client.
 */
if ( (child = fork())<0)
   {perror("Failed to create child.");
    exit(1);
   }
else if (child == 0) /* This is code for the child to execute */
   { close(sockMain); /* The child is not interested in sockMain.*/
     childWork(sockClient);
     close(sockClient);
     exit(0);
   }
/*    7. This is the parent. It is no longer interested in
 *        the client socket, since the child is taking care
 *        of the client. The parent closes its entry to
 *        the client socket and loops back to issue a new accept().
 */
   close(sockClient);
   }
}
/* The child reads one incoming buffer, prints a message and quits.
 */
#define BUFLEN 81
int childWork(sockClient)
int sockClient;
{
char buf[BUFLEN];
int msgLength;
/*    8. Zero out the buffer. Then issue a recv to get a message
 *        from the client.
 */
bzero(buf, BUFLEN);
```

```
if ( (msgLength = recv(sockClient,buf, BUFLEN, 0)) < 0)
    { perror("Bad receive by child.");
      exit(1);
    }
printf("SERVER: Socket used for this client is %d\n", sockClient);
printf("SERVER: Message length was %d\n", msgLength);
printf("SERVER: Message was: %s\n\n", buf);
}
```

Calls Used in the TCP Server Program

1. *sockMain = socket(AF_INET, SOCK_STREAM, 0);*

The socket call has the form:

```
socket_descriptor = socket(address_domain, communications_type,
protocol)
```

Recall that the socket interface can be used for other kinds of communications, such as XNS. *AF_INET* selects the Internet Address Family. *SOCK_STREAM* requests a TCP socket. This variable would be set to *SOCK_DGRAM* to create a UDP socket and *SOCK_RAW* to interface directly to IP.

We do not have to specify any other protocol information for TCP (or for UDP). However, the *protocol* parameter is needed for the raw interface, and for some of the other families that use sockets.

2. *struct sockaddr_in servAddr;*

   ...

bzero((char *) &servAddr, sizeof(servAddr));

servAddr.sin_family = AF_INET;

servAddr.sin_addr.s_addr = htonl(INADDR_ANY);

servAddr.sin_port = 0;

The *servAddr* program structure is used to hold server address information. The *bzero()* call just initializes *servAddr* by putting 0s into all parameters. The first variable in the *servAddr* structure indicates that the rest of the values contain Internet Address Family data.

The next variable holds the local IP address at which this server can be reached. For example, if the server is attached to an Ethernet LAN and to an X.25 network, it might want to restrict access to clients reached through the Ethernet interface. In this program, we don't care. *INADDR_ANY* means that clients can connect through any interface.

The *htonl*(), or host-to-network-long, function is used to translate a 32-bit integer stored in the local computer to the Internet format for a 32-bit IP address. Internet standards represent integers with the most significant byte first. This is called the Big Endian style of data representation. Some computers store data with the least significant byte first, in a Little Endian style. If the local computer is Big Endian, *htonl*() will have no work to do.

If this server were operating at a well-known port, we would fill that port number into the next variable. Since we want the operating system to assign us a port for this test program, we just enter a zero value.

3. *bind(sockMain, &servAddr, sizeof(servAddr))*;
   getsockname(sockMain, &servAddr, &length);

The *bind* call has the form:

```
return_code = bind(socket_descriptor, address_structure,
length_of_address_structure)
```

If the address structure identifies a desired port, *bind* will try to get it for the server. If there is a 0 in the port variable, *bind* will obtain an unused port. *Bind* will enter the port number and IP address into the TCB.

The *getsockname* call has the form:

```
return_code = getsockname(socket_descriptor, address_structure,
length_of_address_structure)
```

We asked *bind* to get us a port, but *bind* does not tell us what port it got. If we want to find out, we have to read it out of the TCB. The *getsockname*() function retrieves information from the TCB and copies it into the address structure where we can read it. The port number is extracted and printed in the statement:

```
printf("SERVER: Port number is %d\n", ntohs(servAddr.sin_port) );
```

The *ntohs*(), or network-to-host-short, function is used to convert the network byte order of the port number to local host byte order.

4. *listen(sockMain,5)*;

The *listen* call is used by connection-oriented servers and has the form:

```
return_code = listen(socket_descriptor, queue_size)
```

The *listen* call indicates that this will be a passive socket and creates a queue of the requested size that will hold incoming connection requests.

5. *sockClient = accept(sockMain, 0, 0)*;

The *accept* call has the form:

```
new_socket_descriptor = accept(socket_descriptor,
client_address_structure, length_of_client_address_structure)
```

By default, the call will block until a client connects to this server. If a *client_address_structure* variable is provided, the client's IP address and port will be entered into this variable when a client connects. In this sample program, since we are not checking up on the client's IP address and port number, we just fill 0s into the last two parameter fields.

6. *child = fork()*;

...

close(sockMain);

This is the C language *fork* command that creates a new child process. The child process will inherit all of the parent program's I/O descriptors and will have access to *sockMain* and *sockClient*. The operating system keeps track of the number of processes that have access to a socket.

A connection is closed when the last process accessing the socket calls *close()*. When the child closes *sockMain,* the parent will still have access to this socket.

7. *close(sockClient)*;

This call is made within the parent part of the program. When the parent closes *sockClient,* the child will still have access to this socket.

8. *msgLength = recv(sockClient,buf, BUFLEN, 0))*;

...

close(sockClient);

The *recv* call has the form:

```
message_length = recv(socket_descriptor, buffer, buffer_length,
flags)
```

By default, the *recv* call blocks. (Either the *fcntl()* or *iocntl()* function could be used to change the status of a socket to nonblocking.)

After the child has received data and printed its messages, it closes its access to *sockClient*. This will cause the connection to enter its termination phase.

A TCP Client Program

The client connects to the server, sends a single message, and terminates. The program steps will be explained in the next section. To run this program, an end user inputs the server host's name and port and a message to be sent to the server. For example:

```
tcpclient plum.cs.yale.edu 1356 hello

/*tcpclient.c
 * Start the server before starting a client. Find out
 * the server's port.
 * To run the client, enter:
 * tcpclient hostname port message
 */
#include <sys/types.h>
#include <sys/socket.h>
#include <netinet/in.h>
#include <netdb.h>
#include <stdio.h>
#include <errno.h>
main(argc, argv) /* The client program has input arguments. */
int argc;
char *argv[];
{
int sock;
struct sockaddr_in servAddr;
struct hostent *hp, *gethostbyname();
/* Args are 0:program-name, 1:hostname, 2:port, and 3:message */
if (argc<4)
    {printf("ENTER tcpclient hostname port message\n");
     exit (1);
    }
/*  1. Create a transmission control block. */
if ( (sock = socket(AF_INET, SOCK_STREAM, 0))<0)
    (perror("Could not get a socket\n");
     exit(1);
    }
/*  2. We will fill the server's address and port into the servAddr.
 *      First we fill the address structure with 0s.
 *      Next we look up the IP address for this host name and
 *      fill it in.
 *      Finally, we fill in the port number, which is in argv[2].
 */
bzero( (char *) &servAddr, sizeof(servAddr) );
servAddr.sin_family = AF_INET;
hp = gethostbyname(argv[1]);
```

```
bcopy(hp->h_addr, &servAddr.sin_addr, hp->h_length);
servAddr.sin_port = htons(atoi(argv[2]) );
/*  3. Connect to the server. We do not have to call bind.
 *      The system will assign a free port while performing the
 *      connect function.
 */
if ( connect(sock, &servAddr, sizeof(servAddr) )<0)
    {perror("Client cannot connect.\n");
     exit(1);
    }
/*  4. The client announces that it is ready to send the message.
 *      It sends and prints a goodbye message.
 */
printf("CLIENT: Ready to send\n");
if (send(sock, argv[3], strlen(argv[3]), 0)<0)
    {perror("problem with send.\n");
     exit(1);
    }
printf("CLIENT: Completed send. Goodbye.\n");
close(sock);
exit(0);
}
```

Calls Used in the TCP Client Program

1. *sock = socket(AF_INET, SOCK_STREAM, 0);*

The client creates a Transmission Control Block ("socket"), just as the server did.

2. The server had to initialize an address structure to use in its *bind* call.

This structure included the server's local IP address and port number. The client also initializes an address structure—and again it contains information about the *server*'s IP address and port. This structure will be used by the *connect* call to identify the destination.

The *bzero()* call below just puts 0s into the server address structure, *servAddr*. Once again, we identify the Address Family as Internet.

Next we must convert the host name entered by the user to an IP address. The *gethostbyname* function does this, returning a pointer to a *hostent* structure. This structure contains the server's name and IP address.

The *bcopy* function is used to copy the IP address (which is in *hp->h_addr*) into *servAddr*.

The second argument entered by the end user was the server's port. This was read in as an ASCII text string, so it must first be converted to an integer via *atoi()* and then converted to network byte order by *htons()*. Finally, the port number is copied into the address variable in *servAddr*.

```
bzero( (char *) &servAddr, sizeof(servAddr) );
servAddr.sin_family = AF_INET;
hp = gethostbyname(argv[1]);
bcopy(hp->h_addr, &servAddr.sin_addr, hp->h_length);
servAddr.sin_port = htons(atoi(argv[2]) );
```

3. *connect(sock, &servAddr, sizeof(servAddr));*

The *connect* call has the form:

```
connect(socket_descriptor, address_structure,
length_of_address_structure)
```

The client will open a connection with the server whose IP address and port are contained in the address structure.

4. *send(sock, argv[3], strlen(argv[3]), 0);*

The *send* call has the form:

```
return_code = send(socket_descriptor, buffer, buffer_length, flags)
```

Recall that the third argument entered by the end user (which appears in the program as *argv[3]*) is a text message. A common use for the flags parameter is to signal urgent data. In this instance, the flags parameter is set to 0.

5. *close(sock);*

The client issues a *close* to terminate the connection.

A Simpler Server

Many servers have the form shown in the earlier example. However, a simpler model can be used when the server needs to perform only a simple task for a client, as was the case in the preceding example.

Instead of creating a child process for each client, the server can directly perform the task and then close the connection to the client. The server queue enables a few other clients to wait until the server is ready for them.

Code for a simpler server follows. This server also can be accessed by clients running the *tcpclient* program discussed earlier.

```c
/* tcpsimp.c
 * To run the program, enter "tcpsimp".
 */
/* First we include a bunch of standard header files.
 */
#include <sys/types.h>
#include <sys/socket.h>
#include <stdio.h>
#include <netinet/in.h>
#include <netdb.h>
#include <errno.h>
main()
{
int sockMain, sockClient, length, child;
struct sockaddr_in servAddr;
/*  1. Create the master socket.
 */
if ( (sockMain = socket(AF_INET, SOCK_STREAM, 0))<0)
    {perror("Server cannot open main socket.");
     exit(1);
    }
/*  2. Enter information into a data structure used to hold the
 *      local IP address and port. The "sin" in the variable names is
 *      short for "socket internet."
 */
bzero( (char *) &servAddr, sizeof(servAddr) );
servAddr.sin_family = AF_INET;
servAddr.sin_addr.s_addr = htonl(INADDR_ANY);
servAddr.sin_port = 0;
/*  3. Call bind. Bind will write a usable port number into servAddr.
 */
if ( bind(sockMain, &servAddr, sizeof(servAddr)) )
    { perror("Server's bind failed.");
      exit(1);
    }
/*  4. We want to look at the port number. We use the
 *      getsockname() function to copy the port into servAddr.
 */
length = sizeof(servAddr);
if ( getsockname(sockMain, & servAddr, &length) )
    { perror("getsockname call failed.");
      exit(1);
    }
printf("SERVER: Port number is %d\n", ntohs(servAddr.sin_port) );
/*  5. Set up a queue that can hold up to five clients.
 */
listen(sockMain,5);
/*  6. Wait for an incoming client. Accept will return
 *      a new socket descriptor that will be used for this client.
 */
for ( ; ; ) {
if ( (sockClient = accept(sockMain, 0, 0))<0)
{ perror("Bad client socket.");
exit(1);
}
/*  7'. Serve the client and close the client's connection.
 */
```

```
        doTask(sockClient);
        close(sockClient);
        }
}
/* Read one incoming buffer, print some information and quit.
 */
#define BUFLEN 81
int doTask(sockClient)
int sockClient;
{
char buf[BUFLEN];
int msgLength;
/*  8'. Zero out the buffer and then issue a recv
 *       to get a message from the client.
 */
bzero(buf, BUFLEN);
if ( (msgLength = recv(sockClient,buf, 80, 0))<0)
    { perror("Bad receive.");
       exit(1);
    }
printf("SERVER: Socket used for this client is %d\n", sockClient);
printf("SERVER: Message length was %d\n", msgLength);
printf("SERVER: Message was: %s\n\n", buf);
}
```

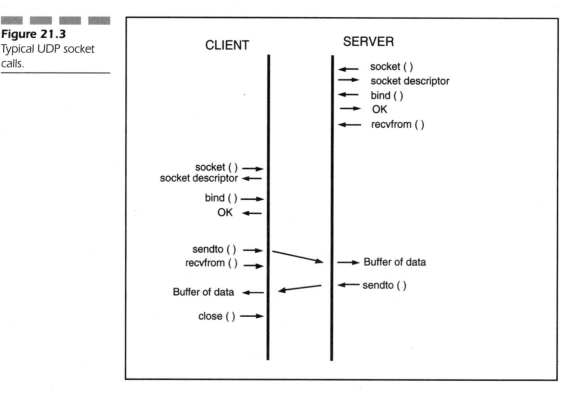

Figure 21.3
Typical UDP socket calls.

UDP Socket Programming Interface

We have tackled the TCP programming interface, which is the most complex, first. Now let's take a look at programming a UDP server and client. Figure 21.3 shows an outline of a UDP dialog between a client and server. The *socket*() and *bind*() calls complete quickly and have an immediate return. The *recvfrom* call is assumed to be blocking, which is its normal default. It can be changed to nonblocking (i.e., asynchronous) mode.

A UDP Server Program

The program that follows creates a UDP socket, binds to a port, and then begins to receive and print messages that are sent to its port:

```
/* udpserv.c
 * To run the program, enter "udpserv".
 *
 * First we include a bunch of standard header files.
 */
#include <sys/types.h>
#include <sys/socket.h>
#include <stdio.h>
#include <netinet/in.h>
#include <netdb.h>
#include <errno.h>
#define BUFLEN 81
main()
{
int sockMain, addrLength, msgLength;
struct sockaddr_in servAddr, clientAddr;
char buf[BUFLEN];
/*  1. Create a UDP socket.
 */
if ( (sockMain = socket(AF_INET, SOCK_DGRAM, 0))<0)
   {perror("Server cannot open UDP socket.");
    exit(1);
   }
/*  2. Enter information into a data structure used to hold the
 *     local IP address and port. We will let bind get a free
 *     port for us.
 */
bzero( (char *) &servAddr, sizeof(servAddr) );
servAddr.sin_family = AF_INET;
servAddr.sin_addr.s_addr = htonl(INADDR_ANY);
servAddr.sin_port = 0;
```

```
/*  3. Call bind. Bind will write a usable port number into the
*TCB.
 */
if ( bind(sockMain, &servAddr, sizeof(servAddr)) )
  { perror("Server's bind failed.");
    exit(1);
  }
/*  4. We want to look at the port number. We use the
 *     getsockname() function to copy the port into servAddr.
 */
addrLength = sizeof(servAddr);
if ( getsockname(sockMain, &servAddr, &addrLength) )
  { perror("getsockname call failed.");
    exit(1);
  }
printf("SERVER: Port number is %d\n", ntohs(servAddr.sin_port) );
/*  5. Loop forever, waiting for messages from clients.
 */
for ( ; ; ) {
    addrLength = sizeof(clientAddr);
    bzero(buf, BUFLEN);
    if ( (msgLength = recvfrom(sockMain, buf, BUFLEN, 0,
                    &clientAddr, &addrLength))<0)
      { perror("Bad client socket.");
        exit(1);
      }
/*  6. Print the client's IP address and port, and the message.
 */
    printf("SERVER: Client's IP address was: %s\n"
                    inet_ntoa( clientAddr.sin_addr) );
    printf("SERVER: Client's port was: %d\n",
                    ntohs(clientAddr.sin_port));
    printf("SERVER: Message length was %d\n", msgLength);
    printf("SERVER: Message was: %s\n\n", buf);
    }
}
```

Calls Used in the UDP Server Program

1. *sockMain = socket(AF_INET, SOCK_DGRAM, 0);*

The Address Family is again Internet.

2. *bzero((char *) &servAddr, sizeof(servAddr));*
servAddr.sin_family = AF_INET;
servAddr.sin_addr.s_addr = htonl(INADDR_ANY);
servAddr.sin_port = 0;

The calls initializing the server address structure are the same as those used in the TCP programs.

3. *bind(sockMain, &servAddr, sizeof(servAddr));*

As before, *bind* will get a port for the server and write values into a Transmission Control Block. Of course, UDP has a very small amount of control information compared to TCP.

4. *getsockname(sockMain, &servAddr, &length);*

We use *getsockname* to extract the port assigned to the socket.

5. *msgLength = recvfrom(sockMain, buf, BUFLEN, 0, &clientAddr, &length);*

The *recvfrom* call has the form:

```
recvfrom(socket_descriptor, receive_buffer, buffer_length,
flags, source_address_structure,
pointer_to_length_of_source_address_structure)
```

The flags parameter can be set to allow the caller to peek at a message without actually receiving it.

On return, the source address structure will be filled with the client's IP address and port number. A pointer to the length of the source address is used because this length may be changed when the actual client address fields are received and filled in.

6. *inet_ntoa(clientAddr.sin_addr);*

This call converts the client's 32-bit Internet address to the familiar dot notation for IP addresses.

A UDP Client Program

The client connects to the server, sends a single message, and terminates. To run this program, an end user inputs the host name, the port of the server, and a message to be sent to the server. For example:

```
udpclient plum.cs.yale.edu 2315 "This is a message."
```

```
/* udpclient.c
 * Start the server before starting a client.
 * Find out the server's port.
 * To run the client, enter:
 *    udpclient hostname port message
 */
#include <sys/types.h>
#include <sys/socket.h>
#include <netinet/in.h>
#include <netdb.h>
#include <stdio.h>
#include <errno.h>]
```

```
main(argc, argv)
int argc;
char *argv[];  /* These are the arguments entered by the enduser. */
      /* argv[0] is the program name. argv[1] points to a hostname. */
      /* argv[2] points to a port, */
      /* and argv[3] points to a text message. */
{
int sock;
struct sockaddr_in servAddr, clientAddr;
struct hostent *hp, *gethostbyname();
/* Should be four args. */
if (argc<4)
   {printf("ENTER udpclient hostname port message\n");
    exit(1);
   }
/*  1. Create a UDP socket. */
if ( (sock = socket(AF_INET, SOCK_DGRAM, 0))<0)
   {perror("Could not get a socket\n");
    exit(1);
   }
/*  2. We will fill the server's address and port into the servAddr.
 *      First we fill the address structure with 0s.
 *      We use the gethostbyname function to look up the host name
 *      and get its IP address. Then we copy the IP address
 *      into servAddr using the bcopy function.
 *      Finally, we fill in the port number, which is in argv[2].
 */
bzero( (char *) &servAddr, sizeof(servAddr) );
servAddr.sin_family = AF_INET;
hp = gethostbyname(argv[1]);
bcopy(hp->h_addr, &servAddr.sin_addr, hp->h_length);
servAddr.sin_port = htons(atoi(argv[2]) );
/*  3. We have to call bind to get a UDP port. The system
 *      will assign a free port.
 */
bzero( (char *) &clientAddr, sizeof(clientAddr) );
clientAddr.sin_family = AF_INET;
clientAddr.sin_addr.s_addr = htonl(INADDR_ANY);
clientAddr.sin_port = 0;
if ( bind(sock, &clientAddr, sizeof(clientAddr))<0)
   {perror("Client cannot get a port.\n");
    exit(1);
   }
/* 4. The client announces that it is ready to send the message.
 * It sends and prints a goodbye message.
 */
printf("CLIENT: Ready to send\n");
if (sendto(sock, argv[3], strlen(argv[3]), 0, &servAddr,
  sizeof(servAddr))<0)
     {perror("problem with sendto.\n");
      exit(1);
     }
printf("CLIENT: Completed send. Goodbye.\n");
/* Close the socket */
close(sock);
}
```

Calls Used in the UDP Client Program

1. *sock = socket(AF_INET, SOCK_DGRAM, 0);*

The UDP client creates a UDP socket.

2. *bzero((char *) &servAddr, sizeof(servAddr));*
servAddr.sin_family = AF_INET;

hp = gethostbyname(argv[1]);

bcopy(hp->h_addr, &servAddr.sin_addr, hp->h_length);

servAddr.sin_port = htons(atoi(argv[2]));

The *servAddr* structure is filled in using values entered by the end user, just as was done for the TCP client.

3. *bind(sock, &clientAddr, sizeof(clientAddr);*

The client calls *bind* to get a port.

4. *sendto(sock, argv[3], strlen(argv[3]), 0, &servAddr, sizeof(servAddr));*

The *sendto* call has the form:

```
sendto(socket_descriptor, buffer, buffer_length, flags,
       destination_address_structure,
       length_of_destination_address_structure)
```

Note that this call contains all of the destination information required to send a User Datagram.

Recommended Reading

Any Unix programmer's manual contains descriptions of socket program calls. *Unix Network Programming* by W. Richard Stevens provides an in-depth discussion of socket programming. TCP/IP programmer's manuals for other operating systems describe the socket calls and often include sample programs. The manual for the TCP/IP product in use should be consulted since there are small variations due to differences between operating systems. The WinSock programming library includes a large number of additional library routines. The C^{++} socket library also provides a greatly enhanced programming interface.

CHAPTER 22

IP Version 6

Introduction

In 1994, the Internet officially changed from a research testbed to a commercial service network. Its growth since then, fueled by the World Wide Web and electronic mail, has been global and phenomenal.

The original IP address system was not designed to be a global numbering system. The number space was small. Unlike the telephone system, which has country and area codes, IP numbering was not hierarchical. Blocks of numbers were assigned to organizations very inefficiently, and much of the number space was wasted.

The result is that the number space is being depleted. In addition, because numbers are not always assigned hierarchically, routing tables are growing too quickly.

The expansion of the Internet is not expected to slow down. There is a steady growth in the spread of personal computers and of their connectivity into the global network. In addition, new challenges are presented by:

- The networking of the coming generations of mobile personal computers—the offsprings of today's pagers and personal digital assistants.

- The anticipated demand for real-time audio and video, which will push the current technology to its limits.

The world of serious commerce has moved onto the Internet, and it also is clear that it is time to build security into the network infrastructure.

There are other problems that plague managers. As the number of IP-enabled devices zooms into the stratosphere, the administration of IP addresses has become a major headache. Many organizations use IP backbones to tie their networks together and tunnel traffic from site to site wrapped in IP headers. Today this is done awkwardly and often without any mechanism for network congestion control.

The development of IP version 6 (IPv6; also called *IP next generation*) has been spurred on by the urgent need to solve these Internet addressing, routing, administration, performance, security, and congestion problems.

Disclaimer

IP version 6 still is under construction. Much of the material in this chapter is taken from drafts that may be (and probably will be) revised.

We present only the major features of IPv6 in this chapter. Implementers should consult the most recent RFCs (and drafts) for up-to-date details.

Overview of IPv6

IPv6 does the following:

- Introduces 128-bit (16-byte) addresses that can be structured hierarchically to simplify address delegation and routing.
- Simplifies the main IP header but defines many optional *extension headers*. This will enable new networking functions to be added as needed.
- Supports authentication, data integrity, and confidentiality at the IP level.
- Introduces *flows,* which can be used to support many new kinds of transmission requirements—such as real-time video.
- Makes it easy to encapsulate other protocols and provides a mechanism for congestion control when carrying "foreign" protocols.
- Provides new automatic address self-configuration methods and builds in a test for IP address uniqueness.
- Improves router discovery and the detection of dead routers or unreachable neighbors on a link.

Terminology

Version 6 makes some adjustments to version 4 nomenclature and standardizes the following terminology:

- A *packet* is an IPv6 header plus payload.
- A *node* is any system that implements IPv6.
- A *router* is a node that forwards IPv6 packets not explicitly addressed to itself.
- A *host* is any node that is not a router.
- A *link* is a medium over which nodes can communicate at the link layer.
- *Neighbors* are nodes attached to the same link.

The term *packet* is one of the most abused in the networking world. People use it to describe Protocol Data Units (PDUs) from the link layer to the application layer.

Why did the version 6 authors switch from *datagram* to *packet?* One of the innovations in IPv6 is that it can be used to carry traffic for many other protocols—hence its payload might not be a PDU from the TCP/IP suite. When the payload is a TCP segment, UDP message, or other TCP/IP native data, the term *datagram* still is appropriate.

In this chapter, we follow the usage in the current IPv6 documents and use the term *packet.*

IPv6 Addresses

IPv6 addresses are 16 bytes (128 bits) long. There are three types of addresses:

1. *Unicast:* Identifies a single interface.
2. *Multicast:* Identifies a set of interfaces. A datagram sent to a unicast address is delivered to all interfaces that have joined the multicast group for this address.
3. *Anycast:* Identifies a set of interfaces, but a datagram sent to an anycast address is delivered to one interface—the nearest one.

Broadcasts are not used in IPv6. This is a significant change. It makes large switched LANs feasible.

IPV6 Address Notation

A fairly compact (if ugly) notation is used to write these addresses. They are represented as eight hexadecimal numbers separated by colons. Each hexadecimal clump represents 16 bits. For example:

   41BC:0:0:0:5:DDE1:8006:2334

Note that leading zeros in a hex field can be dropped (e.g., 0 instead of 0000 and 5 instead of 0005). The format can be compressed further by replacing exactly one contiguous string of 0 fields with ::—for example:

   41BC::5:DDE1:8006:2334

Three clumps are missing, and so :: represents the string :0:0:0:.

Finally, version 4 IP addresses sometimes will be embedded in the last 4 bytes of a version 6 address. These can be written using a mixed address format that uses both the colon and the dot notations, for example:

0:0:0:0:0:FFFF:**128.1.35.201**

Types of IP Addresses

A 128-bit address space allows room for many different types of IP addresses, including:

- Hierarchical addresses that facilitate Internet routing
- Private-site addresses, for use within an organization only
- Local and global multicast addresses

Version 6 has replaced broadcasts with multicasts for control functions such as address resolution and booting. The reasoning behind this is that broadcasting a message causes interrupts at every device on a link. In most cases, only a few devices really need to examine the message.

IPv6 Address Allocations

Table 22.1 shows the suggested overall plan for address space allocation[1]:

- A large block is used for "Aggregatable Global Unicast Addresses." These addresses are designed to facilitate Internet routing.
- There are blocks for stand-alone LANs and private sites. These addresses can be self-administered by an organization.
- All addresses starting with X'FF are multicast addresses.
- Blocks have been allocated for IPX addresses and OSI Network Service Access Point (NSAP) addresses.

Currently, 85 percent of the address space has not been assigned to any use.

---

[1]Allocations have been updated from values assigned in the original IPv6 specifications. Further revisions may be made.

TABLE 22.1

IPv6 Address Space Allocation

Allocation	Prefix (binary)	Fraction of Address Space
Reserved	0000 0000	1/256
Unassigned	0000 0001	1/256
Reserved for NSAP Allocation	0000 001	1/128
Reserved for IPX Allocation	0000 010	1/128
Unassigned	0000 011	1/128
Unassigned	0000 1	1/32
Unassigned	0001	1/16
Aggregatable Global Unicast Addresses	001	1/8
Unassigned (formerly Provider-Based Unicast)	010	1/8
Unassigned	011	1/8
Unassigned (formerly Geographic-Based Unicast)	100	1/8
Unassigned	101	1/8
Unassigned	110	1/8
Unassigned	1110	1/16
Unassigned	1111 0	1/32
Unassigned	1111 10	1/64
Unassigned	1111 110	1/128
Unassigned	1111 1110 0	1/512
Link Local Unicast Addresses	1111 1110 10	1/1024
Site Local Unicast Addresses	1111 1110 11	1/1024
Multicast Addresses	1111 1111	1/256

Aggregatable Global Unicast Addresses

Internet unicast[2] addresses have been given a hierarchical structure. There is a top-level number, second-level number, and third-level number. This structure will simplify routing.

---

[2]Recall that a unicast IP address identifies a single network interface, in contrast to a multicast or broadcast address.

If this were a new numbering scheme for the telephone system, then the numbers would correspond to countries, areas, and localities. The Internet currently is structured as a set of service provider networks. We will treat the addresses as a set of fields that identify the service provider, subscriber, subscriber subnet, and host.

The address format fields are blocked out below:

3	13	8	24	16	64
001	TLA ID	RES	NLA ID	SLA ID	Interface ID

The first 48 bits make up the public part of the address:

- TLA ID: Top-Level Aggregation Identifier. These values identify the top-level service providers.

- RES: 8 bits are reserved for future use. If needed, some bits may be used to expand the top-level field.

- NLA ID: Next-Level Aggregation Identifier. A top-level service provider uses this field to identify its subscribers. The provider can create a subhierarchy, using part of the number for a region, or to identify smaller service providers attached to the big provider.

The next 80 bits belong to the subscriber:

- SLA ID: Site-Level Aggregation Identifier. The organization can use these 2 bytes to number its subnets, or can create a subhierarchy of areas and subnets.

- INTERFACE ID: Interface Identifier. 64 bits are used to identify an individual device interface.

Note that it is easy to route to top-level providers by placing top-level provider prefixes into an Internet routing table. All addresses that start with the routing prefix are aggregated into one routing entry—which explains the title given to these addresses.

A provider can route to its subscribers by placing prefixes for its subscribers into its own routing tables.[3] Individual subscriber site-level addresses do not have to be checked until a datagram has reached the destination service provider.

---

[3]A provider that covers a very large area can create another level of hierarchy by using the first few bits of the Next-Level ID field to identify a particular region.

With this format, a subscriber organization will own sufficient address space to build a convenient internal hierarchy. By the way, all-0 or all-1 fields are not forbidden in version 6 addresses.

Exchanges

Today, some large organizations that are connected to more than one service provider have their own public network numbers. Others assign multiple addresses to their public hosts, so that they can be reached even if one of their providers fails.

The new addressing scheme proposes the use of *exchange* services, which connect a subscriber to multiple long-haul providers. A subscriber could obtain unique addresses from its exchange service and use these addresses with any of its long-haul providers. The subscriber connects to the Internet via its exchange service, which in turn, has connections to long-haul services.

Format of the Subscriber Part

The surprising feature of this address plan is that the subscriber owns the lion's share of an address—80 bits! A subscriber can format the Site-Level part of the address in any convenient way. This 2-byte field can be used to identify up to 64K subnet numbers. As mentioned earlier, a large organization might prefer to break up this field and create a hierarchical structure. The hierarchy would reduce the number of entries needed in the organization's routing tables.

Interface Identifier

The last field of a unicast address is the interface identifier. Each interface to a link must have a different interface identifier. The interface identifier does not have to be globally unique; it has to be unique only on its link. However, the identifier format that was chosen makes global uniqueness possible: it is the IEEE-administered global identifier called *EUI-64*.

For Ethernet, Token-Ring, or FDDI LAN interfaces, an EUI-64 identifier is created by mapping the unique 48-bit MAC address assigned to an interface by its vendor to a 64-bit identifier. Let's look at an example in order to understand how the 48-bit MAC is mapped into the 64-bit field. The hexadecimal MAC address:

34-56-78-9A-BC-DE

is mapped to:

36-56-78-FF-FE-9A-BC-DE

- The last 3 bytes of the MAC address have been placed in the last 3 bytes of the EUI-64 identifier field.
- The middle 2 bytes of the interface ID field have been set to the fixed value FF-FE.
- The first 3 bytes of the MAC address have been placed in the first 3 bytes of the interface ID field, but one bit in the first byte has been changed.

There is a Universal/Local bit in every MAC address. A 0 value indicates that the address is Universal—that is, the address is a globally unique value assigned by the vendor. This bit is mapped to a 1.[4]

Some Asynchronous Transfer Mode (ATM) interfaces have built-in EUI-64 addresses. These contain a Global/Local bit. After setting this bit to 1, the ATM EUI-64 address can be used as its interface ID. Some ATM interfaces are assigned E.164 addresses. There also is a standard mapping between these addresses and EUI-64 interface IDs.

This formulation takes care of LAN and ATM interfaces, but some interfaces—such as leased serial lines—have no built-in identifiers. An identifier can be created manually. If the node has one or more LAN interfaces, it also is acceptable to reuse one of the LAN interface identifiers. Remember, the identifier ID field does not have to be globally unique—it needs to be unique only on its link. The subnet number will be different on each link, so the actual IPv6 addresses will be unique.

Link-Local Addresses

One of the appealing features of IPv6 is that as soon as a system attached to a LAN boots up, it can communicate with other systems on

---

[4]The bit is the next-to-lowest order bit of the first byte. X'34 = 0011 0100. X'36 = 0011 0110.

the LAN. In fact, the system can communicate across any interface that has been assigned its unique interface identifier.

Communication is possible because a system interface automatically expands its unique interface identifier into a *Link-Local* IP address that is unique on its link. Link-Local addresses have the form:

10 bits	54 bits	64 bits
1111111010	00...00	Unique Interface ID

In the previous section, we saw that every Ethernet, Token-Ring, and FDDI interface has a self-assigned 64-bit interface identifier that is derived from its universal MAC address. The automatic self-assignment of a Link-Local address is an example of IPv6's *stateless autoconfiguration*.

A datagram sent to a Link-Local destination address never leaves the link. Although they are limited, Link-Local addresses are very useful. There are many service messages that can be exchanged using these addresses. Link-Local addresses also are used for procedures that enable a system to obtain addresses that have a wider scope.

Site-Local Addresses

A site that has routers, but is not connected to a Service Provider, can use internal addresses of the form:

8 bits	38 bits	16 bits	64 bits
1111111010	00...00	Subnet ID	64-bit Unique Interface ID

A datagram with a Site-Local destination address will not be routed outside the site. Site-Local addresses are obtained very easily:

- A router is configured with the subnet ID of each of its interfaces.
- The router notifies hosts on a link of the subnet ID for the link.

This is another example of stateless autoconfiguration.

Addresses for Stand-Alone Sites

Today, a version 4 LAN or network that is not connected to the Internet uses a special block of addresses, such as 10.0.0.0 or 172.16.0.0, that has been reserved for this purpose. But if the organization subsequently needs to connect to the outside world, it has a big renumbering job on its hands.

As shown in the previous section, IP version 6 takes care of the address assignment problem far more gracefully. The last 80 bits provide a generous set of site-local addresses. The provider part of the address is filled with zeroes.

Note how easy it is to migrate to Service Provider connectivity. Routers simply are configured with a new prefix that includes the external part. The router advertises the new prefix, and hosts start to use it. The site part of an address would not need to change.

Multicast Address Formats

Version 6 multicast addresses have a clearer, more usable definition than version 4 multicast addresses. One glance at the address and you can tell whether the multicast group is permanent or transient, local or global. This is done by using different introducers for each type of multicast.

Specifically, multicast addresses have the format:

8 bits	4 bits	4 bits	112 bits
11111111	000T	Scope	Group ID

T = 0 for a well-known, permanent multicast address.

T = 1 for a transient multicast address.

Scope codes indicate whether the scope is same-node, link-local, site-local, organizational-local, or global. A same-node scope covers the case where a client sends a multicast message to servers that are located at the same host. The specific scope codes are:

0   *reserved*

1   node-local scope

2   link-local scope

3   *unassigned*

4   *unassigned*

5   site-local scope

6   *unassigned*

7   *unassigned*

8   organization-local scope

9   *unassigned*

A   *unassigned*

B   *unassigned*

C   *unassigned*

D   *unassigned*

E   global scope

F   *reserved*

Link-Local Multicast Address Examples

The following are examples of link-local multicast addresses (in hexa-decimal address format):

FF02:0:0:0:0:0:0:1	All-Nodes Address
FF02:0:0:0:0:0:0:2	All-Routers Address
FF02:0:0:0:0:0:0:4	DVMRP Routers
FF02:0:0:0:0:0:0:5	OSPF Routers

Solicited-Node Link-Local Address

A new type of link-local multicast address called the solicited-node address has been introduced for IPv6. It has several useful applica-tions—most notably, it is used in place of a broadcast ARP messages to locate neighbors. A solicited-node multicast address is constructed by adding the last 3 bytes of an IPv6 link-local address to a fixed multicast prefix. These bytes are represented by "XX" below:

FF02:0:0:0:0:1:FFXX:XXXX

Site-Local Multicast Address Examples

The following are examples of site-local multicast addresses:

FF05:0:0:0:0:0:0:2	All Routers Address
FF05:0:0:0:0:0:1:3	All-dhcp-servers
FF05:0:0:0:0:0:1:4	All-dhcp-relays

Multicast Addresses for Any Scope

Many multicast addresses can be used within any desired scope. The scope number is set to the value that is appropriate for the usage. For example, the addresses below can be used within any scope. The scope number is displayed as "X" and can be replaced with any selected value.

FF0X:0:0:0:0:0:0:10B IETF-1-AUDIO

FF0X:0:0:0:0:0:0:10C IETF-1-VIDEO

In general, multicast addresses currently are being restricted to the form:

8 bits	4 bits	4 bits	80 bits	32 bits
11111111	000T	Scope	00...00	Group ID

It is very easy to map an IPv6 multicast address to a 6-byte Ethernet or FDDI MAC multicast address. The mapping is:

X'33-33-(last 4 bytes of IPv6 multicast address)[5]

Anycast Addresses

Sometimes we wish that we could put a destination address into a datagram that says "Go to the nearest node that performs service XYZ." An anycast address is a first step toward this kind of ability. It is used to route to the nearest member of a set of selected nodes. Currently, anycast addresses may be assigned only to routers.

Formally, an anycast address is a unicast address that has been assigned to more than one interface. An interface that has been given an anycast address also has its own real unique address. An anycast address might be used to identify:

- All routers owned by a particular Service Provider
- All routers attached to a particular LAN

An anycast address can be used as a destination address or can be included in a source route. The address means, "Use the nearest router that has this anycast address." For example, if the anycast address identified routers owned by a Service Provider, it would be used to say "Get to this Service Provider using the shortest path."

Usually there is no special format that distinguishes anycast addresses from other unicast addresses. The exception is the Subnet-Router anycast address. It consists of a prefix that identifies a LAN followed by zeros in the unique identifier field, and means "a router on this LAN."

---

[5]For Token-Ring, a mapping to a small set of Token-Ring functional addresses is used.

Special Addresses

Just as was the case for version 4 of IP, there are several special IPv6 address formats.

Unspecified Address

The all-0s address below means "unspecified address."

    0:0:0:0:0:0:0:0

It indicates the absence of an address. It sometimes is used as a source address during initialization, when a system does not yet know its own address.

Version 6 Loopback

The version 6 *loopback* address is:

    0:0:0:0:0:0:0:1

Version 4 Addresses

In a mixed version 4 and 6 environment, the addresses of IP version 4 systems that do *not* support version 6 are mapped to version 6 addresses of the form:

    0:0:0:0:0:FFFF:a.b.c.d

where a.b.c.d is the original IP address.

IPv4-compatible IP Version 6 Addresses

IPv6 will be adopted gradually. The world will consist of islands of IPv6 nodes in a sea of IPv4 systems. These islands will communicate with one another by "tunneling" across the IPv4 sea. That is, a router at one end of the tunnel will wrap each IPv4 packet in a version 4 header addressed to the router at the other end of the tunnel. The remote router will unwrap the IPv6 packet and route it onward.

A special format is used by the version 6 nodes at the ends of the tun-

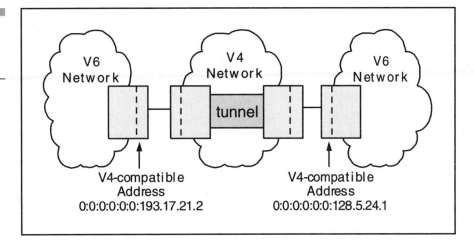

Figure 22.1
IPv4-compatible IPv6 addresses used for tunneling.

nel. As shown in Figure 22.1, the interfaces at the boundaries must be assigned version 4 addresses. These are mapped to the special *IPv4-compatible* IPv6 address format:

0:0:0:0:0:0:a.b.c.d

Thus, these addresses are easily mapped between their version 4 and version 6 representations.

IPv6 Header Format

The basic header is very simple, as shown in Figure 22.2. Note that there are very few fields:

Version	(4 bits) Equals 6 for IP next generation.
Traffic Class	(8 bits) Identifies classes or priorities that affect the handling of a datagram.
Flow label	(20 bits) Identifies traffic that needs a special type of handling (e.g., real-time video).
Payload length	(16 bits) If the length is less than or equal to 64 kilobits, this field reports the length of the part of the packet that follows the initial IPv6 header. If the packet length is greater than 64 kilobits, the payload length is set to zero, and the actual length will be reported in a *Jumbo Payload* option in a later header.

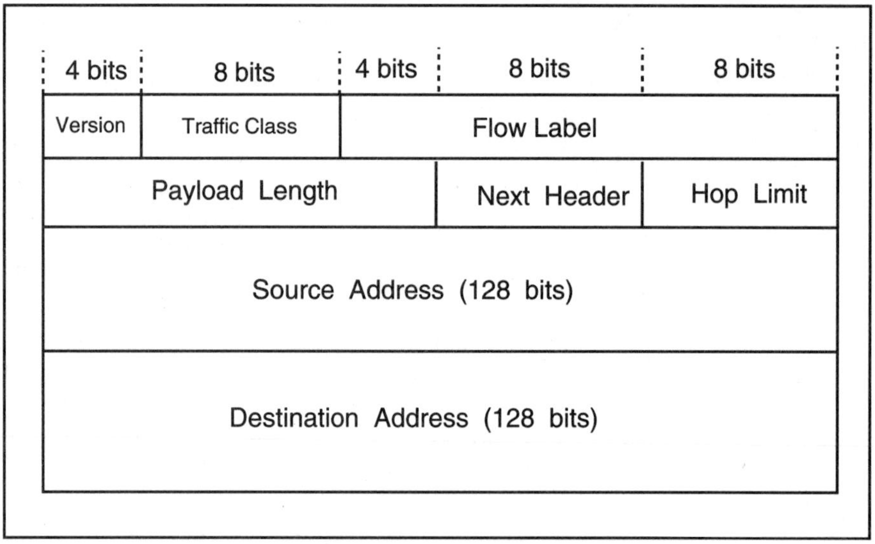

Figure 22.2
IPv6 header.

4 bits	8 bits	4 bits	8 bits	8 bits
Version	Traffic Class	Flow Label		
Payload Length			Next Header	Hop Limit
Source Address (128 bits)				
Destination Address (128 bits)				

Next header	(8 bits) Identifies the type of protocol header that follows (e.g., 6 for a TCP header).
Hop limit	(8 bits) Is decremented by 1 at each router. The packet will be discarded if the value reaches 0 at a router.

Traffic Class

The Traffic Class field will provide functions similar to the IPv4 Type of Service and Precedence fields.

Use of the Flow Label

A *flow* is a sequence of packets from a source to a destination that requires some kind of special treatment. For example, voice or real-time video require different handling from bulk data transfer.

The *flow label* is used to identify a stream of traffic that has a special handling mechanism—such as bandwidth reservation.

A nonzero flow label indicates the fact that packets belong to a flow. Packets belonging to a particular flow all have the same source address, destination address, priority, and flow label.

■ ■ IPv6 Extension Headers

The use of extension headers is a very innovative idea that allows functionality to be added incrementally to IP version 6.

Recall that in an IP version 4 header, the *Protocol* field is used to identify what type of header (e.g., TCP or UDP) follows the IP header. Version 6 uses a more general *Next Header* field. If the next header is a TCP or UDP header, the value in the Next Header field is 6 or 17, the protocol identifier for TCP or UDP.

But several extension headers can be sandwiched between the IPv6 header and a higher-layer header. These are used for options, such as source routing or security. Fragmentation also has been moved into an extension header.

As illustrated in Figure 22.3, each of the extension headers contains a Next Header field, and so headers are chained together. The next layer protocol finally is identified in the last extension header.

This scheme provides great flexibility. New options can be defined as needed at any time, and their overall length need not be restricted. Also note that the final extension header can point to a header that belongs to an entirely different protocol suite (such as ISO or IPX).

The currently defined header identifiers are listed in Table 22.2. The Hop-by-Hop header contains information that must be processed at nodes along the way, whereas others contain information that needs to be processed only at the IPv6 destination address.

■ ■ ■ ■
Figure 22.3
Extension headers.

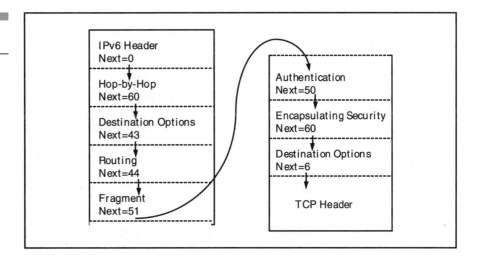

TABLE 22.2

IPv6 Headers

Header	Number In Previous "Next Header" Field
Hop-by-Hop Options	0
Destination Options	60
Routing	43
Fragment	44
Authentication	51
Encapsulating Security Payload	50
No Next Header	59

The order shown in Figure 22.3 reflects the recommended order for whatever headers may be included. Note that two *Destination Options* headers could appear. The first would be placed before a *Routing* header and would be applied to each hop listed in the *Routing* header. The second would appear as the last header and applies only to the final destination.

It is possible that someday there may be a use for sending a packet that consists of a header and no payload. In this case, the final Next Header identifier is 59, which means, "nothing follows."

Routing Header Operation

The Routing header includes a type field. Currently, only type 0 is defined, but new types can be added in the future.

A type 0 Routing header is similar to an IPv4 Loose Source Route header. The format of a type 0 Routing header is shown in Figure 22.4.[6]

As in IP version 4, the final destination is *Address n.* The packet is first forwarded to the address in the main IPv6 header. Then the *Routing* header is consulted. Address 1 is swapped into the IPv6 header's destination address field, the *Segments Left* counter is reduced by 1, and the packet is forwarded. The final address in the *Routing* header is the true destination.[7]

---

[6]In the specification, the "Total Addresses Length" is called the Header Extension length.

[7]If there is a Destination Options header before the Routing header, the Destination Options header must be processed at the initial destination address and the addresses on the list.

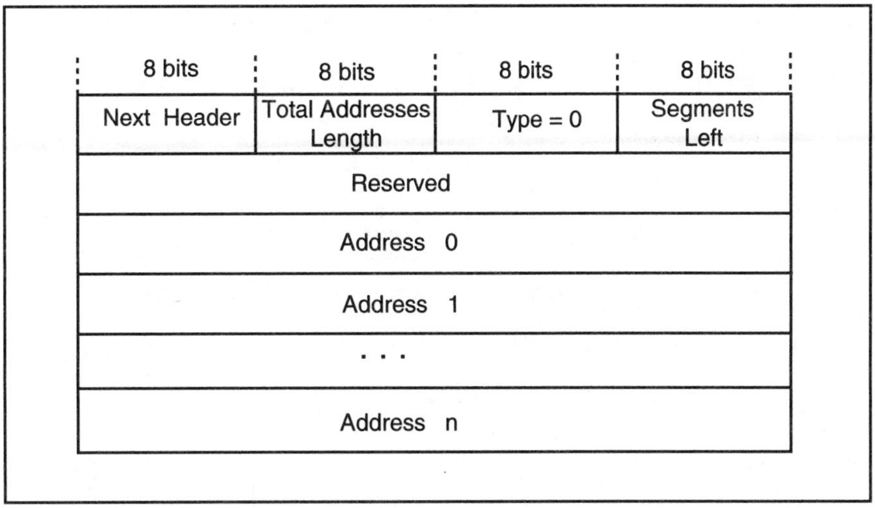

Figure 22.4
Type 0 Routing
header.

8 bits	8 bits	8 bits	8 bits
Next Header	Total Addresses Length	Type = 0	Segments Left
Reserved			
Address 0			
Address 1			
. . .			
Address n			

On arrival, the address list contains addresses for the listed nodes that have been visited. However, unlike the IPv4 Source Route header, it is not necessary to follow the reverse route when sending packets to the source.[8]

Just as for IPv4 loose source routing, there can be intermediate routers between a pair of adjacent nodes on the path.

The Routing header is an interesting feature of version 6. When combined with anycast addresses, it could be used to control paths based on which providers are preferred or on the need to use a specific provider (e.g., to reach a mobile user). Recall that an anycast address can be used to say "Go to the nearest router belonging to Service Provider X."

Options

The Hop-by-Hop header and the Destination Options header carry option information. The headers can carry a variable number of options. Some option values may change along the way. Each option is self-identifying and is encoded in three fields:

Option Type (8 bits)   Option Length (8 bits)   Option Value (n bits)

---

[8]The reverse route should be followed if and only if the responder has verified the integrity and authenticity of the Source Address and Routing header of the received packet.

The *Jumbo Payload* option is an example of a Hop-by-Hop option. It is used to declare the length of a payload that is bigger than 64 kilobits. The payload length (in bytes) is described in a 4-byte value. The payload length reports the total length of the packet excluding the IPv6 header.

Hop-by-Hop Options Header

The format of the Hop-by-Hop header is shown in Figure 22.5.

Fragmentation

Unlike version 4, *fragmentation is never performed by routers.* Fragmentation should be avoided whenever possible, but it will be needed occasionally. It is up to the source node to fragment packets. The destination node must reassemble them.

If a router receives a packet that is too large to forward, it will discard the packet and send back an ICMP message that announces the next-hop Maximum Transmission Unit (MTU).

When a source node creates a fragment, it must include a *Fragment* header. The Fragment header has the form shown in Figure 22.6.

As in version 4, the *Fragment Offset* field is 13 bits long and measures offsets in 8-byte blocks. The *more* bit indicates whether this is the last fragment or not. The *Identification* field has been expanded to 32 bits. Each fragment needs an IPv6 header and must include any extension headers that were part of the original header and need to be

Figure 22.5
The Hop-by-Hop header.

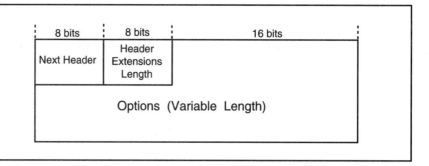

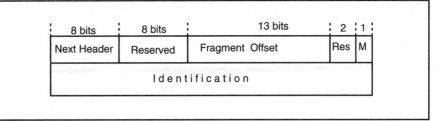

Figure 22.6
Format of a Fragment header.

processed along the way to the final destination, such as a Hop-by-Hop header or a Routing header.

Destination Options

The *Destination Options* header contains options that need to be processed by the packet's destination (or destinations, for multicasts). Currently, no options (other than padding fields) have been defined for this header.

The *Destination Options* header format is shown in Figure 22.7. The length (formally called the Header Extension Length) is the length of the Destination Options header in bytes, not including the first 8 bytes.

Recall that if a *Routing* header is included, the protocol allows two *Destination Options* headers to be included. The first, right before the *Routing* header, contains options that apply to nodes on the route. The second, placed after all other headers, applies only to the final destination.

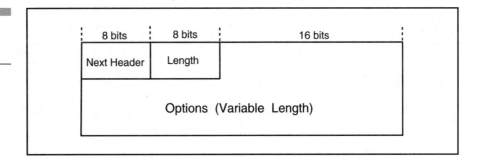

Figure 22.7
The Destination Options header.

Autoconfiguration

In the past, network managers paid for the benefits of having an IP network with a hefty amount of configuration and maintenance. One of the goals of version 6 is to provide a lean, effective automatic initialization procedure. This is important in helping a site migrate to the new address format. It also is vital to automate address changes that may come about because of a change in the choice of Service Provider.

On a LAN, an IPv6 host builds a link-local IP address automatically, using its network interface card address to create an interface identifier field. The host learns one or more prefixes from its neighboring routers and combines these prefixes with its interface identifier field.

Configuration via DHCPv6

Systems still can obtain a full set of configuration parameters from a DHCP server. Some changes are needed in order to migrate DHCP to version 6. Obviously, the updated protocol must support version 6 addresses. Work is proceeding on an updated form of DHCP for IPv6 that includes a number of protocol improvements.

It is hoped that DHCPv6 servers will not only autoconfigure hosts but also will automatically autoregister host names and addresses in the Domain Name System using secure dynamic DNS updates. An initializing host can request a specific host name or else can be assigned a name by the DHCPv6 server.

If the client's lease expires, the DHCPv6 server should then delete the client's DNS record using a secure update.

Neighbor Discovery

Router and prefix autoconfiguration are just a part of a bigger set of "neighbor discovery" functions. These functions include:

Router Discovery: Finding routers on the local link.

Prefix Discovery: Discovering and using prefixes that indicate which destinations are on the link and which are remote. This takes the place of subnet masks.

Parameter Discovery: Discovering parameters such as the link MTU and a default hop count value.

Address Autoconfiguration: Self-configuring IP addresses for link interfaces.

Address Resolution: Mapping a neighbor's IP address to its link-layer address.

Next-hop Determination: Mapping an IP address to the address of the next hop.

Neighbor Unreachability Detection: Detecting dead neighbor hosts and routers.

Duplicate Address Detection: Checking that an IP address that you have been assigned is not already in use.

Redirect: Getting notification that there is a better router to use for a given destination or that a destination is on the local link.

These services are carried out using ICMP messages. Details are presented in Chapter 23.

IPv6 Transition

Given the universality of IP around the world, it will *not* be possible to say, "On such-and-such a day, everybody must cut over to version 6." Clearly transition needs to be gradual:

- Organizations must not be forced to give up their current addresses.

- Organizations should be able to upgrade some nodes, while leaving others unchanged.

- The transition should be easy to understand and easy to do.

One big roadblock stands in the path to transition. Usually, an end user identifies a server by passing the name of the server computer to a client application. The client application performs the name-to-address translation by sending a request to a Domain Name server and expects a 4-byte address in response. Server applications also call on Domain Name servers to perform name-to-address and address-to-name translations. All applications written to use IP version 4 expect to work with 4-byte IP addresses. The application software must be updated before it can use IP version 6 addresses. This is a big job—think of the Year 2000 hassle!

Why Change?

Service Providers need IPv6 in order to perform more efficient backbone routing and provide future subscribers with numbers. But why should an organization with a properly functioning stand-alone IP network switch to version 6? If it is not having problems in managing its IP addresses, and if some of the new services (such as flows) are not needed, the answer is—don't bother. However, as mobile connectivity across the Internet becomes more and more common, there will be increasing pressure on the Internet IP address space. New applications and the expansion of IP addresses to many small devices may turn private IPv4 network administration into a big hassle. The authors of IPv6 believe that eventually, the benefits of IPv6 will outweigh the pain, even for many private networks.

In any case, it is likely that Internet servers will run with dual stacks and dual addresses for a long time.

How to Change

The first step in moving toward version 6 is to upgrade a site's Domain Name Server software so that its DNS servers can respond to queries that use the new address format.

It is very likely that the first private systems to be converted to dual version 4 and 6 protocol stacks will be routers that interface to external networks. Little by little, important servers will add a version 6 stack. In a mixed environment, version 6 traffic sometimes will have to be tunneled across a version 4 network.

During an interim period, IPv6 site-local addresses can be used. When sites attach to a Service Provider, the addresses will be augmented with the appropriate Region, Provider, and Subscriber prefixes.

DNS Changes

A new address resource record type, *AAAA,* maps domain names to IP version 6 addresses. A sample entry is:

MICKEY IN AAAA 4321:0:1:2:3:4:567:89AB

Reverse lookups also have to be supported. A new domain has been added in order to handle IPv6 *address-to-name* mappings. The reverse lookup domain is rooted at *IP6.INT.*

Recall that version 4 IP addresses are reversed to obtain their labels in the *in-addr.arpa* domain. A version 6 address also is reversed and is rewritten as a series of hexadecimal digits separated by dots. For example, a reverse lookup entry for:

4321:0:1:2:3:4:567:89AB

appears in the domain tree as:

B.A.9.8.7.6.5.0.4.0.0.0.3.0.0.0.2.0.0.0.1.0.0.0.0.0.0.0.1.2.3.4.IP6.INT

Tunneling Through a Version 4 Network

During the transition period, datagrams sometimes will traverse a path like the one shown in Figure 22.8. In the figure, Service Providers A and C support version 6, but Service Provider B does not. The boundary router interfaces will be assigned IPv4-compatible IPv6 addresses, which can easily be converted to version 4 addresses by dropping their zero prefixes. Version 6 packets will be wrapped inside a version 4 header and tunneled across the intervening network.

Figure 22.8
Tunneling traffic across a version 4 network.

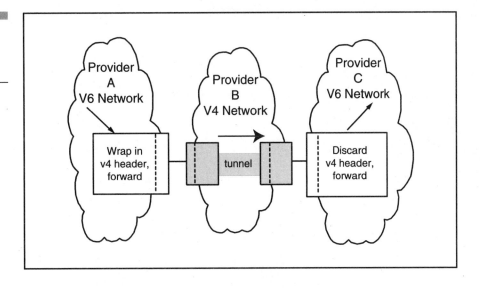

Tunneling also can occur within a site that has converted some of its networks to version 6. Tunneling can be used anywhere that it is convenient to do so. It can be used between routers, between hosts, or on a host/router path.

Summary

The IP next generation working groups have laid the foundation for a version that solves the Internet address space depletion problem and promotes more efficient routing. The new protocol provides attractive options for automatic configuration and enables coexistence and gradual migration. The chained headers allow for fairly painless future updates and also provide a graceful way for other protocols to ride across an IP network.

Recommended Reading

RFC 2373 defines the IP version 6 Addressing Architecture. The IPv6 Aggregatable Global Unicast Address Format is described in RFC 2374. Parts of IP version 6 continue to be revamped. Check the RFC index for current publications.

23

ICMPv6 and Neighbor Discovery

Introduction

Version 6 of the Internet Control Message Protocol (ICMPv6) retains many of the version 4 functions, but there are some major changes:

- As we already have seen, ICMPv6 messages assist in automatic address configuration.
- There are new ICMPv6 messages and procedures that replace the Address Resolution Protocol (ARP).
- Path Maximum Transmission Unit (MTU) discovery is automatic. Since routers no longer fragment packets, whenever a packet is dropped because it is too big, a new *Packet Too Big* message is sent to the source.
- ICMPv6 does not send *Source Quench* messages.
- ICMPv6 incorporates Internet Group Management Protocol multicast membership reporting functions.
- ICMPv6 assists in detecting that a router is not functioning or a communicating partner is no longer active.

ICMPv6 is sufficiently different that it has a new protocol number—it has been assigned Next Header value 58.

Basic ICMP Messages

The basic ICMPv6 error message types are listed below. Error messages have types in the range 0 to 127.

1 Destination Unreachable

2 Packet Too Big

3 Time Exceeded

4 Parameter Problem

5 Redirect

Informational messages have types in the range 128 to 255. The echo request and reply informational messages have types:

128 Echo Request

129 Echo Reply

Figure 23.1
General format of an
ICMPv6 message.

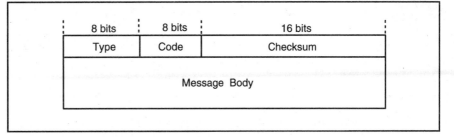

The general ICMP message format is shown in Figure 23.1. The message body field of an error message contains as much of the original IPv6 packet as will fit without making the error message packet exceed 576 bytes. The basic ICMP messages resemble their version 4 counterparts.

Destination Unreachable

The reasons for sending a *Destination Unreachable* message are described by the codes:

0   No route to destination.

1   Communication with destination administratively prohibited.

2   Next destination in Routing header is not a neighbor, and this is a strict route.

3   Address is unreachable.

4   Port is unreachable.

The format of a *Destination Unreachable* message is shown in Figure 23.2.

Figure 23.2
Format of a Destina-
tion Unreachable
message.

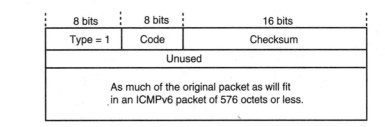

Figure 23.3
Format of a Packet
Too Big message.

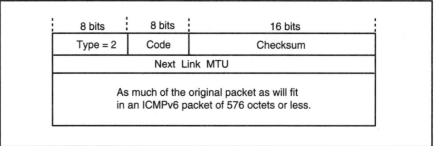

Packet Too Big

A router sends a *Packet Too Big* message when the packet is bigger than the MTU for the next-hop link. The next-hop link's usable MTU is reported in the message. Note that in version 4, this fact was reported in a *Destination Unreachable* message. Figure 23.3 shows the format of a *Packet Too Big* message.

Time Exceeded Message

A *Time Exceeded* message is sent by a router that has decremented the Hop Limit to 0 (code = 0) or by a system whose reassembly timeout has expired (code = 1). The message format is identical to the format of the *Destination Unreachable* message, except that the type is 3.

Parameter Problem Message

A *Parameter Problem* message is sent by a system that cannot process a packet because of a header field. The codes are:

0   Erroneous header field encountered

1   Unrecognized Next Header type encountered

2   Unrecognized IPv6 option encountered

The message format is similar to the format of the *Destination Unreachable* message, except that the "unused" field is replaced by a pointer that indicates the byte offset to the error, and the type is 4.

Echo Request and Reply

The *Echo Request* and *Reply* messages have formats identical to the version 4 messages, except for the fact that type 128 is used for Echo Requests and type 129 is used for Echo Replies.

Group Membership Messages

A separate Internet Group Management Protocol (IGMP) was used to track multicast group memberships for IPv4. The messages used for this protocol were described in Chapter 10.

For IPv6, the functions previously performed by IGMP messages for IPv4 are carried out using ICMPv6 messages. However, the actions of hosts and routers are basically the same.

ICMPv6 messages that contain the same information as the older IGMP messages have been defined. The new group management message format is shown in Figure 23.4. The *Maximum Response Delay* is nonzero only in query messages. It reports the maximum time that responding *Report* messages may be delayed. Message types include:

130 Multicast Listener Query

131 Multicast Listener Report

132 Multicast Listener Done

Figure 23.4
Multicast group message format.

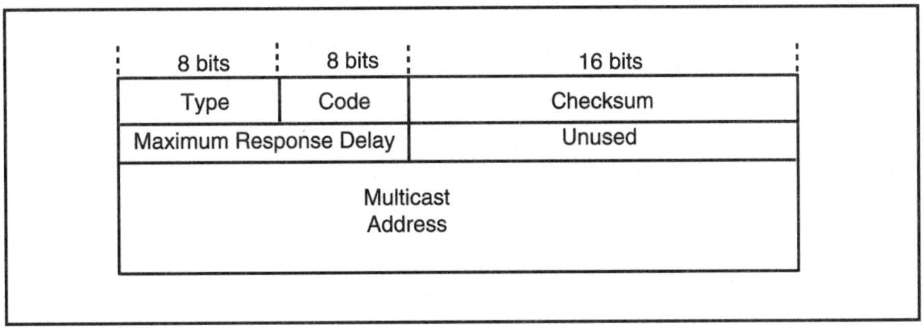

8 bits	8 bits	16 bits	
Type	Code	Checksum	
Maximum Response Delay		Unused	
Multicast Address			

Neighbor Discovery

Recall that ICMPv6 provides a set of "neighbor discovery" functions that assist in:

- Automatic address configuration
- IP parameter configuration
- Location of routers
- Location of other hosts on the link
- Neighbor unreachability detection
- Duplicate address detection

The neighbor discovery functions include:

- *Router Solicitation:* Enables a host to ask neighbor routers to announce their presence and provide link and Internet parameters. This is similar to the ICMPv4 Router Solicitation. The message is sent to the all-routers link-local multicast address.

- *Router Advertisement:* Sent periodically by each router, and also sent in response to a host's solicitation. This is similar to the ICMPv4 Router Advertisement. The message is sent either to the all-nodes multicast address or to the source address of a host that sent a Router Solicitation message.

- *Neighbor Solicitation:* Used (like an ARP request) to discover the link-layer address of a neighbor, to verify that a neighbor still is reachable via a cached link-layer address, or to check that no other node is using a specific IP address. These messages also are used to check whether an unresponsive neighbor no longer can be reached.

- *Neighbor Advertisement:* A response to a Neighbor Solicitation message (similar to an ARP response). A node also can announce a change in its link-layer address by sending unsolicited Neighbor Advertisements.

- *Redirect:* Performs the same function as the ICMPv4 redirect message.

In summary, the ICMPv6 message types used to implement the Neighbor Discovery functions are:

133   Router Solicitation Message

134   Router Advertisement Message

135   Neighbor Solicitation Message

136   Neighbor Advertisement Message

137   Redirect

Role of Routers

When an organization has a routed network or is connected to an Internet Service Provider, routers provide hosts with the basic configuration information. Each router supplies hosts with data that includes:

- The link-layer address of the router.
- A list of all address prefixes that are used on the LAN. More than one prefix might be used on a LAN.[1]
- For each prefix, a prefix length that indicates how many bits need to be matched in order to identify that a system is on the LAN. This takes the place of the subnet mask.
- Which prefixes hosts should use to create their own addresses.
- A default hop value to be used in outgoing IP packets.
- Whether the host should retrieve additional address data from a Dynamic Host Configuration Protocol (DHCP) server.
- Whether the host should retrieve additional configuration parameters from a DHCP server.
- The MTU for a link that has variable MTU.
- Values for various timers.

This is done via the ICMPv6 *Router Advertisement* messages (type 134). Hosts listen for *Router Advertisement* messages on the all-nodes link-local multicast address.

When a host boots, it may not want to wait for a *Router Advertisement*. The host may send out a *Router Solicitation* message (type 133) in order to trigger an advertisement. The router responds by sending an advertisement to the host's link-local address.

---

[1]We use the term "LAN" instead of the more formal term "link" which is used in the standards documents. The same autoconfiguration process could be used on a virtual LAN.

Address Prefix List

Many network managers will be happy to hear of the demise of the loathed subnet mask. Instead, routing decisions are based on comparing address prefixes.

A router advertises the list of address prefixes that are used on the local link. A prefix is expressed as an IPv6 address along with a number that tells how many bits actually belong to the prefix. Hosts listen to the router advertisements and store these prefix lists.

When a host needs to decide whether a destination is on or off the link, the host runs through its list of on-link prefixes and compares the relevant number of bits with the corresponding destination address bits.

IPv6 Interface Addresses

Every version 6 interface has a *list* of addresses associated with it. At minimum, the list includes the unique *link-local address.*

How can a host generate site-local or global addresses automatically? Some of the prefixes advertised by routers are flagged for use in constructing host addresses. A new site-local or global address is constructed by placing an advertised prefix in front of the unique interface identifier. This address is then added to the host's list of addresses for the interface.

The router's advertisement also tells hosts whether they should pick up additional address information from a DHCP server (which can assign administrator-configured addresses). And the advertisement indicates whether additional configuration information should be obtained from a server.

By the way, manual configuration still will be supported for version 6, if anyone wants to use it.

Changing Addresses

The ability to use more than one global prefix can ease a transition from one Service Provider to another. The router's advertisements associate timeouts with each prefix. When switching from one provider to another, the old prefix will simply be allowed to age out. Of course, the timeout values for a new, active prefix are refreshed periodically so that it will not age out.

Timeouts are basically lease times. They make it possible to pick up a host and plug it into a different link at the site. Recall that a prefix includes the subnet identifier as well as global information. Old prefixes will age out, and new ones will be learned.

Neighbor Solicitation and Advertisement

In IP version 4, a host locates a LAN neighbor with a specific IP address by means of an ARP broadcast and its response. ARP messages are link-level frames. In IPv6, ARP frames are replaced with ICMP messages. Since ICMP messages have IP headers, they can be authenticated—or even encrypted, if desired—using IP security.

The new ICMP *Neighbor Solicitation* and *Neighbor Advertisement* messages are sent as multicasts. A *Neighbor Advertisement* is the response to a *Neighbor Solicitation*. In addition to discovering neighbor link-layer addresses, *Neighbor Solicitation* messages also are used to:

- Detect duplicate IP addresses
- Test whether a router is dead
- Test whether a neighbor to whom you are sending packets is dead

Address Resolution

To discover the link-level address for a neighbor, a *Neighbor Solicitation* message is sent to the "solicited-node multicast address" of the target address. Recall that this is constructed by adding the last 3 bytes of an IPv6 link-local address to a fixed multicast prefix. The sender includes its own link-layer address within the message.

Note that using this special multicast cuts down substantially on the number of systems likely to "hear" the request. In fact, it is very likely that only the targeted system will examine the request.

Detecting Duplicate IP Addresses

It is important to avoid the headaches caused by duplicate IP addresses. Before taking possession of a link-local IP address or any other address that is *not* constructed by adding a prefix to the link-local address, a node will send a *Neighbor Solicitation* message asking whether any neighbor has that IP address. (The node uses the unspecified source address as the source address for the message.) If the IP address already is in use, the address-holder will multicast a response. This ensures that the link-local IP address—and every address formed from it by using a different prefix—is unique. In addition, addresses that are manually configured or are learned from a DHCP server are tested for uniqueness before they are used.

Neighbor Unreachability Detection

The detection of a dead router was a chancy business in IPv4. In version 6, if a timeout indicates that a router might be inactive, a system checks by sending a *Neighbor Solicitation* unicast message to the router.

The same procedure is used to check whether a host neighbor has become unreachable.

Redirect Messages

Just as in version 4, when a host has forwarded a datagram to the wrong local router, the router sends back a *Redirect* message indicating the correct first-hop node. A *Redirect* message also is used to notify a sender that the destination is actually on the local link. Perhaps this is why *Redirect* messages are defined in the Neighbor Discovery specification.

Figure 23.5 shows the proposed format for ICMPv6 *Redirect* messages. The target address is the IP address of the next hop that should

Figure 23.5
Format of a Redirect message.

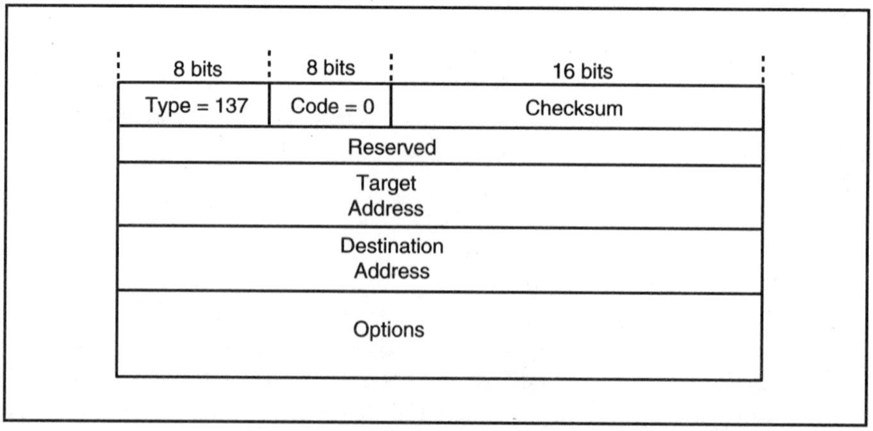

8 bits	8 bits	16 bits
Type = 137	Code = 0	Checksum
Reserved		
Target Address		
Destination Address		
Options		

be used. The destination address is the desired destination. The options field includes the link-layer address for the target system and may also include part of the redirected datagram.

Recommended Reading

At the time of writing, much of ICMP version 6 currently is being revamped in a series of draft documents. Check the RFC index for current publications.

CHAPTER 24

IP Security

Introduction

The need to develop a new version of IP created additional stimulus to the effort to solve TCP/IP's security problems. The proposed mechanisms introduce security into the IP layer. They are designed to be used with both IP versions 4 and 6. For simplicity, the scenarios in this chapter will refer to version 4 addresses and datagrams.

Everyone agrees that there is a need for security, but why build it into the IP layer? Why not use the application layer? In fact, it is likely that many applications *will* add their own security mechanisms. But in an environment where it is easy for snoopers to capture traffic, use all or part of it for later replay, and forge their IP addresses when they do it, you cannot be sure of the validity of any datagram.

Why not use the physical layer? All link traffic could be encrypted. This would solve link eavesdropping problems, but the traffic would need to be automatically decrypted at each router. Today, there is no particular reason to trust all routers.

Also this would not solve authentication problems. It also might cause severe bottlenecks for high-speed traffic, even when encryption and decryption are performed in hardware. Furthermore, every LAN interface card would need to be capable of encryption and decryption, and this would be very costly.

Security Issues

Recall that in Chapter 3 we discussed three security attributes:

Authentication	Validating the identity of a user, client process, or server application
Integrity	Assuring that data has not been changed
Confidentiality	Preventing unwanted disclosure of information

In Chapter 3, we presented several mechanisms for implementing these attributes. In the sections that follow, we see how these mechanisms have been adopted to provide security at the IP layer.

Security Strategy

The integration of security into IP is one of the thorniest jobs that is being tackled by the Internet Engineering Task Force (IETF). The need for authentication, data integrity, and confidentiality is immediate and widespread. The security strategy is:

- To promote interworking, start out with well-known, already implemented mechanisms for authentication, integrity, and confidentiality
- Design the security framework so that it is possible to switch to other mechanisms

The mechanisms selected include:

- Message Digest 5 (MD5) or the Secure Hash Algorithm (SHA-1) for authentication and data integrity.[1]
- Symmetric encryption using the Cipher Block Chaining mode of the U.S. Data Encryption Standard (CBC-DES) for confidentiality.

Public key encryption may be used for key distribution.

Scenarios for Security

There are many different ways to use the security facilities that we will be describing a little later. Let's look at some scenarios in order to understand at least some of the choices.

Scenario 1.   Company XYZ wants to safeguard its internal client/server communications. They want to eliminate the possibility that someone could compromise their data by forging source IP addresses or altering data in transit.

Scenario 2.   There is an administrator at company XYZ who copies highly sensitive files between hosts. Only this administrator is allowed to perform these transfers. It also is important to prevent an eavesdropper from capturing and using these files.

Scenario 3.   Company XYZ connects its manufacturing division to its remote headquarters location via the Internet. The company wishes to make all of its communications opaque to the outside world.

For simplicity, you can think of each client and server host as having a single interface and single IP address. However, all of the security mechanisms work when a system has multiple interfaces and multiple IP addresses.

---

[1]Currently, a problem arises when using MD5 with very high-speed communications because of the time required to perform the calculation.

Figure 24.1
Using a message
digest.

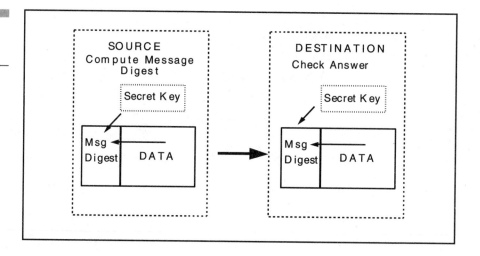

Scenario 1

Message Digest technology is used to satisfy the requirements of scenario 1—that is, authenticate senders and detect whether data has been changed. Let's review how message digests work (see Figure 24.1):

- The source and destination know a secret key.
- The source performs a calculation, using the data and the secret key as input.
- The source sends the answer along with the data.
- The destination performs the same calculation and compares the answers.

Configuring Authentication Information for Scenario 1

Suppose company XYZ has an important server at IP address 130.15.20.2. The server's security administrator numbers the client hosts and assigns a secret authentication key to each client IP address.

The server needs to store this security information. A table such as the one shown in Table 24.1 could be used to store security parameters. The table is indexed by a number assigned to each client host—more formally, the number is called the *Security Parameters Index,* or SPI.[2]

---

[2]If the server has multiple IP addresses, the table also is indexed by its destination IP addresses.

TABLE 24.1

Security Information at Destination 130.15.20.2

SPI (for client host)	Source IP Address	Client's Authentication Key	Client's Authentication Method
301	130.15.24.4	X'2E-41-43-11-5A-5A-74-53-E3-01-88-55-10-15-CD-23	MD5
302	130.15.60.10	X'35-14-4F-21-2B-2C-12-34-82-22-98-44-C0-1C-33-56	MD5
...	...	...	...

Of course, each client would need to be configured with the Security Parameters Index and secret key to be used when accessing this server. Table 24.2 shows configuration data at the second client. Note that the client needs separate entries for each destination that it accesses.

What happens when the client host wants to send an authenticated datagram to the server?

- The client looks up the destination IP address in its table.
- The authentication key is used to calculate a message digest for the datagram.
- The SPI number and message digest answer are put into the Authentication header.
- The datagram is sent.

When the server receives the datagram:

- The server uses the SPI in the Authentication header to look up the client entry in the table.
- The source IP address of the message is compared to the source address in the table.
- The message digest is calculated using the authentication key in the table entry.
- The answer is compared with the value in the Authentication header.

TABLE 24.2

Security Information at Source 130.15.60.10.

Destination IP Address	SPI	Client Source IP Address	Client's Authentication Key	Client's Authentication Method
130.15.20.2	302	130.15.60.10	X'35-14-4F-21-2B-2C-12-34-82-22-98-44-C0-1C-33-56	MD5
130.15.65.4	...	...	...	...

One-Way Security Association

Note that we really have done only half of the job. We have set up authentication in *one direction only*. Datagrams sent from the client to the server are authenticated.

The information that we have described is said to define a one-way *Security Association*. At both the source and destination, the combination of the *destination* IP address for this association and the SPI is sufficient to identify the entry to be used. Thus, a Security Association corresponds to a destination and an SPI.

In order to authenticate data flowing from the server to the client, *we need a separate set of table entries that define the authentication keys for the Security Association in the reverse direction*. That is, each host needs:

- A security table used when the host is the source of datagrams.
- A security table used when the host is the destination of datagrams.

Figure 24.2 shows a pair of Security Associations.

How Many Authentication Keys?

How many authentication keys need to be used by a server when it is sending datagrams to its clients? Intuitively, it might seem natural to

Figure 24.2
A pair of Security
Associations.

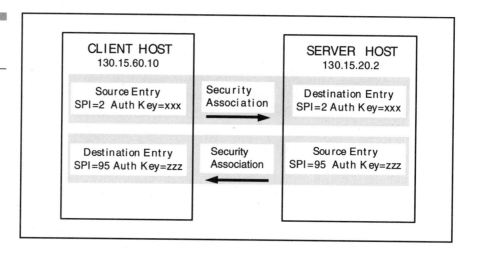

assign a server a single MD5 authentication key, which the server would use to say to all clients "I am server so-and-so."

But then all clients would know that key. A client might use a forged IP address and masquerade as the server. To prevent this from happening, a separate authentication key could be assigned for each client host. The total number of keys could be reduced by using a same key for client-to-server and server-to-client authentication.

Scenario 2

In scenario 1, security was imposed at the host level. But suppose that there is a user or role that requires a different level of security. The security framework provides for user, role, or information sensitivity-based security.

Suppose that the client host that we discussed in scenario 1 is a multiuser system. For scenario 2, a shared host-based authentication key is sufficient for the ordinary users at the client host 130.15.60.10. However, the system administrator's file transfers to the server will need special authentication and will need to be encrypted. Figure 24.3 illustrates the Security Associations that are created.

Figure 24.3
Multiple Security Associations for a client and server.

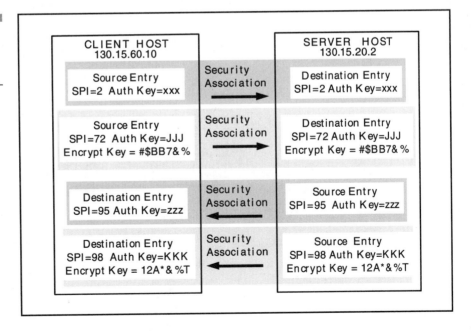

TABLE 24.3

Destination Security Information at 130.15.20.2

SPI	Source IP Address	Client's Authentication Key	Client's Authentication Method	Client's Encryption Key	Client's Encryption Method
301	130.15.24.4	...	MD5	None	None
2	130.15.60.10	..xxx..	MD5	None	None
72	130.15.60.10	..JJJ..	MD5	#$BB7&%	CBC-DES
...	...	...	...	...	...

Let's look at the Security Association tables when they are augmented with an additional entry for the administrator and with encryption keys. Table 24.3 shows destination information at the server, and Table 24.4 shows source information at the client. There are now separate SPIs for the ordinary users at 130.15.60.10 and for the administrator at that address.

Tables 24.3 and 24.4 include security parameters for the one-way Security Associations with the source at client 130.15.60.10 and the destination at server 130.15.20.2. A separate set of parameters would be defined in the reverse direction, with the server acting as the source and the client acting as the destination. Here again, local planners need to decide whether to use the same keys in both directions, or assign different keys for client-to-server and server-to-client traffic.

TABLE 24.4   Source Security Information at 130.15.60.10

Destination IP Address	Role or Userid	SPI	Source IP Address	Client's Authentication Key	Client's Authentication Method	Client's Encryption Key	Client's Encryption Method
130.15.20.2	Host	2	130.15.60.10	..xxx..	MD5	None	None
130.15.20.2	Admin.	72	130.15.60.10	..JJJ..	MD5	#$BB7&%	CBC-DES
130.15.65.4	Host	...	...	...	MD5		...
... ...	...	...	...	...	...		

Figure 24.4
Tunneling traffic
between networks.

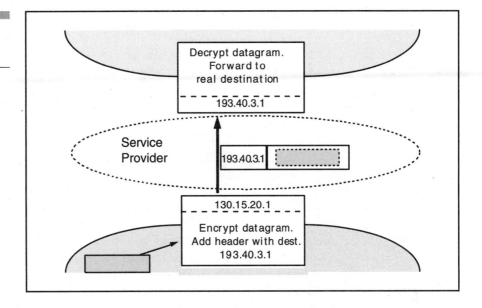

Scenario 3

Scenario 3 is illustrated in Figure 24.4. The goal is to make all of the traffic that company XYZ sends across an untrusted network opaque to the outside world. *Tunnel-mode* encapsulation is used. This means that datagrams are encrypted and encapsulated inside other datagrams.

As shown in the figure, when a datagram whose destination is in network 193.40.3 arrives at the boundary router for network 130.15, the router encrypts the entire datagram, including its headers. The router prepends a temporary (cleartext) IP header[3] and forwards the datagram across the Service Provider network to the boundary router for network 193.40.3. There, the temporary header is removed, the datagram is decrypted, and then the datagram is forwarded to its true destination. In this case, Security Associations are defined between the two boundary routers.

---

[3]In addition to a main header, other headers could also be prepended. For example, a separate Authentication header could be used to authenticate the router-to-router transfer.

Generalizing

We have looked at some specific examples in order to become acquainted with the basic security framework. It is easy to see that in general, a common set of mechanisms can be used to secure traffic when it is transmitted:

- Host to host
- Router to router
- Host to router
- Router to host

If a destination host has more than one IP address, separate Security Association parameter sets could be defined for each destination address. And, there is no barrier to providing authentication, data integrity, and confidentiality for multicast destination addresses.

In scenario 2, we saw that security can be defined at a user- or role-based level. This can be made as fine grained as may be needed. Furthermore, security parameters could be configured based on the sensitivity of information (e.g., unclassified or top secret). Of course, the maintenance of many different parameter sets will depend on having a very good key distribution application.

Security Protocol Elements

Now we are ready to take a more formal look at how security is implemented.

Security Associations

As we have seen, security is handled one direction at a time. To enable a source to communicate securely with a destination, both the source and destination need to store a set of parameters, such as:

- Source address
- The authentication and integrity algorithm(s) to be used
- The confidentiality algorithm to be used
- Secret keys that will be used and any other information needed for the algorithms

- The lifetime limit for the keys
- The lifetime limit for the Security Association
- Sensitivity level (e.g., unclassified or top secret)

A *Security Association* is formally defined as the set of security parameters that supports secure one-way communication between a source and destination. From the scenarios above we can see that:

- A source host might use a single set of parameters when sending data to a destination.
- Alternatively, a host might have several Security Associations that it uses to send data to a given destination host. The association that is selected might be based on source userid, role, or sensitivity.

Recall that a numeric identifier called a Security Parameter Index is assigned to each distinct parameter set *for a given destination.*[4]

The same SPI numbers can be reused for different destinations. The parameter sets for (Destination = A, SPI = 300) and (Destination = B, SPI = 300) are very likely to be different. In other words, sets of parameters are indexed by both destination and SPI.

The IP *Authentication Header* and the IP *Encapsulating Security Payload Header* are used to implement IP version 4 and version 6 security. These headers may be used together or separately.

Authentication Header

When a message digest is used for authentication, the *Authentication Header* serves a double purpose:

- It validates the sender because the sender knows the secret key used to create the computed message digest result.
- It indicates that data has not been changed in transit.

The Authentication Header has the format shown in Figure 24.5. The receiver uses the Security Parameters Index to look up the authentication protocol and authentication key. The receiver uses the authentication key to perform a message digest calculation.

---

[4]Some standard parameter sets will be assigned Security Parameter Indices by the Internet Assigned Numbers Authority (IANA).

Figure 24.5
Format of the
Authentication
Header.

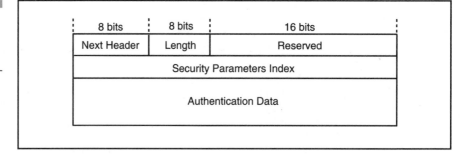

The message digest authentication calculation is performed against all fields in the IP datagram that do not change in transit. (Fields that change, such as the hop counter or IP version 6 routing pointer are treated as zero for the calculation.) The receiver's answer is compared to the value in the *Authentication Data* field. If they differ, the datagram is discarded.

IP Security with Encryption

If data privacy is needed, then data needs to be encrypted. Encryption and decryption of data is enabled by means of an *Encapsulating Security Payload* header. An Encapsulating Security Payload header contains parameters that enable the valid recipient to select the correct decryption key and apply the appropriate decryption algorithm. The recipient might view the fact that the source held key information that enabled it to encrypt correctly as sufficient to authenticate the source and guarantee data integrity. Optionally, an Authentication header could be included to provide authentication and solid data integrity protection.

Transport-Mode and Tunnel-Mode

There are two approaches to the encryption of IP traffic. Within your own organization, you probably would use *Transport-mode,* which is illustrated in Figure 24.6. A normal IP header is used for the datagram. One or more security headers follow the IP header, and the payload is encrypted.

If you were sending data between two private sites across the Internet, you probably would use *Tunnel-mode*. In this case, a router at the sending site's boundary encrypts the entire datagram, including the IP header. As shown in Figure 24.7, the router adds a new IP header whose destination address is the partner boundary router at the remote site. An Encapsulating Security Payload header and optionally, an Authentication header would be inserted after the IP header.

The router at the remote site strips away the tunneling IP header, decrypts the datagram, and forwards it towards its true destination.

Encapsulating Security Payload Header

The IP Encapsulating Security Payload header is used to implement both Transport-mode and Tunnel-mode encryption.

The format of the Encapsulating Security Payload header is shown in Figure 24.8. The recipient will use the Security Parameter Index to look up the algorithm and key(s) to be used. The remainder of the data depends on the algorithm choice.

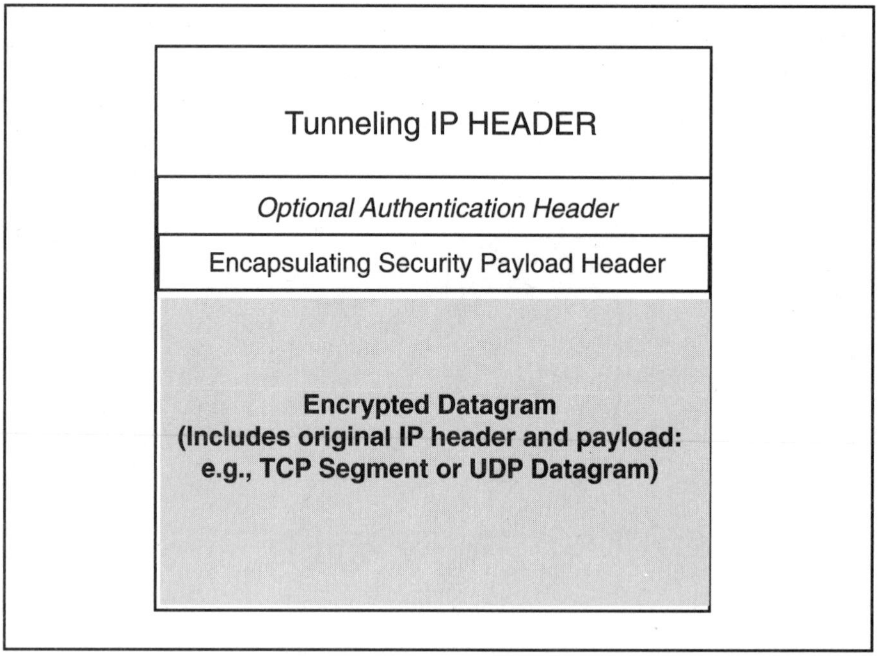

Figure 24.7
Tunnel-mode
encryption.

Tunneling IP HEADER
Optional Authentication Header
Encapsulating Security Payload Header
Encrypted Datagram **(Includes original IP header and payload:** **e.g., TCP Segment or UDP Datagram)**

When using CBC-DES, the format of the Encapsulating Security Payload header and the remainder of the message is as shown in Figure 24.9.

The *Initialization Vector* is a block of data needed to start off the CBC-DES algorithm. The shaded area is transmitted in encrypted form. Type = 4 means that the payload encapsulates a complete datagram (Tunnel-mode).

Although systems are expected to use CBC-DES initially, future Encapsulating Security Payload protocols could combine authentication and data integrity with encryption.

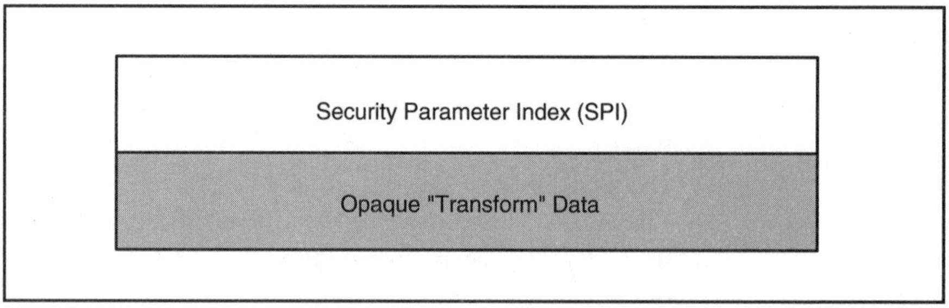

Figure 24.8
An Encapsulating
Security Payload
header.

Security Parameter Index (SPI)
Opaque "Transform" Data

Figure 24.9
Header and payload
when using CBC-
DES.

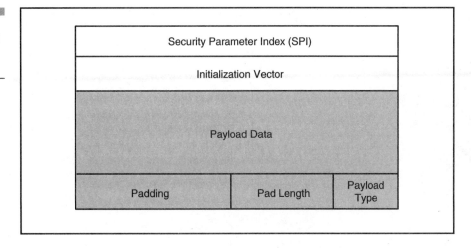

Using Authentication with Tunnel-Mode

Two separate Authentication headers might be included when Tunnel-mode encryption is used between boundary routers. One would be within the *original* datagram header, which would be encrypted and hidden for all or part of the journey. This header would provide end-to-end authentication. The other Authentication header would be part of the cleartext datagram header that is used between boundary routers. This header would provide boundary-to-boundary authentication.

Key Management

As we have seen, wide use of IP security will require the distribution of many secret keys to a large number of nodes. Keys need to be changed periodically, and the use of matching keys needs to be synchronized.

There is a growing literature on key management. No single standard method of key management is mandated, and much experimentation is likely.

The use of asymmetric public/private key pairs instead of symmetric CBC-DES could significantly reduce the number of keys that need to be administered.

Recommended Reading

The following list of RFCs was current at the time of this writing. Check the RFC index for updates.

RFC 1825   *Security Architecture for the Internet Protocol.* The Reference section of this document lists many other publications that relate to security.

RFC 1826   *IP Authentication Header*

RFC 1828   *IP Authentication using Keyed MD5*

RFC 1321   *The MD5 Message-Digest Algorithm*

RFC 1827   *IP Encapsulating Security Payload (ESP)*

RFC 1829   *The ESP DES-CBC Transform*

RFC 1852   *IP Authentication Using Keyed SHA*

RFC 1853   *IP in IP Tunneling.*

RFC 2085   *HMAC-MD5 IP Authentication with Replay Prevention.*

RFCs and Other
TCP/IP Documents

Important RFC Documents

There are numerous archives on the Internet that provide free copies of RFC documents. The authoritative archive is controlled by the RFC Editor and is located at University of Southern California Information Sciences Institute. At each archive, the RFC documents are stored with a master list, which is in a file called *rfc-index.txt*.

Periodically, the official list of standards and their current status is published in an RFC document. This list is itself a standard (STD 1). At the time of writing, RFC 2300 contains the official list of standards. Check the file *rfc-index.txt* for the most current Official Standards document. In STD 1, the protocol *state* indicates progress through the review process. After initial screening, a standard is given *proposed* state. After further examination, improvement, and review, it may be advanced to *draft* state. The protocol becomes a standard after test, usage, and final review. The protocol *status* indicates whether an RFC document is required, recommended, elective, limited use, or not recommended.

There are many interesting RFC documents. The ones in the list below may be helpful:

- rfc2196.txt   Site Security Handbook
- rfc2151.txt   A Primer On Internet and TCP/IP Tools and Utilities
- rfc2132.txt   DHCP Options and BOOTP Vendor Extensions.
- rfc1912.txt   Common DNS Operational and Configuration Errors
- rfc1713.txt   Tools for DNS Debugging
- rfc1536.txt   Common DNS Implementation Errors and Suggested Fixes
- rfc1812.txt   Requirements for IP Version 4 Routers.

■ rfc1700.txt   Assigned Numbers. This is a fairly old RFC that contains Internet parameters. This was the last time that all parameters were gathered into one file. Now they are stored in separate files at the Internet Assigned Numbers Authority. A later section contains retrieval instructions.

Location of RFC Documents

At the time of this writing, Request For Comments (RFC) documents could be obtained from a Web site at University of Southern California Information Sciences Institute. Try the URL:

http://info.internet.isi.edu/7c/in-notes/rfc/.cache

If this becomes invalid, you can start at the page below and follow the pointers to RFCs:

http://www.ietf.org/

Another location that currently works is:

http://nis.nsf.net/internet/documents/

There are several file transfer sites that currently offer RFC documents. Two that work currently are at *nis.nfs.net* and *ftp.isi.edu*. The examples below show how you could retrieve the RFC index and rfc2300 from these sites. Use the same pattern for other documents.

ftp://nis.nfs.net/internet/documents/rfc/rfc-index.txt

ftp://nis.nfs.net/internet/documents/rfc/rfc2300.txt

ftp://ftp.isi.edu/in-notes/rfc-index.txt

ftp://ftp.isi.edu/in-notes/rfc2300.txt

Assigned Numbers

Currently, the Internet Assigned Numbers Authority (IANA) publishes Internet parameter assignments at the public file transfer archive:

ftp://ftp.isi.edu/in-notes/iana/assignments/

Registration Forms

At the time of writing, Internet name registration forms can be obtained from the InterNIC Registration Services, which can be accessed at:

http://www.internic.net/

Address registration forms can be obtained from ARIN, RIPE, or APNIC. See, for example:

http://www/arin/net/

B

Network Information Centers and Other Services

Internet Assigned Numbers Authority

At the time of writing, the Internet Assigned Numbers authority (IANA) performs several very important functions. The IANA:

- Is responsible for administering the global Internet address number space.
- Coordinates the assignment of unique parameter values for Internet protocols.
- Administers domain names under the US naming subtree.

Transition of the IANA to a new nonprofit corporation is currently underway. The responsibilities of the new organization are an expansion of those of the old IANA:

- Coordinating the Internet address space.
- Coordinating the assignment of Internet parameters.
- Managing and performing functions related to the coordination of the Internet Domain Name System.
- Overseeing operation of the authoritative Internet root server system.

Check the following sites for current information:

http://www.isoc.org/, http://www.iana.org/

Registration

Before an organization can connect its network to the Internet, it needs to obtain one or more blocks of IP addresses—either from its Service Provider or directly from an Internet registration service. The organization must register its Domain Name and identify its Domain Name Servers (DNSs).

Address Registration

Currently, overall responsibility for management of the global address space rests with the IANA. The IANA delegates blocks of addresses to three regional registries.

■ **ARIN** The American Registry for Internet Numbers is responsible for administering address blocks for North and South America, the Caribbean, and sub-Saharan Africa.

   http://www.arin.net/

■ **RIPE** Reseaux IP Europeens is responsible for administering address blocks in Europe.

   http://www.ripe.net/

   The RIPE site has pointers to the administrators who are in charge of administering domain names under each country code in Europe and the surrounding region, and can provide information on the administration of these subdomains.

■ **APNIC** The Asia-Pacific Network information Center administers blocks of address for the Asia-Pacific region and can be accessed at:

   http://www.apnic.net/

Registration of Generic Names

In 1993, the National Science Foundation granted a five-year contract to Network Solutions for the purpose of administering the registration of names under the generic top-level names *com, org, net,* and *edu.* Network Solutions also was responsible for managing the root of the Domain Name System database. Network Solutions established the InterNic Registration Services, whose Web site is at:

   http://www.internic.net/

The National Science Foundation contract expired, and there was much debate on how generic name registration and management of the root database should be performed in the future. The new IANA is responsible for overseeing the operation of the authoritative Internet root Domain Name Service system.

Gov and Mil Domains

Registration under *gov* for U.S. federal government civilian agencies is at:

   http://www.registration.fed.gov/

Registrations under *gov* and *mil* for U.S. military agencies is at:

http://www.nic.mil/

US Domain

The US domain is used for local, regional, or state government, K-12 schools, and two-year colleges. It is administered by The US Domain Registry at the Information Sciences Institute of the University of Southern California under the Internet Assigned Numbers Authority. The current Web site is:

http://www.isi.edu/in-notes/usdnr/

Other Registries

There are pointers to other registries at Yahoo:

*http://www.yahoo.com/Computers_and_Internet/Internet/
Domain_Registration/*

Finding Administrators via *Whois*

An organization's name and address registration information includes the names of its administrative and technical points of contact, and information on how to reach them.

This information is made available online by each of the major Network Information Centers in "Whois" databases. There are *whois* database clients that can be pointed at these databases and can retrieve information from them. Below, we use a standard, text-based Unix *whois* client to ask the InterNic database for information on the domain *yale.edu*. The first response gives us Yale's "handle," YALE-DOM, which is used to get more information about the domain.

```
whois -h rs.internic.net yale.edu
Yale University (YALE-DOM)                                    YALE.EDU
Yale University (YALE)      YALE.EDU      128.36.0.1, 130.132.1.1

whois -h rs.internic.net YALE-DOM

Registrant:
Yale University (YALE-DOM)
   175 Whitney Avenue
   New Haven, Connecticut 06520
   US

Domain Name: YALE.EDU

Administrative Contact:
   Paolillo, Joseph     (JP218) joseph.paolillo@YALE.EDU
   ( 203 ) 432.6673
Technical Contact, Zone Contact:
```

```
    George, Jeremy  (JG1823)  jeremy.george@YALE.EDU
      ( 203 ) 432.6679
  Billing Contact:
    Paolillo, Joseph  (JP218) joseph.paolillo@YALE.EDU
      ( 203 ) 432.6673

  Record last updated on 31-May-96.
  Record created on 17-Mar-87.
  Database last updated on 8-Aug-98 04:26:13 EDT.
  Domain servers in listed order:

  SERV1.NET.YALE.EDU          130.132.1.9
  SERV2.NET.YALE.EDU          130.132.1.10
  SERV3.NET.YALE.EDU          130.132.1.11
  SERV4.NET.YALE.EDU          130.132.89.9
  YALE.EDU                    128.36.0.1, 130.132.1.1
```

CERT Security Functions

The CERT Coordination Center was established in 1988 and is located at the Software Engineering Institute, Carnegie Mellon University, Pittsburgh, PA. CERT is an acronym for Computer Emergency Response Team.

CERT publishes notices of security problems found in operating systems or software packages and provides pointers to the solutions. CERT coordinates responses to security attacks upon the Internet. CERT information is available at:

http://www.cert.org/

CERT can be reached at:

CERT Coordination Center
Software Engineering Institute
Carnegie Mellon University
Pittsburgh, Pennsylvania 15213-3890

Via electronic mail: cert@cert.org
Via telephone: (11)-412-268-7090 (24-hour hotline)
Via fax: (11)-412-268-6989

CERT advisories are published in the newsgroup:

comp.security.announce

Advisories are sent to a mailing list that can be joined by sending mail to:

cert-advisory-request@cert.org

C

Variable-Length Subnet Masks

Introduction

The Internet address format has caused many problems for network administrators. The 32-bit address space is just too small and cramped.

Computers work with these addresses using bit boundaries. A computer is happy to accept network, subnet, and host addresses that use any convenient bit boundaries. Humans are not very comfortable with batches of bits.

To add to the confusion, we write addresses by translating *bytes* to decimal numbers—for example, 130.15.1.2. When our subnet boundaries do not fall on byte boundaries, we need to engage in some mental arithmetic to extract the subnet and host parts of an address.

It can be difficult to choose a single subnet mask for an organization. Many enterprise networks are made up of a mixture of communications facilities—long distance lines or frame relay circuits, large headquarters LANs, and small branch office LANs. Fortunately, today you can assign addresses efficiently by using *variable-length subnet masks*. In other words, use several mask sizes, tailored to fit your subnetworks.

The only reason that this was not done in the past was that subnet mask information was not passed between routers by the old routing protocols. Today's routing tables include a subnet mask for each destination, and so we now can match the size of the host and subnet fields to the real requirements of our network topology.

It is the purpose of this appendix to make it easier for you to work with subnet masks that are not aligned on byte boundaries and to demonstrate how a site can use several different subnet sizes. The ability to use variable-length subnet masks is important for sites that have small, medium, and large LANs.

We look at several examples in which we define subnets of the class B network 130.15. Table C.1 at the end of this chapter displays a list of class B subnet sizes. Table C.2 presents Class C subnet sizes.

The official rules of IP say that you should not use an all-0 subnet field, but real implementations use them every day. We use an all-0s subnet in some of the examples that follow. An all-1s subnet field is more problematic, and we do not use it.

A Variable-Length Subnet Mask Plan

Suppose that Company ABCD owns Class B address 130.15 and needs:

4 LANs with 300-500 systems (Large)

20 LANs with 50-100 systems (Medium)

1000 LANs with 10-20 systems (Small)

We will develop the follow plan:

130.15.0-130.15.7	Large LANs
130.15.8-130.15.15	Reserved
130.15.16-130.15.25	Medium-sized LANs
130.15.26-130.15.31	Reserved
130.15.32-130.15.156	Small LANs
130.15.156-130.15.255	Reserved

Large LANs

Checking Table C.1, we can see that we will need to use 9 host bits to provide enough addresses for a LAN whose size ranges up to 500 hosts. The corresponding subnet part of the address must be 7 bits.

When the host part of your address has more than 8 bits, you are opting for fewer subnets with more hosts on each subnet.

We start off with an all-0s subnet field. The display below shows the subnet and host bits for the first and last hosts on the first subnet. It also shows the subnet mask and the first and last addresses in dot notation.

```
S S S S S S S H  H H H H H H H   Mask:  255.255.254.0
0 0 0 0 0 0 0 0  0 0 0 0 0 0 0 1  First: 130.15.0.1
0 0 0 0 0 0 0 1  1 1 1 1 1 1 1 0  Last:  130.15.1.254
```

When translated to dot notation, your first subnet includes addresses:

130.15.0.1 to 130.15.0.255

130.15.1.0 to 130.15.1.254

All addresses starting with 130.15.0 and 130.15.1 are on the same subnet. This makes sense. We needed twice as many addresses as we normally get when using byte boundaries, so we need to use two adjacent third-byte numbers.

Note that host address 130.15.0.255 is legal. This address ends with an all-1s *byte* but not with an all-1s *host field* because of the 0 in the previous byte. Similarly, 130.15.1.0 is legal because we end with an all-0s byte but not with an all-0s host field.

The second subnet will include addresses:

130.15.2.1 to 130.15.2.255

130.15.3.0 to 130.15.3.254

Now we can see the pattern. Each big subnet will start at an even number and stretch across an adjacent pair of even and odd numbers.

This makes sense. An 8-bit host part would give us roughly 250 host addresses. Every time we add a bit to the host field, we double the number of available host addresses. Adding a bit to the host field is equivalent to using two adjacent numbers in the third byte. This doubles the number of host addresses at our disposal.

Using the pairs of numbers (0,1), (2,3), (4,5), and (6,7) in the third byte gives us the four big LANs that we needed. We will skip the numbers from 8 to 15 to allow for possible future requirements.

Medium-Sized LANs

We need 20 LANs that contain up to 100 systems. Checking Table C.1, we see that 7 host bits will cover this number of hosts efficiently. Note that this is equivalent to $\frac{1}{2}$ of a conventional subnet.

We will start numbering the medium-sized LANs at 130.15.16. The subnet and host parts for the first two LANs are shown below:

```
S S S S S S S   S H H H H H H H   Mask:   255.255.255.128
0 0 0 1 0 0 0 0  0 0 0 0 0 0 0 1   First:  130.15.16.1
0 0 0 1 0 0 0 0  0 1 1 1 1 1 1 0   Last:   130.15.16.126

0 0 0 1 0 0 0 0  1 0 0 0 0 0 0 1   First:  130.15.16.129
0 0 0 1 0 0 0 0  1 1 1 1 1 1 1 0   Last:   130.15.16.254
```

Once again, we can apply common sense to these blocks of addresses. An 8-bit host part provides roughly 250 addresses, and a 7-bit host part provides half as many. The first LAN uses the addresses below 128 and the second LAN uses addresses above 128. We had to skip a couple of addresses: 130.15.16.127 because it is an all-1s host address and 130.15.16.128 because it is an all-0s host address.

The range of ten numbers from 130.15.16.0-130.15.25.255 will provide the 20 medium-sized LANs that we need.

Small LANs

As before, it probably is a good idea to leave a gap in the numbers that can be used for future expansion. We will skip to 130.15.32 for our next set of LANs. We want to allow for 1000 LANs with up to 20 systems. Checking Table C.1, five bits provides enough addresses for 30 hosts, which allows for some growth in the LAN size. This is equivalent to roughly $\frac{1}{8}$ of the number of addresses that we would get from an 8-bit host part.

We will start numbering the small LANs at 130.15.32. The display that follows shows the eight LANs that we squeeze out of the number space that starts with 130.15.32.

```
S S S S S S S   S S S H H H H H   Mask:   255.255.255.224
0 0 1 0 0 0 0 0  0 0 0 0 0 0 0 1   First:  130.15.32.1
0 0 1 0 0 0 0 0  0 0 0 1 1 1 1 0   Last:   130.15.32.30

0 0 1 0 0 0 0 0  0 0 1 0 0 0 0 1   First:  130.15.32.33
0 0 1 0 0 0 0 0  0 0 1 1 1 1 1 0   Last:   130.15.32.62

0 0 1 0 0 0 0 0  0 1 0 0 0 0 0 1   First:  130.15.32.65
0 0 1 0 0 0 0 0  0 1 0 1 1 1 1 0   Last:   130.15.32.94

0 0 1 0 0 0 0 0  0 1 1 0 0 0 0 1   First:  130.15.32.97
0 0 1 0 0 0 0 0  0 1 1 1 1 1 1 0   Last:   130.15.32.126

0 0 1 0 0 0 0 0  1 0 0 0 0 0 0 1   First:  130.15.32.129
0 0 1 0 0 0 0 0  1 0 0 1 1 1 1 0   Last:   130.15.32.158

0 0 1 0 0 0 0 0  1 0 1 0 0 0 0 1   First:  130.15.32.161
0 0 1 0 0 0 0 0  1 0 1 1 1 1 1 0   Last:   130.15.32.190

0 0 1 0 0 0 0 0  1 1 0 0 0 0 0 1   First:  130.15.32.193
0 0 1 0 0 0 0 0  1 1 0 1 1 1 1 0   Last:   130.15.32.222

0 0 1 0 0 0 0 0  1 1 1 0 0 0 0 1   First:  130.15.32.225
0 0 1 0 0 0 0 0  1 1 1 1 1 1 1 0   Last:   130.15.32.254
```

Similarly, 130.15.33 gives us eight more LANs. We can generate 1000 small LANs from the number range 130.15.32.0-130.15.156.255.

Subnetting Tables

Table C.1 provides an overview of subnet numbering for a Class B network. It shows what happens when we build a subnet whose host addresses start at 130.15.0.1 for a wide variety of subnet sizes. If you check through some examples, you will see that two numbers are always skipped between usable number ranges. This is because the number after the last usable host number always represents an all-1s host field, and the number after that represents an all-0s host field.

Table C.2 displays ways that a Class C network can be subnetted. We do not display a row for 7 host bits because we are following the guideline that rules out an all-1s subnet field. The result is that we would have only one subnet (with subnet bit value 0), and there would be no point in doing this. We do not

TABLE C.1   **Class B Host and Subnet Bits**

Host Bits	Subnet Bits	Number of Hosts	Sample Range of Numbers on One Subnet	Subnet Mask
14	2	16,382	x.y.0.1 - x.y.63.254	255.255.192.0
13	3	8,190	x.y.0.1 - x.y.31.254	255.255.224.0
12	4	4,094	x.y.0.1 - x.y.15.254	255.255.240.0
11	5	2,046	x.y.0.1 - x.y.7.254	255.255.248.0
10	6	1,022	x.y.0.1 - x.y.3.254	255.255.252.0
9	7	510	x.y.0.1 - x.y.1.254	255.255.254.0
8	8	254	x.y.0.1 - x.y.0.254	255.255.255.0
7	9	126	x.y.0.1 - x.y.0.126	255.255.255.128
6	10	62	x.y.0.1 - x.y.0.62	255.255.255.192
5	11	30	x.y.0.1 - x.y.0.30	255.255.255.224
4	12	14	x.y.0.1 - x.y.0.14	255.255.255.240
3	13	6	x.y.0.1 - x.y.0.6	255.255.255.248
2	14	2	x.y.0.1 - x.y.0.2	255.255.255.252

display a row for 7 subnet bits because we would have no hosts on a subnet with 1-bit host addresses!

More Discussion and Examples

When building big LANs for a Class B network, a clump of numbers in the third byte are used for the same LAN—just as was the case in the preceding "Large LANs" example. For example, if we need to use 14 host bits, there are 2 subnet bits and we could build three enormous LANs. We will not use the fourth subnet number because the subnet field would be all-1s (11). Host addresses for the first LAN would range from 130.15.0.1-130.15.63.254. A second LAN would range from 130.15.64.1-130.15.127.254, and a third LAN would range from 130.15.128.1-130.15.191.254. Note that fresh LANs start at multiples of 64: 0, 64, and 128.

With 13 host bits, there are 3 subnet bits, so we can build seven big LANs. Host addresses for the first LAN would range from 130.15.0.1-130.15.31.254. The second would be 130.15.32.1-130.15.63.254 and the third would be 130.15.64.1-130.15.95.254. Note that fresh LANs start at multiples of 32: 0, 32, 64, 96, 128, 160, and 192.

TABLE C.2   **Class C Host and Subnet Bits**

Host Bits	Subnet Bits	Number of Hosts	Range of Numbers on One Subnet	Subnet Mask
8	0	254	x.y.z.1 - x.y.z.254	255.255.255.0
6	2	62	x.y.z.1 - x.y.z.62	255.255.255.192
5	3	30	x.y.z.1 - x.y.z.30	255.255.255.224
4	4	14	x.y.z.1 - x.y.z.14	255.255.255.240
3	5	6	x.y.z.1 - x.y.z.6	255.255.255.248
2	6	2	x.y.z.1 - x.y.z.2	255.255.255.252

Jumping down to 8-bit host addresses, the range of addresses on a LAN is familiar: 130.15.0.1-130.15.0.254, 130.15.1.1-130.15.1.254, and so forth. A new LAN starts at each number: 0, 1, 2, and so forth.

When we use less than 8 bits for the host part, we get more LANs by dividing up the number space for one third-byte number. For example, with 4-bit host numbers, the ranges are 130.15.0.1-130.15.0.14, 130.15.0.17-130.15.0.30, 130.15.0.33-130.15.0.46, and so on.

With 3-bit host addresses, the ranges would be 130.15.0.1-130.15.0.6, 130.15.0.9-130.15.0.14, 130.15.0.17-130.15.0.22, and so forth.

With 2-bit addresses, the ranges are 130.15.0.1-130.15.0.2, 130.15.0.5-130.15.0.6, 130.15.0.9-130.15.0.10, and so forth.

Put another way, our LANs start out using up 64 adjacent third-byte numbers, then go down to 32, 16, 8, 4, and 2 adjacent numbers. Then we reach the single third-byte number. After that, the LANs are cut to $\frac{1}{2}$, $\frac{1}{4}$, $\frac{1}{8}$, $\frac{1}{16}$, and $\frac{1}{32}$ of the numbers provided by one byte.

Summary

Variable-length masks support the efficient assignment of IP addresses. The first step in using them is to examine a network and identify the subnet sizes that are needed. Next, ranges of numbers can be set aside for use with each mask size. It is a good idea to leave gaps between these ranges, to allow for future expansion.

Abstract Syntax Notation One (ASN.1)   A language used for defining datatypes. ASN.1 is used in OSI standards and also is used in TCP/IP network management specifications.

Access Control   A facility that defines each user's privileges to access computer data.

Acknowledgment   TCP requires that data be acknowledged so that the sender knows that it has been transmitted safely.

Active Open   Action taken by an application to initiate a TCP connection.

Admission Control   An RSVP control function that decides whether the packet scheduler in a node can supply a requested QoS while providing the QoS already reserved for previously admitted requests.

Address Class   Traditional method of assigning blocks of addresses to organizations.

Address Mask   A 32-bit binary number used to identify the parts of an IP address that are used for network and subnet numbers. Every bit in the network and subnet fields is set to 1.

Address Resolution Protocol (ARP)   A protocol that dynamically discovers the physical address of a system, given its IP address.

Agent   In the Simple Network Management Protocol, the process within a device that responds to get and set requests and sends trap messages.

Aggregatable Global Unicast Addresses   Hierarchical addresses designed for use with IP version 6.

American National Standard Code for Information Interchange(ASCII) Seven of the eight bits in a byte are required to define an ASCII character.

American National Standards Institute (ANSI)   Organization responsible for coordinating United States standardization activities. ANSI is a member of ISO.

Anycast Address   An additional address that is assigned to multiple interfaces, such as interfaces for the set of all routers owned by an Internet Service Provider. Sending a message to an anycast address causes it to be delivered to the nearest node that has that address.

Applet A simple function that may be part of a larger package; for example, a Java or ActiveX program that is downloaded from a Web server.

AppleTalk A networking protocol developed by Apple Computer for use with its products.

Application Programming Interface (API) A set of routines that enable a programmer to use computer facilities. The socket programming interface and the Transport Layer Interface are APIs used for TCP/IP programming.

Archie A server that gathers and indexes the locations of files at public file transfer archives and supports user searches.

ARPANET The world's first packet-switching network. For many years it functioned as an Internet backbone.

Asynchronous Link A link on which data is transmitted byte-by-byte, delimited by start and stop bits.

Asynchronous Transfer Mode (ATM) A switch-based technology that transports information in 53-byte cells. ATM may be used for data, voice, and video.

Attribute For a directory entry, a datatype (such as telephone number) and one or more values.

Authentication Verification of the identity of a communications partner.

Authentication Header (AH) An IP-layer header that authenticates a source and protects the integrity of the data. An Authentication Header normally is inserted after the main IP header and before the other information being authenticated.

Autonomous System (AS) An internetwork that is part of the Internet and has a single routing policy. Each Autonomous System is assigned an Autonomous System Number.

Bandwidth The quantity of data that can be sent across a link, typically measured in bits per second.

Base64 An encoding that converts binary data to textual characters.

Basic Encoding Rules (BER) The rules for encoding datatypes specified using ASN.1 into their transmission format.

Baud A unit of signaling speed equal to the number of times per second that a signal changes state. If there are exactly two states, the baud rate equals the bit rate.

Berkeley Software Distribution (BSD) Unix software from the University of California at Berkeley that included TCP/IP support.

Best Current Practices (BCP) A classification applied to a useful RFC that does not define a protocol standard.

Big Endian A format for the storage or transmission of data that places the most significant byte (or bit) first.

BIND Software Domain Name server software from University Of California at Berkeley.

Bootstrap Protocol (BOOTP) Protocol that can be used by booting systems to obtain network configuration information. The Dynamic Host Configuration Protocol is a more recent and more powerful configuration protocol.

Border Gateway Protocol (BGP) A protocol used to advertise the set of networks that can be reached within an Autonomous System. BGP enables this information to be shared with other Autonomous Systems. BGP is newer than EGP, and offers a number of improvements.

Bounce The return of a piece of mail that cannot be delivered.

Bridge A device that connects two or more physical segments of a LAN and forwards frames that have source and destination addresses on different segments.

Broadcast Frame A frame addressed to all systems on a link.

Brouter A device that performs both bridging and routing functions. Some traffic is selected for routing, while the rest is bridged.

Browser A client program that can access Web servers via the hypertext transfer protocol and also can execute other protocols, such as file transfer and network news transfer.

Buffer An area of storage used to hold input or output data.

Canonical Name A host's unique true name.

Carrier Sense Multiple Access with Collision Detection (CSMA/CD) A simple Media Access Control protocol. All stations listen to the medium. A station wanting to send may do so if there is no signal on the medium. When two stations transmit simultaneously, both back off and retry after a random time period.

Certificate A digital block of data issued by a Certificate Authority that binds a public/private key pair to identity information signed by Certificate Authority.

Certificate Authority An entity responsible for checking identities, creating and signing certificates, and for maintaining Certificate Revocation Lists.

Certificate Revocation List A list of certificate identifiers for certificates that have been rendered invalid.

Certification Assigning certificate information that vouches for the identity of the owner of the certificate.

Cipher-Block Chaining A popular option for DES encryption. A block of already encrypted data is fed into the algorithm as it encrypts the next block.

Circuit Proxy Firewall A firewall that maintains separate connections to clients and to servers, and copies bytes from one session to the other.

Classless Inter-Domain Routing (CIDR) A method of routing used to enable the network part of IP addresses to consist of a specified number of bits.

Common Gateway Interface (CGI) A frequently used Web server application programming interface.

Common Management Information Protocol (CMIP)   An OSI network management protocol.

Common Management Information Services and Protocol over TCP/IP (CMOT)   A historic (not recommended) specification for using OSI management protocols on a TCP/IP network.

Community Name   A byte string included in SNMP version 1 and 2 messages that acts as a password.

Computer Emergency Response Team (CERT)   Volunteers at Carnegie-Mellon University who receive reports of security violations, publish alerts, and find solutions.

Confidentiality   Protection of information from disclosure to unintended parties.

Congestion   A network state caused by one or more overloaded network devices. Congestion leads to datagram loss.

Connection   A logical communication path between TCP users.

Control Connection   Used to carry file transfer client requests and server responses.

Core Gateway   Historically, a router on the Internet backbone. Core gateways distributed reachability information among the Autonomous Systems attaching to the Internet backbone.

Counter   A measurement that increases until it wraps around and restarts.

Cracker   Someone who attempts to break into computer systems, often with malicious intent.

Cross Certification   Two certificate authorities certify one another and enable certificates issued by one CA to be accepted by holders of certificates from the other.

Cyclic Redundancy Check (CRC)   The value obtained by applying a mathematical function to the bits in a frame and appended to the frame. The CRC is recalculated when the frame is received. If the result differs from the appended value, the frame is discarded.

Data Circuit-terminating Equipment (DCE)   Equipment required to connect a DTE to a line or to a network.

Data Encryption Standard (DES)   A symmetric encryption protocol officially sanctioned by the United States government. There are several options for the manner in which DES is applied. (See Cipher-Block Chaining)

Data Link Connection Identifier   Circuit identifier used in frame relay.

Data Terminal Equipment (DTE)   A source or destination for data. Often used to denote terminals or computers attached to a wide area network.

DECnet   Digital Equipment Corporation's proprietary network protocol. Versions are identified by their phase number—such as Phase IV and Phase V.

Desktop Management Interface (DMI)   A cooperative system management standards effort.

Digital Signature   A calculation that authenticates the originator of a message.

Directory Access Protocol (DAP)   Client/Server protocol used to access an X.500 directory service.

Directory Information Base (DIB)   The information held in a directory.

Directory System Agent (DSA)   A server that accepts queries from Directory User Agents and extracts information from a database. A DSA interacts with a Directory User Agent by means of the X.500 Directory Access Protocol.

Directory User Agent (DUA)   A client enabling a user to send queries to an X.500 directory server. A DUA interacts with a Directory Service Agent (DSA) via the X.500 Directory Access Protocol.

Distinguished Encoding Rules (DER)   A simplifying alternative to the Basic Encoding Rules (BER). Identical data can be encoded in different ways using BER. DER produces a unique encoding.

Distinguished Name (DN)   The unique name of an X.500 directory entry. For example: person = Jane Jones, ou = sales, o = ACME Widgets, c = us.

Distributed Computing Environment (DCE)   A set of technologies selected by the Open Software Foundation to support distributed computing.

Distributed File Service (DFS)   A file server technology adopted by the Open Software Foundation.

Distributed Management Environment (DME)   A set of technologies selected for network and system management by the Open Software Foundation.

DIX Ethernet   Version of Ethernet developed by Digital, Intel, and Xerox.

Domain Name   Name of a node in the Internet naming tree. Also, a computer name.

Domain Name System (DNS)   A set of distributed databases providing information such as translation between system names and their IP addresses and the location of mail exchangers.

DS1   A frame and interface specification for synchronous T1 lines.

DS3   A frame and interface specification for synchronous T3 lines.

Dynamic Host Configuration Protocol (DHCP)   An updated boot protocol that enables a client to obtain configuration parameters from a server.

Electronic Signature   *See* Digital Signature.

Encryption   Transformation of information into a form that cannot be understood without possession of a secret ("decryption") key.

Encapsulating Security Payload (ESP)   A protocol designed to provide confidentiality (and optionally, authentication and integrity) to IP datagrams. ESP can be used between a pair of hosts, between a pair of routers, or between a host or router and multiple other hosts and routers.

EUI-64   An IEEE-administered global interface identifier.

Extended Binary-Coded Decimal Interchange Code (EBCDIC)   IBM character format.

Extensible Markup Language (XML) A language used to define document formats that meet the needs of many different types of applications. XML is a subset of SGML.

Exterior Gateway Protocol (EGP) Routers in neighboring Autonomous Systems use this protocol to identify the set of networks that can be reached within or via each Autonomous System. EGP is being supplanted by BGP.

eXternal Data Representation (XDR) A standard developed by Sun Microsystems to define datatypes used as parameters and to encode these parameters for transmission.

Federal Information Processing Standard (FIPS) A standard that has been officially adopted by the U.S. government.

Fiber Distributed Data Interface (FDDI) A standard for high-speed data transfer across a dual fiber-optic ring.

File Transfer, Access, and Management (FTAM) The OSI file transfer and management protocol. FTAM allows users to copy whole files or part of a file, such as an individual record.

File Transfer Protocol (FTP) The TCP/IP protocol that enables users to copy files between systems and perform file management functions, such as renaming or deleting files.

Finger A program that displays information about one or more remote users.

Firewall A system that controls what traffic may enter and leave a site.

Fixed Filter An RSVP reservation style that allocates a fixed amount of bandwidth to a sender.

Flow Control A mechanism that allows a receiver to limit the amount of data that a sender may transmit at any time. Flow control prevents a sender from exhausting the receiver's memory buffers.

For Your Information (FYI) A set of documents including useful information, such as answers to frequently asked questions about TCP/IP. FYI documents also are published as RFCs.

Fragmentation Partitioning of a datagram into pieces. This is done when a datagram is too large for a network link that must be traversed to reach the destination.

Frame A link layer Protocol Data Unit.

Frame Check Sequence (FCS) A mathematical function applied to the bits in a frame and appended to the frame. The FCS is recalculated when the frame is received. If the result differs from the appended value, the frame is discarded.

Frame Relay A low-overhead wide area networking technology based on packet switching.

Frequently Asked Questions (FAQ) A document in the form of questions and answers that summarizes information for a newsgroup or mailing list.

Gated A popular free routing toolkit that includes several routing protocols.

Gateway An IP router. Many RFC documents use the term *gateway* rather than *router*.

Gateway-to-Gateway Protocol (GGP)   A protocol formerly used to exchange routing information between Internet core routers.

Gopher   An old protocol that enables clients to access data at a server by means of a series of menus.

Government Open Systems Interconnection Profile (GOSIP)   Specification of a set of OSI protocols to be preferred in government procurements of computer equipment.

Graphics Interchange Format (GIF)   A popular format for graphical image files.

High Level Data Link Control Protocol (HDLC)   A standard that is the basis for several link layer protocols.

High Performance Parallel Interface (HIPPI)   A high-speed communications technology defined in an ANSI standard. Devices communicate via HIPPI across short distances at speeds of 800 and 1600 megabits per second.

Hashing for Message Authentication Code (HMAC)   An authentication method based on performing a message digest calculation on data combined with a secret key.

Hypertext Markup Language (HTML)   A markup language used to write hypertext documents. Tags in the document identify elements such as headers, paragraphs, and lists.

Initial Sequence Number (ISN)   A sequence number defined during TCP connection setup. Data bytes sent over the connection will be numbered starting from this point.

Integrated Services Digital Network (ISDN)   A telephony technology that provides digital voice and data services.

Interior Gateway Protocol (IGP)   Any routing protocol used within an internetwork.

Intermediate System to Intermediate System Protocol (IS-IS)   A protocol that can be used to route both OSI and IP traffic.

International Organization for Standardization (ISO)   An international body founded to promote international trade and cooperative progress in science and technology.

International Telecommunications Union (ITU)   A body that oversees several international organizations devoted to communications standards and cooperation.

International Telecommunications Union Telecommunication Standardization Sector (ITU-T)   An organization that makes recommendations for telephony and data communications standards. Formerly CCITT.

International Telegraph and Telephone Consultative Committee (CCITT)   Former name of an organization formed to facilitate connecting communications facilities into international networks.

Internet   The world's largest network, the Internet is based on the TCP/IP protocol suite.

Internet Architecture Board (IAB)   Formerly the Internet Activities Board. An Internet Society group responsible for promoting protocol development, selecting protocols for Internet use, and assigning state and status to protocols.

Internet Assigned Numbers Authority (IANA)   The authority responsible for controlling the assignment of a variety of parameters, such as well-known ports, multicast addresses, terminal identifiers, and system identifiers.

Internet Control Message Protocol (ICMP)   A protocol that is required for implementation with IP. ICMP specifies error messages to be sent when datagrams are discarded or systems experience congestion. ICMP also provides several useful query services.

Internet Engineering Notes (IEN)   An early set of documents discussing features of the TCP/IP suite.

Internet Engineering Steering Group (IESG)   A group that coordinates the activities of the IETF working groups and performs technical reviews of standards.

Internet Engineering Task Force (IETF)   A set of working groups made up of volunteers who develop and implement Internet protocols.

Internet Gateway Routing Protocol (IGRP)   A proprietary protocol designed for Cisco routers.

Internet Group Management Protocol (IGMP)   A protocol that is part of the multicast specification. IGMP is used to carry group membership information.

Internet Protocol (IP)   The TCP/IP layer 3 protocol responsible for transporting datagrams across an internetwork.

Internet Research Task Force (IRTF)   A group directed by the IAB, charged with long-term research on Internet protocols.

Internet Service Provider (ISP)   An organization that sells Internet connectivity services.

Internet Society (ISOC)   An international organization formed to promote the growth and continued technical enhancement of the Internet.

InterNetNews (INN)   A news server software package maintained by the Internet Software Consortium.

Internetwork   A set of networks connected by IP routers and appearing to its users as a single network.

Internet Security and Key Management Protocol (ISAKMP)   A session-oriented key exchange framework for IP security.

IP Address   A 32-bit quantity that identifies a network interface.

IP Datagram   The unit of data routed by IP.

ISO Development Environment (ISODE)   A research effort that produced software enabling OSI protocols to run on top of TCP/IP.

Joint Photographic Experts Group (JPEG)   A specification for an image compression scheme.

Kerberized Application   An application that can use Kerberos authentication and privacy services.

Kerberos   An authentication service developed at the Massachusetts Institute of

Technology, based on the use of a security server. Kerberos uses encryption to prevent intruders from discovering passwords and gaining unauthorized access to files or services.

KEY Record A DNS record containing a public encryption key.

Lame Delegation A DNS record that identifies a name server that no longer exists.

Lightweight Directory Access Protocol (LDAP) A simplified access protocol designed for X.500 directories, but also able to access other hierarchically structured directories.

Link A medium over which nodes can communicate using a link layer protocol.

Link State Protocol A routing protocol that generates routes using detailed knowledge of the topology of a network.

Listen Queue A memory area controlled by TCP and used to queue clients while their connections to a specific application are being set up.

Little Endian A format for the storage or transmission of data that places the least significant byte (or bit) first.

Local Area Network (LAN) A data network intended to serve an area of only a few square kilometers or less and consisting of a single subnetwork.

Local Management Interface (LMI) Management interface between frame relay customer premise equipment and the network service, used to obtain circuit status information.

Logical Byte A logical byte is a specified number of bits in length. For transferring files for obsolete computer systems, it is sometimes necessary to specify a logical byte size in order to preserve the integrity of data that is transferred.

Logical Link Control (LLC) A layer 2 (data link layer) protocol that governs the exchange of data between two systems connected to the same physical segment or residing on segments that are connected via one or more bridges.

Long Fat Pipes An extension to TCP that increases throughput for links that have large delays or very high bandwidths.

Loopback Address Address 127.0.0.1, used for communications between clients and servers that reside on the same host.

MAC Address A physical address assigned to a LAN interface.

MAC Protocol A Media Access Control protocol defines the rules that govern a system's ability to transmit and receive data on a medium.

Mail Exchanger A system used to relay mail into an organization's network.

Mail Gateway A system that performs a protocol translation between different electronic mail delivery protocols.

Management Information Base (MIB) A set of definitions of network-manageable objects. Also, the configuration, status, and performance information that can be retrieved from a network device.

Manager For the Simple Network Management Protocol, an entity that sends requests to agents in managed systems and receives responses and trap messages.

Maximum Segment Lifetime (MSL) The maximum time that a TCP segment might survive on a network. The MSL for the Internet is assumed to be 2 minutes.

Maximum Segment Size The maximum permissible size for the data part of any segment sent to a partner on a particular TCP connection.

Maximum Transmission Unit (MTU) The largest datagram that can be sent across a particular network medium, such as an Ethernet or Token-Ring.

Media Access Control (MAC) A protocol governing a station's access to a network. For example, CSMA/CD provides a set of MAC rules for sending and receiving data across a local area network.

Message Digest 5 (MD5) A hashing algorithm that calculates a fixed-size quantity on arbitrarily input data. When data is combined with a secret key, a message digest can be used for authentication.

Message Transfer Agent (MTA) An entity that moves messages (such as electronic mail) between computers.

Metropolitan Area Network (MAN) A technology supporting high-speed networking across a metropolitan area. IEEE 802.6 defines a MAN protocol.

Monitor A system that passively watches link traffic, records traffic counts, watches for errors, and checks thresholds that signal that a problem situation may be developing.

Mount Protocol used with the Network File System. Mount commands establish the relationship between a client's file system and the server's file system.

Multicast Transmission of a stream of data to a group of recipients.

Multicast IP Address A destination IP address that can be adopted by multiple hosts. Datagrams sent to a multicast IP address will be delivered to all hosts in the group.

Multihomed Host A host that has multiple IP addresses.

Multipurpose Internet Mail Extensions (MIME) Extensions to Internet mail that enable messages to be made of one or more parts, each of which can contain any content type, such as text, image, sound, or application data.

National Institute of Standards and Technology (NIST) A United States standards organization that has promoted communications standards. NIST formerly was the National Bureau of Standards.

National Science Foundation Network (NSFnet) A network used as part of the old Internet backbone.

Neighbor Discovery A set of ICMP version 6 functions that enable hosts to obtain configuration information, locate neighboring routers and hosts, and detect that a communications partner or neighbor router is defunct.

Neighbors Nodes attached to the same link.

NetBEUI Local area network protocol used for Microsoft LANs.

NETBIOS A network programming interface and protocol developed for IBM-compatible personal computers.

Network Address   The 32-bit IP address of a system.

Network File System (NFS)   A protocol introduced by Sun Microsystems. NFS enables clients to access remote files as if they were local.

Network Information Center (NIC)   An Internet administration facility that supervises network names and network addresses and can provide other information services.

Network Information Service (NIS)   A set of protocols introduced by Sun Microsystems, used to provide a directory service for network information.

Network News Transfer Protocol (NNTP)   A protocol used to transfer news between a client and a server or between two news servers.

Network Service Access Point (NSAP)   An identifier used to distinguish the identity of an OSI host and to point to the transport layer entity at that host to which traffic is directed.

Network Virtual Terminal (NVT)   A set of rules defining a very simple virtual terminal interaction. The NVT is used at the start of a *telnet* session, but a more complex type of terminal interaction can be negotiated.

Nonrepudiation   The ability to prove that a source sent specific data, even if the source later tries to deny that fact.

NXT Record   "Nonexistence" record. A DNS record that announces a range of names for which there are no records.

Object Class   A named set of directory entry attributes.

OBJECT IDENTIFIER   For the Simple Network Management Protocol, a formal identifier for a management variable.

Octet   Eight bits (a byte).

One-Time Password (OTP)   An authentication method based on a challenge that updates S/KEY.

Open Shortest Path First (OSPF)   An Internet routing protocol that scales well, can route traffic along multiple paths, and uses knowledge of an internetwork's topology to make accurate routing decisions.

Open Software Foundation (OSF)   A consortium of computer vendors cooperating to produce standard technologies for open systems. The MOTIF user interface and Distributed Computing Environment (DCE) are OSF technologies.

Open Systems Interconnection (OSI)   A set of ISO standards relating to data communications.

Packet   Originally, a unit of data sent across a packet-switching network. Currently, the term may refer to a communications Protocol Data Unit at any layer.

Packet Assembler/Disassembler (PAD)   Software that converts between a terminal's stream of traffic and X.25 packet format.

Page Structure   A file organization supported in FTP for use with older Digital Equipment Corporation computers.

Passive Open   Action taken by a TCP/IP server to prepare to receive requests from clients.

Path MTU Discovery   A protocol that enables a source to discover the maximum datagram size that can be forwarded to a destination.

Pathname   The character string that must be input to a file system by a user in order to identify a file.

Payload   The information carried in a Protocol Data Unit.

Physical Address   An address assigned to a network interface.

Point-to-Point Protocol (PPP)   A protocol for data transfer across serial links. PPP supports authentication, link configuration, and link monitoring capabilities and allows traffic for several protocols to be multiplexed across the link.

Policy Control   An RSVP (reservation) control function that decides whether a requested Quality of Service meets administrative criteria for acceptance.

Portmapper   A Remote Procedure Call program that acts as a clearinghouse for information about the ports that other RPC server programs use.

Port Number   A 2-byte binary number identifying an upper-level user of TCP or UDP.

Post Office Protocol (POP)   A protocol used to download electronic mail from a server to a client (usually at a desktop system).

Primary DNS Server   A server that holds the definitive database. Updates are carried out at the primary server.

Private Addresses   A set of IP addresses reserved for use within private networks.

Protecting Against Wrapped Sequence numbers (PAWS)   A TCP option that provides a 32-bit timestamp that prevents an old segment from being accepted as a new one.

Protocol Data Unit (PDU)   A formatted unit of data that is transmitted across a network.

Protocol Independent Multicast (PIM)   A method of generating multicast routes using routing information that was gathered by any of the popular unicast routing protocols.

Protocol Interpreter (PI)   An entity that carries out FTP functions. FTP defines two PI roles: user and server.

Protocol Stack   A layered set of protocols that work together to provide communication between applications.

Protocol State   Position on the standards track or classification as informational, experimental, or historic.

Protocol Status   A protocol requirement level.

Protocol Suite   A family of protocols that work together in a consistent fashion.

Proxy ARP   Use of a router to answer ARP requests. This will be done when the originating host believes that a destination is local, when in fact it lies beyond a router.

Proxy Firewall A firewall that forwards requests on behalf of clients and relays responses back to clients.

Public Key Encryption A security technology based on two keys. Data encrypted with one key must be decrypted with the other.

Public Key Infrastructure (PKI) A security framework that includes key distribution and certification.

Push Service A service provided by TCP that lets an application specify that some data should be transmitted and delivered as soon as possible.

Quipu A free implementation of X.500 used at many universities.

Reassembly Timeout The maximum time that IP at a recipient host will attempt to reassemble a fragmented datagram before discarding an incomplete datagram.

Receive Window The valid range of sequence numbers that a sender may transmit at a given time during a connection.

Record Structures Common structure for data files. During a transfer of a file that is organized as a sequence of records, records can be delimited by End-of-Record markers.

Relative Distinguished Name (RDN) The first part of the unique name for an X.500 directory entry.

Relay Agent For BOOTP or DHCP, a system that relays client requests to one or more servers.

Remote Network Monitor (RMON) A device that collects information about network traffic.

Remote Procedure Call (RPC) A protocol that enables an application to call a routine that executes at a server. The server returns output variables and a return code to the caller.

Rendezvous Point (RP) A router that relays data between senders and multicast receivers.

Request For Comments (RFC) A document describing an Internet protocol or related topics. RFC documents are available online at various Network Information Centers.

Reseaux IP Europeens (RIPE) Coordination center for network registration for Europe.

Reset The abrupt termination of a TCP connection.

Resolver A client program capable of looking up information in the Domain Name System.

Resource Record A Domain Name System database record.

Resource Reservation Protocol (RSVP) Enables a data receiver to request reserved network resources that will control delay and improve reliability for an incoming flow of data.

Retransmission Timeout If a TCP segment is not ACKed within the period defined by the retransmission timeout, TCP will retransmit the segment.

Reverse Address Resolution Protocol (RARP)   A protocol that enables a computer to discover its IP address by broadcasting a request on a network.

Reverse Path Forwarding (RPF)   Used in multicast routing. A multicast packet is forwarded only if it arrived on an interface that would be selected to reach the source via a unicast route.

Revocation   Termination of the validity of a certificate.

Round-Trip Time (RTT)   The time elapsed between sending a TCP segment and receiving its ACK.

Router   A system that forwards layer 3 traffic not explicitly addressed to itself. A router is used to connect separate LANs and WANs into an internet and to forward traffic between the constituent networks.

Routing Information Field (RIF)   A field in a Token-Ring frame used to identify the path to a destination that is reached via one or more bridges.

Routing Information Protocol (RIP)   A simple protocol used to exchange information between routers. The original version was part of the XNS protocol suite.

Routing Policy   Rules for which traffic will be routed and how it should be routed.

Routing Registry   A database containing route information, used to forward data along a path that traverses two or more Autonomous Systems.

Routing Table   A table containing information used to forward datagrams toward their destinations.

Rpcbind   An updated version of the portmapper program.

RSA   Refers to protocols developed by Rivest, Shamir, and Adelman, the founders of a company called RSA Data Security.

Schema   The set of attributes and Object Classes selected for use in a directory.

Secondary DNS Server   A server that copies its database from a primary server.

Secure Hash Algorithm (SHA-1)   A U.S. Federal Information Processing Standard message digest function.

Secure Sockets Layer (SSL)   A security technology that provides authentication, data integrity, and privacy.

Security Association   A communication protected by a specific selection of security parameters.

Security Gateway   A system that provides security to datagrams sent between internal systems and untrusted external systems.

Security Parameters Index   An index value that points to IP Security Association information.

Segment   A Protocol Data Unit consisting of a TCP header and optionally, some data. Sometimes used to refer to the data portion of a TCP Protocol Data Unit.

Send Window   The range of sequence numbers between the last byte of data that already has been sent and the right edge of the receive window.

Sequence Number A 32-bit field of a TCP header. If the segment contains data, the sequence number is associated with the first byte of the data.

Serial Line Interface Protocol (SLIP) A very simple protocol used for transmission of IP datagrams across a serial line.

Service Provider An organization that provides TCP/IP connectivity services to a set of customers. Some Service Providers support customers in a small, local area, while others have national or international scope.

Shortest Path First A routing algorithm that uses knowledge of a network's topology in making routing decisions.

SIG Record A DNS record that contains a digital signature computed for one or more other records.

Silly Window Syndrome Inefficient data transfer that results when a receiver reports small window credits and a sender transmits correspondingly small segments.

Simple Key-Management for Internet Protocols (SKIP) A proposed key management scheme for IP security.

Simple Mail Transfer Protocol (SMTP) A TCP/IP protocol used to transfer mail between systems.

Simple Network Management Protocol A protocol that enables a management station to monitor network systems and receive trap (alarm) messages from network systems.

Slow Start A procedure for gradually increasing the rate of data transfer for a TCP connection.

S/KEY An authentication method based on a challenge.

Smoothed Deviation A quantity that measures deviations from the smoothed round-trip time and is used to calculate the TCP retransmission timeout.

Smoothed Round-Trip Time (SRTT) An estimate of the current round-trip time for a segment and its ACK, used in calculating the value of the TCP retransmission timeout.

Socket Address An identifier for the endpoint of a communication, consisting of an IP address and port number.

Socket Descriptor An integer that an application uses to identify a connection. Socket descriptors are used in the Berkeley socket programming interface.

Source Quench An obsolete ICMP message sent by a congested system to the sources of its traffic.

Source Route A sequence of IP addresses identifying the route a datagram must follow. A strict source route contains all routers along the way, while a loose source route contains a subset of the routers to be traversed. A source route may optionally be included in an IP datagram header.

Standard Generalized Markup Language (SGML) A powerful markup language used to describe elements in portable documents.

Stub Network A network that does not carry transit traffic between other networks.

Subnet Address   A selected number of bits from the local part of an IP address, used to identify a set of systems connected to a common link.

Subnet Mask   A configuration parameter that indicates how many bits of an address are used for the host part. It is expressed as a 32-bit quantity, with 1s placed in positions covering the network and subnet part of an IP address and 0s in the host part.

Switch   A layer 2 device that enables many pairs of LAN devices to communicate concurrently.

Switched Multimegabit Data Service (SMDS)   A data transfer service developed by Bellcore, whose access protocol is based on the IEEE 802.6 Metropolitan Area Network protocol.

Symmetric Encryption   An encryption method that uses the same key to encrypt and decrypt.

SYN   A segment used at the start of a TCP connection. Each partner sends a SYN containing the starting point for its sequence numbering, a window size, and, optionally, the size of the largest segment that it is willing to accept.

Synchronous Data Link Protocol (SDLC)   A protocol that is part of IBM's SNA communications protocol suite. SDLC is used for point-to-point and multipoint communications.

Synchronous Optical Network (SONET)   A telephony standard for the transmission of information over fiber-optic channels.

Systems Network Architecture (SNA)   The data communications protocol suite developed and used by IBM.

T1   A digital telephony service that operates at 1.544 megabits per second. DS1 framing is used.

T3   A digital telephony service that operates at 44.746 megabits per second. DS3 framing is used.

TCP Accelerated Open (TAO)   Session opening convention used for brief request/response interactions.

Telnet   The TCP/IP application protocol that enables a terminal attached to one host to login to other hosts and interact with their applications.

Time-To-Live (TTL)   A limit on the length of time that a datagram can remain within an internetwork. The TTL usually is specified as the maximum number of hops that a datagram can traverse before it must be discarded.

TIME-WAIT   The final, prolonged wait state required for the closer of a TCP connection.

Tn3270   A version of Telnet used with options that support IBM 3270 terminal emulation.

Token-Ring   A local area network technology based on a ring topology. Stations on the ring pass a special message, called a token, around the ring. The current token holder has the right to transmit data for a limited period of time.

Traffic Policing (for RSVP)   Forcing a data flow to comply with reservation traffic parameters.

Transactional TCP A TCP extension that enables clients and servers to complete thousands of short TCP sessions per second.

Transmission Control Block (TCB) A data structure used to hold information about a current TCP or UDP communication.

Transmission Control Protocol (TCP) TCP provides reliable, connection-oriented data transmission between a pair of applications.

Transport Class 4 (OSI TP4) An OSI transport layer protocol that is functionally similar to TCP.

Transport Layer Interface (TLI) An application programming interface introduced by AT&T that interfaces to both TCP/IP and OSI protocols.

Transport Service Access Point (TSAP) An identifier that indicates the upper-layer protocol entity to whom an OSI Protocol Data Unit should be delivered.

Trap Message For the Simple Network Management Protocol, a message that reports an important event or a problem.

Trivial File Transfer Protocol (TFTP) A very basic TCP/IP protocol used to upload or download files. Typical uses include initializing diskless workstations or downloading software from a controller to a robot.

Trojan Horse A program that appears to do useful work but also includes secret routines that the perpetrator can use to access the victim's data or to open up access to the victim's computer.

Trunk Coupling Unit (TCU) A hardware element connecting a Token-Ring station to the backbone of a ring.

Tunneling Wrapping a datagram in a new IP header and forwarding it to a specified location. Traffic between sites often is encrypted and tunneled between routers that provide access to the sites.

Unicast Address An address assigned uniquely to a single interface.

Uniform Resource Locator (URL) An identifier for an item that can be retrieved by a World Wide Web browser, which provides a specific location.

Uniform Resource Name (URN) An identifier for an item that can be retrieved by a World Wide Web browser, which provides a generic name. This may map to several locations from which the item may be retrieved.

Universal Resource Identifier (URI) An identifier for an item that can be retrieved by a World Wide Web browser. The identifier may be a Uniform Resource Locator or a Uniform Resource Name.

Universal Time Coordinated (UTC) Formerly known as Greenwich Mean Time.

Urgent Service A service provided by TCP that lets an application indicate that specified data is urgent and should be processed by the receiving application as soon as possible.

Usenet Thousands of bulletin-board-like newsgroups whose information is available on the Internet.

User Agent (UA)   An electronic mail application that helps an end user to prepare, save, and send outgoing messages and view, store, and reply to incoming messages.

User Datagram Protocol   A simple protocol enabling an application to send individual messages to other applications. Delivery is not guaranteed, and messages need not be delivered in the same order as they were sent.

Virtual Circuit   A term derived from packet-switching networks. A virtual circuit is supported by facilities that are shared between many users, although each circuit appears to its users as a dedicated end-to-end connection.

Virus   A routine that attaches to other, legitimate programs and usually harms local data or program execution.

WebNFS   A version of the Network File System that supports ad hoc file access and also can operate efficiently across wide area networks.

Well-known Port   An application port number in the range 0-1023 that has been assigned to a widely used application by the Internet Assigned Numbers Authority.

Whois Database   A database containing information about a network, such as its administrators and technical support personnel, the addresses owned by an organization, and identifiers assigned to the organization.

Wide Area Network (WAN)   A network that covers a large geographical area. Typical WAN technologies include point-to-point, X.25, and frame relay.

Wildcard Filter (for RSVP)   A method of specifying that several senders will share some reserved bandwidth.

Window   The amount of buffer space available to receive data.

Winsock   Windows version of socket programming interface. Also, a program library that implements this interface.

World Wide Web   A set of Internet servers that enable clients to access many types of information, including documents that include data extracted from a database, images, sounds, or links to other documents.

Worm   A program that replicates itself at other networked sites.

X11   A windowing system invented at MIT.

X.121   A CCITT standard describing the assignment of numbers to systems attached to an X.25 network. These numbers are used to identify a remote system so that a data call can be set up over a virtual circuit.

X.25   A CCITT standard for connecting computers to a network that provides reliable, virtual circuit-based data transmission.

X.400   A series of protocols defined by the CCITT for message transfer and interpersonal messaging. These protocols were later adopted by ISO.

X.500   A series of protocols that describe directory services that can have global scope.

X.509   A standard that specifies a format for public key certificates. Version 3 is current.

Xerox Network System (XNS)   A suite of networking protocols developed at Xerox Corporation.

X/Open   A consortium of computer vendors that cooperate to provide a common application environment.

X-Window System (see also X11)   A set of protocols developed at MIT that enable a user to interact with applications that may be located a several different computers. The input and output for each application occurs in a window at the user's display. Window placement and size are controlled by the user.

Zone   A subtree of the DNS naming tree that is under the control of an administrator.

Zone File   A file that contains database information for a zone.

Abbreviations and Acronyms

AAL	ATM Adaptation Layer
ACI	Access Control Information
ACK	Acknowledgment
ACL	Access Control List
AF	Address Family
AH	Authentication Header
ANSI	American National Standards Institute
API	Application Programming Interface
APNIC	Asia-Pacific Network Information Center
ARIN	American Registry for Internet Numbers
ARP	Address Resolution Protocol
ARPA	Advanced Research Projects Agency
ARPANET	Advanced Research Projects Agency Network
AS	Autonomous System
ASA	American Standards Association
ASCII	American National Standard Code for Information Interchange
ASN.1	Abstract Syntax Notation 1
ATM	Asynchronous Transfer Mode
AXFR	"All" (complete) Zone Transfer
BBN	Bolt, Beranek, and Newman, Incorporated
BCP	Best Current Practices
BECN	Backward Explicit Congestion Notification (Frame Relay)
BER	Basic Encoding Rules

BGP	Border Gateway Protocol
BIND	Berkeley Internet Name Domain
BOG	BIND Operations Guide
BOOTP	Bootstrap Protocol
BPDU	Bridge Protocol Data Unit
BRI	Basic Rate Interface
BSD	Berkeley Software Distribution
CA	Certificate Authority
CBC	Cipher-Block Chaining
CC	Connection Count
CCITT	International Telegraph and Telephone Consultative Committee, now ITU-T (Comite Consultatif International de Telegraphique et Telephonique)
CERT	Computer Emergency Response Team
CGI	Common Gateway Interface
CHAP	Challenge Handshake Authentication Protocol
CIDR	Classless Inter-Domain Routing
CLNP	Connectionless Network Protocol
CMIP	Common Management Information Protocol
CMIS	Common Management Information Services
CMOT	Common Management Information Services and Protocol over TCP/IP
CNAME	Common Name
CPU	Central Processing Unit
CR	Carriage Return
CRC	Cyclic Redundancy Check
CRL	Certificate Revocation List
CSLIP	Compressed SLIP
CSMA/CD	Carrier Sense Multiple Access with Collision Detection
CSO	Computer Services Organization
CSU	Channel Service Unit
DAP	Directory Access Protocol
DARPA	Defense Advanced Research Projects Agency
DCA	Defense Communications Agency
DCE	Data Circuit-terminating Equipment
DCE	Distributed Computing Environment
DDN	Defense Data Network
DDN NIC	Defense Data Network Network Information Center
DE	Discard Eligibility (Frame Relay)

DEC	Digital Equipment Corporation
DER	Distinguished Encoding Rules
DES	Data Encryption Standard
DEV	Deviation
DFS	Distributed File Service
DHCP	Dynamic Host Configuration Protocol
DIB	Directory Information Base
DISA	Defense Information Systems Agency
DIT	Directory Information Tree
DIX	Digital, Intel, and Xerox Ethernet protocol
DLCI	Data Link Connection Identifier
DLL	Dynamic Link Library
DME	Distributed Management Environment
DMI	Desktop Management Interface
DMTF	Desktop Management Task Force
DN	Distinguished Name
DNS	Domain Name System
DOD	Department of Defense
DOS	Disk Operating System
DSA	Digital Signature Algorithm
DSA	Directory System Agent
DSAP	Destination Service Access Point
DSE	DSA Specific Entry
DSU	Data Service Unit
DTE	Data Terminal Equipment
DUA	Directory User Agent
DUAL	Diffusing Update Algorithm
DVMRP	Distance Vector Multicast Routing Protocol
DXI	Data Exchange Interface
EBCDIC	Extended Binary-Coded Decimal Interchange Code
EGP	Exterior Gateway Protocol
EIGRP	Enhanced Internet Gateway Routing Protocol
EOF	End of File
EOR	End of Record
ESMTP	Extensions to SMTP
ESP	Encapsulating Security Payload
FAQ	Frequently Asked Questions
FCS	Frame Check Sequence

FDDI	Fiber Distributed Data Interface
FECN	Forward Explicit Congestion Notification (Frame Relay)
FF	Fixed Filter
FIN	Final Segment
FIPS	Federal Information Processing Standard
FTAM	File Transfer, Access, and Management
FTP	File Transfer Protocol
FYI	For Your Information
GGP	Gateway-to-Gateway Protocol
GIF	Graphics Interchange Format, used for graphic files
GMT	Greenwich Mean Time
GOSIP	Government Open Systems Interconnection Profile
GUI	Graphical User Interface
HDLC	High Level Data Link Control Protocol
HINFO	Host Information
HIPPI	High Performance Parallel Interface
HMAC	Hashing for Message Authentication Code
HSSI	High-Speed Serial Interface
HTML	Hypertext Markup Language
HTTP	Hypertext Transfer Protocol
IAB	Internet Architecture Board (Internet Activities Board)
IAC	Interpret As Command
IANA	Internet Assigned Numbers Authority
IBM	International Business Machines
ICMP	Internet Control Message Protocol
ID	Identifier
IDRP	OSI Inter-Domain Routing Protocol
IEEE	Institute of Electrical and Electronics Engineers
IEN	Internet Engineering Notes
IESG	Internet Engineering Steering Group
IETF	Internet Engineering Task Force
IGMP	Internet Group Management Protocol
IGP	Interior Gateway Protocol
IGRP	Internet Gateway Routing Protocol (Cisco proprietary)
ILMI	Interim Local Management Interface
IMAP	Internet Mail Access Protocol
INN	InterNetNews
I/O	Input/Output
IP	Internet Protocol

IPng	IP next generation (version 6)
IPSO	IP Security Option
IPX	Internetwork Packet eXchange (for NetWare)
IRQ	Interrupt Request
IRTF	Internet Research Task Force
ISAKMP	Internet Security and Key Management Protocol
ISDN	Integrated Services Digital Network
IS-IS	Intermediate System to Intermediate System
ISN	Initial Sequence Number
ISO	International Organization for Standardization
ISOC	Internet Society
ISODE	ISO Development Environment
ISP	Internet Service Provider
ITU	International Telecommunications Union
ITU-T	Telecommunication Standardization Sector of the ITU
IXFR	Incremental Zone Transfer
JPEG	Joint Photographic Experts Group
LAN	Local Area Network
LAPB	Link Access Procedures Balanced
LAPD	Link Access Procedures on the D-channel
LDAP	Lightweight Directory Access Protocol
LF	Line Feed
LLC	Logical Link Control
LMI	Local Management Interface
MAC	Media Access Control
MAN	Metropolitan Area Network
MBONE	Multicast Backbone
MD5	Message Digest 5
MIB	Management Information Base
MIME	Multipurpose Internet Mail Extensions
MOSPF	Multicast Extensions to OSPF
ms	Millisecond
MSL	Maximum Segment Lifetime
MSS	Maximum Segment Size
MTA	Message Transfer Agent
MTU	Maximum Transmission Unit
MX	Mail Exchanger
NAP	Network Access Point
NCSA	National Center for Supercomputing Applications

NDIS	Network Device Interface Specification
NETBIOS	Network Basic Input Output System
NFS	Network File System
NIC	Network Information Center
NIS	Network Information System
NISI	Network Information Service Infrastructure
NIST	National Institute of Standards and Technology
NLPID	Network Level Protocol ID
NNTP	Network News Transfer Protocol
NOC	Network Operations Center
NREN	National Research and Education Network
NS	Name Server
NSAP	Network Service Access Point
NSF	National Science Foundation
NTP	Network Time Protocol
NVT	Network Virtual Terminal
NXT	Non-Existent Record
ODI	Open Device Interface
ONC	Open Network Computing
OSF	Open Software Foundation
OSI	Open Systems Interconnect
OSPF	Open Shortest Path First
OTP	One-Time Password
OUI	Organizationally Unique Identifier
PAD	Packet Assembler/Disassembler
PAP	Password Authentication Protocol
PASV	Passive (File Transfer)
PAWS	Protecting Against Wrapped Sequence numbers
PC	Personal Computer
PDU	Protocol Data Unit
PGP	Pretty Good Privacy
PI	Protocol Interpreter
PIM	Protocol Independent Multicast
PING	Packet Internet Groper
PKI	Public Key Infrastructure
PNG	Portable Network Graphic
POP	Point Of Presence
POP	Post Office Protocol
POTS	Plain Old Telephone Service

PPP	Point-to-Point Protocol
PTR	Pointer
PTT	Postal Telegraph and Telephone
PVC	Permanent Virtual Circuit
QoS	Quality of Service
RA	Routing Arbiter
RARP	Reverse Address Resolution Protocol
RBOC	Regional Bell Operating Company
RDN	Relative Distinguished Name
RFC	Request For Comments
RIF	Routing Information Field
RIP	Routing Information Protocol
RIPE	Reseaux IP Europeens
RMON	Remote Network Monitor
ROM	Read Only Memory
RP	Rendezvous Point
RPB	Reverse Path Broadcasting
RPC	Remote Procedure Call
RPF	Reverse Path Forwarding
RPM	Reverse Path Multicasting
RR	Resource Record
RR	Routing Registry
RSA	Rivest, Shamir, and Adelman, the founders of a company called RSA Data Security
RST	Reset
RSVP	Resource Reservation Protocol
RTO	Retransmission Timeout (for TCP)
RTT	Round-Trip Time
SAP	(Multicast) Session Announcement Protocol
SASL	Simple Authentication and Security Layer
SDEV	Smoothed Deviation
SDLC	Synchronous Data Link Control
SDP	(Multicast) Session Description Protocol
SEI	Software Engineering Institute
SGML	Standard Generalized Markup Language
SHA-1	Secure Hash Algorithm 1
SIP	SMDS Interface Protocol
SIP	(Multicast) Session Initiation Protocol
SKIP	Simple Key-Management for Internet Protocols

SLIP	Serial Line Interface Protocol
SMDS	Switched Multimegabit Data Service
SMI	Structure of Management Information
S/MIME	Secure MIME
SMTP	Simple Mail Transfer Protocol
SNA	Systems Network Architecture
SNAP	Sub-Network Access Protocol
SNMP	Simple Network Management Protocol
SOA	Start of Authority
SONET	Synchronous Optical Network
SPF	Shortest Path First
SPI	Security Parameters Index
SPX	Sequenced Packet Exchange (for NetWare)
SRTT	Smoothed Round-Trip Time
SSAP	Source Service Access Point
SSL	Secure Sockets Layer
SVC	Switched Virtual Circuit
SWS	Silly Window Syndrome
SYN	Synchronizing Segment
TAO	TCP Accelerated Open
TCB	Transmission Control Block
TCP	Transmission Control Protocol
TCU	Trunk Coupling Unit
TELNET	Terminal Networking
TFTP	Trivial File Transfer Protocol
TGS	(Kerberos) Ticket Granting Service
TLI	Transport Layer Interface
TOS	Type of Service
TP4	OSI Transport Class 4
TSAP	Transport Service Access Point
T/TCP	Transactional TCP
TTL	Time-To-Live
UA	User Agent
UDP	User Datagram Protocol
ULP	Upper Layer Protocol
URI	Universal Resource Identifier
URL	Uniform Resource Locator
URN	Uniform Resource Name
UTC	Universal Time Coordinated

VCC	Virtual Channel Connection
VLSM	Variable-Length Subnet Masks
VPC	Virtual Path Connection
W3	World Wide Web
W3C	World Wide Web Consortium
WAIS	Wide Area Information Service
WAN	Wide Area Network
WF	Wildcard Filter
WWW	World Wide Web
WYSIWYG	What You See Is What You Get
XDR	eXternal Data Representation
XML	Extensible Markup Language
XNS	Xerox Network Systems

Binary/Decimal Tables

To translate a binary number to decimal, you need to multiply each binary digit by an appropriate power of 2. Below, we show the multipliers that are used to convert 10010111 to decimal.

```
  1   0   0   1   0  1  1  1
128  64  32  16   8  4  2  1
```

Thus 10010111 is (128)(1) + (64)(0) + (32)(0) + (16)(1) + (8)(0) + (4)(1) + (2)(1) + (1)(1) which equals 128 + 16 + 4 + 2 + 1 = 151.

Table F.1 below lists the binary to decimal translations that are used to write subnet masks. In this case, just the set of binary numbers that have contiguous 1s on the left are translated. Note that the decimal numbers start at 128 and increase by 64, 32, 16, 8, 4, 2, and 1. Table F.2 on the pages that follow displays all 8-bit translations between binary and decimal numbers.

TABLE F.1   Subnet Mask Translation

Binary	Decimal
10000000	128
11000000	192
11100000	224
11110000	240
11111000	248
11111100	252
11111110	254
11111111	255

TABLE F.2 Binary to Decimal Translation

Binary	Decimal	Binary	Decimal	Binary	Decimal	Binary	Decimal
00000000	0	00100000	32	01000000	64	01100000	96
00000001	1	00100001	33	01000001	65	01100001	97
00000010	2	00100010	34	01000010	66	01100010	98
00000011	3	00100011	35	01000011	67	01100011	99
00000100	4	00100100	36	01000100	68	01100100	100
00000101	5	00100101	37	01000101	69	01100101	101
00000110	6	00100110	38	01000110	70	01100110	102
00000111	7	00100111	39	01000111	71	01100111	103
00001000	8	00101000	40	01001000	72	01101000	104
00001001	9	00101001	41	01001001	73	01101001	105
00001010	10	00101010	42	01001010	74	01101010	106
00001011	11	00101011	43	01001011	75	01101011	107
00001100	12	00101100	44	01001100	76	01101100	108
00001101	13	00101101	45	01001101	77	01101101	109
00001110	14	00101110	46	01001110	78	01101110	110
00001111	15	00101111	47	01001111	79	01101111	111
00010000	16	00110000	48	01010000	80	01110000	112
00010001	17	00110001	49	01010001	81	01110001	113
00010010	18	00110010	50	01010010	82	01110010	114
00010011	19	00110011	51	01010011	83	01110011	115
00010100	20	00110100	52	01010100	84	01110100	116
00010101	21	00110101	53	01010101	85	01110101	117
00010110	22	00110110	54	01010110	86	01110110	118
00010111	23	00110111	55	01010111	87	01110111	119
00011000	24	00111000	56	01011000	88	01111000	120
00011001	25	00111001	57	01011001	89	01111001	121
00011010	26	00111010	58	01011010	90	01111010	122
00011011	27	00111011	59	01011011	91	01111011	123
00011100	28	00111100	60	01011100	92	01111100	124
00011101	29	00111101	61	01011101	93	01111101	125
00011110	30	00111110	62	01011110	94	01111110	126
00011111	31	00111111	63	01011111	95	01111111	127
10000000	128	10100000	160	11000000	192	11100000	224
10000001	129	10100001	161	11000001	193	11100001	225
10000010	130	10100010	162	11000010	194	11100010	226
10000011	131	10100011	163	11000011	195	11100011	227
10000100	132	10100100	164	11000100	196	11100100	228
10000101	133	10100101	165	11000101	197	11100101	229
10000110	134	10100110	166	11000110	198	11100110	230
10000111	135	10100111	167	11000111	199	11100111	231

TABLE F.2 **Binary to Decimal Translation**

Binary	Decimal	Binary	Decimal	Binary	Decimal	Binary	Decimal
10001000	136	10101000	168	11001000	200	11101000	232
10001001	137	10101001	169	11001001	201	11101001	233
10001010	138	10101010	170	11001010	202	11101010	234
10001011	139	10101011	171	11001011	203	11101011	235
10001100	140	10101100	172	11001100	204	11101100	236
10001101	141	10101101	173	11001101	205	11101101	237
10001110	142	10101110	174	11001110	206	11101110	238
10001111	143	10101111	175	11001111	207	11101111	239
10010000	144	10110000	176	11010000	208	11110000	240
10010001	145	10110001	177	11010001	209	11110001	241
10010010	146	10110010	178	11010010	210	11110010	242
10010011	147	10110011	179	11010011	211	11110011	243
10010100	148	10110100	180	11010100	212	11110100	244
10010101	149	10110101	181	11010101	213	11110101	245
10010110	150	10110110	182	11010110	214	11110110	246
10010111	151	10110111	183	11010111	215	11110111	247
10011000	152	10111000	184	11011000	216	11111000	248
10011001	153	10111001	185	11011001	217	11111001	249
10011010	154	10111010	186	11011010	218	11111010	250
10011011	155	10111011	187	11011011	219	11111011	251
10011100	156	10111100	188	11011100	220	11111100	252
10011101	157	10111101	189	11011101	221	11111101	253
10011110	158	10111110	190	11011110	222	11111110	254
10011111	159	10111111	191	11011111	223	11111111	255

Bibliography

Albitz, Paul, and Cricket Liu, *DNS and BIND,* O'Reilly & Associates, 1993.

American National Standards Institute, *Fiber Distributed Data Interface (FDDI)—Token Ring Physical Layer Protocol (PHY),* ANS X3.148-1988, (also ISO 9314-1, 1989).

——, *Fiber Distributed Data interface (FDDI)—Token Ring Media Access Control (MAC),* ANS X3.139-1987, (also ISO 9314-2, 1989).

——, *T1.602—Telecommunications—ISDN—Data Link Layer Signaling Specification for Application at the Network Interface,* 1990.

——, *T1.606—Frame Relaying Bearer Service—Architectural Framework and Service Description,* 1990.

——, *T1S1/90-175—Addendum to T1.696—Frame Relaying Bearer Service—Architectural Framework and Service Description,* 1990.

——, *T1S1/90-214—DSS1—Core Aspects of Frame Protocol for Use with Frame Relay Bearer Service—Architectural Framework and Service Description,* 1990.

Bellcore TA-TSV-00160, *Exchange Access SMDS Service Generic Requirements,* December 1990.

Bellovin, S., and M. Merritt, "Limitations of the Kerberos Authentication System," *Computer Communications Review,* October 1990.

Black, Uyless D., *Data Communications, Networks, and Distributed Processing,* Reston, 1983.

Bolt, Beranek, and Newman, *A History of the ARPANET: The First Decade,* Technical Report, 1981.

Borman, D., "Implementing TCP/IP on a Cray Computer," *Computer Communication Review,* April 1989.

Brand, R., *Coping with the Threat of Computer Security Incidents: A Primer from Prevention through Recovery,* at cert.sei.cmu.edu in /pub/info/primer, June 1990.

Callon, Ross, "An Overview of OSI NSAP Addressing in the Internet," *ConneXions,* The Interoperability Report, December 1991.

CCITT Recommendation I.22, *Framework for providing additional packet mode bearer services,* Blue Book, ITU, Geneva, 1988.

CCITT Recommendation X.25, *Interface between data terminal equipment (DTE) and data-circuit-terminating equipment (DCE) for terminals operating in the packet mode on public data networks,* 1980 and 1984.

CCITT Recommendation X.400, *Message Handling System,* 1984 and 1988.

CCITT Recommendation X.500, *The Directory,* 1988.

Cerf, V., "A History of the ARPANET," *ConneXions,* The Interoperability Report, October 1989.

Cerf, V., and R. Kahn, "A Protocol for Packet Network Intercommunication," *IEEE Transactions on Communication,* May 1974.

Cheswick, B., "The Design of a Secure Internet Gateway," *Proceedings of the Summer Usenix Conference,* Anaheim, CA, June 1990.

Checswick, William R., and Steven M. Bellovin, *Firewalls and Internet Security,* Addison-Wesley, 1994.

Cisco, StrataCom, Digital Equipment Corporation, *Frame Relay Specification with Extensions,* Draft, 1990.

Cisco Systems, *Gateway System Manual,* 1991.

Coltun, Rob, "OSPF: An internet routing protocol," *ConneXions,* August 1989.

Comer, Douglas E., *Internetworking With TCP/IP, Volume I Principles, Protocols, and Architecture,* 2d ed., Prentice Hall, 1991.

Comer, Douglas E., and David L. Stevens, *Internetworking With TCP/IP, Volume II, Design, Implementation, and Internals,* Prentice Hall, 1991.

Cooper, J., *Computer and Communications Security: Strategies for the 1990s,* McGraw-Hill, 1989.

Deering, S., "IP Multicasting," *ConneXions,* February 1991.

Dern, Daniel P., "Standards for Interior Gateway Routing Protocols," *ConneXions,* July 1990.

Digital Equipment Corporation, Intel Corporation, and XEROX Corporation, *The Ethernet: A Local Area Network Data Link Layer and Physical Layer Specification,* September 1980.

Feit, Sidnie, *SNMP: A Guide to Network Management,* McGraw-Hill, 1995.

———, *The LAN Manager's Internet Connectivity Guide,* McGraw-Hill, 1997.

Frey, Donnalyn, and Rick Adams, *!%@:: A Directory of Electronic Mail Addressing and Networks,* 2d ed., O'Reilly & Associates, 1989.

FRICC, *Program Plan for the National Research and Education Network,* Federal Research Internet Coordinating Committee, U.S. Department of Energy, Office of Scientific Computing Report ER-7, May 1989.

FTP Software, *PC/TCP Kernel Installation and Reference Guide,* Version 2.05 for DOS, 1990.

———, *PC/TCP User's Guide,* Version 2.05 for DOS, 1990.

Garcia-Luna-Aceves, J. J., *A Unified Approach to Loop-Free Routing Using Distance Vectors or Link States,* ACM 089791-332-9/89/0009/0212, pages 212-223, 1989.

———, "Loop-Free Routing using Diffusing Computations," *IEEE/ACM Transactions on Networking,* vol. 1, no. 1, 1993.

GOSIP, *U.S. Government Open Systems Interconnection Profile Version 2.0,* Advanced Requirements Group, National Institute of Standards and Technology (NIST), April 1989.

Green, James Harry, *The Dow Jones-Irwin Handbook of Telecommunications,* Dow Jones-Irwin, 1986.

Hoffman, L., *Rogue Programs: Viruses, Worms, and Trojan Horses,* Van Nostrand Reinhold, 1990.

Huitema, Christian, *Routing in the Internet,* Prentice Hall, 1995.

IBM GG24-3442, *IBM AS/400 TCP/IP Configuration and Operation,* 1991.

IBM GG24-3696, *Managing TCP/IP Networks Using NetView and the SNMP Interface,* 1991.

IBM GG24-3816, *High-Speed Networking Technology, An Introductory Survey,* 1992.

IBM SC31-6081, *TCP/IP Version 2 Release 2 for VM: User's Guide,* 1991.

IBM SC31-6084, *TCP/IP Version 2 Release 2 for VM: Programmer's Reference,* 1991.

IBM, *Vocabulary for Data processing, Telecommunications, and Office Systems,* 1981.

Institute of Electrical and Electronics Engineers, *Draft Standard P802.1A—Overview and Architecture,* 1989.

———, *Local Area Networks—CSMA/CD Access Method,* ANSI/IEEE 802.3, (ISO 8802-3).

———, *Local Area Networks—Distributed Queue Dual Bus (DQDB) Subnetwork of a Metropolitan Area Network (MAN),* ANSI/IEEE 802.6 (ISO DIS 8802-6, 1991).

———, *Local Area Networks—Higher Layers and Interworking,* ANSI/IEEE 802.1, 1990 (ISO DIS 8802-1D, 1990).

———, *Local Area Networks—Logical Link Control,* ANSI/IEEE 802.2, 1989 (ISO 8802-2, 1989).

———, *Local Area Networks—Network Management.* Draft IEEE 802.1B, 1990.

———, *Local Area Networks—Token-Bus Access Method,* ANSI/IEEE 802.4 (ISO 8802-3).

———, *Local Area Networks—Token Ring Access Method,* ANSI/IEEE 802.5, 1989 (ISO 8802-5,1989).

International Organization for Standardization, *Information Processing Systems—Common Management information Protocol (CMIP),* ISO 9596, 1990.

———, *Information Processing Systems—Common Management information Service (CMIS),* ISO 9595, 1990.

———, *Information Processing Systems—Data Communications—Addendum to the Network Service Definition,* ISO 8348 AD1.

———, *Information Processing Systems—Data Communications—High-Level Data Link Control Procedures—Consolidation of Classes of Procedures,* ISO 7809.

———, *Information Processing Systems—Data Communications—High-Level Data Link Control Procedures—Consolidation of Elements of Procedures,* ISO 4335.

———, *Information Processing Systems—Data Communications—High-Level Data Link Control Procedures—Frame Structure,* ISO 3309.

———, *Information Processing Systems—Data Communications—Network Service Definition,* ISO 8348.

———, *Information Processing Systems—Data Communications—Protocol for Providing the Connectionless-Mode Network Service,* ISO 8473.

———, *Information Processing Systems—Open Systems Interconnection—Basic Connection Oriented Session Protocol Specification,* ISO 8327.

———, *Information Processing Systems—Open Systems Interconnection—Basic Connection Oriented Session Service Definition,* ISO 8326.

———, *Information Processing Systems—Open Systems Interconnection—Connection Oriented Presentation Protocol Specification,* ISO 8823.

———, *Information Processing Systems—Open Systems Interconnection—Connection Oriented Presentation Service Definition,* ISO 8822.

———, *Information Processing Systems—Open Systems Interconnection—Connection Oriented Transport Protocol,* ISO 8073.

———, *Information Processing Systems—Open Systems Interconnection—Intermediate System to Intermediate System Intra-Domain Routing Exchange Protocol for use in Conjunction with the Protocol for Providing the Connectionless-Mode Network service,* ISO DIS 10589.

———, *Information Processing Systems—Open Systems Interconnection—Message Handling System,* ISO 10021/CCITT X.400.

———, *Information Processing Systems—Open Systems Interconnection—Protocol Specification for the Association Control Service Element,* ISO 8650.

———, *Information Processing Systems—Open Systems Interconnection—Remote Operations: Model, Notation, and Service Definition,* ISO 9072-1.

———, *Information Processing Systems—Open Systems Interconnection—Remote Operations: Protocol Specification,* ISO 9066-2.

———, *Information Processing Systems—Open Systems Interconnection—Service Definition for the Association Control Service Element,* ISO 8649.

———, *Information Processing Systems—Open Systems Interconnection—Specification of Abstract Syntax Notation One (ASN.1),* ISO 8824.

———, *Information Processing Systems—Open Systems Interconnection—Specification of Basic Encoding Rules for Abstract Syntax Notation One (ASN.1),* ISO 8825.

———, *Information Processing Systems—Open Systems Interconnection—Transport Service Definition,* ISO 8072.

———, *OSI Routing Framework,* ISO TC97/SC6/N4616, June 1987.

Jacobson, V., "Berkeley TCP Evolution from 4.3-Tahoe to 4.3-Reno," *Proceedings of the Eighteenth Internet Engineering Task Force.*

———, *Congestion Avoidance and Control,* ACM SIGCOMM-88, August 1988.

Jain, R., K. Ramakrishnan, and D-M. Chiu, *Congestion Avoidance in Computer Networks With a Connectionless Network Layer,* Technical Report, DEC-TR-506, Digital Equipment Corporation, 1987.

Kapoor, Atul, SNA, *Architecture, Protocols, and Implementation,* McGraw-Hill, 1992.

Karn, P., and C. Partridge, "Improving Round Trip Time Estimates in Reliable Transport Protocols," *Proceedings of the ACM SIGCOMM,* 1987.

Kernighan, Brian W., and Dennis M. Ritchie, *The C Programming Language:* Second Edition, Prentice-Hall, 1988.

Kessler, Gary C., and David A. Train, *Metropolitan Area Networks,* McGraw-Hill, 1992.

Kessler, Gary C., and Peter Southwick, *ISDN,* McGraw-Hill, 1998.

Kochan, Stephen G., and Patrick H. Wood, Consulting Editors, *UNIX Networking,* 1989.

Laquey, T. L., *User's Directory of Computer Networks,* Digital Press, 1989.

Lippis, Nick, and James Herman, "Widening Your Internet Horizons," *ConneXions,* October 1991.

Liu, Cricket, Jerry Peek, Russ Jones, Bryan Buus, and Adrian Nye, *Managing Internet Information Services,* O'Reilly & Associates, Inc., 1995.

Malamud, Carl, *DEC Networks and Architectures,* McGraw-Hill, 1989.

———, *STACKS_The INTEROP Book,* Prentice-Hall, 1991.

McKenney, P., "Congestion Avoidance," *ConneXions,* February 1991.

Medin, Milo, "The Great IGP Debate—Part Two: the Open Shortest Path First (OSPF) Routing Protocol," *ConneXions,* October 1991.

Microsoft Windows NT Networking Guide, Microsoft Press, 1996.

Mills, D., and H-W. Braun, "The NSFNET Backbone Network," *Proceedings of the ACM SIG-COMM,* 1987.

Mogul, Jeffrey C., "Efficient Use Of Workstations for Passive Monitoring of Local Area Networks," *Proc. SIGCOMM '90 Symposium on Communications Architectures and Protocols,* September 1990.

Narten, T., "Internet Routing," *Proceedings of the ACM SIGCOMM,* 1989.

Nemeth, Evi, Garth Snyder, and Scott Seebass, *UNIX System Administration Handbook,* Prentice-Hall, 1989.

Odlyzko, A. M., *The future of integer factorization,* CryptoBytes (The technical newsletter of RSA Laboratories), 1994.

Perlman, Radia, and Ross Callon, "The Great IGP Debate—Part One: IS-IS and Integrated Routing," *ConneXions,* October 1991.

Pfleeger, C., *Security in Computing,* Prentice-Hall, 1989.

Postel, J. B., "Internetwork Protocol Approaches," *IEEE Transactions on Communications,* 1980.

Postel, J. B., C. A. Sunshine, and D. Chen, "The ARPA Internet Protocol," *Computer Networks,* 1981.

Postel, J, B., C. A. Sunshine, and D. Cohen, "The ARPA Internet Protocol," *Computer Networks,* vol. 5, no. 4, July 1981.

Quarterman, John S., and J. C. Hoskins, "Notable Computer Networks," *Communications of the ACM,* October 1986.

Quarterman, John S., *The Matrix,* Computer Networks and Conferencing Systems Worldwide, Digital Press, 1990.

Romkey, John, "The Packet Driver," *ConneXions,* July 1990.

Rose, Marshall T., *The Little Black Book: Mail Bonding with OSI Directory Services,* Prentice-Hall, 1990.

———, *The Open Book: A Practical Perspective on OSI,* Prentice-Hall, 1990.

———, *The Simple Book: An Introduction to Management of TCP/IP-based Internets,* Prentice-Hall, 1990.

Sackett, George C., *IBMs Token-Ring Networking Handbook,* McGraw-Hill, 1993.

St. Amand, Joseph V., *A Guide to Packet-Switched, Value-Added Networks,* Macmillan, 1986.

Schneier, Bruce, *Applied Cryptography,* John Wiley & Sons, 1996.

Schwartz, Michael F., "Resource Discovery and Related Research at the University of Colorado," *ConneXions,* May 1991.

Seeley, D., "A Tour of the Worm," *Proceedings of 1989 Winter USENIX Conference,* Usenix Association, San Diego, CA, February 1989.

Sijan, Karanjit, and Chris Hare, *Internet Firewalls and Network Security,* New Riders Publishing, 1995.

Simmons, G. J., ed., "Contemporary Cryptology," *IEEE,* 1991.

Spafford, E., "The Internet Worm Program: An Analysis," *Computer Communication Review,* vol. 19, no. 1, ACM SIGCOM, January 1989.

Stallings, William, *Data and Computer Communications,* Macmillan, 1984.

———, *Handbook of Computer Communications Standards,* Department of Defense Protocol Standards, 1988.

Stern, Hal, *Managing NFS and NIS,* O'Reilly and Associates, 1991.

Stevens, W. Richard, *TCP/IP Illustrated, Volume 1,* Addison Wesley, 1994.

———, *TCP/IP Illustrated, Volume 3,* Addison Wesley, 1996.

———, *UNIX Network Programming,* Prentice Hall, 1990.

Stevens, W. Richard, and Gary Wright, *TCP/IP Illustrated, Volume 2,* Addison Wesley, 1995.

Stoll, C., *The Cuckoo's Egg,* Doubleday, 1989.

Tannenbaum, Andrew S., *Computer Networks,* Prentice Hall, 1981.

Vitalink, *Building and Managing Multivendor Networks using Bridge and Router Technologies,* 1990.

Tsuchiya, Paul F., "Inter-domain Routing in the Internet," *ConneXions,* January 1991.

XEROX, *Internet Transport Protocols, Report XSIS 028112,* Xerox Corporation, 1981.

X/Open specification, *X/Open CAE Specification: Protocols for X/Open Internetworking: XNFS,* X/Open Company, Ltd., 1991.

INDEX

A

AAL (*see* ATM Adaptation Layer)
Abandon (LDAP operation), 700
Abstract Syntax Notation 1 (ASN.1), 751
accept(), 774, 776
Accept headers (HTTP), 675
Accept-Ranges header (HTTP), 677
Access control, 721–724, 763–764
Acknowledgments (ACKs), 31, 291–292, 297–298, 316–317
Active content, 652
Active open, 294
Add (LDAP operation), 701
Address Mask request and reply messages (ICMP), 204–205
Address records, 478
Address Resolution Protocol (ARP), 132–136, 144
   message contents, 134–135
   proxy, 138
   reverse, 136
   table, ARP, 135–136
Addresses, 107–132
   in BOOTP, 436
   classes of, 110–113, 115
   classless, 124–128
   configuration of, 130–132
   in DHCP, 444–445
   examples of, 112–113
   formats for, 109–110
   in IPv6, 128–129, 796–807
      allocations, 797–798
      anycast addresses, 805
      Link-Local addresses, 801–802
      multicast addresses, 803–805
      notation, 796–797
      Site-Local addresses, 802
      special addresses, 806–807
      types of addresses, 797

Addresses, in IPv6 (*Cont.*):
      unicast addresses, 798–801
   and multihoming, 130
   multiple, 137–138
   names vs., 132
   non-Internet, 111–112
   reserved, 119–124
   subnet addressing, 115–119
   translating names to, 113–115
   unicast, 85
Address-to-name translations, 465–468, 480–481
Administrative attributes, 718–719
Advanced Research Projects Agency (ARPA), 10
Advanced Research Projects Agency Network (ARPANET), 10–13
Advertisement address, 207
Agents:
   desktop news, 643–645
   in SNMP, 729
Alias names, 114–115, 695–696
Allman, Eric, 606
All-routers multicast address, 207
All-systems multicast address, 207
American National Standard Code for Information Interchange (ASCII), 32, 551–552
American Registry for Internet Numbers (ARIN), 109
Andreessen, Marc, 651
Anycast addresses, 796, 805
API (Application Programming Interface), 667
APNIC (*see* Asia-Pacific Network Information Center)
Application port numbers:
   in TCP, 285
   in UDP, 275–278
Application Programming Interface (API), 667

ABOUT THE AUTHOR

Sidnie Feit is Chief Scientist for the Standish Group, leading middleware consultants. She has had extensive experience in both academe and industry, including five years with the ITT System Design and Architecture Grpoup. Dr. Feit is the author and director of several Phelps Group courses dealing with TCP/IP and the Internet. She also is the author of McGraw-Hill's *SNMP: A Guide to Network Management* and *The LAN Manager's Internet Connectivity Guide.*